ESSENTIALS OF MANAGEMENT

McGRAW-HILL SERIES IN MANAGEMENT

Fred Luthans and Keith Davis, Consulting Editors

ALLEN   The Management Profession

ARNOLD AND FELDMAN   Organizational Behavior

BENTON   Supervision and Management

BUCHELE   The Management of Business and Public Organizations

CASCIO   Managing Human Resources: Productivity, Quality of Work Life, Profits

CLELAND AND KING   Management: A Systems Approach

CLELAND AND KING   Systems Analysis and Project Management

DALE   Management: Theory and Practice

DAVIS AND FREDERICK   Business and Society: Management, Public Policy, Ethics

DAVIS AND NEWSTROM   Human Behavior at Work: Organizational Behavior

DAVIS AND NEWSTROM   Organizational Behavior: Readings and Exercises

DEL MAR   Operations and Industrial Management: Designing and Managing for Productivity

DOBLER, LEE, AND BURT   Purchasing and Materials Management: Text and Cases

DUNN AND RACHEL   Wage and Salary Administration: Total Compensation Systems

FELDMAN AND ARNOLD   Managing Individual and Group Behavior in Organizations

FINCH, JONES, AND LITTERER   Managing for Organizational Effectiveness: An Experiential Approach

FLIPPO   Personnel Management

GERLOFF   Organizational Theory and Design: A Strategic Approach for Management

GLUECK AND JAUCH   Business Policy and Strategic Management

GLUECK AND JAUCH   Strategic Management and Business Policy

GLUECK AND SNYDER   Readings in Business Policy and Strategy from Business Week

HICKS AND GULLETT   Management

HICKS AND GULLETT   Modern Business Management: A Systems and Environmental Approach

HICKS AND GULLETT   Organizations: Theory and Behavior

JAUCH AND TOWNSEND   Cases in Strategic Management and Business Policy

JOHNSON, KAST, AND ROSENZWEIG   The Theory and Management of Systems

KARLINS   The Human Use of Human Resources

KAST AND ROSENZWEIG   Experiential Exercises and Cases in Management

KAST AND ROSENZWEIG   Organization and Management: A Systems and Contingency Approach

KNUDSON, WOODWORTH, AND BELL   Management: An Experiential Approach

KOONTZ, O'DONNELL, AND WEIHRICH   Essentials of Management

KOONTZ, O'DONNELL, AND WEIHRICH   Management

KOONTZ, O'DONNELL, AND WEIHRICH
Management, A Book of Readings

KOPELMAN   Managing Productivity in
Organizations: A Practical, People-
Oriented, Perspective

LEVIN, McLAUGHLIN, LAMONE, AND
KOTTAS   Production/Operations
Management: Contemporary Policy for
Managing Operationg Systems

LUTHANS   Introduction to Management:
A Contingency Approach

LUTHANS   Organizational Behavior

LUTHANS AND THOMPSON   Contemporary
Readings in Organizational Behavior

McNICHOLS   Executive Policy and Strategic
Planning

McNICHOLS   Policymaking and Executive
Action

MARGULIES AND RAIA   Conceptual
Foundations of Organizational
Development

MAYER   Production and Operations
Management

MILES   Theories of Management:
Implications for Organizational Behavior
and Development

MILES AND SNOW   Organizational Strategy,
Structure, and Process

MILLS   Labor-Management Relations

MITCHELL   People in Organizations: An
Introduction to Organizational Behavior

MOLANDER   Responsive Capitalism: Case
Studies in Corporate Social Conduct

MONKS   Operations Management: Theory
and Problems

NEWSTROM, REIF, AND MONCZKA   A
Contingency Approach to Management:
Readings

PORTER, LAWLER, AND HACKMAN
Behavior in Organizations

PRASOW AND PETERS   Arbitration and
Collective Bargaining: Conflict Resolution
in Labor Relations

RUE AND HOLLAND   Strategic Management:
Concepts and Experiences

QUICK AND QUICK   Organizational Stress
and Preventive Management

REDDIN   Managerial Effectiveness

RUGMAN, LECRAW, AND BOOTH
International Business: Firm and
Environment

SARTAIN AND BAKER   The Supervisor and
the Job

SAYLES   Leadership: What Effective
Managers Really Do . . . and How They
Do It

SCHLESINGER, ECCLES, AND GABARRO
Managing Behavior in Organizations:
Text, Cases, Readings

SCHROEDER   Operations Management:
Decision Making in the Operations
Function

SHARPLIN   Strategic Management

SHORE   Operations Management

STEERS AND PORTER   Motivation and
Work Behavior

STEINHOFF AND BURGESS   Small
Business Management Fundamentals

SUTERMEISTER   People and Productivity

VANCE   Corporate Leadership: Boards,
Directors, and Strategy

WALKER   Human Resource Planning

WEIHRICH   Management Excellence:
Productivity through MBO

WERTHER AND DAVIS   Personnel
Management and Human Resources

WOFFORD, GERLOFF, AND CUMMINS
Organizational Communications: The
Keystone to Managerial Effectiveness

FOURTH EDITION

ESSENTIALS OF MANAGEMENT

Harold Koontz

Late Mead Johnson Professor of Management
Graduate School of Management
University of California, Los Angeles

Cyril O'Donnell

Late Professor of Management
Graduate School of Management
University of California, Los Angeles

Heinz Weihrich

Professor of Management
McLaren College of Business Administration
University of San Francisco

McGraw-Hill Book Company

New York St. Louis San Francisco Auckland Bogotá Hamburg
Johannesburg London Madrid Mexico Montreal New Delhi
Panama Paris São Paulo Singapore Sydney Tokyo Toronto

Library of Congress Cataloging-in-Publication Data

Koontz, Harold, date
   Essentials of management.

   McGraw-Hill series in management)
   Includes bibliographical references and indexes.
    1. Management. I. O'Donnell, Cyril,   date–
II. Weihrich, Heinz. III. Title. IV. Series.
HD31.K62 1986   658.4   85-18834
ISBN 0-07-035516-9

ESSENTIALS OF MANAGEMENT

1 2 3 4 5 6 7 8 9 0 HALHAL 8 9 8 7 6

ISBN 0-07-035516-9

This book was set in Plantin by Waldman Graphics, Inc.
The editor was John R. Meyer;
the design was done by INK, Graphic Design;
the production supervisor was Diane Renda.
New drawings were done by Danmark & Michaels, Inc.
Halliday Lithograph Corporation was printer and binder.

About
the Authors

HEINZ WEIHRICH is Professor of Management at the University of San Francisco. He received his doctorate degree from the University of California, Los Angeles (UCLA), where he conducted the first research study on management by objectives (MBO) as a comprehensive, integrated management system. He taught at Arizona State University, at the University of California at Los Angeles, and in France and Austria. He has published seven books, including *Management Excellence: Productivity through MBO*; *Management,* eighth edition, with Professors Harold Koontz and Cyril O'Donnell; and *Executives Skills: A Management by Objectives Approach,* with Professors George S. Odiorne and Jack Mendleson. Over eighty of his articles have been published in the United States and abroad. His extensive business and consulting experience in the United States and Europe includes work with firms such as Kodak, Volkswagen, and Hughes Aircraft Company.

The late HAROLD KOONTZ was active as a business and government executive, university professor, company board chairman and director, management consultant, worldwide lecturer to top management groups, and author of many books and articles. From 1950 he was Professor of Management and from 1962 Mead Johnson Professor of Management at the University of California, Los Angeles; from 1978 to 1982 he was World Chancellor at The International Academy of Management. He was author or coauthor of nineteen books and ninety journal articles, and his *Principles of Management* (now in its eighth edition as *Management*) has been translated into sixteen languages. His *Board of Directors and Effective Management* was given the Academy of Management Book Award in 1968. After taking his doctorate at Yale, Professor Koontz served as Assistant to the Trustees of the New Haven Railroad, Chief of the Traffic Branch of the War Production Board, Assistant to the Vice President of the Association of American Railroads, Assistant to the President of Trans

World Airlines, and Director of Sales for Convair. He acted as management consultant for, among others, Hughes Tool Company, Hughes Aircraft Company, Purex Corporation, KLM Royal Dutch Airlines, Metropolitan Life Insurance Company, Occidental Petroleum Corporation, and General Telephone Company. Professor Koontz's honors included election as a Fellow of the American and the International Academies of Management, and a term of service as President of the American Academy of Management. He received the Mead Johnson Award in 1962 and the Society for Advancement of Management Taylor Key Award in 1974 and is listed in *Who's Who in America, Who's Who in Finance and Industry,* and *Who's Who in the World.* Harold Koontz passed away in 1984.

The late CYRIL O'DONNELL was educated at the University of Alberta and the University of Chicago, where he received a Ph.D. in management. His last position was Professor of Business Organization and Policy and Director, Case Development Program, at the Graduate School of Business Administration, University of California, Los Angeles. He was previously chairman of the Department of Economics at DePaul University. He had extensive business and professional experience, having been affiliated with the War Labor Board and private business enterprises. Professor O'Donnell was a consultant to several domestic and foreign firms and government agencies and was an active director of several business corporations. In addition to contributing to numerous professional journals, he was the author of *Business Management, Cases in General Management,* and *The Strategy of Corporate Research.*

Contents

Preface   xix

Part I   The Basis of Management Theory and Science

Chapter 1   Management: Science, Theory, and Practice   3
Why Management?   4
The Aim of All Managers   5
Managing: Science or Art?   7
The Elements of Science   8
The Evolution of Management Thought   9
The Situational, or Contingency, Approach to Managing   12
Seeing the Organization as a System   13
The Systems Approach to Operational Management   13
Summary   17
Key Ideas and Concepts for Review   18
For Discussion   18
Case 1-1 Hart Electronics   18
Case 1-2 The Paragon Radar Corporation   19
For Further Information   21

Chapter 2   Patterns of Management Analysis   22
The Various Approaches to Management   23
Implementing the Operational Approach   35
Functions of Managers   35
The Management Theory Jungle: Tendencies toward Convergence of
    Theory Approaches   38

Summary   **44**

Key Ideas and Concepts for Review   **45**

For Discussion   **45**

Case 2-1 Carlton Plywood Company   **46**

Case 2-2 LMT, Incorporated   **47**

For Further Information   **47**

Chapter 3   **The External Environment and International Management**   **48**

Managers in Their Environments   **49**

Japanese Management and Theory Z   **56**

International Management and Multinational Corporations   **60**

Summary   **64**

Key Ideas and Concepts for Review   **66**

For Discussion   **66**

Case 3-1 The Social Responsibility of Business   **67**

Case 3-2 Consolidated Computers, Inc.   **68**

For Further Information   **69**

Part II   **Planning**

Chapter 4   **The Nature and Purpose of Planning**   **73**

The Nature of Planning   **74**

Types of Plans   **76**

Steps in Planning   **84**

The Planning Process: A Rational Approach to Goal Achievement   **89**

Summary   **93**

Key Ideas and Concepts for Review   **93**

For Discussion   **94**

Case 4-1 Eastern Electric Corporation   **94**

Case 4-2 International Machine Corporation   **95**

For Further Information   **96**

Chapter 5   **Objectives**   **97**

The Nature of Objectives   **97**

Evolving Concepts in Management by Objectives   **102**

The Process of Managing by Objectives   **104**

How to Set Objectives   **107**

Benefits and Weaknesses of Management by Objectives and Some
     Recommendations   **110**

Summary   **113**

Key Ideas and Concepts for Review   **113**

For Discussion   **114**

Case 5-1 Developing Verifiable Goals   **114**

Case 5-2 The Municipal Water District   **115**

For Further Information   **116**

Chapter 6	**Strategies and Policies**	**118**
	Strategies and Policies to Give Direction to Plans	119
	Requirements for Effective Strategies	120
	The Major Kinds of Strategies	122
	A Tool for Allocating Resources: The Portfolio Matrix	124
	The Strategic Planning Process	126
	Effective Implementation of Strategies	128
	Summary	130
	Key Ideas and Concepts for Review	131
	For Discussion	131
	Case 6-1 The General Savings and Loan Association	132
	Case 6-2 The Penn Central Transportation Company	132
	For Further Information	133

Chapter 7	**Decision Making**	**135**
	The Importance and Limitations of Rational Decision Making	136
	Development of Alternatives	137
	The Nature and Process of Evaluation of Alternatives	138
	Selecting an Alternative: Three Approaches	140
	Programmed and Nonprogrammed Decisions	143
	Modern Approaches to Decision Making Under Uncertainty	144
	Evaluating the Importance of a Decision	150
	The Systems Approach and Decision Making	150
	Summary	151
	Key Ideas and Concepts for Review	152
	For Discussion	152
	Case 7-1 Olympic Toy Company	153
	Case 7-2 King's Supermarkets	153
	For Further Information	154
	Summary of Major Principles of Planning	156

Part III	**Organizing**	

Chapter 8	**The Nature and Purpose of Organizing**	**161**
	Formal and Informal Organization	162
	Organizational Division: The Department	164
	Organization Levels and the Span of Management	164
	Factors Determining an Effective Span	168
	Organizing as a Process	172
	Basic Questions for Effective Organizing	175
	Summary	175
	Key Ideas and Concepts for Review	175
	For Discussion	176
	Case 8-1 Measurement Instruments Corporation	176
	Case 8-2 American Aircraft Company	178
	For Further Information	178

Chapter 9   **Basic Departmentation**   **180**

Departmentation by Simple Numbers   181
Departmentation by Time   181
Departmentation by Enterprise Function   182
Departmentation by Territory or Geography   184
Departmentation by Product   186
Customer Departmentation   188
Market-Oriented Departmentation   190
Process or Equipment Departmentation   192
Matrix Organization   192
Strategic Business Units (SBUs)   197
Choosing the Pattern of Departmentation   199
Summary   200
Key Ideas and Concepts for Review   201
For Discussion   201
Case 9-1 Agricultural Fertilizer Division of the Northern Chemical Corporation   202
Case 9-2 Universal Food Products Company   203
For Further Information   204

Chapter 10   **Line and Staff Authority Relationship**   **205**

Authority and Power   206
Line and Staff Concepts   207
Functional Authority   209
Staff and the Small Business   215
Benefits of Staff   216
Limitations of Staff   216
Making Staff Work Effectively   218
Summary   220
Key Ideas and Concepts for Review   220
For Discussion   220
Case 10-1 ABC Airlines   221
Case 10-2 Controllership at International Supermarkets, Inc.   222
For Further Information   223

Chapter 11   **Decentralization of Authority**   **224**

Delegation of Authority   226
The Art of Delegation   231
Factors Determining the Degree of Decentralization of Authority   234
Recentralization of Authority   240
Obtaining the Desired Degree of Decentralization   241
Clarifying Decentralization: Chart of Approval Authorization   242
Balance: The Key to Decentralization   243
Summary   247
Key Ideas and Concepts for Review   247
For Discussion   247

Case 11-1 Decentralization at American Business Computers and
        Equipment Company   248
Case 11-2 The Miracle Products Company   249
For Further Information   250

Chapter 12   Making Organizing Effective   **251**
Some Mistakes in Organizing   252
Avoiding Mistakes by Planning   256
Avoiding Organizational Inflexibility   257
Avoiding Conflict by Clarification   258
Ensuring Understanding of Organizing   262
Promoting an Appropriate Organization Culture   263
Summary   265
Key Ideas and Concepts for Review   265
For Discussion   266
Case 12-1 Staff and Service Domination of Line Operations   266
Case 12-2 The VGI Company   267
For Further Information   268
Summary of Major Principles of Organizing   269

Part IV   Staffing

Chapter 13   The Nature and Purpose of Staffing   **275**
Defining the Managerial Job   276
The Systems Approach to Staffing: An Overview of the Staffing Function   277
Situational Factors Affecting Staffing   283
Summary   289
Key Ideas and Concepts for Review   289
For Discussion   290
Case 13-1 Belden Electronics Company   290
Case 13-2 Texas Oil Company   291
For Further Information   292

Chapter 14   Selection: Matching the Person with the Job   **293**
Systems Approach to the Selection of Managers: An Overview   294
Position Requirements and Job Design   294
Skills and Personal Characteristics Needed by Managers   298
Matching Manager Qualifications with Position Requirements   301
Selection Process, Techniques, and Instruments   304
Orienting and Socializing New Employees   308
Summary   309
Key Ideas and Concepts for Review   310
For Discussion   310
Case 14-1 Carl Wendover   311
Case 14-2 The Denied Promotion   311
For Further Information   312

Chapter 15	**Performance Appraisal and Career Strategy**	**313**
	The Problem of Management Appraisal	314
	Choosing the Appraisal Criteria	314
	Traditional Trait Appraisals	315
	Appraising Managers against Verifiable Objectives	317
	Appraising Managers as Managers: A Suggested Program	319
	Formulating the Career Strategy	324
	Summary	328
	Key Ideas and Concepts for Review	328
	For Discussion	329
	Case 15-1 Hardstone Corporation	329
	Case 15-2 Foresite Incorporated	330
	For Further Information	332
Chapter 16	**Manager and Organization Development**	**333**
	The Need for Effective Manager Development	334
	Manager Development Process and Training	336
	Approaches to Manager Development: On-the-Job Training	338
	Approaches to Manager Development: Internal and External Training	340
	Organizational Conflict	342
	Organization Development	344
	Summary	349
	Key Ideas and Concepts for Review	349
	For Discussion	349
	Case 16-1 Aerospace, Inc.	350
	Case 16-2 Management Development at the Pendleton Department Stores Corporation	351
	For Further Information	351
	Summary of Major Principles of Staffing	354

Part V Leading

Chapter 17	**Managing and the Human Factor**	**359**
	The Human Factors in Managing	360
	Behavioral Models	361
	Creativity and Innovation	364
	Harmonizing Objectives: The Key to Leading	367
	Summary	367
	Key Ideas and Concepts for Review	368
	For Discussion	368
	Case 17-1 What Do We Know for Sure?	369
	Case 17-2 Customer's Electric Appliance Company	369
	For Further Information	370

Chapter 18   **Motivation**   372

Motivation and Motivators   373

Motivation: The Carrot and the Stick   375

The Hierarchy of Needs Theory   376

The Motivation-Hygiene Approach to Motivation   378

The Expectancy Theory of Motivation   378

Reinforcement Theory   382

McClelland's Needs Theory of Motivation   383

Special Motivational Techniques   384

Job Enrichment   387

A Systems and Contingency Approach to Motivation   389

Summary   391

Key Ideas and Concepts for Review   392

For Discussion   392

Case 18-1 Motivation at the Bradley Clothing Company   393

Case 18-2 Consolidated Motors Corporation   393

For Further Information   394

Chapter 19   **Leadership**   396

Defining Leadership   397

Ingredients of Leadership   398

Trait Approaches to Leadership   399

Leadership Behavior and Styles   400

Situational, or Contingency, Approaches to Leadership   408

Summary   414

Key Ideas and Concepts for Review   415

For Discussion   415

Case 19-1 Leaders in Government Departments and Agencies   416

Case 19-2 Palmer Machinery Company   416

For Further Information   417

Chapter 20   **Communication**   419

The Communication Function in an Organization   419

The Communication Process   421

Communication in the Enterprise   424

Barriers and Breakdowns in Communication   428

Toward Effective Communication   431

Summary   436

Key Ideas and Concepts for Review   437

For Discussion   437

Case 20-1 Haynes Fashion Stores, Incorporated   438

Case 20-2 Home Radio and Television Company   439

For Further Information   440

Summary of Major Principles of Leading   442

Part VI Controlling

Chapter 21 **The System and Process of Controlling** 447
The Basic Control Process 448
Critical Control Points and Standards 450
Control as a Feedback System 452
Real-Time Information and Control 452
Feedforward Control 454
Requirements for Adequate Controls 459
Summary 462
Key Ideas and Concepts for Review 463
For Discussion 463
Case 21-1 The Kappa Corporation 464
Case 21-2 Hanover Space and Electronics Corporation 464
For Further Information 465

Chapter 22 **Control Techniques and Information Technology** 466
Control Techniques: The Budget 467
Traditional Nonbudgetary Control Devices 474
Time-Event Network Analyses 477
Program Budgeting 481
Information Technology 483
The Use of Computers in Managing Information 484
Summary 485
Key Ideas and Concepts for Review 486
For Discussion 487
Case 22-1 Anchor Consolidated Industries, Inc. 487
Case 22-2 The Electrical Construction Company 488
For Further Information 488

Chapter 23 **Planning and Controlling Production and Operations Management** 490
Production and Operations Management 491
Operations Management Systems 491
Operations Research for Planning and Controlling 497
Other Tools and Techniques 505
The Future of Operations Management 507
Summary 508
Key Ideas and Concepts for Review 509
For Discussion 509
Case 23-1 Lampert & Sons Company 510
Case 23-2 Manufacturing Requirements Planning (MRP) 511
For Further Information 512

Chapter 24   **Control of Overall Performance**   513
Budget Summaries and Reports   514
Profit and Loss Control   515
Control Through Return on Investment (ROI)   517
Summary   522
Key Ideas and Concepts for Review   522
For Discussion   522
Case 24-1 Western Petroleum Corporation   523
Case 24-2 Hospital Services, Inc.   525
For Further Information   526

Chapter 25   **Preventive Control: Ensuring Effective Managing**   527
Direct Control   528
The Principle of Preventive Control   530
Management Audit and Enterprise Self-Audit   532
Managerial Obsolescence   535
Developing Excellent Managers   536
Summary   539
Key Ideas and Concepts for Review   540
For Discussion   540
Case 25-1 McAllister–Strong Publishing Company   541
Case 25-2 Furniture Stores, Inc.   542
For Further Information   542
Summary of Major Principles of Controlling   544

Indexes   549
Name Index   551
Subject Index   555

Preface

You as students, teachers, managers, and those aspiring to managerial success are invited to apply the principles, concepts, and theories of managing discussed in this book to make you more effective as a person and as a managerial leader, or to prepare you for the challenging task of managing.

Essentials of Management is a concise version of the eighth edition of *Management,* whose prior editions and translations into fifteen languages have been well accepted around the world by readers and educators for more than thirty years. The success of both books can be attributed, in part, to the continuous efforts of the authors to update the contents by adding important new managerial knowledge. While we do not pretend that this version is as comprehensive as the larger *Management,* we do believe that it deals with the essential aspects of managing.

Who Will Benefit from This Book?

All persons who work in enterprises will benefit from learning about managing. This book is for students in universities and continuing education courses, participants in management development programs, and anyone interested in self-improvement. It is for managers at all levels and in all kinds of organizations, both business and nonbusiness.

The functions of managers, as managers, are essentially the same whether they are first-line supervisors or top executives of an enterprise. You will find, therefore, no basic distinction made among managers, executives, administrators, or supervisors. To be sure, there may be considerable variation in environment, scope of authority, and types of problems dealt with. But the fact remains that managers undertake the same basic functions to obtain results by establishing an environment for effective and efficient performance of individuals operating in groups.

Moreover, the essentials related to the task of managing apply to any kind of enterprise in any kind of culture. The purposes of different enterprises may vary, but all organized enterprises rely on effective group operation for efficient attainment of whatever goals they may have.

Organization of This Book

Managerial knowledge is classified in this book under the functions of planning, organizing, staffing, leading, and controlling. Then the components of each function are discussed.

Part I covers the basis of management, with chapters on management science, theory and practice, the various approaches to managing, and the external environment, including domestic and international situations. Parts II to VI focus on the managerial functions of planning, organizing, staffing, leading, and controlling. Each of these parts is introduced by a model that shows the systems nature of managing; the model, which is the framework for the organization of the book, is also shown on the inside of the front and back covers.

Revision Work in This Edition

In writing this and earlier editions of *Essentials of Management,* we have tried to respond to two major influences. One is the continuing help from comprehensive surveys of teachers and scholars. The other is the burgeoning volume of research, new ideas, and techniques, particularly those from the behavioral and physical sciences that are now being applied to management.

Although not all changes can be mentioned here, certain major revisions should be pointed out. All chapters have been updated, many have been considerably revised, one new chapter has been added ("Planning and Controlling Production and Operations Management"), while another one has been deleted. Specifically, much of the third-edition material discussed in the chapter "Making Planning Effective" has now been integrated with other chapters.

Chapter 2, "Patterns of Management Analysis," has been expanded to include McKinsey's 7-S framework, which has many similarities with the managerial functions discussed in this and previous editions of *Essentials.* Chapter 3, "The External Environment and International Management," has been completely rewritten and includes the important topics of ethics, Japanese management, and Theory Z.

Chapter 6, "Strategies and Policies," now adds coverage of a new strategic planning process model and the portfolio matrix. Although the important role of women in management and the equal employment opportunity provisions have been discussed throughout the book, special attention has been given to these topics in the chapters on staffing. Chapter 15, "Performance Appraisal and Career Strategy," now includes a model helpful for formulating career strategy.

Organizational conflicts and what to do about them are discussed in Chapter 16, "Manager and Organization Development."

The chapter on communication (Chapter 20) has been expanded to include discussions of the electronic media and communication in committees. Information technology and the application of computers are also discussed in Chapter 22, "Control Techniques." The new Chapter 23, "Planning and Controlling Production and Operations Management," has been added in response to the request of schools that do not have a separate course on production and operations management.

Other new or expanded features of this book are:

- A table summarizing the various approaches to management based on Harold Koontz's famous article, "The Management Theory Jungle"
- Extensive discussion of motivation theories
- New coverage of job design and quality of working life
- Frequent references to nonbusiness organizations
- Many figures, tables, and other illustrations
- Real-life examples
- Comprehensive name and subject indexes

Learning Aids

Each chapter begins with learning objectives, and marginal notes have been added in this edition as an aid to reviewing the chapter contents. The summary and the listing of key ideas and concepts also facilitate the learning of material in the chapter. There are two cases at the end of each chapter, for a total of 50 cases in the book. Finally, a list of significant books and articles, "For Further Information," is given at the end of each chapter for additional study or for preparing term papers.

The summary sections at the end of Parts II to VI, those dealing with the five managerial functions, are reviews of the major principles, or propositions, related to planning, organizing, staffing, leading, and controlling.

Instructional Aids

Because this and the comprehensive *Management* text have been successfully used in the classroom for over thirty years, several teaching aids are available.

- *Instructor's manual.* The comprehensive instructor's manual by Heinz Weihrich and Stephen Funk contains sample syllabi, notes on the discussion questions and cases in the textbook, and a wide selection of teaching aids, films, videotapes, management journals, and magazines.

- *Transparency masters.* A set of transparency masters is included in the instructor's manual.

- *Test bank.* Instructors can request a comprehensive test file to prepare examinations. The test bank is available in a booklet and on computer disks.

- *Book of readings.* The fifth edition of *Management: A Book of Readings,* by Harold Koontz, Cyril O'Donnell, and Heinz Weihrich (McGraw-Hill Book Company), has 80 readings organized like the text.

Acknowledgments

With very deep regret we note that Dr. Harold Koontz passed away in 1984. He will be sorely missed by those who knew him. His inspiration and guidance popularized the classification of management knowledge according to the managerial functions, a framework now used by most authors of major management texts. At the memorial session at the Academy of Management meeting in 1984, Professor Ronald Greenwood stated that Howdy Koontz was many years ahead of his time. He will never be forgotten for his contributions to management and by those who read his many books, especially his book with Cyril O'Donnell which was originally published with the title *Principles of Management* in 1955 and has been continuously updated in its eight editions. Dr. O'Donnell, a highly respected colleague, passed away in 1976. *Essentials of Management* still carries his name as a token of appreciation for his contributions to earlier editions.

As might be expected in a book of this kind, we are indebted to so many persons that a complete acknowledgment would be encyclopedic. Some managers and scholars are acknowledged through references in the text. Many managers with whom we have served in business, government, education, and other enterprises have contributed by word and by precept. Thousands of managers at all levels in all kinds of enterprises have honored us over the years by allowing us to test our ideas in executive training classes and lectures. To the executives of the various companies with whom we have been privileged to work as directors or consultants, we are grateful for the opportunity to gain the clinical practice of managing.

Many able teachers and scholars have freely given us their time and the benefit of their teaching experience. We are especially indebted to those who reviewed this book and who made many suggestions. They include: Richard D. Babcock, University of San Francisco; Keith Davis, Arizona State University; Ronald G. Greenwood, General Motors Institute; Donald Hucker, Cypress College; Gary D. Law, Cuyahoga Community College; Kathryn Lewis, California State University, Chico; Bernard L. Martin, University of San Francisco; Andrew

J. Papageorge, California State College; Eugene Seyna, Eastman Kodak Company; Tom Shaughnessy, Illinois Central; Wm. Bruce Storm, University of Southern California; and Philip A. Weatherford, Embry-Riddle Aeronautical.

Finally, my wife Ursula has helped greatly with her critique and her cooperative spirit.

Heinz Weihrich

ESSENTIALS OF MANAGEMENT

The Basis of Management Theory and Science

1

Management: Science, Theory, and Practice

CHAPTER OBJECTIVES After reading this chapter, you should understand:

1 The purpose of this book
2 The aim of all managers
3 Whether managing is a science or an art
4 The elements of science and the role of management theory
5 The evolution of management thought
6 The nature of the situational, or contingency, approach to managing
7 The systems approach to managing

Definition of managing

One of the most important human activities is **managing,** for all managers at all levels and in all kinds of enterprises have the basic task of designing and maintaining an environment in which individuals, working together in groups, can accomplish selected missions and objectives. In other words, managers are charged with the responsibility of taking actions that will make it possible for individuals to make their best contributions to group objectives. Although we emphasize managers' tasks in designing an internal environment for performance, it must never be overlooked that managers must operate in the external environment of an enterprise as well as in the internal environment of the various departments within an enterprise. Clearly, managers cannot perform their tasks well unless they have an understanding of, and are responsive to, the many elements of the

Internal and external environment

external environment—economic, technological, social, political, and ethical factors that affect their areas of operations.

The way managers perform their tasks and the available basic knowledge that underlies their performance are the focus of this book. As many scholars and managers in all kinds of organizations have found, we can most easily study management by breaking it down into a number of primary functions and then organizing basic knowledge—concepts, theory, principles, and techniques—around these functions.

Functions of managers

We have used the five **functions of managers**—planning, organizing, staffing, leading, and controlling—as a first step in studying management. Although others may prefer a slightly different classification, this one is comprehensive (we believe that all significant management knowledge can be placed within it); it is divisible into enough parts to permit logical analysis; and it is practical in the sense that it portrays functions as managers themselves see them. Moreover, this classification sharply distinguishes managerial tasks from nonmanagerial ones, such as finance, production, and marketing (which are enterprise functions), and allows us to concentrate on what managers do as managers.

Why Management?

Cause of business failures

Analyses of business failures made over many years have shown that a high percentage of these failures have been the fault of unqualified or inexperienced management. The prominent investor magazine, *Forbes*, which has studied American businesses for a number of years, has found that companies succeed almost invariably to the extent that they are well managed. The Bank of America has said in its publication, *Small Business Reporter*, "In the final analysis more than 90 percent of business failures are due to managerial incompetence and inexperience." The importance of management is nowhere better dramatized than in many developing countries. Review by economic development specialists has shown that providing money or technology does not ensure development. The limiting factor in many cases has been managerial know-how.

While our culture is characterized by revolutionary advances in the physical and biological sciences, the social sciences have lagged far behind. Yet, unless we can learn to harness human resources and coordinate the activities of people, inefficiency and waste in applying technical discoveries will continue. We have only to look at the incredible waste of human and material resources to realize that the social sciences are far from doing their job of guiding social policy and action.

Critics of management

Not all groups believe that they need managing. In fact, certain critics of modern management feel that people would work together better and with more personal satisfaction if there were no managers. They refer to the ideal group operation as a "team effort." They apparently do not realize that in the most elementary form of team play, individuals have clear group goals as well as personal ones, are assigned to positions, follow play patterns, allow someone to call the plays, and follow certain rules and guidelines. Indeed, every effective group effort designed to attain group goals at the least cost of time, money, material, and discomfort adopts the basic processes, principles, and techniques of management.

Managing in all organizations at all levels

Managing is essential in all organized cooperation, as well as at all levels of organization in an enterprise.[1] It is the function not only of the corporation president and the army general but also of the shop supervisor and the company commander. In working with various enterprises, we have often heard it said that the "trouble" with the enterprise is the "management." Even vice-presidents of a company have made this observation. While weaknesses and difficulties may appear at any level of management, effective and perceptive management demands that all those responsible for the work of others, at all levels and in any type of enterprise, regard themselves as managers. It is in this sense that we use the term "management" in this book.

No basic distinction between managers

This book draws no basic distinction among managers, executives, administrators, and supervisors. A given situation may be considerably different at various levels in an organization or enterprise, the scope of authority may vary, the types of problems dealt with may differ widely, and a person in a managerial role may also be a salesperson, an engineer, or a financier; but the fact remains that, as managers, all those who obtain results by establishing an environment for effective group efforts perform the same functions.

Managerial and nonmanagerial tasks

Even so, those in a managerial role seldom devote all their time and talents to managing, and the organization roles which individuals fill almost invariably involve nonmanagerial duties. We have only to look at the duties associated with perhaps the most complex managerial position in our society—that of the President of the United States—to realize that much of the chief executive's work is nonmanagerial. Even in business corporations, company presidents find themselves doing a considerable amount of nonmanagerial work. And, as one goes down the organization ladder, the number of nonmanagerial duties tends to increase. Nevertheless, this fact of life should not detract in any way from the significance of managing.

The Aim of All Managers

The aim: surplus

Nonbusiness executives sometimes say that the aim of business managers is simple—to make a profit. But *profit* is really only a measure of a surplus of sales dollars over expense dollars. In a very real sense, in all kinds of organizations, whether business or nonbusiness, the logical and publicly desirable aim of all managers should be a surplus—managers must establish an environment in which people can accomplish group goals with the least amount of time, money, materials, and personal dissatisfaction, or where they can achieve as much as possible of a desired goal with available resources. In a nonbusiness enterprise such as a police department, as well as in units of a business (such as an accounting department) that

---

[1]The word "enterprise" is used in this book to refer to businesses, government agencies, hospitals, universities, and other organizations, since almost everything said here refers to nonbusiness as well as business organizations.

are not responsible for total business profits, managers still have goals and should strive to accomplish them with the minimum of resources or to accomplish as much as possible with available resources.

Deceleration of U.S. productivity growth

Another way to view the aim of all managers is to say that they must be productive. After World War II the United States was the world leader in productivity. But in the late 1960s the deceleration of productivity growth began. Today the urgent need for productivity improvement is recognized by government, private industry, and universities. Often we look to Japan to find answers to our productivity problem and indeed we will do so in Chapter 3 of this book, but what we often overlook is the importance of performing effectively the basic managerial and nonmanagerial activities. In their search for excellent companies, Thomas J. Peters and Robert H. Waterman identified the following eight attributes of successful firms. These firms:

Successful companies

- Were oriented toward action

- Learned about the needs of their customers

- Promoted managerial autonomy and entrepreneurship

- Achieved productivity by paying close attention to the needs of their people

- Were driven by a company philosophy often based on the values of their leaders

- Focused on the business they knew best

- Had a simple organization structure with a lean staff

- Were centralized as well as decentralized, depending on appropriateness[2]

Successful companies create a surplus and they are productive. Although there is no agreement on the true meaning of productivity, we will define it as:

Definition of productivity

The output-input ratio within a time period with due consideration for quality.

$$\text{Productivity} = \frac{\text{outputs}}{\text{inputs}} \text{ (within a time period, quality considered)}$$

Effectiveness

Efficiency

Productivity, then, implies effectiveness and efficiency in individual and organizational performance. **Effectiveness** is the achievement of objectives. **Efficiency** is the achievement of the ends with the least amount of resources. To know whether they are productive, managers must know their goals and those of the organization, a topic that will be discussed in Chapter 5.

The aim of managers is fundamentally the same in business and nonbusiness enterprises. It is also the same at every level: that of the corporation president,

[2]T. J. Peters and R. B. Waterman, Jr., *In Search of Excellence* (New York: Harper & Row, Publishers, 1982), chap. 1. For a critical evaluation of the book see D. T. Carroll, "A Disappointing Search of Excellence," *Harvard Business Review*, vol. 61. no. 3 (November–December 1983), pp. 78–88.

the chief of police, the hospital department head, the business or government supervisor, the scout leader, the bishop, the baseball manager, and the university dean or president. All, as managers, have the same aim. The purposes of their operations may differ, and these purposes may be more difficult to define and accomplish in one situation than in another, but the basic managerial aim remains the same.

Managing: Science or Art?

Although this question is often raised, a moment's reflection will show that it is really meaningless. Managing, like all other practices (whether of medicine, music composition, engineering, accountancy, or even baseball), is an art. It is know-how. It is doing things in the light of the realities of a situation. Yet managers can work better by using the organized knowledge about management, and it is this knowledge, whether crude or advanced, whether exact or inexact, that, to the extent it is well organized, clear, and pertinent, comprises a science. Thus, managing as practice is an art; the organized knowledge underlying the practice may be referred to as a science. In this context science and art are not mutually exclusive but are complementary.

Managing as
art and science

As science improves so should art, as has happened in the physical and biological sciences. To be sure, the science underlying managing is fairly crude and inexact. This is true because the many variables with which managers deal are extremely complex, and partially because there has been relatively little research in the field of management. But such management knowledge as is available can certainly improve managerial practice. Physicians without the advantage of science would be little more than witch doctors. Executives who attempt to manage without such management science must trust to luck, intuition, or what they did in the past.

In managing, as in any other field, unless practitioners are to learn by trial and error (and it has been said that managers' errors are their subordinates' trials), there is no other place they can turn for meaningful guidance than the accumulated knowledge underlying their practice. As we shall soon see, this does not mean that a manager should manage "by the book." In their best-selling book, *In Search of Excellence*, Peters and Waterman identified eight attributes of successful companies, many of them examples of the art of managing. For example, the preference of excellent companies for action rather than for endless analyses implies the importance of art. One company that became less than excellent is Revlon, which overemphasized numbers rather than paying sufficient attention to the customer.[3] Another attribute of excellent companies is their emphasis on improving productivity by paying close attention to their people's needs; this also suggests that art is critical to managerial and organizational success. The editors of *Business Week* go even further, stating that "good management is a human art and not science."[4]

---

[3]"Who's Excellent Now?" *Business Week*, Nov. 5, 1984, pp. 76–88.
[4]Ibid., p. 144.

We maintain, however, that effective managing is an art that applies underlying science.

The Elements of Science

Science is organized knowledge. The essential feature of any science is the application of the scientific method to the development of knowledge. Thus, we speak of a science as having clear concepts, theory, and other accumulated knowledge developed from hypotheses (assumptions that something is true), experimentation, and analysis.

The Scientific Approach

Scientific methods

Principles

The scientific approach first requires clear **concepts**—words and terms that are exact, relevant to the things being analyzed, and informative to the scientist and practitioner alike. From this base, the **scientific method** involves determining facts through observation. After classifying and analyzing these facts, scientists look for causal relationships. When these generalizations or hypotheses are tested for accuracy and appear to be true, that is, to reflect or explain reality, and therefore to have value in predicting what will happen in similar circumstances, they are called **principles.** This designation does not always imply that they are unquestionably or invariably true, but that they are believed to be valid enough to be used for prediction.

Theory is a systematic grouping of interdependent concepts and principles which give a framework to, or tie together, a significant area of knowledge. Scattered data, such as what we may find on a blackboard after a group of engineers has been discussing a problem, are not information unless the observer has knowledge of the theory which will explain relationships. Theory is, as Homans has said, "in its lowest form a classification, a set of pigeon holes, a filing cabinet in which fact can accumulate. Nothing is more lost than a loose fact."[5]

The Role of Management Theory

Principles: descriptive or predictive

In the field of management, then, the role of theory is to provide a means of classifying significant and pertinent management knowledge. In the area of designing an effective organization structure, for example, there are a number of principles that are interrelated and that have a predictive value for managers. Some principles give guidelines for delegating authority; these include the principle of delegating by results expected, the principle of equality of authority and responsibility, and the principle of unity of command. Likewise, decision making, while at the heart of planning, is meaningless unless related to desired objectives, done in the light of the expected future setting in which a decision will be implemented, and made with proper analysis of the most promising alternatives.

Principles in management, like those in the physical sciences, are **descriptive** or **predictive,** and not prescriptive. This is, they describe how one variable relates to another—what will happen when these variables interact. They do not prescribe

[5]G. C. Homans, *The Human Group* (New York: Harcourt, Brace & World, Inc., 1958), p. 5.

Parkinson's Law

what we *should* do. For example, in physics, if gravity is the only force acting on a falling body, the body will fall at an increasing speed; this principle does not tell us whether anyone *should* jump off the roof of a high building. Or take the example of Parkinson's Law: Work tends to expand to fill the time available. Even if Parkinson's somewhat frivolous principle is correct (as it probably is), it does not mean that a manager *should* lengthen the time available for people to do a job. To take another example, in management, the principle of unity of command states that the more often an individual reports to a single superior, the more that individual is likely to feel a sense of loyalty and obligation and the less likely it is that there will be confusion about instructions. The principle merely predicts. It in no sense implies that individuals should *never* report to more than one person. Rather, it implies that if they do so, their managers must be aware of the possible dangers and should take these risks into account in balancing the advantages and disadvantages of multiple command.

Like engineers who apply physical principles to the design of an instrument, managers who apply theory to managing must usually blend principles with realities. An engineer is often faced with the necessity of combining considerations of weight, size, conductivity, and other factors in designing an instrument. Likewise, a manager may find that the advantages of giving a controller authority to prescribe accounting procedures throughout an organization outweigh the possible costs of multiple authority. But if they know theory, these managers will know that such costs as conflicting instructions and confusion may exist, and they will take steps (such as making the controller's special authority crystal clear to everyone involved) to minimize disadvantages.

Management Techniques

Techniques are essentially ways of doing things, methods of accomplishing a given result. In all fields of practice they are important. They certainly are in managing, even though few really important managerial techniques have been invented. Among them are budgeting, cost accounting, network planning and control techniques like the Program Evaluation and Review Technique (PERT) or the Critical Path Method (CPM), rate-of-return-on-investment control, various devices of organizational development, and managing by objectives, all of which will be discussed in later chapters. Techniques normally reflect theory and are a means of helping managers undertake activities most effectively.

The Evolution of Management Thought

Although modern operational-management theory dates primarily from the early twentieth century with the works of Frederick Taylor and Henri Fayol, as shown in Table 1-1, there was serious thinking and theorizing about managing many years before. Indeed, the development of thought on management dates back to the days when people working together in groups first attempted to accomplish goals.

TABLE 1-1 The Emergence of Management Thought

Name and approximate year of major contribution	Major contribution to management
Scientific management	
Frederick W. Taylor *Shop Management* (1903) *Principles of Scientific Management* (1911) Testimony before the Special House Committee (1912)	Acknowledged as "the father of scientific management." His primary concern was to increase productivity through greater efficiency in production and increased pay for workers through the application of the scientific method. His principles emphasized using science, creating group harmony and cooperation, achieving maximum output, and developing workers.
Modern operational-management theory	
Henry Fayol *Administration Industrielle et Generale* (1916)	Referred to as "the father of modern management theory." Divided industrial activities into six groups: technical, commercial, financial, security, accounting, managerial. Recognized the need for teaching management. Developed fourteen principles of management such as authority and responsibility, unity of command, scalar chain, and esprit de corps.
Behavioral sciences	
Elton Mayo and F. J. Roethlisberger (1933)	Conducted famous studies at the Hawthorne plant of the Western Electric Company. Studied influence of social attitudes and relationships of work groups on performance.

Frederick Taylor and Scientific Management[6]

Taylor is generally acknowledged as "the father of scientific management." Probably no other person has had a greater impact on the development of management. His principal concern throughout most of his life was that of increasing efficiency in production, not only to lower costs and raise profits, but also to make possible increased pay for workers through their higher productivity.

The fundamental principles that Taylor saw underlying the scientific approach to managing may be summarized as follows:

1 Replacing rules of thumb with science (organized knowledge)

2 Obtaining harmony in group action, rather than discord

3 Achieving cooperation of human beings, rather than chaotic individualism

4 Working for maximum output, rather than restricted output

5 Developing all workers to the fullest extent possible for their own and their company's highest prosperity

---

[6]See for example, Frederick Taylor, *Scientific Management* (New York: Harper & Brothers, 1947).

You will note that these basic precepts by Taylor are not far from the fundamental beliefs of the modern manager.

Henri Fayol: Father of Modern Operational-Management Theory[7]

Perhaps the real father of modern management theory is the French industrialist Henri Fayol. He recognized a widespread need for principles and management teaching. Consequently, he identified fourteen such principles, noting that they are flexible, not absolute, and must be usable regardless of changing conditions. Let us look at some of these principles.

1 **Authority and responsibility.** Fayol suggests that authority and responsibility are related, with the latter the corollary of the former and arising from it. He sees authority as a combination of official—deriving from the manager's position—and personal factors that are "compounded of intelligence, experience, moral worth, past experience, etc."

2 **Unity of command.** This means that employees should receive orders from one superior only.

3 **Scalar chain.** Fayol thinks of this as a "chain of superiors" from the highest to the lowest ranks, which, while not to be departed from needlessly, should be short-circuited when to follow it scrupulously would be detrimental.

4 **Esprit de corps.** This is the principle that "in union there is strength," as well as an extension of the principle of unity of command, emphasizing the need for teamwork and the importance of communication in obtaining it.

Fayol regarded the elements of management as the functions of planning, organizing, commanding, coordinating, and controlling. These will be discussed later in this book.

Elton Mayo and F. J. Roethlisberger and the Hawthorne Studies[8]

Mayo and Roethlisberger undertook the famous experiments at the Hawthorne plant of the Western Electric Company between 1927 and 1932. Earlier, the National Research Council made a study in collaboration with Western Electric to determine the effect of illumination and other conditions upon workers and their productivity. Finding that, when illumination was either increased or decreased for a test group, productivity improved, the researchers were about to declare the whole experiment a failure until Elton Mayo of Harvard saw in it something unusual and, with Roethlisberger and others, continued the research.

What Mayo and his colleagues found, based partly on the earlier thinking of Pareto, was to have a dramatic effect on management thought. Changing illumination for the test group, modifying rest periods, shortening workdays, and varying incentive pay systems did not seem to explain changes in productivity. Mayo and his researchers then came to the conclusion that other factors were responsible.

---

[7]H. Fayol, *General and Industrial Administration* (London, Sir Isaac Pitman & Sons, Ltd., 1949).
[8]For a full description of these experiments see E. Mayo, *The Human Problems of an Industrial Civilization* (New York: The Macmillan Company, 1933); and F. J. Roethlisberger and W. J. Dickson, *Management and the Worker* (Cambridge, Mass. Harvard University Press, 1939).

They found them in the social attitudes and relationships of work groups. Changing illumination—up and down—resulted in increased productivity because the test group began to be noticed by management and people felt important. It was found that, in general, improvement in productivity was due to such social factors as morale, satisfactory interrelationships among members of a work group (a "sense of belonging") and effective management—a kind practiced by managers who would understand human behavior, especially group behavior. Such managers would serve through such interpersonal skills as motivating, counseling, leading, and communicating. This phenomenon, arising basically from people being "noticed," has been known as the "Hawthorne effect."

The Situational, or Contingency, Approach to Managing

By its very nature, managerial practice requires that managers take into account the realities of a situation when they apply theory, principles, or techniques. Management science and theory does not advocate the one best way to do things in every situation, as some writers seem to believe, any more than the science of astrophysics or mechanics tells an engineer how to design a single best instrument for all kinds of applications. How management theory and science is applied in practice naturally depends on the situation.

Contingency and situational management

Contingency management is akin to **situational management** and the terms are often used synonymously. But whether we regard a managerial approach as situational or contingency, we must recognize that the application of science and theory to practice must necessarily take into account a given set of circumstances. This means that managers must alter their practices as factors change in the environment. We can say that there is science and there is art, and there is knowledge and there is practice. One does not need much experience to understand that a corner grocery store could scarcely be organized in the same way as General Motors; or that the technological realities of petroleum exploration, production, and refining make independently organized product divisions for gasoline, lubricating oils, or asphalt impracticable.

Another way of stating this is to say that studying management will not give you the specific answers as to what should be done in every kind of managerial situation. Knowing management theory, principles, and techniques, however, should help you become a better manager. This is true in other fields also. Our best design engineers are those who have considerable knowledge of the underlying sciences. Our best financial analysts are those who understand, among other things, the theory and science of accountancy. This does not mean, however, that an engineer well trained in underlying sciences will always be a good instrument designer, or that any person who knows the theory and science of accountancy will be an astute financial analyst. More than knowledge is needed. Practitioners also must know how to apply their knowledge in the areas in which they operate.

It never has been the task of theory and science to prescribe what *should* be done. The role of theory and science is to search for fundamental relationships, for basic techniques, and for organization of available knowledge—all, it is hoped, based on clear concepts. How these are applied in practice depends on the situation. We would not expect physicians to give all patients penicillin regardless of the ailment. Nor would we expect engineers, although using basic principles of physics and metallurgy, to design automobiles the way they would design airplanes, or chemists to use the same formulas for mixing detergents that they would use for compounding drugs. But we would expect all these practitioners to understand and utilize in their work the science and theory underlying their practice.

Definition of management

In the same way, effective management is always contingency, or situational, management. The very concept of **management** used in this book—the design of an environment in which people working together in groups can accomplish objectives—implies this. Used in this sense, design is the application of knowledge to a practical problem for the purpose of determining the best possible results for that situation. This is what managing and management are all about—the application of knowledge to realities in order to attain desired results.

Seeing the Organization as a System

Definition of a system

Management theory and practice require, as a matter of common sense, a systems approach. A **system** is essentially a set or assemblage of interconnected, interdependent things that form a complex whole. These things may be physical, like the parts of an automobile engine; or they may be biological, like the components of the human body; or they may be theoretical, like a well-integrated assemblage of concepts, principles, and techniques related to managing.

Although systems are assigned boundaries so that we can analyze them, there are no systems (except possibly the universe) which are "closed," that is, completely independent of others. An automobile engine can be looked on as a system, but it is really a subsystem of an automobile, which in turn is a subsystem—when driven on a highway—of driver- and traffic-control systems, and so on.

In the same way, although we arbitrarily limit management science and theory to the establishment of knowledge underlying the managerial job, they, as well as what managers do, must be related to and interact with many environmental variables. Thus, when managers plan, they have no choice but to take into account such external variables as markets, technology, social forces, and laws and regulations. When managers design an organizational system to help people to perform in an enterprise, they cannot help but be influenced by the pattern of behavior

Organizations as open systems

people bring to their jobs from a variety of family, school, church, and other influences. In short, organizations are "open" systems.

The concept of the system plays an important part in management theory and practice. We will discuss organization systems, planning systems, control systems, and many others. And within these we can find subsystems, such as systems of delegation, budgeting, and feedback of information for control.

The Systems Approach to Operational Management

An organized enterprise does not, of course, exist in a vacuum. Rather, it is dependent on its external environment; it is a part of larger systems such as the industry to which it belongs, the economic system, and society. Thus the enter-

FIGURE 1-1

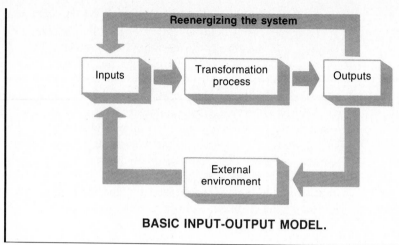

BASIC INPUT-OUTPUT MODEL.

prise receives inputs, transforms them, and exports the outputs to the environment, as shown by the very basic model in Figure 1-1. However, this simple model needs to be expanded and developed into a model of operational management that indicates how the various inputs are transformed through the managerial functions of planning, organizing, staffing, leading, and controlling. The nature of operational-management theory is discussed and the managerial functions are defined in Chapter 2, pages 33 to 38. Clearly, any business or other organization must be described by an open-system model that includes interactions between the enterprise and its external environment.

Inputs and Claimants

Conflicting claims

The inputs from the external environment (see Figure 1-2) may include people, capital, and managerial skills, as well as technical knowledge and skills. In addition, various groups of people make demands on the enterprise. Unfortunately, many of the goals of these claimants are incongruent, and it is the manager's job to reconcile these divergent needs and goals. For example, employees want higher pay, more benefits, and job security. On the other hand, consumers demand safe and reliable products at a reasonable price. Suppliers want assurance that their products will be bought. Stockholders want not only a high return on their investment but also security for their money. Federal, state, and local governments depend on taxes paid by the enterprise, but they also expect the enterprise to comply with their laws. Similarly, the community demands that enterprises be "good citizens," providing the maximum number of jobs with a minimum of pollution. Other claimants to the enterprise may include financial institutions and labor unions; even competitors have a legitimate claim for fair play. It is clear that many of these claims are incongruent, and it is management's job to integrate the legitimate objectives of the claimants.

The Managerial Transformation Process

It is the task of managers to transform the inputs in an effective and efficient manner into outputs. Of course, the transformation process can be viewed from different perspectives. Thus, one can focus on such diverse enterprise functions

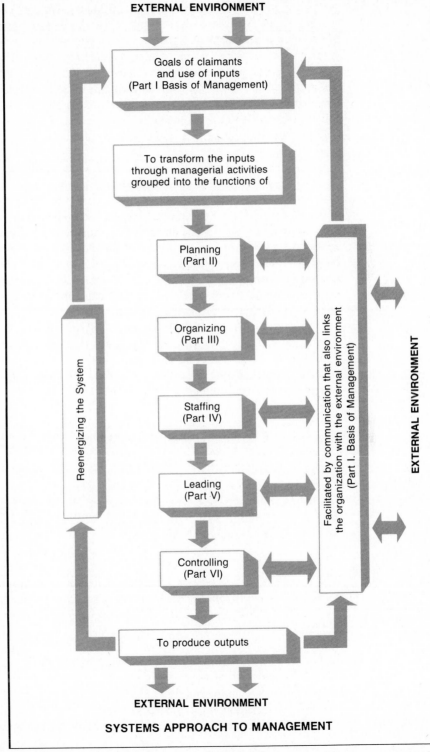

SYSTEMS APPROACH TO MANAGEMENT

as finance, production, personnel, and marketing. Writers on management, as you will see in Chapter 2, look on the transformation process in terms of their particular approaches to management. Specifically, as you will see, writers belonging to the human behavior school focus on interpersonal relationships; social systems theorists analyze the transformation by focusing on social interactions; and those advocating decision theory see the transformation as sets of decisions. We will suggest in Chapter 2 that the most comprehensive and useful approach to discussing the job of managers is to use the managerial functions of planning, organizing, staffing, leading, and controlling as a framework (see Figure 1-2).

The Communication System

Communication is essential to all phases of the managerial process: it integrates the managerial functions and it links the enterprise with its environment. For example, the objectives set in planning are communicated so that the appropriate organization structure can be devised. Communication is essential in the selection, appraisal, and training of managers to fill the roles in this structure. Similarly, effective leadership and the creation of an environment conducive to motivation depend on communication. Moreover, it is through communication that one determines whether events and performance conform to plans. Thus, it is communication which makes managing possible.

The second function of the communication system is to link the enterprise with its external environment, where many of the claimants are. For example, one should never forget that the customer, who is the reason for the existence of virtually all businesses, is outside a company. It is through the communication system that the needs of customers are identified; this knowledge enables the firm to provide products and services at a profit. Similarly, it is through an effective communication system that the organization becomes aware of competition and other potential threats and constraining factors.

External Variables

Effective managers will constantly scan the external environment. While it is true that managers may have little or no power to change the external environment, they have no alternative but to respond to it. The forces acting in the external environment are discussed in Chapter 3.

Outputs

It is the task of managers to secure and utilize inputs to the enterprise, transforming them through the managerial functions of planning, organizing, staffing, leading, and controlling—with due consideration for external variables—to produce outputs.

Although the kinds of outputs will vary with the enterprise, they usually include at least one or more of the following: products, services, profits, satisfaction, and integration of the goals of various claimants to the enterprise. Most of these require no elaboration, and only the last two will be discussed.

The organization must indeed provide many "satisfactions" if it hopes to retain and elicit contributions from its members. It must contribute to the satisfaction not only of basic material needs (for example, earning money to buy food and shelter, having job security) but also of needs for affiliation, acceptance, esteem, and perhaps even self-actualization.

Another output is goal integration. As noted above, the different claimants to the enterprise have very divergent—and often directly opposing—objectives. It is the task of managers to resolve conflicts and integrate these aims. This is not easy, as one former Volkswagen executive discovered. Economics dictated the construction of a Volkswagen assembly plant in the United States. However, this plan was opposed by an important claimant, German labor, because of fear of the elimination of some jobs. The conflict was so deep that it contributed to executive resignation and a change in leadership. After a costly delay, the Volkswagen assembly plant was eventually built in the United States. This example indicates that the integration of the goals of the various claimants to the enterprise is an important task of any manager.

Reengergizing the System

Finally, we should notice that in the systems model of operational management, some of the outputs become inputs again. Thus, the satisfaction of employees becomes an important human input. Similarly, profits, the surplus of income over costs, are reinvested in cash and capital goods, such as machinery and equipment, buildings, and inventory.

Summary

Management is an essential activity; it ensures the coordination of individual efforts to achieve group goals. Knowledge is organized and grouped into the managerial functions of planning, organizing, staffing, leading, and controlling. The aim of all managers is to establish an environment in which people can achieve group goals with the least amount of time, money, material, and personal dissatisfaction. Managers must also aim at productivity, which is outputs divided by inputs within a time period with consideration given to quality. Productivity implies effectiveness and efficiency. Effectiveness is the achievement of ends; efficiency is the achievement of the ends with the least amount of resources.

Managing as practice is art; organized knowledge about management is science. In applying theory to management, managers always deal with real situations. Many have contributed to management thought, but the contributions of Frederick Taylor, Henri Fayol, and Mayo and Roethlisberger were especially noted in this chapter. This is sometimes called contingency, or situational, management.

The organization is an open system that operates within and interacts with the environment. The systems model of operational management includes inputs from the external environment and from claimants, the managerial transformation process, the communication system, external variables, outputs, and a way to reenergize the system.

Key Ideas and Concepts for Review

Managing	Theory
Managerial functions	Principles: descriptive, predictive,
Aim of all managers	not prescriptive
Attributes of successful companies	Parkinson's Law
Productivity	Frederick Taylor
Effectiveness	Henri Fayol
Efficiency	Elton Mayo and F. J. Roethlisberger
Managing—science or art?	Contingency, or situational, management
Scientific method	System
Concepts	Closed and open systems
Principles	Systems model of operational management

For Discussion

1 Is managing a science or an art? Could the same explanation apply to engineering or accounting?

2 In what fundamental way are the basic goals of all managers at all levels and in all kinds of enterprises the same?

3 Look up the terms "science," "theory," and "principle," in a dictionary and determine how they are used. Compare these definitions with the usage of these terms as applied to management in this book. What advantages are there in attempting to identify science, theory, and principles in a book on management?

4 Why do management analysis and practice require a systems approach? Do managers operate in an open or a closed system? Explain.

5 What is the contingency, or situational, approach to management? Could a manager operate in any other way?

CASE 1-1

HART ELECTRONICS

Hart Electronics, Incorporated, was built up to design and manufacture special instruments for the Apollo moon-landing program. Its founders were two eminent physicians, Dr. Smith Lane and Dr. Raymond Morey. Adequately financed by Robert Hart, well-known multimillionaire, the two founders soon attracted a large group of scientists who developed acceleration instruments and test equipment useful in space programs and in airborne missile systems. Within a few years, they found themselves the designers and producers of entire space control systems. The company prospered and within 10 years reached $100 million in annual sales with some 2000 employees.

The company was neither well-organized nor well-managed during its rapid growth, but, because of its new and imaginative products, it did succeed in making reasonable profits. However, as it grew, competition entered the field and Mr. Hart became worried about the company's ability to market and produce efficiently. On discussing this problem with his consultant, Mr. Hart was told that the top scientists in the company's managerial positions must learn to become more effective managers. At this point, Mr. Hart asked the consultant to start a management development program. With the approval of the company's top officers, who felt compelled to follow the suggestions of their major owner, a management development committee was established with the consultant as chairperson. The committee's task was to design and implement a development program for the company. The consultant was given a committee comprising the company's financial vice-president, the director of personnel, and two top scientific leaders who headed major divisions of the company.

At the first meeting of the committee, the two top scientists were clearly unsympathetic toward the program, feeling, with some justification, that managers of a company that had experienced such rapid and successful growth could scarcely need any management training. One of them, obviously trying to stop the whole program, said at the start of the meeting: "How can we even be talking about instituting a management development program? No one has even been able to tell me what management is. I have heard it said that it is getting things done through people. If that is all it is, I have been doing this in my work for years. How can we be taking our time to develop a program for something as simple as this?"

1 Does the scientist have an accurate idea of what managing is?

2 Exactly how would you respond to him and convince him of the desirability of having a management development program?

CASE 1-2
THE PARAGON RADAR CORPORATION

The Paragon Radar Corporation was organized and managed by three engineers who had formerly worked for the McDonnell Aircraft Company. They were instrumental in developing a radar capable of handling transmissions over distances far greater than those formerly permitted by the curvature of the earth. The Paragon people were adequately financed and decided upon a market policy of dealing only with government agencies, especially the Air Force, Navy, Army, and National Aeronautics and Space Administration (NASA). The budgets of these agencies grew steadily as the years passed, and business was very good.

The Paragon people did not have a marketing department in the usual sense. The heads of each department were expected to develop their own business. Consequently, the engineers would keep in close touch with their counterparts in the several agencies, help them identify their needs, help them "sell" these needs to relevant policymaking executives and contracting officers, and would write the proposals as soon as the requests came through.

Then the federal government drastically cut back the budget for the Department of Defense and NASA. Business was scarce and hard to get. The Paragon people bid more and more contracts with less and less success. This state of affairs became the subject of a staff meeting at the corporate level.

"Ladies and gentlemen," said the president, "you all know the causes for the decline in our business. The corporation is gradually approaching a precarious posture. We do have excellent technical abilities, and there is still some $100 billion being spent on national defense; so our potential is still there. I have pointed out to the department heads that you must get new business if you are to remain part of the organization. It seems that my words have fallen on deaf ears. But I assure you that I am really serious. The time has come when we must either get well or be acquired by another firm."

James Simpson, one of the department heads, spoke up, saying, "You may think that there is something lacking in my loyalty, but I really believe that we are not organized in an effective way to do what we must do. In the good years we did very well. Business was good, our bids were highly successful, indeed so much so that department managers would turn down business if the technical content did not interest them. Now that we need business we don't have the contacts. The way we have approached the problem, no one is responsible for getting business: we all are, but no one can say how much. Authority is widely diffused. We all share the blame and yet no one accepts it."

The members of the staff were shocked. The president had the good sense to remain silent for a time while each examined his or her position. One member eventually reached for his alibis. "I don't view the matter in that light. Here we have been successful for going on two decades, we get

business like other aerospace companies do, and you can't expect a department head to accept and work on a contract that he is not interested in. You know, the defense business is not like selling soap."

"I know," said Simpson. "I used to believe that too. Recently I have been looking at the management literature to see if there is some principle we have overlooked. These chaps seem to be saying that the best results occur when a man has a definite objective to achieve, when he is personally held responsible for achieving it, when he has the authority to make the decisions that must be made in order to achieve it. We operate this way in everything except marketing. Why is this an exception?"

The meeting adjourned at this point. The president said he would reexamine the matter and try to bring a proposal to the next meeting. Two weeks later, after many hours of study and consultation, he opened the regular staff meeting with an announcement.

"Ladies and gentlemen," he said, "I think it is time we stop fighting management principles; let's use them for our own benefit. I think we should have a 'business-getting' activity centralized in the hands of one person and reporting to me. We might call it 'advanced program development.' I visualize this activity comprising three functions. One would be staffed by engineers with marketing ability, another with engineers who will write the proposals, and another with market research capability. The head of this whole group would be responsible for bringing in new business and would have the necessary decision-making authority. The head would be expected to run a tight ship. I do not want an expanding bureaucracy. We will borrow technical people as needed from the operating departments. In order that the technical people in the new department will not grow stale and useless, I feel that whoever is head of a proposal committee should be made program manager when and if the contract is secured. Thus, I can see a great deal of lateral movement among the engineers in all our activities."

The proposal was so revolutionary that no

one could be expected to take a position on its feasibility. The staff was dismissed with the injunction to study it and bring back suggestions that would make it more viable.

1   Do you believe that the president's proposal for an "advanced program development" department would work at Paragon? What do you see to be the strengths and weaknesses of this proposal?

2   Can you suggest anything else that could be done to solve Paragon's problem?

For Further Information

Barnard, C. I. *The Functions of the Executive* (Cambridge, Mass.: Harvard University Press, 1938).

Buehler, V. M., and Y. K. Shetty (eds.). *Productivity Improvement* (New York: AMACOM, 1981).

Donnelly, J. H., Jr., G. L. Gibson, and J. M. Ivancevich (eds.). *Perspectives on Management*, 5th ed. (Plano, Tex.: Business Publications, Inc., 1984).

Dublin, R. "Management: Meanings, Methods, and Moxie," *Academy of Management Review*, vol. 7, no. 3 (July 1982), pp. 372–379.

Hurst, D. K. "Of Boxes, Bubbles, and Effective Management," *Harvard Business Review*, vol. 60, no. 6 (November–December 1982), pp. 156–167.

Lorsch, J. W., and P. R. Lawrence. *Studies in Organization Design* (Homewood, Ill.: The Dorsey Press and Richard D. Irwin, Inc., 1970).

March, J. G., and H. A. Simon. *Organizations* (New York: John Wiley & Sons, Inc., 1958).

Matteson, M. T., and J. M. Ivancevich (eds.). *Management Classics* (Santa Monica, Calif.: Goodyear Publishing Company, Inc., 1981).

Peters, T. J., and R. H. Waterman, Jr. *In Search of Excellence* (New York: Harper & Row Publishers, Incorporated, 1982).

Weihrich, H. *Management Excellence: Productivity through MBO* (New York: McGraw-Hill Book Company, 1985).

2

Patterns of Management Analysis

CHAPTER OBJECTIVES   After reading this chapter, you should understand:

1 What the "management theory jungle" is
2 Eleven approaches to the analysis of management
3 The details of the operational approach around which this book is built
4 The five managerial functions—planning, organizing, staffing, leading, and controlling
5 That coordination is the essence of managership
6 That approaches to management theory may be converging

Confusion

Because of the extraordinary interest in management, a number of approaches have developed to explain the concepts, theory, and techniques underlying managerial practice. Although academic writers and theorists contributed notably little to the study of management until the early 1950s, previous writing having come largely from practitioners, the past three decades have seen a veritable deluge of writing from the academic halls. The variety of approaches to management analysis, the welter of research, and the number of differing views have resulted in much confusion as to what management is, what management theory and science are, and how managerial events should be analyzed. As a matter of fact, the senior author some years ago called this situation the **management theory jungle.**[1] Since that time, the vegetation in this jungle has changed somewhat, new approaches have developed, and older approaches have taken on some new meanings with some new words attached, but the developments of management science and theory still have the characteristics of a jungle.

The Various Approaches for Management

Eleven approaches to management

The various approaches to management analysis—summarized in Figure 2-1—are grouped here into the following categories: (1) the empirical, or case, approach; (2) the interpersonal behavior approach; (3) the group behavior approach; (4) the cooperative social systems approach; (5) the sociotechnical systems approach; (6) the decision theory approach; (7) the systems approach; (8) the mathematical or "management science" approach; (9) the contingency, or situational, approach; (10) the managerial roles approach; and (11) the operational approach. Although we cannot treat the aproaches here in much detail, we can sketch the nature of each so that you can at least identify the point of view from which any book or article on management has probably been written. As we shall note later in this chapter, there are a number of currently popular approaches with attractive new names like "organizational behavior" and "organization development"; they are really not new, basic approaches to management analysis but are, rather, special areas of knowledge or techniques attempting to improve managerial practice.

The Empirical, or Case, Approach

The empirical, or case, approach analyzes management by studying experience, usually through cases. It is based on the belief that, through the study of managers' successes and mistakes in individual cases and of their attempts to solve specific problems, students and practitioners will somehow come to know how to manage effectively in similar situations.

Limitations

However, unless a study of experience is aimed at determining *why* something happened or did not happen, in many cases it is likely to be a useless and even a dangerous approach to understanding management. What happened or did not happen in the past is not likely to offer a solution for the problems of what will almost certainly be a different future. Experience may be a helpful guide if it is distilled to reveal the basic reasons why an action succeeded or failed and if the differing circumstances of the past are taken into account.

If this distillation of experience takes place with a view to generalizations, the empirical, or case, approach can be a useful way to develop principles of manage-

---

[1]See Harold Koontz, "The Management Theory Jungle," *Journal of the Academy of Management*, vol. 4, no. 3 (December 1961), pp. 174–188. See also Harold Koontz, "Making Sense of Management Theory," *Harvard Business Review*, vol. 40, no. 4 (July–August 1962), p. 24ff.; and "The Management Theory Jungle Revisited," *Academy of Management Review*, vol. 5, no. 2 (April 1980), pp. 175–187. Much of the material in this chapter is drawn from these articles.

FIGURE 2-1

APPROACHES TO MANAGEMENT

CHARACTERISTICS/ CONTRIBUTIONS	LIMITATIONS	ILLUSTRATION
EMPIRICAL, OR CASE, APPROACH		
Studies experience through cases. Identifies successes and failures	Situations are all different. No attempt to identify principles. Limited value for developing management theory.	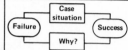
INTERPERSONAL BEHAVIOR APPROACH		
Focus on interpersonal behavior, human relations, leadership, and motivation. Based on individual psychology.	Ignores planning, organizing, and controlling. Psychological training is not enough to become an effective manager.	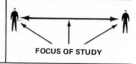
GROUP BEHAVIOR APPROACH		
Emphasis on behavior of people in groups. Based on sociology and social psychology. Primarily study of group behavior patterns. The study of large groups is often called "organization behavior."	Often not integrated with management concepts, principles, theory, and techniques. Need for closer intergration with organization structure design, staffing, planning, and controlling.	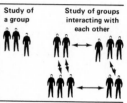
COOPERATIVE SOCIAL SYSTEMS APPROACH		
Concerned with both interpersonal and group behavioral aspects leading to a system of cooperation. Expanded concept includes any cooperative group with a clear purpose.	Too broad a field for the study of management. At the same time, it overlooks many managerial concepts, principles, and techniques.	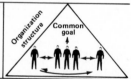
SOCIOTECHNICAL SYSTEMS APPROACH		
Technical system has great effect on social system (personal attitudes, group behavior). Focus on production, office operations, and other areas with close relationships between the technical system and people.	Emphasis only on blue-collar and lower-level office work. Ignores much of other managerial knowledge.	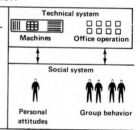
DECISION THEORY APPROACH		
Focus on the making of decisions, persons or groups making decisions, and the decision-making process. Some theorists use decision making as a springboard to study all enterprise activities. The boundaries of study are no longer clearly defined.	There is more to managing than making decisions. The focus is at the same time too narrow and too wide.	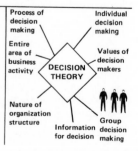

CHARACTERISTICS/ CONTRIBUTIONS	LIMITATIONS	ILLUSTRATION
SYSTEMS APPROACH		
Systems concepts have broad applicability. Systems have boundaries, but they also interact with the external environment; i.e., organizations are open systems. Recognizes importance of studying interrelatedness of planning, organizing, and controlling in an organization as well as the many subsystems.	Analyses of the interrelatedness of systems and subsystems as well as the interactions of organizations with their external environment. Can hardly be considered a new approach to management.	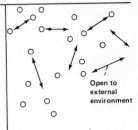 Open to external environment
MATHEMATICAL OR "MANAGEMENT SCIENCE" APPROACH		
Managing is seen as mathematical processes, concepts, symbols, and models. Looks at management as a purely logical process, expressed in mathematical symbols and relationships.	Preoccupation with mathematical models. Many aspects in managing cannot be modeled. Mathematics is a useful tool, but hardly a school or an approach to management.	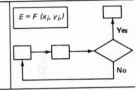
CONTINGENCY OR SITUATIONAL APPROACH		
Managerial practice depends on circumstances (i.e., a contingency or a situation). Contingency theory recognizes the influence of given solutions on organizational behavior patterns.	Managers have long realized that there is *no* one best way to do things. Difficulty in determining all relevant contingency factors and showing their relationships. Can be very complex.	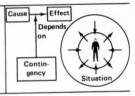
MANAGERIAL ROLES APPROACH		
Original study consisted of observations of five chief executives. On the basis of this study, ten managerial roles were identified and grouped into (1) interpersonal, (2) informational, and (3) decision roles.	Original sample was very small. Some activities are not managerial. Activities are evidence of planning, organizing, staffing, leading, and controlling. But some important managerial activities were left out (e.g., appraising managers).	
OPERATIONAL APPROACH		
Draws together concepts, principles, techniques, and knowledge from other fields and managerial approaches. The attempt is to develop science and theory with practical application. Distinguishes between managerial and nonmanagerial knowledge. Develops classification system built around the managerial functions of planning, organizing, staffing, leading, and controlling.	Does not, as some authors do, identify "representing" or "coordination" as a separate function. Coordination, for example, is the essence of managership and is the purpose of managing.	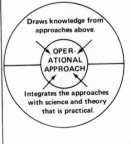

ment. Also, there can be no doubt that cases can provide a laboratory situation for introducing, explaining, and testing management knowledge. But this approach has serious limitations in developing management theory and techniques simply because experience has definite limitations in a subject as complex and broad as management.

The Interpersonal Behavior Approach

The interpersonal behavior approach is based on the idea that managing involves getting things done through people, and therefore, its study should be centered on interpersonal relationships. Variously called the **human relations, leadership, or behavioral science approach,** this school concentrates on the human aspect of management. Its proponents believe that when people work together to accomplish objectives, "people should understand people."

Focus

The writers and scholars using this approach are heavily influenced by psychological theory and, indeed, most are trained as psychologists. Their focus is the individual and his or her motivations and relationships with others. In this school are those who seem to emphasize human relations as an art which a manager, perhaps even acting as an amateur psychiatrist, should understand and practice. There are those who focus attention on the manager as a leader and who sometimes equate managership with leadership, thus, in effect, treating all "led" activities as "managed" situations. Linked to these are specialists who see leadership as largely a matter of understanding and developing means of obtaining response to human motivations.

No one can deny that managing involves human behavior or dispute that the study of human interactions, whether in the context of managing or elsewhere, is useful and important. It would likewise be a mistake not to regard leadership and the ability to motivate others as important for effective managing. On the contrary, effective managers do tend to become good leaders. In creating and maintaining an environment for performance, managers will almost surely develop situations where people will find it advantageous to follow them.

Limitations

The field of interpersonal behavior scarcely encompasses all there is to management. It is entirely possible for all the managers of a company to understand psychology and yet not be effective in managing. As a matter of fact, a fairly large company undertook extensive psychological training of managers at all levels only to find that this training did not guarantee effective managing. The company quickly found that managers need to know something of planning, control and control techniques, and devising a suitable organization structure, as well as other matters, in order to accomplish the entire managerial task.

Moreover, many members of the interpersonal behavior school are finding that they must extend their views far beyond psychological matters. For example, in the area of leadership, research has shown that the entire organizational climate has much to do with effective leading. And in understanding human motivations, psychologically oriented specialists are finding that such operational-management techniques as setting meaningful and verifiable objectives, designing organization structures showing clearly who is responsible for what, and giving accurate and prompt feedback on how well a person is doing are among the most important arousers of human interest and effort.

**The Group
Behavior Approach**

The group behavior approach is closely related to the interpersonal behavior approach and is often confused or combined with it. But it is concerned primarily with behavior of people in groups rather than behavior of individuals. It thus tends to be based on sociology and social psychology rather than on individual psychology. Its supporters include those writers and scholars who look on the study of management as primarily a study of group behavior patterns.

The group behavior approach varies all the way from the study of small groups with their cultural and behavioral patterns to the study of the behavioral composition of large groups. This latter is often called the **organization behavior approach,** and an "organization" may mean the system, or pattern, of any set of group relationships in a company, a government agency, a hospital, or any other kind of undertaking. But sometimes, as Chester Barnard employed the terms, "organization" is used to mean the "cooperation of two or more persons"[2] and "formal organization" to mean an organization with conscious, deliberate, joint purpose.[3] Chris Argyris has even used the term "organization" to include "*all* the behavior of *all* the participants" in a group undertaking.[4]

*Organization
behavior*

Contributions

Proponents of this approach have made many worthwhile contributions to management. The recognition that any organized enterprise is a social arrangement, made up in turn of many social units within it, with a complex of interacting attitudes, pressures, and conflicts arising from people's cultural backgrounds, has been helpful to both theorists and practicing managers. Many of our problems in managing stem from group behavior patterns, attitudes, and desires, some arising within a company or some other enterprise, but many coming from people's backgrounds.

Limitations

Group behaviorists acknowledge that basic management techniques and theory are an important part of their approach. But some have drawn a line between "organization behavior" and "management." In organizing management knowledge, all behavioral sciences related to managing should be interwoven logically with management concepts, principles, theory, and techniques. Fortunately, some authors understand that study of behavioral elements in group operations must be more closely integrated with study of organizational structure design, staffing, planning, and control. As important as the analysis of group behavior is, it is not all there is to management.

**The Cooperative
Social Systems
Approach**

The interpersonal and group behavior approaches have instigated an increased focus on the study of human relationships as cooperative social systems. This change has been due in part to the vogue of looking at everything from a systems point of view. It is also the result of a desire to refine the group behavior approach by giving emphasis to well-organized cooperation.

Almost 50 years ago, seeking to explain the work of executives in his notable book, *The Functions of the Executive*, Chester Barnard saw executives as operating

[2]C. I. Barnard, *The Functions of the Executive* (Cambridge, Mass.: Harvard University Press, 1938), p. 65.
[3]Ibid., p. 4.
[4]C. Argyris, *Personality and Organization* (New York: Harper & Brothers, 1957), p. 239.

Organizations as cooperative social systems

in, and maintaining, cooperative social systems which he referred to as "organizations." In other words, Barnard saw social systems as the cooperative interaction of the ideas, forces, desires, and thinking of two or more people. He therefore was concerned with both interpersonal and group behavior elements, and he saw their interaction as leading to systems of cooperation.

The Barnard concept of cooperative social systems pervades the work of many social scientists concerned with management. For example, Herbert Simon at one time defined organizations as "systems of interdependent activity, encompassing at least several primary groups and usually characterized at the level of consciousness of participants by a high degree of rational direction of behavior towards ends that are objects of common knowledge."[5] Simon and an increasing number of writers in recent years have expanded this concept to apply to any system of cooperative group interrelationships or behavior where a clear purpose exists, and they have given the field the rather general title of "organization theory."

Limitations

The cooperative social systems approach is pertinent to the study of management. All managers do, of course, operate in a cooperative social system. But we do not find people who are generally referred to as managers in *all* kinds of cooperative social systems. We would hardly think of a group of motorists sharing a main highway as being managed. We would not regard the leaders of a mob as managers. Nor would we think of a family group gathering to celebrate a birthday as being managed. Therefore, we can conclude that this approach is broader than the field of management but that, at the same time, it also tends to overlook many concepts, principles, and techniques that are important to managers.

The Sociotechnical Systems Approach

Impact of technical system on social system

One of the newer schools of management identifies itself as the sociotechnical systems approach. Its development is generally credited to E. L. Trist and his associates at the Tavistock Institute in England. In studies of production problems in coal mining, this group found that merely to study social problems was not enough. Instead, it found, in dealing with problems of productivity, that the technical system (machines and methods) had a strong effect on the social system. In other words, personal attitudes and group behavior are influenced by the technical system in which people work.

It is, therefore, the position of this school that social systems and technical systems must be made harmonious. If they are found not to be, changes should be made, usually in the technical systems. Most of the work of this school has consequently been concentrated on production, office operations, and other areas where the technical systems have a close relationship to people. It therefore tends to be heavily oriented to industrial engineering.

This relatively new school has made some interesting contributions to management practice. However, technology in such fields as transportation, product assembly, and chemical processing has long been known to influence the ways in which managers organize and manage their operations.

At the same time, particularly where technology has a great effect on group

[5]"Comments on the Theory of Organizations," *American Political Science Review*, vol. 46, no. 4 (1952), p. 1130.

behavior patterns, as it does in so much blue-collar and lower-level white-collar work, the orderly analysis and coordination of social and technical systems can have great managerial benefits. But as promising as this approach is in such areas, there is much pertinent management knowledge not encompassed in this approach.

The Decision Theory Approach

Focus

The decision theory approach to management is based on the belief that, since managers make decisions, those studying management must concentrate on decision making—the selection from among possible alternatives of a course of action. Decision theorists concentrate primarily on the making of decisions, on the persons or organized groups making decisions, and on an analysis of the decision process. Study of the process of evaluating alternatives has become, for some decision theorists, a springboard for examining the entire area of enterprise activity, including the psychological and social reactions of individuals and groups, the nature of organization structure, the need for and development of information for decisions, and the analysis of values.

The result has been that decision theory no longer concentrates narrowly on decisions but, rather, has tended to take a broader view of companies or other enterprises as social systems. As one prominent decision theorist informed the authors when accused of looking at management through a narrow keyhole, his school of thought is concerned not only with the making of decisions, but also with everything that precedes a decision and everything that follows one. Thus, nothing is left out. Nor has a clear area for this approach been defined.

Limitations

It is not surprising that many theorists believe that, since managing is characterized by decision making, the central focus of management theory can be decision making and the rest of management thought can be built around it. This argument has a degree of reasonableness. But it does seem to overlook the fact that there is much more to managing than making decisions and that, for most managers, the actual making of a decision is a fairly easy thing—if goals are clear, if adequate information is available, if the organization structure provides a clear understanding of responsibility for decisions, and if many of the other requirements of the managerial task are present. In fact, managers report that they spend a very small percentage of their time actually making decisions.

Important as it is in managing, decision making appears to be too narrow a focus for a total theory of management or, if its implications are considerably extended, too wide a focus. For, as most decision theorists recognize, decision theory could be applied to the thinking and problems of a Robinson Crusoe as well as of the United States Steel Corporation.

The Systems Approach

Definition of a system

During recent years, many management scholars and writers have emphasized the systems approach to the study and analysis of management.

A **system** is essentially a set or assemblage of things interconnected, interdependent, things that form a complex unity. As we mentioned in Chapter 1, these things may be physical, such as the parts of an automobile engine; or they may be biological, like components of the human body; or they may be theoretical, as is a set of concepts, principles, theory, and techniques in an area such as managing. All systems, except perhaps that of the universe, interact with and are influenced by their environments, although we define boundaries for them so that we can see them more clearly and analyze them.

The use of systems theory and analysis in the physical and biological sciences has given rise to a considerable body of systems knowledge. Systems theory has been found applicable to management. Although management theory, as a system, does have boundaries in order to make it convenient to study, it is a system open to the environment. Thus, when managers plan, they have no choice but to take into account such external variables as markets, technology, social forces, laws, and regulations. When they design an organizational system to provide an environment for performance, they cannot help but be influenced by the behavior patterns people bring to their jobs from the environment external to an enterprise.

Systems boundaries

Systems also play an important part within the area of managing itself. There are planning systems, organizational systems, and control systems. And within these we can perceive many subsystems, such as systems of delegation, network planning, and budgeting.

Managerial systems

Intelligent and experienced practicing managers and many management writers with practical experience, accustomed as they are to seeing their problems and operations as a network of interrelated elements with daily interaction between environments inside or outside their companies or other enterprises, are often surprised to find that many writers regard the systems approach as something new. To be sure, conscious study of, and emphasis on, systems have forced many managers and scholars to consider more perceptively the various interacting elements affecting management theory and practice. But this can hardly be regarded as a new approach to management thought.

The Mathematical, or "Management Science," Approach

There are theorists who see managing primarily as an exercise in mathematical processes, concepts, symbols, and models. Perhaps the most widely known of these theorists are the operations researchers, many of whom have called themselves "management scientists." This group believes that if managing or organizing or planning or decision making is a logical process, it can be expressed in mathematical symbols and relationships. The primary focus of this school is the mathematical model. Through this device, problems can be expressed in terms of basic relationships, and where a given goal is sought, the model can often be constructed so as to suggest a decision as to the best thing to do. An example of a mathematical model will be given in Chapter 23, in which we discuss operations research. There is often an almost complete absorption with mathematics, and some members of this school have even taken the extreme position that "if you cannot express it mathematically, it is not worth expressing."

The journal *Management Science*, published by the Institute of Management Sciences, carries on its cover the statement that the purpose of the Institute is to "identify, extend, and unify scientific knowledge pertaining to management." But, as judged by this journal and the hundreds of papers presented by members of the Institute at its many meetings all over the world, the school's almost complete preoccupation has been with mathematical models and developing elegant mathematical solutions to certain enterprise and managerial problems. As many critics

Limitations

both inside and outside the ranks of the so-called management scientists have observed, the narrow mathematical focus on management can hardly be called an approach to a true management science.

No one interested in any scientific field can overlook the great usefulness of mathematical analyses. Mathematical analysis makes us define problems first and allows us to use symbols for unknown quantities. Mathematics also provides a powerful logical tool for simplifying and solving complex problems. But it is as difficult to see mathematics as a separate approach to management as it is to see it as a separate approach to physics, chemistry, or engineering.

The Contingency, or Situational, Approach

One approach to management thought and practice which has taken management academicians by storm is the contingency, or situational, approach. Proponents of this approach emphasize that what managers do in practice depends upon a given set of circumstances (a contingency or a situation). According to some scholars, contingency theory takes into account not only situations but also the influence of given solutions on behavior patterns of an enterprise. For example, an organization structured around operating functions, such as finance, engineering, production, and marketing, might be most suitable for a given situation; however, managers using this approach should consider that it may foster patterns of group loyalty to the function rather than to the company.

As we pointed out earlier, by its very nature, managerial practice requires that managers take into account the realities of a given situation when they apply theory or techniques. It is not the task of science and theory to prescribe what should be done in a given situation. As we emphasized in Chapter 1, management science and theory does not advocate a best way to do things in every situation, any more than the science of astrophysics or mechanics tells an engineer how to design a single best instrument for all kinds of applications. How theory and science are applied in practice naturally depends upon the situation.

This is to say that there is science and there is art, that there is knowledge and there is practice. These are matters that any experienced manager has long known. As we said earlier, one does not need much experience to understand that a corner grocery store could hardly be organized like General Motors, or that the technical realities of petroleum exploration, production, and refining make impracticable autonomously organized product divisions for gasoline, jet fuel, and lubricating oils.

The Managerial Roles Approach

Perhaps the newest approach to management theory to catch the attention of academics and practitioners alike is the managerial roles approach, popularized by Professor Henry Mintzberg of McGill University.[6] Essentially, his approach is to observe what managers actually do and from such observations come to conclusions as to what managerial activities (or roles) are. Although many researchers

---

[6]Especially in his award-winning article "The Manager's Job: Folklore and Fact," *Harvard Business Review*, vol. 53, no. 4 (July–August 1975), pp. 49–61, and his book *Nature of Management Work* (New York: Harper & Row, Publishers, Incorporated, 1973).

have studied the actual work of managers from chief executives to line supervisors, Mintzberg has given this approach higher visibility.

After systematically studying the activities of five chief executives in a variety of organizations, Mintzberg came to the conclusion that executives do not act out the classical classification of managerial functions—planning, organizing, coordinating, and controlling. Instead, they engage in a variety of other activities.

From his research and the research of others who have studied what managers actually do, Mintzberg has come to the conclusion that managers really fill a series of ten roles. These are:

*Mintzberg's
ten roles*

A **Interpersonal roles**

1 The figurehead role (performing ceremonial and social duties as the organization's representative)

2 The leader role

3 The liaison role (particularly with outsiders)

B **Informational roles**

1 The recipient role (receiving information about the operation of an enterprise)

2 The disseminator role (passing information to subordinates)

3 The spokesperson role (transmitting information to those outside the organization)

C **Decision roles**

1 The entrepreneurial role

2 The disturbance-handler role

3 The resource allocator role

4 The negotiator role (dealing with various persons and groups of persons)

Mintzberg refers to the usual way of classifying managerial functions as "folklore." As we will see in the following discussion on the operational-management approach, operational theorists have used such managerial functions as planning, organizing, staffing, leading, and controlling as the means of classifying the growing body of managerial knowledge. While the functions are believed to be real, they are not intended to describe all activities of managers. If Mintzberg has

Limitations

intended to sweep away this first-level classification (he has denied this in conversations with one of the authors), he can hardly be taken seriously. In the first place, the sample used in his research is far too small to support so sweeping a conclusion. In the second place, in analyzing the actual activities of managers—from chief executives to supervisors—any researcher must realize that all managers do some work that is not purely managerial; one would expect even presidents of large companies to spend some of their time in public and stockholder relations, in raising money, perhaps in dealer relations, marketing, and so on.

In the third place, many of the activities Mintzberg found are, in fact, evidences of planning, organizing, staffing, leading, and controlling. For example, what is resource allocation but planning? The entrepreneurial role is certainly an element of planning. And the interpersonal roles are mainly instances of leading. In addition, the informational roles can be fitted into a number of the functional areas.

Nevertheless, looking at what managers really do can have considerable value. In analyzing activities, an effective manager might wish to ascertain how activities and techniques fall into the various fields of knowledge reflected by the basic functions of managers. However, the roles Mintzberg identifies appear to be incomplete. Where does one find such unquestionably important managerial activities as structuring organization, selecting and appraising managers, and determining major strategies? Omissions such as these make one wonder whether the executives in his sample were really effective managers. It certainly raises a serious question as to whether the managerial roles approach, at least as put forth by Mintzberg, is an adequate one on which to base a practical, operational theory of management.

The Operational Approach

The operational approach to management theory and science attempts to draw together the pertinent knowledge of management by relating it to the managerial job—what managers do. Like other operational sciences, it tries to put together the concepts, principles, and techniques that underlie the task of managing.

The operational approach recognizes that there is a central core of knowledge about managing pertinent only to the field of management. Such matters as line and staff, departmentation, managerial appraisal, and various managerial control techniques involve concepts and theory found only where managers are involved.

Integration of knowledge

But, in addition, this approach draws on and absorbs knowledge from other fields, including systems theory, decision theory, theories of motivation and leadership, individual and group behavior, social systems, and cooperation and communications, and the application of mathematical analyses and concepts.

The nature of the operational approach can be seen in Figure 2-2. As this diagram shows, the operational management school recognizes the existence of a central core of science and theory peculiar to managing and also draws important contributions from various other schools and approaches. As the circle shows, the operational theorist is not interested in *all* the important knowledge in these various fields, but only that which is deemed most useful and relevant to managing.

Those who subscribe to the operational approach do so with the hope of developing a science and theory which has practical application to managing and yet is not so broad as to apply to everything that might have any relationship to the managerial task. They recognize that managing is a difficult task with an immense number of variables affecting it. They realize that any field as complex as managing, which deals with the production and marketing of anything from bread to money, with religion, and with government services, can never be isolated from the physical, biological, or social environment. But they also recognize that

FIGURE 2-2

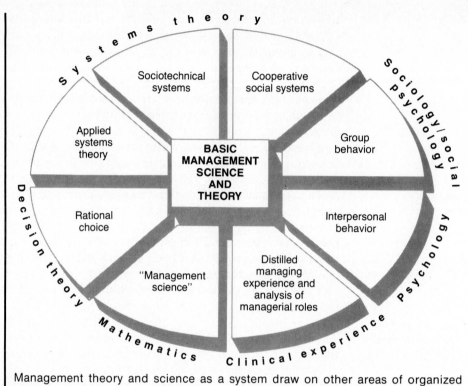

Management theory and science as a system draw on other areas of organized knowledge. The figure shows how operational-management theory and science, here enclosed in the circle, have a core of basic science and theory and draw from other fields of knowledge pertinent to understanding management. Basic management is thus, in part, an eclectic science and theory.

some partitioning of knowledge is necessary and that some boundaries must be set if meaningful progress is to be made there or in any other field.

Because the functions of managers are emphasized in the operational approach, it is often called the "management process" school. Because the great French industrialist and management pioneer Henri Fayol first attempted to organize management knowledge around managerial functions, the school is also often referred to as the "classical" or the "traditional" school. But it is really merely an approach that has been found useful to, and understandable by, practicing managers and that also furnishes a means of distinguishing between managerial knowledge and the special knowledge and expertise of such nonmanagerial fields as marketing or production. In addition, it is a way of integrating into management useful and pertinent knowledge from all schools and approaches.

Management process school

Although the operationalists generally believe that the fundamentals of management are universal, theorists of this school would readily admit that the problems managers face and the situations in which they operate vary among managerial levels in an enterprise and among different enterprises, and that the application of concepts, theories, and techniques will naturally vary. But, as indicated in Chapter 1, this diversity is characteristic of the difference between theory and practice in any field.

Implementing the Operational Approach

Functions of managers

To organize any field of knowledge and make it more useful, a classification system is necessary. In the field of management, a variety of first-order classifications, or "pigeonholes," might be used. Those who subscribe to the operational school of management believe that it is both realistic and helpful to practitioners to use as this **first-order classification** the functions of managers—planning, organizing, staffing, leading, and controlling. A useful **second-order classification** builds knowledge in each functional area by looking at the following aspects: (1) the nature and purpose of each function; (2) the key concepts applicable to each; (3) the way each is structured; (4) the way each is undertaken; (5) the theory and principles underlying each; (6) the most useful techniques that have been developed in each area; (7) the difficulties encountered in applying knowledge in practice; and (8) the way managers might develop an environment for performance in each area.

These primary classifications are not airtight and there are many overlaps. Thus, a manager plans an organization structure and may also organize a planning function. But this overlapping is a characteristic of all fields of science. For example, we speak of the fields of chemistry and physics but recognize the existence of physical chemistry.

Functions of Managers

The functions of managers provide a useful framework for organizing management knowledge. There have been no new ideas, research findings, or techniques that cannot readily be placed in these classifications. For this reason, then, the basic functional areas of management selected are planning, organizing, staffing, leading, and controlling. The essentials of management dealt with in this book are organized around these functions.

Planning

Planning involves decision making; it is selecting the courses of action that a company or other enterprise, and every department of it, will follow. As we will see in Chapter 4, there are various types of plans, ranging from overall purposes and objectives to the most detailed action to be taken to order a special stainless steel bolt for an instrument or to hire and train workers for an assembly line. No real plan exists until a decision—a commitment of human or material resources or reputation—has been made. Before a decision is made, all we have is a planning study, an analysis, or a proposal, but not a real plan.

What, how, when, who

Planning is deciding in advance *what* to do, *how* to do it, *when* to do it, and *who* is to do it. Planning bridges the gap from where we are to where we want to be in a desired future. It strongly implies not only the introduction of new things, but also sensible and workable implementation. It makes it possible for things to occur that would not otherwise happen. Although the future can seldom be predicted with accuracy and unforeseen events may interfere with the best-laid plans, unless there is planning, actions tend to be aimless and left to chance. There is no more important and basic element in establishing an environment for performance than enabling people to know their purposes and objectives, the tasks to be performed, and the guidelines to be followed in performing them. If group effort is to be effective, people must know what they are expected to accomplish. the various aspects of planning are discussed in Part II of this book.

Organizing

People working together in groups to achieve some goal must have roles to play, much like the parts actors fill in a drama, whether these roles are ones they develop themselves, are accidental or haphazard, or are defined and structured by someone who wants to make sure that people contribute in a specific way to group effort. The concept of a "role" implies that what people do has a definite purpose or objective; they know how their job objective fits into group effort, and they have the necessary authority, tools, and information to accomplish the task.

This can be seen in as simple a group effort as setting up camp on a fishing expedition. Everyone could do anything he or she wanted to do, but activity would almost certainly be more effective and certain tasks would be less likely to be left undone if one or two persons were given the task of gathering firewood, others the assignment of getting water, others the task of making a fireplace and starting a fire, others the job of cooking, and so on.

Organizing, then, is that part of managing that involves establishing an intentional structure of roles for people to fill in an enterprise. It is intentional in the sense of making sure that all the tasks necessary to accomplish goals are assigned and, it is hoped, assigned to people who can do them best. Imagine what would have happened if such assignments had not been made in the programs to put people on the moon or to land Viking I on Mars! Thus, organizing involves:

1   Determination of what activities are required to achieve goals

2   Grouping of these activities into departments or sections

Steps in organizing

3   Assignment of such groups of activities to a manager

4   Delegation of authority to carry them out

5   Provision for horizontal and vertical coordination of activities, authority, and communication

The purpose of an organization structure is to help in creating an environment for human performance. It is, then, a management tool and not an end in and of itself. Although the structure must define the tasks to be done, the roles so established must also be designed in the light of the abilities and motivations of people available.

To design an effective organization structure is not an easy managerial task. Many problems are encountered in making structures fit situations, including both defining the kind of jobs that must be done and finding the people to do them. These problems and the essential theory, principles, and techniques of handling them are the subjects of Part III of this book.

Staffing

Staffing involves filling, and keeping filled, the positions in the organization structure. It involves setting requirements for the job to be done, and it includes inventorying, recruiting, appraising, and selecting candidates for positions; compensating; and training or otherwise developing both candidates and current job holders to accomplish their tasks effectively. Since this book is devoted to managers, we will deal with the staffing function primarily as it concerns managers rather than nonmanagers, but the principles involved apply in most instances to both groups. This is in no way meant to imply that the first-level supervisor is not a manager. This subject is dealt with in Part IV of this book.

Leading

Leading is influencing people so that they will strive willingly and enthusiastically toward the achievement of organization and group goals; it has to do predominantly with the interpersonal aspect of managing. All managers would agree that their most important problems arise from people—their desires and attitudes, their behavior as individuals and in groups—and that effective managers also need to be effective leaders. Since leadership implies followership and people tend to follow those who offer a means of satisfying their own needs, wishes, and desires, it is understandable that leading involves motivation, leadership styles and approaches, and communication. The essentials of these subjects are dealt with in Part V of this book.

Controlling

Controlling is the measuring and correcting of activities of subordinates to ensure that events conform to plans. It measures performance against goals and plans, shows where negative deviations exist, and, by putting in motion actions to correct deviations, helps ensure accomplishment of plans. Although planning must precede controlling, plans are not self-achieving. The plan guides managers in the use of resources to accomplish specific goals. Then activities are checked to determine whether they conform to plans.

Control activities generally relate to the measurement of achievement. Some means of controlling, like the budget for expense, inspection records, and the record of labor-hours lost, are generally familiar. Each measures; each shows whether plans are working out. If deviations persist, correction is indicated. But what is corrected? Activities, through persons. Nothing can be done about reducing scrap, for example, or buying according to specifications, or handling sales returns unless one knows who is responsible for these functions. Compelling events to conform to plans means locating the persons who are responsible for results that differ from planned action and then taking the necessary steps to improve performance. Thus, outcomes are controlled by controlling what people do. This subject is treated in Part VI.

**Coordination,
the Essence of
Managership**

Many authorities consider coordination to be a separate function of the manager. It seems more accurate, however, to regard it as the essence of managership, for the achievement of harmony of individual efforts toward the accomplishment of group goals is the purpose of managing. Each of the managerial functions is an exercise contributing to coordination.

Even in the case of a church or a fraternal organizaiton, individuals often interpret similar interests in different ways, and their efforts toward mutual goals do not automatically mesh with the efforts of others. It thus becomes the central task of the manager to reconcile differences in approach, timing, effort, or interest, and to harmonize individual goals to contribute to organization goals.

*Importance of
well-defined
enterprise goals*

The best coordination occurs when individuals see how their jobs contribute to the goals of an enterprise. They are able to see this only when they know what those goals are. If, for example, managers are not sure whether the goal of their firm is sales volume, quality, advanced techniques, or customer service, they cannot coordinate their efforts to achieve any objective. Each would be guided by his or her own ideas of what is in the interest of the firm or, without any such conviction, might work for self-enrichment. To avoid such splintering of efforts, the domdinant goal of the enterprise should be clearly defined and communicated to everyone concerned. And, naturally, goals of subordinate departments should be designed to contribute to the goals of the enterprise.

The Management Theory Jungle:
Tendencies Toward Convergence of Theory Approaches

There is evidence that the management theory jungle not only continues to flourish but gets more dense, with nearly twice as many schools or approaches as were found over 20 years ago. It is no wonder that useful operational-management theory and science has been so tardy in arriving. It is no wonder that we still do not have a clear notion of the scientific underpinnings of managing; nor have we been able to identify clearly what we mean by competent managers.

The varying approaches, each with its own gurus, each with its own semantics, and each with a fierce determination to protect its concepts and techniques from attack or change, make the theory and science of management extremely difficult for the intelligent practitioner to understand and utilize. If the persistence of the jungle were only an evidence of competing academic thought and research, it would not much matter. But when it retards the development of a useful theory and science and confuses practicing managers, the problem becomes serious. Effective managing at all levels and in all kinds of enterprises is too important to any society to allow it to fail through lack of available and understandable knowledge.

At the same time, there are signs indicating tendencies of the various schools of thought to converge and blend. While the process is by no means complete, we hope that, as scholars and writers become more familiar with what managers really do and the situations in which they act, more and more of them will adopt, and even expand, the basic thinking and concepts of the operational school of management.

Realizing that these are only signs along the road to a more unified and operational theory of management, and that there is much more of this road to travel, let us briefly examine some of these tendencies toward convergence.

Distilling Basics with the Empirical Approach

In reviewing the many programs which utilize cases as a means of educating managers, the authors have found that there appears to be much greater emphasis on distilling fundamentals than there was two decades ago. Likewise, in the field of business policy, by which term these case approaches have tended to be known, there has been increased emphasis in teaching and research on going beyond recounting what happened in a given situation to analyzing the underlying causes. One major result of all this has been a new emphasis on strategy and strategic planning. This has led many empiricists to come up with distilled knowledge that fits neatly into the operational classification of planning.

Recognizing that Systems Thinking Is Not a Separate Approach

When systems theory was introduced into the management field some two decades ago, it was hailed by many as a new way of analyzing and classifying management knowledge. But in recent years, as people have come to understand systems theory *and* the job of managing better, two things have become increasingly clear: first, that there is little that is new about systems theory, and second, that practicing managers as well as the operational theorists had been utilizing its basics (although not always its jargon) for a number of years. Nonetheless, as operational theorists have more consciously utilized the concepts and theory of systems, their attempts to develop a scientific field have been aided.

Recognizing that Situational and Contingency Approaches Are Not New or Separate Approaches

It is now clear that the concepts of situational, or contingency, management are merely a way of distinguishing between science and art—knowledge and practice. This is surprising neither to perceptive and intelligent managers nor to many management theorists. As pointed out in Chapter 1 and earlier in this chapter, science and art are two different things, albeit complementary. Those writers and scholars who have emphasized situational, or contingency, approaches have done the field of management theory and practice a great service by stressing that what the intelligent manager actually does depends on the realities of a situation. But this has long been true of the *application* of any science.

That contingency theory is really "application in the light of a situation" has been increasingly recognized. This is evidenced by a recent statement of one of the founders of contingency theory, Professor Jay Lorsch of Harvard, who admitted that his use of the term "contingency" was "misleading."[7] Even he appeared to recognize that an operational-management theorist would necessarily become a situationalist when it came to applying management concepts, principles, and techniques.

---

[7]"Organization Design: A Situational Perspective," *Organizational Dynamics*, vol. 6, no. 2 (Autumn 1977), pp. 2–14, at p. 2.

Finding that "Organization Theory" Is Too Broad an Approach

Largely because of the influence of Chester Barnard and his broad concept of "organization" as referring to almost any kind of interpersonal relationship, it has become customary, particularly in academic circles, to use the term "organization theory" to refer to theory pertaining to almost any kind of interpersonal relationship. While many scholars attempted to equate "organization theory" with management theory, it is now fairly well-agreed that managing is a narrower activity and that management theory pertains only to theory related to managing. Management theory is often thought of as being a subset of organization theory, and there is now fairly wide concurrence that the general concept of organization theory is too broad. This is an encouraging sign; it means that some of the underbrush of the jungle may soon be cleared away.

Gaining New Understanding of Motivation

As we will see in Chapter 18, the more recent research into motivation in organizational settings has tended to emphasize the importance of the organizational climate in curbing or arousing motivation. The oversimplified explanations of motives by Maslow and Herzberg may identify human needs fairly well, but much more emphasis must be given to rewards and expectations of rewards. These, along with a climate which arouses and supports motivation, depend to a very great extent on the nature of managing in an organization.

The interaction between motivation and organizational climate not only underscores the systems aspects of motivation but also emphasizes how motivation depends on what managers do to create and maintain an environment for performance. These researchers move the problem of motivation from a purely behavioral matter to one closely related to and dependent upon what managers do. The theory of motivation, then, fits nicely into the operational approach to management theory and science.

Merging of Motivation and Leadership Theory

Another interesting sign that we may be moving toward a unified operational theory of management is the way that research and analysis have tended to merge motivation and leadership theory. As will be seen in Chapters 18 and 19, especially in recent years, leadership research and theory have tended to emphasize the rather elementary proposition that the job of leaders is to know and appeal to needs and desires that motivate people and to recognize the simple truth that people tend to follow those who offer them a means of satisfying their own desires. Thus, explanations of leadership have been increasingly related to motivation.

Leadership

The blending of motivation and leadership theories has also led to an emphasis on the importance of organization climate and styles of leaders. Most current studies and theories tend to underscore the importance of making managers effective leaders. Implied by most recent research and theory is the clear message that effective leaders design a system that takes into account the expectations of subordinates; the variability of motives between individuals; and, from time to time, situational factors, the need for clarity of role definition, interpersonal relations, and types of rewards.

Climate for performance

Knowledgeable and effective managers develop exactly this kind of system when they design a climate for performance, when goals and means of achieving them are planned, when organizational roles are defined and well-structured, when roles are intelligently staffed, and when control techniques and information are designed to make control by self-control possible. In other words, leadership theory and research are, like motivation theory, fitting neatly into the scheme of operational-management theory, rather than remaining a separate branch of theory.

The New, Managerially Oriented "Organization Development"

Both "organization development" and the field ordinarily referred to as "organization behavior" have grown out of the interpersonal and group behavior approaches to management. For a while, these fields seemed unrelated to operational-management theory. But many specialists in these areas are now beginning to see that basic management theory and techniques, such as managing by objectives and clarifying organization structure, fit well into their programs of behavioral intervention.

Fortunately, a review of the latest organization behavior books indicates that many authors in this field are beginning to understand that study of behavioral elements in group operations must be more closely integrated with study of organization structure design, staffing, planning, and control. In so doing, certain members of this behavioral school of thought are beginning to see the deficiencies of their narrow approach. This is a hopeful sign. It is a recognition that analysis of individual and group behavior, at least in managed situations, easily and logically falls into place in the scheme of operational-management theory.

The Impact of Technology: Researching an Old Problem

That technology has an important impact on organizational structure, behavior patterns, and other aspects of managing has been recognized by intelligent practitioners for many years. However, primarily among academic researchers, there has seemed to be in recent years a "discovery" that the impact of technology is important and real. To be sure, some of this research has been helpful to managers, especially that of the sociotechnical school of management. Also, while perceptive managers have known for many years that technology has important impacts, some of this research has tended to clarify the nature and implications of these impacts.

Defections among "Management Scientists"

You will recall that in the earlier discussion of schools of, or approaches to, management, one of them was identified as the mathematical, or "management science," approach. You have undoubtedly noticed that "management science" was put in quotation marks. This was done because this group does not really deal with a total science of management, but rather with mathematical models, symbols, and elegance.

Among the so-called management scientists, there are defectors who realize that their interests go far beyond the use of mathematics, models, and the computer. These defectors are primarily in the ranks of operations researchers in industry and government, who are faced daily with practical management problems. A small but growing number of academics are also coming to this realization. In fact, one of the leading and most respected academics, widely regarded as one of the pioneers in operations research, Professor C. West Churchman (in conversations with one of the authors), has been highly critical of the excessive absorption with models and mathematics and, for this reason, has even resigned from the Operations Research Society.

There is no doubt that operations research and similar mathematical and modeling techniques fit nicely into the planning and controlling areas of operational-management theory and science. Most operational-management theorists recognize this. All that is really needed is for the few "management science" defectors to become a horde, moving their expertise and research to the service of a practical and useful management science.

Converts among Consultants: McKinsey's 7-S Framework

In recent years, the 7-S framework for management analysis developed by the respected consulting firm of McKinsey & Company has gained in popularity, partly because it became the basis for the research of two best-selling books, *The Art of Japanese Management*[8] and *In Search of Excellence*.[9] The Seven S's are: strategy, structure, systems, style, staff, shared values, and skills, as summarized in Table 2-1. However, the author of one of the above-mentioned books admitted that in the attempt to make the key aspects of the model begin with an s (to serve as a memory hook), the meaning of some of the terms had to be stretched. For example, in traditional management literature the term "skills" is generally applied to personal skills (e.g., technical, human, conceptual) while in the 7-S framework "skills" means the capabilities of the organization as a whole. Organizational capabilities, or the lack of them, are generally referred to in management literature as strengths and weaknesses of the firm.

The outstanding feature of the 7-S model is that it has been tested extensively by McKinsey consultants in their studies of many companies. At the same time, this framework has been used by respected business schools, such as Harvard and Stanford. Thus, theory and practice seem to support each other in the study of management. Perhaps the most surprising fact about the 7-S framework is that it supports, and is similar to, the framework of the managerial functions (planning, organizing, staffing, leading, and controlling) used in this book, as shown in Table 2-1.

By using the term "shared values," also sometimes called "superordinate goals," 7-S theorists emphasize that goal statements are very important in determining the destiny of the enterprise, as emphasized in Chapter 5 in our book; they also point out that values must be shared by organization members. Therefore, special attention is given to personal and organizational values in Chapter 12, where we discuss organizational effectiveness.

Identifying key aspects of the management system and showing the interrelatedness of the variables is a positive contribution to management theory. A simple, easy-to-remember framework, such as that suggested by McKinsey, is

---

[8]R. T. Pascale and A. G. Athos, *The Art of Japanese Management* (New York: Warner Books, Inc., 1981).

[9]T. J. Peters and R. H. Waterman, Jr., *In Search of Excellence* (New York: Harper & Row, Publishers, Incorporated, 1982).

TABLE 2-1   Comparison of 7-S Framework and the Operational-Management Approach

McKinsey's 7-S framework for management analysis	Textbook reference
Strategy: Systematic action and allocation of resources to achieve company aims	Strategies and Policies (Chap. 6)
Structure: Organization structure and authority/responsibility relationships	Part III: Organizing, especially: Basic Departmentation (Chap. 9) Line and Staff Authority Relationships (Chap. 10) Decentralization (Chap. 11)
Systems: Procedures and processes such as information systems, manufacturing processes, budgeting and control processes	Part VI: Controlling, especially: The System and Process of Controlling (Chap. 21) Control Techniques (Chap. 22) Planning and Controlling Production and Operations Management (Chap. 23)
Style: The way management behaves and collectively spends its time to achieve organizational goals	Part V: Leading (Chaps. 17–20)
Staff: The people in the enterprise and their socialization into the organizational culture	Part IV: Staffing (Chaps. 13–16)
Shared values (superordinate goals): The values shared by the members of an organization	Various parts of the book, especially: Making Organizing Effective (Chap. 12) Leadership (Chap. 19)
Skills: Distinctive capabilities of an enterprise	Strategies and Policies (Chap. 6)

Source: R. T. Pascale and A. G. Athos, *The Art of Japanese Management* (New York: Warner Books, Inc., 1981); R. H. Waterman, Jr., "The Seven Elements of Strategic Fit," in A. A. Thomson, Jr., A. J. Strickland III, and W. E. Fulmer (eds.), *Readings in Strategic Management* (Plano, Tex.: Business Publications, Inc., 1984), pp. 333–339.

certainly an effort to be welcomed by practitioners and academicians, but at this point it cannot be considered a new approach to management. Although the terminology it employs is, at times, not quite clear, and may have somewhat increased the semantic jungle, the positive contributions of this framework must be recognized.

Clarifying Semantics: Some Hopeful Signs

One of the greatest obstacles to disentangling the jungle has been the problem of semantics. Those writing and lecturing on management and related fields have tended to use the same terms in different ways. This is exemplified by the variety of meanings given to such terms as "organization," "line and staff," "authority," "responsibility," and "policies," to mention a few. While this semantics swamp still exists and we are a long way from general acceptance of meanings of key terms and concepts, there are some hopeful signs on the horizon.

It has become rather common now for leading management texts to include a glossary of key terms and concepts, and an increasing number of textbooks are beginning to use terms in a similar way. Of interest also is the fact that the Fellows of the International Academy of Management, a group comprising some 180 management scholars and leaders from thirty-two countries, have responded to the demands of members and have undertaken to develop a glossary of management concepts and terms to be published in a number of languages and given wide circulation in many countries.

Although it is too early even to hope, it does appear that we may be moving in the direction necessary for the development of a science—the acceptance of clear definitions of key terms and concepts.

Summary

There are many theories about management, and each contributes something to our knowledge of what managers do. The empirical approach applies the experience of the past to present situations. The interpersonal behavior approach concentrates on the manager's understanding of people as people and their relationships. By contrast, the group behavior approach focuses on the behavior of people acting in groups. The study of human relationships as "cooperative social systems" forms the basis of another approach, which emphasizes the systems aspects of group behavior and its relationship to technical systems.

The sociotechnical systems school emphasizes that social systems and technical systems (machines and methods) must be harmonious. Decision theorists concentrate on decision making as the manager's most important activity. The systems approach views management as a system that is itself made up of subsystems and that operates within the total environment.

Mathematical models and analysis are the basis of the mathematical, or "management science," approach. The contingency approach says that what managers do depends on circumstances, or contingencies. Another school views managers as people who fill a number of roles as decision makers, leaders, and receivers and disseminators of knowledge, among other functions. The operational approach draws on knowledge from a number of fields, including psychology, sociology, and mathematics, that is relevant to management and recognizes a core of knowledge generally unique to managing.

Basically, there are five main functions that managers fulfill. These are planning, organizing, staffing, leading, and controlling, and they may be used as a basic classification of managerial knowledge. The essence of managing is the coordination, through these five functions, of the efforts of people.

Key Ideas and Concepts for Review

Management theory jungle
Empirical, or case, approach
Interpersonal behavior approach
Group behavior approach
Cooperative social systems approach
Sociotechnical systems approach
Decision theory approach
Systems approach
Mathematical, or "management science,"
    approach
Contingency, or situational, approach

Managerial roles approach
Operational approach
Planning
Organizing
Staffing
Leading
Controlling
Coordination
Convergence of approaches to
    management theory

For Discussion

1   Do the various approaches to the analysis of management represent a management theory jungle, or do they represent simply an intellectual division of labor?

2   Taking each approach except the operational one, identify its major elements and probable biases, and show how it can be integrated into an operational approach to management.

3   To what extent is the "management science" approach truly management science?

4   Why and how is the problem of semantics so important in explaining the confusion arising from the various approaches to management? Taking any four books or articles on management that you like, ascertain what approach to management each author takes and the extent of the semantic differences among them.

5   Does using the functions of the manager as a first-order classification of management knowledge constitute a closed-system approach to management?

6   How are the various functions of managers, as defined in this chapter, both independent and interdependent?

7   Why has coordination not been included as one of the major functions of the manager?

8   As you read the following chapters of this book, watch for signs of convergence of the various approaches to management theory and science. Is it reasonable to refer to the various approaches as the "management theory jungle"?

CASE 2-1

CARLTON PLYWOOD COMPANY

The Carlton Plywood Company is a medium-sized company in the Pacific Northwest that buys logs, peels them, and makes plywood, which is marketed through independent sales agents. Frank Carlton, now 55 years old, inherited the company from his father, who founded it 40 years ago. An astute purchaser of logs who is also able to anticipate market trends and run an efficient operation, Frank Carlton built the company to an annual sales level of $10 million, with profits after taxes averaging $750,000, with 200 stockholders (although he and his family hold 60 percent of the stock), and with some 300 employees in three mills. His son James, having just graduated from a business school with an M.B.A. degree, joined his father as assistant to the president, with the plan that he would become president in a few years, when his father took early retirement.

After a few weeks in his new position, James told his father that he must modernize his management style and manage the company more in accordance with the new theories of contingency management. His father listened patiently and with great expectations as James explained that the company should not be managed and organized in accordance with "classical" theories—that there was no best way to organize it, to develop or carry out plans, or to promote and compensate employees. Instead, the company should be managed by taking into account contingencies, that is, the various situations which exist from time to time.

Frank Carlton then questioned his son as to what he would have done differently over the past 30 years, pointing out that the plywood industry had always been subject to many variables, such as changing prices and availability of logs, changing price and demand for finished plywood as markets changed (especially as demand for plywood for housing and commercial construction and for exports to Japan changed so often), and large variations in labor rates and availability of skilled labor from year to year. He asked his son how the new contingency theory would change what he was doing and what he had been doing.

1 If you were Frank Carlton, how would you have answered James when he said that the company should not be managed according to "classical" theory, and that there is no one best way to manage?

2 How would you apply contingency theory? How would it change the way effective managers, who may never have heard about contingency theory, carry out their jobs?

CASE 2-2
LMT, INCORPORATED

Frank W. Bates was president of LMT, Incorporated, a large company making wheels, brakes, springs, radios, and other components for the automobile manufacturing companies. The firm also had a division developing and manufacturing components for the space program. LMT's space program activities were in a division headed by a general manager, Julia Sanders. Her personnel manager, Lewis Lemke, recommended that the way to develop managers at all levels in the division was to give them courses and exercises in psychology and human relations. He made the point that, after all, managing is a "people" problem, and the only way people can be good managers is to thoroughly understand themselves and their fellow managers and employees.

Ms. Sanders, impressed with this idea, told Mr. Lemke to go ahead with the program. The personnel manager did so with great energy and thoroughness. After a few years, every manager from top to bottom of the division had gone through a number of courses and exercises to make them understand themselves and other people as well as the entire area of human relations.

But then Ms. Sanders found that the quality of management in the division had not improved, even though it was clear that people did better understand people. In fact, it became apparent that the other divisions of LMT were performing far better than the space division. President Bates had also noted this and asked Ms. Sanders to explain how her division developed managers. After hearing about the program, Mr. Bates said, "I wonder if you have been on the right track."

1 What do you think of the space division's approach to training managers in the essentials of management?

2 If you were Mr. Bates, what would you suggest that Ms. Sanders should have done?

For Further Information

Fayol, H. *General and Industrial Management* (New York: Pitman Publishing Corporation, 1949).

Koontz, H., C. O'Donnell, and H. Weihrich (eds.). *Management—A Book of Readings*, 5th ed. (New York: McGraw-Hill Book Company, 1980).

Matteson, M. T., and J. M. Ivancevich (eds.). *Management Classics*, 2d ed. (Santa Monica, Calif.: Goodyear Publishing Co. Inc., 1981).

Richards, M. D. (ed). *Readings in Management*, 6th ed. (Cincinnati: South-Western Publishing Company, 1982).

Scott, W. G. "Organization Theory: An Overview and an Appraisal," *Academy of Management Journal*, vol. 4, no. 1 (April 1961), pp. 7–26.

Shafritz, J. M., and P. H. Whitbeck (eds.). *Classics of Organization Theory* (Oak Park, Ill.: Moore Publishing Company, Inc., 1978).

3

The External Environment and International Management

After reading this chapter, you should understand:

1 The nature of operating in a pluralistic society
2 The social responsibility of managers
3 The nature and importance of ethics in managing
4 The practice of Japanese management and Theory Z
5 The application of management thought and practice in international and multinational corporations

Much of this book deals with interaction of managers and their subordinates with the environment inside the enterprise, but in most instances the effective manager must also deal with the outside environment. Every time managers plan, they take into account the needs and desires of members of society outside the organization, as well as their own needs for material and human resources, technology, and other inputs from the external environment. They do likewise to some degree with almost every other kind of managerial activity.

All managers, whether they operate in a business, a government agency, a church, a charitable foundation, or a university, must, to varying degrees, take

FIGURE 3-1

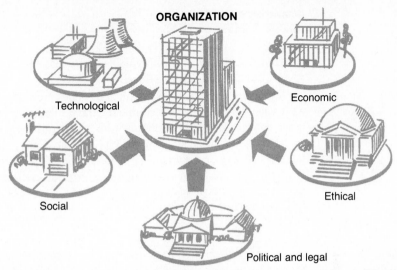

ORGANIZATION

Technological

Economic

Social

Ethical

Political and legal

An organization must operate in, and be responsive to, a number of different external environments.

into account their external environment. While they may be able to do little or nothing to change it, they have no alternative but to respond to it. They must identify, evaluate, and react to the forces outside the enterprise that may affect its operations.

The constraining influences of external factors on the enterprise are even more crucial in international management. As we will show later in this chapter, external constraints are similar for domestic and international enterprises. The impact of external constraints on managing, however, is likely to be more severe. Executives operating in a foreign country need to learn a great deal about the country's educational, economic, legal, and political systems, and especially its sociocultural environment. The impact of the external environment on the organization is illustrated in Figure 3-1.

This chapter deals with the impact of the external environment on the organization and the relationships between business and the society in which it operates. First, the focus is on the domestic environment—particularly the United States. Then the discussion extends to the international environment.

Managers in Their Environments

The relationships between the enterprise and its environment can be examined in several ways. First, we can view the enterprise as importing various kinds of inputs—human, capital, managerial, technical, etc. These inputs are then transformed to produce outputs, such as services and profits. A second approach to the study of the relationships between the enterprise and society is to focus on the demands and legitimate rights of different claimants, such as employees, consumers, suppliers, stockholders, governments, and the community. A third approach is to view the enterprise as operating in an external environment of opportunities and constraints, which can be classified as economic, technological, sociocultural, political, or ethical.

Any single approach is insufficient. The three approaches are not inconsistent with each other; they are complementary. Thus business enterprises—and any other enterprises for that matter—are a part of a larger system. This means that external events affect all organizations. Conversely, the operations of organizations—business or nonbusiness—affect at least to some extent the external environment. The result is a delicate and complex relationship between business and nonbusiness enterprises and society. This section deals with these relationships. Specifically, our discussion focuses on the pluralistic society, social responsibility, and ethics.

Operating in a Pluralistic Society

Managers in the United States operate in a pluralistic society with many organized groups representing various interests. Each group has an impact on other groups but no one group exerts an inordinate amount of power. Many groups exert some power over business. As we have seen in Chapter 1, there are many claimants on the organization (employees, consumers, suppliers, etc.) with divergent goals, and it is the task of the manager to integrate those aims.

Working within a pluralistic society has several implications for business.[1] First, business power is kept in balance by various groups, such as environmental groups. Second, business interests can be expressed by joining groups such as the Chamber of Commerce. Third, business participates in projects with other responsible groups for bettering society; an example might be working toward the renewal of inner cities. Fourth, in a pluralistic society there can be conflict or agreement among groups. Finally, in such a society one group is quite aware of what other groups are doing.

The Social Responsibility of Managers

In the early 1900s the mission of business firms was exclusively economic. Today, partly due to the interdependencies of the many groups in our society, the social involvement of business has increased. There is indeed a question as to what the social responsibility of business really is. Moreover, this same question, orginally asked of business, is now being addressed with increasing frequency to the people in government, universities, nonprofit foundations, charitable organizations, and even churches. Thus, we talk about the social responsibility and social responsiveness (terms we use interchangably) of all organizations, although the focus of our discussion is on business. Society, awakened and vocal with respect to the urgency of social problems, is asking managers, particularly those at the top, what they are doing to discharge their social responsibilities and why they are not doing more. Although there are arguments for business involvement in social activities, there are also arguments against it.[2]

---

[1] G. A. Steiner, *Business and Society* (New York: Random House, Inc., 1975), chap. 5.
[2] The arguments for and against social involvement are based on K. Davis and W. C. Frederick, *Business and Society* (New York: McGraw-Hill Book Company, 1984), chap. 2.

Arguments for social involvement of business

1 Public needs have changed, leading to changed expectations. Business, it is suggested, received its charter from society and consequently has to respond to the needs of society.

2 The creation of a better social environment benefits both society and business. Society gains through better neighborhoods and employment opportunities; business benefits from a better community, since the community is the source of its work force and the consumer of its products and services.

3 Social involvement discourages additional government regulation and intervention. The result is greater freedom and more flexibility in decision making for business.

4 Business has a great deal of power which, it is reasoned, should be accompanied by an equal amount of responsibility.

5 Modern society is an interdependent system, and the internal activities of the enterprise have an impact on the external environment.

6 Social involvement may be in the interest of stockholders.

7 Problems can become profits. Items that may once have been considered waste (for example, empty soft drink cans) can be profitably used again.

8 Social involvement creates a favorable public image. Thus, a firm may attract customers, employees, and investors.

9 Business should try to solve the problems which other institutions have not been able to solve. After all, business has a history of coming up with novel ideas.

10 Business has the resources. Specifically, business should use its talented managers and specialists, as well as its capital resources, to solve some of society's problems.

11 It is better to prevent social problems through business involvement than to cure them. It may be easier to help the hard-core unemployed than to cope with social unrest.

Arguments against social involvement of business

1 The primary task of business is to maximize profit by focusing strictly on economic activities. Social involvement could reduce economic efficiency.

2 In the final analysis, society must pay for the social involvement of business through higher prices. Social involvement would create excessive costs for business, which cannot commit its resources to social action.

3 Social involvement can create a weakened international balance of payments situation. The cost of social programs, the reasoning goes, would have to be added to the price of the product. Thus, American companies selling in international markets would be at a disadvantage when competing with companies in other countries which do not have these social costs to bear.

4 Business has enough power and additional social involvement would further increase its power and influence.

5 Business people lack the social skills to deal with the problems of society. Their training and experience is with economic matters and their skills may not be pertinent to social problems.

6 There is a lack of accountability of business to society. Unless accountability can be established, business should not get involved.

7 There is not complete support for involvement in social actions. Consequently, disagreements among groups with different viewpoints will cause frictions.

Trend toward greater responsiveness

Today many businesses are involved in social action. A decision as to whether companies should extend their social involvement requires a careful examination of the arguments for and against such actions. Certainly society's expectations are changing and the trend seems to be toward greater social responsiveness. In fact, most respondents in a study of *Harvard Business Review* readers consider social responsibility a legitimate and achievable aim for business.[3] Still, the mission of the organization must be taken into account.

Differing enterprise missions

The mission of the enterprise Various kinds of organized enterprises have different missions, entrusted to them by society. The mission of business is the production and distribution of goods and services. The mission of a police department is protection of the safety and welfare of the people. The mission of a state highway department is the design and construction of highways. The mission of a university is teaching and research. And so on.

We should not hold business managers, for example, responsible for solving all social problems. There can hardly be any sense in making it the job of business to furnish public school education or the many other things, like police and fire protection, that the government provides. But business, like any other type of organized enterprise, must interact with, and live in, its environment.

Whether managers achieve their missions, and how they do so, are matters of great social importance. A society expects and deserves the accomplishment of the missions of approved enterprises. In striving to fulfill these expectations, managers know that they must interact with, and live within, an existing environment. This means that they must take into account elements in their surroundings that are important to their success and important to others who may be affected by the actions they take. In other words, managers respond to their environment and become active participants in the community to improve the quality of life. This is what they must do, since the survival of their enterprise depends upon successful interaction with all environmental elements.

---

[3]S. N. Brenner and E. A. Molander, "Is the Ethics of Business Changing?" *Harvard Business Review*, vol. 55, no. 1 (January–February 1977), pp. 57–71.

Reaction or proaction   But to live within an environment and be responsive to it does not mean that managers should merely react in the face of stress. There is a positive aspect as well. For example, there may be a question of whether to react to or to take positive action to modify some environmental elements. To respond requires first of all that we know what aspects in our total environment have or will have a significant influence on our operations. Since no enterprise can be expected to react very quickly to unforeseen developments, an enterprise must *Proaction vs.* practice ways of anticipating developments through forecasts. An alert company, *reaction* for example, does not wait until its product is obsolete and sales have fallen off before coming out with a new or improved product. A government agency should not wait until its regulations are obsolete and discredited before looking for another way to achieve its objectives. No enterprise should wait for problems to develop before preparing to face them. Proaction, as we shall see in Part II on planning, is an essential part of the planning process.

Role of the government   There are many instances where social changes can be implemented only by the enactment of legislation. However, many managers in business and elsewhere have found it to their advantage to do something about pressing social problems. For example, many businesses have profited by filtering smokestack pollutants and selling or utilizing these recovered wastes. Some companies have made a profit by building low-cost apartment buildings in ghetto areas. The Internal Revenue Service learned that it increased tax collection efficiency and effectiveness by simplifying or eliminating certain burdensome reports and forms. In other words, contributing to the solution of social problems does not always involve net expense. But we may need the bludgeoning force of legislation to get improvements under way.

The influence of values and performance criteria on behavior   Even if individual managers have full freedom to act in accordance with the currently conceived social responsibilities, they may not do so because of standards applied in evaluating their performance. Managers, like everyone else, want their performance positively appraised—they seek approval. Therefore, if their success is measured *Performance criteria* in terms of profit, living within a budget, tax collection as a percentage of income, the volume of blood contributed to a blood bank, or the number of communicants in a church, managers will tend to strive to achieve excellence in these regards. If success is measured in terms of pollution control, the number of convicts returned successfully to society, the dollar support for employees seeking university degrees, the ratio of "disadvantaged" to total number of employees, achievements in raising the productivity of subordinates, or combinations of these and similar goals, then managers will strive to achieve them.

Social values   In other words, managers will respond to socially approved values and will give priority to those held in highest esteem. If we want to make sure that organizations respond to social forces, we must clarify social values and then, within a system of varied organizations with a variety of missions, reward managers for their success in responding to them.

The Ethical Environment

All persons, whether in business, government, a university, or any other enterprise are concerned with ethics. In *Webster's Ninth New Collegiate Dictionary*, ethics is defined as "the discipline dealing with what is good and bad and with moral duty and obligation." Business ethics is concerned with truth and justice and has a variety of aspects such as expectations of society, fair competition, advertising, public relations, social responsibilities, consumer autonomy, and corporate behavior in the home country as well as abroad.[4]

Institutionalizing Ethics

Three ways to institutionalize ethics

Managers often have problems with the application of ethical concepts to everyday corporate life. Integrating concepts into daily action is what is meant by institutionalizing ethics. Purcell and Weber suggest that this can be accomplished in three ways: through (1) company policy or a code of ethics; (2) a formally appointed ethics committee; and (3) the teaching of ethics in management development programs.[5] The most common way to institutionalize ethics is to establish a code of ethics; much less common is the use of ethics board committees. Management development programs dealing with ethical issues are very seldom used although companies such as Allied Chemical, International Business Machines, and General Electric have instituted such programs.

Code of Ethics and Its Implementation through Formal Committees

Ethical codes in government

A code is a statement of policies, principles, or rules that guide behavior.

Certainly codes of ethics do not apply only to business enterprises; they should guide the behavior of persons in all organizations and in everyday life. The federal government, for example, has established the following code:[6]

Code of Ethics for Government Service
Any person in Government service should:

I Put loyalty to the highest moral principles and to country above loyalty to persons, party, or Government department.

II Uphold the Constitution, laws, and regulations of the United States and of all governments therein and never be a party to their evasion.

III Give a full day's labor for a full day's pay; giving earnest effort and best thought to the performance of duties.

IV Seek to find and employ more efficient and economical ways of getting tasks accomplished.

V Never discriminate unfairly by the dispensing of special favors or privileges to anyone, whether for remuneration or not; and never accept, for himself or herself or for family members, favors or benefits under circumstances which might be construed by reasonable persons as influencing the performance of governmental duties.

---

[4]C. Walton, *The Ethics of Corporate Conduct* (Englewood Cliffs, N.J.: Prentice-Hall, Inc., 1977), p. 6.
[5]Much of this discussion is based on J. Weber, "Institutionalizing Ethics into the Corporation," *MSU Business Topics*, vol. 29, no. 2 (Spring 1981), pp. 47–52; and T. V. Purcell, S.J., and J. Weber, *Institutionalizing Corporate Ethics: A Case History* (New York: The Presidents Association, The Chief Executive Officers' Division of American Management Association, 1979), Special Study no. 71.
[6]Source: Public Law 96-303, July 3, 1980.

VI Make no private promises of any kind binding upon the duties of office, since a Government employee has no private word which can be binding on public duty.

VII Engage in no business with the Government, either directly or indirectly, which is inconsistent with the conscientious performance of governmental duties.

VIII Never use any information gained confidentially in the performance of governmental duties as a means of making private profit.

IX Expose corruption wherever discovered.

X Uphold these principles, ever conscious that public office is a public trust.

Simply stating a code of ethics is not enough, and the appointment of an ethics committee, consisting of internal and external directors, is considered essential for institutionalizing ethical behavior.[7] The functions of such a committee may include (1) regular meetings to discuss ethical issues, (2) dealing with "gray areas," (3) communicating the code to all members of the organization, (4) checking for possible violations of the code, (5) enforcing the code, (6) rewarding compliance and punishing violations, (7) reviewing and updating the code, and (8) reporting activities of the committee to the board of directors.

Factors That Raise Ethical Standards

In the study cited earlier, the two factors that raise ethical standards the most, according to the respondents, are (1) public disclosure and publicity and (2) the increased concern of a well-informed public. These factors are followed by government regulations and by education to increase the professionalism of business managers.[8]

Enforcement of ethical codes

To make ethical codes effective, provisions must be made for their enforcement. Unethical managers should be held responsible for their actions. This means that privileges and benefits have to be withdrawn and sanctions have to be applied. Although the enforcement of ethical codes may not be easy, the mere existence of such codes can increase ethical behavior by clarifying expectations. On the other hand, one should not expect ethical codes to solve all problems. In fact, they can create a false sense of security. To enforce codes effectively requires consistent ethical behavior and support from top management.

Differing Ethical Standards of Various Societies

Any person in business, government, a university, a church, or some other organization is aware that ethical, as well as legal, standards do differ, particularly among nations and societies. This has long been true. For example, many nations with privately owned companies permit corporations to make contributions to political parties, campaigns, and candidates. (The United States does not.) In countries, payments to government officials and other persons with political influence to assure expedited or favorable handling of a business transaction are not regarded as unethical bribes but as proper payment for services rendered. In many

[7]Weber, op. cit.
[8]Brenner and Molander, op. cit., p. 63.

cases, payments made to assure the landing of a contract are even looked upon as a normal and acceptable way of doing business. Or consider the Quaker Oats Company, which was faced with a situation in which foreign officials threatened to close the operation if the demand for "payouts" was not met. Or what should a company do when the plant manager's safety is in question in case payoffs are not made?[9]

Difficult decisions

The question facing responsible American business managers is: What ethical standards should they follow? There is no question of what to do in the United States, and American executives have had to refuse the suggestion of putting money in a "paper bag." But in a country where such practices are expected and common, American executives are faced with a difficult problem. With the passage of laws by the United States Congress and the adoption of regulations by the Securities and Exchange Commission, not only must American firms report anything that could be called a payoff, but anything else that can be construed as a bribe is now unlawful. Thus we have attempted to export our standards for doing business to other countries.

Japanese Management and Theory Z

Japan, one of the leading industrial nations in the world, has adopted managerial practices that are quite different from those of other economically advanced countries in the Western world. We will discuss two common Japanese practices: lifetime employment and consensus decision making.

Lifetime Employment

Important features of Japanese management practice are lifelong employment (related to the staffing function), great concern for the individual employee, and emphasis on seniority. Typically, employees spend their working life with a single enterprise, which in turn provides employees with security and a feeling of belonging. This practice brings the culturally induced concept of *wa* (harmony) to the enterprise, resulting in employee loyalty and close identification with the aims of the company.

Harmony and loyalty

However, it also adds to business costs because employees are kept on the payroll even though there may be insufficient work. Consequently, firms are beginning to question the practice of lifelong employment. Indeed, changes appear to be in the making, but they are slow—very slow. What is often overlooked, however, is that this permanent employment practice, known as *nenko*, is used only by large firms. In fact, it is estimated that the job security system applies to only about one-third of the labor force.[10]

Lifelong employment

Closely related to lifelong employment is the seniority system, which has

---

[9]Walton, op. cit., chap. 7.
[10]T. K. Oh, "Japanese Management—A Critical Review," *Academy of Management Review*, vol. 1, no. 1 (January 1976), pp. 14–25.

Seniority

provided privileges for older employees who have been with the enterprise a long time. But there are indications that the seniority system may be superceded by a more open approach that provides opportunities for advancement for young people. For example, the relatively new Sony Corporation has team leaders (a point is made of not calling them supervisors) who are often young women 18 or 19 years of age. There is practically no age difference between these leaders and the operators they lead.

Decision Making

The managerial practice of decision making is also considerably different from that in the United States. It is built on the concept that change and new ideas should come primarily from below. Thus, lower-level employees prepare proposals for higher-level personnel. Supervisors, rather than simply accepting or rejecting suggestions, tactfully question proposals, make suggestions, and encourage subordinates. If necessary, proposals are sent back to the initiator for more information.

Consensus decision making

Japanese management, then, uses decision making by consensus; lower-level employees initiate the idea and submit it to the next higher level until it reaches the desk of the top executive. If the proposal is approved, it is returned to the initiator for implementation. Although the decision-making process is time-consuming, the implementation of the decision—because of the general consensus at various levels of management—is swift and does not require additional "selling."

An important characteristic of Japanese decision making is the large amount of effort that goes into defining the question or problem; there is a great deal of communication *before* a decision is actually made. American managers are often accused of making decisions before defining the problem. In contrast, Japanese management makes a decision only after long discussions of the issue.

In summary, Japanese managerial practice still emphasizes (although changes are occurring) lifetime employment, concern for the individual, seniority, and a sense of loyalty to the firm. Furthermore, in decision making there is open communication among people at different levels of the organizational hierarchy, a great deal of collaboration, and a recognition of mutual dependence.

Japanese vs. U.S. Management Practices and Theory Z

Of great concern is the declining growth rate in productivity in the United States. Thus, we increasingly look at Japanese management—rightly or wrongly—to find answers to our productivity crisis. In the above discussion we focused on two characteristics of Japanese management: lifetime employment and consensus decision making. But there are other characteristics that distinguish Japanese from American management practices; these are summarized in Table 3-1. A word of caution must be added as to the interpretation of this table. It is obvious that not all American firms are managed the same way; the same is true of Japanese firms. We also must realize that very few empirical studies exist on the subject and most of the available literature is descriptive. Therefore, the contrasting managerial approaches are suggestive and need to be substantiated by additional research.

Theory Z

In Theory Z, selected Japanese managerial practices are adapted to the environment of the United States and practiced by companies such as IBM, Hewlett-

TABLE 3-1 Comparison of Japanese and United States Management Approaches*

Japanese management	United States management
Planning	
1 Long-term orientation	1 Primarily short-term orientation
2 Collective decision making (*ringi*) with consensus	2 Individual decision making
3 Involvement of many people in preparing and making the decision	3 Involvement of a few people in making and "selling" the decision to persons with divergent values
4 Decision flow from bottom to top and back	4 Decisions initiated at the top, flowing down the organization
5 Slow decision making; fast implementation of the decision	5 Fast decision making; slow implementation requiring compromise, often resulting in suboptimal decisions
Organizing	
1 Collective responsibility and accountability	1 Individual responsibility and accountability
2 Ambiguity of decision responsibility	2 Clarity and specificity of decision responsibility
3 Informal organization structure	3 Formal, bureaucratic organization structure
4 Well-known common organization culture and philosophy; competitive spirit toward other enterprises	4 Lack of common organization culture; identification with profession rather than with company

*Japanese managerial practices are widely discussed in the literature and at professional meetings such as the Japanese-United States Business Conference held in Tokyo, Japan, April 4–8, 1983, and the Pan-Pacific Conference held in Honolulu, Hawaii, March 26–28, 1984.
Source: Adapted from H. Koontz, C. O'Donnell, and H. Weihrich, *Management*, 8th ed. (New York: McGraw-Hill Book Company, 1984).

Packard, and the diversified retail company Dayton-Hudson.[11] One of the characteristics of Type Z organization is an emphasis on the interpersonal skills that are needed for group interaction. Yet, despite the emphasis on group decision making, responsibility remains with the individual (which is quite different from the Japanese practice, which emphasizes collective responsibility). There is also an emphasis on informal and democratic relationships based on trust. Yet, the hierarchical structure still remains intact as illustrated by IBM, where not only goals but also authority, rules, and discipline guide corporate behavior.[12]

Participative management facilitates the free flow of information needed to reach consensus. Formal planning and objectives are important but numerical measures are not overly emphasized. Instead a corporate philosophy and corporate

---

[11]This discussion is based on W. G. Ouchi, *Theory Z* (Reading, Mass.: Addison-Wesley Publishing Company, Inc., 1981).
[12]"Life At IBM—Rules and Discipline and Praise Shape IBMer's Taut World," *Wall Street Journal*, April 8, 1982, pp. 1, 14.

Japanese management	United States management
Staffing	
1 Young people hired out of school; hardly any mobility of people among companies	1 People hired out of schools and from other companies; frequent company changes
2 Slow promotion through the ranks	2 Rapid advancement highly desired and demanded
3 Loyalty to the company	3 Loyalty to the profession
4 Very infrequent performance evaluation for new (young) employees	4 Frequent performance evaluation for new employees
5 Appraisal of long-term performance.	5 Appraisal of short-term results
6 Promotions based on multiple criteria	6 Promotions based primarily on individual performance
7 Training and development considered a long-term investment	7 Training and development undertaken with hesitation (employee may switch to another firm)
8 Lifetime employment common in large companies	8 Job insecurity prevailing
Leading	
1 Leader acting as a social facilitator and group member	1 Leader acting as decision maker and head of the group
2 Paternalistic style	2 Directive style (strong, firm, determined)
3 Common values facilitating cooperation	3 Often divergent values; individualism sometimes hindering cooperation
4 Avoidance of confrontation, sometimes leading to ambiguities; emphasis on harmony	4 Face-to-face confrontation common; emphasis on clarity
5 Bottom-up communication	5 Communication primarily top-down
Controlling	
1 Control by peers	1 Control by superior
2 Control focus on group performance	2 Control focus on individual performance
3 Saving face	3 Fixing blame
4 Extensive use of quality control circles	4 Limited use of quality control circles

values guide managerial actions. People are seen as whole human beings, not simply as factors in production. However, the Japanese practice of very infrequent performance evaluations and promotions is not emphasized by Theory Z-type companies. In short, these companies selectively use some Japanese managerial practices, but make adjustments for the environment prevailing in the United States.

Japanese Companies Operating in the United States

In an attempt to demonstrate the effectiveness of Japanese managerial approaches, success stories of Japanese companies operating in the United States are often cited. Workers at Sony's television plant in San Diego are said to produce as well as workers in Japan. But other experiences are not quite as convincing. YKK,

Inc., a manufacturer of zippers, has experienced labor-management confrontations similar to those experienced by U.S. companies. Let us look at a more positive example.

Bridgestone Tire Company

Bridgestone Corporation, a Japanese tire firm that took over the Firestone Tire & Rubber Company plant in Tennessee, was able not only to smooth the stormy labor relations that had plagued the company for years, but also to improve both productivity and quality.[13] Some of the methods used to achieve these results were indeed rather traditional. They included investing in new equipment, setting high quality standards, and using a disciplined managerial approach that required employees to work harder and to give up some seniority provisions, thus allowing the company to fill key positions with the most suitable employees. Moreover, employees were also asked to participate in decisions that affect them and their jobs. For example, workers, not just inspectors, now have responsibility for the quality of the products. And this was done with the cooperation of the union. Bridgestone also used a management-by-objectives approach which is built on the concept of self-control and self-direction as will be discussed in a later chapter.

Japanese firms investing in the U.S.

The trend of Japanese firms investing in manufacturing facilities in the United States is probably going to continue. In 1983, 31 Japanese firms were established here bringing the total of Japanese-owned companies to 309 in 1984, employing 73,000 workers.[14] These firms often demand less costly labor contracts. Although Japanese firms generally resist unions, 23 percent of the 163 companies responding to a 1982 survey were unionized.

International Management and Multinational Corporations

International management

The study of *international management* focuses on the operation of international firms in host countries. It is concerned with managerial problems related to the flow of people, goods, and money, with the ultimate aim being to manage better in situations that involve crossing national boundaries.

The environmental factors that affect domestic firms usually are more critical for international corporations operating in foreign countries. Managers involved in international business are faced with many factors that are different from those of the domestically oriented firm. Managers have to interact with employees who have different educational backgrounds and value systems; they also must cope with different legal, political, and economic factors. Thus, these environments understandably influence the way managerial and enterprise functions are carried out.

[13]"The Japanese Manager Meets the American Worker," *Business Week*, Aug. 20, 1984, pp. 128–129.
[14]Ibid.

The Nature and Purpose of International Business

International businesses

Although business has been conducted on an international scale for many years, international business has gained greater visibility and importance in recent years because of the growth of large multinational corporations. *International businesses* engage in transactions across national boundaries. These transactions include the transfer of goods, services, technology, managerial knowledge, and capital to other countries.

Kinds of interactions

The interaction of a firm with the host country can take many forms, as illustrated in Figure 3-2. One is the *exportation* of goods and services. Another is a *licensing* agreement for producing goods in another country. The parent company may also engage in *management contracts* that provide for operating foreign companies. Still another form of interaction is the *joint venture* with a firm in the host country. Finally, multinationals may set up wholly owned *subsidiaries* or *branches* with production facilities in the host country. Thus, in developing a global strategy, an international firm has many options.

The contact between the parent firm and the host country is affected by several factors; some are unifying, others can cause conflicts.

Unifying effects   Unifying influences occur when the parent company provides and shares technical and managerial know-how, thus assisting the host company in the development of human and material resources. Moreover, the parent corporation and the firm in the host country may find it advantageous to be integrated into a global organization structure. Whatever the interaction, policies must provide for equity and result in benefits for both the parent firm and the host company. Only then can one expect a long-lasting relationship.

Sources of conflict

Potentials for conflict   Many factors can cause conflicts between the parent firm and the host country. Nationalistic self-interest may overshadow the benefits obtained through cooperation. Similarly, sociocultural differences can lead to breakdowns in communication and subsequent misunderstandings. Also, a large multinational firm may have such overpowering economic effects on a small country that the host country feels overwhelmed. Some international corporations have been charged with making excessive profits, hiring the best local people away from local firms, and operating contrary to social customs. The international corporation must develop social and diplomatic skills in its managers in order to prevent such conflicts and to resolve those that unavoidably occur.

The Multinational Corporations

Ethnocentric outlook

Multinational corporations (MNCs) have their headquarters in one country, but their operations in many countries. As illustrated in Table 3-2, managers involved in international business are faced with many factors that are different from those confronting the domestically oriented firm. Managers have to interact with employees who have different educational backgrounds and value systems; they also must cope with different legal, political, and economic factors. Thus, environments do influence the way managerial and enterprise functions are carried out.

In its early stages, international business was conducted with an *ethnocentric* outlook; that is, the orientation and type of operation was based on that of the

FIGURE 3-2

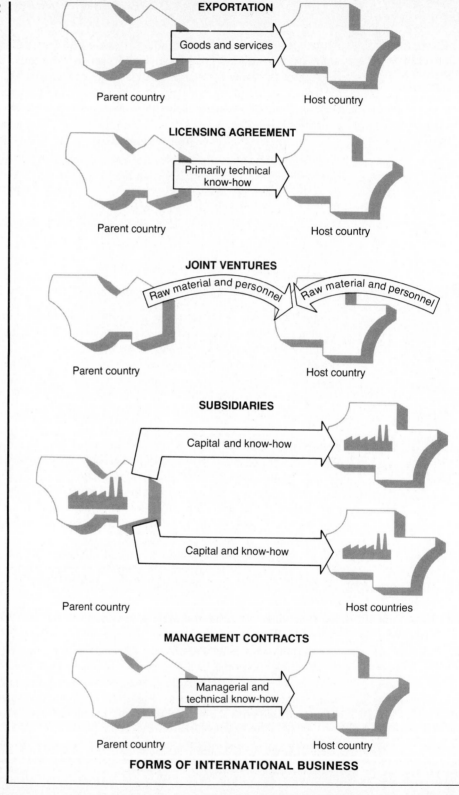

EXPORTATION

Goods and services

Parent country   Host country

LICENSING AGREEMENT

Primarily technical know-how

Parent country   Host country

JOINT VENTURES

Raw material and personnel   Raw material and personnel

Parent country   Host country

SUBSIDIARIES

Capital and know-how

Capital and know-how

Parent country   Host countries

MANAGEMENT CONTRACTS

Managerial and technical know-how

Parent country   Host country

FORMS OF INTERNATIONAL BUSINESS

Geocentric outlook

parent company.[15] In contrast, the modern multinational corporation has a *geocentric* orientation. This means that the total organization is viewed as an interdependent system operating in many countries. The relationships between headquarters and subsidiaries are collaborative, with communication flowing in both directions. Furthermore, key positions are filled by managers of different nationalities. In short, the orientation of the multinational corporation is truly international and goes beyond a narrow nationalistic viewpoint.

Advantages of multinationals Multinational corporations have several advantages over firms that have a domestic orientation. Obviously, the MNC can take advantage of business opportunities in many different countries. It can also raise money for its operations throughout the world. Moreover, multinational firms benefit by being able to establish production facilities in countries where their products can be produced most effectively and efficiently. Companies with worldwide operations sometimes have better access to natural resources and materials that may not be available to domestic firms. Finally, the large MNCs can recruit management and other personnel from a worldwide labor pool.

Women in management and the worldwide labor pool

To illustrate the demand for managers with an international background, let us consider Marisa Bellisario, one of the most sought-after executives in Europe in 1984.[16] She was the first woman to head a major industrial firm in Italy, the state-controlled Italtel Societa Italiana (Iltaltel), the biggest Italian firm making telecommunications equipment. Her background, however, is international. After receiving her degree in economics and business administration from Turin University, she worked at Olivetti in the electronics division. When Olivetti sold its data processing unit to General Electric, she spent time in Miami working on GE's worldwide marketing strategy for computers. She left GE to head corporate planning at Olivetti. As the CEO at Iltaltel, she turned the company around, showing a small profit. (The firm had experienced huge losses in the past.) Her managerial approach has been characterized as "straight out of the textbook" and companies such as GTE Corporation, IBM, AT&T, and other European and Japanese firms are interested in recruiting her.

Threats to MNCs

Challenges for the multinationals The advantages of multinational operation must be weighed against the challenges and risk associated with operating in foreign environments. One problem is the increasing nationalism in many countries. Years ago, developing countries lacked managerial, marketing, and technical

---

[15]D. A. Heenan and H. V. Perlmutter, *Multinational Organization Development* (Reading, Mass.: Addison-Wesley Publishing Company, Inc., 1979), chap. 2.

[16]"Iltaltel's New Chief Gets What She Wants," *Business Week*, Apr. 30, 1984, p. 51; Robert Ball, "Italy's Most Talked-About Executive," *Fortune*, Apr. 2, 1984, pp. 99–102.

**TABLE 3-2 Characteristics and Practices of
Domestic and International Enterprises**

	Domestic enterprise (industrialized country)	International enterprise
The environment		
1 *Educational environment*		
(a) Language (spoken, written, official)	One	Multiple
(b) Education system (quality, level, extent)	No or little constraint	Great constraint
2 *Sociocultural environment*		
(a) Values, attitudes (toward achievement, risk taking, scientific method, work)	Homogeneous	Heterogeneous
(b) Social organization (authority, status, roles, institutions, mobility, social systems)	Similar	Different
3 *Political-legal environment*		
(a) Political orientation (power, ideologies)	Country-centered	Transnational
(b) Legal environment (laws, codes, regulations)	Fairly uniform	Different
(c) National sovereignties	One	Many
(d) Government policies, regulations	Same	Different
4 *Economic environment*		
(a) Economic development (underdeveloped, industrialized)	At similar stages	At different stages
(b) Economic system (capitalistic, mixed, Marxist)	Similar	Different

skills. Consequently, they welcomed the multinationals. But the situation is changing, with people in developing countries acquiring those skills. In addition, countries not only become aware of the value of their natural resources, but they also become more skilled in international negotiations. Finally, multinationals must maintain good relations with the host country, a task that may prove difficult because governments frequently change, and corporations must deal with and adapt to these changes.

Summary

This chapter focuses on the influences of external factors on enterprises operating within their home country and abroad. In the United States, managers operate in a pluralistic society in which many organized groups represent different interests. There are many arguments for and against the social involvement of business. At

	Domestic enterprise (industrialized country)	International enterprise
Managerial functions		
1 *Planning*		
Scanning the environment for threats and opportunities	National market	Worldwide market
2 *Organizing*		
(*a*) Organization structure	Structure for domestic operations	Global structure
(*b*) View of authority	Similar	Different
3 *Staffing*		
(*a*) Sources of managerial talent	National labor pool	Worldwide labor pool
(*b*) Manager orientation	Often ethnocentric	Geocentric
4 *Leading*		
(*a*) Leadership and motivation	Influenced by similar culture	Influenced by many different cultures
(*b*) Communication lines	Relatively short	Network with long distances
5 *Controlling*		
Reporting system (e.g., accounting and tax)	Similar requirements	Many different requirements
Enterprise functions		
1 *Engineering and production*		
State of the art, technology	Similar technology	Different levels of technology
2 *Marketing*		
Consumer needs and preferences	Local market	Global market
3 *Financing*		
Sources, capital transfer	Primarily domestic	Global

any rate, the mission of the enterprise, proaction rather than reaction, the role of the government, and values and performance criteria must all be taken into account in making decisions about social involvement. Ethics is concerned with what is good, moral, true, and just. Some authors have suggested that businesses institutionalize ethics and develop codes of ethics. But there are also other factors that raise ethical standards.

Japanese managerial practices differ greatly from those in the United States. Theory Z are selected managerial practices that have been adapted by some U.S. companies. International business extends its operations across national boundaries. Many factors help to unify the parent company and the firm in the host country. However, there is also the potential for conflict. Multinational corporations have certain advantages over firms operating solely in the domestic market. More recently, however, multinational firms have been challenged by host countries.

Key Ideas and Concepts for Review

Pluralistic society
Arguments for social involvement of
  business
Arguments against social involvement
  of business
Ethics
Institutionalizing ethics
Code of ethics for government service
Factors raising ethical standards
Lifetime employment

Decision making in Japan
Theory Z
International management
Forms of international business
  interaction
Ethnocentric orientation
Geocentric orientation
Advantages of MNCs
Women in international management
Challenges to MNCs

For Discussion

1 Why is the environment external to an enterprise so important to all managers? Can any manager avoid being influenced by the external environment? Identify the elements of the external environment that are likely to be the most important to each of the following: a company president, a sales manager, a production manager, a controller, and a personnel manager.

2 What effects do the external social, political, and legal environments have on the enterprise? How do managers respond to these influences?

3 What are the major social responsibilities of business managers? Of government managers? Have these responsibilities changed over the years? How?

4 List and discuss benefits of some codes of ethics. What additional ethical codes would you recommend for your enterprise, your university, your class, your family? How should these codes be enforced?

5 Do you think managerial concepts and practices we know and apply in the United States can be transferred to England, France, or West Germany?

6 What are some typical management practices in Japan and how do they compare with those in the United States?

7 What are likely to be the differences between the operation of a domestic firm and that of a multinational corporation? Select five differences and discuss their importance.

8 What advantages do multinational corporations have? What challenges must they meet? Give examples.

CASE 3-1

THE SOCIAL RESPONSIBILITY OF BUSINESS

In a conference held in Washington to consider the social responsibility of business managers, among the many statements made were the following.

By a leader of a consumer group: "The trouble with business managers is that they talk a lot about social responsibility but they do little or nothing about it. Look at the problem of air pollution caused by automobiles that our manufacturers have produced. Look at the problem of energy shortages caused by businesses with their manufacture and sale of energy-eating air conditioners, electrical appliances, and automobiles. Look at the unwillingness of our oil companies to find more oil and gas, on the excuse that they cannot afford to do so, especially when the government tightly limits the prices of oil and gas. Look at the problems of poverty and unemployment caused by the unwillingness of business to pay higher wages and hire more people. I could mention more things, but they all add up to an unwillingness of business managers to meet their social responsibilities."

By a prominent economist: "There is one and only one social responsibility of business—to use its resources in activities designed to increase its profits—so long as it stays within the rules of the game, which is to say, engages in open and free competition, without deception or fraud. Few trends could so thoroughly undermine the very foundations of our free society as the acceptance by corporate officials of a social responsibility other than to make as much money for their stockholders as possible."

By a corporation president: "We speak constantly of the social responsibility of business. Why not speak also of the social responsibility of our governments, our hospitals, our universities, and our other organizations? Our federal, state, and local governments spend around 40 percent of our nation's entire spendable income; are they socially responsible in taking so much from all of us and then often spending even more than they take in? Cities with poor sewage disposal systems are polluting our oceans, lakes, and rivers. Our hospitals are charging, for a little room, from $175 to $300 per day for their portion of health care; is this being socially responsible? Our universities continue to increase the costs of education every year and show no signs of increasing their productivity; is this being socially responsible? And so on. No, ladies and gentlemen, social responsibility is not only a business manager's problem. It is far more."

1 What do you see to be the social responsibility of business managers?

2 How does this concern fit into the need for managers in nonbusiness as well as business enterprises to take into account their total external environment?

3 How should managers meet their social responsibilities?

CASE 3-2

CONSOLIDATED COMPUTERS, INC.

James Pruitt was ushered into the president's office. Three months ago he had been appointed manager of the first foreign plant of Consolidated Computers, Inc. A division manager of many proven talents, he appeared to be the ideal person for this assignment. He was an innovator and very much interested in a foreign appointment. Now he was calling on his superior just before catching the plane for Riyadh.

"I wanted to talk to you," the president began, "about some issues you will be facing when you reach Saudi Arabia. I guess you might call what I want to say a matter of my search for a business philosophy. We have not had to experience here the new issues that you will face, and we simply do not have a set of policies and procedures to cover such matters. Perhaps out of your experience we can move in that direction in case we later establish operations in other countries.

"I am not concerned about your encountering new principles of management. They are universal, you have developed great skill in applying them to domestic operations, and I have no doubt about your skill in applying them in a foreign environment. You will soon discover, however, that managing is different abroad because the cultural environment is so different.

"I think our best position is to realize that we are going into Saudi Arabia as a guest. We each need the other at this time, but there may come a time when their political forces will require us to give up ownership of our plant. It is up to you to develop the rapport with all interested parties which will most benefit our long-run interests.

"Since all of your employees will be, or soon will be, Saudis, it is vital to learn as quickly as possible something about their culture. Perhaps your best move is to perfect your skill in the use of their language and really learn to think and act as a native. I am not sure anyone from the United States can do this. You and I were raised in the folds of Western civilization, which has very different institutions and behavior patterns from those you will encounter in the Near East. For instance, does one adhere to the ethical principles of the Saudis or to our own? Do they have the same trust and reliance on people that we do? Will they always react as we here are accustomed to do? Is social responsibility thought of in the same terms? What intentions and actions on your part will be well received by your suppliers, your customers, your competitors, and public figures?

"You know, I suppose that what is really on my mind is that we don't really know at what point there may be a conflict between our two cultures, or when it occurs, what choice you will make."

1 If you were James Pruitt, how would you go about finding out what the local business customs in Saudi Arabia are? What other environmental factors would you look for? How would you respond to them?

2 Suppose you found that it is customary not to lay off employees when work slackens. What would you do?

3 Suppose you found that it is normal business practice to give government employees a small amount of money when they help your people to get something through a department or clear up some paperwork jams. Would you do the same thing? Why, or why not?

For Further Information

"Are Foreign Partners Good for U.S. Companies?" *Business Week*, May 28, 1984.

"Catholic Social Teaching and the U.S. Economy: First Draft—Bishops' Pastoral," *Origins*, vol. 14, no. 22/23 (Nov. 15, 1984), pp. 337–383.

Davis, K., and W. C. Frederick. *Business and Society*, 5th ed. (New York: McGraw-Hill Book Company, 1984).

Diebold, J. *The Role of Business in Society* (New York: AMACOM, 1982).

Gladwin T. N., and I. Walter. *Multinationals Under Fire: Lessons in the Management of Conflict* (New York: John Wiley & Sons, Inc., 1980).

Jones, T. M. "An Integrating Framework for Research in Business and Society: A Step Toward the Elusive Paradigm?" *Academy of Management Review*, vol. 8, no. 4 (October 1983), pp. 559–564.

Koontz, H. "A Model for Analyzing the Universality and Transferability of Management," in H. Koontz, C. O'Donnell, and H. Weihrich (eds.), *Management—A Book of Readings*, 5th ed. (New York: McGraw-Hill Book Company, 1980), pp. 88–97.

Kujawa, D. "Technology Strategy and Industrial Relations: Case Studies of Japanese Multinationals in the United States," *Journal of International Business Studies*, vol. 14, no. 3 (Winter 1983), pp. 9–22.

Main, J. "The Trouble With Managing Japanese-Style," *Fortune*, Apr. 2, 1984, pp. 50–56.

Magaziner, I. C., and R. B. Reich. *Minding America's Business* (New York: Harcourt Brace Jovanovich, 1982).

McCoy, B. H. "The Parable of the Sadhu," *Harvard Business Review*, vol. 61, no. 5 (September–October 1983), pp. 103–108.

McFarland, D. E. *Management and Society: An Institutional Framework* (Englewood Cliffs, N.J.: Prentice-Hall, Inc., 1982).

Schonberg, R. J. *Japanese Manufacturing Techniques: Nine Hidden Lessons in Simplicity* (New York: The Free Press, 1982).

Sullivan, J. "A Critique of Theory Z," *Academy of Management Review*, vol. 8, no. 1 (January 1983), pp. 132–142.

Yang, C. Y. "Management Styles: American Vis-A-Vis Japanese," in H. Koontz, C. O'Donnell, and H. Weihrich (eds.), *Management—A Book of Readings*, 5th ed. (New York: McGraw-Hill Book Company, 1980), pp. 98–104.

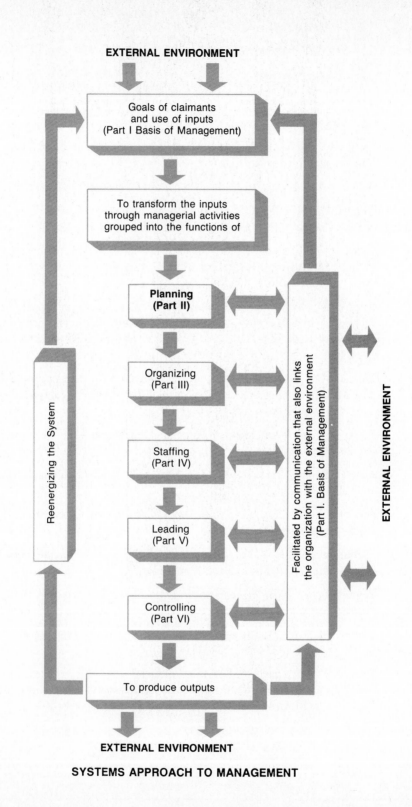

EXTERNAL ENVIRONMENT

Goals of claimants
and use of inputs
(Part I Basis of Management)

To transform the inputs
through managerial activities
grouped into the functions of

**Planning
(Part II)**

Organizing
(Part III)

Staffing
(Part IV)

Leading
(Part V)

Controlling
(Part VI)

Reenergizing the System

Facilitated by communication that also links
the organization with the external environment
(Part I. Basis of Management)

EXTERNAL ENVIRONMENT

To produce outputs

EXTERNAL ENVIRONMENT

SYSTEMS APPROACH TO MANAGEMENT

Planning

4

The Nature and Purpose of Planning

CHAPTER OBJECTIVES

After reading this chapter, you should understand:

1 What planning involves
2 The nature of planning
3 The various types of plans
4 The steps in planning
5 The meaning of the commitment principle

You are now familiar with basic management theory and have been introduced to the five essential managerial functions: planning, organizing, staffing, leading, and controlling. The following four chapters on planning form Part II of the book.

In designing an environment for the effective performance of individuals working together in groups, a manager's most essential task is to see that everyone understands the group's purposes and objectives and its methods of attaining them. If group effort is to be effective, people must know what they are expected to accomplish. This is the function of planning. It is the most basic of all the managerial functions. **Planning** involves selecting from among alternative future courses of action for the enterprise as a whole and for every department or section within it. It requires selecting enterprise objectives and departmental goals and determining ways of achieving them. Plans thus provide a rational approach to preselected objectives. Planning also strongly implies managerial innovation.

Definition of planning

Planning bridges the gap from where we are to where we want to go. It makes it possible for things to occur which would not otherwise happen. Although we can seldom predict the exact future and although factors beyond our control may interfere with the best-laid plans, unless we plan, we are leaving events to chance. Planning is an intellectually demanding process; it requires that we consciously determine courses of action and base our decisions on purpose, knowledge, and considered estimates.

The Nature of Planning

We can highlight the essential nature of planning by examining its four major aspects: (1) its contribution to purpose and objectives (2) its primacy among the manager's tasks; (3) its pervasiveness; and (4) the efficiency of resulting plans.

Contribution of Planning to Purpose and Objectives

The purpose of every plan and all its supporting plans is to contribute to the accomplishment of enterprise purpose and objectives. This principle derives from the nature of organized enterprise, which exists for the accomplishment of group purpose through deliberate cooperation.

Primacy of Planning

As you can see in Figure 4-1, since managerial operations in organizing, staffing, leading, and controlling are designed to support the accomplishment of enterprise objectives, *planning logically precedes* the execution of all other managerial functions. Although in practice all the functions mesh as a system of action, planning is unique in that it involves establishing the objectives necessary for all group effort. Besides, a manager must plan in order to know what kind of organization relationships and personal qualifications are needed, along which course subordinates are to be led, and what kind of control is to be applied. And, of course, all the other managerial functions must be planned if they are to be effective.

Planning precedes other functions

Planning and **control** are inseparable—the Siamese twins of management (see Figure 4-2). Unplanned action cannot be controlled, for control means keeping activities on course by correcting deviations from plans. Any attempt to control without plans is meaningless, since there is no way for people to tell whether they are going where they want to go (the result of the task of control) unless they first know where they want to go (part of the task of planning). Plans thus furnish the standards of control.

Planning and controlling are closely related

Pervasiveness of Planning

Planning is a function of all managers, although the character and breadth of planning will vary with each manager's authority and with the nature of policies and plans outlined by superiors. It is virtually impossible to limit managers' jobs so that they can exercise no discretion, and unless they have some planning responsibility, they are not truly managers.

If we recognize the pervasiveness of planning, we can more easily understand why some people distinguish between policy making (the setting of guidelines for decision making) and administration, or between the "manager" and the "administrator" or "supervisor." One manager, because of his or her authority or position in the organization, may do more—or more important—planning than another,

FIGURE 4-1

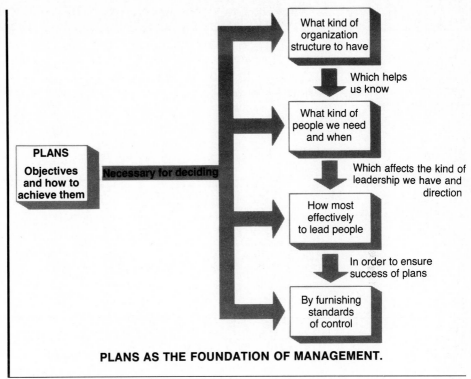

PLANS AS THE FOUNDATION OF MANAGEMENT.

or the planning of one may be more basic and applicable to a larger portion of the enterprise than that of another. However, all managers—from presidents to first-level supervisors—plan. Even the head of a road gang or a factory crew plans in a limited area under fairly strict rules and procedures. Interestingly, in studies of work satisfactions, a principle factor in the success of supervisors at the lowest organization level was the extent of their ability to plan.

All managers plan

Although all managers plan, the work schedule of the first-line supervisor differs from the strategic plan developed by top managers. Roger Smith, the chief executive officer at General Motors planned the grand strategy of producing small cars in Japan and Korea. Chairman Fauber of K-Mart, a retailer known for its no-frills discount stores, planned to "upscale" the operation by offering a wider selection and higher-margin apparel. Thornton Bradshaw of the RCA Corporation redirected strategy, moving the company away from videodiscs and selling unrelated businesses. He focused instead on the company's strengths in communication satellites and radar display systems produced for the Navy. While top executives plan the general direction of the firm, managers at all levels must prepare their plans so that they contribute to the overall aims of the organization.

Top managers plan the strategy

Managers at all levels contribute to the organization's aims

Efficiency of Plans

We measure the *efficiency* of a plan by its contribution to our purpose and objectives, offset by the costs and other factors required to formulate and operate it. A plan may enhance the attainment of objectives, but at unnecessarily high cost. Plans are efficient if they achieve their purpose at a reasonable cost, when cost is

FIGURE 4-2

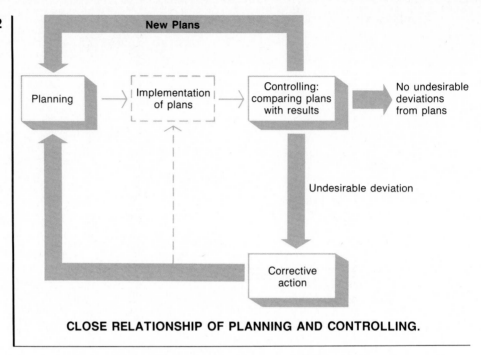

CLOSE RELATIONSHIP OF PLANNING AND CONTROLLING.

measured not only in terms of time or money or production, but also in the degree of individual and group satisfaction.

Many managers have followed plans whose costs were greater than the revenue that could be obtained. For example, one airline acquired certain aircraft with costs exceeding revenues. Companies have also tried to sell products that were unacceptable to the market; an example is an auto manufacturer that tried to capture a market by emphasizing engineering without making competitive advances in style. Plans can even make it impossible to achieve objectives if they make enough people in an organization dissatisfied or unhappy. The new president of a company that was losing money attempted to reorganize and cut expenses quickly by wholesale and unplanned layoffs of key personnel. The resulting fear, resentment, and loss of morale led to productivity so much lower as to defeat the new executive's objective of eliminating losses and making profits. And some attempts to install management appraisal and development programs have failed because of group resentment of the methods used, regardless of the basic soundness of the programs.

Types of Plans

The failure of some managers to recognize that there are a number of different types of plans has often caused difficulty in making planning effective. It is easy to see that a major program, such as one to build and equip a new factory, is a plan. But a number of other courses of future action are also plans. Keeping in

FIGURE 4-3

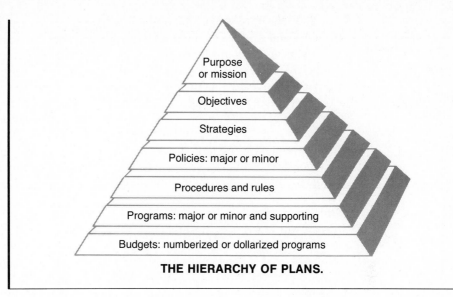

THE HIERARCHY OF PLANS.

mind that a plan encompasses any course of future action, we can see that plans are varied. They are classified here as (1) purposes or missions, (2) objectives, (3) strategies, (4) policies, (5) procedures, (6) rules, (7) programs, and (8) budgets. To some extent, they are a hierarchy, as illustrated in Figure 4-3.

Purposes or Missions

Every kind of organized operation has, or at least should have if it is to be meaningful, purposes or missions. In every social system, enterprises have a basic function or task which is assigned to them by society. The purpose of a business generally is the production and distribution of goods and services. The purpose of a state highway department is the design, building, and operation of a system of state highways. The purpose of the courts is the interpretation of laws and their application. The purpose of a university is teaching and research. And so on.

Although we do not do so, some writers distinguish between purposes and missions. While a business, for example, may have a social purpose of producing and distributing goods and services, it can accomplish this by fulfilling a mission of producing certain lines of products. The missions of an oil company, like Exxon, are to search for oil and to produce, refine, and market petroleum and a wide variety of petroleum products, from diesel fuel to chemicals. The mission of the Du Pont Company has been expressed as "better things through chemistry," and Kimberly-Clark (noted for its Kleenex trademark) regards its business mission as the production and sale of paper and paper products. In the 1960s, the mission of NASA was to get a person to the moon before the Russians. Hallmark, which has expanded its business beyond greeting cards, defines its mission as "the social expression business."[1]

Examples

---

[1]W. L. Glueck and L. R. Jauch, *Business Policy and Strategic Management* (New York: McGraw-Hill Book Company, 1984), chap. 2.

It is true that in some businesses and other enterprises, the purpose or mission often becomes fuzzy. In some of the larger conglomerates, such as Litton Industries, missions related to the product line do not appear to exist. However, many of the conglomerates have regarded their mission as synergy,[2] which is accomplished through the combination of a variety of companies.

Synergy

People sometimes think that the mission of a business, as well as its objective, is to make a profit. It is true that every kind of enterprise must have, as we pointed out in Chapter 1, a "surplus"—in business, a "profit"—goal or objective if it is to survive and do the task society has entrusted to it. But this basic objective is accomplished by undertaking activities, going in clearly defined directions, achieving goals, and accomplishing a mission.

Objectives

Objectives or **goals**—terms we use interchangeably in this book—are the ends toward which activity is aimed. They represent not only the end point of planning but the end toward which organizing, staffing, leading, and controlling are aimed. While enterprise objectives are the basic plan of the firm, a department may also have its own objectives. Its goals naturally contribute to the attainment of enterprise objectives, but the two sets of goals may be entirely different. For example, the objective of a business might be to make a certain profit by producing a given line of home entertainment equipment, while the goal of the manufacturing department might be to produce the required number of television sets of a given design and quality at a given cost. These objectives are consistent, but they differ in that the manufacturing department alone cannot ensure accomplishing the company's objective.

Strategies

For years the military used the word "strategies" to mean grand plans made in the light of what is believed an adversary might or might not do. While the term "strategies" still usually has a competitive implication, managers increasingly use it to reflect broad areas of an enterprise operation.

Three definitions of strategy

Three definitions are indicative of the most common usages of the term **"strategies"**: (1) general programs of action and deployment of resources to attain comprehensive objectives; (2) the program of objectives of an organization, resources used to attain these objectives, and policies governing the acquisition, use, and disposition of these resources; and (3) the determination of the basic long-term objectives of an enterprise and the adoption of courses of action and allocation of resources necessary to achieve these goals.

Basic questions

Thus, a company has to decide what kind of business it is going to be in. Is it a transportation or a railroad company? Is it a container or a paper box manufacturer? The firm also has to decide on its growth goal and its desired profitability. A strategy might include such major policies as to market directly rather than through distributors, or to concentrate on proprietary products, or to have a full line of autos, as General Motors decided to have many years ago.

---

[2]Expressed simply as a situation where 2 plus 2 becomes equal to 5, or where the whole is greater than the sum of the parts.

The purpose of strategies, then, is to determine and communicate, through a system of major objectives and policies, a picture of what kind of enterprise is envisioned. Strategies do not attempt to outline exactly how the enterprise is to accomplish its objectives, since this is the task of countless major and minor supporting programs. But they furnish a framework for guiding thinking and action. Their usefulness in practice and their importance in guiding planning do, however, justify the separation of strategies as a type of plan for purpose of analysis.

GM's strategy

Strategies have become increasingly complex and internationally oriented.[3] Take General Motors, which has been threatened by foreign competitors, especially the Japanese. For decades, GM had a "do-it-yourself" strategy. But now some GM cars are made by Asian rival companies such as Suzuki Motors Company and Isuzu Motors Ltd. of Japan. In addition, GM engaged in a joint venture with Toyota Motor Corporation to produce subcompacts in California. Equally surprising is GM's strategic move into nonautomotive businesses such as information processing and robotics. To implement this strategy, GM bought Electronic Data Systems Corporation and engaged in a joint venture with the Japanese robot maker Fanuc Ltd. But a change in strategy usually requires a reorganization, and GM is currently in the process of changing the organization structure that served the company well for over 60 years.

Policies

Policies also are plans in that they are general statements or understandings which guide or channel thinking and action in decision making. All policies are not "statements;" they are often merely implied from the actions of managers. The president of a company, for example, may strictly follow—perhaps for convenience rather than as policy—the practice of promoting from within; the practice may then be interpreted as policy and carefully followed by subordinates. In fact, one of the problems of managers is to make sure that subordinates do not interpret as policy minor managerial decisions that are not intended to serve as patterns.

Policies define an area within which a decision is to be made and ensure that the decision will be consistent with, and contribute to, an objective. Policies help decide issues before they become problems, make it unnecessary to analyze the same situation every time it comes up, and unify other plans, thus permitting managers to delegate authority and still maintain control over what their subordinates do. For example, a certain railroad has the policy of acquiring industrial land to replace all company acreage sold along its right of way. This policy permits the manager of the land department to develop acquisition plans without continual reference to top management, while at the same time furnishing a standard of control.

Policies ordinarily exist on all levels of the organization and range from major

---

[3]U. C. Lehner, "With His Bid for EDS, GM's Smith Continues to Make Bold Changes," *Wall Street Journal*, July 2, 1984; "GM Moves into a New Era," *Business Week*, July 16, 1984, pp. 48–54.

Policies at
all levels

company policies through major department policies to minor policies applicable to the smallest segment of the organization. They may be related to functions such as sales and finance, or merely to a project such as the design of a new product to meet a specified competition.

Types of
policies

There are many types of policies. Examples include policies to hire only university-trained engineers or to encourage employee suggestions for improved cooperation, to promote from within, to conform strictly to a high standard of business ethics, to set competitive prices, or to insist on fixed, rather than cost-plus, pricing.

Since policies are guides to decision making, it follows that they must allow for some discretion. Otherwise, they would be rules. Too often, policies are interpreted as a kind of "ten commandments" that leave no room for discretion. Although discretion, in some instances, is quite broad, it can be exceedingly narrow. For example, a policy to buy from the lowest of three qualified bidders leaves to discretion only the question of which bidders are qualified; a requirement to buy from a certain supplier, regardless of price or service, would, however, be a rule.

To see how policies are often misunderstood, let us look at examples from a company's policy manual. In each case, there is room for a person in a decision-making capacity to use discretion.

Examples
of policies

1 **Gifts from suppliers.** Except for token gifts of purely nominal or advertising value, no employee shall accept any gift or gratuity from any supplier at any time. [What is "token" or "nominal"?]

2 **Entertainment.** No officer or employee shall accept favors or entertainment from an outside organization or agency which are substantial enough to cause undue influence in the selection of goods or services for the company. [What is "substantial" or "undue"?]

3 **Outside employment.** It is improper for any employee to work for any company customers, or for any competitors, or for any vendors or suppliers of goods or services to the company; outside employment is further prohibited if it (*a*) results in a division of loyalty to the company or a conflict of interest, or (*b*) interferes with or adversely affects the employee's work or opportunity for advancement in the company. [What is meant by "division of loyalty," "conflict of interest," and "adversely"?]

4 **Pricing.** Territorial division managers may each establish such prices for the products under their individual control as they deem in the division's interest so long as (*a*) these prices result in gross profit margins for any line of products which are consistent with the approved profit plan; (*b*) price reductions will not result in detrimental effects on prices of similar products of another company division in another state or country; and (*c*) prices meet the legal requirements of the state or country in which the prices are effective. [What are "consistent profit margins," "detrimental effects," and "legal requirements"?]

Policy is a means of encouraging discretion and initiative, but within limits. The amount of freedom will naturally depend upon the policy and in turn reflects

FIGURE 4-4

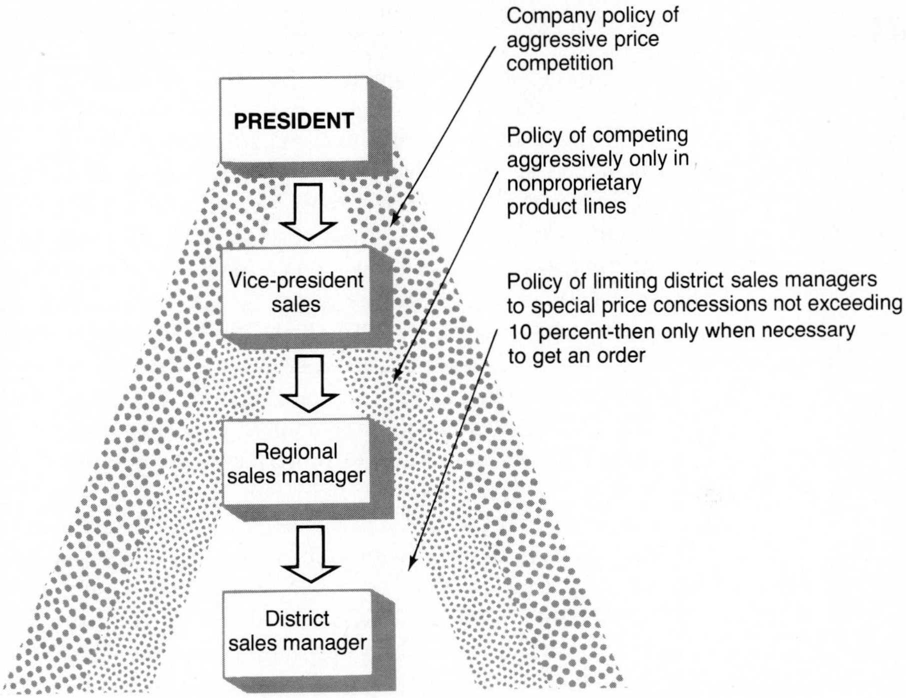

Company policy of aggressive price competition

Policy of competing aggressively only in nonproprietary product lines

Policy of limiting district sales managers to special price concessions not exceeding 10 percent-then only when necessary to get an order

PRESIDENT

Vice-president sales

Regional sales manager

District sales manager

SUCCESSIVE LIMITING OF POLICY BY HIERARCHICAL LEVEL.

position and authority in the organization. The president of a company with a policy of aggressive price competition has a broad area of discretion and initiative in which to interpret and apply this policy. The district sales manager (who reports to the regional sales manager) abides by the same basic policy, but the interpretations made by the president, the vice-president for sales, and the regional sales manager become derivative policies that might narrow the district manager's scope to the point of being, for example, only wide enough to approve a special sale price not exceeding a 10 percent reduction to meet competition. (See Figure 4-4).

Making policies consistent and integrated enough to realize enterprise objectives is difficult for many reasons. First, policies are too seldom defined in writing and their exact interpretations are too little known. Second, the very delegation of authority that policies are intended to implement leads, through its decentralizing influence, to widespread participation in policy making and interpretation, with almost certain variations among individuals. Third, it is not always easy to control policy because actual policy may be difficult to ascertain and intended policy may not always be clear.

Procedures

Procedures are plans that establish a required method of handling future activities. They are guides to action, rather than to thinking, and they detail the exact manner in which a certain activity must be accomplished. They are chronological sequences of required actions.

*Chronological
sequence*

Procedures are found in every part of an organization. The board of directors follows many procedures quite different from those of the supervisor; the expense account of the vice-president may go through quite different approval procedures than that of the salesperson; the procedures for carrying out vacation and sick leave provisions may differ considerably at various levels of the organization. But the important fact is that procedures exist throughout an organization, even though, as we might expect, they become more exacting and more numerous at the lower levels, largely because of the necessity for more careful control, the economic advantages of spelling out actions in detail, the lower-level managers' lesser need for leeway, and the fact that many routine jobs can be performed most efficiently when management prescribes the best way to carry them out.

Like other types of plans, procedures exist in a hierarchy. Thus, in a typical corporation, we may find a manual called "Corporation Standard Practice," outlining procedures for the corporation as a whole; a manual called "Division Standard Practice"; and special sets of procedures for a department, a branch, a section, or a unit.

*Crossing
department lines*

Procedures often cut across department lines. For example, in a manufacturing company, the procedure for handling orders will almost certainly involve the sales department (for the original order), the finance department (for acknowledgement of receipt of funds and for customer credit approval), the accounting department (for recording the transaction), the production department (for the order to produce goods or authority to release them from stock), and the traffic department (for determination of shipping means and route).

*Policy vs.
procedure*

Let us look at a few examples of the relationship between procedures and policies. Company policy may grant employees vacations; procedures established to implement this policy will provide for scheduling vacations to avoid disruption of work, setting methods and rates of vacation pay, maintaining records to assure each employee of a vacation, and spelling out the means for applying for a vacation. A company may have a policy of shipping orders quickly; particularly in a large company, careful procedures will be necessary to ensure that orders are handled in a specific way. Company policy may require the public relations department to clear its employees' public utterances; to implement this policy, managers must establish procedures for obtaining clearance with minimum inconvenience and delay.

Rules

Rules spell out specific required action or nonaction, allowing no discretion. They are usually the simplest type of plan.

People frequently confuse rules with policies or procedures. Rules are unlike procedures in that they guide action without specifying a time sequence. In fact, a procedure might be looked upon as sequence of rules. A rule, however, may or may not be part of a procedure. For example, "No smoking" is a rule quite unrelated to any procedure; but a procedure governing the handling of orders may incorporate the rule that all orders must be confirmed the day they are received. This rule allows no deviation from a stated course of action and in no way interferes with the rest of the procedure for handling orders. It is comparable to a rule that all fractions of weight of over half an ounce are to be counted as a full ounce or that receiving inspection must count or weigh all materials against the purchase order. The essence of a rule is that it reflects a managerial decision that some certain action must—or must not—be taken.

Rules: no discretion

Be sure you can distinguish rules from policies. The purpose of policies is to guide decision making by marking off areas in which managers can use their discretion. Although rules also serve as guides, they allow no discretion in their application. Many companies and other organizations think they have policies when they really have spelled-out rules. The result is confusion as to when people may use their own judgment, if at all. This can be dangerous. Rules and procedures, by their very nature, are designed to repress thinking; we should use them only when we do not want people in an organization to use their discretion.

Programs

Programs are complexes of goals, policies, procedures, rules, task assignments, steps to be taken, resources to be employed, and other elements necessary to carry out a given course of action; they are ordinarily supported by budgets. They may be as major as an airline's program to acquire a $400 million fleet of jets or the five-year program embarked upon by the Ford Motor Company several years ago to improve the status and quality of its thousands of foremen. Or they may be as minor as a program formulated by a single supervisor to improve the morale of workers in a parts-manufacturing department of a farm machinery company.

A primary program may call for many supporting programs. To cite an airline again, its program to invest in new jets, costing many millions of dollars for the aircraft and the necessary spare parts, requires many supporting programs if the investment is to be properly used. A program for providing the maintenance and operating bases with spare parts and components must be developed in detail. Special maintenance facilities must be prepared and maintenance personnel trained. Pilots and flight engineers must also be trained, and, if the new jets mean a net addition to flying hours, flight personnel recruited. Flight schedules must be revised, and ground station personnel trained to handle the new airplanes and their schedules as service is expanded to new cities in the airline's system. Advertising programs must give adequate publicity to the new service. Plans to finance the aircraft and provide for insurance coverage must be developed.

These and other programs must be devised and implemented before any new aircraft are received and placed in service. Furthermore, all these programs call for coordination and timing, since the failure of any part of this network of supporting plans means delay for the major program as well as unnecessary costs and loss of profits. Some programs, particularly those involving hiring and training of personnel, can be accomplished too soon as well as too late, and needless expense results from employees' being available and trained before their services are required.

Thus a program of any importance seldom stands by itself. It is usually one part of a complex system of programs, depending upon some and affecting others. This interdependence makes planning very difficult. The results of poor or inadequate planning are seldom isolated, for a plan is only as strong as its weakest link. Even a seemingly unimportant procedure or rule, if badly conceived, may wreck an important program. Coordinated planning requires extraordinary managerial skill. It truly requires the most rigorous application of systems thinking and action.

Budgets

A **budget** is a statement of expected results expressed in numerical terms. It may be referred to as a "numberized" program. In fact, the financial operating budget is often called a "profit plan." It may be expressed either in financial terms or in terms of labor-hours, units of product, machine-hours, or any other numerically measurable term. It may deal with operations, as the expense budget does; it may reflect capital outlays, as the capital expenditures budget does; or it may show cash flow as the cash budget does.

Since budgets are also control devices, we reserve our principal discussion of them for Chapters 22 and 24 on control. However, making a budget is clearly planning. The budget is the fundamental planning instrument in many companies. A budget forces a company to make in advance—whether for a week or five years— a numerical compilation of expected cash flow, expenses and revenues, capital outlays, or labor- or machine-hour utilization. The budget is necessary for control, but it cannot serve as a sensible standard of control unless it reflects plans.

Although a budget usually implements a program, it may in itself be a program. One company in difficult financial straits installed an elaborate budgetary control program designed not only to control expenditures but also to instill cost consciousness in mangement. In fact, one of the major advantages of budgeting is that it makes people plan; because a budget is in the form of numbers, it forces precision in planning. Moreover, since budgets are usually developed for an entire company, budgeting is an important device for consolidating plans of an enterprise. We shall discuss various types of budgets in Chapter 22 on control techniques.

Different kinds of budgets

Budgets vary considerably in accuracy, detail, and purpose. Some budgets vary according to the organization's level of output; these are called **variable** or **flexible** budgets. Government agencies often develop **program** budgets in which the agency (and each department within the agency) identifies goals, develops detailed programs to meet the goals, and estimates the cost of each program. To plan an effective program budget, a manager must do some fairly detailed and thorough planning.

Still another type, really a combination of the variable and the program budget, is the **zero-base** budget. A manager using this approach thinks of the goals and the programs needed to achieve them as a "work package," as though the programs were started from scratch, or "base zero."

Steps in Planning

Although we present the steps in planning here in connection with major programs such as the acquisition of a plant or a fleet of jets or the development of a product, managers would follow essentially the same steps in any thorough planning. As minor plans are usually simpler, certain of the steps are more easily accomplished, but the practical steps we list below are of general application. These steps are diagramed in Figure 4-5. Obviously, a discriminating manager would not use $100

FIGURE 4-5

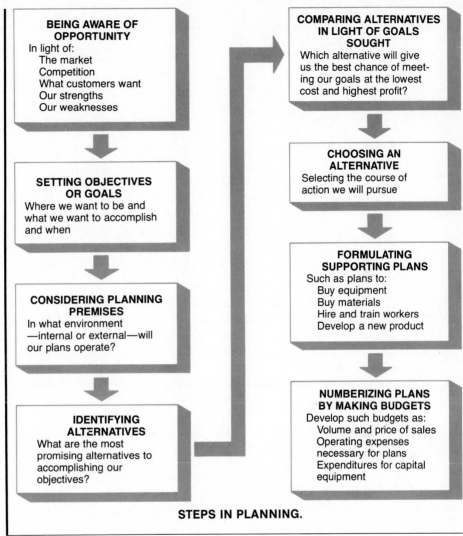

STEPS IN PLANNING.

worth of time to make a decision worth 50 cents, but it is shocking to see 50 cents worth of time used to make a planning decision involving millions of dollars.

**Step 1:
Being Aware of
Opportunities**

Although it precedes actual planning and is therefore not strictly a part of the planning process, being aware of an opportunity[4] is the real starting point for planning. We should take a preliminary look at possible future opportunities and see them clearly and completely, know where we stand in the light of our strengths

---

[4]The word "problem" might be used instead of "opportunity." A state of disorder or confusion and a need for a solution to gain a given goal can more constructively be regarded as an opportunity. In fact, one very successful and astute company president does not permit his colleagues to speak of problems, but only of opportunities.

and weaknesses, understand what problems we wish to solve and why, and know what we expect to gain. Our setting realistic objectives depends on this awareness. Planning requires realistic diagnosis of the opportunity situation.

Step 2: Establishing Objectives

In planning a major program, the second step is to establish objectives for the entire enterprise and then for each subordinate work unit. Objectives specify the expected results and indicate the end points of what is to be done, where the primary emphasis is to be placed, and what is to be accomplished by the network of strategies, policies, procedures, rules, budgets, and programs.

Enterprise objectives give direction to the major plans which, by reflecting these objectives, define the objective of every major department. Major department objectives, in turn, control the objectives of subordinate departments, and so on down the line. The objectives of lesser departments will be better framed, however, if subdivision managers understand the overall enterprise objectives and the implied derivative goals, and if they are given an opportunity to contribute their ideas to setting their own goals and those of the enterprise.

Step 3: Developing Premises

Principle of planning premises

A third logical step in planning is to establish, circulate, and obtain agreement to utilize critical planning premises. Planning premises are forecasts, applicable basic policies, and existing company plans. They are assumptions about the environment in which the plan is to be carried out. It is important for all the managers involved in planning to agree on the premises. In fact, one of the major principles of planning is this: *The more thoroughly individuals charged with planning understand and agree to utilize consistent planning premises, the more coordinated enterprise planning will be.*

Forecasting is important in premising: What kind of markets will there be? What volume of sales? What prices? What products? What technical developments? What costs? What wage rates? What tax rates and policies? What new plants? What policies with respect to dividends? How will expansion be financed? What political or social environment? What are the long-term trends?

Information sources for forecasting

Managers have a number of sources to draw from when preparing a forecast for their enterprise. The government publishes a wealth of information that can be useful. Here are just a few examples: *Business Cycle Developments*, *Survey of Current Business*, and *Economic Indicators*. Most large banks publish newsletters on current economic conditions, often on a monthly basis. *Business Week* magazine prepares outlooks for specific industries such as basic manufacturing (autos, chemicals, machinery, steel), natural resources (agriculture, energy, forest products, nonferrous metals), high technology (drugs, electronics, information, telecommunications), services and consumer products (entertainment, food processing, health care, personal care).[5] Many universities, such as UCLA, make national and regional economic forecasts. Managers interested in long-term trends will find John Naisbitt's bestselling book *Megatrends* useful. (See Table 4-1.)

---

[5]See for example, "Industrial Outlooks," *Business Week*, Jan. 9, 1984.

TABLE 4-1   Long-Term Trends

1 From industrial to information society
2 From forced technology to high tech/high touch (which means that technology is counterbalanced by a human response, such as relating to people)
3 From a national to a world economy
4 From a short-term to a long-term orientation
5 From centralization to decentralization (transformations in politics, business, and culture)
6 From institutional assistance to self-help (e.g., self-care, self-education, and so on)
7 From representation to participation (in politics and in organizations)
8 From organizational hierarchies to networking (which means sharing of information, resources, and ideas)
9 A shift of population and activity from the North to the South and the Southwest
10 From simple and limited options to multiple options

Source: J. Naisbitt, *Megatrends* (New York: Warner Books, Inc., 1982). Used with permission.

Some premises forecast policies not yet made. For instance, if a company has no pension plan and no policy with respect to one, planning premises sometimes must forecast whether such a policy will be set and, if so, what it will contain. Other premises naturally grow out of existing policies or other plans. For example, if a company has a policy of paying out no more than 2 percent of its profits, before taxes, for contributions and if there is no reason to believe that this policy will be changed, the policy becomes a planning premise. Or, if a company has made large investments in special purpose fixed plant and machinery, this fact also becomes an important planning premise.

Premising in the organization hierarchy

Since agreement about a given set of premises is important to coordinated planning, managers, starting with those at the top, must make sure that subordinate managers understand the premises upon which they are expected to plan. It is not unusual for chief executives in well-managed companies to force top managers with differing views, through group deliberation, to arrive at a set of major premises that all can accept. But whether they are acceptable to all or not, chief executives cannot afford to have their managers planning portions of the company's future on substantially different premises.

As we move down the organization hierarchy, the composition of planning premises changes somewhat. The basic process is the same, but old and new major plans will materially affect the future against which managers of lower-level departments must plan. A superior's plans affecting a subordinate manager's area of authority become premises for the latter's planning.

Because the future is so complex, it would not be profitable or realistic to make assumptions about every detail of the future environment of a plan. Therefore, premises are, as a practical matter, limited to assumptions that are critical, or strategic, to a plan, that is, those which most influence its operation.

Step 4: Determining Alternative Courses

The fourth step in planning is to search for and examine alternative courses of action, especially those not immediately apparent. There is seldom a plan for which reasonable alternatives do not exist, and quite often an alternative that is not obvious proves to be the best.

The more common problem is not finding alternatives, but reducing the number of alternatives so that the most promising may be analyzed. Even with mathematical techniques and the computer, there is a limit to the number of alternatives that can be thoroughly examined. The planner must usually make a preliminary examination to discover the most fruitful possibilities.

Step 5: Evaluating Alternative Courses

Having sought out alternative courses and examined their strong and weak points, we must next evaluate them by weighing them in the light of premises and goals. One course may appear to be the most profitable but require a large cash outlay and a slow payback; another may look less profitable but involve less risk; still another may better suit the company's long-range objectives.

If the only objective were to maximize immediate profits in a certain business, if the future were not uncertain, if cash position and capital availability were not worrisome, and if most factors could be reduced to definite data, this evaluation would be relatively easy. But planners typically encounter many uncertainties, problems of capital shortage, and various intangible factors, and so evaluation is usually very difficult, even with relatively simple problems. A company may wish to enter a new product line primarily for purposes of prestige; the forecast may show a financial loss; but the question is still open as to whether the loss is worth the gain in prestige.

Because there are so many alternative courses in most situations and there are numerous variables and limitations to be considered, evaluation can be exceedingly difficult. Because of these complexities, the newer methodologies and applications of operations research and analysis, discussed in Chapter 23 are helpful. Indeed, it is at this step in the planning process that operations research and mathematical and computing techniques have their primary application to the field of management.

Step 6: Selecting a Course

This is the point at which the plan is adopted—the real point of decision making. Occasionally an analysis and evaluation of alternative courses will disclose that two or more are advisable, and the manager may decide to follow several courses rather than the one best course.

Step 7: Formulating Derivative Plans

At the point when a decision is made, planning is seldom complete, and a seventh step is indicated. There are, almost invariably, derivative plans required to support the basic plan. When an airline decided to acquire a fleet of new planes, this decision was the signal for the development of a host of derivative plans, for the hiring and training of various types of personnel, the acquisition and positioning of spare parts, the development of maintenance facilities, scheduling, and advertising, financing, and insurance.

Step 8: Numberizing Plans by Budgeting

After decisions are made and plans are set, the final step to give them meaning, as was indicated in the discussion of types of plans, is to numberize them by converting them to budgets. The overall budgets of an enterprise represent the sum total of income and expenses, with resultant profit or surplus, and budgets of major balance sheet items such as cash and capital expenditures. Each department or program of a business or other enterprise can have its own budgets, usually of expenses and capital expenditures, which tie into the overall budget.

If done well, budgets become a means of adding together the various plans and also important standards against which planning progress can be measured. We will discuss budgets in connection with managerial control in Chapter 22.

Information System Needed

The planning model, Figure 4-5, shows sequentially the steps in planning. In practice, however, we must study the *feasibility* of possible courses of action at each stage. For example, in establishing objectives we must have some idea about the premises underlying the plans. An ambitious objective of increasing sales by 200 percent may be unrealistic in an environment with a projected economic recession. Similarly, *feedback* is also essential. In formulating supportive plans we may have to reevaluate and change the overall objectives set earlier.

The Planning Process: A Rational Approach to Goal Achievement

As we saw in the planning steps above, planning is a rational approach to accomplishing objectives. The process can be illustrated as shown in Figure 4-6. In this diagram, progress (toward more sales, more profits, lower costs, and so forth) is on the vertical axis, and time is on the horizontal axis. Here x indicates where we are (at t_0 or "time zero") and y where we want to be, at a future time (at t_n). In short, we are at x and want to go to y. Often we do not have all the data, but we

FIGURE 4-6

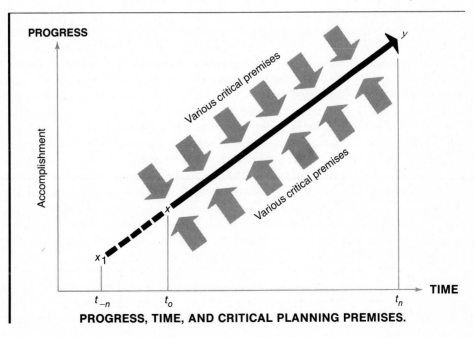

PROGRESS, TIME, AND CRITICAL PLANNING PREMISES.

start planning anyway. We may even have to start our planning study at x_1 (at t_{-n}). The line xy is the decision path.

If the future were completely certain, the line xy would be relatively easy to draw. However, in actuality, a myriad of factors may push us away from or toward the desired goal. These are the planning premises. Again, because we cannot forecast or consider everything, we try to develop our path from x to y in the light of the most critical premises.

The essential logic of planning applies regardless of the time interval between t_0 and t_n, whether it is 5 minutes or 20 years. However, the clarity of premises, the attainability of goals, and the simplification of planning are almost certain to be inversely related to the time span. That is, if the time span is long, premises may be unclear, goals may be more difficult to set, and other planning complexities may be great.

Decision making may be the easiest part of planning, although it involves techniques of evaluation and considerable skill in applying them. The real difficulties arise primarily in sharpening and giving meaning to objectives and critical premises, seeing the nature and relationships of the strengths and weaknesses of alternatives, and communicating goals and premises to those throughout the enterprise who must plan.

The Planning Period

Shall plans be for a short period or a long one? How shall short-range plans be coordinated with long-range plans? These questions suggest multiple horizons of planning—in some cases, planning a week in advance may be ample, and in others, the desirable period may be a number of years. Even within the same firm at the same time, various planning periods may exist for various matters.

The Commitment Principle

Commitment principle defined

Some criteria must be used in selecting the time range for company planning. In general, since planning and the forecasting that underlies it are costly, a company or any other organization should probably not plan for a longer period than is economically justifiable; yet it is risky to plan for a shorter period. The key to choosing the right planning period seems to lie in the **commitment principle**: *Logical planning encompasses a future period of time necessary to fulfill, through a series of actions, the commitments involved in decisions made today.*

Perhaps the most obvious application of this principle is the setting of a planning period long enough to anticipate, as well as we can, the recovery of costs sunk into a project. But, since other things than costs can be committed for various lengths of time and because a commitment to spend often precedes an expenditure and may be as unchangeable as sunk costs, it seems inadequate to refer to recovery of costs alone. Thus a company may commit itself for varying lengths of time to a personnel policy, such as promotion from within, or to other policies or programs involving commitments of direction not immediately measurable in terms of dollars.

We can readily grasp the logic of planning far enough in the future to foresee, as well as possible, the recovery of capital sunk in a building or a machine. Since capital is the lifeblood of an enterprise and is normally limited in relation to the firm's needs, its expenditure must be accompanied by a reasonable possibility of recovering it, plus a return on investment, through operations. For example, when Lever Brothers sank $35 million into a new factory on the West Coast, it, in effect, decided that the detergent business would permit the recovery of this investment over a period of time. If this period was 20 years, then logically the plans should have been based on a 20-year projection of business. Of course, the company might have introduced some flexibility and reduced its risk (as it did) by spending extra funds to make the plant modifiable for other purposes.

What the Commitment Principle Implies

The commitment principle implies that long-range planning is not really planning for future decisions but, rather, planning for the future impact of *today's* decisions. In other words, a decision is a commitment, normally of funds, direction of action, or reputation. And decisions lie at the core of planning. While studies and analyses precede decisions, any type of plan implies that some decision has been made. Indeed, a plan does not really exist as such until a decision has been made. Knowing this, the astute manager will recognize the validity of gearing longer-term considerations to present decisions. To do otherwise is to overlook the basic nature of both planning and decision making.

Application of the Commitment Principle

There is no uniform or arbitrary length of time for which a company should plan or for which a given program or any of its parts should be planned. An airplane company embarking on a new commercial jet aircraft project should probably plan this program for at least 12 years ahead, with 5 or 6 years for engineering and development and at least as many more years for production and sales, in order to recoup total costs and make a reasonable profit. An instrument manufacturer with a product already developed might need to plan revenues and expenses only 6 months ahead, since this period may represent the cycle of raw-materials purchasing, production, inventorying, and sales. But the same company might wish to see much further into the future before assuming a lease for specialized manufacturing facilities, undertaking a program of management training, or developing and promoting a new product. Other examples, showing that different planning areas require different time periods are illustrated in Figure 4-7.

Although the commitment principle indicates that various plans call for various planning periods, those used are often compromises. The short range tends to be a number of quarters or a year because of the practical need to make plans conform to accounting periods. The somewhat arbitrary selection of 5 years or so for the long range is often based on the probably mistaken belief that the degree of uncertainty over longer periods makes planning of questionable value.

Coordination of Short- and Long-Range Plans

Often short-range plans are made without reference to long-range plans. This is plainly a serious error. The importance of integrating the two types can hardly be overemphasized, and no short-run plan should be made unless it contributes to the achievement of the relevant long-range plan. Much waste arises from decisions about immediate situations that fail to consider their effect on more remote objectives.

Sometimes short-range decisions not only fail to contribute to a long-range plan but actually impede, or require changes in, the long-range plan. For example,

FIGURE 4-7 | EXAMPLE OF KINDS OF COMMITMENTS FOR A MANUFACTURING FIRM

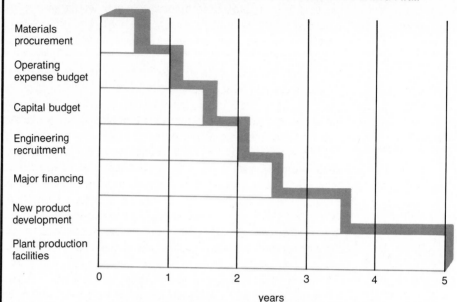

PLANNING AREAS AND TIME PERIODS.

Various management decision areas typically involve planning ahead for differing periods of time. These periods also vary according to the kind of business. For example, a large public utility may plan new power-production plants twenty-five or thirty years into the future, whereas a small garment manufacturer may plan new production facilities only one year ahead.

if a small company accepts a large order without reckoning the effect of the order on its capacity to produce or its supply of cash, it may hamper its future ability to finance a systematic expansion enough to require changes in its long-range program. Or, in another company, small additions to the plant (which may be urgently needed) may utilize vacant property so haphazardly as to thwart the land's longer-range use as the site for a large new plant. In other instances, the decision of a plant superintendent to discharge workers without adequate cause may interfere with the company's long-range objective of developing a fair and successful personnel program. The short-range decision of Sewell Avery, chairman of Montgomery Ward, to curtail expansion of the business after World War II because he believed that a serious recession was at hand interfered with the long-range program of enhancing the profitability of the company.

Responsible managers should continually review and revise immediate decisions to determine whether they contribute to long-range programs, and subordinate managers should be regularly briefed on long-range plans so that they will make decisions consistent with the company's long-range goals. It is far easier to do this than to correct inconsistencies, especially since short-term commitments tend to lead to further commitments along the same line.

Summary

The function of planning, the most basic of all managerial functions, is to make sure that all members of a group know what they will be expected to accomplish in order to reach the group's goal. Planning involves selecting from among alternative future courses of action.

The many types of plans can be arranged in a hierarchy, starting with purposes or missions, which define the basic task of an organization. Objectives are the ends toward which activity is aimed; strategies determine the purpose and kind of an operation and the means of achieving the aims of the enterprise. Policies are general statements or understandings that guide thought and action, while procedures outline chronological sequences of required actions. Rules spell out specific required action (or nonaction) and are thus a type of plan that allows no discretionary action. Programs are complexes of goals, policies, procedures, rules, and assignments of resources—usually supported by a budget—that are needed to carry out a course of action. Budgets express in numeric terms the resources that are to be spent or gained in accomplishing a project.

Once aware of an opportunity, a manager plans rationally by establishing objectives, making assumptions about (premising) the present and future environment, finding and evaluating alternative courses of action, and choosing a course to follow. Next the manager must make supporting plans and devise a budget. These activities must be carried out with attention to the total environment; good planning cannot occur in a vacuum.

The commitment principle says that plans should cover a period of time long enough to fulfill the commitments involved in a decision made today. Long-range planning is planning for the future impact of decisions made today. Short-range plans must take long-range plans into account for everyone's actions to be coordinated.

Key Ideas and Concepts for Review

Planning
Contribution of planning to purpose and objectives
Primacy of planning
Pervasiveness of planning
Efficiency of plans
Purpose or mission
Objectives or goals
Strategies
Policies

Procedures
Rules
Programs
Budgets
Variable budgets
Program budgets
Zero-base budgeting
Planning steps
Rational approach to planning
Commitment principle

For Discussion

1 "Planning is looking ahead, and control is looking back." Comment.

2 If planning involves a rational approach to selected goals, how can goals or objectives be a type of plan?

3 Draw up a statement of policy and devise a brief procedure that might be useful in implementing it. Are you sure your policy is not a rule?

4 If all decisions involve commitments and if the future is always uncertain, how can a manager guard against costly mistakes?

5 Taking a planning problem which is now facing you, proceed to deal with it in accordance with the planning steps outlined in this chapter.

6 Using as an example a planning decision with which you are familiar, show to what extent, and how, the commitment principle applies to it.

7 "Planning theory illustrates the open-system approach to management." Comment.

CASE 4-1

EASTERN ELECTRIC CORPORATION

Margaret Quinn, the president of Eastern Electric Corporation, one of the large electric utilities operating in the Eastern United States, had long been convinced that effective planning in the company was absolutely essential to success. For more than 10 years she had tried to get a company planning program installed without seeing much result. Over this time she had consecutively appointed three vice-presidents in charge of planning and, although each had seemed to work hard at the job, she noticed that individual department heads kept going their own ways. They made decisions on problems as they came up, and they prided themselves on doing an effective job of "fighting fires."

But the company seemed to be drifting, and individual decisions of department heads did not always jibe with each other. The executive in charge of regulatory matters was always pressing state commissions to allow higher electric rates without having very much luck, since the commissions felt that costs, although rising, were not justified. The head of public relations was constantly appealing to the public to understand the problems of electric utilities, but electric users in the various communities felt that the utility was making enough money and that the company should solve its problems without raising rates. The vice-president in charge of operations, pressed by many communities to expand electric lines, to put all lines underground to get rid of unsightly poles and lines, and to give customers better service, felt that costs were secondary to keeping customers off his back.

When a consultant called in at the request of Ms. Quinn looked over the situation, he found that the company really was not planning very well. The vice-president—planning and his staff were working hard making studies and forecasts and submitting them to the president. There they stopped, since all the department heads looked on the studies as impractical paperwork that had no importance for their day-to-day operations.

1 If you were the consultant, what steps would you suggest to get the company to plan effectively?

2 What advice would you give the company as to how far in the future to plan?

3 How would you suggest to the president that your recommendations be put into effect?

CASE 4-2

INTERNATIONAL MACHINE CORPORATION

Gilbert Brown, the president of International Machine Corporation (IMC), leaned back in his chair and reflected with well-deserved satisfaction on the success of his company, which produces and distributes a line of farm machinery. That afternoon, at a meeting of distributors from various parts of the world, Mr. Brown had been urged to introduce new models to satisfy the changing demands of customers.

The president, who had an engineering background, recognized the implications of the distributors' suggestion. It would require greater investments in research and development. Furthermore, the changes in the highly automated production line would be very costly indeed. Also, having a greater variety of models would require stocking many more spare parts. Depending on the kinds of changes, mechanics also might need to be retrained.

Reflecting on previous staff meetings, the president realized that sales and marketing people always wanted a greater variety of models but never

acknowledged the costs involved in changing models. After all, the company had been extremely successful with just a few models. Consequently, the president decided against the introduction of new models. Instead, he considered improving the current models and reducing the cost and price. He felt that what the customer really wants is value. Nevertheless, to test his judgment, the president asked a consultant for an opinion.

1 How would you state the mission of the enterprise?

2 What do you think are the opportunities and threats in the external environment?

3 How would you go about evaluating the strengths and weaknesses of the firm? What factors are critical for success or failure?

4 It is often said that to be successful, an organization must be an open system. What does this mean, and how does it apply to this case?

For Further Information

Hall, W. K. "Survival Strategies in a Hostile Environment," *Harvard Business Review*, vol. 53, no. 6 (September–October 1980), pp. 75–85.

Hout, T., M. E. Porter, and E. Rudder. "How Global Companies Win Out," *Harvard Business Review*, vol. 60, no. 2 (September–October 1982), pp. 98–108.

Lorange, P. *Corporate Planning* (Englewood Cliffs, N.J.: Prentice-Hall, Inc., 1980).

Mace, L. M., "The President and Corporate Planning," in *Harvard Business Review on Management*. (New York: Harper & Row, Publishers, Incorporated, 1975), pp. 119–142.

Makridakis, S., and S. C. Wheelwright. "Forecasting: Issues and Challenges for Marketing Management," in H. Koontz, C. O'Donnell, and H. Weihrich (eds.), *Management—A Book of Readings*, 5th ed. (New York: McGraw-Hill Book Company, 1980), pp. 136–151.

Naisbitt, J. *Megatrends—Ten Directions Transforming Our Lives* (New York: Warner Books, Inc., 1982).

Pearce, J. A. "An Executive-Level Perspective on the Strategic Management Process," *California Management Review*, vol. 24, no. 1 (Fall 1981), pp. 39–48.

Steiner, G. A. *Strategic Planning* (New York: The Free Press, 1979).

5

Objectives

After reading this chapter, you should understand:

1 What objectives are
2 The nature of enterprise objectives
3 The development of managing by objectives
4 That management by objectives is a systematic process of managing
5 The nature of managing by verifiable objectives
6 The process of managing by objectives
7 That objectives can be set in government
8 The benefits and weaknesses of managing by objectives

In the previous chapter we stated that *objectives* are the important ends toward which organizational and individual activities are directed. Since writers and practitioners make no clear distinction between the terms "goals" and "objectives" we will use them interchangeably. Within the context of our discussion it will become clear whether they are long-term or short-term, broad or specific. The emphasis in this chapter is on *verifiable* objectives; that is, at the end of the chapter one should be able to determine whether or not the objective has been achieved. The goal of every manager is to create a surplus, and clear and verifiable objectives facilitate measurement of the effectiveness and efficiency of managerial actions.

Verifiable objectives

The Nature of Objectives

Objectives state end results and overall objectives need to be supported by subobjectives. Thus, objectives form a hierarchy as well as a network. Moreover, organizations and managers have multiple goals which are sometimes incompatible and may lead to conflicts within the organization, within the group, and even within individuals. A manager may have to choose between short-term and long-term performance, and personal interests may have to be subordinated to organizational objectives.

**A Hierarchy of
Objectives**

As you can see in Figure 5-1, objectives form a hierarchy, ranging from the broad aim to specific individual objectives. At the zenith of the hierarchy is the purpose, which has two dimensions. First, there is the purpose of society, such as regarding the organization to contribute to the welfare of the people by providing goods and services at a reasonable cost. Second, there is the purpose of the business, which might be to furnish convenient, low-cost transportation for the average person. The stated mission might be to produce, market, and service automobiles. As you will notice, the distinction between purpose and mission is a fine one and therefore many writers and practitioners do not differentiate between the two terms. At any rate, these aims are, in turn, translated into general objectives and strategies (discussed in the next chapter) such as designing, producing, and marketing reliable, low-cost, fuel-efficient automobiles.

Key result areas

At the next level of the hierarchy, we find more specific objectives such as those in the key result areas. These are the areas in which performance is essential for the success of the enterprise. Although there is no complete agreement on what the key result areas of a business should be—and they may differ for various enterprises—Peter F. Drucker suggests the following: market standing; innovation; productivity; physical and financial resources; profitability; manager performance and development; worker performance and attitude; public responsibility.[1] Some examples of objectives for key result areas are the following: to obtain 10 percent return on investment by the end of calendar year 1988 (profitability); to increase the number of units of product X by 7 percent without an increase in cost or a reduction of current quality level by June 30, 1987 (productivity).

The objectives have to be further translated into division, department, and unit objectives down to the lowest level of the organization.

**The Process
of Setting
Objectives and
the Organizational
Hierarchy[2]**

As you can see in Figure 5-1, managers at different levels in the organizational hierarchy are concerned with different kinds of objectives. The board of directors and top managers are very much involved in determining the purpose, the mission, the overall objectives of the firm, and also the more specific overall objectives in the key result areas. Middle-level managers, such as the vice-president or manager of marketing, or the production manager, are involved in the setting of key-result-area objectives, division as well as department objectives. The primary concern of lower-level managers is the setting of objectives on the department and unit level as well as the objectives of their subordinates. Although we show individual objectives, consisting of performance and development goals, at the bottom of the hierarchy, managers at higher levels also should set objectives for their own performance and development.

---

[1]In *The Practice of Management* (New York: Harper & Brothers, 1954), p. 63.
[2]Parts of this discussion are based on H. Weihrich, "A Hierarchy and Network of Aims," *Management Review*, vol. 71, no. 1 (January 1982), pp. 47–54.

FIGURE 5-1

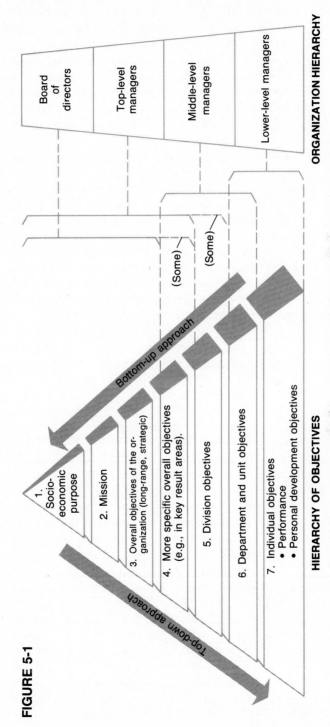

HIERARCHY OF OBJECTIVES

RELATIONSHIP OF OBJECTIVES AND THE ORGANIZATIONAL HIERARCHY.

Adapted from H. Weihrich and J. Mendleson, Management: An MBO Approach (Dubuque, Iowa: Wm. C. Brown. Co., 1978), p. xi. Used with permission.

There is some controversy about whether an organization should use the top-down or the bottom-up approach in setting objectives, as indicated by the arrows in Figure 5-1. In the top-down approach, upper-level managers determine the objectives for subordinates while in the bottom-up approach subordinates initiate the setting of objectives for their position and present them to their superior.

Proponents of the top-down approach suggest that the total organization needs direction through corporate objectives provided by the chief executive officer (in conjunction with the board of directors). Proponents of the bottom-up approach, on the other hand, argue that top management needs to have information from lower levels in the form of objectives. In addition, subordinates are likely to be highly motivated by and committed to goals which they initiate. Our experience has been that the bottom-up approach is underutilized, but also that either approach alone is insufficient. Both are essential but the emphasis should depend on the situation, including such factors as the size of the organization, the organizational culture, the preferred leadership style of the executive, and the urgency of the plan.

A Network of Objectives

Both objectives and planning programs normally form a network of desired results and events. If goals are not interconnected and if they do not support one another, people very often pursue paths that may seem good for their own department but may be detrimental to the company as a whole.

Goals and plans are seldom linear; that is, when one objective is accomplished, it is not neatly followed by another, and so on. Goals and programs form an interlocking network. Figure 5-2 depicts the network of contributing programs (each of which has appropriate objectives) that constitute a typical new product program. Each of the programs could itself be broken down into an interlocking network. Thus the product research program shown in Figure 5-2 as a single event might involve within it a network of such goals and programs as development of preliminary schematic design, development of a breadboard model (such as a design that focuses on the product's function but disregards its appearance), simplification of electronic and mechanical elements, packaging design, and other events.

Managers must make sure that the components of the network "fit" one another. Fitting is a matter not only of having the various programs carried out, but also of timing their completion, since undertaking one program often depends upon first completing another.

Conflicts among departments

It is easy for one department of a company to set goals that may seem entirely appropriate for it, only to be operating at cross-purposes with another department. The manufacturing department may find its goals best served by long production runs, but this might interfere with the marketing department's desire to have all products in the line readily available, or the finance department's goal of maintaining investment in inventory at a certain low level.

It is bad enough when goals do not support and interlock with one another. It may be catastrophic when they interfere with one another. What is needed is what one executive described as a matrix of mutually supportive goals.

FIGURE 5-2

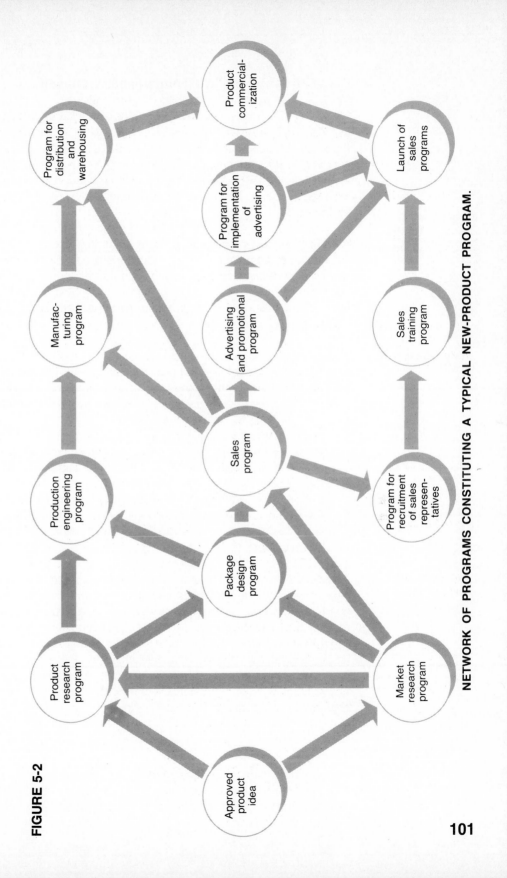

NETWORK OF PROGRAMS CONSTITUTING A TYPICAL NEW-PRODUCT PROGRAM.

Evolving Concepts in Management by Objectives

Management by objectives (MBO) is now practiced around the world. Yet, despite its wide applications, it is not always clear what is meant by MBO. Some still think of it as an appraisal tool; others see it as a motivational technique; still others consider MBO a planning and control device. In other words, definitions and applications of MBO differ widely, and it is therefore important to highlight the evolving concepts. Before we do that, however, we will define management by objectives as:

A comprehensive managerial system that integrates many key managerial activities in a systematic manner, and is consciously directed toward the effective and efficient achievement of organizational and individual objectives.

Our view of MBO as a system of managing is not shared by all. Some still define MBO in a very narrow, limited way.

Early Impetus to MBO

No one person can be called the originator of an approach that emphasizes objectives. Common sense has told people for many centuries that groups and individuals expect to accomplish some end results. However, certain individuals have long placed emphasis on management by objectives and, by doing so, have speeded its development as a systematic process.

Peter F. Drucker

One of these is Peter F. Drucker. In 1954 he acted as a catalyst by emphasizing that objectives must be set in all areas where performance affects the health of the enterprise. He laid down a philosophy that emphasizes self-control and self-direction. About the same time, if not earlier, the General Electric Company was using elements of MBO in its reorganization efforts to decentralize managerial decision making. The company implemented this philosophy of appraisal by identifying key result areas and undertaking considerable research on the measurement of performance.

Emphasis on Performance Appraisal

In 1957, in his classic article in the *Harvard Business Review*, Douglas McGregor, a major contributor to the behavioral sciences, criticized traditional appraisal programs that focused on personality trait criteria for evaluating subordinates.[3] In this approach, managers are required to pass judgment on the personal worth of subordinates. Consequently, McGregor suggested a new approach to appraisal based on Drucker's concept of management by objectives. Specifically, subordinates assume the responsibility of setting short-term objectives for themselves and review them with their superior. Of course, the superior has veto power over those objectives, but in the appropriate environment it will hardly need to be used.

---

[3]"An Uneasy Look at Performance Appraisal," *Harvard Business Review*, vol. 35, no. 3 (May–June 1957), pp. 89–94. In more recent writings the emphasis in MBO is still on goal setting and appraisal as shown by M. L. McConkie, "A Clarification of the Goal Setting and Appraisal Process in MBO," *Academy of Management Review*, vol. 4, no. 1 (January 1979), pp. 29–40.

Performance is then evaluated against the preset objectives, primarily by subordinates themselves. In this new approach, which encourages self-appraisal and self-development, the emphasis is where it ought to be, on performance rather than on personality. The active involvement of subordinates in the appraisal process leads to commitment and creates an environment for motivation.

Emphasis on Short-Term Objectives and Motivation

Researchers, consultants, and practitioners have long recognized the importance of individual goal setting. One of the early field studies on an MBO program, as well as a follow-up study, found "a significant upward movement in the overall average level of goals."[4] Also, an improvement in the attainment of goals and a continuing increase in productivity was noted in this firm. However, productivity had tapered off when the follow-up study was made. Although goal setting is not the only factor in motivating employees, it is an important one (other factors are incentives, participation, and autonomy. Certainly the importance of goal setting as a motivational technique is not restricted to business, but is also useful in public organizations. The general vagueness of objectives in many public organizations is a challenge for managers, but there is evidence that this challenge can be met.[5]

Inclusion of Strategic Planning in the MBO Process

In MBO programs that emphasize performance appraisal and motivation, the focus tends to be on short-term objectives. This orientation, unfortunately, may result in undesirable managerial behavior. For example, a production manager, in an effort to reduce maintenance costs, may neglect the necessary expenses for keeping the machines in good working order. The breakdown of machinery may not be evident at first, but can result in costly repairs much later. In an effort to show a good return on investment in a given year, the nurturing of good customer relations may be neglected. Similarly, a manager may not invest in new products that would take several years before contributing to profit. Recognizing these shortcomings, some managers now include long-range and strategic planning in MBO programs.

The Systems Approach to MBO

Management by objectives has undergone many changes; it has been used in performance appraisal, as an instrument for motivating individuals, and more recently in strategic planning. But there are still other managerial subsystems that can be integrated into the MBO process; they include design of organizational structures, portfolio management, management development, career development, compensation programs, and budgeting. These various managerial activities need to be integrated into a system. For example, George Odiorne, the most vocal spokesperson for MBO today, considers it to be a system of managerial leadership. Others discuss the systematic relationships of MBO and many other key managerial activities in different environments.

---

[4]A. P. Raia, "A Second Look at Management Goals and Controls," *California Management Review*, vol. 8, no. 4 (Summer 1966), pp. 49–58.

[5]H. Weihrich, "The Application of Management by Objectives in Government," Faculty Working Paper MG 76-3, Arizona State University, Tempe, 1976.

A research study

One of the early research studies that investigated MBO as a comprehensive system of managing indicates that most key managerial activities can and should be integrated with the MBO process. The degree of integration, however, differs for individual activities. It was found, for example, that the highest degree of integration of MBO with managerial functions was in controlling, planning, and directing. But several key managerial activities in staffing and organizing also were well integrated into the MBO process. These findings suggest that MBO, to be effective, has to be viewed as a comprehensive system. In short, it must be considered a way of managing, and not an addition to the managerial job.[6]

The Process of Managing by Objectives

The MBO process

We can best see the practical importance of objectives in management by summarizing how successful managing by objectives works in practice.[7] Figure 5-3 graphically portrays this process. Ideally, the process starts at the top of an organization and has the active support of the chief executive, who gives direction to the organization. It is not essential that objective setting starts at the top, however. It can start at division level, at marketing-manager level, or even lower. For example, in one company the system was first started in a division where it was carried down to the lowest level of supervision with an interlocking network of goals. Under the personal leadership and tutelage of the division general manager, it succeeded in areas of profitability, cost reduction, and improved operations. Soon, some other division managers and the chief executive became interested in, and attempted to implement, similar programs. In another case, the head of an accounting section developed a system for his group; his success not only earned him recognition (and promotion) but served as the starting point for a companywide program.

As in all planning, one of the critical needs in MBO is the development and dissemination of consistent planning premises. No manager can be expected to set goals or establish plans and budgets without guidelines.

Preliminary Setting of Objectives at the Top

Given appropriate planning premises, the first step in setting objectives is for the top manager concerned to determine what he or she perceives to be the purpose and the more important goals of the enterprise for a given period ahead. These goals can be set for any period—a quarter, a year, five years, or whatever is appropriate in given circumstances. In most instances, objectives are set to coincide with the annual budget or the completion of a major project. But this is not necessary and often not desirable. Certain goals should be scheduled for accomplishment in a much shorter period and others for a much longer period. Also,

---

[6]H. Weihrich, "A Study of the Integration of Management by Objectives with Key Managerial Activities and the Relationship to Selected Effectiveness Measures," unpublished doctoral dissertation, University of California, Los Angeles, 1973.

[7]Some of the material in this section is drawn from H. Koontz, *Appraising Managers as Managers* (New York: McGraw-Hill Book Company, 1971), chaps. 3–4.

FIGURE 5-3

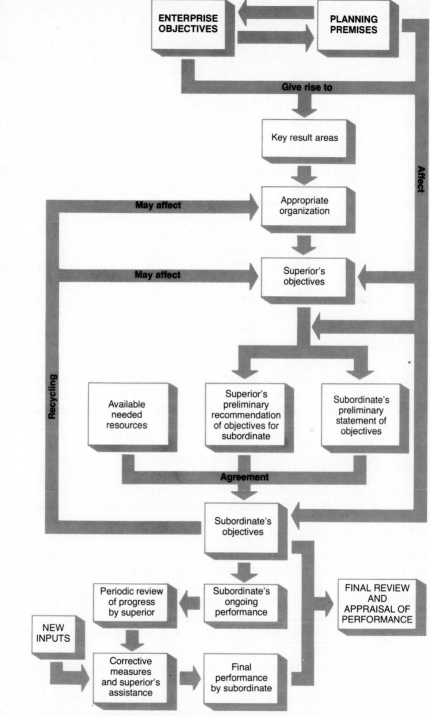

THE PROCESS OF MANAGING AND APPRAISING BY OBJECTIVES.

Source: *H. Koontz*, Appraising Managers as Managers (*New York: McGraw-Hill, 1971*), *p. 78.*

typically, as one proceeds down the organizational hierarchy, the length of time set for accomplishing goals tends to get shorter. It is seldom feasible or wise for first-level supervisors, for example, to set many annual goals since their goal span on most operating matters, such as cost or scrap reduction, rearrangement of facilities, or instituting of special personnel programs, is short (most of these goals may be accomplished in weeks or months).

Tentative goals

The goals set by the superior are preliminary, based on an analysis and judgment as to what can and should be accomplished by the organization within a certain period. This requires taking into account the company's strengths and weaknesses in the light of available opportunities and threats. These goals must be regarded as tentative and subject to modification as the entire chain of verifiable objectives is worked out by subordinates. It is usually not advisable to force objectives on subordinates since force can scarcely give rise to a sense of commitment. Most managers also find that the process of working out goals with subordinates reveals both problems to be dealt with and opportunities they were not previously aware of.

When setting objectives, the manager also establishes measures of goal accomplishment. If verifiable objectives are developed, these measures, whether in sales dollars, profits, percentages, cost levels, or program execution, will normally be built into the objectives.

Clarification of Organizational Roles

The relationship between expected results and the responsibility for attaining them is often overlooked. Ideally, each goal and subgoal should be some one person's clear responsibility. By analyzing an organization's structure, however, we often find that responsibility is vague and that clarification or reorganization is needed. Sometimes it is impossible to structure an organization so that a given objective is someone's personal responsibility. In setting goals for launching a new product, for example, the managers of research, marketing, and production must carefully coordinate their activities. Their separate functions can be centralized by putting a product manager in charge. But, if this is not desirable, at least the specific parts of each coordinating manager's contribution to the program goal can and should be clearly identified.

Setting of Subordinates' Objectives

After making sure that subordinate managers have been informed of pertinent general objectives, strategies, and planning premises, the superior can then proceed to work with subordinates in setting their objectives. The superior first asks what goals the subordinates believe they can accomplish, in what time period, and with what resources. They will then discuss some preliminary thoughts about what goals seem feasible for the company or department.

Role of the superior

The superior's role at this point is extremely important. Questions that she or he should ask include: What can you contribute? How can we improve your operation to help me improve mine? What stands in the way; what obstructions keep you from a higher level of performance? What changes can we make? How can I help? It is amazing how many things can be identified that might obstruct performance and how many constructive ideas can be dredged up from the experience and knowledge of subordinates.

Superiors must also be patient counselors, helping their subordinates develop consistent and supportive objectives and being careful not to set goals that are impossible to achieve. It is human nature to believe that anything can be accomplished a year hence, but that much less can be done next week. And one of the things that can weaken a program of managing by objectives is to allow managers to set unrealistic objectives.

Final decision

At the same time, when subordinates set goals, it does not mean that people can do whatever they want to do. Superiors must listen to, and work with, their subordinates, but in the end they must take responsibility for approving subordinates' goals. The superior's judgment and final approval must be based upon what is reasonably attainable with "stretch" and "pull," what is fully supportive of upper-level objectives, what is consistent with goals of other managers in other functions, and what is consistent with the longer-run objectives and interests of the department and company.

One of the major advantages of carefully setting up a network of verifiable goals and a requirement for doing so effectively is tying in the need for capital, material, and human resources at the same time. All managers at all levels require these resources to accomplish their goals. By relating these resources to the goals themselves, superiors can better see the most effective and most economical way of allocating them. It helps to avoid the bane of any upper-level manager's existence—"nickel and diming" by subordinates who need "one more" technician or engineer or "one more" piece of equipment, requests that are easy for them to "sell" to their boss and difficult for the superior to refuse.

Recycling Objectives

Objectives can hardly be set by starting at the top and dividing them up among subordinates. Nor should they be started from the bottom. A degree of recycling is required. Recycling is indicated by the arrows in Figures 5-1 and 5-3. Top managers may have an idea as to what their subordinates' objectives should be—but they will almost certainly change these preconceived goals as the contributors of the subordinates come into focus. Thus, objectives setting is not only a joint process but also one of interaction. For example, a sales manager may realistically set a goal to achieve much higher sales of a product than what top management has believed possible. In this event, the goals of the manufacturing and finance departments will surely be affected.

How to Set Objectives

Without clear objectives, managing is haphazard. No individual and no group can expect to perform effectively and efficiently unless there is a clear aim. Table 5-1 illustrates some objectives and how they can be restated in a way that allows measurement.

Quantitative and Qualitative Objectives

To be measurable, objectives must be verifiable. This means one must be able to answer the question: At the end of the period, how do I know if the objective has been accomplished? For example, the objective of making a reasonable profit can

TABLE 5-1 Examples of Nonverifiable and Verifiable Objectives

Nonverifiable objectives	Verifiable objectives
1 To make a reasonable profit	1 To achieve a return on investment of 12% at the end of the current fiscal year
2 To improve communication	2 To issue a two-page monthly newsletter beginning July 1, 1986, involving not more than 40 working hours of preparation time (after the first issue)
3 To improve productivity of the production department	3 To increase production output by 5% by December 31, 1986, without additional costs and while maintaining the current quality level
4 To develop better managers	4 To design and conduct a 40-hour in-house program on the "fundamentals of management," to be completed by October 1, 1987, involving not more than 200 working hours of the management development staff and with at least 90% of the 100 managers passing the exam (specified)
5 To install a computer system	5 To install a computerized control system in the production department by December 31, 1986, requiring not more than 500 working hours of systems analysis and operating with not more than 10% downtime during the first 3 months

at best indicate whether the company made a profit or had a loss (see Table 5-1), but it does not state how much profit is to be made. Also, what is reasonable to the subordinate may not be at all acceptable to the superior. In case of such a disagreement it is, of course, the subordinate who loses the argument. In contrast, a return of investment of 12% at the end of the fiscal year can be measured; it gives answers to the questions: How much? and When?

At times it is more difficult to state results in verifiable terms. This is especially true for staff personnel and also in government. For example, installing a computer system is an important task; but "to install a computer system" is not a verifiable goal. But suppose we say "to install a computerized control system (with certain specifications) in the production department by December 31, 1987, with an expenditure of not more than 500 working hours. Then, goal accomplishment can be measured. Moreover, quality can also be specified (in terms of computer downtime).

Setting Objectives in Government

The need for managing by objectives in government has been recognized by Frederic V. Malek, a former special assistant to the President and one of the driving forces in the implementation of MBO in the federal government.[8] He stated: "If the executive branch of government is to be managed effectively, it clearly needs

---

[8]This discussion is based on Malek's book *Washington's Hidden Tragedy* (New York: The Free Press, 1978), chaps. 7–9. It provides one of the best insights into the operation of MBO in the federal government.

Need for MBO in government

a system for setting priorities, pinpointing responsibility for their achievement, requiring follow-through, and generating enough feedback that programs can be monitored and evaluated from the top." The MBO program initiated in the federal government in the early 1970s had indeed some successes. For example the Department of Health, Education, and Welfare set an objective of training and placing 35,000 welfare recipients in meaningful jobs, an objective that seemed almost impossible to achieve. The goal was not only achieved but was exceeded; 40,000 welfare recipients were trained and on payrolls.

Special problems

To be sure, the management of government has some special problems. Many expenditures are uncontrollable because they are mandated by law. There is also the tendency to perpetuate ineffective programs for political reasons, and congressional members have a political rather than a managerial orientation. Finally, the traditional budgeting process is not conducive to managerial productivity.

Improving management in government

Improving the operation of the federal government, and other governments as well, requires:

1 Identifying ineffective programs by comparing performance against preestablished objectives

2 Using zero-base budgeting (discussed later Chapter 22)

3 Applying MBO concepts for measuring individual performance

4 Preparing short- and long-range objectives and plans

5 Installing effective controls

6 Designing sound organization structures with clear responsibilities and decision-making authority at appropriate levels

7 Developing and preparing government officials for managerial responsibilities

We can conclude that the setting of objectives, as in MBO programs, is not only essential to make line managers in business organizations more effective, but is equally important to improve the performance of staff personnel and public administrators.

Guidelines for Setting Objectives

Setting objectives is indeed a difficult task. It requires intelligent coaching by the superior and extensive practice by the subordinate. We have prepared some guidelines, shown in Table 5-2, that will help managers in setting their objectives.

The list of objectives should not be too long, yet it should cover the main features of the job. We have emphasized that objectives should be verifiable, and should state what is to be accomplished and when. If possible, the quality desired and the projected cost of achieving the objectives should be indicated. Furthermore, objectives should present a challenge, indicate priorities, and promote personal and professional growth and development. These and other criteria for good objectives are summarized in Table 5-2. Testing objectives against the criteria shown in the checklist is a good exercise for managers and aspiring managers.

TABLE 5-2   Checklist for Manager Objectives

If the objectives meet the criteria, write "+" in the box at the right of the statement. If they do not, mark "−" in the box.

1   Do the objectives cover the main features of my job? ☐
2   Is the list of objectives too long? If so, can I combine some objectives? ☐
3   Are the objectives verifiable, i.e., will I know at the end of the period whether or not they have been achieved? ☐
4   Do the objectives indicate
    (*a*) Quantity (how much)? ☐
    (*b*) Quality (how well, or specific characteristics)? ☐
    (*c*) Time (when)? ☐
    (*d*) Cost (at what cost)? ☐
5   Are the objectives challenging, yet reasonable? ☐
6   Are priorities assigned to the objectives (ranking, weighing, etc.)? ☐
7   Does the set of objectives also include
    (*a*) Improvement objectives? ☐
    (*b*) Personal development objectives? ☐
8   Are the objectives coordinated with those of other managers and organizational units? Are they consistent with the objectives of my superior, my department, the company? ☐
9   Have I communicated the objectives to all who need to be informed? ☐
10 Are the short-term objectives consistent with long-term aims? ☐
11 Are the assumptions underlying the objectives clearly identified? ☐
12 Are the objectives expressed clearly, and in writing? ☐
13 Do the objectives provide for timely feedback so that I can take any necessary corrective steps? ☐
14 Are my resources and authority sufficient for achieving the objectives? ☐
15 Have I given the individuals who are expected to accomplish objectives a chance to suggest their objectives? ☐
16 Do my subordinates have control over aspects for which they are assigned responsibility? ☐

Benefits and Weaknesses of Management by Objectives and Some Recommendations

Although management by objectives is now the most widely practiced managerial approach, its effectiveness is sometimes questioned. Often faulty implementation is blamed, but another reason is that MBO is applied as a mechanistic technique focusing on selected aspects of the managerial process without integrating them into a system. To provide a realistic view, we will analyze some of the benefits and weaknesses of MBO.

Benefits of Management by Objectives

As pointed out earlier, there is considerable research evidence, much of it from laboratory studies, that points at the motivational aspects of clear goals. But there are other benefits.

Better managing   We could summarize all the advantages of management by objectives by saying that it results in much-improved management. Objectives cannot be established without planning, and results-oriented planning is the only kind that makes sense. Management by objectives forces managers to think about planning for results, rather than merely planning activities or work. To ensure that objectives are realistic, it also requires managers to think of the way they will accomplish results, the organization and personnel they will need to do so, and the resources and assistance they will require. Also, there is no better incentive for control and no better way to know the standards for control than a set of clear goals.

Clarified organization   Another major benefit of managing by objectives is that it forces managers to clarify organizational roles and structures. To the extent possible, positions should be built around the key results expected of people occupying them.

Companies that have effectively embarked on MBO programs have often discovered deficiencies in their organization. Managers often forget that to get results, they must delegate authority according to the results they expect. As an executive of Honeywell is reported to have said: "There are two things that might also be considered fundamental creed at Honeywell: decentralized management is needed to make Honeywell work and management by objectives is needed to make decentralization work."

Personal commitment   One of the great advantages of management by objectives is that it encourages people to commit themselves to their goals. No longer are people just doing work, following instructions, and waiting for guidance and decisions; they are now individuals with clearly defined purposes. They have had a part in actually setting their objectives; they have had an opportunity to put their ideas into planning programs; they understand their area of discretion—their authority—and they have been able to get help from their superiors to ensure that they can accomplish their goals. These are the elements that make for a feeling of commitment. People become enthusiastic when they control their own fate.

Development of effective controls   In the same way that management by objectives sparks more effective planning, it also aids in developing effective controls. Recall that control involves measuring results and taking action to correct deviations from plans in order to ensure that goals are reached. As we will see in Chapter 21 on the system and process of management control, one of the major problems is knowing what to watch; a clear set of verifiable goals is the best guide.

Weaknesses in Managing by Objectives and Some Recommendations

With all its advantages, a system of management by objectives has a number of weaknesses. Most are due to shortcomings in applying the MBO concepts.

Failure to Teach the Philosophy of MBO   As simple as management by objectives may seem, managers who would put it into practice must understand and appreciate a good deal about it. They in turn must explain to subordinates what it is, how it works, why it is being done, what part it will play in appraising performance, and above all, how participants can benefit. The philosophy is built on concepts of self-control and self-direction aimed at making managers professionals.

Failure to give guidelines to goal setters   Management by objectives, like any other kind of planning, cannot work if those who are expected to set goals are not given needed guidelines. Managers must know what the corporate goals are and how their own activity fits in with them. If corporate goals are vague, unreal, or inconsistent, it is virtually impossible for managers to tune in to them.

Managers also need planning premises and a knowledge of major company policies. People must have some assumptions as to the future, some understanding of policies affecting their areas of operation, and an awareness of the objectives and programs with which their goals interlock in order to plan effectively. Failure to fill these needs can result in a fatal vacuum in planning.

Difficulty of setting goals   Truly verifiable goals are difficult to set, particularly if they are to have the right degree of stretch or pull, quarter in and quarter out, year in and year out. Goal setting may not be much more difficult than any other kind of effective planning, although it will probably take more study and work to establish verifiable objectives that are formidable but attainable than to develop many plans, which tend only to lay out work to be done. Participants in MBO programs report at times that the excessive concern with economic results puts pressure on individuals that may encourage questionable behavior.[9] To reduce the probability of selecting unethical means for achieving results, top management must agree to reasonable objectives, clearly state behavioral expectations, and give a high priority to ethical behavior, rewarding it as well as punishing unethical behavior.

Emphasis on short-run goals   In most management-by-objectives programs, managers set goals for the short term, seldom for more than a year, and often for a quarter or less. There is clearly the danger of emphasizing the short run, perhaps at the expense of the longer range. This means, of course, that superiors must always assure themselves that current objectives, like any other short-run plan, are designed to serve longer-range goals.

Danger of inflexibility   Managers often hesitate to change objectives. Although goals may cease to be meaningful if they are changed too often and do not represent a well-thought-out and well-planned result, it is nonetheless foolish to expect a manager to strive for a goal that has been made obsolete by revised corporate objectives, changed premises, or modified policies.

Other dangers   There are some other dangers and difficulties in management by objectives. In their desire to make goals verifiable people may overuse quantitative goals and attempt to use numbers in areas where they are not applicable, or they may downgrade important goals that are difficult to state in terms of end results. A favorable company image may be the key strength of an enterprise, yet it is

---

[9]C. D. Pringle and J. G. Longenecker, "The Ethics of MBO," *Academy of Management Review*, vol. 7, no. 2 (April 1982), pp. 305–312.

difficult to state this in quantitative terms. Sometimes managers fail to use objectives as a constructive force even with the full participation and assistance of their superiors. There is also the danger of forgetting that there is more to managing than goal setting.

But with all the difficulties and dangers of managing by objectives, this system emphasizes in practice the setting of goals, long known to be an essential part of planning and managing.

Summary

Objectives are the end points toward which activities are aimed. Objectives are verifiable if we can look back later and say whether or not they have been accomplished.

Objectives form both a hierarchy, reaching from corporate purposes and missions down to individual goals, and a network as they are reflected in interlocking programs. Managers can best determine the number of objectives they should realistically set for themselves by determining the nature of the job and how much they can do themselves and how much they can delegate. In any case, managers should know the relative importance of each of their goals.

Managing by objectives (MBO) has been widely used for performance appraisal and employee motivation, but in reality it is a system of managing. The MBO process consists of setting goals at the highest level of the organization, clarifying the specific roles of those responsible for achieving the goals, and setting and modifying objectives for subordinates. Goals can be set for staff managers as well as for line managers. Goals can be qualitative or quantitative.

Among other benefits, MBO results in better managing, often forces managers to clarify the structure of their organizations, encourages people to commit themselves to their goals, and helps develop effective controls.

Some of its weaknesses are that managers sometimes fail to explain the philosophy of MBO to subordinates and to give them guidelines for their goal setting. In addition, goals themselves are difficult to set, tend to be short-run, and may become inflexible despite changes in the environment of plan operation. People, in their search for verifiability, may too often overemphasize quantifiable goals.

Key Ideas and Concepts for Review

Objectives
Hierarchy of objectives
Network of objectives
Evolving concepts in MBO
Systems approach to managing by
   objectives
MBO process

Quantitative objectives
Qualitative objectives
Verifiability
MBO in the government
MBO benefits
MBO weaknesses

For Discussion

1 To what extent do you believe that managers you have known in business or elsewhere have a clear understanding of their objectives? If, in your opinion, they do not, how would you suggest that they go about setting them?

2 Make a list of goals you wish to achieve in the next 5 years. Are they verifiable? Are they attainable?

3 Some people object to defining long-term goals because they think it is impossible to know what will happen over a long period. Do you believe that this is an intelligent position to take?

4 Take any program of any kind that you would like to see accomplished and draw a network of contributing programs and goals necessary for its accomplishment.

5 "The only planning tool we need in this company is the budget. If everyone meets his or her budget, we need nothing else, and management by objectives would be an unnecessary frill." Comment.

6 Why do you suspect that, although so many business enterprises talk about and introduce programs of management by objectives, the actual record of performance under these programs has been so poor?

7 Do you believe that managing by objectives could be introduced in a government agency? A church? A university? A college fraternity or sorority?

8 What are your five most important personal objectives? Are they long or short range? Do they conflict with each other? Are the objectives verifiable?

9 In your organization, what does your superior expect from you in respect to the level of performance? Is it stated in writing? If you wrote your job objectives on a sheet of paper and your boss wrote down what he or she expects of you, would the two be consistent?

CASE 5-1

DEVELOPING VERIFIABLE GOALS

The division manager had recently heard a lecture on management by objectives. His enthusiasm, kindled at that time, tended to grow the more he thought about it. He finally decided to introduce the concept and see what headway he could make at his next staff meeting.

He recounted the theoretical developments in this technique, cited the advantages to the division of its application, and asked his subordinates to think about adopting it.

It was not as easy as everyone had thought. At the next meeting, several questions were raised.

"Do you have division goals assigned by the president to you for next year?" the finance manager wanted to know.

"No, I do not," the division manager replied. "I have been waiting for the president's office to tell me what is expected, but they act as if they will do nothing about the matter."

"What is the division to do, then?" the manager of production asked, rather hoping that no action would be indicated.

"I intend to list my expectations for the division," the division manager said. "There is not much mystery about them. I expect $30 million in sales, a profit on sales before taxes of 8 percent, a return on investment of 15 percent, an ongoing program in effect by June 30, with specific characteristics I will list later, to develop our own future managers, completed development work on our XZ model by the end of the year, and employee turnover stabilized at 5 percent."

The staff was somewhat stunned that their superior had thought through to these verifiable objectives and stated them with such clarity and assurance. They were also surprised about his sincerity in wanting to achieve them.

"During the next month I want each of you to translate these objectives into verifiable goals for your own functions. Naturally they will be different for finance, marketing, production, engineering, and administration. However you state them, I will expect them to add up to the realization of the division goals."

1 Can a division manager develop verifiable goals, or objectives, when they have not been assigned to him or her by the president? How? What kind of information or help do you believe is important for the division manager to have from headquarters?

2 Do you believe the division manager was going about setting goals in the best way? What would you have done?

CASE 5-2
THE MUNICIPAL WATER DISTRICT

The district proposed an incentive program for its higher-level managers to be tried for one year. The program, based on MBO concepts, was a response to criticism from citizens in the community. Here is a summary of the proposed program.

The objectives are to be set to represent higher than normal performance. Furthermore, the emphasis will be on verifiable objectives against which performance can be measured. One of the objectives, for example, will be to keep the average water bill increase at 75 percent or less of the inflation rate. The participating managers will receive only half of the cost-of-living increases granted to other employees. To be eligible for the other half they will have to achieve *some* of the objectives. If, on the other hand, *most* of the above-normal objectives are achieved, their pay increases will be above the inflation rate. No lump sum bonuses will be granted, but the performance of the managers will be reflected in their wages.

It was figured that the program would result in $15,000 to $25,000 savings for the district if none of the objectives were met. On the other hand, if all objectives were met the cost to the company would be between $25,000 and $35,000 in salary increases. But the indirect savings were estimated at $1 million or more. This incentive program was submitted to the public through a poll with arguments for and against the plan.

The arguments *for* the incentive program were as follows:

1 It would stop the rise in water rates.

2 Rewards would be based on performance.

3 Turnover of management personnel would be reduced.

4 The cost for outstanding performance would be low compared with the potential savings.

The arguments *against* the incentive program were as follows:

1 The program would only raise the current objectives to what would normally be expected of the managers.

2 The company has one of the highest water costs in the state.

3 If the general manager were to meet all the objectives, he would get paid more than a United States senator. If three other high-level managers were to achieve all of their objectives, they would get paid more than the governor of the state.

4 Since the budget is prepared by the same persons who would be the beneficiaries of the incentives, there would be the temptation to "pad" the budget.

5 The past performance was considered substandard; no bonus should be offered to managers for improving their substandard performance and doing what they are supposed to in the first place.

6 The policy of the company states that it should supply adequate water at the lowest possible cost. If the managers are not capable of performing their job, they should seek employment elsewhere.

1 What do you think about the incentive program?

2 Do you think that the public should be polled on such a program? Why, or why not?

3 As a consultant, what would you recommend?

For Further Information

Humble, J. W. *Improving Business Results* (Maidenhead, England: McGraw-Hill Book Company (U.K.) Ltd., 1968).

Koontz, H. *Appraising Managers as Managers* (New York: McGraw-Hill Book Company, 1971).

Mark, M. A. "Productivity Measurement of Government Services—Federal, State, and Local," *White House Conference on Productivity*, Panel Background Papers, 1983.

Morrisey, G. L. *Management by Objectives and Results in the Public Sector* (Reading, Mass.: Addison-Wesley Publishing Company, Inc., 1976).

Odiorne, G. S. *MBO II* (Belmont, Calif.: Fearon Pitman Publishers, 1979).

Odiorne, G. S., H. Weihrich, and J. Mendleson (eds.). *Executive Skills—A Management by Objectives Approach* (Dubuque, Iowa: Wm. C. Brown Company Publishers, 1980).

Raia, A. P. *Managing by Objectives* (Glenview, Ill.: Scott, Foresman and Company, 1974).

Weihrich, H. "An Uneasy Look at the MBO Jungle—Toward a Contingency Approach to MBO," *Management International Review*, vol. 16, no. 4 (1976), pp. 103–109.

Weihrich, H. *Management Excellence—Productivity through MBO* (New York: McGraw-Hill Book Company, 1985).

6

Strategies and Policies

CHAPTER OBJECTIVES

After reading this chapter, you should understand:

1 The nature of strategies and policies
2 The importance of strategies and policies
3 The requirements for effective strategies
4 Major kinds of strategies
5 The Portfolio Matrix for allocating resources
6 Key aspects of the strategic planning process
7 Requirements for effectively implementing strategies

Definition of strategies

Definition of policies

Strategies and policies are closely related. **Strategies** are general programs of action toward the attainment of comprehensive objectives. The major strategies of an enterprise imply objectives, the commitment of resources to attain these objectives, and the main policies to be followed in using these resources. **Policies** guide our thinking in decision making. They ensure that decisions fall within certain boundaries. They usually do not require action but are intended to guide managers in their decision commitments when they do make decisions.

The essence of policy is discretion. Strategy, on the other hand, concerns the direction in which human and material resources will be applied in order to increase the chance of achieving selected objectives.

Certain major policies and strategies may be essentially the same. A policy to develop only those new products that fit into a company's market structure or one to distribute only through retailers may be an essential element of a company's strategy for new product development or marketing. One company may have a policy of growth through acquisition of other companies, while another may have a policy of growing only by expanding present markets and products. While these

*Guide to thinking
vs. commitment
of resources*

are policies, they are also essential elements of major strategies. Perhaps the way to draw a meaningful distinction is to say that policies will guide our thinking in decision making—if a decision is to be made—while strategies imply that an enterprise has made the decision to commit resources in a given direction.

People sometimes say that there is a policy-making level of management and an administrative or operating level. This is not strictly true. Not all policy making is reserved for top management. To be sure, the higher a manager is in an organization structure, the more important his or her role in policy making is likely to be. And top managers do have the major role in making overall policy for an enterprise. This is understandable, since the purpose of policies is to guide decision making by subordinates. But even though managers at lower levels carry out policies mainly determined by their upper-level superiors, they may occasionally make policies on their own to guide themselves and their subordinates.

Strategies and Policies to Give Direction to Plans

The key function of strategies and policies is to unify and give direction to plans. In other words, they influence the direction in which an enterprise is trying to go. But, standing alone, they do not ensure that an organization will, in fact, go where it wants to go.

**Strategies
and Policies
Furnishing the
Framework of
Plans**

Strategies and policies help managers plan by guiding operating decisions and often premaking them. The underlying *principle* is, then, that *the more carefully developed and clearly understood strategies and policies are, the more consistent and effective the ensuing plans will be.* For example, if a company has a major policy of developing only new products that fit its marketing organization, it will avoid wasting energy and resources on new products that do not meet this test.

**The Need for
Operational
Planning: Tactics**

To be effective, strategies and policies must be put into practice by means of plans, increasing in detail until they get down to the nuts and bolts of operations. **Tactics,** then, are the action plans through which strategies are executed. Strategies must be supported by effective tactics.

IBM's tactics

When IBM ventured into the retail market, setting up IBM product centers to sell personal computers (PCs) and typewriters, it decorated the sales offices in red. However, the bright colors alarmed customers and irritated salespeople. Also, these centers were staffed by IBM personnel who often did not have retail experience. Their thorough product knowledge—reflected in their sales discussions—intimidated many customers with little computer knowledge. But IBM corrected both tactical mistakes by switching to subdued colors for decor and giving formal sales training to their personnel.[1] This case illustrates that a strategy, to be successful, must be supported by carefully developed tactics.

---

[1]P. Petre, "IBM's Misadventures in the Retail Jungle," *Fortune*, vol. 110, no. 2 July 23, 1984, p. 80.

Strategy and Policy Affecting All Areas of Managing

Since strategies and policies affect planning, they also greatly affect other areas of managing. For example, major strategies and policies will naturally influence organization structure and, through this, other functions of the manager. In his extraordinary analysis of the history of some of the nation's largest companies, Alfred Chandler, Jr., depicts in detail how strategy affected organization structure.[2] In the Du Pont Company, the organization around product lines, with centralized control, followed the strategy of product diversification. General Motors had essentially the same situation. In Du Pont, the strategy of diversification was dictated by the need to use resources made surplus by the post-World War I decline in the explosives business. In General Motors, on the other hand, the strategy was one of integration and expansion of a large, disparate group of companies acquired by W. C. Durant in his formation of the company during the two decades before 1920. While the strategies of these two companies were based on different premises and situations, they led to essentially the same organization structures.

Effects of strategy on structure

Requirements for Effective Strategies[3]

To develop major strategies, we need to meet a number of key requirements: (1) assessment of the present and future environment, (2) corporate self-appraisal, (3) an organization structure that ensures planning, (4) consistency among strategies, and (5) development of contingency strategies. We shall now consider each of these.

Assessment of the Present and Future External Environment

Since strategies are intended to operate in the future, we must make the best possible estimate of the future environment. Often, we start with a situational analysis of the present environment, then forecast the future for 3, 5, 7, or more years. But forecasting the future is difficult. Few people would have forecasted the impact of the oil-producing nations' cartel on overall price levels (inflation) in the 1970s. Similarly, few economists foresaw the strong, sustained economic growth of the early 1980s.

Forecasting

Clearly, the better an enterprise can foresee its future environment, the better it can prepare for the future by establishing strategies and supporting plans that take advantage of its capabilities in that environment. However, except for economic and market forecasts, it has been difficult to put the forecast and assessment of environmental factors to practical use. While this can be done by developing and actually using planning premises as the background for decision making, it is one type of planning that has not been done very well.

---

[2]A. D. Chandler, Jr., *Strategy and Structure* (Cambridge, Mass.: The M.I.T. Press, 1962). In this excellent historical study, the author analyzes the history of Du Pont, General Motors, Standard Oil Company (New Jersey), and Sears, Roebuck and shows how in each case organization structure followed and reflected strategy.

[3]Much of this section is drawn from H. Koontz, "Making Strategic Planning Work," *Business Horizons*, vol. 19, no. 2 (April 1976), pp. 37–47.

Reactions of competitors

An important element of any future environment, of course, is the probable action of competitors. Too often, we premise our planning on what competitors have been doing and not on what we might expect them to do. Good planners never assume that their competitors are asleep.

The Internal Environment: Corporate Self-Appraisal

Making a corporate self-appraisal essentially involves asking these two questions: What is our business? What kind of business are we in? These simple questions are not always easy to answer, as many businesses have found out. In fact, many nonbusiness enterprises could and should ask these questions. Universities could gain insights, as could virtually every government agency. The classic case of an industry that did not consider its identity is the railroad industry, which too long overlooked the fact that its companies were in the transportation business, not just the railroad business, with the result that they did not expand early enough into trucking, pipelines, water transport, and air transportation.

Glass bottle manufacturers in the United States almost missed their opportunities by seeing themselves for too long as glass bottle makers rather than as liquid container manufacturers, while plastic and metal containers came to replace glass in many cases. Likewise, many feel that steel companies have too long believed that they are steelmakers rather than firms in the structural materials business, which includes many materials not made of steel.

Analysis of strengths and weaknesses

To answer questions about its identity, a company must look at itself as a whole, analyzing strengths and weaknesses in each functional area—marketing, product development, production and other operations areas, finance, and public relations. It must focus attention on its customers and what they want and can buy, on its technological capabilities and financial resources.

Although the corporate appraisal is based on subjective judgments, it is, nevertheless, a starting point for analyzing the firm's situation. Besides making this analysis, top executives must also examine their values, their aspirations, and their prejudices, because managers determine the strategy by matching the external threats and opportunities with the internal weaknesses and strengths. Many companies have spent so much time and effort shoring up weaknesses that they did not capitalize on their strengths. To be sure, weaknesses should be corrected to the extent possible. But identifying strengths and taking advantage of them in formulating strategies offer the most promise.

Organization Structure Ensuring Planning

Companies should make organizational arrangements to ensure the development and implementation of strategies. Especially in large companies, top management may have the assistance of a planning staff for forecasting, establishing premises, and developing various kinds of analyses. However, the planning studies made by staff personnel are not enough. The great need is for line managers to integrate this information into the decision-making process.

Planning staff

To avoid useless or impractical staff efforts, we need to do several things. A planning staff should be given the tasks of developing major objectives, strategies, and planning premises and submitting them to top management for review and approval. It should be given the responsibility for making approved premises and strategies known and for helping operating people to understand them. Also, before major decisions, especially those of long-range or strategic impact, are made, the staff group should be given the task of reviewing them and making recommendations. These steps can force managers to consider environmental factors and can keep the advisers from becoming a detached and impractical group.

Review

Another major organizational device is the regular, formal, and rigorous review of planning programs and performance, preferably by an appropriate committee. This has long been done in well-managed divisionalized companies where division general managers are called before a top executive committee. Perhaps it should be done at lower levels. Review has the advantages of forcing people to plan, of making sure that strategies are being followed by programs and, where strategies do not exist or are unclear, of making this deficiency apparent.

Consistency in Strategies

One of the important requirements of effective strategic planning is to make sure that strategies are consistent, that they "fit" each other. For example, one medium-sized company had a successful sales record as the result of a strategy of putting out quality products at lower prices than its larger competitors, which had done their selling through heavy and expensive advertising. Pleased with this success, and after adding to its product line through acquisitions, the company then embarked on an additional strategy of trying to sell through costly advertising, which, combined with price-cutting, had a disastrous effect on profits.

The Need for Contingency Strategies

Because every strategy must operate in the future and the future is always subject to uncertainty, we should have contingency strategies. If a regulated telephone company, for example, suddenly faces competition (as happened recently in the United States when other companies were allowed to furnish telephone facilities that were once the monopoly of the telephone companies) and adopts a strategy of aggressive competition on the assumption that regulatory commissions will allow competitive pricing, the strategy will become useless if the commissions do not actually allow such pricing. Or if a company develops a strategy based on a certain state of technology and a new discovery materially changes the technological environment, that company is faced with a major change.

Where events might occur to render a strategy obsolete, and they often can without warning, it is wise to develop an alternate strategy based on a different set of premises. These are the "what if" kinds of strategies, supported by contingency plans that can be put into effect quickly, thus avoiding "crisis management."

The Major Kinds of Strategies

For a business enterprise (and, with some modification, for other kinds of organizations as well), the major strategies that give an overall direction to operations are likely to be in the following areas:

New or changed products and services. A business exists to furnish products or services. In a very real sense, profits are merely a measure—although an important one—of how well a company serves its customers.

Marketing. Marketing strategies are designed to guide managers in getting products or services to customers and encouraging customers to buy.

Growth. Growth strategies give answers to such questions as how much growth should occur, and how fast, where, and how it should occur.

Finance. Every business enterprise, and for that matter, any nonbusiness enterprise, must have a clear strategy for financing its operations. There are various ways of doing this and usually many serious limitations.

Organization. Organizational strategy has to do with the type of organizational pattern an enterprise will use. It answers such practical questions as how centralized or decentralized decision-making authority should be, what kinds of departmental patterns are most suitable, whether to develop integrated divisions with profit responsibility, whether to use matrix organization structures, and how to design staff positions. Naturally, organization structures furnish the system of roles and role relationships that help people to accomplish objectives.

Personnel. There can be many major strategies in the area of human resources and relationships. They deal with such topics as union relations, compensation, selection, hiring, training, and appraisal, as well as with special areas such as job enrichment.

Public relations. Strategies in this area can hardly be independent but must support other major strategies and efforts. They must also be designed in the light of the company's type of business, its closeness to the public, and its susceptibility to regulation by government agencies.

To develop strategies in any area, we must ask the right questions. While no set of strategies can be formulated that will fit all organizations and situations, certain key questions will help any company to discover what its strategies should be.

To show how the right questions can lead to answers, we will raise some key questions in only two major strategic areas: new products and services, and marketing. With a little thought, you can devise key questions for other major strategic areas.

Products or Services

New products or services, more than any other single factor, determine what an enterprise is or will be. The key questions in this area can be summarized as follows:

What is our business?

Who are our customers?

What do our customers want?

How much will our customers buy and at what price?

Do we wish to be a product leader?

Do we wish to develop our own new products?

What advantages do we have in serving customer needs?

How should we respond to existing and potential competition?

How far can we go in serving customer needs?

What profits can we expect?

What basic form should our strategy take?

Marketing

Marketing strategies are closely related to product strategies; they must be interrelated and mutually supportive. As a matter of fact, Peter Drucker regards the two basic business functions as innovation (for example, the creation of new goods or services) and marketing. A business can scarcely survive without at least one of these functions and preferably both. A company can succeed by copying products, but it can hardly succeed without effective marketing. And, as the world has grown increasingly competitive, marketing has become the tail that wags the company dog.

The key questions that serve as guides for establishing a marketing strategy are:

Where are our customers and why do they buy?

How do our customers buy?

How is it best for us to sell?

Do we have something to offer that competitors do not?

Do we wish to take legal steps to discourage competition?

Do we need, and can we supply, supporting services?

What are the best pricing strategy and policy for our operation?

A Tool For Allocating Resources: The Portfolio Matrix

Business
Portfolio Matrix

Strategists have been aided by a number of tools that help them decide how to allocate resources. We will focus on one such tool, the Business Portfolio Matrix, which was developed by the Boston Consulting Group (BCG).[4] Figure 6-1, a simplified version of the matrix, shows the linkages between the growth rate of the business and the relative competitive position of the firm, identified by the market share. Businesses in the "question mark" quadrant, with a weak market share and a high growth rate, usually require cash investment so that they can

---

[4]B. D. Henderson, "The Product Portfolio," in *Perspectives* (Boston Consulting Group, 1970); B. D. Henderson, "The Experience Curve Revisited" (Boston Consulting Group, undated); B. Headly, "Strategy and the 'Business Portfolio,' " *Long Range Planning*, vol. 10 (February 1977), pp. 9–15.

FIGURE 6-1

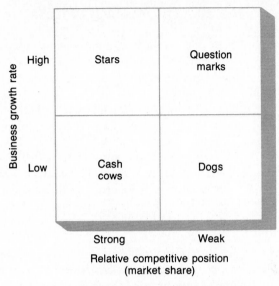

BUSINESS PORTFOLIO MATRIX.

Adapted from The Product Portfolio Matrix, *copyright © 1970, The Boston Consulting Group, Inc.*

become "stars," the businesses in the high-growth quadrant with strong competitive position. These kinds of businesses have opportunities for growth and profit. The "cash cows," with a strong competitive position and a low growth rate, are usually well established in the market, and such enterprises are in the position of making the products at low cost. Therefore, the products of such enterprises provide the cash needed for their operation. The "dogs" are businesses with a low growth rate and a weak market share position. These businesses are usually not profitable and generally should be disposed of.

The Portfolio Matrix was developed for large corporations with several divisions often organized around strategic business units (SBUs). (SBUs will be discussed in Chapter 9 of this book.) While portfolio analysis was popular in the 1970s, it is not without its critics, who contend that it is too simplistic. Also the growth rate criterion has been considered insufficient for the evaluation of an industry's attractiveness. Similarly, the market share as a yardstick for estimating the competitive position may be inadequate.[5]

Criticism

[5]C. W. Hofer and D. Schendel, *Strategy Formulation: Analytical Concepts* (St. Paul: West Publishing Company, 1978); W. Kiechel III, "Oh Where, Oh Where Has My Little Dog Gone? or My Cash Cow? or My Star?" *Fortune*, November 1981, pp. 148–154; R. G. Hammermesh and R. E. White, "Manage Beyond Portfolio Analysis," *Harvard Business Review*, vol. 62, no. 1 (January–February 1984), pp. 103–109.

The Strategic Planning Process

Let us put the above discussion into a more comprehensive framework. Although the specific steps of strategic planning may vary, the process is usually structured, at least conceptually, around the key elements shown in Figure 6-2.

1 Inputs

The various organizational *inputs*, including the goal inputs of the claimants, were discussed in Chapter 1 and need no elaboration.

2 The Enterprise Profile

The *enterprise profile* is usually the starting point for determining where the company is and where it should go. Thus, top managers determine the basic purpose of the enterprise and clarify the firm's geographic orientation, such as whether it should operate in selected regions, in all states in the United States, or internationally. In addition, managers assess the competitive situation of their firm.

3 Orientation of Top Managers

The enterprise profile is shaped by people, especially *top managers*, and their *orientation* is an important influence on strategy. They create the organizational climate, and they determine the direction of the firm. Consequently, their values, their preferences, and their attitudes toward risks have to be carefully examined because they impact on the strategy.

4 Purpose and Objectives

The *purpose* and the basic *objectives* are the end points toward which the activities of the enterprise are directed. These topics were dealt with at length in the previous chapter.

5 The External Environment

The present and future *external environment* must be assessed in terms of threats and opportunities. The evaluation focuses on economic, social, political, legal, demographic, and geographic factors. In addition, the environment is scanned for technological developments, products and services offered by competitors, and other factors affecting the competitive situation of the enterprise.

6 The Internal Environment

Similarly, the firm's *internal environment* should be evaluated in respect to its weaknesses and strengths in research and development, production, operations, procurement, marketing, products, and services. Other internal factors that are important to assess when formulating a strategy include human resources, financial resources, the company image, the organization structure and climate, the planning and control system, and relations with customers.

7 Alternative Strategies

Specialization, or concentration

Diversification

Strategic *alternatives* are *developed* on the basis of analysis of the external and internal environment. An organization may pursue many different kinds of strategies. It may *specialize*, or *concentrate*, as American Motors did by producing lower-priced cars (in contrast to General Motors which has a complete product line ranging from economy to luxury cars).

Another strategy is *diversification*, extension of the operation into new and profitable markets. Sears not only is in retailing, but now also provides many financial services.

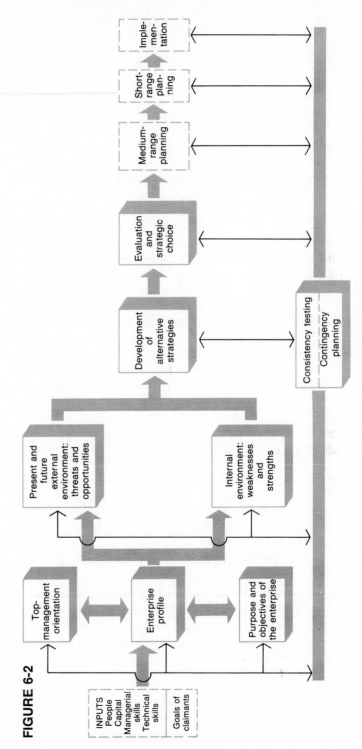

FIGURE 6-2

STRATEGIC PLANNING PROCESS .

Internationalization

Joint ventures

Liquidation

Retrenchment

Still another strategy is to go *international*, expanding the operation into other countries. The multinational firms discussed in Chapter 3 provide many examples. In the same chapter we also saw that *joint ventures* may be appropriate, especially for big undertakings in which firms have to pool their resources, such as the joint venture of General Motors and Toyota to produce small cars in California.

Under certain circumstances, a company may have to adopt a *liquidation* strategy, terminating an unprofitable product line or even dissolving the firm. But in some cases liquidation may not be necessary and a *retrenchment* strategy may be appropriate. In such a situation the company may curtail its operations temporarily.

These are just a few examples of possible strategies. In practice, companies, especially large ones, pursue a combination of strategies.

8 Evaluation and Choice of Strategies

The various strategies have to be carefully *evaluated* before the *choice* is made. Strategic choices must be considered in light of the risks involved. Some profitable opportunities may not be pursued because a failure in a risky venture could result in bankruptcy. Another critical element in choosing a strategy is timing. Even the best product may fail if it is introduced to the market at an inappropriate time. Moreover, the reaction of competitors must be taken into consideration. When IBM reduced the price of its personal computer (the IBM PC) in reaction to the high sales of Apple's Macintosh computer, other IBM-compatible computer firms had little choice but to reduce their prices as well. This illustrates the interconnections of the strategies of several firms in the same industry.

9 Medium- and Short-Range Planning and Implementation

Although not a part of the strategic planning process (and therefore shown by broken lines in Figure 6-2), *medium-* and *short-range planning* as well as the *implementation* of the plans must be considered during all phases of the process. The importance of feedback is shown by the loops in the model.

10 Consistency and Contingency

The last key aspect of the strategic planning process is the testing for *consistency* and the preparation of *contingency plans;* both topics are discussed earlier in this chapter.

Effective Implementation of Strategies

It is one thing to develop clear and meaningful strategies. It is another matter, and one of very great practical importance, to implement strategies effectively. If strategic planning is to be successful, we must take certain steps to implement it. Following are eight steps that should be followed by managers who wish to put their strategies to work.

Communication of Strategies to All Key Decision-Making Managers

It does little good to formulate meaningful strategies unless we communicate them to all those managers who are in a position to make decisions on programs and plans designed to implement them. Nothing has been communicated unless it is clear to the receiver. Strategies may be clear to the executive committee members and the chief executive who participate in developing them. But they should be in writing, and top executives and their subordinates must make sure that everyone involved in implementing strategies understands them.

Developing and Communicating Planning Premises

We have stressed the importance of planning premises. Managers must develop premises critical to plans and decisions, explain them to all those in the decision-making chain, and give instructions to develop programs and make decisions in line with them. Too few organizations do this. But if premises do not include key assumptions about the environment in which plans will operate, decisions are likely to be based on personal assumptions and predilections. This will almost certainly lead to a collection of uncoordinated plans.

Action Plans Contributing to and Reflecting Major Objectives and Strategies

Action plans are tactical or operational programs and decisions, major or minor, that take place in various parts of an organization. If they do not reflect desired objectives and strategies, the result will be vague hopes or useless intentions. If care is not taken in this area, strategic planning is not likely to have a bottom-line impact, that is, to have an important effect on company profits.

There are various ways of making sure that action plans contribute to major goals. If every manager understands strategies, all managers can certainly review the recommendations of staff advisers and line subordinates to see that they contribute something and are consistent. It might even be a good idea for major decisions to be reviewed by an appropriate small committee, such as one including a subordinate's superior, the superior's superior, and a staff specialist. This would lend an atmosphere of formality to the program decision, and important influences on implementation of strategies might become clear. Budgets likewise should be reviewed with objectives and strategies in mind.

Regular Review of Strategies

Even carefully developed strategies may cease to be suitable if conditions change. Therefore, they should be reviewed from time to time, certainly not less than once a year for major strategies and perhaps more often.

Development of Contingency Strategies and Programs

Where considerable change in competitive factors or other elements in the environment may occur, strategies for such contingencies should be formulated. No one, of course, can wait to make plans until a future is certain. Even where there is considerable uncertainty and events may occur that make a given set of objectives, strategies, or programs obsolete, we have no choice but to proceed on the most credible set of premises we can come up with at a given time. But even then, we need not find ourselves totally unprepared if certain possible contingencies do occur. Contingency plans can give us this degree of preparation.

Making Organization Structure Fit Planning Needs

The organization structure with its system of delegations should be designed to help managers accomplish goals and make the decisions necessary to put plans into effect. If possible, one person should be responsible for the accomplishment of each goal and for implementing strategies to achieve this goal. In other words, end-result areas and key tasks should be identified and assigned to a single position as far down the organization structure as is feasible. Since this assignment sometimes cannot be made, there may be no alternative but to utilize a form of matrix organization, a type of organization structure discussed in Chapter 9. But, where this is done, the responsibilities of the various positions in the matrix should be clearly defined.

The role of staff analysts in an organization structure should be so defined as to make it clear that the job of people in a staff position is to advise. Staff studies and recommendations then enter the decision system at the various points where decisions are actually made. Unless they do so, we end up with independent staff work of no value for planning.

Continuing Stress on Planning and Implementing Strategy

Even where we may have a workable system of objectives and strategies and their implementation, it can easily fail unless responsible managers continue to stress the nature and importance of these elements. This process may seem tedious and unnecessarily repetitious, but it is the best way to make sure that members of an organization learn about them. Teaching does not necessarily mean attending seminars; rather, much of the teaching can take place in the day-to-day interaction between superiors and subordinates.

Creating a Company Climate that Forces Planning

People tend to allow problems and crises that arise today to interfere with effective planning for tomorrow. The only way to ensure that planning of all kinds will be done is to develop strategies carefully and to take pains to implement them. In fact, if a company or any other kind of organization is to be successful over a period of time, it really has no other alternative.

Summary

Strategies are general programs of action that imply commitment of resources for the purpose of reaching objectives. Policies guide managers in using discretion in decision making. Strategies and policies give direction to plans. They furnish a framework for plans and serve as the basis for the development of tactics and other managerial activities.

Effective strategies require the assessment of the present and the future external environment. Similarly, the internal environment of the enterprise must be evaluated. The firm's position in the industry, its organization structure, the consistency of its strategy, and the adequacy of contingency strategies should be considered.

Major strategies need to be developed in the areas of (1) new or changed products and services, (2) marketing, (3) growth, (4) finance, (5) organization, (6) personnel, and (7) public relations. Developing strategies requires asking the right questions about the firm's purpose, product or service, customers, circumstances, capabilities, and so on.

Resource allocation can be aided by the Portfolio Matrix, which links the growth rate of the business and the relative competitive position of the firm (as measured by market share).

The strategic planning model provides a framework for understanding how the process works. It shows the critical elements of this process and how they relate to each other.

To effectively put strategies to work, managers must communicate the strategies and planning premises to all who should know them, make sure that the plans contribute to and reflect the strategies and goals they serve, review strategies regularly, develop contingency strategies, and be sure that the organization structure of the firm fits its planning programs. Managers also need to make learning about planning and implementing strategy an ongoing process.

Key Ideas and Concepts for Review

Strategies	Major kinds of strategies
Policies	Portfolio Matrix
Principle of strategy and policy framework	Key aspects of the strategic planning process
Tactics	Requirements for implementing strategies
Requirements for effective strategies	

For Discussion

1 How can you distinguish between strategies and policies?

2 Most middle managers are anxious for a business or other organization to develop and publish clear policies. Can you see any reason why this should be the case?

3 Are strategies and policies as important in a nonbusiness enterprise (such as a labor union, the State Department, a hospital, or a city fire department) as in a business? Why and how?

4 Why are contingency strategies important?

5 How would you go about formulating a company's major strategies?

6 How can strategies be effectively implemented?

7 Choose an organization you know and identify its strengths and weaknesses. What are its special opportunities and threats in the external environment?

8 How would you make an organizational appraisal of your college or university? What is the kind of "business" the school is in?

9 Take the concepts of strategic planning and relate them to your life. What are your personal strengths and weaknesses? Based on this analysis, what would be a suitable (for you) "mission" in this world?

CASE 6-1

THE GENERAL SAVINGS AND LOAN ASSOCIATION

A large savings and loan association with offices throughout the state had a problem many financial institutions would like to have: It was very successful and was growing. But top executives recognized that the management system used in the past was insufficient to cope with the new demands. Consequently, the president called a meeting to discuss the future direction of the company.

Soon the need for a planning system became evident. However, since the firm never did systematic planning, the managers did not know how to go about developing a planning system. Therefore, the president thought of hiring a consultant. The vice-president concerned with finances argued against the hiring of such a consultant. She said, "We have been successful in the past without outside help and I doubt whether the benefits of the consultant would outweigh his high fees." "Furthermore," she contended, "the firm's budgetary process is a planning system and as such is sufficient."

The president, however, overruled the vice-president of finance and contacted a consultant to design a strategic planning system and integrate it with management by objectives. The vice-president of finance wondered what this comprehensive system would be like.

1 Assuming that you were the consultant, how would you convince the vice-president of finance of the value of strategic planning?

2 How would you go about evaluating the external environment? What factors would you consider? What is the importance of these factors for the savings and loan association?

3 How would you go about assessing the internal environment of the firm?

4 What kind of planning system would you suggest? Draw a planning model that shows the important variables and their relationships.

CASE 6-2

THE PENN CENTRAL TRANSPORTATION COMPANY

One of the most shocking failures of American history was the bankruptcy of the Penn Central in 1970, only 2 years after a merger was completed between two of the country's largest Eastern railroads, the New York Central and the Pennsyl-

vania Railroad. During the short period of 2 years its stock dropped from a high of $86.50 per share to $5.50. It fell to $1 per share shortly thereafter, and many thousands of investors in bonds as well as stocks lost most of their investment. And this was in a company once regarded as one of the largest and most promising in the United States!

This failure has been ascribed to many causes. Among these are the cost and revenue problems of most Eastern railroads, obsolete and costly labor practices, accounting deficiencies that did not accurately disclose earnings or cash flows, the foolish policy of deferring railroad maintenance, poor service to shippers and passengers, the payment of cash dividends when cash losses were occurring in operations, and "gross mismanagement."

However, many financial analysts believe that the fundamental cause of Penn Central's failure was the company's strategy of diversification. It is stated by these analysts that the company lost sight of its business and that the top executives became intent on making Penn Central a con-

glomerate. It is true that the company did invest heavily in real estate, amusement parks, construction companies, coal fields, hotels, pipelines, oil refineries, investment companies, and even some sports teams.

When one of the most vocal critics, who declared that "diversification disease" was the cause of the Penn Central fiasco, was asked what the company's strategy should have been, the only reply he could readily make was, "That is something I would have to study in some depth."

1 What was the business of Penn Central? Should it have been changed? Identify the mission or purpose of the firm.

2 What opportunities and threats can you identify in the external environment?

For Further Information

Ansoff, H., R. P. Declerck, and R. L. Hayes (eds.). *From Strategic Planning to Strategic Management* (New York: John Wiley & Sons, Inc., 1976).

Chandler, A. D., Jr. *Strategy and Structure* (Garden City, N. Y.: Doubleday Company, Inc., 1962).

Fredrickson, J. W. "Strategic Process Research: Questions and Recommendations," *Academy of Management Review*, vol. 8, no. 4 (October 1983), pp. 565–575.

Glueck, W. F., and L. R. Jauch. *Business Policy and Strategic Management*, 4th ed. (New York: McGraw-Hill Book Company, 1984).

Harrigan, K. R., and M. E. Porter. "End-Game Strategies for Declining Industries," *Harvard Business Review*, vol. 61, no. 4 (July–August 1983), pp. 111–120.

Leontiades, M. *Policy, Strategy, and Implementation—Readings and Cases* (New York: Random House Business Division, 1983).

Lorange, P. *Corporate Planning* (Englewood Cliffs, N.J.: Prentice-Hall, Inc., 1980).

Paine, F. T., and C. R. Anderson. *Strategic Management* (New York: The Dryden Press, 1983).

Robinson, R. B., Jr., and J. A. Pearce II. "Research Thrusts in Small Firm Strategic Planning," *Academy of Management Review*, vol. 9, no. 1 (January 1984), pp. 128–137.

Steiner, G. A., and J. B. Miner. *Management Policy and Strategy* (New York: Macmillan Publishing Company, Inc., 1982).

Thompson, A. A., Jr., and A. J. Strickland III. *Strategy Formulation and Implementation* (Plano, Texas: Business Publications, Inc., 1983).

Thurston, P. H. "Should Smaller Companies Make Formal Plans?" *Harvard Business Review*, vol. 61, no. 5 (September–October 1983), pp. 162–168 and 170–188.

Weihrich, H. "The TOWS Matrix—A Tool for Situational Analysis," *Long Range Planning*, vol. 15, no. 2 (April 1982), pp. 52–64.

Wheelen, T. L., and J. D. Hunger. *Strategic Management* (Reading, Mass.: Addison-Wesley Publishing Company, Inc., 1984).

7

Decision Making

CHAPTER OBJECTIVES

After reading this chapter, you should understand:

1 What decision making is
2 The principle of the limiting factor
3 The nature and process of evaluation of alternatives
4 Three bases for selecting from among alternative courses
5 Programmed and nonprogrammed decisions
6 Modern approaches to decision making in light of uncertainties
7 Factors influencing the importance of the decision
8 The system approach to decision making
9 Major principles for planning

Decision making

Decision making—the selection from among alternatives of a course of action—is at the core of planning. A plan cannot be said to exist unless a decision—a commitment of resources, direction, or reputation—has been made. Until that point, we have only planning studies and analyses. Managers sometimes see decision making as their central job because they must constantly choose what is to be done, who is to do it, and when, where, and occasionally even how it will be done. Decision making is, however, only a step in planning, even when done quickly and with little thought or when it influences action for only a few minutes. It is also part of everyone's daily living. A course of action can seldom be judged alone because virtually every decision must be geared to other plans. The stereotype of the finger-snapping, button-pushing managerial mogul fades as the requirements of systematic research and analysis preceding a decision come into focus.

The Importance and Limitations of Rational Decision Making

In outlining and discussing the steps in planning in Chapter 4, we were really considering decision making as a major part of planning. As a matter of fact, given an awareness of an opportunity and a goal, the core of planning is really the **decision process.** Thus, in this context, decision making might be thought of as (1) premising, (2) identifying alternatives, (3) the evaluation of alternatives in terms of the goal sought, and (4) the choosing of an alternative, that is, making a decision. As you will note, the discussion of decision making in this chapter, although emphasizing the logic and techniques of choosing a course of action, really places decision making as one of the steps in planning.[1]

The decision process

Effective decision making must be rational. But what is rationality? When is a person thinking or deciding rationally?

People acting or deciding rationally are attempting to reach some goal that cannot be attained without action. They must have a clear understanding of alternative courses by which a goal can be reached under existing circumstances and limitations. They also must have the information and the ability to analyze and evaluate alternatives in the light of the goal sought. And, finally, they must have a desire to come to the best solution by selecting the alternative that most effectively satisfies goal achievement.

Partial rationality

We seldom achieve complete rationality, particularly in managing. In the first place, since no one can make decisions affecting the past, decisions must operate for the future, and the future almost invariably involves uncertainties. In the second place, all the alternatives that might be followed to reach a goal can scarcely be recognized; this is particularly true when decision making involves opportunities to do something that has not been done before. Moreover, in most instances, not all alternatives can be analyzed, even with the newest available analytical techniques and computers.

Bounded rationality

A manager must settle for **limited rationality,** or **"bounded" rationality.** In other words, limitations of information, time, and certainty limit rationality even though a manager tries earnestly to be completely rational. Since we cannot be completely rational in practice, managers sometimes allow their dislike of risk—the desire to "play it safe"—to interfere with the desire to reach the best solution under the circumstances. Herbert Simon has called this **"satisficing,"** that is, picking a course of action that is satisfactory or good enough under the circumstances. Although many managerial decisions are made with a desire to "get by" as safely as possible, most managers do attempt to make the best decisions they can within the limits of rationality and in the light of the size and nature of risks involved.

Satisficing

We will now consider the steps of the decision process in detail.

---

[1]The attempts by a number of management specialists to bring logical order to the decision process are outlined and explained in E. R. Archer, "How To Make a Business Decision: An Analysis of Theory and Practice," *Management Review*, vol. 69, no. 2 (February 1980) pp. 30–37.

Development of Alternatives

Assuming that we know what our goals are and agree on clear planning premises, the first step of decision making is to develop alternatives. There are always alternatives to any course of action; indeed, if there seems to be only one way of doing a thing, that way is probably wrong. If we can think of only one course of action, clearly we have not thought hard enough.

Generating Alternatives in an Adverse Situation

A certain firm once desperately needed some new equipment. Without this equipment, the company could not increase its production or expand its market, and thus it would continue to lose money. The company had lost so much money already, however, that it could not afford to buy new machinery, nor could it borrow the money to do so. It looked as if the only thing to do was to do nothing; but this meant certain bankruptcy.

The officers of the company set out to find alternatives. They located a manufacturer who had the equipment they needed and had not been able to sell it to anyone. He in turn owed money borrowed from a bank to purchase the equipment. The bank agreed to let the manufacturer sell the machines to the firm without taking a down payment on them and arranged for the manufacturer and the firm both to sign a note for the money owed to the bank. The officers also found a competitor who had ordered some new equipment and was willing to sell his old machinery, also without requiring a down payment. Thus, in an apparently hopeless situation, the firm found two reasonable alternatives.

The ability to develop alternatives is often as important as selecting correctly from among them. On the other hand, ingenuity, research, and common sense will often unearth so many choices that all of them cannot be adequately evaluated. The manager needs help in this situation, and this help, as well as assistance in choosing the best alternative, is found in the concept of the limiting or strategic factor.

The Principle of the Limiting Factor

A **limiting factor** is something that stands in the way of accomplishing a desired objective. If we recognize the limiting factors in a given situation, we can narrow our search for alternatives to those that will overcome the limiting factors. In the example above, the objective was to turn a loss into a profit. The means for doing so was to acquire some equipment. The limiting factor was the lack of cash and credit. The managers' alternatives were confined to those that would overcome the limiting factor. Their search was accurate, direct, and successful. The **principle of the limiting factor** is as follows: *Only when we recognize and solve for those factors that stand critically in our way to our goal can we select the best alternative course of action.*

The principle

It may not be easy to discover the limiting factor or factors, since they are often obscure. For example, if a company were considering a profit sharing program, the limiting factors might be tax deductibility and the attitude of employees toward the plan. In deciding whether to expand operations, a company might find its limiting factor to be availability of capital, the problems of managing the firm if it got too large, or the attitude of the government antimonopoly agencies.

The search for, and recognition of, limiting factors in planning never end. For one program at one time, a certain factor may be critical, but, at a later time and for a similar decision, the limiting factor may be something that was relatively unimportant in the earlier planning. Thus, a company might decide to acquire new equipment when the limiting factor was capital availability, only to have the limiting factor become delivery or, later, the training of people to operate the equipment.

The Nature and Process of Evaluation of Alternatives

Once appropriate alternatives have been found, the next step in planning is to evaluate them and select the one that will best contribute to the goal. This is the point of ultimate decision making, although decisions must also be made in the other steps of planning—in selecting goals, in choosing critical premises, and even in selecting alternatives.

Quantitative and Qualitative Factors

As we compare alternative plans for achieving an objective, we are likely to think exclusively of **quantitative factors.** These are factors that can be measured in numerical terms, such as time or the various types of fixed and operating costs. No one would question the importance of this analysis, but the success of the venture would be endangered if intangible, or qualitative, factors were ignored. **Qualitative** or **intangible factors** are those that are difficult to measure numerically, such as the quality of labor relations, the risk of technological change, or the international political climate. There are all too many instances where the best of quantitative plans were destroyed by an unforeseen war, a fine marketing plan was made inoperable by a long transportation strike, or a rational borrowing plan was hampered by an economic recession. These illustrations point up the importance of giving attention to both quantitative and qualitative factors when comparing alternatives.

To evaluate and compare the intangible factors in a planning problem and make decisions, we must first recognize these factors and then determine whether a reasonable quantitative measurement can be given them. If not, we should find out as much as possible about them, perhaps rate them in terms of their importance, compare their probable influence on the outcome with that of the quantitative factors, and then come to a decision. This decision may give predominant weight to a single intangible.

Such a procedure allows the manager to decide upon the weight of the total evidence. It does involve fallible personal judgments; however, few managerial decisions can be so accurately quantified that judgment is unnecessary. Decision making is seldom so simple. It is not without some justification that the successful executive has been cynically described as a person who guesses right.

Evaluating Alternatives: Marginal Analysis

In evaluating alternatives, we may utilize the techniques of marginal analysis to compare additional revenues arising from additional costs. Where the objective is to maximize profits, this goal will be reached, as elementary economics teaches us, when the additional revenues and additional costs are equal. In other words, if additional revenues are greater than additional costs with a larger quantity, more profits can be made by producing more. However, at the point where additional volume costs more than additional revenues, the profit will be larger at a lesser volume.

Different uses

Marginal analysis can be used in comparing factors other than costs and revenues. For example, to find the best output of a machine, we could vary inputs against outputs until the additional input equals the additional output. This would then be the point of maximum efficiency of the machine. Or the number of subordinates reporting to a manager might conceivably be increased to the point where additional savings in costs, better communication and morale, and other factors equal additional losses in effectiveness of control, leadership, and similar factors.

Evaluating Alternatives: Cost Effectiveness Analysis

An improvement on, or variation of, traditional marginal analysis is cost effectiveness, or cost benefit, analysis. **Cost effectiveness** analysis seeks the best ratio of benefits and costs; this means, for example, finding the least costly way of reaching an objective, or, getting the greatest value for given expenditures. Similarly, **cost benefit analysis** pertains to the ratio of the benefits to costs; it is often not possible, however, to measure benefits of a program accurately. Thus, it is the technique of weighing alternatives that cannot be conveniently reduced to dollars or some other specific measure, as in the case of normal marginal analysis, which is similar to a traditional form of cost benefit analysis.

In its simplest terms, cost effectiveness analysis is a technique for choosing the best plan when the objectives are less specific than sales, costs, or profits. For example, defense objectives may be to deter or repel enemy attack; social objectives may be to reduce air pollution or retrain the unemployed; and business objectives may be to participate in social objectives through a program of training unemployables.

Nonquantifiable objectives can sometimes be given some fairly specific measures of effectiveness. In a program with the general objectives of improving employee morale, for example, we can measure effectiveness by such verifiable factors as employee turnover, absenteeism, or volume of grievances and also supplement these measurements by such subjective inputs as the judgment of qualified experts.

The major features of cost effectiveness analysis are that it makes us focus on the results of a program, helps us weigh the potential benefits of each alternative against its potential cost, and makes us then compare the alternatives in terms of the overall advantages. This was apparently the reasoning that led to the selection of the F-111 combat airplane some years ago for both the Navy and the Air Force. As wrong as many military officers believed this decision to have been (and the Defense Department itself clearly recognized that the airplane was not the best for either service), the plane's effectiveness, considering the estimated costs of undertaking two combat aircraft programs when resources were needed for other defense requirements, appeared to justify the same aircraft program for both the Navy and the Air Force.

Although the decision on cost effectiveness involves the same steps as any planning decision, its major distinguishing features are:

Major features

1 Objectives are normally oriented to output or end result and usually are not precise.

2 Alternatives ordinarily represent total systems, programs, or strategies for meeting objectives.

3 The measures of effectiveness must be relevant to objectives and set in terms as precise as possible, although some may not be subject to quantification.

4 Cost estimates are usually traditional and normal, but may include nonmonetary as well as monetary costs, even though the former may be eliminated by expressing them as negative factors of effectiveness.

5 Decision standards, while definite but not usually as specific as cost or profit, may include achieving a given objective at least cost, achieving it with resources available, or providing for a trade-off of cost for effectiveness, particularly in the light of the claims of other programs.

Cost effectiveness analysis can be made most systematic through the use of models and other operations research techniques, which we will describe in Chapter 23. We can develop models to show cost estimates for each alternative, and effectiveness models to show the relationship between each alternative and its effectiveness. Then, models combining these results can be made to show the relationships of costs and effectiveness for each alternative.

Selecting an Alternative: Three Approaches

When selecting from among alternatives, managers can use three basic approaches: (1) experience, (2) experimentation, and (3) research and analysis. (See Figure 7-1.)

Experience

Reliance on past experience probably plays a larger part than it deserves in decision making. Experienced managers usually believe, often without realizing it, that the things they have successfully accomplished and the mistakes they have made furnish almost infallible guides to the future. This attitude is likely to be more pronounced the more experience a manager has had and the higher in an organization he or she has risen.

To some extent, experience is the best teacher. The very fact that managers have reached their position appears to justify their past decisions. Moreover, the process of thinking problems through, making decisions, and seeing programs

FIGURE 7-1

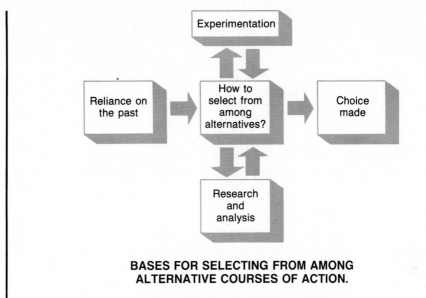

**BASES FOR SELECTING FROM AMONG
ALTERNATIVE COURSES OF ACTION.**

succeed or fail does make for a degree of good judgment (at times bordering on intuition). Many people, however, do not profit by their errors, and there are managers who seem never to gain the seasoned judgment required by modern enterprise.

Relying on our past experience as a guide for future action can be dangerous, however. In the first place, most of us do not recognize the underlying reasons for our mistakes or failures. In the second place, the lessons of experience may be entirely inapplicable to new problems. Good decisions must be evaluated against future events, while experience belongs to the past.

On the other hand, if we carefully analyze experience rather than blindly follow it and if we distill from experience the fundamental reasons for success or failure, then experience can be useful as a basis for decision analysis. A successful program, a well-managed company, a profitable product promotion, or any other decision that turns out well may furnish useful data for such distillation. Just as scientists do not hesitate to build upon the research of others and would be foolish indeed merely to duplicate it, managers can learn much from others.

Experimentation

An obvious way to decide among alternatives is to try one of them and see what happens. Experimentation is often used in scientific inquiry. People often argue that it should be employed more often in managing and that the only way a manager can make sure some plans are right—especially in view of the intangible factors—is to try the various alternatives and see which is best.

Costliness

The experimental technique is likely to be the most expensive of all techniques, especially where a program requires heavy expenditures in capital and personnel and where the firm cannot afford to vigorously attempt several alternatives. Besides, after an experiment has been tried, we may still doubt what it proved, since the future may not duplicate the present. This technique, therefore, should be used only after considering other alternatives.

On the other hand, there are many decisions that cannot be made until the best course of action can be ascertained by experiment. Even reflections on experience or the most careful research may not assure managers of correct decisions. This is nowhere better illustrated than in the planning of a new airplane. The manufacturer may draw from personal experience and that of other plane manufacturers and of new plane users. Engineers and economists may make extensive studies of stresses, vibrations, fuel consumption, speed, space allocations, and other factors. But all these studies do not give every answer to questions about the flight characteristics and economics of a successful plane; therefore, some experimentation is almost always involved in the process of selecting the right course to follow. Ordinarily, a first production, or prototype, airplane is constructed and tested, and, on the basis of these tests, production airplanes are made on a somewhat revised design.

Experimentation is used in other ways. A firm may test a new product in a certain market before expanding its sale nationwide. Organizational techniques are often tried in a branch office or plant before being applied over an entire company. A candidate for a management job may be tested in the job during the incumbent's vacation.

Research and Analysis

The most generally used, and almost certainly the most effective, technique for selecting from alternatives when major decisions are involved is research and analysis. This approach means solving a problem by first comprehending it. It thus involves a search for relationships among the more critical of the variables, constraints, and premises that bear upon the goal sought. It is the pencil-and-paper (or, better, the computer-and-printout) approach to decision making.

To solve a planning problem we must break it into its component parts and study the various quantitative and qualitative factors. Study and analysis are likely to be far cheaper than experimentation. Hours of time and reams of paper used for analyses usually cost much less than trying the various alternatives. In building airplanes, if careful research has not preceded the building and testing of the prototype airplane and its parts, we can hardly imagine the resulting costs.

Model building

A major step in the research and analysis approach is to develop a model simulating the problem. Thus we often make models of buildings in the form of extensive blueprints or three-dimensional renditions. We test models of airplane wings and missiles in a wind tunnel. But the most useful simulation is likely to be a representation of the variables in a problem situation by mathematical terms and relationships. If we can thereby conceptualize a problem, we have taken a major step toward its solution. The physical sciences have long relied on mathematical models to do this, and it is encouraging to see this method being applied to managerial decision making.

FIGURE 7-2

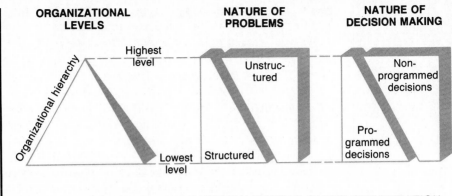

NATURE OF PROBLEMS AND DECISION MAKING IN THE ORGANIZATION.

One of the most comprehensive research-and-analysis approaches to decision making is operations research. Since this is an important tool for production and operations management, we will discuss it in Chapter 23.

Programmed and Nonprogrammed Decisions

Programmed decisions

We can make a distinction between programmed and nonprogrammed decisions. A *programmed* decision, as shown in Figure 7-2, is applied to structured or routine problems. Lathe operators have specifications and rules that tell them when the part they made can be accepted, when it has to be discarded, and when it can be reworked. Another example of a programmed decision is the reordering of standard items in the inventory. In fact, there is a formula for doing this as you will see in Chapter 23. This kind of decision is for routine and repetitive work, relying primarily on previously established criteria. You might say that it is decision making by precedent.

Nonprogrammed decisions

Nonprogrammed decisions are used for unstructured, novel, and ill-defined situations of a nonrecurring nature. Examples are the introduction of the Macintosh computer by Apple Computer, Inc., the development of the four-wheel-drive passenger car by Audi, and the marketing of a small video camera by Kodak. In fact, strategic decisions, in general, are nonprogrammed decisions, requiring subjective judgments.

Combination of both types

Most decisions are neither completely programmed nor completely nonprogrammed, but are a combination of both.

As you can see from Figure 7-2, nonprogrammed decisions are mostly made by upper-level managers because upper-level managers have to deal with unstructured problems. Problems on lower levels of the organization are often routine and well-structured, requiring less decision discretion by managers and nonmanagers.

Modern Approaches to Decision Making Under Uncertainty

A number of modern techniques improve the quality of decision making under the normal conditions of uncertainty. Among the most important of these are (1) risk analysis, (2) decision trees, and (3) preference theory.

Risk Analysis

All intelligent decision makers dealing with uncertainty like to know the size and nature of the risk they are taking in choosing a course of action. One of the deficiencies in using the traditional approaches of operations research for problem solving is that many of the data used in a model are merely estimates, and others are based upon probabilities. The ordinary practice is for staff specialists to come up with "best estimates." But these might be like the best estimate that, on a given roll of the dice, the number 7 is more likely to come up than any other number, even though there is only 1 chance in 6 that it will. Consequently, to give a more precise view of risk, new techniques have been developed.

Estimating probability

Virtually every decision is based on the interaction of a number of important variables, many of which have an element of uncertainty but, perhaps, a fairly high degree of probability. Thus, the wisdom of launching a new product might depend upon a number of critical variables: how much it will cost to introduce the product, how much it will cost to produce it, how much of a capital investment will be required, what price can be set for the product, the size of the potential market for it, and the share of total market that it will represent. A best estimate might be that the new product has a high (say, 80 percent) chance of yielding a return of 30 percent on the total investment made in it.

But, suppose that further analysis of each critical variable shows that the introduction, operating, and investment cost estimates each have a 90 percent probability of being accurate, the price estimate a 70 percent chance of being correct, and the market quantity estimate a 60 percent probability of being correct. In this case, the calculated probability of the entire program estimate being right would almost certainly be less than 80 percent; exactly how much less would depend upon the values of each variable and the extent to which probabilities less or more than 80 percent would affect costs or revenues. It can be said that the probability of *all* the estimates of the various important variables being correct, however, is only 30.6 percent ($.90 \times .90 \times .90 \times .70 \times .60$).

Probability distribution curve

Risk analysis attempts to develop for every critical variable in a decision problem a probability distribution curve. Usable ones can be derived by asking each specialist who estimated a variable to estimate what the range and probability of each variable are. For example, the sales manager might be asked to estimate what the probability would be of a selling price exceeding or falling below the best estimate, and by how much. No matter what these estimates may be, a range of values and probabilities will be better than a single best estimate. With the aid of computer programs, a range of expectancies for the "rightness" of any total estimate can be derived.

In the example of the new product investment program noted above, the range of probabilities for a return on investment might be based on different estimates as follows:

Rate of return (percent)	Probability of achieving at least rate of return shown
0	.90
10	.80
15	.70
20	.65
25	.60
30	.50
35	.40
40	.30

In other words, there is a 90 percent (.90) chance that the rate of return (or the rate at which the company earns money from its investment) will be at least zero, an 80 percent (.80) chance that it will be at least 10 percent, and so on.

Given such data as these, a manager is better able to assess the probability of accomplishing a best estimate and can see the chances of success that he or she might have if a lesser rate of return would be sufficient. The manager can also see there is a 10 percent chance of losing on the original investment and other costs on the project. Had the risk analysis shown a 50 percent chance of making the 30 percent return on investment, but a 25 percent probability of losing a considerable amount, the manager might even decide that undertaking the project would not be worth the risk.

Decision Trees

One of the best ways to analyze a decision is to use so-called decision trees. **Decision trees** sketch in the form of a "tree" the decision points, the chance events, and the probabilities involved in various courses that might be undertaken. A common problem occurs in business when a new product is introduced. Managers must decide whether to install expensive permanent equipment so as to ensure production at the lowest possible cost or to undertake cheaper temporary tooling involving a higher manufacturing cost but lower capital investments and lower losses if the product does not sell as well as estimated. In its simplest form, a tree showing the decision a manager faces in this situation might be similar to that in Figure 7-3.

A simple decision tree

The tree shows a manager what the chance events are and what their values are (in terms of profits and losses) for each of the two tooling alternatives. For example, at the far left of the tree the manager decides either to install temporary tooling or to buy permanent tooling. Each course of action entails a set of possible future events. But this alone is not enough. What we need is an assessment of the probability that each course of possible events will occur. If the probability that product sales will be as much as estimated is 60 percent, that they will be slow is 20 percent, and that the product may fail to sell is 20 percent, the manager can make a decision much more easily. Using these probabilities, we can see that there is a 60 percent chance that an investment of $2 million (for the permanent tooling option) will yield a net profit of $1 million per year for the assumed product life of 5 years and a similar chance that an investment of $100,000 (for temporary

FIGURE 7-3

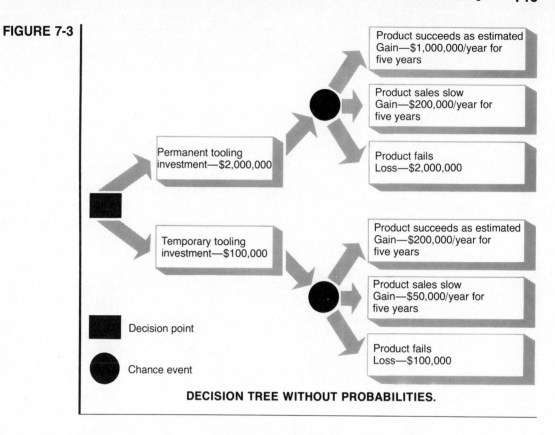

Product succeeds as estimated
Gain—$1,000,000/year for
five years

Product sales slow
Gain—$200,000/year for
five years

Product fails
Loss—$2,000,000

Permanent tooling
investment—$2,000,000

Temporary tooling
investment—$100,000

Product succeeds as estimated
Gain—$200,000/year for
five years

Product sales slow
Gain—$50,000/year for
five years

Product fails
Loss—$100,000

Decision point

Chance event

DECISION TREE WITHOUT PROBABILITIES.

tooling) will yield a net profit of $200,000 per year. Taking into account these probabilities, the $2-million investment has a predicted worth of $600,000 per year for the 5 years of product life assumed, and the $100,000 temporary tooling alternative a worth of $120,000 per year for 5 years. On consideration of rate of return on investment only, the temporary tooling approach would seem to be preferable. But, depending on the availability of capital, a 30 percent return on $2 million over 5 years would normally be regarded as greatly preferable to a 120 percent return on $100,000 over the same period.

There is also the possibility that if we drew a decision tree for a longer period and took into account a further chance event, such as that one or more competitors would enter the market, thus putting a squeeze on prices and sales values, the larger investment might look much better. Using the probabilities mentioned above and the further probability that a vigorous competitor would enter the field, a longer-range and more complete decision tree might look like that in Figure 7-4.

If we calculate the value of each probability over a 5-year period (what we assume the life of the product will be) and disregard the cost of interest and the discounting of future income, the total return on the permanent tooling option, modified by these probabilities, would be $1,918,000, and on the temporary tooling $360,000. While the temporary tooling approach still looks better in terms of

Decision tree with probabilities and competition

FIGURE 7-4

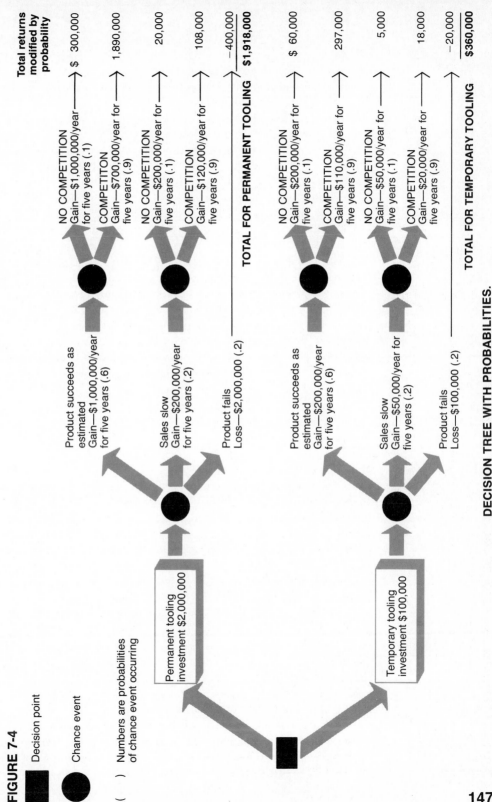

DECISION TREE WITH PROBABILITIES.

rate of return on investment, the higher total expected profits plus the possibility of a product life exceeding 5 years and considerations of better meeting competition might indicate that the permanent tooling program would be preferred. Whether we take this course, however, would depend in large part on the extent to which we might be willing to take the risk of investing $2 million before a product proved itself on the market.

Complexity in real life

As the number of chance events increases, the decision tree becomes more complicated, and the compounding of various probabilities makes the solution much more difficult. In many real-life cases, a computer may even be necessary to calculate them. Also, in real life, the tree would show various decision points in the future. For example, the firm might have the option, in case it initially followed the temporary tooling approach, to invest later in permanent tooling (at the loss of the $100,000 for temporary tooling) if product demand justified doing so. Also, it might make a decision later to reduce price, adopt a new marketing strategy, or develop a substitute improved product.

The decision tree approach makes it possible to see at least the major alternatives and the fact that subsequent decisions may depend upon events in the future. By incorporating probabilities of various events in the tree, we can also comprehend the true probability of a decision leading to the desired results. The "best estimate" may really turn out to be quite risky. One thing is certain: Decision trees and similar decision techniques do replace broad judgments with a focus on the important elements in a decision, bring out into the open premises that are often hidden, and disclose the reasoning process by which decisions are made under uncertainty.

Preference Theory

Preference, or **utility, theory** is based on the notion that individual attitudes toward risk will vary, with some individuals being willing only to take lower risks than indicated by probabilities ("risk averters") and others being willing to take greater risks ("gamblers"). While referred to here as "preference theory," this technique is more classically called "utility theory." Purely statistical probabilities, as applied to decision making, rest upon the assumption that decision makers will follow them. In other words, it might seem reasonable that if there were a 60 percent chance of a decision being the right one, we would take it, but this is not necessarily true, since the risk of being wrong is 40 percent and we might not wish to take this risk. Managers avoid risk, particularly if the penalty for being wrong is severe, whether it be in terms of monetary losses, reputation, or job security. If we doubt this, we might ask ourselves whether we would risk, say, $40,000 on the 60 percent chance that we might make $100,000, realizing that there is still a 40 percent chance that we might lose $40,000. We might readily risk $4 on a chance of making $10, and gamblers have been known to risk much more on a lesser chance of success.

Attitudes toward risk

Therefore, in order to give probabilities practical meaning in decision making, we need better understanding of the individual decision maker's aversion to, or acceptance of, risk. This varies not only with the individual but also with the size of the risk, with the level of the manager in an organization, and according to whether the funds involved are personal or belong to a company.

FIGURE 7-5

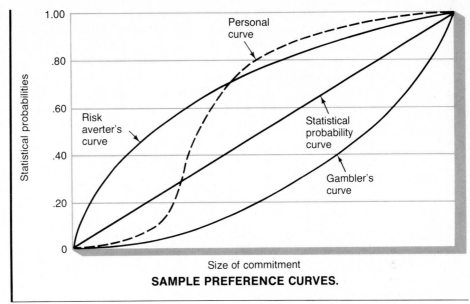

SAMPLE PREFERENCE CURVES.

Higher-level managers are accustomed to taking larger risks than lower-level managers, and their decision areas tend to involve larger elements of risk. A company president may have to take great risks in launching a new product, in selecting an advertising program, or in choosing a vice-president, while a first-level supervisor may have risk taking limited to hiring or promoting semiskilled workers or approving vacation schedules for subordinates.

Also, the same top managers who may make a decision involving risks of millions of dollars for a company in a given program with a chance of success of, say, 75 percent would not be likely to do that with their own personal fortunes, at least unless they were very large. Moreover, the same manager willing to take a 75 percent risk in one case might not be willing to do so in another. Furthermore, a top executive might "go for" a large advertising program where the chances of success are 70 percent, but might not decide in favor of an investment in plant and equipment unless the probability of success were higher. In other words, attitudes toward risk vary with events, as well as with people and positions.

Personal risk or preference curves

While we do not know much about attitudes toward risk, we do know that some people are risk averters in some situations and gamblers in others and that some people have by nature a high aversion to risk, and others a low one. Typical personal risk or preference curves may be drawn as in Figure 7-5. This graph shows both risk averter's and gambler's curves as well as what is referred to as a "personal" curve. The latter, of course, implies that most of us are gamblers when small stakes are involved but that we soon become risk averters when the stakes rise.

Most managers (understandably influenced by the dangers of failure), tend to be risk averters to some extent and do not in fact play the averages. Therefore, statistical probabilities are not good enough for practical decision making.

Although perhaps too many managers are risk averters and thereby miss opportunities, few are players of pure statistical averages, at least in important decisions. Therefore, individual preference curves could be substituted for statistical probabilities in decision trees. We can do this, at least roughly, by assessing our willingness to take risks in a variety of real or imaginary situations and by developing our own preference curve. Even where we do not do so systematically, those of us who receive recommendations on courses of action from subordinates gain an important advantage if we are aware of the effect of our subordinates' attitude toward risk in making decisions or decision recommendations.

Evaluating the Importance of a Decision

Since managers not only must make correct decisions but also must make them as needed and as economically as possible, and since they must do this often, guidelines to the relative importance of decisions are useful. Decisions of lesser importance need not require thorough analysis and research, and they may even be safely delegated without endangering an individual manager's basic responsibility. The importance of a decision also depends upon the extent of responsibility, so that what may be of practically no importance to a corporation president may be of great importance to a section head.

Size or length of commitment

If a decision commits the enterprise to heavy expenditure of funds or to an important personnel program, such as a program for management appraisal and training, or if the commitment can be fulfilled only over a long period, such as by the construction of a new chemical plant, it should be subjected to suitable attention at an upper level of management.

Flexibility of plans

Some plans can be easily changed; some have built into them the possibility of a future change of direction; and others involve action difficult to reverse. Clearly, decisions involving inflexible courses of action must carry a priority over decisions that can be easily changed.

Certainty of goals and premises

If goals and premises are fairly certain, a decision resting on them tends to be less difficult and to require less judgment and analysis than when they are highly uncertain.

Quantifiability of variables

Where the goals, inputs, restrictions, and variables can be accurately measured, like definite inputs in a production machine shop, the importance of the decision, other things remaining the same, tends to be less than where the inputs are difficult to quantify, as in pricing a new consumer product or deciding on its style.

Human impact

Where the impact of a decision on people is great, its importance is high. No one making a decision that affects other people can afford to overlook the need for those people to accept the decision.

The Systems Approach and Decision Making

Decisions cannot, of course, usually be made in a closed-system environment. As we have emphasized, many elements of the environment of planning lie outside the enterprise. In addition, every department or section of an enterprise is a subsystem of the entire enterprise; managers of these organizational units must be responsive to the policies and programs of other organization units and of the total enterprise. Moreover, people within the enterprise are a part of the social system, and their thinking and attitudes must be taken into account whenever a manager makes a decision.

Furthermore, even when managers construct a closed-system model, as they may do with operations research decision models, they do so simply to have a workable program to solve. But in doing so, they make certain assumptions as to environmental forces that heavily influence their decision, they enter inputs into their calculations as they are or appear to be at any given time, and they change the construction of their model when forces and developments beyond its boundaries so require.

To say that managers take into account the various elements in the system environment of their problem does not mean, however, that they abdicate their role as decision makers. Someone must select a course of action from among alternatives. Even though that person does take account of all events and forces in the environment of a decision, he or she does not democratize the decision process by taking a vote from subordinates or the many other persons who may have some immediate or remote interest in the decision.

Summary

Decision making is at the core of planning. Managers must make choices based on limited or bounded rationality, that is, in light of everything they can learn about a situation, which may not be everything that should be known. "Satisficing" is a term sometimes used to describe picking a course of action that is satisfactory under the circumstances.

Because there are always alternatives to a course of action, and usually a very large number, managers need to narrow them down to those few that deal with the limiting factors in a situation. These alternatives are then evaluated in terms of quantitative and qualitative factors. Other decision-making techniques include marginal analysis and cost effectiveness analysis. Experience, experimentation, and research and analysis also come into play in making decisions.

There is a distinction between programmed and nonprogrammed decisions. The former are suited to structured problems and routine decisions. These kinds of decisions are made especially by lower-level managers and nonmanagers. Nonprogrammed decisions are used for unstructured problems and nonroutine decisions and are made especially by upper-level managers.

Some modern approaches to decision making are risk analysis, which assigns mathematical probabilities to the outcomes of decisions; decision trees, which physically illustrate the decision points, chance events, and probabilities of each possible course of action; and preference theory, which takes into account managers' willingness or unwillingness to take certain risks.

The factors that determine how much time and attention should go into making a decision are the size of the commitment involved, the flexibility or inflexibility of the plans to be put into effect, the certainty or uncertainty of goals and premises, the degree to which variables can be measured, and the impact of the decision on people. Finally, decisions must be made with the recognition that organizations are open systems.

Key Ideas and Concepts for Review

Decision making	Experimentation in decision making
Limited rationality, or bounded rationality	Research and analysis in decision making
Satisficing	Programmed decisions
Principle of the limiting factor	Nonprogrammed decisions
Marginal analysis	Risk analysis
Cost effectiveness	Decision trees
Cost benefit analysis	Preference, or utility, theory
Experience in decision making	Systems approach to decision making

For Discussion

1 Why is experience often referred to not only as an expensive basis for decision making but also as a dangerous one? How can a manager make best use of experience?

2 In a decision problem you now know of, how and where would you apply the principle of the limiting factor?

3 Identify five decision problems and recommend programmed or nonprogrammed decisions. If the examples are from an organizational setting, did they occur on upper or lower levels?

4 Draw a decision tree for a decision problem you face.

5 Could you conceptualize an operations research problem in broad terms without the use of mathematics?

6 "Decision making is the primary task of the manager." Comment.

7 How does risk aversion affect your own life? Given a situation, can you draw your preference curve?

8 Your boss offers you a promotion to a position in a location your family does not like. Make the necessary assumptions and then state how and what you would decide.

CASE 7-1

OLYMPIC TOY COMPANY

"I expect all the managers in my department to act completely rationally in every decision they make," declared Eleanor Johnson, vice-president of marketing for the Olympic Toy Company. "Every one of us, no matter what his or her position, is hired to be a professional rationalist and I expect all of us not only to know what they are doing and why, but to be right in their decisions. I know that someone has said that a good manager needs only to be right in more than half of his or her decisions. But that is not good enough for me. I would agree that you may be excused for occasionally making a mistake, especially if it is a matter beyond your control, but I can never excuse you for not acting rationally."

"I agree with your idea, Eleanor," said Jill Goldberg, her advertising manager, "and I always try to be rational and logical in my decisions. But would you mind helping me be sure of this by explaining just what 'acting rationally' is?"

1 Explain how the vice-president of marketing might describe what is involved in making rational decisions.

2 If Jill Goldberg then declares that there is no way she can be completely rational, what would you suggest as a reply?

CASE 7-2

KING'S SUPERMARKETS

King's Supermarkets was a chain of twenty-five highly successful supermarkets located in medium-sized cities in New England, New York, and New Jersey. It had always been the company's policy to have only one leading store in each of a number of cities of approximately 25,000 to 50,000 population. In each city, the best possible location was sought out and very large stores were developed with attractive buildings, large parking lots, and complete product lines of food and food-related products sold at advertised competitive prices. Although the company had had to close a few poorly located markets over the years, it relied almost entirely for its choice of cities

and locations on the instincts of the founder-president, Walter King. The company's record of profits indicated that his judgment had been generally correct over the 25 years since he had opened his first market.

After Walter King's daughter Donna graduated from the university with a degree in business administration and joined the company as assistant to the president, the researching of new city locations was made one of her major assignments. Ms. King felt that the techniques of operations research might be applied to this problem. She pointed out that there must be a "best" city and a "best" location for expansion at any given time and for the future, if only this could be discovered. She insisted that all a company needed to do was to clarify its goals; identify the constraints such as cash available, existing competition, and distance from company warehouses; look at such variables as cost of real estate, money costs, market size and characteristics, local labor markets, and local taxes and regulations; and then put these into a model to come up with a means of identifying the best location.

Her father and the other officers of the company maintained that operations research might be all right for an oil company, a large aerospace company, or even a large bank, but it was too complicated an approach and there were too many intangibles in a matter of a supermarket location. Moreover, for 25 years the company had been successful in relying on the president's judgment,

and anyway, neither Mr. King nor any of the other top officers or managers understood advanced mathematics. In addition, they felt that they wanted no part of a company where such major decisions were made by a computer. They pointed out emphatically that they were merchandisers and not computer experts.

Ms. King was not convinced. She was sure that operations research would be a great help in such decisions. But she did not know what to do under the circumstances.

1 Making some reasonable assumptions, show Ms. King and her father how operations research might apply in this case.

2 Draw a rough diagram which shows what factors should be included in an operations research model for this case.

For Further Information

Barnard, C. I. *The Functions of the Executive* (Cambridge, Mass.: Harvard University Press, 1964).

Bass, B. M. *Organizational Decision Making* (Homewood, Ill.: Richard D. Irwin, Inc., 1983).

Duncan, J. *Decision Making and Social Issues* (Hinsdale, Ill.: Dryden Press, 1973).

Kepner, C. H., and B. B. Tregoe. *The Rational Manager* (New York: McGraw-Hill Book Company, 1965).

March, J. M., and H. A. Simon. *Organizations* (New York: John Wiley & Sons, Inc., 1958).

McCreary, E. A. "How to Grow a Decision Tree," in H. Koontz, C. O'Donnell, and H. Weihrich (eds.), *Management—A Book of Readings*, 5th ed. (New York: McGraw-Hill Book Company, 1980), pp. 182–187.

Meyer, Alan D. "Mingling Decision Making Metaphors," *Academy of Management Review*, vol. 9, no. 1 (January 1984), pp. 6–17.

Mintzberg, H., D. Raisinghani, and A. Theoret. "The Structure of 'Unstructured' Decision Processes," *Administrative Science Quarterly*, vol. 21 (June 1976), pp. 246–275.

Oxenfeldt, A. R. "Effective Decision Making for the Business Executive," in H. Koontz, C. O'Donnell, and H. Weihrich (eds.), *Management—A Book of Readings,* 5th ed. (New York: McGraw-Hill Book Company, 1980), pp. 170–174.

Shull, F., A. Delbecq, and L. L. Cummings. *Organizational Decision Making* (New York: McGraw-Hill Book Company, 1970).

Simon, H. A. *Administrative Behavior* (New York: The Free Press, 1947).

Staw, B. M. "The Escalation of Commitment to a Course of Action," *Academy of Management Review,* vol. 6, no. 4 (October 1981), pp. 577–587.

Ulvila, J. W. and R. V. Brown. "Decision Analysis Comes of Age," *Harvard Business Review,* vol. 60, no. 5, (September–October 1982), pp. 130–141.

Summary of Major Principles of Planning

Perhaps the best way to summarize Part II on planning, is to list some of the major principles, or guidelines, that may be used in planning. While others might be added, the most essential guiding principles are the following.

The Purpose and Nature of Planning
The purpose and nature of planning may be summarized by reference to the following principles.

Principle of contribution to objective The purpose of every plan and all supporting plans is to promote the accomplishment of enterprise objectives.

Principle of objectives If objectives are to be meaningful to people, they must be clear, attainable, and verifiable.

Principle of primacy of planning Planning logically precedes all other managerial functions.

Principle of efficiency of plans Efficiency of a plan is measured by the amount it contributes to purpose and objectives as offset by the costs required to formulate and operate it and by unsought consequences.

The Structure of Plans
Two major principles dealing with the structure of plans can go far in tying plans together, making supporting plans contribute to major plans, and ensuring that plans in one department harmonize with those in another.

Principle of planning premises The more thoroughly individuals who are charged with planning understand and agree to utilize consistent planning premises, the more coordinated enterprise planning will be.

Principle of strategy and policy framework The more strategies and policies are clearly understood and implemented in practice, the more consistent and effective will be the framework of enterprise plans.

The Process of Planning

Within the process of planning, there are four principles that help in the development of a practical science of planning.

Principle of the limiting factor In choosing from among alternatives, the more accurately individuals can recognize and solve for those factors which are limiting or critical to the attainment of the desired goal, the more easily and accurately they can select the most favorable alternative.

The commitment principle Logical planning should cover a period of time in the future necessary to foresee as well as possible, through a series of actions, the fulfillment of commitments involved in a decision made today.

Principle of flexibility The more that flexibility can be built into plans, the less will be the danger of losses incurred through unexpected events, but the cost of flexibility should be weighed against its advantages.

Principle of navigational change The more planning decisions commit us to a future path, the more important it is that we periodically check on events and expectations and redraw plans as necessary to maintain a course toward a desired goal.

The commitment principle and the principles of flexibility and navigational change are aimed at a contingency approach to planning. Although it makes sense to forecast and draw plans far enough into the future to make reasonably sure of meeting commitments, often it is impossible to do so or the future is so uncertain that it is too risky to fulfill those commitments.

The principle of flexibility deals with that ability to change which is built into plans. The principle of navigational change, on the other hand, implies reviewing plans from time to time and redrawing them if that is required by changed events and expectations. Unless plans have built-in flexibility, navigational change may be difficult or costly.

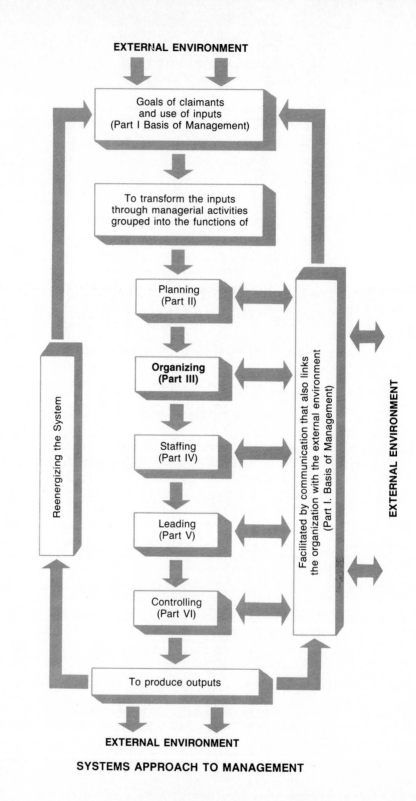

SYSTEMS APPROACH TO MANAGEMENT

PART

Organizing

8

The Nature and Purpose of Organizing

CHAPTER OBJECTIVES

After reading this chapter, you should understand:

1 That the purpose of an organization structure is to establish a formal system of roles that people can perform so that they may best work together to achieve enterprise objectives
2 The meaning of "organizing" and "organization" as used in this book
3 How to draw a distinction between formal and informal organization
4 How organization structures and their levels are due to limitations of span of management and how the exact number of people a manager can effectively supervise depends on a number of underlying variables and situations
5 The logic of organizing and its relationship to other managerial functions
6 That the application of structural organization theory must necessarily take situations into account and that principles and theory do not imply that there is a single best way to organize

It is often said that good people can make any organization pattern work. Some even assert that vagueness in organization is a good thing in that it forces teamwork, since people know that they must cooperate to get anything done. However, there can be no doubt that good people and those who want to cooperate will work together most effectively if they know the parts they are to play in any team operation and how their roles relate to one another. This is as true in business or government as it is in football or in a symphony orchestra. To design and maintain these systems of roles is basically the managerial function of organizing.

Organizational role

For an **organizational role** to exist and to be meaningful to people, it must incorporate (1) verifiable objectives, which, as we indicated in Part II, are a major part of planning; (2) a clear idea of the major duties or activities involved; and (3) an understood area of discretion or authority, so that the person filling the role knows what he or she can do to accomplish goals. In addition, to make a role work out effectively, provision should be made for supplying needed information and other tools necessary for performance in that role.

Definition of organizing

It is in this sense that we think of **organizing** as the grouping of activities necessary to attain objectives, the assignment of each grouping to a manager with authority necessary to supervise it, and the provision for coordination horizontally and vertically in the enterprise structure. An organization structure should be designed to clarify who is to do what and who is responsible for what results; to remove obstacles to performance caused by confusion and uncertainty of assignment; and to furnish decision-making and communications networks reflecting and supporting enterprise objectives.

Uses of the term "organization"

Organization is a word many use loosely. Some would say it includes *all* the behavior of *all* participants. Others would equate it with the total system of social and cultural relationships. Still others refer to an enterprise, such as the United States Steel Corporation or the Department of Defense, as an "organization." But for most practicing managers, the term implies a formalized intentional structure of roles or positions. This meaning is generally used in this book, although we sometimes use the term to denote an enterprise.

What do we mean by an "intentional structure of roles"? In the first place, as we implied in defining the nature and content of organizational roles, people working together must fill certain roles. In the second place, the roles people are asked to fill should be intentionally designed to provide that required activities be done and to make sure that activities fit together so that people can work smoothly, effectively, and efficiently in groups. Certainly most managers believe they are organizing when they establish such an intentional structure.

Formal and Informal Organization

Many writers on management distinguish between formal and informal organization. Both types are found in organizations, as shown in Figure 8-1. Let us look at them in more detail.

Formal Organization

In this book, generally, **formal organization** means the intentional structure of roles in a formally organized enterprise. While we speak of an organization as "formal," there is nothing inherently inflexible or unduly confining about it. If the manager is to organize well, the structure must furnish an environment in which individual performance, both present and future, contributes most effectively to group goals.

Formal organization must be flexible. There should be room for discretion, for taking advantage of creative talents, and for recognition of individual likes and

FIGURE 8-1

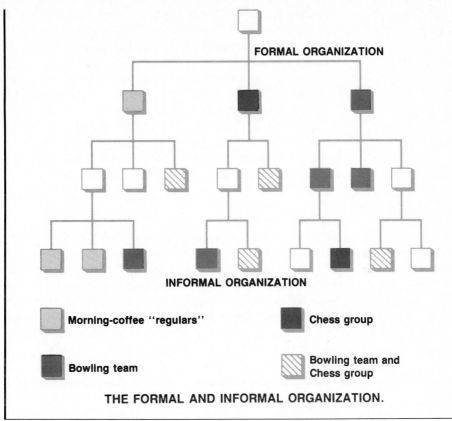

THE FORMAL AND INFORMAL ORGANIZATION.

capacities in the most formal of organizations. Yet, individual effort in a group situation must be channeled toward group and organization goals.

Although the attainment of goals must be the reason for any cooperative activity, we must look further for principles to guide the establishment of effective formal organization. These principles—summarized at the end of Part III—pertain to the unity of objectives and organizational efficiency.

Informal Organization

Chester Barnard, author of the management classic, *The Functions of the Executive,* regarded as informal organization any joint personal activity without conscious joint purpose, even though contributing to joint results. Thus, the informal relationships established in the group of people playing chess during lunchtime may aid in the achievement of organizational goals. It is much easier to ask for help on an organizational problem from a person you know, and who may be even in a different department, than from a person you know only as the name on an organization chart. More recently, Keith Davis of Arizona State University, who has written extensively on the topic and whose definition will be used in this book, described the **informal organization** as "a network of personal and social relations not established or required by the formal organization but arising spontaneously

Definition of informal organization

as people associate with one another."[1] Thus informal organizations—relationships not appearing on an organization chart—might include the machine-shop group, the sixth-floor crowd, the Friday evening bowling gang, and the morning coffee "regulars."

An inquiry into why and how these informal organizations exist is a special study in social psychology. The manager knows that these interpersonal relationships are important in managing. These dynamic interpersonal relationships are influenced by the number of people in the group, the actual personnel involved, what the group is concerned with, its changing leadership, and the continuing process of change. Managers must be aware of the informal organization and avoid antagonizing it, and they will find it advantageous to use it as they manage subordinates.

Organizational Division: The Department

Definition of department

One aspect of organizing is the establishment of departments. The word **department** designates a distinct area, division, or branch of an enterprise over which a manager has authority for the performance of specified activities. A department, as the term is generally used, may be the production division, the sales department, the West Coast branch, the market research section, or the accounts receivable unit. In some enterprises, departmental terminology is loosely applied; in others, especially large ones, a stricter terminology indicates hierarchical relationships. Thus a vice-president may head a division; a director, a department; a manager, a branch; and a chief, a section. This relationship of terminology to status is often found in the federal government, where, in the typical executive department, the hierarchy runs from office or bureau to divisions, branches, sections, units, and subunits.

In an enterprise requiring successive subordinate groupings, exact definitions may become imperative, since certain designations carry implications of authority, prestige, and salary. If the vice-president of production heads a *division*, the vice-president in charge of sales will hardly be satisfied to head a *department*. Some large organizations run out of appropriate designations; then they invent such terms as "group," "activity," or "component."

Organization Levels and the Span of Management[2]

Reason for levels

While the reason for organizing is to make human cooperation effective, we find the reason for levels of organization in the limitations of the span of management. In other words, organization levels exist because there is a limit to the number of

---

[1]K. Davis and J. Newstrom, *Human Behavior at Work* (New York: McGraw-Hill Book Company, 1985), p. 308.

[2]In much of the literature of management, this is referred to as the "span of control." Despite the widespread use of this term, we prefer to use "span of management," since the span is one of management and not merely of control, which is only one function of managing.

FIGURE 8-2 | **Organization with Narrow Spans**

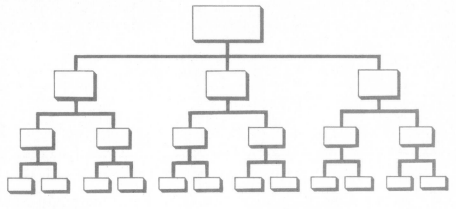

ADVANTAGES

- Close supervision
- Close control
- Fast communication between subordinates and superiors

DISADVANTAGES

- Superiors tend to get too involved in subordinates' work
- Many levels of management
- High costs due to many levels
- Excessive distance between lowest level and top level

Organizations with Wide Spans

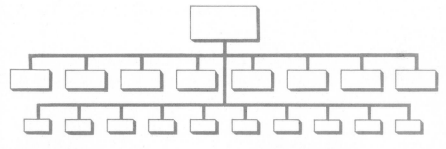

ADVANTAGES

- Superiors are forced to delegate
- Clear policies must be made
- Subordinates must be carefully selected

DISADVANTAGES

- Tendency of overloaded superiors to become decision bottlenecks
- Danger of superior's loss of control
- Requires exceptional quality of managers

ORGANIZATION STRUCTURES WITH NARROW AND WIDE SPANS.

persons a manager can supervise effectively, even though this limit varies depending on situations. The relationships between the span and organizational levels are shown in Figure 8-2. A wide span of management is associated with few organizational levels; a narrow span results in many levels.

That the problem of span management is as old as organization itself is apparent from the passages of the Bible dealing with Moses organizing the exodus of the Israelites. The difficulties that he met and the departmentation he employed to meet them are recounted in Exodus 18:17-26, which records that Moses' father-in-law, noting that Moses was spending so much time supervising so many individuals, advised him as follows:

> The thing thou doest is not good. Thou will surely wear away, both thou and this people that is with thee: for this thing is too heavy for thee; thou art not able to perform it thyself alone. Hearken now unto my voice, I will give thee counsel. . . . Thou shalt provide out of the people able men . . . and place such over them [the people], to be rulers of thousands, and rulers of hundreds, rulers of fifties, and rulers of tens. And let them judge the people at all seasons; and it shall be, that every great matter they shall bring unto thee, but every small matter they shall judge: so shall it be easier for thyself, and they shall bear the burden with thee. If thou shalt do this thing, and God command thee so, then thou shall be able to endure, and all this people shall also go to their place in peace.

Moses thereupon followed his father-in-law's advice. He:

> . . . chose able men out of all Israel, and made them heads over the people, rulers of thousands, rulers of hundreds, rulers of fifties, and rulers of tens. And they judged the people at all seasons: the hard causes they brought unto Moses, but every small matter they judged themselves.

Choosing the Span

In every organization, it must be decided how many subordinates a superior can manage. Students of management have found that this number is usually four to eight subordinates at the upper levels of organization and eight to fifteen or more at the lower levels. For example, the prominent British consultant Lyndall Urwick found "the ideal number of subordinates for all superior authorities . . . to be four," while "at the lowest level of organization, where what is delegated is responsibility for the performance of specific tasks and not for the supervision of others, the number may be eight or twelve."[3] Others find that a manager may be able to manage as many as twenty to thirty subordinates.

Variations in practice

In actual experience, one finds a wide variety of practices, even among admittedly well-managed enterprises. In the General Motors Corporation in 1980, the president had three executive vice-presidents reporting to him, but one group vice-president had eight persons reporting to him. The president of a railroad that is generally regarded as one of the best managed in the industry had ten top executives reporting to him in 1980, and one of these had nine subordinates. Yet, the head of another large carrier, not regarded as so well managed, had only seven major subordinates. The president of one well-managed department store had four

---

[3]Lyndall Urwick, "Axioms of Organization," *Public Administration Magazine* (London, October 1955), pp. 348–349. However, in other writings, Urwick modified this position by saying that "no person should supervise more than five, or at the most, six, direct subordinates *whose work interlocks.*" See *Notes on the Theory of Organization* (New York: American Management Association, 1952), p. 53 (emphasis in quotation added).

key executives reporting to him, none of whom had more than five subordinates, whereas an equally large and successful store showed twelve key executives reporting to the president and an equally large number of subordinates reporting to most of them.

In a survey of 100 large companies made by the American Management Association, the number of executives reporting to the presidents varied from one to twenty-four, and only twenty-six presidents had six or fewer subordinates. The median number was nine.[4] In forty-one smaller companies surveyed, twenty-five of the presidents supervised seven or more subordinates, and the most common number was eight. Comparable results were found in other studies.

In a very real sense, none of these studies is truly indicative of the actual span of management. For one thing, they measure the span only at or near the top of an enterprise. This is hardly typical of what the span may be throughout the enterprise, particularly since every organizer has experienced the tremendous pressure for a large number of the functions to report to the top executive. It is probable that spans below the top executive are much narrower. Indeed, in a study of more than 100 companies of all sizes, we found a much narrower span in the middle levels of management than at the top.

In addition, the fact that apparently well-managed companies have, among them and certainly within them, widely varying spans indicates that merely counting the numbers in existing spans is not enough to establish what a span *ought* to be. And this is true even if it could be assumed that, through trial and error, each company has reached the best number. That might prove only that underlying conditions vary.

Problems with Organization Levels

There is a tendency to regard organization and departmentation as ends in themselves and to gauge the effectiveness of organization structures in terms of clarity and completeness of departments and department levels. Division of activities into departments, and hierarchical organization and the creation of multiple levels, are not completely desirable in themselves.

Expense

In the first place, levels are expensive. As they increase, more and more effort and money are devoted to managing because of the additional managers, staffs to assist them, and the necessity of coordinating departmental activities, plus the costs of facilities for such personnel. Accountants refer to such costs as "overhead," or "burden," or "general and administrative," in contrast to so-called direct costs. Real production is accomplished by factory, engineering, or sales employees who are, or could logically be accounted for as, "direct labor." Levels above the "firing line" are predominantly staffed with managers who are not directly productive and whose cost it would be desirable to eliminate, if that were possible.

---

[4]As summarized in *Business Week*, Aug. 18, 1951, pp. 102–103. Healey found similar variations in his study of 409 manufacturing companies in Ohio, although the median was six subordinates. See J. H. Healey, *Executive Co-ordination and Control* (Columbus: Ohio State University Press, 1956), p. 66.

Complication in communication

In the second place, departmental levels complicate communication. An enterprise with many levels has greater difficulty communicating objectives, plans, and policies downward through the organization structure than the firm in which the top manager communicates directly with employees. Omissions and misinterpretations occur as information passes down the line. Levels also complicate communication from the "firing line" to the commanding superiors, which is every bit as important as downward communication. It has been well said that levels are "filters" of information.

Complication in planning and controlling

Finally, numerous departments and levels complicate planning and control. A plan that may be definite and complete at the top level loses coordination and clarity as it is subdivided at lower levels. Control becomes more difficult as levels and managers are added, while at the same time the complexities of planning and difficulties of communication make this control more important.

Operational-Management Position: A Situational Approach

The classical school approach to the span of management deals with specifying numbers of subordinates for an effective span. Actual experience does support the classical school opinion that at upper- and top-levels the span is of from three to seven or eight subordinates. However, more recent operational-management theorists have taken the position that there are too many underlying variables in a management situation for us to specify any particular number of subordinates that a manager can effectively supervise. *There is a limit to the number of subordinates a manager can effectively supervise, but the exact number will depend upon underlying factors that affect the difficulty and time requirements of managing.*

Span-of-management principle

In other words, the dominant current guideline is to look for the causes of limited span in individual situations, rather than to assume that there is a widely applicable numerical limit. If we can examine what it is that consumes the time of managers in their handling of their superior-subordinate relationships, and also ascertain what devices can be used to reduce these time pressures, we have an approach that will be helpful in determining the best span in individual cases and also a powerful tool for finding out what can be done to extend the span without destroying effective supervision. There can be no argument that the costs of levels of supervision are such as to make it highly desirable for every individual manager to have as many subordinates as can be *effectively* supervised.

Factors Determining an Effective Span

In searching for the answer as to how many subordinates a manager can effectively manage, we discover that—aside from such personal capacities as comprehending quickly, getting along with people, and commanding loyalty and respect—the most important determinant is the manager's ability to reduce the time the superior spends with subordinates. This ability naturally varies with managers and their jobs, but eight factors materially influence the number and frequency of such contacts and therefore the span of management (see Table 8-1).

Table 8-1   Factors Influencing the Span of Management

Narrow span (a great deal of time spent with subordinates) related to:	Wide spans (very little time spent with subordinates) related to:
No or little training	Thorough training
Inadequate or unclear authority delegation	Clear delegation to undertake well-defined tasks
Unclear plans for nonrepetitive operations	Well-defined plans for repetitive operations
Nonverifiable objectives and standards	Verifiable objectives used as standards
Fast changes in external and internal environments	Slow changes in external and internal environments
Use of poor or inappropriate communication techniques, including vague instructions	Use of appropriate techniques such as proper organization structure, written and oral communication
Ineffective interaction of superior and subordinate	Effective interaction between superior and subordinate
Ineffective meetings	Effective meetings
Incompetent and untrained manager	Competent and trained manager
Complex task	Simple task
Greater number of specialties at lower and middle levels	Number of specialties at upper levels (top managers concerned with external environment)

1 Subordinate Training

The better the training of subordinates, the less the impact of necessary superior-subordinate relationships. Well-trained subordinates require not only less of their managers' time but also less contact with them.

Training problems increase in new and more complex industries. Managers in the railroad industry, for example, would—because the technology does not change much—tend to be more completely trained than those in the aerospace industry. The rapid changes in policy and procedures in the complex electronics and missile industries would increase training problems.

2 Clarity of Delegation of Authority

Although training enables managers to reduce the frequency and extensiveness of time-consuming contacts, the principal cause of the heavy time burdens of superior-subordinate relationships is to be found in poorly conceived and confused organization. The most serious symptom of poor organization affecting the span of management is inadequate or unclear authority delegation. If a manager clearly delegates authority to undertake a well-defined task, a well-trained subordinate can get it done with a minimum of the superior's time and attention. But if the subordinate's task is not one that can be done, if it is not clearly defined, or if the subordinate does not have the authority to undertake it effectively, either the task will not be performed or the manager will have to spend a disproportionate amount of time supervising and guiding the subordinate's efforts.

3 Clarity of Plans

Much of the character of a subordinate's job is defined by the plans to be put into effect. If these plans are well defined, if they are workable, if the authority to undertake them has been delegated, and if the subordinate understands what is expected, little of a supervisor's time will be required. Such is often the case with a production supervisor responsible for largely repetitive operations. Thus, in one large-volume work-clothing manufacturer's plant, production supervisors operated satisfactorily with as many as thirty subordinates.

On the other hand, where plans cannot be drawn accurately and where subordinates must do much of their own planning, they may require considerable guidance. However, if the superior has set up clear policies to guide decisions and has made sure they are consistent with the operations and goals of a department, and if the subordinate understands them, there will certainly be fewer demands on the superior's time than there would be if these policies were indefinite, incomplete, or not understood.

4 Use of Objective Standards

A manager must find out, either by personal observation or through use of objective standards, whether subordinates are following plans. Obviously, good objective standards, revealing with ease any deviations from plans, enable managers to avoid many time-consuming contacts and to direct attention to exceptions at points critical to the successful execution of plans.

5 Rate of Change

Certain enterprises change much more rapidly than others. The rate of change is an important determinant of the degree to which policies can be formulated and the stability of policies maintained. It may explain the organization structure of companies—railroad, banking, and public utility companies, for example—operating with wide spans of management or, on the other hand, the very narrow span of management used by General Eisenhower during World War II.

The effect of slow change on policy formulation and on subordinate training is dramatically shown in the organization of the Roman Catholic Church. This organization, in terms of durability and stability, can probably be regarded as the most successful in the history of Western civilization. Yet the organization levels are few: in most cases, bishops report directly to the Pope, and parish priests to bishops, although in some instances bishops report to archbishops. Thus, there are generally only very few levels in this worldwide organization and a consequent wide span of management at each level. Even though it is unquestionably too broad, this extraordinarily wide span is apparently tolerable, partly because of the degree of training possessed by the bishops and, even more, because the rate of change in the Church has been slow. Changes in procedures or policies are developments of decades, and major objectives have remained the same for almost 2000 years.

6 Communication Techniques

The effectiveness with which communication techniques are used also influences the span of management. Objective standards of control are a kind of communications device, but many other techniques reduce the time spent with subordinates.

If every plan, instruction, order, or direction has to be communicated by personal contact and every organization change or staffing problem handled orally, a manager's time will obviously be heavily burdened. Some executives use "assistant-to" positions or administrative staff personnel as a communications device to help them solve their problems with key subordinates. Written recommendations by subordinates, summarizing important considerations, frequently speed decision making. We have seen busy top executives widen their span of management by insisting upon summary presentation of written recommendations, even when these involved enormously important decisions. A carefully reasoned and presented recommendation helps an executive reach a considered decision in minutes, when even the most efficient conference would require an hour.

An ability to communicate plans and instructions clearly and concisely also tends to increase a manager's span. The subordinate who, after leaving a superior's desk or receiving instructions, is still in doubt as to what is wanted or what has been said is sure to request further meetings sooner or later. One of the pleasures of being a subordinate is to have superiors who can express themselves well. A manager's casual, easy style may please subordinates, but where this easiness degenerates into confusion and wasted time, the effect is to reduce sharply the effective span of management and often to lower morale as well.

7 Amount of Personal Contact Needed and Other Factors

In many instances, face-to-face meetings are necessary. Many situations cannot be completely handled with written reports, memorandums, policy statements, planning documents, or other communications not calling for personal contact. An executive may find it valuable and stimulating to subordinates to meet and discuss problems in the give-and-take of a conference. There may also be problems of such political delicacy that they can be handled only in face-to-face meetings. This is also true when it comes to appraising people's performance and discussing it with them. And there are other situations where the best way of communicating a problem, instructing a subordinate, or for "getting a feel" for how people really think on some matter is to spend time in personal contact.

We wonder, however, whether the high percentage of executive time spent in meetings and committees might be reduced somewhat by better training, better policy making and planning, clearer delegation, more thorough staff work, better control systems and objective standards, and, in general, better application of sound principles of management. We wonder, also, whether much of the time spent in personal contact might not be much better spent in thought and study.

At the other extreme, many companies seem somewhat unaware of how newer personnel techniques affect first-line supervisors, many of whom appear to have spans of management far beyond their abilities to handle. Merit rating, insurance programs, grievance procedures, and other personnel matters now requiring supervisors' time in face-to-face relationships have reduced their traditionally wide spans. This is not to say that these innovations are not worth their cost, but span-of-management limitations must be evaluated in the light of these factors. Perhaps we have reached the point where first-level supervisors, with a traditionally large number of people reporting to them, are the most overworked of all managers.

Besides the listed factors, there are others that influence the span of management. For example, a competent and trained manager can effectively supervise more people than one not having these attributes. Furthermore, simple tasks allow for a wider span than tasks that are complex and include a great variety of activities.

8   Variation by Organization Level

Several research projects have found that the size of the most effective span differs by organization level. In one major study, the researchers developed and tested a model to take into account this variable and found that the degree of specialization by individuals ("person specialization") was the most important variable affecting span, although technology and size also were tested since previous research had concentrated on these.[5] It was found that (1) when a greater number of specialties was supervised, effective spans were less at lower and middle levels of organization but were increased at upper levels, primarily because top-level managers were most concerned with the interface of the enterprise with its external environment, strategic planning, and major policy matters; (2) routineness of an operation appeared to have little effect at any level; and (3) size had little effect at lower levels but a positive effect at middle levels.

Actually, this study is consistent with the impact of variables outlined above. It found what many practitioners have long known, that neither size nor technology has had much to do with an effective span at upper levels of an organization although the variables outlined above in this section have.

Need for Balance

There can be no doubt that, despite the desirability of a flat organization structure, the span of management is limited by real and important restrictions. Managers may have more subordinates than they can manage effectively, even though they delegate authority, carry on training, formulate plans and policies clearly, and adopt efficient control and communication techniques. It is equally true that as an enterprise grows, the span-of-management limitations force an increase in the number of levels simply because there are more people to supervise.

What is required is more precise balancing, in a given situation, of all pertinent factors. Widening spans and reducing the number of levels may be the answer in some cases; the reverse may be true in others. One must balance all the costs of adopting one course or the other, not only the financial costs but costs in morale, personal development, and the attainment of enterprise objectives. In military organization, perhaps the attainment of objectives quickly and without error would be most important. On the other hand, in a department store operation, the long-run objective of profit may be best served by forcing initiative and personal development at the lower levels of the organization.

Organizing as a Process

In looking at organizing as a process, we can clearly see that several fundamentals must be considered. In the first place, the structure must reflect objectives and plans because activities derive from them. In the second place, it must reflect the

---

[5]R. D. Dewar and D. P. Simet, "A Level Specific Prediction of Spans of Control Examining the Effects of Size, Technology, and Specialization," *Academy of Management Journal*, vol. 24, no. 1 (March 1981), pp. 5–24.

authority available to an enterprise's management. Authority in a given organization is a socially determined right to exercise discretion; as such, it is subject to change.

In the third place, organization structure, like any plan, must reflect its environment. Just as the premises of a plan may be economic, technological, political, social, or ethical, so may those of an organization structure. It must be designed to work, to permit contributions by members of a group, and to help people gain objectives efficiently in a changing future. In this sense, a workable organization structure can never be static. There can be no single best organization structure that will work in all kinds of situations. An effective organization structure depends on the situation.

In the fourth place, the organization is staffed with people. The groupings of activities and the authority relationships of an organization structure must take into account people's limitations and customs. This is not to say that the structure must be designed around individuals instead of around goals and accompanying activities. But an important consideration is the kind of people who are to staff it. Just as engineers consider the performance strengths and weaknesses of materials going into their projects, so must organizers consider their materials—people.

The Logic of Organizing

There is a fundamental logic to organizing, as shown in Figure 8-3. Noting that steps 1 and 2 are actually part of planning, we suggest the following six steps:

1 Establishment of enterprise objectives

2 Formulation of supporting objectives, policies, and plans

3 Identification and classification of activities necessary to accomplish these

4 Grouping of these activities in the light of human and material resources available and the best way, under the circumstances, of using them

5 Delegation to the head of each group the authority necessary to perform the activities

6 Tying together of the groups horizontally and vertically, through authority relationships and information flows

Some Misconceptions

Organizing does not imply any extreme occupational specialization, which in many instances makes labor uninteresting, tedious, and unduly restrictive. There is nothing in organization itself that dictates this. To say that tasks should be specific is not to say they must be limited and mechanical. Whether they should be broken down into minute parts—as on a typical assembly line—or be broad enough to encompass the design, production, and sale of a machine is for the organizer to consider in light of the results desired. In any organization, jobs can be defined to allow little or no personal leeway or the widest possible discretion. One must not forget that the application of structural organization theory must take into account the situation and that there is no best way to organize.

FIGURE 8-3

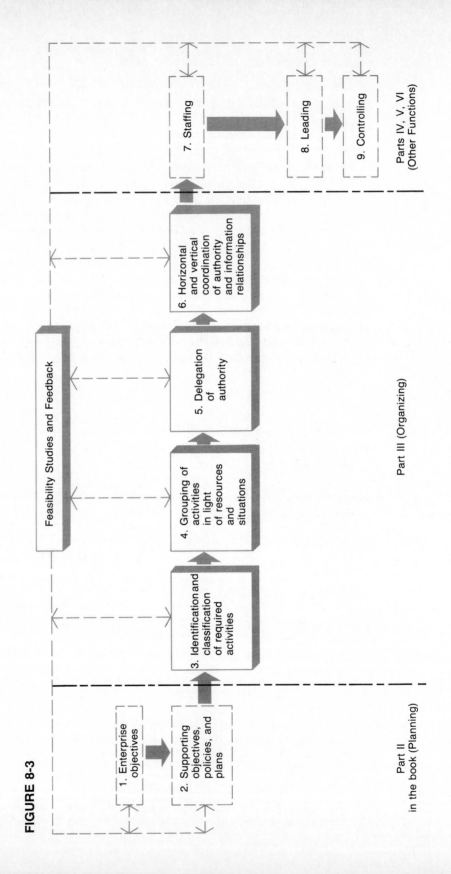

174

ORGANIZING PROCESS

Basic Questions for Effective Organizing

It is useful to analyze the managerial function of organizing by raising and answering the following questions:

1   What determines the span of management and hence the levels of organization?

2   What determines the basic framework of departmentation, and what are the strengths and weaknesses of the basic forms?

3   What kinds of authority relationships exist in organizations?

4   How should authority be dispersed throughout the organization structure, and what determines the extent of this dispersion?

5   How should the manager make organization theory work in practice?

The answers to these questions form a basis for a theory of organizing. When considered along with similar analyses of planning, staffing, leading, and controlling, they constitute an operational approach to management.

Summary

Organizing consists of identifying and grouping activities, assigning authority to managers, and providing for coordination. Formal organization is the intentional structure of roles. Informal organization is a network of personal and social relations not established or required by formal authority but created spontaneously as people interact with each other. The term "span of management" refers to the number of people a manager can effectively supervise. A wide span of management results in few organizational levels, and a narrow span results in many levels. There is no definite number of people a manager can always effectively supervise: the number depends on several underlying factors. These include the degree of subordinate training required and possessed, the clarity of authority delegated, the clarity of plans, the rate of change, the use of objective standards, the effectiveness of communication techniques, the amount of personal contact needed, and the level in the organization. The steps in organizing include formulating objectives, subobjectives, policies, and plans to achieve the ends (strictly speaking, these steps are carried out in planning), identifying and classifying activities, grouping these activities, delegating authority, and coordinating authority as well as information relationships.

Key Ideas and Concepts for Review

Structure of roles	Organizational levels
Organization	Factors determining the span of management
Formal organization	
Informal organization	Logical steps of organizing
Span of management	Basic questions for effective organizing

For Discussion

1 Since people must occupy organization positions and an effective organization depends on people, it is often said that the best organization arises when a manager hires good people and lets them do a job in their own way. Comment.

2 A formal organization is often conceived of as a communications system. Is it? How?

3 Construct a diagram depicting the formal organizations of some enterprises or activity with which you are familiar. How does this organization structure help or hinder the establishment of an environment for performance?

4 Using the same enterprise or activity as in question 3, chart the informal organization. Does it help or hinder the formal organization? Why?

5 Urwick and other writers seem to say that at top levels, the number of persons in the span of management should not exceed six. Some 750 bishops and some 1200 other persons report directly to the Pope. At one time in the Bank of America organization, over 600 bank managers reported to the chief executive officer. How do you fit these facts with the idea that there is a limit to the number of subordinates a manager can supervise?

6 When you become a manager, what criteria will you favor to determine your span?

7 Does the application of principles recommend, as many critics insist, a "tall" organization structure with a limited span of management?

8 Organize a family picnic using the steps suggested in this chapter.

CASE 8-1

MEASUREMENT INSTRUMENTS CORPORATION

William B. Richman, president of the Measurement Instruments Corporation, was explaining his organizational arrangements to the board of directors. His organization chart is on the following page.

When asked by a board member whether he thought he had too many people reporting to him, Mr. Richman replied: "I do not believe in the traditional principle of span of control, or management, that managers should have only four or five persons reporting to them. This is what makes waste and bureaucracy. All my subordinates are good people and know what they are doing. All can reach me readily with their problems when they have them. All feel close to the top because they *are* close to the top. Moreover, I want to know firsthand how every person is doing and to detect any weaknesses or errors as soon as possible. Furthermore, if a store manager at Sears, Roebuck can have twenty-five to thirty persons reporting to him, I ought to be able to handle nineteen. In addition, too few reporting to a manager doesn't give him enough to do, and I assume that you hired me to give the company my full time."

1 How would you respond to Mr. Richman's arguments?

2 If you were a member of the board of directors, what would you suggest that Mr. Richman do?

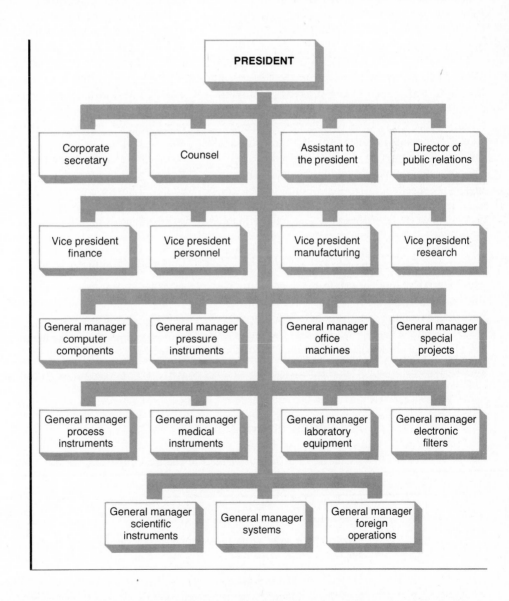

CASE 8-2

AMERICAN AIRCRAFT COMPANY

The management consultant was lunching with Allen Murray, the president of American Aircraft Corporation. She did this quite often, largely in order to facilitate communication between them.

"This just isn't my day," she told the president. "For instance, I was out in the factory an hour ago. I happened to run into the plant manager, so I asked him, 'Why do you have that conference room filled with people every morning? 'Well,' the plant manager replied, 'the people in there, some twenty-two of them, represent assembly, production control, shipping, and accounting. They meet each day for 3 hours. They iron out the problems we have in coordinating effort around here. It is effective as a means of maintaining our shipping schedule.'

"Then," she continued, "just as I reached the administration building, I met the sales manager. He really looked wrung out like a rag. He told me that the weekly Tuesday meeting of department managers had just concluded. It appears that it was my friend's turn to be at the center of the stage explaining the performance reports of his department. Every week his division manager holds a staff meeting given over to reviewing the performance of one of the departments. My friend did say with a spark of malice that next week it will be the turn of engineering."

"I don't see why you are depressed by these events," Mr. Murray remarked.

"Well, it is just this way. I think that these techniques of communication are all wrong. They are expensive, they tend to expose individual managers to criticism before their associates, and they create the wrong circumstances for corrective action. There are other and better means of control. It seems managers agree with theory but never let it influence their practices."

1 Was the consultant right in being depressed about what she had found?

2 What do you believe was wrong with the methods of communication being used?

3 What would you have done to solve the communications problem without having so many long staff meetings?

For Further Information

Barnard, C. I. *The Functions of the Executive* (Cambridge, Mass.: Harvard University Press, 1964).

Bartlett, C. A. "MNCs: Get Off the Reorganization Merry-Go-Round," *Harvard Business Review*, vol. 61, no. 2 (March–April 1983), pp. 138–146.

Chandler, A. D. *Strategy and Structure* (Cambridge, Mass.: The M.I.T. Press, 1962).

Drucker, P. F. *Management—Tasks, Responsibilities, Practices* (New York: Harper & Row, Publishers, Incorporated, 1974).

Jackson, J. H., and C. P. Morgan. *Organization Theory* (Englewood Cliffs, N. J.: Prentice-Hall, Inc., 1982).

Katz D., and R. L. Kahn. *The Social Psychology of Organizations*, 2nd ed. (New York: John Wiley & Sons, Inc., 1978).

Koontz, H. "Making Theory Operational: The Span of Management," in H. Koontz, C. O'Donnell, and H. Weihrich (eds.), *Management—A Book of Readings*, 5th ed. (New York: McGraw-Hill Book Company, 1980), pp. 232–240.

Kuhn, A., and R. D. Beam. *The Logic of Organization* (San Francisco: Jossey-Bass Inc., Pubs., 1982).

Lawrence, P. R., and J. W. Lorsch. *Organization and Environment* (Homewood, Ill.: Richard D. Irwin, Inc., 1969).

March, J. G., and H. A. Simon. *Organizations* (New York: John Wiley & Sons, Inc., 1958).

Miner, J. B. *Theories of Organizational Structure and Process* (Chicago: Dryden Press, 1982).

Mintzberg, H. *Structure in Fives—Designing Effective Organizations* (Englewood Cliffs, N.J.: Prentice-Hall, Inc., 1983).

Pearce, J. A., II, and F. R. David. "A Social Network Approach to Organizational Design-Performance," *Academy of Management Review*, vol. 8, no. 3 (July 1983), pp. 436–444.

Scott, W. G., T. R. Mitchell, and P. H. Birnbaum. *Organization Theory—A Structural and Behavioral Analysis*, 4th ed. (Homewood, Ill.: Richard D. Irwin, Inc., 1981).

Van Fleet, D. D., and A. G. Bedeian. "A History of the Span of Management," *Academy of Management Review*, vol. 2, no. 3 (July 1977), pp. 356–372.

9

Basic Departmentation

After completing this chapter, you should understand:

1 The basic patterns of departmentation, and the advantages and disadvantages of each
2 Matrix organization, and the steps that can be taken to avoid the dangers of disunity of command
3 That there is no single best pattern of departmentation and that responsible managers must select patterns that will assist in accomplishing objectives in the light of the particular situation

The limitation on the number of subordinates that can be directly managed would restrict the size of enterprises if it were not for the device of departmentation. Grouping activities and people into departments makes it possible to expand organizations to an indefinite degree. Departments, however, differ with respect to the basic patterns used to group activities. We will deal with the nature of these patterns, developed out of logic and practice, and their relative merits in the following sections.

No single best way

At the outset, let us emphasize that there is no single best way of departmentizing applicable to all organizations or to all situations. The pattern that will be used will depend on given situations and what managers believe will yield the best results for them in the situation they face.

Departmentation by Simple Numbers

Departmentation by simple numbers was once an important method in the organization of tribes, clans, and armies. Although it is rapidly falling into disuse, it still may have certain applications in modern society.

The simple-numbers method of departmentizing is achieved by tolling off persons who are to perform the same duties and putting them under a manager. It is, as you recall from the previous chapter, what Moses did in organizing his large group. The essential fact is not what these people do, where they work, or what they work with, but that the success of the undertaking depends only upon the number of people involved in it.

Reasons for decline in usefulness

Even though a quick examination may impress an investigator with the number of people departmentized on a human resource basis, the usefulness of this organizational device has declined with each passing century. For one thing, technology has advanced, demanding more specialized and different skills. In the United States, the last stronghold of common labor was agriculture, and even here it is restricted more and more to the harvesting of fewer and fewer crops as farming operations become larger and more specialized.

A second reason for the decline of departmentizing purely by number is that groups composed of specialized personnel are frequently more efficient than those based on mere numbers. The reorganization of the defense forces of the United States on this basis is a case in point. Many ways have been found to combine people skilled in the use of different types of weapons into single units. For example, the addition of artillery and tactical air support to the traditional infantry division makes it a much more formidable fighting unit than if each were organized separately.

A third and long-standing reason for the decline of departmentation by numbers is that it is useful only at the lowest level of the organization structure. As soon as any other factor besides pure human power becomes important, the simple-numbers basis of departmentation fails to produce good results.

Departmentation by Time

One of the oldest forms of departmentation, generally used at lower levels of the organization, is to group activities on the basis of time. The use of shifts is common in many enterprises where for economic, technological, or other reasons the normal workday will not suffice. Examples of this kind of departmentation can be found in hospitals where around-the-clock patient care is essential. Similarly, the fire department has to be ready to respond to emergencies at any time. But there are also technological reasons for the use of shifts. A steel furnace, for example, can not be started and turned off at will. Instead, the process of making steel is continuous and requires workers to work in three shifts.

Advantages

From these few illustrations you can see a number of *advantages* of departmentation by time. First, services can be rendered that go beyond the typical 8-hour day, often extending to 24 hours a day. Second, it makes possible processes that cannot be interrupted but that require a continuing cycle. Third, expensive capital equipment can be used more than 8 hours a day when workers in several shifts use the same machines. Fourth, some people, students attending classes during the day for instance, find it convenient to work at night.

Disadvantages

But departmentation by time also has *disadvantages*. First, supervision may be lacking during the night shift. Second, there is the fatigue factor, it is difficult for most people to switch, for instance, from day to night shift and vice versa. Third, the changing of the shifts may cause problems in coordination and communication. In a hospital, for example, nurses from different shifts attending a patient may not be familiar with the patient's particular problems. In a factory, the night shift may not clean up the machines to be used by the day shift people. Third, the payment of overtime rates can increase the cost of the product or service.

Departmentation by Enterprise Function

The grouping of activities in accordance with the functions of an enterprise—functional departmentation—embodies what enterprises typically do. Since all enterprises undertake the creation of something useful and desired by others, the basic enterprise functions are production (creating utility or adding utility to a good or service), selling (finding customers, patients, clients, students, or members who will agree to accept the good or service at a price or for a cost), and financing (raising and collecting, safeguarding, and expending the funds of the enterprise). It has been logical to group these activities into such departments as engineering, production, sales or marketing, and finance. Figure 9-1 shows a typical functional grouping for a manufacturing company.

Terminology

Often, these particular terms do not appear in the organization chart. First, there is no generally accepted terminology: manufacturing enterprises employ the terms "production," "sales," and "finance"; a wholesaler is concerned with such activities as "buying," "selling," and "finance"; and a railroad is involved with "operations," "traffic," and "finance."

A second reason for variance of terms is that basic activities often differ in importance: hospitals have no selling departments; churches, no production departments. This does not mean that these activities are not undertaken, but merely that they are unspecialized or of such minor importance that they are combined with other activities.

A third reason for the absence of sales, production, or finance departments on many organization charts is that other methods of departmentation may have been deliberately selected. Those responsible for the enterprise may decide to organize on the basis of product, customer, territory, or marketing channel (the way goods or services reach the user).

Functional departmentation is the most widely employed basis for organizing activities and is present in almost every enterprise at some level in the organization structure. The characteristics of the selling, production, and finance functions of

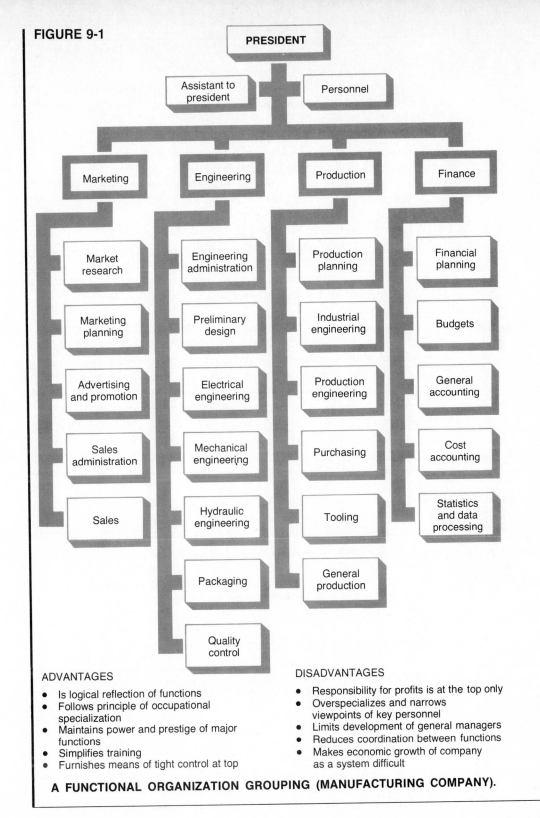

FIGURE 9-1

PRESIDENT

Assistant to president

Personnel

Marketing
- Market research
- Marketing planning
- Advertising and promotion
- Sales administration
- Sales

Engineering
- Engineering administration
- Preliminary design
- Electrical engineering
- Mechanical engineering
- Hydraulic engineering
- Packaging
- Quality control

Production
- Production planning
- Industrial engineering
- Production engineering
- Purchasing
- Tooling
- General production

Finance
- Financial planning
- Budgets
- General accounting
- Cost accounting
- Statistics and data processing

ADVANTAGES

- Is logical reflection of functions
- Follows principle of occupational specialization
- Maintains power and prestige of major functions
- Simplifies training
- Furnishes means of tight control at top

DISADVANTAGES

- Responsibility for profits is at the top only
- Overspecializes and narrows viewpoints of key personnel
- Limits development of general managers
- Reduces coordination between functions
- Makes economic growth of company as a system difficult

A FUNCTIONAL ORGANIZATION GROUPING (MANUFACTURING COMPANY).

enterprises are so widely recognized and thoroughly understood that they are the basis not only of departmental organization but also most often of departmentation at the top level.

Advantages

The most important advantage of functional departmentation is that it is a logical and time-proven method. It is also the best way of making certain that the power and prestige of the basic activities of the enterprise will be defended by the top managers. This is an important consideration among functional managers, for they see on every side the encroachments of staff and service groups, which sometimes threaten the security of the principal line executives. Another advantage is that functional departmentation follows the principle of occupational specialization, thereby making for efficiency in the utilization of people. Still other advantages are that it simplifies training and, because the top managers are responsible for the end results, furnishes a means of tight control at the top.

Disadvantages

In spite of the advantages of functional departmentation, there are times when the claims of other methods seem even stronger. The size of the geographic area over which an enterprise operates may call for territorial grouping of activities; the production or purchase of numerous product lines, or of products designed for certain buyer classifications, may call for grouping along product or customer lines. In addition, functional departmentation may tend to deemphasize overall enterprise objectives. Accountants, production experts, and sales people, growing up in specialized departments, often have difficulty seeing the business as a whole, and coordination among them is frequently difficult to achieve. They develop attitudes and other behavior patterns involving loyalty to a function and not to the enterprise as a whole. Such "walls" between functional departments are common and it requires considerable effort to break them down.

Another disadvantage is that only the chief executive officer can be held responsible for profits. In small firms, this is as it should be, but in large firms the burden becomes too heavy for one person to bear. What is perhaps most important is that since the lowest general managerial position is that of the president or the executive vice-president, the functionally organized company is not the best training ground for promotable top-management people.

Departmentation by Territory or Geography

Departmentation based on territory is rather common in enterprises that operate over wide geographic areas. In this case, it may be important that activities in a given area or territory should be grouped and assigned to a manager, for example, as shown in Figure 9-2.

Extent of Use

Territorial departmentation is especially attractive to large-scale firms or other enterprises whose activities are physically or geographically spread. However, a plant may be local in its activities and still assign the personnel in its security department on a territorial basis, placing two guards, for example, at each of the south and west gates. Department stores assign floorwalkers on this basis, and it

FIGURE 9-2

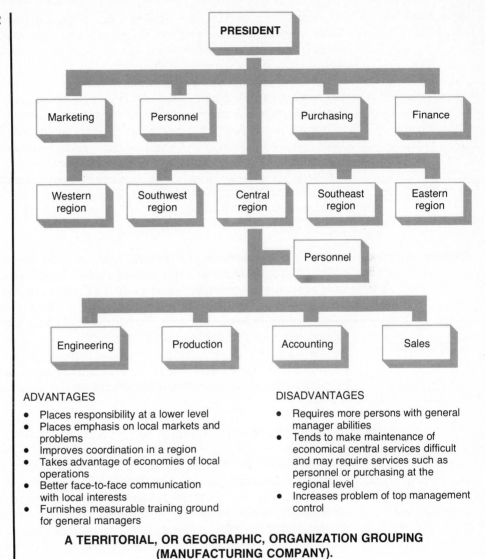

ADVANTAGES

- Places responsibility at a lower level
- Places emphasis on local markets and problems
- Improves coordination in a region
- Takes advantage of economies of local operations
- Better face-to-face communication with local interests
- Furnishes measurable training ground for general managers

DISADVANTAGES

- Requires more persons with general manager abilities
- Tends to make maintenance of economical central services difficult and may require services such as personnel or purchasing at the regional level
- Increases problem of top management control

**A TERRITORIAL, OR GEOGRAPHIC, ORGANIZATION GROUPING
(MANUFACTURING COMPANY).**

is a common way to assign janitors, window washers, and the like. Business firms resort to this method when similar operations are undertaken in different geographic areas, as in automobile assembly, chain retailing and wholesaling, and oil refining. Many government agencies—the Internal Revenue Service, the Federal Reserve Board, the federal courts, and the Postal Service, among others—adopt this basis of organization in their efforts to provide like services simultaneously across the nation. Territorial departmentation is most often used in sales and in production; it is not used in finance, which is usually concentrated at the headquarters.

Advantages

Departmentation by territory, or geography, offers a number of advantages. It places responsibility at a lower level, encourages local participation in decision making, and improves coordination of activities in a region. Managers can give special attention to the needs and problems of local markets. Thus, they may recruit local salespeople who are familiar with the special situation in the area. Moreover, these salespeople can spend more time selling and less time traveling.

Production may also be organized on a territorial basis by establishing plants in a particular region. This can reduce transportation costs and delivery time. Moreover, labor rates may be lower in certain regions, and producing things locally may create jobs and goodwill in the local community.

Geographic departmentation improves face-to-face communication with local people. Also, since the manager in a territory has to carry out many different functional and managerial activities, this type of organization provides a good training ground for general managers.

Disadvantages

There are also disadvantages in organizing territorially. This kind of departmentation requires more persons with general managerial abilities, and a shortage of them is often a factor limiting the growth of an enterprise. Moreover, geographic departmentation tends to lead to duplication of services. Thus, managers of a territory want to have their own purchasing, personnel, accounting, and other services, services that are also carried out in the home office. This duplication, naturally, can be costly. Finally, geographic departmentation may increase the problem of control by top managers who, at the headquarters, may find it difficult to monitor the activities of the departments located in various territories.

Departmentation by Product

Organizational growth

The grouping of activities on the basis of product or product lines has long been growing in importance in multiline, large-scale enterprises. It can be seen as an evolutionary process. Typically companies and other enterprises adopting this form were organized by enterprise functions. With the growth of the firm, production managers, sales and service managers, and engineering executives encountered problems of size. The managerial job became complex, and the span of management limited their ability to increase the number of immediate subordinate managers. At this point, reorganization on a product division basis became necessary. This structure permits top management to delegate to a division executive extensive authority over the manufacturing, sales, service, and engineering functions that relate to a given product or product line and to exact a considerable degree of profit responsibility from each of these managers. Figure 9-3 shows an example of a typical product organization grouping for a manufacturing company.

Advantages

Product or product line is an important basis for departmentation because it facilitates the use of specialized capital, facilitates a certain type of coordination, and permits the maximum use of personal skills and specialized knowledge. For example, the sales effort of a particular person may be most effective when con-

FIGURE 9-3

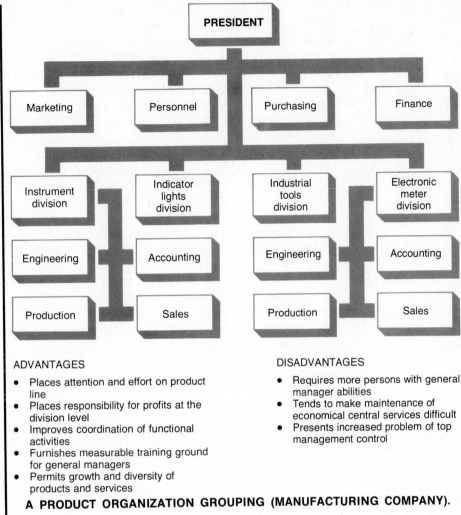

ADVANTAGES

- Places attention and effort on product line
- Places responsibility for profits at the division level
- Improves coordination of functional activities
- Furnishes measurable training ground for general managers
- Permits growth and diversity of products and services

DISADVANTAGES

- Requires more persons with general manager abilities
- Tends to make maintenance of economical central services difficult
- Presents increased problem of top management control

A PRODUCT ORGANIZATION GROUPING (MANUFACTURING COMPANY).

fined to lubricants, or conveyors, or power plants, each of which is best sold by the expert thoroughly familiar with the product. Where the potential volume of business is high enough to fully employ such salespeople, the advantages of product departmentation are significant.

This basis for grouping activities may help in using highly specialized machinery, equipment, or buildings. If production of an item, or closely related items, is sufficiently large to employ fully specialized facilities, strong pressure may be felt for product departmentation in order to realize economic advantages in manufacturing, assembly, or handling.

If it is important for activities relating to a particular product to be coordinated, then product departmentation may be preferred. Better timing and customer service can thus sometimes be provided. If sales and engineering efforts are also located in the plant, cooperation with production can be exceptionally good. We will consider later other factors that may reduce this advantage.

Finally, profit responsibility can be exacted from product department managers. Where they supervise the sales, production, engineering, service, and cost functions, they may be held responsible for certain profit goals. They have the responsibility for producing a profit along with other similarly organized groups and this enables top managers to evaluate more intelligently the contribution of each product line to total profit.

Avoidance of oversimplification

In considering these advantages, however, it is essential to avoid oversimplification. Even product-line managers may be saddled with heavy overhead costs, allocated from the expense of operating the headquarters office, perhaps a central research division, and, frequently, many central service divisions. Accountants will realize that these problems are similar to those found when establishing profit centers within the primary functional departments. Also, similar problems arise when one attempts to identify responsibilities for product-line costs within functional divisions. In these cases, the guesswork in making allocations is greater than in the case of true product departmentation. And product managers understandably resent being charged with costs over which they have no control.

Disadvantages

The disadvantages of product deparmentation are similar to those of territorial departmentation. They include the necessity of having more persons with general managerial abilities available, the dangers of increased cost through duplication of central service and staff activities, and the problem of maintaining top-management control. The latter becomes especially important because a product division manager is, to a very great extent, in the same position as the chief executive of a single-product-line company. Enterprises that operate with product divisions must take care, as the General Motors Corporation has done, to place enough decision making and control at the headquarters level that the entire enterprise does not disintegrate.

Customer Departmentation

The grouping of activities to reflect a primary interest in customers is common in a variety of enterprises. Customers are the key to the way activities are grouped when the different things an enterprise does for them are each managed by one department head. The industrial sales department of a wholesaler who also sells to retailers is a case in point. Business owners and managers frequently arrange activities on this basis to cater to the requirements of clearly defined customer groups, and educational institutions offer regular and extension courses to serve different groups of students.

There are difficult decisions to be made in separating some types of customer departments from product departments. For example, in the great central cash markets for agricultural products, the loan officers of commercial banks frequently specialize in fruit, vegetables, or grain even to the point where an individual officer will make loans only on wheat or oranges. This is a case of customer departmentation, since loan service is provided by type of customer. Figure 9-4 illustrates a typical customer departmentation in a large bank.

Advantages

The special and widely varied needs of customers for clearly defined service lead many suppliers to departmentize on this basis. The manufacturer who sells to both wholesalers and industrial buyers frequently finds that the needs of each can best be met by specialized departments. The wholesaler requires a product of dependable quality, available on a continuous-reorder basis, and suited to the ultimate consumer. The industrial buyer wants a product that will save money, which frequently means a high-quality product, and training of employees.

Nonbusiness groups follow similar practices. The extension services of universities, such as night-school divisions, are arranged, with respect to time, subject matter, and sometimes instructors, to appeal to an entirely different group of students from those who attend on a full-time day basis. The operations of a United Way drive are arranged on the basis of different "customer" classifications. And departments of the federal government are set up to care for farmers, business people, industrial workers, the elderly and other specific groups.

FIGURE 9-4

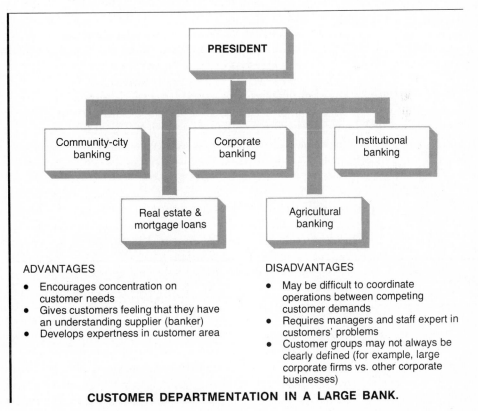

ADVANTAGES

- Encourages concentration on customer needs
- Gives customers feeling that they have an understanding supplier (banker)
- Develops expertness in customer area

DISADVANTAGES

- May be difficult to coordinate operations between competing customer demands
- Requires managers and staff expert in customers' problems
- Customer groups may not always be clearly defined (for example, large corporate firms vs. other corporate businesses)

CUSTOMER DEPARTMENTATION IN A LARGE BANK.

Disadvantages

Customer departmentation is not without certain drawbacks. There is, for instance, the difficulty of coordination between this type of department and those organized on other bases, with constant pressure from the managers of customer departments for special treatment.

Another disadvantage is the possibility of underemployment of facilities and labor-specialized workers in customer groups. In periods of recession, some customer groups may all but disappear, for example, machine-tool buyers; in periods of expansion, the unequal development of customer groups and demands is characteristic.

Market-Oriented Departmentation

Marketing channels

Market-centering

Newer forms of basic departmentation involve organizing an enterprise around markets served or around marketing channels used. While both these approaches to departmentation are designed to emphasize marketing and make it more effective, there are some differences between them. Organizing around marketing channels requires making an organization structure reflect the ways a company reaches an ultimate customer, whether through wholesale channels direct to grocery stores or direct to supermarkets, through channels designed to serve hardware stores, or through those that reach drugstores. Market-centered organization, on the other hand, groups activities to support marketing efforts in such key markets as hospitals, aerospace companies, computer operations, and brokerage firms.

Both approaches may sound like customer departmentation, and they are similar to it. However, the essential considerations in these market-oriented forms are the marketing channel and the market, as shown in Figure 9-5.

Purex Corporation

The Purex Corporation, for example, found some years ago, when it moved from a functional to a divisional organization, that neither product nor territorial departmentation patterns would work. Various soaps and detergents moved to the ultimate customers through supermarkets as well as through drugstores and drug chains. On investigating these channels, the company found that the ways of doing business, the kinds of buyers, and the methods of sales and promotion were so different in grocery markets and in drug chains and drugstores that it was wise to establish a grocery products division and a drug and toiletries division. While this may sound like product departmentation, it was not. The grocery products division manufactured the various soap and detergent items that were marketed through the drug and toiletries division.

The more purely market-centered approach to organizing has grown in importance as businesses have become more market-oriented. Data processing operations of International Business Machines Corporation have been organized around such key markets as supermarkets and hospitals. The Xerox Information Systems Group has organized around various copier markets. Hewlett Packard has organized sales and service around electrical manufacturing and aerospace markets. Other companies have taken similar steps. This means, of course, that organizational patterns must change in response to specific situations since it is the task of an organization structure to help in making possible the kind of performance desired.

FIGURE 9-5

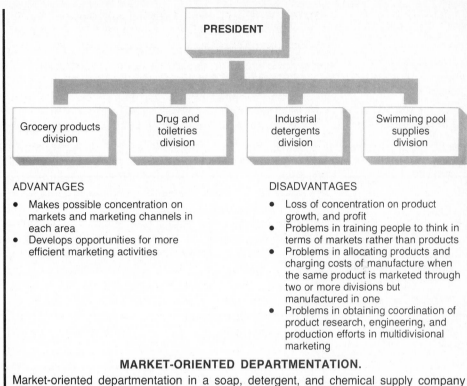

ADVANTAGES

- Makes possible concentration on markets and marketing channels in each area
- Develops opportunities for more efficient marketing activities

DISADVANTAGES

- Loss of concentration on product growth, and profit
- Problems in training people to think in terms of markets rather than products
- Problems in allocating products and charging costs of manufacture when the same product is marketed through two or more divisions but manufactured in one
- Problems in obtaining coordination of product research, engineering, and production efforts in multidivisional marketing

MARKET-ORIENTED DEPARTMENTATION.
Market-oriented departmentation in a soap, detergent, and chemical supply company organizes the company around markets served or marketing channels used.

Advantages

The advantages of market-oriented departmentation are not difficult to perceive. In this day of trying to reach customers through effective selling, good marketing is "the name of the game" for most business enterprises. There is even some merit in being more concerned than we are with our "markets" in government, education, and churches. It is the different publics served by government, by colleges and universities, and by churches that must be served, and served efficiently, if such organizations are to survive.

Disadvantages

But market-oriented organization does have its problems. A company usually needs a manager with strong entrepreneurial skills to head up the division or department. There may be duplication of many top organization services, such as sales, advertising, accounting, purchasing, and personnel. Duplication and confusion may arise in product research and development activities as well as in manufacturing, as the market-oriented managers demand special attention and service. The demands for market and other information are likely to be greater and more costly. For these reasons, departmentizing on a market-oriented basis does not mean that all activities necessary for producing for, and serving, a given market will be included. Economics is likely to demand that companies centralize such activities as accounting, production, engineering, purchasing, and even sales.

Process or Equipment Departmentation

Manufacturing firms often group activities around a process or a type of equipment. Such a basis of departmentation is illustrated by a paint or electroplating process grouping or by the arrangement in one plant area of punch presses or automatic screw machines. People and materials are brought together in such a department in order to carry out a particular operation.

One common example of equipment departmentation is the electronic data processing department. As installations for data processing have become expensive and complex, with ever-increasing capacities, they have tended to be organized in a separate department. Most large and even medium-sized companies have such departments. In some cases, computer stations connected to an enterprise's central computer (or an outside one under a time-sharing or leasing basis), minicomputers, and electronic desk computers have tended to slow the growth of centralized computer departments. However, major data processing departments will unquestionably continue to exist and to be placed fairly high in the organization structure.

Matrix Organization

The essence of matrix organization

An interesting and increasingly used form of organization is variously referred to as **matrix** or **grid** organization or **project** or **product** management, although, as we will later see, pure project management need not imply a grid or matrix. The essence of matrix organization normally is the combining of functional and product departmentation in the same organization structure. As is shown in Figure 9-6, which depicts matrix organization in an engineering department, there are functional managers in charge of engineering functions with an overlay of project managers responsible for the end product. While this form has been common in engineering and in research and development, it has also been widely used, although seldom drawn as a matrix, in product marketing organization.

Why Matrix Management Is Used

Project organization in engineering

As companies and customers have become increasingly interested in end results, that is, in the final product or completed project, there has been pressure to establish responsibility for ensuring such end results. Of course, this could be accomplished by organizing along traditional product department lines. This is often done, even in engineering, where a project manager is put in charge of all the engineering and support personnel necessary to accomplish an entire project. This kind of organization is depicted in Figure 9-7.

But pure project organization may not be feasible for a number of reasons. For example, the project may not be able to utilize certain specialized engineering personnel or equipment full time; a solid-state physicist may be needed only occasionally; or the project may need only part-time use or an expensive environmental test laboratory or a prototype shop. Also, the project may be of relatively

FIGURE 9-6

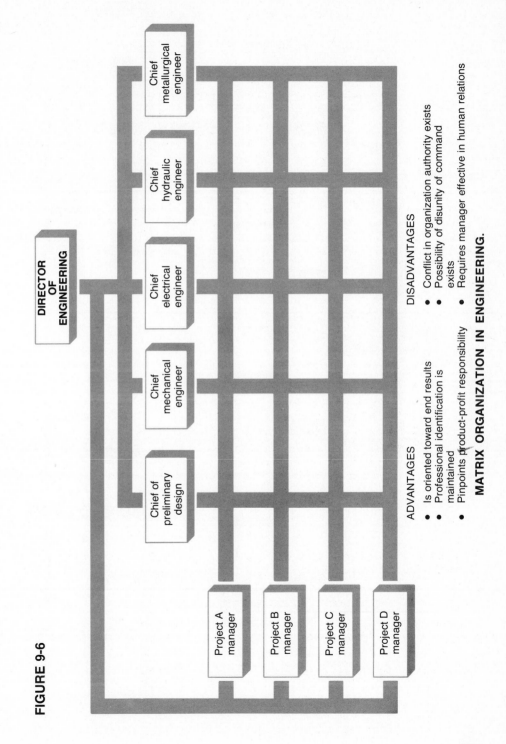

DIRECTOR OF ENGINEERING

Chief of preliminary design

Chief mechanical engineer

Chief electrical engineer

Chief hydraulic engineer

Chief metallurgical engineer

Project A manager

Project B manager

Project C manager

Project D manager

ADVANTAGES

- Is oriented toward end results
- Professional identification is maintained
- Pinpoints product-profit responsibility

DISADVANTAGES

- Conflict in organization authority exists
- Possibility of disunity of command exists
- Requires manager effective in human relations

MATRIX ORGANIZATION IN ENGINEERING.

194

FIGURE 9-7

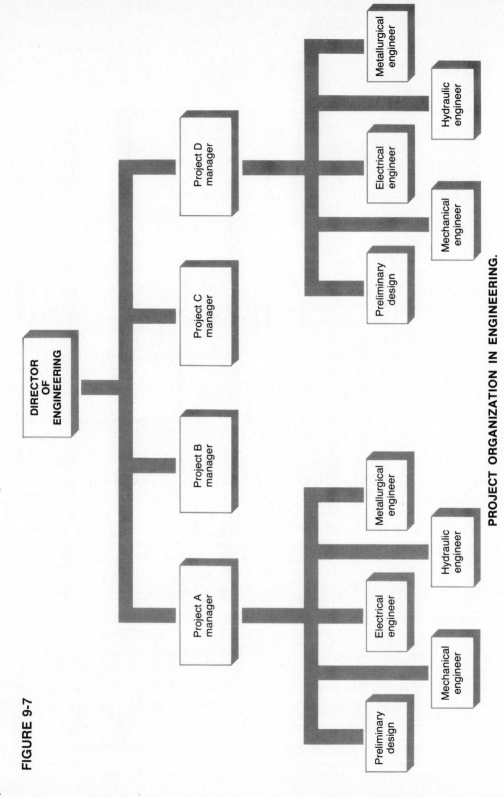

PROJECT ORGANIZATION IN ENGINEERING.

short duration. Although there is no *logical* reason why an organization structure should not be changed daily or monthly, there is the practical reason that people, particularly highly trained professionals, simply may not tolerate the insecurity of frequent organization change. Another reason why pure project organization may not be feasible is that highly trained professionals (and some that are not so highly trained) generally prefer to be allied organizationally with their professional group. They feel more at home; they feel that their professional reputation and advancement will be better served by belonging to such a group than by being allied with a project; and they believe that their superiors, if they are professionals in the same field, will be more likely to appreciate their expertise at times of salary advances, promotions, or layoffs. These feelings ordinarily exist not only among engineers and scientists but also among lawyers, accountants, and university professors.

Matrix organization in product management

The reasons for existence of a matrix organization in commercial or industrial product management may be somewhat different. In a soap and detergent company, for example, the top management may want individual responsibility for profit to exist for a given product or brand. If the company had only one product or brand, there would obviously be no problem; the chief executive would have profit responsibility. If the company could organize through the use of an integrated (research, marketing, manufacturing) product division, then the division manager would have profit responsibility. But where, as in a multiproduct soap and detergent company, technology and economics dictate that the company can hardly have separate manufacturing facilities or sales forces for each product, the only way to get a degree of profit responsibility is to overlay, in some way, a product manager with responsibility for profit for a given brand or product.

Variations in Practice

There are many variations of the project or product manager role. In some cases, the project or product managers have no authority to tell any functional department to do anything. In these cases, they may be only information gatherers, keeping tabs on how their project or product is proceeding and reporting to a top executive when significant deviations from plans occur. Their role might be that of a persuader, using knowledge and personal persuasiveness to get results. Obviously, these roles have some very serious drawbacks, particularly if the manager without any organization power whatsoever is actually held responsible for end results. No wonder that turnover among those who hold such positions has been high!

Another variation in practice is to simply draw a grid or matrix, like Figure 9-6, showing certain managers in charge of functional departments and others in charge of projects or products. This grid is usually intended to represent a pure case of dual command. The results are predictable. If something goes wrong with a project or product, it is often difficult for a top superior to know whose fault it is and where the difficulties really lie. A superior faced with this kind of situation would do just as well not to know that the deviation exists since, if responsibility cannot be traced, little can be done to correct the problem. Also, in such cases, there tend to arise the usual friction, buck-passing, and confusion one would expect to result from disunity of command.

Solution in Engineering and Research and Development

Role of project manager

The more sophisticated companies in high-technology industries that have found no alternative to matrix management have solved the problem of confused authority and multiple subordination largely by clarification of the authorities and responsibilities of the functional and project managers. Project managers are normally given authority over the integrity of a total design; they usually have the task of dealing with customers, although in many instances this responsibility will be passed on to the marketing department; they are given authority over budget and in this case become essentially buyers of services from the functional managers; and they are given the authority to work out schedules and priorities for their projects with the functional departments. If they cannot work out priorities because of the claims of other project managers and if they and the other project managers cannot compromise, the matter of priorities goes to a higher authority, usually the manager who has primary responsibility for relationships with all customers.

Under this sytem, functional managers are given authority over the people in their area and over the integrity of engineering or research work done by them. Thus, between the project manager and the functional manager, much of the problem of disunity of command is eliminated, although there still may be a degree of conflict and uncertainty in such borderline areas as total project design accuracy and integrity.

Solution in Product Management

Varying role of product manager

Although the Procter & Gamble Company and Libby, McNeil & Libby have successfully used product management in the marketing of their products for many years and although other prominent companies like Lever Brothers and General Foods have long used it, most of the development of its use has occurred in the past three decades.

As might be expected, the term **product manager** is used in many ways; it may be applied to the general manager of an integrated product division or to someone who is little more than a staff assistant in the marketing head's organization who gathers information and makes recommendations. But a matrix form of organization does not occur until product managers have some degree of authority over functional departments that do not report to them.

Research on the degree of authority granted to product managers shows that in most companies, they may be held to some degree responsible for the success of the brands assigned to them, but may be given either little or no authority to accomplish these results; they may merely be assigned the ambiguous role of "charming persuader." It is interesting that this promising organizational device, aiming as it does in a functionally organized company toward giving responsibility for end results to product managers, should repeat the history of vagueness and lack of authority experienced for years in engineering.

However, a number of companies have begun to solve this problem of authority in a way that makes this a real and reasonably workable matrix organization. One of the best solutions is the one that has been used by Procter & Gamble for many years. In this company, a brand manager (located in the advertisting department, since the company has long had a policy of preselling through advertising and promotion) derives authority in an interesting way. The brand manager develops the plan for a brand, covering not only advertising but also use of the field sales force, research assistance, packaging, and manufacturing programs, and then negotiates with the various functional departments on the part they will play in the program and the costs involved. After such a comprehensive brand program has been developed, it goes up the line in the company until it and other brand programs are finally approved by the chief executive. Armed with such an approved plan, the brand manager hardly needs any other authority. While the organization chart would not show grid, the fact is that one exists through authority derived from plans approved at the top.

Matrix Organization and the Future

Matrix, or project, organization will gain greater emphasis in the future because of the rapidly changing environment with its many uncertainties. This kind of departmentation facilitates quick responses to changes in the dynamic environment. Also, with increased emphasis on end results and goal accomplishment, there can hardly be any doubt that increasing use will be made of some form of matrix organization, especially since it is often not possible to give a manager direct line authority over all the activities necessary to accomplish major end results. This trend also results from a recognition of the fact that programs represent interacting networks and systems.

But if modern managers are to meet the challenge involved in matrix organization and get the results desired, they must face up better than they have to the task of clarifying authority. As we noted earlier, good people may make an unclear structure work, but they can certainly work better where their roles are clarified.

Strategic Business Units (SBUs)

More recently, companies have been using an organizational device generally referred to as a strategic business unit (SBU). These are distinct little businesses set up as units in a larger company to assure that a certain product or product line is promoted and handled as though it were an independent business. One of the earlier users of this organizational device was the General Electric Company. This special organization unit was introduced to ensure that each product or product line of the hundreds offered by the company got the same attention it would if it were developed, produced, and marketed by an independent company. The device has also been used in some cases by companies for a major product line. Occidential Chemical Company, for example, used it for such products as phosphates, alkalis, and resins.[1]

---

[1]For a discussion of SBUs, see W. K. Hall, "SBUs: Hot, New Topic in the Management of Diversification," *Business Horizons*, vol. 21, no. 1 (February 1978), pp. 13–23.

FIGURE 9-8

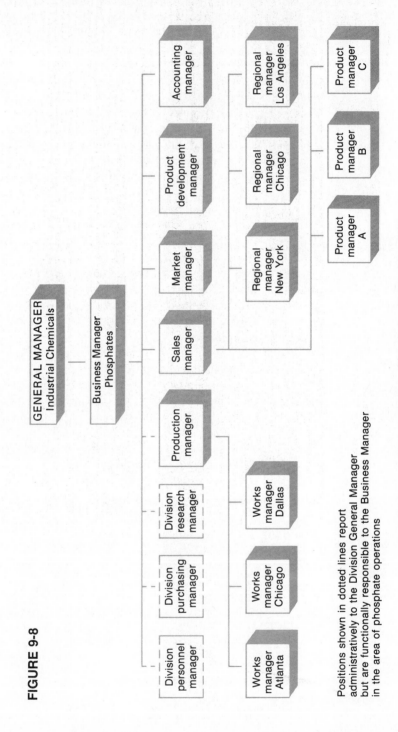

Positions shown in dotted lines report administratively to the Division General Manager but are functionally responsible to the Business Manager in the area of phosphate operations

TYPICAL STRATEGIC BUSINESS UNIT ORGANIZATION IN A LARGE INDUSTRIAL CHEMICAL COMPANY.

GENERAL MANAGER
Industrial Chemicals

Business Manager
Phosphates

Division personnel manager

Division purchasing manager

Division research manager

Production manager

Sales manager

Market manager

Product development manager

Accounting manager

Works manager Atlanta

Works manager Chicago

Works manager Dallas

Regional manager New York

Regional manager Chicago

Regional manager Los Angeles

Product manager A

Product manager B

Product manager C

For each SBU a manager (usually a "business manager") is appointed with responsibility for guiding and promoting the product from the research laboratory through product engineering, market research, production, packaging, and marketing, and with bottom-line responsibility for its profitability. Thus, an SBU is given its own missions and goals and a manager with the assistance of a full-time or part-time (people from other departments assigned to the SBU on a part-time basis) staff to develop and implement strategic and operating plans for the product. The organization of a typical SBU, that for phosphate of the Occidental Chemical Company, is shown in Figure 9-8. You will note that the business manager for phosphates has all the functions reporting to him or her that would be found necessary in a separate company.

Obviously, the major benefit of utilizing an SBU organization is to provide assurance that a product will not get "lost" among other products (usually those with larger sales and profits) in a large company. It preserves the attention and energies of a manager and a staff whose job it is to guide and promote a product or product line. It is thus an organizational technique to preserve the entrepreneurial attention and drive so characteristic of the small company. In fact, it is an excellent means of promoting entrepreneurship which is likely to be so lacking in the large company.

Choosing the Pattern of Departmentation

As we said at the beginning of this chapter, there is no one best way of departmentizing applicable to all organizations and all situations. Managers must determine what is best by looking at the situation they face—the jobs to be done and the way they should be done, the people involved and their personalities, the technology employed in the department, the users being served, and other internal and external environmental factors in the situation. However, if they know the various patterns, their advantages, disadvantages, and dangers, practicing managers should be able to design the organization structure most suitable for their particular operations.

The Aim: Achieving Objectives

Departmentation is not an end in itself but is simply a method of arranging activities to facilitate the accomplishment of objectives. It is not even an unmixed good, for the separation of activities on any basis creates problems of coordination that are difficult to solve. Each method has its advantages and disadvantages. Consequently, the process of selection involves a consideration of the relative advantages of each type at each level in the organization structure. In all cases, the central question concerns the type of organizational environment that the manager wishes to design and the situation being faced. In our discussion of the alternative methods of departmentation, we showed that each method yields certain gains and involves certain costs.

**Mixing Types of
Departmentation**

Another point to be highlighted concerns the mixing of types of departmentation with a functional area. For example, a wholesale drug firm has grouped the buying and selling activities relating to beverages in one product department, but has grouped, on the same level, all other selling activities on a territorial basis. A manufacturer of plastic goods has territorialized both the production and the sale of all its products except dinnerware, which is itself a product department. A functional department manager may, in other words, employ two or more bases for grouping activities on the same organizational levels. Such practices may be justified on logical grounds because the objective of departmentation is not to build a rigid structure, balanced in terms of levels and characterized by consistency and identical bases. The purpose is to group activities in the manner which will best contribute to achieving enterprise objectives. If variety of bases does this, there is no reason why managers should not take advantage of the alternatives before them.

The logic of this view is frequently ignored by those who design organization structures. For some reason, possibly to make an organization chart look pretty or to maintain control, specialists often insist that all departmentized activities below the primary level of organization be grouped in exactly the same manner. For instance, the organization structure of the Internal Revenue Service at the regional and district levels is essentially the same, despite tremendous variation in district sizes. Firms with multiplants often organize them in the same way; thus, the same departments will be found in virtually all Sears, Roebuck and Company stores.

Creating an identical organization structure in similar enterprise groupings merely to make an organizational chart look nice is really not good practice. The organization planner may think it "looks better," but this is a poor reason for organizing in a particular way. The matter of control, however, is quite different. There may be very important reasons for comparing the operation of similarly organized plants, stores, and agencies. They all may be comparable profit centers; their managers can be more readily compared within this organization structure. Even though these, and others, are important arguments for similarity of organization structure, we must remember that no one organizes to control; people organize to produce efficiently and effectively. If the latter purpose is sacrificed for the former, the cost of control is too great to allow.

Summary

The grouping of activities and people into departments makes organizational expansion possible. Departmentation can be done by simple numbers, by time, by enterprise function, by territory, by product, by the kind of customer served, by market, and by process or equipment required. Relatively new kinds of departmentation are the hybrid, matrix, or project, organization, and the strategic business unit.

There is no single best way to organize. Instead, the pattern to be selected depends on various factors in a given situation. These factors include the kind of job to be done, the way the task must be done, the kinds of people involved, the technology, the people being served, and other internal and external considerations. At any rate, the selection of the specific departmentation should be done so that organizational and individual objectives can be achieved effectively and efficiently. To accomplish this goal often requires mixing forms of departmentation.

Key Ideas and Concepts for Review

Departmentation by simple numbers
Departmentation by time
Departmentation by enterprise function
Departmentation by territory
Departmentation by product

Customer departmentation
Market-oriented departmentation
Process or equipment departmentation
Matrix organization
Strategic business unit

For Discussion

1 Some sociologists tell us that organization structuring is a social invention. What do you think they mean? Do they imply that there is a "right" or "wrong" way to organize? What test of whether an organization structure is "right" would you suggest?

2 If you were the president of a company that was organized along functional lines and a consultant suggested that you organize along territorial or product lines, what might concern you in following this recommendation?

3 Why do you think that many large companies have organized along product lines (for example, General Motors or Du Pont), while other large companies have territorial departments (for example, Prudential Life Insurance Company)?

4 Why do most large department-store and supermarket chains organize their stores on a territorial basis and then organize the internal store units by products? Give examples from your own experience.

5 Why do most small companies use functionally organized departments?

6 Why are so many federal government agencies organized primarily on a territorial basis?

7 Do you see any reasons why managing by objectives may result in increased use of matrix organizational structures?

8 How does this chapter illustrate a situational approach to management?

CASE 9-1

AGRICULTURAL FERTILIZER DIVISION OF THE NORTHERN CHEMICAL CORPORATION

At the end of a busy day, a group of middle-level managers of the Agricultural Fertilizer Division of the Northern Chemical Corporation gathered to reflect on their problems. The headquarters of Northern Chemical had recently set up a central data processing department in Houston, where all the corporation's data processing would be done for its various divisions located over the entire United States. At that time, the data processing equipment of every division had been taken away from it, each division headquarters office was given a terminal connected to Houston, and each division was required to get any report processing it needed from the Houston facility.

The headquarters of the Agricultural Chemicals Division was located in Sacramento, California. This division had long concentrated on developing and selling fertilizers to the large agricultural growers in the West and on distributing its garden and house plant fertilizers to stores throughout the country. It had been very successful, with sales growing rapidly and profits even faster. But the line managers of the division were quite unhappy about not being able to have their own computer facilities to give them the analyses and reports they needed.

Bill Jacobs, production planning and control supervisor, was particularly disturbed about this move to centralize data processing. "There is no way," said Jacobs, "that I can plan our production, especially with our many products and customers and the demands of our large growers for good service, if Houston runs our programs. They do not always have the data needed in their data bank, and, by the time I get it worked out with them, I have lost much valuable time."

Barry Hill, district sales manager for Northern California, was even unhappier. He pointed out that he often needed to run productivity and profitability studies for large growers and he could not do so unless the division had a computer operation in its own offices in Sacramento. "The growers will never understand why I cannot make these analyses for them quickly and will never understand why they must be made in Houston; they will soon tell me that there are other companies that can serve their needs," moaned Hill.

"You do have a problem," said Mona Fredericks, head of statistical analyses and reports in the division controller's office. "But yours is a small one compared with mine. I have to get many special and regular reports to headquarters, to the division managers, and to all you people in sales, market research, product development, and production. You always want them right now and in the form you can use most easily. How can I do that for you now?"

The frustration reached its peak when Joe Morey, cost control supervisor, startled the group by saying: "Did you know that all the departments in our division are being charged fees each month for Houston's services and that these are higher than the costs when we each had our own little computer system?"

1 Do you agree that these people had a serious problem?

2 If you were one of them, what would you do about it?

3 If you were to look at this purely as an organization problem, what conclusions would you draw?

CASE 9-2

UNIVERSAL FOOD PRODUCTS COMPANY

Alexander Owen, president of the Universal Food Products Company, was tired of being the only one in his company actually responsible for profits. While he had good vice-presidents in charge of finance, sales, advertising, manufacturing, purchasing, and product research, he realized he could not hold any of them responsible for company profits, as much as he would like to. He often found it difficult even to hold them responsible for the contribution of their various areas to company profits. The sales vice-president, for example, had rather reasonably complained that he could not be fully responsible for sales when the advertising was ineffective, when the products customer stores wanted were not readily available from manufacturing, or when he did not have the new products he needed to meet competition. Likewise, the manufacturing vice-president had some justification when he made the point that he could not hold costs down and still be able to produce short runs so as to fill orders on short notice; moreover, financial controls would not allow the company to carry a large inventory of everything.

Mr. Owen had considered breaking his company down into six or seven segments by setting up product divisions with a manager over each with profit responsibility. But he found that this would not be feasible or economical since many of the company's branded food products were produced on the same factory equipment and used the same raw materials, and a salesperson calling on a store or supermarket could far more economically handle a number of related products than one or a few.

Consequently, Mr. Owen came to the conclusion that the best thing for him to do was to set up a system with six product managers reporting to a product marketing manager. Each product manager would be given responsibility for one or a few products and would oversee, for each product, all aspects of product research, manufacturing, advertising, and sales, thereby becoming the person responsible for the performance and profits of the products.

Mr. Owen realized that he could not give these product managers actual line authority over the various operating departments of the company since that would cause each vice-president and his or her department to report to six product managers and the product marketing manager, as well as the president. He was concerned about this problem, but he knew that some of the most successful large companies in the world had used the product manager system. Moreover, one of his friends on a university faculty had told him that he must expect some lack of clearness and some confusion in any organization and that this result might not be bad since it forced people to work together as teams.

Mr. Owen resolved to put in the product manager system as outlined and hope for the best. But he wondered how he could avoid the problem of confusion in reporting relationships.

1 Do you agree with Mr. Owen's program? Would you have done it differently?

2 Exactly what would you do to avoid any confusion in this organization?

For Further Information

Dalton, D. R., W. D. Todor, M. J. Spendolini, G. J. Fielding, and L. W. Porter. "Organization Structure and Performance: A Critical Review," *Academy of Management Review*, vol. 5, no. 1 (January 1980), pp. 49–64.

Galbraith, J. R. "Matrix Organization Designs: How to Combine Functional and Project Forms," in H. Koontz, C. O'Donnell, and H. Weihrich, (eds.), *Management—A Book of Readings*, 5th ed. (New York: McGraw-Hill Book Company, 1980), pp. 282–300.

Herbert, T. T. "Strategy and Multinational Organization Structure: An Interorganizational Relationships Perspective," *Academy of Management Review*, vol. 9, no. 2, (April 1984), pp. 259–271.

Jackson, J. H., and C. P. Morgan. *Organization Theory*, 2nd ed. (Englewood Cliffs, N.J.: Prentice-Hall, Inc., 1982).

Mintzberg, H. *Structures in Fives—Designing Effective Organizations* (Englewood Cliffs, N.J.: Prentice-Hall, Inc., 1983).

Stieglitz, H. "On Concepts of Corporate Structure," in H. Koontz, C. O'Connell, and H. Weihrich (eds.), *Management—A Book of Readings*, 5th ed. (New York: McGraw-Hill Book Company, 1980), pp. 266–272.

10

Line and Staff Authority Relationships

After completing this chapter, you should understand:

1 The different kinds of power
2 Line and staff in organization, recognizing their nature as authority relationships rather than as positions or people
3 The importance of distinguishing line and staff authority relationships.
4 The nature and use of functional authority, which is a special kind of line authority application
5 How the dangers of confusion of line and staff relationships can be avoided
6 The problems encountered in the use of staff
7 How to make staff effective in practice

We have discussed the patterns of departmentation. We now consider another essential question: What *kind* of authority do we find in an organizational structure? The question has to do with the nature of authority relationships—the problem of line and staff.

Without authority—the power to exercise discretion in making decisions—properly placed in managers, various departments cannot become smoothly working units harmonized for the accomplishment of enterprise objectives. Authority relationships, whether vertical or horizontal, are the factors that make organization possible, harness departmental activities, and bring coordination to an enterprise.

Authority and Power

Power

Authority

Before concentrating in this and the next chapter on authority in organization, it will be useful to distinguish between authority and power. **Power** is a much broader concept. It is the ability of individuals or groups to induce or influence the beliefs or actions of other persons or groups: **Authority** in organization is the power in a position (and through it the person occupying the position) to exercise discretion in making decisions affecting others. It is, of course, power, but power in an organization setting.

Legitimate power

Although there are many different bases of power, the power we are most concerned with in this book is *legitimate* power. It normally arises from position and derives from our cultural system of rights, obligations, and duties whereby a "position" is accepted by people as being "legitimate." In a privately owned business, authority of position arises primarily from the social institution (a "bundle of rights") of private property. In government, this authority arises basically from the institution of representative government. A traffic officer who gives you a traffic ticket gets the power to do so because we have a system of representative government in which we have elected legislators to make and provide for the enforcement of laws.

Expert power

Referent power

Power may also come from the *expertness* of a person or a group. This is the power of knowledge. Physicians, lawyers, and university professors may have considerable influence on others because they are respected for their special knowledge. Power may further exist as *referent* power, that is, influence which people or groups may exercise because people believe in them and their ideas. Thus, Martin Luther King had very little legitimate power but, by the force of his personality, his ideas, and his ability to preach, he strongly influenced the behavior of many people. Likewise, a movie star or a military hero might possess considerable referent power.

Reward power

In addition, power arises from the ability of some people to grant rewards. Purchasing agents, with little position power, might be able to exercise considerable influence by their ability to expedite or delay a much-needed spare part. Or university professors have considerable *reward* power; they can grant or withhold high grades.

Coercive power

Coercive power is still another type. Although closely related to reward power and normally arising from legitimate power, it is the power to punish, whether by firing a subordinate or withholding a merit increase.

As you can see, then, while organization authority is the power to exercise discretion in decision making, it almost invariably arises from the power of position, or legitimate power. However, as we have noted, when we speak of authority in managerial settings, we usually refer to the power of positions. At the same time, other factors, such as personality and style of dealing with people, are involved in leadership.

Line and Staff Concepts

Much confusion has arisen both in literature and among managers as to what line and staff are; as a result, there is probably no area of management that causes more difficulties, more friction, and more loss of time and effectiveness. Yet line and staff relationships are important as an organizational way of life, and the authority relationships of members of an organization must necessarily affect the operation of the enterprise.

One widely held view

One widely held concept of line and staff is that line functions are those that have direct responsibility for accomplishing the objectives of the enterprise, while staff functions to help the line to work most effectively in accomplishing the objectives. Those who hold to this view almost invariably classify production and sales (and sometimes finance) as line functions, and purchasing, accounting, personnel, plant maintenance, and quality control as staff functions.

Confusion

The confusion arising from such a concept is immediately apparent. It is argued that purchasing, for example, merely helps in achieving the main goals of business because, unlike the production departments, such as painting or parts assembly, it is not directly essential. But is purchasing really any less essential to the achievement of company objectives? Could the company not store up painted or assembled parts and get along without these departments for a while as well as it could get along for a while without purchasing? And could not the same question be asked about other so-called staff and service departments, such as accounting, personnel, and plant maintenance? And, there is probably nothing that could stop the satisfactory production and sale of most manufactured goods more completely than the failure of quality control.

The Nature of Line and Staff Relationships

Scalar principle

A more precise and logically valid concept of line and staff is that they are simply a matter of relationships. Line authority gives a superior a line of authority over a subordinate. It exists in all organizations as an uninterrupted scale or series of steps. Hence, the **scalar principle** in organization: *The clearer the line of authority from the ultimate management position in an enterprise to every subordinate position, the clearer will be the responsibility for decision making and the more effective organization communication will be.* In many large enterprises, the steps are long and complicated, but even in the smallest, the very fact of organization introduces the scalar principle.

Line authority

It therefore becomes apparent from the scalar principle that **line** authority is that relationship in which a superior exercises direct supervision over a subordinate—an authority relationship in direct line or steps.

Staff authority

The nature of the **staff** relationship is advisory. The function of people in a pure staff capacity is to investigate, research, and give advice to line managers to whom they report.

Figure 10-1 shows a typical organization chart for a manufacturing company.

Line and Staff: Relationship or Departmentation?

Frequently, line and staff are regarded as types of departments. Although a department may stand in a predominantly line or staff position with respect to other departments, we distinguish line and staff by authority relationships and not by what people do.

FIGURE 10-1

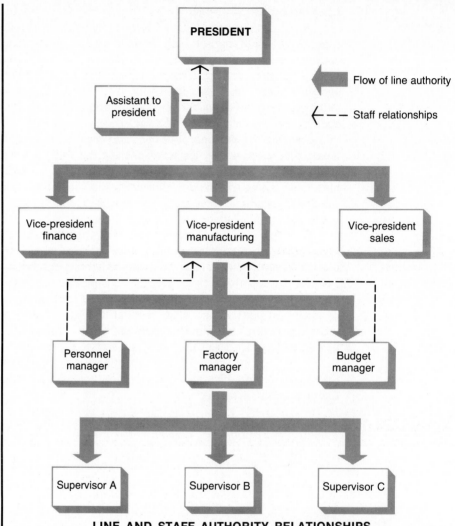

LINE AND STAFF AUTHORITY RELATIONSHIPS.
Note: In certain instances, such as personnel and budgets, these departments often have operating activities as well as responsibilities in a staff
capacity.

Examples

For example, we may think of the public relations department, to the extent
that it is primarily advisory to the top executives, as a staff department. But within
the department are line relationships; the director will stand in a line authority
position with respect to his or her immediate subordinates. On the other hand,
the vice-president in charge of production may head what is clearly and generally
known as a line department. His or her job is *not primarily* advisory to the chief
executive officer. If, however, the vice-president counsels the chief executive on

overall company production policy, this relationship becomes one of staff. Within the production department there may be many subordinates, among them a number having an advisory role and, therefore, having a staff relationship to the whole department or any of its parts.

When one looks at an organization structure *as a whole*, the general character of line and staff relationships for the total organization emerges. Certain departments are predominantly staff in their relationship to the entire organization. Other departments are primarily line.

Figure 10-2 portrays a simplifed organization chart of a manufacturing company. The activities of the director of research and the director of public relations are apt to be mainly advisory to the mainstream of corporate operations and are consequently often considered staff activities. The finance, production, and sales departments, with activities generally related to the main corporate functions, are ordinarily considered line departments.

Relationships distinguishing line from staff

Although it is often convenient and even correct to refer to one department as a line department and to another as a staff department, *their activities do not so characterize the departments. Line and staff are characterized by relationships and not by departmental activities.* Should research be a principal function of the company—as in aerospace manufacturing, where the engineering department produces ideas for sale to military and commercial customers—it will stand in an operating relationship to the organization as a whole and take on the authority characteristics of a factory department in a typical manufacturing enterprise.

Functional Authority

Functional authority

Functional authority is the right which is delegated to an individual or a department to control specified processes, practices, policies, or other matters relating to activities undertaken by personnel in other departments. If the principle of unity of command were followed without exception, authority over these activities would be exercised only by their line superiors, but numerous reasons—including a lack of special knowledge, lack of ability to supervise processes, and danger of diverse interpretations of policies—explain why they occasionally are not allowed to exercise this authority. In such cases, line managers are deprived of some authority. It is delegated by their common superior to a staff specialist or a manager in another department.

Functional authority is not restricted to managers of a particular type of department. It may be exercised by line, service, or staff department heads, more often the latter two, because they are usually composed of specialists whose knowledge becomes the basis for functional controls.

Delegation of Functional Authority

We can better understand functional authority if we think of it as a small slice of the authority of a line superior. A corporation president, for example, has complete authority to manage a corporation, subject only to limitations placed by such superior authority as the board of directors, the corporate charter and bylaws, and government regulations. In the pure staff situation, the advisers on personnel,

FIGURE 10-2

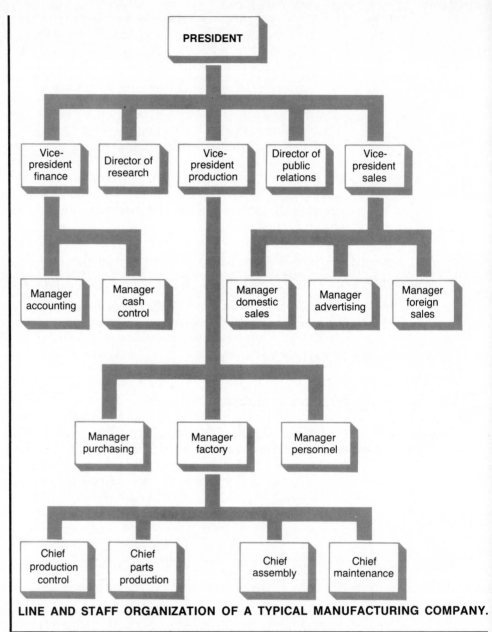

LINE AND STAFF ORGANIZATION OF A TYPICAL MANUFACTURING COMPANY.

accounting, purchasing, or public relations have no part of this line authority, their duty being merely to offer counsel. But when the president delegates to these advisers the right to issue instructions directly to the line organizations, as shown in Figure 10-3, that right is called "functional authority."

The four staff and service executives have functional authority over the line

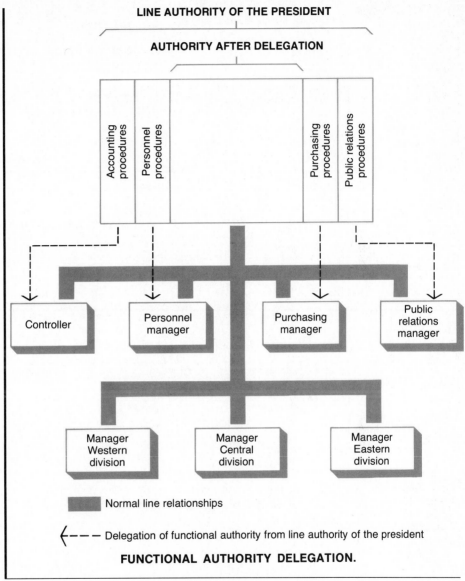

FIGURE 10-3

LINE AUTHORITY OF THE PRESIDENT

AUTHORITY AFTER DELEGATION

Accounting procedures

Personnel procedures

Purchasing procedures

Public relations procedures

Controller

Personnel manager

Purchasing manager

Public relations manager

Manager Western division

Manager Central division

Manager Eastern division

Normal line relationships

Delegation of functional authority from line authority of the president

FUNCTIONAL AUTHORITY DELEGATION.

organization with respect to procedures in the fields of accounting, personnel, purchasing, and public relations. What has happened is that the president, feeling it unnecessary that such specialized matters be cleared through him or her, has delegated line authority to staff assistants to issue their own instructions to the operating departments. Of course, subordinate managers can use the same device, as when a factory superintendent sets up cost, production control, and quality control supervisors with functional authority to prescribe procedures for the operating supervisors.

FIGURE 10-4

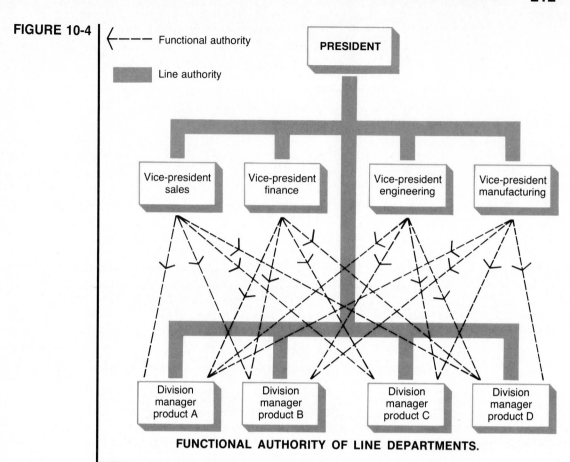

Functional authority
Line authority

PRESIDENT

Vice-president sales

Vice-president finance

Vice-president engineering

Vice-president manufacturing

Division manager product A

Division manager product B

Division manager product C

Division manager product D

FUNCTIONAL AUTHORITY OF LINE DEPARTMENTS.

Functional Authority as Exercised by Operating Managers

Operating department heads sometimes have good reason to control some method or process of another operating department. For example, the vice-president in charge of sales may be given functional authority over the manufacturing executives in such sales-related areas as scheduling customer orders, packaging, or making service parts available.

Where a company is organized along product lines, the exercise of functional authority over the product division managers by other executives is rather commonplace. All functions of sales, production, finance, or other operating functions may be placed under a division or product manager. In this case, certain top line officials in charge of a major function of the business might not have a direct line of authority over the product managers. But, to make sure that sales or financial policy is properly followed in the divisions, these officers may be given functional authority, as illustrated in Figure 10-4.

The Area of Functional Authority

Functional authority should be carefully restricted. A purchasing manager's functional authority, for example, is generally limited to setting the procedures to be used in divisional or departmental purchasing and does not include telling these departments what they can purchase or when. When these managers conduct certain purchasing activities that relate to the whole company, they are acting as heads of service departments. The functional authority of the personnel manager over the general line organization is likewise ordinarily limited to prescribing procedures for handling grievances, for sharing in the administration of wage and salary programs, and for handling vacation procedures and similar matters.

"How" and "when"

Functional authority is usually limited to the area of "how" and sometimes "when"; it seldom applies to "where," "what," or "who." The reason for this limitation is not found in any logical division between normal line authority and functional authority, since the latter can be made to apply to any aspect of operations. Functional authority would destroy the manager's job if carried to extremes; that is why it is usually limited.

Complications in Exercising Functional Authority

Limiting the area of functional authority is, then, important in preserving the integrity of managerial positions. If a company had, as some do, executives with functional authority over procedures in the fields of personnel, purchasing, accounting, traffic, budgets, engineering, public relations, law, sales policy, and real estate, the complications of authority relationships could be great indeed. A factory manager or a sales manager might have, in addition to an immediate line superior, five, ten, or even fifteen functional bosses. In one case, a factory superintendent was found to be subject to functional authority from eighteen different places. When asked whether, on occasion, some of these instructions were conflicting and confusing, he replied, "Every day!" When asked what he did when this happened, he said that he followed the "decibel system" of management—he paid attention only to those persons who made the most noise.

Although such complexity is often necessary, you can see that it can create serious confusion. Some degree of unity of command is needed, and top-level managers ensure this by delegating functional authority so that it can be exercised at only one level below that of the appointed manager. Thus, in Figure 10-5, the functional authority of the personnel or public relations director should not extend beyond the level of the vice-presidents in charge of finance, sales, and manufacturing. In other words, functional authority should be exercised at the nearest possible point to which it applies in the organization structure, in order to preserve the unity of command of the line executives.

This rule is often violated. Top managers with functional authority sometimes issue instructions directly to personnel throughout the organization. Where policy or procedure determination is so important that there must be no deviation, both the prestige of the top manager and the necessity for accurate communication may make it necessary and wise to issue such instructions. Issuing them to the responsible line subordinate, as well as to the functional counterpart at the lower level, may not seem to harmfully increase the multiplicity of command. There are needs for centralizing authority that may make this kind of exercise of functional authority unavoidable.

Clarifying Functional Authority

To achieve the best results from delegating functional authority, top managers should make sure that the extent of the authority is clearly spelled out to both the person who will use it and the person who will be subject to it. An example of

FIGURE 10-5

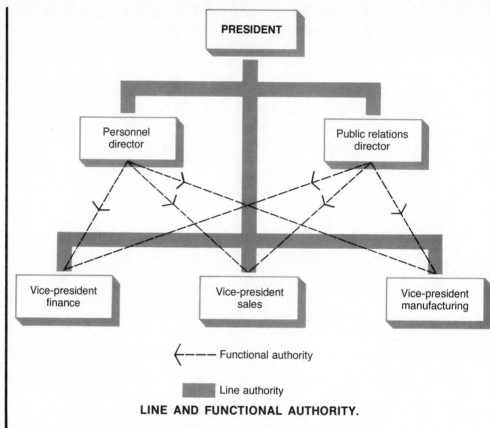

LINE AND FUNCTIONAL AUTHORITY.

one company's attempt to define the authority of the vice-president-controller is the following specific delegations to that officer, which were thoroughly discussed with her and her subordinates and with key operating managers and their subordinates over whom the controller was expected to exercise such authority.

The V-P–controller

Authority delegations to vice-president–controller

1   Authority to prescribe the corporate chart of accounts and the divisions' charts of accounts so far as they are supportive to and necessary for the corporation chart of accounts; authority to direct the development and maintenance of necessary procedures to ensure the integrity of the company's accounts and statements; authority to see that the company's accounting policies and procedures are followed in the division

2   Authority to prescribe policies and procedures in the handling of cash, including banking arrangements, methods of handling receipts and disbursements, and the requirements for bonding throughout the company

3 Authority to prescribe policies, standards, and procedures with respect to inventory control matters which affect the integrity of accounting records

4 Authority to prescribe the necessary form, procedures, and timing for the preparation and submission of profit plans

5 Authority to require from the various divisions and departments of the company financial, accounting, and statistical reports and forecasts in a form and at the times necessary to ensure proper company planning and control

6 Authority to approve the selection of the chief accounting officer of any division or affiliate

7 Authority to prescribe and undertake a program of internal auditing of financial, cash, credit, and accounting transactions and an audit of corporate and divisional financial and accounting policies and procedures

Staff and the Small Business

Since the staff department represents a refinement in specialization resulting from division of labor, the use of staff is usually proportional to the size of the enterprise. Just how large a business must be before it will gain by regrouping certain activities into staff departments cannot be stated generally. However, the organization need not be very large before it feels the necessity for specialized assistance on such matters as taxation, government procurement, personnel policy and procedures, accounting, financing, contracts and legal matters, and even management itself.

Even without being able to develop extensive staff departments, the small company can benefit from staff assistance in many ways. Indeed, in the present economic, social, and political environment, the price of error in such matters as determining costs and taxes, maintaining labor relations, meeting environmental regulations, and planning and control is so great that the small firm cannot afford to do without the best possible counsel. Heads of companies of thirty or even fewer employees can frequently afford a general staff assistant. No matter how small the company, one of its essential costs is for legal and tax advice on a retainer, hourly, or job basis.

Outside counsel for small business

Any company can receive accounting counsel at moderate cost from its auditing firm, and audit of a company's books is usually a necessity in connection with income taxes and bank loans. Other advisory services include those of bankers and those relatively untapped but available resources in universities and colleges. Just as medical schools contribute to the community, so can university faculty be available, at a reasonable cost, to small businesses in such areas as engineering, accounting, economics, and management. The small corporation, furthermore, can use its board of directors as a source of advice and assistance. Sitting on boards of directors has attractions for individuals who are challenged by the opportunity for interesting service and wish to contribute to the free enterprise system.

In the small firm, managers often operate in both line and staff capacities.

Inside counsel

The production manager may be the president's chief adviser on present and future manufacturing costs and even on product design. The treasurer or controller may be the counselor on taxes, prices and availability of materials, or wage levels. But this fact does not change the essential nature of line and staff relationships, which are the same in small as in large firms. However, a staff organization suitable for the Ford Motor Company would bankrupt a medium-sized company, and a staff organization suitable for a medium-sized company would be too expensive for a small firm. Thus, one of the arts of good managing is to tailor the application of the various management techniques to the resources available. Practice depends on situations.

Benefits of Staff

Advice on operations

There are, of course, many important benefits in using staff. The necessity of having the advice of well-qualified specialists in various areas of an organization's operations can scarcely be overestimated, especially as operations become more complex. The United States Army learned this the hard way in 1898: in the Spanish-American War, troops were sent into Cuba in woolen uniforms despite the tropical heat and were expected to take territory although they lacked accurate road and topographic maps.

Information about external environment

Staff advice is far more critical for business, government, and other enterprises today, when operating managers are faced with making decisions requiring expert knowledge in economic, technical, political, legal, and social areas. Moreover, it may be necessary, in many instances where highly specialized knowledge is required, to give specialists some functional authority to make decisions for their bosses.

Time for thinking and research

Another major advantage of staff is that these specialists may be allowed the time to think, to gather data, and to analyze, when their superiors, busy managing an operation, cannot do so. It is a rare operating manager, especially at top levels, who has the time, or will take the time, to do those things that a staff assistant can do so well.

Therefore, not only can a staff help line managers to be effective, but, as problems become more complex, staff analysis and advice becomes an urgent necessity. Moreover, despite the dangers of multiple command, even functional authority delegated to staff specialists is often imperative.

Limitations of Staff

Although staff relationships are usually necessary to an enterprise and can do much to make it successful, the nature of staff authority and the difficulty of understanding it lead to certain problems in practice.

Danger of Undermining Line Authority

Operating managers often view staff personnel with skepticism. Too frequently, a president brings in staff executives, clothes them with authority (frequently very vague), and commands all other managers to cooperate. The proposals of staff specialists are received by the president with enthusiasm, and pressure is brought to bear upon the managers involved to put them into effect. What is actually taking place here is that the authority of department managers is being undermined; yet, grudgingly and resentfully, the proposals will be accepted because all will recognize the high tide of the staff specialists' prestige. A continuation of this situation might harm or even destroy operating departments. Capable managers, not willing to submit to indignity or wait until the tide ebbs, might resign; or they might put the matter bluntly to their boss—fire the staff specialists or get along without the line managers!

Operating departments represent the main line of the enterprise, and their managers gain a degree of indispensability. If staff advisers forget that they are to counsel and not to order, if they overlook the fact that their value lies in the extent to which they strengthen line managers, and if—worse yet—they undermine line authority, they risk becoming expendable. If there is an expendable person in an organization, it is likely to be the staff assistant.

Example

In one company, a personnel manager extended his service activities and advisory functions to encompass control over the actual staffing and much of the supervision of subordinates in line departments. For a time, the line managers welcomed this assistance with their personnel problems. But when they realized they no longer controlled their subordinates and when the personnel manager was unwilling to give up control, the resultant outcry forced the president to request his resignation.

Lack of Staff Responsibility

Advisory departments only propose a plan. Others must make the decision to adopt the plan and put it into operation. This creates an ideal situation for shifting blame for mistakes. The staff will claim that it was a good plan and that if failed because the operating manager was unqualified, uninterested, or intent on sabotage. The manager who must make the plan work will claim that it was a poor plan hatched by inexperienced and impractical theorists.

Thinking in a Vacuum

The argument that a staff position gives planners time to think is appealing, but it overlooks the possibility that staff may think in a vacuum because staff people do not implement what they recommend. The alleged impracticality of staff recommendations often results in friction, loss of morale, and even sabotage.

Another weakness in the suggestion that planners must be set off from line departments in order to think is the implication that operating managers are without creative ability. They may, indeed, be without specialized knowledge, but this can be furnished by able staff assistants. Good operating managers can analyze plans, see long-range implications, and spot fatal weaknesses far better than most staff assistants. An intelligent manager will not delegate managerial functions, and it is fatal to managership to strip away real responsibility for activities such as planning and to assign them to a staff assistant.

Managerial Problems

Few would deny the importance of maintaining unity of command. It is not easy for a department head to be responsible to two or more people; at the worker level, it may be disastrous to attempt multiple responsibility. Some disunity in

Multiple authority

command may be unavoidable, since functional authority relationships are often unavoidable. But managers should remain aware of the difficulties of multiple authority and should either limit it—even with the loss of some uniformity or of the fruits of specialization—or else carefully clarify it.

Furthermore, too much staff activity may complicate a line executive's job of leadership and control. A corporation president may be so busy dealing with the recommendations of a large number of staff assistants and straightening twisted lines of authority that time and attention may not be available for operating departments; or a business may become so intent on making policies and setting procedures that there is little time left to make instruments or provide transportation service.

Making Staff Work Effectively

The line-staff problem is not only one of the most difficult that organizations face but also the source of an extraordinarily large amount of inefficiency. Solving this problem requires great managerial skill, careful attention to principles, and patient teaching of personnel.

Understanding Authority Relationships

Line: tell
Staff: sell

Managers must understand the nature of authority relationships if they want to solve the problems of line and staff. So long as managers regard line and staff as groups of people or groupings of activities (for example, service departments), confusion will result. Line and staff are authority relationships and many jobs have elements of both. Line means making decisions and acting on them. Staff relationship, on the other hand, implies the right to assist and counsel. In short, the line may "tell," but the staff must "sell" (its recommendations).

Making Line Listen to Staff

If staff counsel and advice are justifiable at all, it is because of the need for assistance either from experts or from those freed from more pressing duties to give such assistance. Obviously, if staff help is not used, it would make sense to abolish it. Line managers should realize that competent staff assistants offer suggestions to aid and not to undermine or criticize. Although line-staff friction may stem from ineptness or overzealousness on the part of staff people, trouble also arises when line executives too carefully guard their authority and resent the very assistance they need.

Compulsory staff assistance

Line managers should be encouraged or required to consult with staff. Enterprises would do well to adopt the practice of compulsory staff assistance wherein the line must *listen* to staff. At General Motors, for example, product division managers consult with the headquarters staff divisions before proposing a major program or policy to the top executive or the finance committee. They may not be *required* to do so, but they are likely to find that this practice results in smoother sailing for their proposals; and if they can present a united front with the staff division concerned, there will unquestionably be a better chance for the adoption to their proposals.

Keeping Staff Informed

Common criticisms of staff are that specialists operate in a vacuum, fail to appreciate the complexity of the line manager's job, or overlook important facts in making recommendations. To some extent, these criticisms are warranted because specialists cannot be expected to know all the fine points of a manager's job. Specialists should take care that their recommendations deal only with matters within their competence, and operating managers should not lean too heavily on a recommendation if it deals only with part of a problem.

Many criticisms arise because staff assistants are not kept informed on matters within their field. Even the best assistant cannot advise properly in such cases. If line managers fail to inform their staff of decisions affecting its work or if they do not pave the way—through announcements and requests for cooperation—for staff to obtain the requisite information on specific problems, the staff cannot function as intended. In relieving their superiors of the necessity for gathering and analyzing such information, staff assistants largely justify their existence.

Requiring Completed Staff Work

Many staff persons overlook the fact that in order to be most helpful, their recommendations should be complete enough to make possible a simple positive or negative answer by a line manager. Staff assistants should be problem solvers and not problem creators. They create problems for managers when their advice is indecisive or vague, when their conclusions are wrong, when they have not taken into account all the facts or have not consulted the persons seriously affected by a proposed solution, or when they do not point out to superiors the pitfalls as well as the advantages in a recommended course of action.

Completed staff work implies presentation of a clear recommendation based upon full consideration of a problem, clearance with persons importantly affected, suggestions about avoiding any difficulties involved, and, often, preparation of the paperwork—letters, directives, job descriptions, and specifications—so that a manager can accept or reject the proposal without further study, long conferences, or unnecessary work. Should a recommendation be accepted, thorough staff work provides line managers with the machinery to put it into effect. People in staff positions who learn to do these things can find themselves highly valued and appreciated.

Making Staff Work as a Way of Organizational Life

An understanding of staff authority lays the foundation for an organizational way of life. Wherever staff is used, its responsibility is to develop and maintain a climate of favorable personal relations. Essentially, the task of staff assistants is to make responsible line managers "look good" and to help them do a better job. A staff assistant should not attempt to assume credit for an idea. Not only is this a sure way of alienating line teammates who do not like being shown up by a staff assistant, but operating managers who accept ideas actually bear responsibility for implementation of the proposals.

Even under the best of circumstances, it is difficult to coordinate line and staff authority, for people must be persuaded to cooperate. Staff persons must gain and hold the confidence of their fellow workers. They must keep in close touch with operating departments, know their managers and staffs, and understand their problems. They must, through precept and example, convince their line teammates that their prime interest is the welfare of operating managers, and they must downgrade their own contributions while embellishing those of the persons they assist. People in a staff capacity have succeeded in their role when line executives seek their advice and ask them to study their problems.

Summary

There are a number of different bases of power. Power can be: legitimate, expert, referent, reward, or coercive. There are also various ways to conceptualize line and staff. We characterize line and staff by relationships and not by people or by departments. Line is the authority relationship in which the superior is directly responsible for the activities of subordinates. The staff relationship, on the other hand, consists of giving advice and counsel. Functional authority is the right to control *selected* processes, practices, policies, or other matters in departments other than the person's own. Functional authority is a small slice of a line manager's authority and should be used sparingly.

Using staff has limitations because of the danger of undermining line, and the lack of responsibility of staff. There are possibilities of making impractical recommendations and of undermining the unity of command. The managers to whom staff personnel report are responsible for developing an understanding of authority relationships, for making line listen to staff, for keeping staff informed, for demanding completed staff work, and for utilizing staff as a way of organizational life.

Key Ideas and Concepts for Review

Legitimate power	Functional authority
Expert power	Unity of command and functional
Referent power	authority
Reward power	Practice of line and staff
Coercive power	Problems in using staff
Line	Effective staff work
Staff	Completed staff work

For Discussion

1 Select four articles or books in which the terms "line" and "staff" are used. How are they defined? To what extent are the concepts you find the same as or different from those in this book?

2 Why has there been a conflict between line and staff for so long and in so many companies? Can this conflict be removed?

3 Take as examples a number of positions in any kind of enterprise (business, church, government, or elsewhere). Classify them as line or staff.

4 If the task of a person in a purely staff position is to offer advice, how can another individual receiving this advice make sure that it is independent, well researched, and realistic?

5 How many cases of functional authority in organization have you seen? Analyzing a few, do you agree that they could have been avoided? If avoidance had been possible, would you have eliminated them? If they could not have been avoided or if you had not wanted to eliminate them, how would you remove most of the difficulties which might arise?

6 If you were asked to advise a young college graduate who has accepted a staff position as assistant to a factory manager, what suggestions would you make?

CASE 10-1
ABC AIRLINES

The president of ABC Airlines, seeing that costs were getting out of control as the company grew, brought in as an assistant a brilliant young man who was a certified public accountant. The assistant was told about the company's problem of rising costs and asked for his help in solving the problem.

The new assistant gathered a staff of high-quality industrial engineers, financial analysts, and recent top graduates from one of the nation's best-known graduate schools of business administration. After laying out the company's problem, he assigned them to investigate cost problems and management methods in the airline's operations, maintenance, engineering, and sales departments. After a number of studies, the president's assistant found many sources of inefficiency in the various departments and initiated a number of changes in operating practices. In addition, he made many reports to the president outlining in detail the inefficiencies his staff had found and the measures being taken to correct them. These reports also showed, with ample supporting detail, the millions of dollars which his actions were saving the company.

Just as these cost savings programs were being implemented, the vice-presidents in charge of operations, maintenance, engineering, and sales descended on the president and insisted that the assistant be discharged.

1 Why should the assistant who was doing so well be so much resented by the vice-presidents? What went wrong?

2 Assuming that the findings of the assistant and his staff were accurate, what should have been done by the president, the assistant, the vice-presidents, and others to make these findings useful?

CASE 10-2

CONTROLLERSHIP AT INTERNATIONAL SUPERMARKETS, INC.

George Evans is the corporate controller of International Supermarkets, Inc., a position he has held for some 15 years. International is a profitable chain of eighty-eight large supermarkets located in major cities in the United States and Canada. These supermarkets are organized into eight territorial divisions with eleven stores in each region and each division reporting to a regional vice-president to whom the store managers report.

The founder, chairman of the board, and president of International is Allan Adams, who had, over the past 30 years, founded and brilliantly developed seventy of the supermarkets and had acquired in exchange for International common stock eighteen supermarkets, usually from their founders. At headquarters in Los Angeles, Adams has reporting to him the eight regional vice-presidents, the corporate controller (George Evans), and vice-presidents in charge of purchasing, marketing, finance, store development, and personnel. Adams is a typical entrepreneur who had seen the opportunities for lower costs and profits through common purchasing of major items, much television and newspaper advertising, and uniform marketing and personnel policies.

Adams believed in running a tightly disciplined company with careful control over operating expenses, purchases, and capital expenditures. Every store was a profit center and every store budget was personally approved by Adams or his corporate controller, Evans. He and Evans held meetings each month with the group of regional vice-presidents and every 3 months with these officers and the eighty-eight store managers. In setting up budgets and reviewing performance

against them, Adams relied heavily on Evans, with whom he believed very strongly that the job of the corporate controller is to control. He even felt that the corporate controller must be held responsible for profitable performance of the company.

Evans reacted to this responsibility with aggressiveness and care. He insisted that every store budget be personally approved by him and that he approve every store operating expense or capital expenditure above $2000. Because of the heavy burden of being responsible for so many expenditures and for the budgets of eighty-eight large supermarkets, Evans hired eight staff assistants to the corporate controller and vested in each of them authority in one of the eight regions. Each was assigned to act for him in the less important matters in his or her region.

The regional vice-presidents and the store managers understandably felt that Evans was exercising too much authority and that, since each store averaged over $3 million in sales monthly, the corporate controller should not have so much authority.

When Virginia Tilley, an outside director and a long-time friend of Allan Adams, heard of the unhappiness and frustrations of the regional vice-presidents and store managers who felt that the corporate controller should not exercise so much power, she asked Evans why he held such tight rein on these managers and why he vested so much power in his eight staff assistants. Evans' response was that, after all, if he did not exercise this control, the regional vice-presidents and store managers might run their operations with too free a hand and profits would suffer. Moreover, since Mr. Adams held him responsible for profits and since he needed the help of his staff assistants, whom he had hand-picked, he could not meet his responsibilities without exercising tight control over all important expenditures and programs.

1 Who was right in this case, the corporate controller or the vice-presidents and store managers?

2 If you were Virginia Tilley, what would you suggest be done?

3 What was the basic problem here?

For Further Information

Cobb, A. T. "An Episodic Model of Power: Toward an Integration of Theory and Research," *Academy of Management Review*, vol 9, no. 8 (July 1984), pp. 482–493.

Dale, E. *The Great Organizers* (New York: McGraw-Hill Book Company, 1960).

Flax, S. "The Toughest Bosses in America," *Fortune*, Aug. 6, 1984, pp. 18–23.

Gabarro, J. J., and J. P. Kotter. "Managing Your Boss," *Harvard Business Review*, vol. 58, no. 1 (January–February 1980), pp. 92–100.

Henning, D. A., and R. L. Moseley. "Authority Role of a Functional Manager: The Controller," in H. Koontz, C. O'Donnell, and H. Weihrich (eds.), *Management—A Book of Readings*, 5th ed. (New York: McGraw-Hill Book Company, 1980), pp. 340–346.

Kiechel, W. "How to Manage Your Boss," *Fortune*, Sept. 17, 1984, pp. 207–210.

Laurent, A. "Managerial Subordinancy: A Neglected Aspect of Organizational Hierarchies," *Academy of Management Review*, vol. 3, no. 2 (April 1978), pp. 220–230.

Logan. H. H. "Line and Staff: An Obsolete Concept?" in H. Koontz, C. O'Donnell, and H. Weihrich (eds.), *Management—A Book of Readings*, pp. 322–325.

March, J. G., and H. A. Simon. *Organizations* (New York: John Wiley & Sons, Inc., 1958).

Mintzberg, H. "Power and Organization Life Cycles," *Academy of Management Review*, vol. 9, no. 2 (April 1984), pp. 207–224.

Scott, W. G., T. R. Mitchell, and P. H. Birnbaum. *Organization Theory—A Structural and Behavioral Analysis*, 4th ed. (Homewood, Ill: Richard D. Irwin, Inc., 1981).

11

Decentralization of Authority

After reading this chapter, you should understand:

1 The nature of delegation of authority and of centralization and decentralization of authority in organization structures
2 The principles underlying delegation of authority and important factors underlying the practice of delegation
3 The factors that normally determine the degree of decentralization and actions that can and should be undertaken in various circumstances
4 The means of ensuring the degree of decentralization desired and the importance of clarifying delegations
5 The special importance of obtaining balance in practice in the centralization and decentralization of authority.

Definition of decentralization

Organization authority is merely the discretion conferred on people to use their judgement to make decisions and issue instructions. **Decentralization** is the tendency to disperse decision-making authority in an organized structure. It is a fundamental aspect of delegation; to the extent that authority is not delegated, it is centralized. How much should authority be concentrated or dispersed through the organization? There could be absolute centralization of authority in one person. But that implies no subordinate managers and therefore no structured organization. Some decentralization exists in all organizations. On the other hand, there cannot be absolute decentralization, for if managers should delegate *all* their authority, their status as managers would cease, their position would be eliminated, and there would, again, be no organization. Centralization and decentralization

FIGURE 11-1

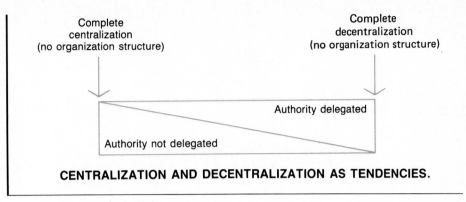

CENTRALIZATION AND DECENTRALIZATION AS TENDENCIES.

are tendencies; they are qualities like "hot" and "cold" as indicated in Figure 11-1.

Degree of decentralization

The **degree of decentralization** is greater:

1 The greater the number of decisions made at lower levels of an organization.

2 The more important the decisions made at lower levels of an organization. For example, the greater the amount of capital expenditure that the plant manager can approve without consulting any superior, the greater the degree of decentralization.

3 The more functions affected by decisions made at lower levels of an organization. Thus companies that permit only manufacturing decisions to be made at separate branch plants are less decentralized than those that also permit financial and personnel decisions to be made at branch plants.

4 The less checking of a decision with others a manager must do. Decentralization is greater when no check at all must be made; it is less when superiors have to be informed of the decision after it has been made; and it is still less if superiors have to be consulted before the decision is made. The fewer people to be consulted, and the lower they are in the management hierarchy, the greater the degree of decentralization.[1]

Centralization

Centralization has been used to describe tendencies other than the dispersal of authority, such as centralization of performance (discussed on page 238). This is a problem of geography: a business characterized by centralized performance operates in a single location or under a single roof. Centralization often refers, furthermore, to departmental activities; service divisions centralize similar or specialized activities in a single department. But when centralization is discussed as

[1]E. Dale, "Planning and Developing the Company Organization Structure," (New York: American Management Association, 1952), Research Report no. 20, p. 107.

an aspect of management, it refers to the tendency of management to restrict delegation of decision making in an organization structure, usually holding authority at or near the top of the organization structure.

*Decentralization
as philosophy
and policy*

Decentralization implies more than delegation: It reflects a philosophy of organization and management. It requires careful selection of which decisions to push down into the organization structure and which to hold near the top, specific policy making to guide the decision making, proper selection and training of people, and adequate controls. A policy of decentralization affects all areas of management and can be looked upon as an essential element of a managerial system. In fact, without it, managers could not use their discretion to handle the ever-changing situations they face.

Delegation of Authority

As simple as delegation of authority appears to be, studies have shown that many managers fail because of poor delegation. For anyone going into any kind of organization, it is worthwhile to study the science and art of delegation.

The primary purpose of delegation is to make organization possible. Just as no one person in an enterprise can do all the tasks necessary for accomplishing a group purpose, so is it impossible, as an enterprise grows, for one person to exercise all the authority for making decisions. As we saw in Chapter 8, there is a limit to the number of persons managers can effectively supervise and for whom they can make decisions. Once this limit has been passed, authority must be delegated to subordinates, who will make decisions within the area of their assigned duties.

**How Authority
Is Delegated**

Authority is delegated when a superior gives a subordinate discretion to make decisions. Clearly, superiors cannot delegate authority they do not have, whether they are board members, presidents, vice-presidents, or supervisors. Nor can superiors delegate all their authority without, in effect, passing on their positions to their subordinates.

The process of delegation involves:

Steps in delegation

1 Determination of results expected from a position

2 Assignment of tasks to a position

3 Delegation of authority for accomplishing these tasks

4 The holding of people in positions responsible for accomplishment of tasks

In practice, it is impossible to split this process, since expecting a person to accomplish goals without the authority to achieve them is unfair, as is the delegation of authority without knowing for what end results it will be used. Moreover, since his or her responsibility cannot be delegated, a boss has no practical alternative but to hold subordinates responsible for completing their assignments.

Clarity of Delegation

Delegations of authority can be specific or general, written or unwritten. If the delegation is unclear, a manager may not understand the nature of the duties or the results expected. The job assignment of a company controller, for example, may specify such functions as accounting, credit control, cash control, financing, export-license handling, and preparation of financial statistics, and these broad functions may even be broken down into more definite duties. Or a controller may be told merely that he or she is expected to do what controllers generally do.

Written delegation

Specific written delegations of authority are extremely helpful both to the manager who receives them and to the person who delegates. The latter will more easily see conflicts or overlaps with other positions and will also be better able to identify those things for which a subordinate can and should be held responsible.

Oral delegation

One top executive claims he never delegates authority but merely tells his subordinate managers to take charge of a department or plant and then holds them responsible for doing so. This particular executive is actually making an extremely broad delegation—that of full discretion to operate as the subordinates see fit. However, in too many cases where such nonspecific delegations are made, subordinates are forced to feel their way and—by testing what the superior will permit—define authority delegation by trial and error. Unless they are very familiar with top company policies and traditions, know the personality of the boss, and exercise sound judgment, they may be placed at a disadvantage. An executive will do well to balance the costs of uncertainty against the effort to make the delegation specific.

Preventing inflexibility

On the other hand, there are those who argue that, especially at the upper levels of management, it is too difficult to make authority delegations specific and that the subordinate, robbed of flexibility, will be unable to develop in the best way. Sometimes, particularly for new top jobs, delegations cannot be very specific, at least at the outset. If a large company hires for the first time a traffic manager at its various plants, the president may be unclear about the amount of authority called for. But this situation should be remedied as soon as possible. One of the first duties of the new appointee should be to establish a description of the job and to clear the description with the superior and, ideally, with those other managers on the same level whose cooperation is necessary. Otherwise, organizational frictions, unnecessary meetings and negotiations, jealousies, and numerous other disadvantages are likely to follow. Too many top executives believe they have a happy team of subordinates who do not need specific authority delegations, when, in fact, they have a jealous group of frustrated managers.

If executives fear that specific delegations will result in inflexibility, they can best meet that fear by developing a tradition of flexibility. It is true that if authority delegations are specific, a manager may regard his or her job as a staked claim with a high fence around it. But executives can eliminate this attitude by making necessary changes in organization structure an accepted and expected thing. When there is resistance to change through definite delegations, much of it comes from managerial laziness and failure to reorganize often enough for the smooth accomplishment of objectives.

Recovery of Delegated Authority

A manager who delegates authority does not permanently dispose of it; delegated authority can always be regained. Reorganization inevitably involves some recovery and redelegation of authority. In a shuffle in an organization, rights are recovered by the responsible head of the firm or a department and then redelegated to managers of new or modified departments; the head of a new department may receive the authority formerly held by other managers. For example, when a reorganization takes quality control responsibility away from a works manager and assigns it to a new manager of quality control reporting to the vice-president in charge of manufacturing, the vice-president has recovered some of the authority formerly delegated to the works manager and has redelegated it, with or without modification, to the new quality control executive.

Principles of Delegation

The following principles are guides to delegation of authority. When they are not carefully practiced, delegation may be ineffective, organization may fail, and poor managing may result.

Principle of delegation by results expected   Since authority is intended to furnish managers with a tool for managing so as to ensure that objectives are achieved, *authority delegated to all individual managers should be adequate to ensure their ability to accomplish results expected.* Too many managers try to partition and define authority on the basis of the rights to be delegated or withheld, rather than looking first at the goals to be achieved and then determining how much discretion is necessary to achieve them. In no other way can a manager delegate authority in accordance with the responsibility exacted.

Principle of functional definition   In order to set up departments, executives must group activities to facilitate accomplishment of goals, and managers of each subdivision must have authority to coordinate subdivision activities with those of the organization as a whole. These requirements give rise to the **principle of functional definition:** *The more a position or a department has clear definitions of results expected, activities to be undertaken, organization authority delegated, and authority and informational relationships with other positions, the more adequately the responsible individuals can contribute toward accomplishing enterprise objectives.* To ignore this principle is to risk confusion as to what is expected of whom. This principle—which involves both delegation and departmentation—although simple, is often difficult to apply. To define a job and delegate authority to do it requires, in most cases, patience, intelligence, and clear objectives and plans. It is obviously difficult to define a job if the superior does not know what results are desired.

Scalar principle   The **scalar principle** refers to the chain of direct authority relationships from superior to subordinate throughout the organization. *The clearer the line of authority from the ultimate management position in an enterprise to every* *subordinate position, the clearer will be the responsibility for decision making and the more effective organization communication will be.*

A clear understanding of the scalar principle is necessary for proper organization functioning because subordinates must know who delegates authority to them and to whom matters beyond their own authority must be referred. Although the chain of command may be safely detoured for purposes of obtaining information, departure for purposes of decision making tends to destroy the decision-making system and, by doing so, to undermine managership itself.

Authority-level principle   Functional definition plus the scalar principle gives rise to the authority-level principle. Clearly, at some organization level, authority exists for making a decision within an organization's power. Therefore, the **authority-level principle** we can derive is: *Maintenance of intended delegation requires that decisions within the authority of individuals be made by them and not be referred upward in the organizations structure.* In other words, managers at each level should make whatever decisions are within their delegated authority, and only matters that they cannot decide because of limitations on their authority should be referred to superiors.

A fairly common complaint among top executives is that while they know the importance of delegating downward, they are concerned with the practice of subordinates delegating upward. In other words, as chief executives, they assign a problem only to find it back on their desks in a few days or weeks. The answer is, of course, not to permit these problems to come upward. If discretion to make a decision has been properly delegated, superiors must resist the temptation to make that decision. Subordinates can quickly see when a boss is willing to make decisions that should have been made by the subordinates themselves (see Figure 11-2).

It is obvious from the authority-level principle that if managers wish to make effective authority delegations and thereby to be relieved from some of the burden of decision making, they must make sure that delegations are clear and that subordinates understand them. They should also avoid the temptation to make decisions for subordinates.

Principle of unity of command   A basic management principle is the **principle of unity of command:** *The more complete an individual's reporting relationship to a single superior, the less the problem of conflicting instructions and the greater the feeling of personal responsibility for results.* In discussing delegation of authority, it has been assumed that the power of exercising discretion over a particular activity will flow from a single superior to a subordinate. Although it is possible for a subordinate to receive authority from two or more superiors and, therefore, to be held responsible by them, the practical difficulties of serving two or more masters are obvious. An obligation is essentially personal, and authority delegation by more than one person to an individual is likely to result in conflicts in both authority and responsibility.

The principle of unity of command is useful in the clarification of authority-responsibility relationships. A company president, for example, does not normally

FIGURE 11-2

Once authority has been delegated to a manager . . .

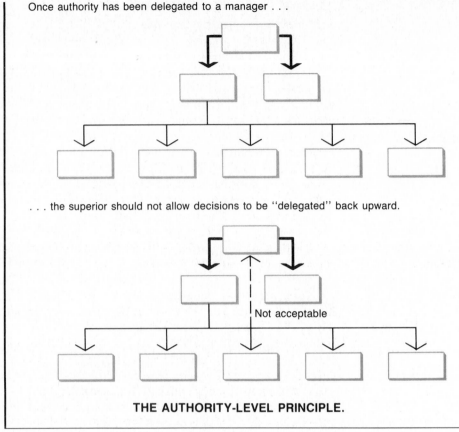

. . . the superior should not allow decisions to be "delegated" back upward.

Not acceptable

THE AUTHORITY-LEVEL PRINCIPLE.

divide sales activities among sales, manufacturing, public relations, finance, accounting, and personnel, with no single person responsible for the activities. Instead, since selling activities are a cohesive activity, assignment is made to the sales manager. Unity of command would not exist if, instead of a single sales manager, the president appointed an executive committee to run the department. To force every major subordinate in the sales department to owe full obligation to each committee member rather than to one manager would produce confusion, buck-passing, and general inefficiency. Similarly, it is undesirable to have several managers assign duties to one employee, who would then be obligated to each of the several bosses for each specific assignment. The principle of unity of command is sometimes disregarded for what are believed to be compelling reasons. (Note, in Chapter 10, the case of functional authority.)

Principles of absoluteness of responsibility   Since responsibility, being an obligation owed, cannot be delegated, no superior can escape, through delegation, responsibility for the activities of subordinates, for it is the superior who has delegated authority and assigned duties. *The responsibility of subordinates to their superiors for performance is absolute, once they have accepted an assignment and the right to carry it out, and superiors cannot escape responsibility for the organization activities of their subordinates.* The terms "responsibility" and "accountability" are often used interchangeably. Strictly speaking, as the military agencies are well aware, accountability is used to denote a special kind of responsibility. In the military, an officer is said to be "accountable" for material and equipment, but "responsible" for the actions of troops reporting to him or her.

Principle of parity of authority and responsibility   Since authority is the discretionary right to carry out assignments and responsibility is the obligation to accomplish them, it logically follows that the amount of authority should correspond to the amount of responsibility. From this rather obvious logic is derived the principle that *the responsibility for actions cannot be greater than that implied by authority delegated, nor should it be less.* The president of a firm may, for example, assign duties, such as buying raw materials and machine tools and hiring subordinates in order to meet certain goals, to the manufacturing vice-president. The vice-president will be unable to perform these duties unless given enough discretion to meet this responsibility.

Managers often try to hold subordinates responsible for duties for which they do not have the necessary authority. This is, of course, unfair. Sometimes sufficient authority is delegated, but the delegant is not held responsible for its proper use. This is, obviously, a case of poor managerial direction and control and has no bearing upon the principle of parity.

Managers are sometimes said to be given authority to do that for which they cannot be held responsible; thus, sales managers are given authority to sell, but cannot be responsible for making people buy. However, sales managers have authority to use certain material and human resources to obtain sales wherever possible. Here, parity consists of their responsibility as executives for managing the sales force in the best possible way, equated with the authority to sell.

The Art of Delegation

Most failures in effective delegation occur not because managers do not understand the nature and principles of delegation but because they are unable or unwilling to apply them. Delegation is, in a way, an elementary act of managing. Yet, as pointed out at the start of this chapter, studies of managerial failures almost invariably find that poor or inept delegation is at or near the top of the list of causes. Much of the reason lies in personal attitudes toward delegation.

Personal Attitudes toward Delegation   Although charting an organization and outlining managerial goals and duties will help in making delegations, and knowledge of the principles of delegation will furnish a basis for it, certain personal attitudes underlie the making of real delegations.

1 Receptiveness   An underlying attribute of managers who will delegate authority is a willingness to give other people's ideas a chance. Decision making always involves some discretion, and a subordinate's decision is not likely to be exactly the one a superior would have made. The manager who knows how to delegate must have a minimum of the "NIH (not invented here) factor" and must be able not only to welcome the ideas of others but also to help others and to compliment them on their ingenuity.

2 Willingness to let go   A manager who will effectively delegate authority must be willing to release the right to make decisions to subordinates. A great fault of some managers who move up the executive ladder—or of the pioneer who has built a large business from the small beginning of, say, a garage machine shop—is that they want to continue to make decisions for the positions they have left. Corporate presidents and vice-presidents who insist upon confirming every purchase or the appointment of every laborer or secretary do not realize that doing so takes their time and attention from far more important decisions.

Where the size or complexity of the organization forces delegation of authority, managers should realize that there is a kind of law of comparative managerial advantage, somewhat like the law of comparative economic advantage that applies to nations. Well known to economists and logically sound, the law of comparative economic advantage states that a country's wealth will be enhanced if it exports what it produces most efficiently and imports what it produces least efficiently, even though it could produce such imports more cheaply than any other nation. Likewise, managers will enhance their contributions to the firm if they concentrate on tasks that contribute most to the firm's objectives and assign to subordinates other tasks, even though they could accomplish the latter better themselves. This rule is hard to practice, but failure to do so defeats the very purpose of delegation.

3 Willingness to let other make mistakes   Although no responsible manager would sit idly by and let a subordinate make a mistake that might endanger the company or the subordinate's position in the company, continual checking on the subordinate to ensure that no mistakes are ever made will make true delegation impossible. As everyone makes mistakes, a subordinate must be allowed to make some, and their cost must be considered an investment in personal development.

Serious or repeated mistakes can be largely avoided without nullifying delegation or hindering development of a subordinate. Patient counseling, asking leading or discerning questions, and carefully explaining the objectives and policies are among the tools available to the manager who would delegate well. None of these techniques involves discouraging subordinates with intimidating criticism or harping on their shortcomings.

4 Willingness to trust subordinates   Superiors have no alternative to trusting their subordinates, for delegation implies a trustful attitude between the two. This trust is sometimes hard to come by. A superior may put off delegation with the thought that subordinates are not well enough seasoned, that they cannot handle people, that they have not yet developed judgment, or that they do not appreciate all the facts bearing on a situation. Sometimes these considerations are true, but then a superior should either train subordinates or else select others who are prepared to assume the responsibility. Too often, however, bosses distrust their subordinates because they do not wish to let go, do not delegate wisely, or do not know how to set up controls to assure proper use of the authority.

5 Willingness to establish and use broad controls   Since superiors cannot delegate responsibility for performance, they should not delegate authority unless they are willing to find means of getting feedback, that is, of assuring themselves that the authority is being used to support enterprise or department goals and plans. Obviously, controls cannot be established and exercised unless goals, policies, and plans are used as basic standards for judging the activities of subordinates. More often than not, reluctance to delegate and to trust subordinates comes from the superior's not having planned carefully enough and having an understandable fear of loss of control.

Guides for Overcoming Weak Delegations

Unclear delegations, partial delegations, delegations inconsistent with the results expected, and the hovering of superiors who refuse to allow subordinates to use their authority are among the many widely found weaknesses in delegation of authority.

Combine with these weaknesses untrained, inept, or weak subordinates who go to their bosses for decisions and subordinates who will not accept responsibility, plus lack of plans, planning information, and incentives, and the frequent failure of delegation is partly explained. All that this means, as is so generally the case in managing, is that delegation does not stand alone, but is related to other things in the whole system of managing. But most of the responsibility for weak delegation lies with superiors and, primarily, with top managers. The following are five practical guides to making delegation real:

1   Define assignments and delegate authority in the light of results expected. Or, to put it another way, grant sufficient authority to make possible the accomplishment of goal assignments.

2   Select the person in the light of the job to be done. Although the good organizer will approach delegation primarily from the standpoint of the task to be accomplished, in the final analysis, staffing as a part of the total system of delegation cannot be ignored.

3   Maintain open lines of communication. Since the superior does not delegate all authority or abdicate responsibility and since managerial independence therefore does not exist, decentralization should not lead to insulation. There should be a free flow of information between superior and subordinate, furnishing subordinates information with which to make decisions and to interpret properly authority delegated. Delegations, then, do depend on situations.

4   Establish proper controls. Because no manager can relinquish responsibility, delegations should be accompanied by techniques to make sure the authority

is properly used. But if controls are not to interfere with delegation, they must be relatively broad and designed to show deviations from plans rather than interfere with routine actions of subordinates.

5 Reward effective delegation and successful assumption of authority. Managers should be ever-watchful for means of rewarding both effective delegation and effective assumption of authority. Although many of these rewards will be monetary, the granting of greater discretion and prestige—both in a given position and by promotion to a higher position—is often even more of an incentive.

Factors Determining the Degree of Decentralization of Authority

Managers cannot ordinarily be for or against decentralization of authority. They may *prefer* to delegate authority, or they may like to make all the decisions. A despot in a certain large enterprise in this country, who would like to make all the decisons, finds that he cannot. Even the autocrat in a smaller enterprise is often forced to delegate some authority.

Although the temperament of individual managers influences the extent of authority delegation, other factors also affect it. Most of them are beyond the control of individual managers. Managers may resist their influence, but no successful manager can ignore them.

1 Costliness of the Decision

Perhaps the overriding factor determining the extent of decentralization is, as in other aspects of policy, costliness. As a general rule, the more costly the action to be decided on, the more probable it is that the decision will be made at the upper levels of management. Cost may be reckoned directly in dollars and cents or in such intangibles as the company's reputation, its competitive position, or employee morale. Thus, an airline decision to purchase airplanes will be made at the top levels, while the decision to purchase desks may be made in the second or third echelon of an operating department. Quality control in drug manufacturing, where a mistake might endanger lives, to say nothing of the company's reputation, would normally report at a high level, while the quality inspection in toy manufacturing might report much lower.

The fact that the cost of a mistake affects decentralization is not necessarily based on the assumption that top managers make fewer mistakes than subordinates. They *may* make fewer mistakes, since they are probably better trained and in possession of more facts, but the controlling reason is the weight of responsibility. As we have already discussed, delegating authority is not delegating responsibility; therefore, managers typically prefer not to delegate authority for crucial decisions.

The need for top control depends on the area of decision. In the typical large business, top managers may reasonably feel that they cannot delegate authority over the expenditure of capital funds. The financial aspects of General Motors' operations are centralized under an executive vice-president, who reports to the chairman or vice-chairman of the board of directors rather than to the president. This is a living example of the importance of centralization in this area.

2 Desire for Uniformity of Policy

Those who value consistency above all invariably favor centralized authority, since this is the easiest road to such a goal. They may wish to ensure that customers will be treated alike with respect to quality, price, credit, delivery, and service; that the same policies will be followed in dealing with suppliers; or that public relations policies will be standardized.

Uniform policy also has certain internal advantages. For example, standardized accounting, statistics, and financial records make it easier to compare relative efficiencies of departments and keep down costs. The administration of a union contract is facilitated by uniform policy with respect to wages, promotions, vacations, dismissals, and similar matters. Taxes and government regulation entail fewer worries and less chance of error with uniform policies.

Yet many enterprises go to considerable length to make sure that some policies will not be completely uniform. Many companies encourage variety in all except major matters, hoping that out of such nonuniformity may come managerial innovation, progress, competition among organizational units, improved morale and efficiency, and a supply of promotable managers.

3 Size of the Organization

The larger the organization, the more decisions to be made, and the more places in which they must be made, the more difficult it is to coordinate them. These complexities of organization may require policy questions to be passed up the line and discussed not only with many managers in the chain of command but also with many managers at each level, since horizontal agreement may be as necessary as vertical clearance.

Slow decisions—slow because of the number of specialists and managers who must be consulted—are costly. To minimize this cost, authority should be decentralized wherever feasible. Indeed, the large enterprise that prides itself on the right kind of decentralization is recognizing the inevitable, although the extent and effectiveness of decentralization may differ widely among companies, depending largely upon the quality of their management.

The costs of large size may be reduced by organizing an enterprise into a number of units, such as product or territorial divisions. Considerable increases in efficiency are likely to result from making the unit small enough for *its* top executives to be near the point where decisions are made. This makes speedy decisions possible, keeps executives from spending time coordinating their decisions with many others, reduces the amount of paperwork, and improves the quality of decisions by reducing them to manageable proportions.

Exactly what this unit size is cannot be arbitrarily stated. Some managers believe it to be 1000 persons, others believe it to be closer to 100 or 250, and some would hold that 2500 employees can be grouped into manageable divisions, each with considerable decentralized authority. In any case, there is evidence that where the unit exceeds a certain size the distance from top to bottom may impair the quality and speed of decision making.

Also important in determining size is the character of a unit. For decentralization to be thoroughly effective, a unit must possess a certain economic and managerial self-sufficiency. Functional departments, such as sales or manufacturing or engineering, cannot be independent units, while product or territorial departments of the same size can be, encompassing as they do nearly all the functions of an enterprise. It therefore follows that if the uneconomic aspects of size are to be reduced, it is preferable to departmentize along product, territorial, or distribution channel lines.

In the zeal to overcome the disadvantages of size by reducing the size of the decision-making unit, certain shortcomings of decentralization should not be overlooked. When authority is decentralized, a lack of policy uniformity and of coordination may follow. The branch, product division, or other self-sufficient unit may be so preoccupied with its objectives as to lose sight of those of the enterprise as a whole.

4 History and Culture of the Enterprise

Whether authority will be decentralized frequently depends upon the way the business has been built. Those enterprises which, in the main, expand from within—such as Marshall Field and Company and International Harvester Company—show a marked tendency to keep authority centralized, as do those which expand under the direction of their owner-founders. The Ford Motor Company was, under its founder, an extraordinary case of centralized authority; Henry Ford, Sr., prided himself on having no organizational titles in the top management except that of president and general manager, insisting, to the extent he could, that every major decision in that vast company be made by himself.

On the other hand, enterprises that result from mergers and consolidations are likely to show, at least at first, a definite tendency to retain decentralized authority, especially if the unit acquired is already operating profitably. To be sure, this tendency not to rock the boat may be politically inspired rather than based purely on managerial considerations. Certainly, the claim to independence of the once-independent units is especially strong, and many years may have to pass before the chief executive of the consolidated company dares materially to reduce the degree of decentralization.

In some cases, the first influence of a merger or an acquisition may be toward increased centralization. If the controlling group wishes to put in its own management or take immediate advantage of the economies of combined operation, the requirements of policy uniformity and quick action may necessitate centralization.

5 Management Philosophy

The character and philosophy of top executives have an important influence on the extent to which authority is decentralized. Sometimes top managers are despotic, tolerating no interference with the authority they jealously hoard. At other times, top managers keep authority not merely to gratify a desire for status or power but because they simply cannot give up the activities and authorities they enjoyed before they reached the top or before the business expanded from an owner-manager shop.

In many cases, top managers may see decentralization as a way of organizational life that takes advantage of the innate desire of people to create, to be free, and to have status. Many successful top managers find in it a means to harness the desire for freedom to economic efficiency, much as the free enterprise system has been responsible for this country's remarkable industrial progress. To give an example of this attitude, General Robert E. Wood, former chairman of the Board of Sears, Roebuck and Company, said:

Wood's philosophy at Sears

> We complain about government in business, we stress the advantages of the free enterprise system, we complain about the totalitarian state, but in our industrial organizations, in our striving for efficiency, we have created more or less of a totalitarian organization in industry—particularly in large industry.[2]

Retaining efficiency and discipline while allowing people to express themselves, to exercise initiative, and to have some voice in the affairs of the organization is the greatest problem large organizations have to solve.

6 Desire for Independence

Individuals and groups often desire a degree of independence from bosses who are far away. It is not at all unusual for West Coast divisions or subsidiaries of companies headquartered in New York to feel somewhat hostile toward directives coming from headquarters managers who are believed not to know West Coast conditions. For example the American Telephone and Telegraph Corporation, headquartered in New York, has found it difficult at times to control the actions of its subsidiary, the Pacific Telephone and Telegraph Corporation.

Individuals may become frustrated by delay in getting decisions, by long lines of communication, and by the great game of passing the buck. This frustration can lead to dangerous loss of good people, to jockeying by the office politician, and to an attitude of "not rocking the boat" by the less competent seeker of security.

7 Availability of Managers

A real shortage of managers would limit decentralization of authority, since in order to delegate, superiors must have qualified managers to whom to give authority. But too often the scarcity of good managers is used as an excuse for centralizing authority; executives who complain that they have no one to whom they can delegate authority are often trying to magnify their own value to the firm or are confessing a failure to develop subordinates.

There are also managers who believe that a firm should centralize authority because it will then need very few good managers. One difficulty is that the firm that so centralizes authority may not be able to train managers to take over the duties of the top executives, and external sources must be relied upon to furnish necessary replacements.

The key to safe decentralization is adequate training of managers. By the same token, decentralization is perhaps the most important key to training. Many large firms whose size makes decentralization a necessity consciously push decision making down into the organization for the purpose of developing managers; they

---

[2]Dale, op. cit., p. 116.

feel that the best training is actual experience. Since this policy usually carries with it chances for mistakes by a novice, it is good practice to limit, at least initially, the importance of the decisions so delegated.

8 Control Techniques

Another factor affecting the degree of decentralization is the state of development of control techniques. A good manager at any level of the organization cannot delegate authority without having some way of knowing whether it will be used properly. Because some managers do not know how to control, they are unwilling to delegate authority. They may think that it takes more time to correct a mistake than to do the job themselves.

Improvements in statistical devices, accounting controls, and other techniques have helped make possible the current trend toward considerable managerial decentralization. Even the most ardent supporters of decentralization, such as General Motors, Du Pont, and Sears, could hardly take so favorable a view without adequate techniques to show managers, from the top down, whether performance is conforming to plans. To decentralize is not to lose control, and to push decision making down into the organization is not to walk away from responsibility.

9 Decentralized Performance

"Decentralized performance" refers to the situation where the operators of a company or other organization are spread over a geographic area. This is basically a technical matter depending upon such factors as the economies of division of labor, the opportunities for using machines, the nature of the work to be performed (a railroad has no choice but to spread its performance), and the location of raw materials, labor supply, and consumers. This geographic decentralization influences the centralization of authority.

Authority tends to be decentralized when performance is decentralized, if for no other reason than that the absentee manager is unable to manage, although there are exceptions. For example, some of the large chain store enterprises are characterized by widely decentralized performance, and yet the local manager of a store may have little or no authority over pricing, advertising and merchandising methods, inventory and purchasing, or product line, all of which may be controlled from a central or regional office. The head of a local manufacturing plant of a large organization may have little authority beyond the right to hire and fire, and even then action may be limited by company policy and procedure and by the authority of a centralized personnel department. At the same time, the decentralization of performance limits the ability to centralize authority. The most dictatorial top manager of a national organization based in New York cannot supervise the San Francisco plant as closely as if it were adjacent to the home office.

It does not follow that when performance is centralized, authority is centralized. True, authority can be more easily centralized if performance is, and if a company wishes tight control over decision making, centralized performance will aid this. But there are too many other factors for geographic concentration to have a controlling influence in centralization. Here, again, what is done depends on situations, or contingencies.

10 Business Dynamics: The Pace of Change

The pace of change of an enterprise also affects the degree to which authority may be decentralized. If a business is growing fast and facing complex problems of expansion, its managers, particularly those responsible for top policy, may be forced to make a large share of the decisions. But, strangely enough, this very dynamic condition may force these managers to delegate authority and take a calculated risk on the costs of error. Generally this dilemma is resolved in the direction of delegation, and, in order to avoid delegation to untrained subordinates, close attention is given to rapid formation of policies and the acceleration of training in management. An alternative often adopted is to slow the rate of change, including the cause of fast change, expansion. Many top managers have found that the critical factor limiting their ability to meet change and expand a business or other enterprise is the lack of trained personnel to whom authority may be delegated.

In old, well-established, or slow-moving businesses, there is a natural tendency to centralize or recentralize authority. When few major decisions must be made, the advantages of uniform policy and the economies of having a few well-qualified persons make the decisions cause authority to be centralized. This may explain why, in some banks and insurance companies and in certain railroads, decentralization is not extensive. Nevertheless, in slow-moving businesses too much centralization may carry danger. New discoveries, vigorous competition from an unexpected source, and political change are only a few of the factors that might introduce conditions requiring change, and if they occur, an overcentralized firm may not be able to meet a situation as well as if authority were decentralized.

11 Environmental Influences

The factors determining the extent of decentralization that we have dealt with so far are largely factors within the enterprise. However, the economics of decentralization of performance and the character of change include elements well beyond the control of an enterprise's managers. In addition, there are definite external forces affecting the extent of decentralization. Among the most important of these are governmental controls, national unionism, and tax policies.

Government regulations

Government regulation of many facets of business policy makes decentralization difficult and sometimes impossible. If prices are regulated, sales managers cannot be given much real freedom in determining them. If materials are allocated and restricted, purchasing and factory managers are not free to buy or use any they might wish. If labor may be asked to work only a limited number of hours at a given rate of pay, the local division manager cannot freely set hours and wages.

But restriction on decentralization goes further. Top management itself no longer has authority over many aspects of policy and cannot, therefore, delegate authority it does not have. Much authority in areas controlled by government action could still be decentralized. But managers often do not dare trust subordinates to interpret government regulations, especially since the penalties and the public criticism for breaking laws are so serious and since interpretation of most laws is a matter for the specialist.

National unions

In the same way, the rise of national unions in the past decades has had a centralizing influence on business. So long as department or division managers can negotiate the terms of a labor contract by dealing either with local unions or with employees directly, authority to negotiate may be delegated by top management to these subordinates. But where, as is increasingly the case, a national union enters into a collective bargaining contract with headquarters management, with the terms of the contract applicable to all workers of a company wherever located, a company cannot chance decentralization of certain decision making any more than it can in the case of government controls.

Tax systems

The tax systems of the national, state, and local governments have had a marked regulatory effect on business. The tax collector, especially the federal income tax collector, sits at the elbow of every executive who makes a decision involving funds. The impact of taxation is often a policy-determining factor that overshadows such traditional business considerations as plant expansion, marketing policies, and economical operations. Uniformity of tax policy becomes of primary importance to company management. This spells centralization because managers without appropriate tax advice cannot be expected to make wise decisions. It may even require a central tax department acting not only in an advisory capacity and as a tax service agency but also with a high degree of functional authority over matters with tax implications.

Recentralization of Authority

At times an enterprise can be said to recentralize authority—to centralize authority once decentralized. **Recentralization** is normally not a complete reversal of decentralization, for the authority delegations are not wholly withdrawn by the managers who made them. The process is a centralization of authority over a certain type of activity or a certain kind of function, wherever in the organization it may be found.

Thus, the growing importance of taxes, the requirements of uniform labor policy, and the realities of government regulation may dictate that authority over these areas be recentralized or managed by a department with functional authority over them. This recentralization may also occur when, through growth and extensive decentralization, top managers feel that they have lost control over the business. Or, if a business falls on difficult times, managers may wish to reinforce their authority over the expenditure of funds, the level of costs, or the character of the sales effort. As the president of highly decentralized Boise Cascade Company said when the company got in trouble several years ago: "In a storm, the captain must be at the helm." Such recentralization, sometimes intended to be temporary, often becomes permanent. Many top managers take pride in their cost control, budget, or internal auditing departments and in the authority of these departments not only to advise but also to supervise many powers previously vested in lower managers.

Obtaining the Desired Degree of Decentralization

To this point we have assumed that managers can obtain the degree of decentralization upon which they have decided. In other words, we have emphasized how much decentralization to have, rather than whether the desired degree can be realized and maintained.

Many managers who believe that authority should be pushed down in an organization as far as it will go are faced with the practical problem of how to push it down there. It is a rare top manager who does not find in the organization somewhere an authority hoarder who simply will not delegate. In one company, a division controller once had an office piled high with major policy matters requiring attention, while he engaged in minute examination of employees' expense accounts, excusing himself with the statement that none of this work could be entrusted to his subordinates.

Understanding decentralization

In order to obtain the degree of decentralization they want, top managers must understand decentralization; understanding is based upon the knowledge that decentralization cannot mean independence, that it requires establishment of policies to guide decision making along desired courses, that it needs careful delegation of authority by managers who know how and who want to delegate, and that it must be accompanied by controls designed to ensure that delegated authority is used properly. Although the art of authority delegation is basic to proper decentralization, it is apparent that the mere act of delegation is not enough to ensure decentralization.

Verifiable objectives

No manual can indicate how to ensure that authority is properly decentralized or appropriately withheld, but several techniques may be used with some chance of success. One of the most effective of these is to ensure that a system of verifiable objectives is established, that each person is held responsible for achieving certain goals, and that each is given the necessary authority for doing so. Another is merely a technique of organization—providing a statement of each manager's duties and of the responsibility and the degree of authority delegated to that manager. Besides being clear and, preferably, written, the statements should be issued in such a way that any employees may know what they contain if they need to know.

Teaching

Another important technique is the example and teaching of a superior, starting at the top of the organization. The character of top leadership in an enterprise affects everyone in an organization. There are in every firm of any size those who will reach out for power, intrude upon activities assigned to others, and bully the timid. Rules and job descriptions are often subject to differences in interpretation, which can be conveniently stretched or limited depending upon the politics in an organization. Their unreliability, despite their obvious usefulness, stands as a warning to executives that the most dependable foundation for achieving a desired degree of decentralization is the education of subordinate managers in the rights of others—teaching them restraint as well as aggressiveness.

One of the means of forcing delegation of authority, particularly in middle and lower levels of organization, is to require managers to have a large number of subordinates and, at the same time, to hold them to a high standard of per-

Span of
management

formance. When the span of management is stretched, there is no alternative but to delegate authority. In order to protect their own performance, managers learn to select good subordinate managers, train them well, establish clear-cut policies, and find efficient means of control. This is said to be the longtime practice of Sears, Roebuck and Company, where store managers are encouraged to have many department managers reporting to them.

Promotion policy

Another technique used to force decentralization has been the policy of promoting managers only when they have subordinates able to take their places. To accomplish this end, managers are forced to delegate authority. Moreover, this policy removes a major cause of hoarding authority, the desire of managers to become indispensable by making sure that their duties cannot be handled by any of their subordinates.

Occasionally the problem is how to retain a predetermined degree of authority. Division and branch managers—because they are far away from the home office, often wish to build empires, or want to do a complete job—may assume too much authority and resent the outside auditor, sabotage centralized controls, and oppose central management. The answer to this problem, of course, is primarily one of leadership, clear policy determination, and delegation of authority to and proper training of subordinate managers. But perhaps the principal problem lies in the character of the top executives. If they sit on the fence, do not support the authority delegations they have made, ignore the organization structure, overlook serious deviations from policy, and neglect in other ways to do a thorough managerial job, little can be done to retain any predetermined degree of decentralization.

Clarifying Decentralization: Chart of Approval Authorization

As in so many areas of managing, conflict, friction, and inefficiencies result from lack of clarification of individual roles. This is nowhere more true in practice than in clarifying the extent and nature of decentralization. This problem can be greatly simplified by means of a chart of executive approval authorizations. The chart is a technique by which the various authority delegations of a company are specified. Since most of these delegations have to do with the right to commit the company for money, most of the chart has to do with expenditure limits. However, there are other matters, such as certain policies and programs, which can be and often are shown on such a chart.

An excerpt of a chart of approval authorization for a small to medium-sized company is shown in Table 11-1. A list of major decisions (*nature of transaction* in the table) appears on the left-hand side of the chart. This company found it useful to group these decisions under the classifications of personnel, operating expenses, capital expenditures and commitments, prices and sales commitments, and general. Table 11-1 illustrates the first and the last categories. Across the top of the chart are listed the various managers who have authority to make these decisions along with certain staff or operating personnel who have functional authority or whose consultation is required for advice or information.

The authority and responsibility for developing a chart must rest at the top of a company. Because the chart even distinguishes between decisions that the board of directors reserves for itself and those delegated to operating management, the board must necessarily be called upon to approve at least this area of delegation. An effective board may wish to do more. If its organizational policy is really one of decentralization, with centralized decision making in only certain matters at the top, it may wish to approve the entire chart, or at least enough of it to assure itself that its policy is being followed.

Advantages

In addition to promoting clarity, the chart has other advantages. It acts as a means of communicating the entire structure of decision making in a company so that people down the line, or in departments whose coordination in a decision is necessary, can see what the decision-making relationships are. Also, in a multi-division company, if there are separate divisional charts as well as a corporate chart, authority may be delegated in varying degrees. Thus, in a large division, more authority may be delegated; or in a division staffed by less experienced managers, a smaller degree of authority could be delegated. A further advantage is that authority delegations can be changed with greater ease than when they are included in a number of individual position descriptions.

Although the chart of approval authorizations is only a tool, it is an essential one. If it is to work, it should be made a way of life in an enterprise; it must be updated whenever there is any significant change in organization structure or authority delegation and must be communicated to all those in decision making positions. Along with position descriptions and the formulation of verifiable goals for each position in an enterprise, it helps define the roles which individuals must fill.

Balance: The Key to Decentralization

To avoid pitfalls, any program for decentralization of authority must take into consideration the advantages and limitations summarized in Table 11-2. There are, in addition, several other matters to be considered.

Forces favoring decentralization

Strong forces favor the practice of decentralization. The nature of organized effort requires coordination of people at every level, and most of the managers responsible for coordination are employed at middle and lower organization levels; they cannot function without the authority to manage. The growing size of the average organized activity requires an increasing number of managers. And while enterprises do not decentralize in order to develop managers, it is nevertheless quite true that managers will not be developed internally unless they have an opportunity to exercise authority. Moreover, the presence of large numbers of well-educated and ambitious young people in an enterprise provides a steady pressure on top managers to decentralize.

Limitations of decentralization

At the same time, extensive decentralization is not to be blindly undertaken. In many organizations, the size and complexity of operations do not require it. Decentralization is not without cost, even in larger companies. In addition to the dangers from nonuniform policy and the problems of control, there are often real

TABLE 11-1 Chart of Approval Authorization (excerpt)*

Nature of transaction	Department manager	Staff manager	Division director	President (corporate, domestic), board chairperson (international)	Board of directors
Personnel					
Employment of new personnel:					
Hourly	All	Personnel manager to process and review for consistency with company policy	All exceptions to company policy		
Salaried	All	Personnel manager to process	All over $2000 per month	All over $3000 per month	All over $5000 per month
Wage and salary increases:					
Hourly	All	Personnel manager to process and review for consistency with company policy	All exceptions to company policy		
Salaried	All	Personnel manager to process	All	All resulting in salary over $3000 per month	All resulting in salary over $5000 per month
Moving expenses		To be processed by controller	All	All over $2000 in cost	
Leaves of absence	All	Personnel manager to process	All	All over 30 days	All over 60 days

Operating expenses

Procurement of materials and services (approval of manufacturing and engineering schedule by vice president of manufacturing and engineering):		
In accordance with approved schedules	Manager of purchasing on all	All
Not in accordance with approved schedules	Vice-president of manufacturing and engineering on all. Controller on all exceeding $10,000	

General

Bank loans for company operations		
Line of credit	Vice-president—finance on all	All
Loans within line	Vice-president—finance on all	
Loan for buildings and land	Vice-president—finance on all	All
Acquisition of financial interest in or loan to any company	Vice-president—finance	All

*A person required to approve transactions as outlined in the above chart may authorize another person to sign in case of his or her absence. The person so authorized must affix the proper signature showing his or her initials under such signatures.

Source: H. Koontz, *The Board of Directors and Effective Management* (New York: McGraw-Hill Book Company, 1967), pp. 46–49. (Certain limits revised in 1983.)

TABLE 11-2 Advantages and Limitations of Decentralization

Advantages of decentralization

1 Relieves top management of some burden of decision making and forces upper-level managers to let go.
2 Encourages decision making and assumption of authority and responsibility.
3 Gives managers more freedom and independence in decision making.
4 Promotes establishment and use of broad controls which may increase motivation.
5 Makes comparison of performance of different organizational units possible.
6 Facilitates setting up of profit centers.
7 Facilitates product diversification.
8 Promotes development of general managers.
9 Aids in adaptation to fast-changing environment.

Limitations of decentralization

1 Makes it more difficult to have a uniform policy
2 Increases complexity of coordination of decentralized organizational units.
3 May result in loss of some control by upper-level managers.
4 May be limited by inadequate control techniques.
5 May be constrained by inadequate planning and control systems.
6 Can be limited by the availability of qualified managers.
7 Involves considerable expenses for training managers.
8 May be limited by external forces (national labor unions, governmental controls, tax policies).
9 May not be favored by economies of scale of some operations.

financial costs. As authority is decentralized, managers become more and more like independent operators of small businesses. They may acquire their own accounting force, statisticians, and engineering staff, and these people may soon be duplicating specialized services of the top company organization.

Principal problem

Perhaps the principal problem of decentralization is loss of control. No enterprise can decentralize to the extent that its existence is threatened and the achievement of its goals is frustrated. If organizational disintegration is to be avoided, decentralization must be tempered by selective centralization in certain major policy areas. The company with well-balanced decentralization will probably centralize decisions at the top on such things as financing, overall profit goals and budgeting, major facilities and other capital expenditures, important new product programs, major marketing strategies, basic personnel policies, and the development and compensation of managerial personnel.

But, judging from experience, a proper balance is not easy to achieve. Many prominent enterprises have had serious problems in this area. Even the large General Electric Company lived too long with a highly centralized functional organization structure; then, when it reorganized after 1954, it decentralized too much, giving far more discretion than later proved to be wise to some 120 integrated and highly independent departments.

The achievement of balance is perhaps one of the greatest accomplishments of Alfred Sloan in his management of General Motors over the years. Although practicing and preaching decentralization, he and his top management team realized that no department or division could be given complete freedom. As a result, this company, as large as it has been, has always continued to hold at the very top its major policy and program decisions on matters affecting the soundness and success of the entire company. Yet, as pointed out above, once major program and strategy decisions are made at the top, the countless decisions involving their execution have been decentralized to operating divisions. The company has become a model for good centralization and decentralization.

Summary

Decentralization is the tendency to disperse decision-making authority. Centralization is the concentration of authority; the term may also refer to enterprises operating in a single location and to centralized departmental activities. The process of delegation of authority includes determining the results to be achieved, assigning tasks, delegating authority, and holding people responsible for results.

The principles of delegation are: delegation by results expected, functional definition, scalar chain, authority-level, unity of command, absoluteness of responsibility, and parity of authority and responsibility.

Delegation, which is an art, is influenced by personal attitudes. We have listed five guides helpful in overcoming weak delegation. Decentralization is influenced by many other factors a manager should recognize when determining the degree of authority delegation. Previously decentralized authority may be recentralized. To reduce conflicts, decentralization should be clarified. This may be done, for example, by a chart of executive approval authorization. Balance is the key to proper decentralization.

Key Ideas and Concepts for Review

Centralization
Decentralization
Process of delegation
Principle of delegation by results expected
Principle of functional definition
Scalar principle
Authority-level principle
Principle of unity of command
Principle of absoluteness of responsibility
Principle of parity of authority and responsibility

Attitudes toward delegation
Guides for overcoming weak delegation
Factors determining the degree of decentralization
Means for obtaining desired degree of decentralization
Chart of executive approval authorization
Balance in delegation

For Discussion

1 Why is poor delegation of authority often found to be the most important single cause of managerial failure?

2 If you had a subordinate who failed to delegate necessary authority in his or her department, what would you do?

3 What is the distinction between decentralizing "some of all authority" and "all of some authority"? What is actually done in each case?

4 In many foreign countries where companies have grown from within and are often family-owned, very little authority is decentralized. What do you think would explain this? What effect does it have?

5 If you were a manager, would you decentralize authority? State several reasons for your answer. How would you make sure that you did not decentralize too much?

6 There is considerable justification for the claim of some top managers that they do not have a free choice in deciding upon the extent of decentralization of authority. Comment.

7 Should authority be pushed down into an organization as far as it will go?

CASE 11-1

DECENTRALIZATION AT AMERICAN BUSINESS COMPUTERS AND EQUIPMENT COMPANY

Because of its excellent new products, imaginative marketing, and fine service to company customers, the American Business Computers and Equipment Company grew to be a leader in its field, with sales over $1 billion annually, high profit margins, and continually rising stock prices. It became one of the favorites of investors, who enjoyed its fast growth rate and high profits. But the president soon realized that the organization structure, which had served the company so well, no longer fit the company's needs.

For years the company had been organized along functional lines, with vice-presidents in charge of finance, marketing, production, personnel, purchasing, engineering, and research and development. As it grew, the company had expanded its product lines beyond business computers to include electric typewriters, photocopying machines, motion-picture cameras and projectors, computer controls for machine tools,

and electric accounting machines. As time went on, concern had arisen that its organization structure did not provide for profit responsibility below the office of the president, did not appear to fit the far-flung nature of the business now being conducted in many foreign countries, and seemed to accentuate the "walls" impeding effective coordination between the functional departments of marketing, production, and engineering. There seemed to be too many decisions that could not be made at any level lower than the president's office.

As a result, the president decentralized the company into fifteen independent domestic and foreign divisions, each with complete profit responsibility. However, after this reorganization was in effect, he began to feel that the divisions were not adequately controlled. There developed considerable duplication in purchasing and personnel functions, each division manager ran his or her operations without regard to company policies and strategies, and it became apparent to the president that the company was disintegrating into a number of independent parts.

Having seen several large companies get into trouble when a division manager made mistakes and the division suffered large losses, the president concluded that he had gone too far with decentralization. As a result, he withdrew some of the authority delegations to the division managers and required them to get top corporate management approval on such important matters as (1) any capital expenditures over $10,000, (2) the introduction of any new products, (3) marketing and pricing strategies and policies, (4) plant expansion, and (5) changes in personnel policies.

The division general managers were understandably unhappy when they saw some of their independence taken away from them. They openly comlained that the company was on a "yo-yo" course, first decentralizing and then centralizing.

The president, worried about his position, calls you in as a consultant to advise him on what to do.

1   In your opinion, what did the president do wrong when he set up the fifteen independent divisions?

2   Do you agree that what the president did to regain control was correct?

3   What would you have done under the circumstances?

CASE 11-2
THE MIRACLE PRODUCTS COMPANY

Adam Stonebridge inherited from his father a small regional household cleaning products company. Through seeing that the three large companies in the field could not compete for quality products on a price basis because of their high advertising and promotional costs and by his extraordinary talent in setting up an imaginative sales program, Mr. Stonebridge succeeded in profitably developing the company's sales from $2 million to $20 million per year from 1957 to 1965. Because of the attractiveness of his shares to investors and their high market price, he was then able to acquire a number of smaller companies throughout the country so that by 1973, his company grew to $80 million of sales with six plants, a national sales organization, and approximately 2500 employees.

Throughout the company's growth, Mr. Stonebridge found it difficult to delegate authority. Following the pattern adopted when the company was much smaller, Mr. Stonebridge continued to make all final decisions on new products, advertising, pricing, sales plans and organization, hiring, operating budgets, production plans, capital expenditures, purchase orders above $1000, credits given to stores, union agreements, production plans, and many other matters. As the controller, who had been with the company for many years, said to a new executive who asked what the company's policy was in a given area: "We don't need any policies here; whenever we want to know what to decide, we ask Adam."

Long before the company grew to its present size, the key executives—vice-presidents, plant managers, sales managers—became frustrated by bottlenecks in the president's office. They finally approached one of the outside directors whom they trusted and knew to be a close friend of the president and asked his aid in solving the problem.

When the director investigated their complaints, he found them to be justified. He also found the president to be receptive to the idea of delegation, knowledgeable in the principles of delegation, and aware of the importance of delegating. He finally came to the conclusion that the president's unwillingness to delegate was due to a justifiable fear of losing control over the company's operations.

1 What would you do in order to get Mr. Stonebridge to delegate authority?

2 Exactly what kinds of authority would you suggest be delegated?

For Further Information

Brown, A. *Organization of Industry* (Englewood Cliffs, N.J.: Prentice-Hall, Inc., 1947).

Dale, E. *Planning and Developing the Company Organization Structure* (New York: American Management Association, 1952), Research Report no. 20.

Fayol, H. *General and Industrial Administration* (New York: Pitman Publishing Corporation, 1949).

Krein, T. J. "How to Improve Delegation Habits," *Management Review*, vol. 71, no. 5 (May 1982), pp. 58–61.

Perrow, C. "The Bureaucratic Paradox: The Efficient Organization Centralizes in Order to Decentralize," *Organizational Dynamics*, vol. 5 (Spring 1977), pp. 3–14.

Staiger, J. G. "What Cannot be Decentralized," in H. Koontz, C. O'Donnell, and H. Weihrich (eds.), *Management—A Book of Readings*, 5th ed. (New York: McGraw-Hill Book Company, 1980), pp. 319–321.

12

Making Organizing Effective

After reading this chapter, you should understand:

1 Some common mistakes made in organizing
2 The importance of planning organization structures
3 How organizing can be made more effective by maintaining flexibility, clarifying relationships and structure, and ensuring understanding by people who fill the position within the structure
4 That effective organizing requires adaptation to the specific requirements of the situation
5 The importance of the organization culture
6 Some major principles or guidelines for designing organization structures

Organizing involves developing an intentional structure of roles for effective performance. Organizing requires a network of decision and communication centers for coordinating efforts toward group and enterprise goals. To work, an organization structure must be understood, and principles must be put into practice. As we emphasized at the outset, in organizing, as elsewhere in managing, there is no one best way. What works will always depend on the specific situation.

Some Mistakes in Organizing

Despite their obvious nature and their interference with personal and enterprise goals, the persistence of certain mistakes of organizing is striking evidence of the difficulty of managing, the lack of sophistication of managers, or both.

1 Failure to Plan Properly

It is not unusual to find an enterprise continuing with a traditional organization structure long after its objectives, plans, and external environment have changed. For example, a company may keep its product research department under the control of the manufacturing division long after the business environment has changed from being production-oriented (as in a typical sellers' market) to being marketing-oriented (as in a typical buyers' market). Or a company may continue its functional organization structure when product groupings and the need for integrated, decentralized profit responsibility demand decentralized product divisions.

Also, a company may need managers of a kind not currently available, or, just as likely, may find that certain managers have not grown with the company or do not fit current needs. Small, growing businesses often make the mistake of assuming that original employees can grow with the company, only to find that a good engineering designer, made a vice-president—engineering, cannot fill the larger role of the engineering chief or that a once-adequate production superintendent cannot head a larger manufacturing department.

Another guideline for planning involves properly organizing around people. Organization structure must normally be modified to take people into account, and there is much to be said for trying to take full advantage of employee strengths and weaknesses. But managers organizing *primarily* around people overlook several facts. In the first place, managers organizing in this way cannot be assured that all bases will be covered and all the necessary tasks will be undertaken. In the second place, there is danger that different people will desire to do the same things, resulting in conflict or multiple command. In the third place, people have a way of coming and going in an enterprise—through retirement, resignation, promotion, or death—which makes organizing around them risky and their positions, when vacated, hard to describe accurately and to fill adequately.

Such mistakes occur when an enterprise fails to plan properly toward a future materially different from the past or present. By looking forward, a manager should determine what kind of organization structure will best serve future needs and what kinds of people will best serve an organization.

2 Failure to Clarify Relationships

The failure to clarify organization relationships, probably more than any other mistake, accounts for friction, politics, and inefficiencies. Since both the authority and the responsibility for action are critical, lack of clarity about them means lack of knowledge of the part members are to play on an enterprise team. This does not imply the need for detailed job descriptions or the possibility that people cannot operate as a team. Although some enterprise leaders have prided themselves on having a team of subordinates without specified tasks and authority lines, any sports coach could tell them that such a team is likely to be a group of jealous, insecure, buck-passing individuals jockeying for position and favor.

3 Failure to Delegate Authority

A common complaint in organization life is that managers are reluctant to push decision making down into the organization. In some businesses where uniformity of policy is necessary and decision making can be handled by one or a few managers, there may be neither the need nor desire to decentralize authority. But decision-making bottlenecks, excessive referral of small problems to upper echelons, overburdening of top executives with detail, continual "firefighting" and "meeting of crises," and underdevelopment of managers in the lower levels of organization give evidence that failing to delegate authority to the proper extent is decidedly a mistake.

4 Failure to Balance Delegation

Another mistake made in organizing is failure to maintain balanced delegation. In other words, some managers—in their zeal for decentralization—may push decision making too far down in the organization. It may reach down to the very bottom of the structure a system of independent organizational satellites may develop. Even when it is not taken to this extreme, excessive delegation may cause organization failures.

As we pointed out in Chapter 11 on decentralization, top managers must retain some authority, particularly over decisions of companywide impact and at least enough to review the plans and performance of subordinates. Managers must not forget that there is some authority they should not delegate. Nor should they overlook the fact that they must maintain enough authority to ensure that when they do delegate authority to a subordinate, it will be used in the way and for the purposes intended.

5 Confusion of Lines of Authority with Lines of Information

The problems and costs of levels of organization and departmentation can be reduced by opening wide the channels of information. Unless information is confidential (and businesses and government, as well as other enterprises, overuse this classification), there is no reason why lines of information should follow lines of authority. In other words, relevant information should be widely available to people at all levels of the organization. Information gathering should be separated from decision making, since only the latter requires managerial authority. Enterprises often force lines of information to follow lines of authority when the only reason for following a chain of command is to preserve the integrity of decision-making authority and the clarity of responsibility.

6 Granting Authority without Exacting Responsibility

A significant cause of mismanagement is the assignment of authority without holding a person responsible. Authority delegation is not responsibility delegation; superiors remain responsible for the proper exercise of authority by their subordinates. Any other relationship would lead to organizational chaos. But all those to whom authority is delegated must be willing to be held responsible for their actions.

7 Holding People Responsible Who Do Not Have Authority

A common complaint of subordinates is that superiors hold them responsible for results without giving them the authority to accomplish them. Some of these complaints are unjustified and based on misunderstanding of the fact that subordinates can seldom have unlimited authority in any area because their actions must be coordinated with those of people in other positions and must conform to policy. Subordinates often see their jobs as all-encompassing and forget that their authority must be limited to their own departments and must be within controlling policy guidelines.

Too often, however, complaints are justified; managers, sometimes without realizing they are doing so, hold subordinates responsible for results they have no power to accomplish. This does not happen so frequently where organization lines and duties have been clearly set forth, but where a structure of roles is unclear or confused, it does occur.

8 Careless Application of the Staff Device

There are many valid reasons for using a staff assistant or staff specialist and even building entire advisory departments. However, there is danger that staff people will be used by their superiors to undermine the authority of the very managers they are intended merely to advise.

There is an ever-present danger that top managers may surround themselves with staff specialists and become so preoccupied with the specialists' work as to exclude from their schedule the time and attention needed for their line subordinates; or they may assign problems to their staff that would be more appropriately assigned to line managers.

In other instances, staff personnel exercise line authority that has not been delegated to them. It is easy to understand the impatience of staff specialists who see clearly how a situation should be handled, while the line officer in charge of it seems to be slow and clumsy. The very quality that makes staff specialists valuable—specialized knowledge—also makes them impatient of command. Yet, if they were to exercise authority without clear delegation, they would not only be undermining the authority of the responsible line official but also breaking down the unity of command.

9 Misuse of Functional Authority

Perhaps even more dangerous to good managing are the problems arising from undefined and unrestricted delegation of functional authority. This is especially common because the complexities of modern enterprise often create instances where it is desirable to give a predominantly staff or service department functional authority over activities in other parts of the organization.

In the search for economies of specialization and for advantages of technically expert opinion, managers often unduly exalt staff and service departments at the expense of operating departments. Many line officers—from the vice-president in charge of operations to a first-level supervisor—feel, with justice, that the business is being run by the staff and service departments through their exercise of functional authority.

10 Multiple Subordination

The principal danger of too much functional authority is the breakdown of unity of command. We have only to look at the various departments of a typical medium-sized or large business to see how such a breakdown occurs. The controller prescribes accounting procedures throughout the company. The purchasing director prescribes how and where purchases are to be made. The personnel manager dictates (often according to union contracts or government regulations) how employees shall be classified for pay purposes, how vacations shall be scheduled, and how many hours are to be worked. The traffic manager controls the routing of all freight. The general counsel insists that all contracts bear his or her approval and be made in prescribed form. The public relations director requires that all public utterances of managers and other employees be cleared or meet a prescribed policy line. And the tax director reviews all program decisions for clearance on their tax aspects.

Thus, with all these staff and service specialists having some degree of line authority over other parts of the organization, plus similar groups in divisions and regions, operating managers find themselves subject to the direction of a number of people with functional authority in addition to their principal superiors, who usually have the final decision concerning their pay scales and chances for promotion. It is no wonder that many managers, especially those at lower levels where there are so many functional authorities, feel frustrated.

11 Misunderstanding of the Function of Service Departments

Service departments are often looked upon as rather unconcerned with the accomplishment of major enterprise objectives, when they are, in fact, just as immediately concerned as any operating department. Sometimes people, particularly in so-called line departments, regard a service department as relatively unnecessary, unimportant, and therefore something to be ignored when possible.

On the other hand, many service departments mistakenly look upon their function as an end unto itself rather than a service to other departments. Thus, a purchasing department may not realize that its purpose is to purchase efficiently items ordered by authorized departments; or a statistics department may forget that it exists to furnish data desired by others, rather than to produce reports of its own choosing.

"Efficient inefficiency"

Perhaps the greatest misuse of service departments is summed up in the words "efficient inefficiency." When managers establish service departments, looking more to cost savings than to the efficiency of the entire enterprise, a highly "efficient" service may do an inefficient job of servicing. For example, little is gained in setting up a low-cost central recruiting section if the employees recruited do not meet organization needs.

12 Overorganization and Underorganization

Too many levels

Overorganization usually results from failure to put into practice the idea that the structure of the enterprise is merely a system for making possible efficient performance of people. Managers unduly complicating the structure through creating too many levels ignore the fact that efficiency demands that managers supervise as many subordinates as they can. Narrow spans may reflect misunderestanding of the span-of-management principle, managerial inability to minimize the time requirements of necessary human relationships, or lack of time to manage—a lack often caused by poor assignments and authority delegations. Likewise, the multiplication of staff and service activities or departments may be caused by inadequate delegation to line subordinates and the tendency to regard service specialization and efficiency so narrowly that larger enterprise operations are overlooked.

Unnecessary assistants

Managers also overorganize by appointing unnecessary line assistants (for example, assistant or deputy managers). Having a line assistant is justified when managers wish to devote their time to matters outside their department, during their long absences from the office, when they wish to delegate line authority in a given area such as engineering, or during a limited training period for a subordinate to whom full managerial status is soon to be given. Otherwise, the separation of managers from their other subordinates and the confusion as to who is really the superior that result from this practice lead us to conclude that it should be undertaken carefully and sparingly.

Excessive procedures

Sometimes, excessive procedures are confused with overorganization. Overorganization—particularly if interlaced with functional authority—can lead to excessive procedures. But much of the red tape often blamed on overorganization really results from poor planning. The failure to regard procedures as plans—and to treat them with the respect given other kinds of plans—often results in bewilderingly complex and even unnecessary procedures.

Too many committees

Similarly, too many committees, sapping the time and energies of managers and their staffs, are often blamed on overorganization rather than on *poor* organization (particularly when committees make decisions better made by individuals). An excess of committees often results from having authority delegated to too many positions or from vague delegation. Such an excess may actually point to underorganization.

Avoiding Mistakes by Planning

As with the other functions of managing, establishment of objectives and orderly planning are necessary for good organization. As Urwick said in his classic book, "Lack of design [in organization] is illogical, cruel, wasteful, and inefficient."[1] It is illogical because good design, or planning, must come first, whether one speaks of engineering or social practice. It is cruel because "the main sufferers from a lack of design in organization are those individuals who work in an undertaking." It is wasteful because "unless jobs are clearly put together along lines of functional specialization, it is impossible to train new men [or women] to succeed to positions as the incumbents are promoted, resign or retire." And it is inefficient because, unless based on principles, management will be based on personalities, with the resultant rise of company politics, for "a machine will not run smoothly when fundamental engineering principles have been ignored in construction."

Planning for the Ideal

The search for an ideal organization to reflect enterprise goals under given circumstances is the impetus to planning. The search entails charting the main lines of organization, considering the organizational philosophy of the enterprise managers (for example, whether authority shall be centralized as much as possible or whether the company should divide its operations into semi-independent product

---

[1]L. Urwick, *The Elements of Administration* (New York: Harper & Row, Publishers, Incorporated, 1944), p. 38.

or territorial divisions), and sketching out consequent authority relationships. The ultimate form established, like all plans, seldom remains unchanged, and continuous remolding of the ideal plan is normally necessary. Nevertheless, an ideal organization plan constitutes a standard, and, by comparing present structure with it, enterprise leaders know what changes should be made when possible.

An organizer must always be careful not to be blinded by popular notions in organizing, because what may work in one company may not work in another. Principles of organizing have general application, but the background of each company's operations and needs must be considered in applying these principles. Organization structure needs to be tailor-made. It requires a contingency approach.

Modification for the Human Factor

If available personnel do not fit into the ideal structure and cannot or should not be pushed aside, the only choice is to modify the structure to fit individual capabilities, attitudes, or limitations. This modification may seem like organizing around people; the difference is that in this case, one is organizing *first* around the goals to be met and activities to be undertaken, and only *then* making modifications for the human factor. Thus, planning will reduce compromising the necessity for principle whenever changes occur in personnel.

Advantages of Planning

Planning the organization structure helps determine future personnel needs and required training programs. Without knowing what managerial personnel will be needed and what experience to demand, an enterprise cannot intelligently recruit people and train them.

Furthermore, organization planning can disclose weaknesses. Duplication of effort, unclear lines of authority, overlong lines of communication, excessive red tape, and obsolete practices show up best when desirable and actual organization structures are compared.

Avoiding Organizational Inflexibility

One basic advantage of organization planning is avoidance of organizational inflexibility. Many enterprises, especially those which have been in operation for many years, become too rigid to meet the first test of effective organization structure—ability to adapt to changing environment and meet new contingencies. This resistance to change can cause considerable loss of efficiency in organizations.

Signs of Inflexibility

Some older companies provide ample evidence of inflexibilities: an organization pattern no longer suited to the times; a district or regional organization that could be either abolished or enlarged because of improved communications; or a too highly centralized structure for an enlarged enterprise requiring decentralization.

Avoiding Inflexibility through Reorganization

Although reorganization is intended to respond to changes in the enterprise environment, there may be other compelling reasons for reorganization. Those related to the business environment include changes in operations caused by acquisition or sale of major properties, changes in product line or marketing methods, business cycles, competitive influences, new production techniques, labor union policy, government regulatory and fiscal policy, or the current state of knowledge about organizing. New techniques and principles may become applicable, such as that of developing managers by allowing them to manage decentralized semi-independent units of a company, or new methods may come into use, such as that of gaining adequate financial control with a high degree of decentralization.

Moreover, a new chief executive officer and new vice-presidents and department heads are likely to have some definite organizational ideas of their own. Shifts may be due merely to the desire of new managers to make changes based on ideas formulated through their previous experience or to the fact that their methods of managing and their personalities require a changed organization structure.

Furthermore, reorganization may be caused by demonstrated deficiencies in an existing structure. Some of these arise from organizational weaknesses: excessive spans of management, too many levels, inadequate communication, poor interdepartmental coordination, an excessive number of committees, lack of uniform policy, slow decision making, failure to accomplish objectives, inability to meet schedules, excessive costs, or breakdown of financial control. Other deficiencies may stem from inadequacies of managers. Lack of knowledge or skill on the part of a manager who for some reason cannot be replaced may be avoided by organizing so as to move much of the authority for decision making to another position.

Personality clashes between managers also may be solved by reorganization. Staff-line conflicts may develop to such an extent that they can be resolved only by reorganization.

Need for Readjustment and Change

In addition to pressing reasons for reorganization, there is a certain need for moderate and continuing readjustment merely to keep the structure from becoming stagnant. "Empire building" (i.e., building up a large organization to make the manager appear to be more important) is not so attractive when all those involved know that their positions are subject to change. As a company president told his subordinates: "Don't bother to build any empires, because I can assure you that you won't be in the same position three years from now." Some managers, realizing that an organization structure must be a living thing, make structural changes merely to accustom subordinates to change.

Much can be said for developing a tradition of change. People who are used to change tend to accept it without the frustration and demoralization that result when need for reorganization is allowed to reach the stage at which change must be revolutionary. On the other hand, a company continually undertaking major reorganization may damage morale, and people may spend much of their time wondering what will happen to them because of organizational changes.

Avoiding Conflict by Clarification

A major reason for conflict in organizations is that people do not understand their assignments and those of their coworkers. No matter how well conceived an organization structure, people must understand it to make it work. Understanding is aided materially by proper use of organization charts, accurate job descriptions, the spelling out of authority and informational relationships, and the introduction of specific goals for specific positions.

Organization Charts

Every organization structure, even a poor one, can be charted, for a chart merely indicates how departments are tied together along the principal lines of authority (see Chapter 9). It is therefore somewhat surprising to occasionally find top managers taking pride in not having an organization chart or feeling that the charts should be kept a secret.

Advantages A prominent manufacturer once said that although he could see some use for an organization chart for his factory, he had refused to chart the organization above the level of factory superintendent. His argument was that charts tended to make people overly conscious of being superiors or inferiors, tended to destroy team feeling, and gave persons occupying a box on the chart too great a feeling of "ownership." Another top executive once said that if an organization is left uncharted, it can be changed more easily, and that the absence of a chart also encourages a competitive drive for higher executive positions on the part of the uncharted middle-management group.

These reasons for not charting organization structures are clearly unsound. Subordinate-superior relationships exist not because of charting but, rather, because of essential reporting relationships. As for a chart's creating a too-comfortable feeling and causing a lack of drive on the part of those who have "arrived," these are matters of top leadership—of reorganizing whenever the enterprise environment demands, of developing a tradition of change, and of making subordinate managers continue to meet adequate and well-understood standards of performance. Managers who believe that team spirit can be produced without clearly spelling out relationships are fooling themselves and preparing the way for politics, intrigue, frustration, buck-passing, lack of coordination, duplicated effort, vague policy, uncertain decision making, and other evidences of organizational inefficiency.

Since a chart maps lines of decision-making authority, sometimes merely charting an organization can show inconsistencies and complexities and lead to their correction. A chart also reveals to managers and new personnel how they tie into the entire structure. It has been generally found that firms that have comprehensive organization charts appear to have sounder organization structures than those that do not.

Limitations Organization charts are subject to important limitations. In the first place, a chart shows only formal authority relationships and omits the many significant informal and informational relationships. Figure 12-1 shows many, but not nearly all, of the informal relationships found in a typical organized enterprise. It shows also the major line, or formal, relationships. It does not show *how much* authority exists at any point in the structure. While it would be interesting to chart an organization with lines of different widths to denote formal authority of varying degrees, authority is not subject to such measurement. And if the multiple

FIGURE 12-1

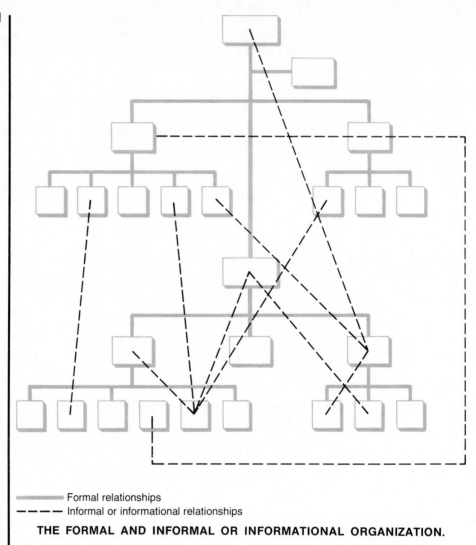

▬▬▬ Formal relationships
— — — Informal or informational relationships

THE FORMAL AND INFORMAL OR INFORMATIONAL ORGANIZATION.

lines of informal relationships and of communication were drawn, they would so complicate a chart that it could not be understood.

Many charts show structures as they are supposed to be or used to be, rather than as they really are. Managers hesitate or neglect to redraft charts, forgetting that organization structures are dynamic and that charts should not be allowed to become obsolete.

Another difficulty with organization charts is that individuals may confuse authority relationships with status. The staff officer reporting to the corporation president may be shown at the top of the organization chart, while a regional line officer may be shown one or two levels lower. Although good charting attempts to make levels on the chart conform to levels of enterprise importance, it cannot always do so. This problem can be handled by clearly spelling out authority relationships and by that best indicator of status—salary and bonus levels. No one is likely, for example, to hear that the general manager of Chevrolet in General Motors feels a sense of inferiority because his position on the chart is below that of the company secretary.

Position Descriptions and Charts of Approval Authorizations

Every managerial position should be defined. A good position description informs everyone what the incumbent is supposed to do. A modern position description is not a detailed list of all the activities an individual is expected to undertake and it certainly does not specify *how* to undertake them. Rather, it states the basic function of the position, the major end-result areas for which the manager is responsible, and the reporting relationships involved; it makes reference to the current chart of approval authorizations in order to clarify the position's authority and to the current set of verifiable objectives for the end-result areas.

In this way, position descriptions may be made far less detailed than they once were. Also, by merely referring to the current authority chart and set of objectives, managers can make the description much more flexible as authority delegations and objectives change. For example, the basic function of one vice-president in charge of marketing was described as being responsible to the president for effectively and efficiently planning, organizing, staffing, directing, and controlling company activities in market research, advertising and promotion, and sales. The vice-president was given authority in accordance with a separately published chart of executive approval authorizations (an example of such a chart appears in Chapter 11) and was held responsible for setting and achieving approved objectives as they were developed from time to time in consultation with the president.

Benefits

Such descriptions have many benefits. As jobs are analyzed, duties and responsibilities are brought into focus and areas of overlapping or neglected duties come to light. Forcing people to consider what should be done and who should do it is more than worth the effort. Further benefits of job descriptions include the guidance they provide in training new managers, in drawing up candidate requirements, and in setting salary levels. Finally, as a means of control over organization, the position description furnishes a standard against which to judge whether a position is necessary and, if so, what its organization level and exact location in the structure should be.

Because it reveals vague authority relationships, inappropriate or misunderstood communication lines, and inefficiencies of organization levels or management spans, the spelling out of a position's duties and its relationships is a major step toward removing conflict. As with organization charts, the very spelling out furnishes a standard against which effectiveness of organization can be measured. Perhaps the most powerful tool for defining and clarifying relationships is the chart of executive approval authorizations, discussed in Chapter 11. The authority relationships are clarified by describing organizational positions, showing who has the authority for approving and making commitments, and indicating the functional authority for individual positions.

Ensuring Understanding of Organizing

All the members of an enterprise must understand the structure of their organization in order for that structure to work. This requires teaching. Also, since formal organization is supplemented by informal organization, members of an enterprise must understand the general working of informal as well as formal organization.

Teaching the Nature of Organizing

Many soundly conceived organization plans fail because organization members do not understand them. A well-written organization manual—containing a statement of organization philosophy, programs, charts, and an outline of job descriptions—goes far toward making organizing understandable. If an organization structure is put into written words and charts, it has a better chance of being clear than if it is not. However, because even the best-written words and charts do not always clearly convey the same meaning to every reader, effective managers cannot stop with written clarification. They must teach those in their operation the meaning of the organization structure, their position in it, and the relationships involved.

Managers may do this by individual coaching, through staff or special meetings, or by simply watching how the structure works. If subordinates pass decisions up the line that they should be making themselves, managers can take this opportunity to clarify authority. Likewise, if communication among members of a group seems to be inadequate, managers can look for causes in either a poorly conceived or a poorly understood organization structure. Too many group meetings or too much committee work is a signal for managers to do some investigating. Thus, managers are obligated continually to teach the fundamentals of organizing, for if they do not, their enterprise or department is likely to fail.

Recognizing the Importance of Informal Organization

Another way of making the formal organization work effectively is to recognize and take full advantage of informal organization. The nature of informal organizations and their distinction from formal organizations were discussed in Chapter 8. Many informal organizations arise from the formal organization in which they operate. They include interrelationships that are not usually charted, such as the unwritten rules of organizational conduct, the way to "learn the ropes," who in an enterprise has power not implied by or coming from an organization position, and gossip. One of the best-known examples of an important informal organization, one which seems to exist in every department and organization, is the "grapevine."

The grapevine   Informal organization tends to exist when members of a formal organization (perhaps a company department) know one another well enough to pass on information—sometimes only gossip—in some way connected with the enterprise. In the typical enterprise—the members of which spend many hours a day deriving material security and status, as well as social satisfaction, from the grapevine—the desire for information concerning the organization and its people is strong enough that such information is rapidly transmitted between persons who know and trust one another.

The grapevine, of course, thrives on information not openly available to the entire group, whether because that information is regarded as confidential, or because formal lines of communication are inadequate to spread it, or because it is of the kind, like much gossip, that would never be formally disclosed. Even a management that conscientiously informs employees through company bulletins or newspapers never so completely or quickly discloses all information of interest as to make the grapevine purposeless.

Since all informal organization serves essential human communication needs, the grapevine is inevitable and valuable. Indeed, an intelligent top manager would probably be wise to feed it accurate information, since it is very effective for quick communication. There is much to be said for a manager getting a place—personally or through a trusted staff member or secretary—on the company grapevine.

Benefits   Informal organization brings a kind of cohesiveness to formal organization. It imparts to members of a formal organization a feeling of belonging, of status, of self-respect, and of satisfaction. The great management writer Chester Barnard observed that informal organizations are an important "means of maintaining the personality of the individual against certain effects of formal organizations which tend to disintegrate personality." Many managers, understanding this fact, consciously use informal organizations as channels of communication and molders of employee morale.

Promoting an Appropriate Organization Culture

The effectiveness of an organization is also influenced by the organization culture, which affects the way the managerial functions of planning, organizing, staffing, leading, and controlling are carried out. (See illustration in Table 12-1.) In their search for excellent companies, Peters and Waterman, the authors of a best-selling book on management, found that the dominance of a coherent culture characterized these organizations.[2]

Defining Organization Culture

As it relates to organizations, **culture** is the general pattern of behavior, shared beliefs, and values that members have in common.[3] Culture can be inferred from what people say, do, and think within an organizational setting. It involves the learning and transmitting of knowledge, beliefs, and patterns of behavior over a period of time. This also means that an organization culture is fairly stable and does not change fast. It often sets the tone for the company and establishes implied rules for how people should behave. Many of us have heard slogans that give us a general idea what the company stands for.[4] Here are some examples:

---

[2]T. J. Peters and Robert H. Waterman, Jr., *In Search of Excellence* (New York: Harper & Row, Publishers, Incorporated, 1982).

[3]V. Sathe, "Some Action Implications of Corporate Culture: A Manager's Guide to Action," *Organizational Dynamics*, vol. 12, no. 2 (Autumn 1983), pp. 4–23.

[4]T. E. Deal and A. A. Kennedy, *Corporate Cultures* (Reading, Mass.: Addison-Wesley Publishing Company, Inc., 1982), chap. 2.

TABLE 12-1 Illustrations of Organization Culture and Management Practice

Environment A	Environment B
Planning	
Goals are set in an autocratic manner. Decision making is centralized.	Goals are set with a great deal of participation. Decision making is decentralized.
Organizing	
Authority is centralized. Authority is narrowly defined.	Authority is decentralized. Authority is broadly defined.
Staffing	
People are selected on the basis of friendship.	People are selected on the basis of performance criteria.
Training is in a narrowly defined specialty.	Training is in many functional areas.
Leading	
Managers exercise directive leadership. Communication flow is primarily top-down.	Managers practice participative leadership. Communication flow is top-down, bottom-up, horizontal, and diagonal.
Controlling	
Superiors exercise strict control. Focus is on financial criteria.	Individuals exercise a great deal of self-control. Focus is on multiple criteria.

Examples

For General Electric, it is, "Progress is our most important product."

American Telephone & Telegraph Company is proud of its "universal service."

DuPont makes "better things for better living through chemistry."

Delta Airlines describes its internal climate with the slogan, "the Delta family feeling."

Similarly, IBM wants to be known for its service, Sears for quality and price, Caterpillar for its 24-hour parts service, Polaroid for its innovation, Maytag for its reliability, and so on. Indeed, the orientation of these companies, often expressed in slogans, contributes to the successful conduct of their businesses.

The Influence of the Leader on Organization Culture

Managers, and especially top managers, create the climate for the enterprise. Their values influence the direction of the firm. Although the term "value" is usually used differently, we like to think of a **value** as a fairly permanent belief about what is appropriate and what is not that guides the actions and behavior of employees in fulfilling the organization's aims. Values can be thought of as forming an ideology that permeates everyday decisions.

*Impact
of values*

In many successful companies, value-driven corporate leaders serve as role models, set the standards for performance, motivate employees, make the company special, and are a symbol to the external environment. It was Edwin Land, the founder of Polaroid, who created a favorable organizational environment for research and innovation. It was Jim Treybig of Tandom in the "Silicon Valley" near San Francisco who made it a point that every person is a human being and deserves to be treated accordingly. It was William Cooper Proctor of Proctor & Gamble who ran the company with the slogan: "Do what is right." It was Theodore Vail of AT&T who addressed the needs of customers by emphasizing service. The organization culture created by corporate leaders can result in managerial functions being carried out in quite different ways.

Summary

Organizing involves developing an intentional structure of roles in a formally organized enterprise. Common mistakes in organizing are the failure of proper planning, unclear relationships and delegation of authority, and unbalanced delegation. Other failures include the confusion of lines of authority with lines of information, the granting of authority without holding the recipient responsible, the careless application of staff, the inappropriate use of functional authority, multiple subordination, the wrong use of service departments, and overorganization.

Many mistakes in organizing can be avoided by first planning the ideal organization for goal achievement and then making modifications for the human or other situational factors. Organization planning identifies staffing needs and helps to overcome staffing deficiencies. It also discloses duplication of effort, unclear authority and communication lines, and obsolete ways of doing things. An effective organization remains flexible and adjusts for changes in the environment.

Organizational conflict can be reduced by the use of organization charts, position descriptions, and charts of approval authorizations. Organizing is improved by teaching its nature and by recognizing the informal organization and the grapevine. Moreover, effective enterprises develop and nurture an appropriate organization culture.

Key Ideas and Concepts for Review

Mistakes in organizing	Position description
Avoiding mistakes by planning	Understanding of organizing
Avoiding organizational inflexibility	Informal organization
Avoiding organizational conflict by clarification	The grapevine
	Organization culture
Organization charts	Values

For Discussion

1 Many psychologists have pointed to the advantages of "job enlargement"—assignment of tasks that are not so specialized that an individual loses a sense of doing things which are meaningful. Assuming that managers wish to limit specialization of tasks and "enlarge" jobs, can they do so and still apply the basic principles of organizing?

2 Taking an organized enterprise with which you have some familiarity, can you find any of the deficiencies commonly found in organization structures?

3 It is sometimes stated that the typical organization chart is undemocratic in that it emphasizes the superiority and inferiority of people and positions. Comment.

4 What, in your judgment, makes an organization structure "good"? How do "good" organization structures support leadership?

5 What would you need to know to plan an organization structure? How far ahead should you plan it? How would you go about making such a plan?

6 Take an organization you know and discuss its culture. Is the culture helping or hindering the organization in achieving its goals?

CASE 12-1

STAFF AND SERVICE DOMINATION OF LINE OPERATIONS

Several members at an American Management Association conference were discussing informally the tendency of staff and service departments to dominate line operations.

"I remember one case," said Henry Lorenz, a chief of audit in one of the Internal Revenue districts, "where many complaints from line managers were registered concerning the autocratic way the facilities and financial management people handled requests. In our business we had to make the annual fiscal budget some 2 years before it became operable. I'm afraid we did not anticipate our needs for equipment very well, perhaps because we thought no one could see that far ahead. Anyway, some of us would become distraught when

the facilities department turned down our requests with the remark, 'Why didn't you put that in your budget request?' At first it seemed to be rather high-handed that a service group could deny a request by a line manager. Then we finally figured out that we could get most of the things we really needed if we got them approved in the budget."

"We had a different problem in our company," said George Marshall, engineering director for an aerospace company. "We really try to make plans in a democratic fashion for the following year's operation. We start early, have several reviews at group level, and eventually acquire a quite firm grasp on next year's expense, capital, and work-force budgets. I notice that in allocating indirect labor and G&A (general and administration) money to the divisions, our group executive uses ratios provided by the controller or the vice-president for administration. This never sits well with us line managers, and we have often chided the group chief about using rules of thumb rather than business sense. I never get very far in my protests, however, because the group executive always says, 'Give me a better guide and I'll use it.' I have never been able to devise a substitute."

"In our business we are concerned about the arbitrary decisions of service departments," said Helen Lester, marketing director, Argon Manufacturing Corp. "For instance, their charges to our department are outrageous. I can get outside service for half the price. When these people submit a budget they seem to look at last year's fig-ures, the profit projection for next year, and add 10 percent. Then they palm off a lot of services we don't want. Personnel is particularly effective in this game. Maintenance has a monopoly on service, so we get it when it suits them, not us."

Other participants added their experiences. Finally someone remarked, "These examples do make the picture seem quite bleak. But I would suggest that we still have need of service and staff departments. The salient issue would appear to be how we can use them efficiently. Lorenz appears to have solved his problem. The rest of us have not. Can we generalize an effective approach?"

1 What is the basic problem being discussed? What is the issue that needs solution?

2 How do you suggest that this problem be solved?

CASE 12-2

THE VGI COMPANY

Egon Schnell was a bright young engineer working for an electronics firm. Although he was very successful as an engineer with the company, and liked his job, which involved developing video games, he decided to leave his job and start his own company. He borrowed money wherever he could get it. Despite his enormous efforts and his good ideas, he failed and almost went bankrupt. Finally, he succeeded after a large retail chain gave him a big order. But success was followed by failure and failure was succeeded by renewed success.

Employees liked to work at Schnell's company, VGI, where the atmosphere was casual. This climate was conducive for developing new ideas. Yet the competition from large, well-managed companies grew. Still, some brilliant ideas resulted in a great demand for several of the prod-ucts. In fact, the demand was such that the company could not keep up with production, and there were shortages. But an expansion required capital. Consequently, Mr. Schnell decided to go public and to link up with a large company. This made the owner-entrepreneur several million dollars richer. Mr. Schnell remained as the head of VGI, but his interest in running the company visibly diminished and observers described the firm's state of affairs as "chaotic." Mr. Schnell admitted that he was not a good executive and agreed to a reorganization in which Mr. Newsome assumed the leadership of the company as president. One of the first decisions of the new president was to appoint a new marketing manager to overcome the weakness of the VGI company, which in the past had been dominated by people with technical backgrounds.

Mr. Newsome also exerted strong managerial leadership, developed many new procedures, set specific objectives, and installed strict financial controls. The change from a free-reign to a rather tight managerial approach annoyed many of the old-time engineers. Since there was a great demand for their services, many left the company. Some even established their own software company and became direct competitors to their former firm.

1 Why do you think Mr. Schnell was successful at the beginning?

2 Why did employees, and especially the engineers, like to work under the free-reign management of Mr. Schnell?

3 Why did Mr. Schnell fail and what would you have done in his place?

4 Do you agree with Mr. Newsome's approach to managing? Why or why not?

For Further Information

Cavanagh, G. P., D. J. Moberg, and M. Velasquez. "The Ethics of Organizational Politics," *Academy of Management Review*, vol. 6, no. 3 (July 1981), pp. 363–374.

Davis, K., and J. Newstrom. *Human Behavior at Work—Organizational Behavior*, 7th ed. (New York: McGraw-Hill Book Company, 1985).

Davis, S. M. "Corporate Culture and Human Resource Management: Two Keys to Implementing Strategy," *Human Resource Planning*, vol. 6, no. 3 (1983), pp. 159–167.

Deal, T. E., and A. A. Kennedy. *Corporate Cultures—The Rites and Rituals of Corporate Life* (Reading, Mass.: Addison-Wesley Publishing Company, Inc., 1982).

Deal, T. E., and A. A. Kennedy. "Culture: A New Look through Old Lenses," *Journal of Applied Behavioral Science*, vol. 19, no. 4 (1983), pp. 497–505.

Donaldson, L. "Woodward, Technology, Organizational Structure and Performance—A Critique of the Universal Generalization," in H. Koontz, C. O'Donnell, and H. Weihrich (eds.), *Management—A Book of Readings*, 5th ed. (New York: McGraw-Hill Book Company, 1980), pp. 369–380.

Lawrence, P. R., and J. W. Lorsch. *Organization and Environment* (Homewood, Ill.: Richard D. Irwin, Inc., 1969).

Luce, S. R. "Managing Corporate Culture," *Canadian Business Review*, vol. 11, no. 1 (Spring 1984), pp. 40–43.

Matthews, G. H. "Run Your Business or Build an Organization?" *Harvard Business Review*, vol. 62, no. 2 (March–April 1984), pp. 34–44.

Peters, T. J., and R. H. Waterman, Jr. *In Search of Excellence* (New York: Harper & Row Publishers, Incorporated, 1982).

Summary of Major Principles of Organizing

Although the science of organizing has not yet developed to the point where principles are infallible laws, there is considerable agreement among management scholars and practitioners about a number of them. These principles are truths (or are believed to be truths) of general applicability, although their application is not so precise as to give them the exactness of the laws of pure science. They are more in the nature of essential criteria for effective organizing. The most essential guiding principles of organizing are summarized in this section.

The Purpose of Organizing
The purpose of organizing is to aid in making objectives meaningful and to contribute to organizational efficiency.

Principle of unity of objective An organization structure is effective if it enables individuals to contribute to enterprise objectives.

Principle of organizational efficiency An organization is efficient if it is structured to aid the accomplishment of enterprise objectives with a minimum of unsought consequences or costs.

The Cause of Organizing
The basic cause of organization structure is the limitation of the span of management. If there were no such limitation, we might have an unorganized enterprise with only one manager.

Span-of-management principle In each managerial position, there is a limit to the number of persons an individual can effectively manage, but the exact number will depend on the impact of underlying variables.

The Structure of Organization: Authority

Authority is the cement of organization structure, the thread that makes it possible, the means by which groups of activities can be placed under a manager and coordination of organizational units can be promoted. It is the tool by which a manager is able to exercise discretion and to create an environment for individual performance. Some of the most useful principles of organizing are related to authority.

Scalar principle The clearer the line of authority from the ultimate management position in an enterprise to every subordinate position, the clearer will be the responsibility for decision making and the more effective organization communication will be.

Principle of delegation by results expected Authority delegated to all individual managers should be adequate to ensure their ability to accomplish results expected.

Principle of absoluteness of responsibility The responsibility of subordinates to their superiors for performance is absolute, and superiors cannot escape responsibility for the organization activities of their subordinates.

Principle of parity of authority and responsibility The responsibility for actions cannot be greater than that implied by the authority delegated, nor should it be less.

Principle of unity of command The more complete an individual's reporting relationship to a single superior, the less the problem of conflicting instructions and the greater the feeling of personal responsibility for results.

The authority-level principle Maintenance of intended delegation requires that decisions within the authority of individual managers should be made by them and not be referred upward in the organization structure.

The Structure of Organization: Departmentized Activities

Organization involves the design of a departmental framework. Although there are several principles in this area, one is of major importance.

Principle of functional definition The more a position or a department has clear definition of results expected, activities to be undertaken, organization authority delegated, and authority and informational relationships with other positions understood, the more adequately the responsible individual can contribute toward accomplishing enterprise objectives.

The Process of Organizing

The various principles of authority delegation and of departmentation are fundamental truths about the process of organizing. They deal with phases of the two primary aspects of organizing—authority and activity groupings. There are other principles that deal with the process of organizing. It is through their application that we gain a sense of proportion or a measure of the total organizing process.

Principle of balance In every structure there is need for balance. The application of principles or techniques must be balanced to ensure the overall effectiveness of the structure in meeting enterprise objectives.

The principle of balance is common to all areas of science and to all functions of the manager. The inefficiencies of broad spans of management must be balanced against the inefficiencies of long lines of communication. The losses from multiple command must be balanced against the gains from expertness and uniformity in delegating functional authority to staff and service departments. The savings of functional specialization in departmentalizing must be balanced against the advantages of establishing profit-responsible, semi-independent product or territorial departments. We see again that the application of management theory depends on the specific situation.

Principle of flexibility The more provisions are made for building flexibility in an organizational structure, the more adequately an organization structure can fulfill its purpose.

Devices and techniques for anticipating and reacting to change must be built into every structure. Every enterprise moves toward its goal in a changing environment, both external and internal. The enterprise that develops inflexibilities, whether these are resistance to change, too-complicated procedures, or too-firm departmental lines, is risking inability to meet the challenges of economic, technical, biological, political, and social change.

Principle of leadership facilitation The more an organization structure and its delegations of authority enable managers to design and maintain an environment for performance, the more they will help the leadership abilities of those managers.

Since managership depends to a great extent upon the quality of leadership of those in managerial positions, it is important for the organization structure to do its part in creating a situation in which a manager can most effectively lead. In this sense, organizing is a technique of promoting leadership. If the authority allocation and the structural arrangements create a situation in which heads of departments tend to be looked upon as leaders and in which their task of leadership is aided, organization structuring has accomplished an essential task.

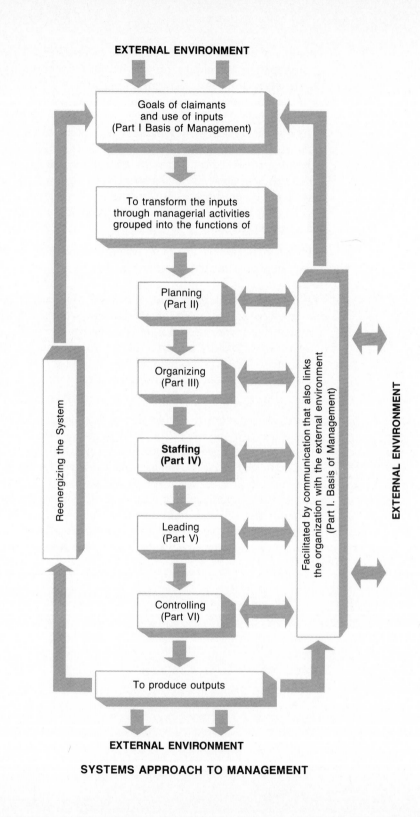

SYSTEMS APPROACH TO MANAGEMENT

IV

Staffing

13

The Nature and Purpose of Staffing

CHAPTER OBJECTIVES

After reading this chapter, you should understand:

1 What it means to be a manager
2 The logic and importance of the systems approach to staffing
3 The nature and use of the management inventory as a staffing tool
4 The importance of the laws on equal employment opportunity to staffing
5 The role of women in management
6 The advantages and problems associated with promotion from within and from outside the organization
7 The policy of open competition

Definition of staffing

The managerial function of **staffing** is defined as filling positions in the organization structure through identifying work-force requirements, inventorying the people available, recruitment, selection, placement, promotion, appraisal, compensation, and training of needed people.[1] It is clear that staffing must be closely linked to organizing, that is, to the setting up of intentional structures of roles and positions. Many writers on management theory discuss staffing as a phase of organizing.

---

[1] Another term now frequently used for the managerial function of staffing is "Human resource management."

We, however, have identified staffing as a separate managerial function for several reasons. First, the staffing of organizational roles includes knowledge and approaches not usually recognized by practicing managers, who often think of organizing as just setting up a structure of roles and give little attention to filling these roles. Second, making staffing a separate function allows us to give even greater emphasis to the human element in selection, appraisal, and manager development. Third, an important body of knowledge and experience has been developed in the area of staffing. The fourth reason for separating staffing is that managers often overlook the fact that staffing is *their* responsibility—not that of the personnel department. To be sure, this department provides valuable assistance, but it is the job of managers to fill the positions in their organization and keep them filled with qualified people.

Defining the Managerial Job

Different views

There is not complete agreement about what exactly the job of manger consists of. In fact, the nature of managerial tasks has been studied from several different perspectives.[2] One group of writers, known as the *great man school*, studied successful managers and described their behaviors and habits. Although the stories about these people are interesting, the authors usually do not provide an underlying theory to explain the success of their subjects. Other writers—primarily economists—focus on the *entrepreneurial* aspects of managing. Their main concern is profit maximization, innovation, risk taking, and similar activities. Yet another group of writers emphasizes *decision making*, especially the kinds of decisions that cannot be easily programmed. An additional view of the managerial job draws attention to *leadership*, with an emphasis on particular traits and managerial styles. Closely related to this approach is the discussion about *power* and *influence*, that is, the leader's control of the environment and subordinates. Other writers focus their attention on the *behavior of leaders* by examining the content of the manager's job. Finally, the approach favored by Henry Mintzberg is based on observing the *work activities* of managers. It is interesting that the extensive research of the literature by Mintzberg resulted in a grouping of management "schools" which is not altogether different from the approaches to management discussed in Chapter 2 of this book.[3] He found through observations of five executives that their work was characterized by brevity, variety, discontinuity, and action orientation. He also found that executives favor oral communication and that they engage in many activities that link the enterprise with its environment.

The author's view

We have found it useful as we have made clear, to organize the key tasks of managers into the five functions of planning, organizing, staffing, leading, and controlling, and these constitute the framework of this book.

---

[2]For a comprehensive review see H. Mintzberg, *The Nature of Managerial Work* (New York: Harper & Row, Publishers, Incorporated, 1973), chap 2.

[3]H. Mintzberg, "The Manager's Job: Folklore and Fact," *Harvard Business Review*, vol. 53, no. 4 (July–August 1975), pp. 49–61.

The Systems Approach to Staffing: An Overview of the Staffing Function

An overview

Figure 13-1 shows how the managerial function of staffing relates to the total management system.[4] Specifically, *enterprise plans* (discussed in Part II) become the basis for *organization plans* (Part III) which are necessary to achieve enterprise objectives. The present and projected organization structure determines the *number and kinds of managers required*. These demands for managers are compared with available talent through the *management inventory*. Based on this analysis, *external and internal sources* are utilized in the processes of *recruitment, selection, placement, promotion, and separation*. Other essential aspects of staffing are *appraisal* and *training and development* of managers.

Staffing, as seen in the model, affects *leading and controlling*. For instance, well-trained managers create an environment in which people, working together in groups, can achieve enterprise objectives and at the same time accomplish personal goals. In other words, proper staffing facilitates leading (Part V). Similarly, selecting quality managers affects controlling by, for example, preventing many undesirable deviations from becoming major problems (Part VI).

An open-system approach

Staffing requires an open-system approach. It is carried out within the enterprise, which, in turn, is linked to the external environment. Therefore, internal factors of the firm—such as personal policies, the organizational climate, and the reward system—must be taken into account. Clearly, without adequate rewards it is impossible to attract and keep quality managers. The external environment cannot be ignored either; high technology demands well-trained, well-educated, and highly skilled managers. Inability to meet the demand for such managers may well prevent an enterprise from growing at a desired rate.

Factors Affecting the Number and Kinds of Managers Required

The number of managers needed in an enterprise depends not only upon its size but also upon the complexity of the organization structure, plans for expansion, and the rate of turnover of managerial personnel. The ratio between the number of managers and the number of employees does not follow any law. It is possible, by enlarging or contracting the delegation of authority, to modify a structure so that the number of managers in a given instance will increase or decrease regardless of the size of an operation.

The annual rate of appointments to managerial positions can be determined by a review of past experience and future expectations. Analysis will also reveal the relative importance of age for retirement, vacancies created by ill health, demotions and separations, and the steady demand of other enterprises for able young subordinates whom the firm has trained but is unable to hold.

Although the need for determining the number of managers required has been stressed here, clearly numbers are only part of the picture. Specifically, the qualifications for individual positions must be identified so that the best-suited

---

[4]Figure 13-1 is an overview of the staffing function. The variables not discussed in this chapter, but which also focus on staffing, are enclosed with broken lines.

FIGURE 13-1

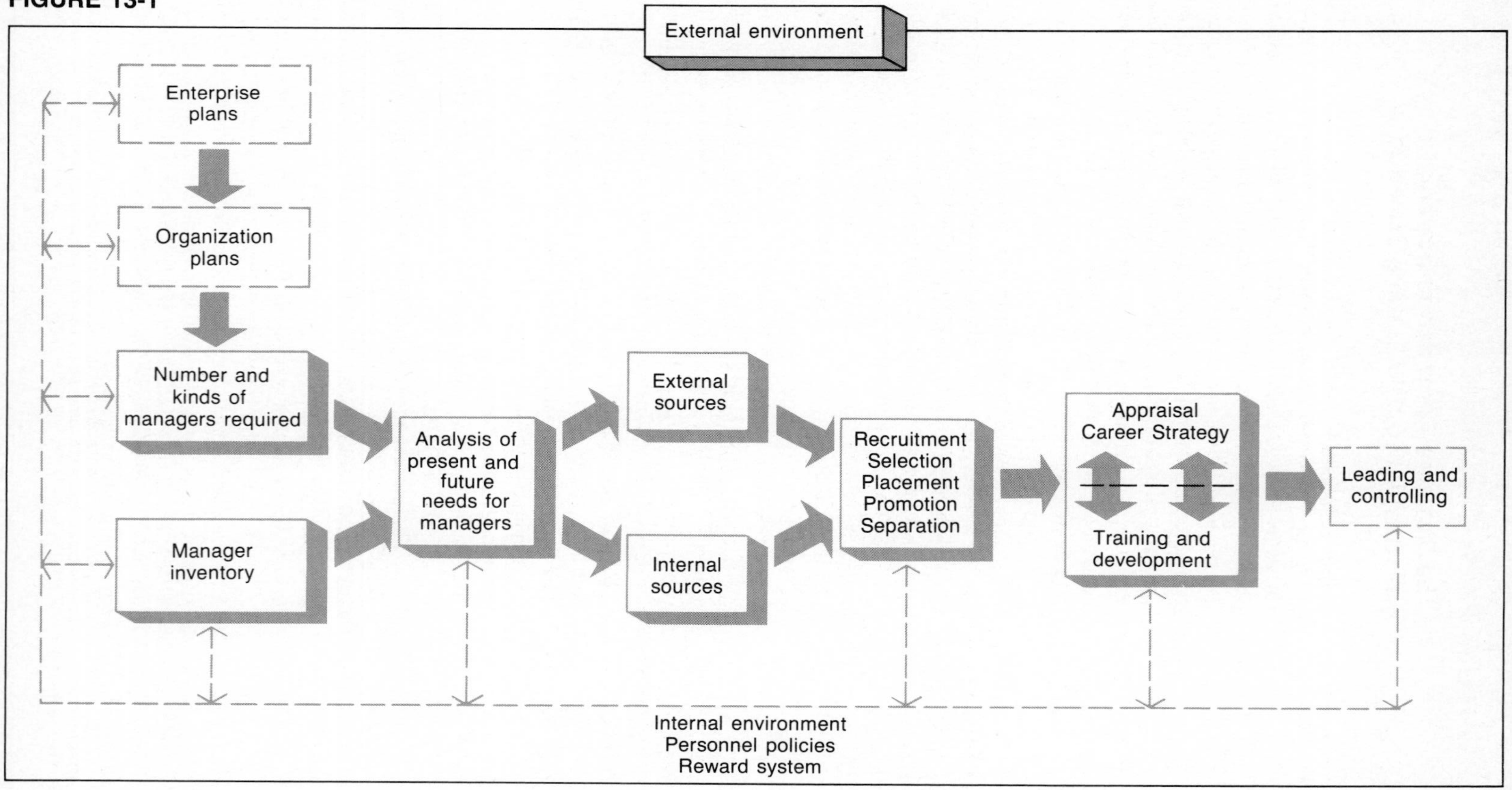

SYSTEMS APPROACH TO STAFFING.

managers can be chosen. This kind of detailed analysis of position requirements will be discussed in the next chapter on selection of managers.

Determination of Available Managerial Resources: The Management Inventory

It is common for any business, as well as for most nonbusiness enterprises, to keep an inventory of raw materials and goods on hand to enable it to carry on its operations. It is far less common for enterprises to keep an inventory of available human resources, particularly managers, despite the fact that the required number of competent managers is a vital requirement for success. Keeping abreast of the management potential within a firm can be done by the use of an *inventory chart*,[5] which is simply an organization chart of a unit with all managerial positions indicated and keyed as to the promotability of each incumbent.

Figure 13-2 depicts a typical inventory chart. At a glance the controller can see where he or she stands with respect to the staffing function. The controller's successor is probably the manager of general accounting, and this person in turn has a successor ready for promotion. Supporting that person in turn is a subordinate who will be ready for promotion in 1 year, but below that position are one person who does not have potential and two newly hired employees.

The cost accounting manager represents the all-too-frequent case of a person who is acceptable but not promotable. This individual stands in the way of one subordinate who is promotable now. The remaining people in this department represent extremes of nonpromotability and good potential. Overall, the staffing pattern in this department is not satisfactory.

The manager of budget and analysis has considerable development to accomplish before being ready for promotion. There is no immediately promotable successor. And to complicate matters, no further potential exists among the remaining two subordinates.

Contract pricing portends some problems. Its manager is not promotable, but there is good potential in the subordinates.

Advantages and Limitations of the Manager Inventory Chart

The manager inventory chart, as seen from the above discussions, has certain general *advantages*:

1 The chart gives an overview of the staffing situation of an organization.

2 Managers who are ready for promotion can now be easily identified. Prompt action in finding a suitable position within the organization may reduce the propensity of managers to seek employment outside the company.

3 The chart also shows the future internal supply of managers by indicating who is promotable in a year or more.

4 Managers who do not perform satisfactorily are identified and the need for replacement is indicated.

5 If the organization has insufficient "depth," recruitment and training plans can be initiated immediately to ensure the future supply of managers.

---

[5]Another term for "inventory chart" is "management replacement chart."

FIGURE 13-2

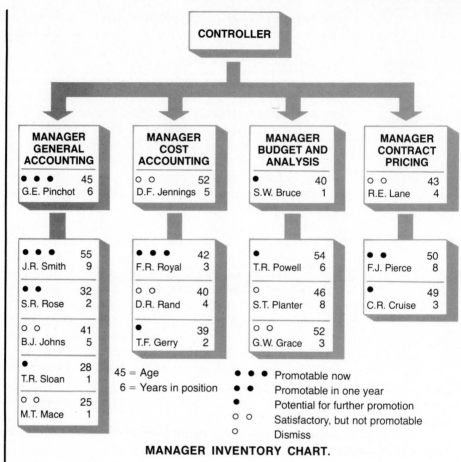

MANAGER INVENTORY CHART.

Note: The age shown on the inventory chart must not be used to discriminate against employees on the basis of their age.

6 Managers who are close to retirement can be identified and preparations can be made for their replacement.

7 The chart facilitates the transfer of managers not only to strengthen weak departments but also to broaden the managers' experience.

8 One can identify and prevent the hoarding of promotable people by their immediate superiors, a practice quite common especially in large enterprises. Naturally, superiors dislike depriving themselves of able subordinates by letting them transfer to other organizational units. But the overall interest of the enterprise is more important than the self-interest of an individual manager.

9 Managers can counsel subordinates about their career paths and relate them to employment opportunities within the company.

Despite its many advantages the manager inventory chart also has *limitations:*

1   The chart does not show to what position the manager may be promotable. If an opening occurs in another organizational unit, the person who is "promotable now" will not necessarily be able to fit this position since knowledge or skills may be required in specialized areas. A promotable manager in a production department can hardly fill the job of vice-president of sales.

2   The data shown on the chart are not sufficient to make a fair assessment of all the capabilities of individuals. It is still necesary to keep records of the individual's skills, performance, and other biographical information.

3   Although the chart is useful for counseling subordinates, it is often not practical to share the information with all employees. Instead, only the top manager of a division or a department may have this information available.

4   It takes time and effort to keep the chart up to date.

5   Upper-level managers may hesitate to make their charts available to other upper-level managers because they may be afraid they will lose competent subordinates to other organizational units.

Analysis of Need for Managers: External and Internal Information Sources

As shown in Figure 13-2, the need for managers is determined by enterprise and organizational plans and, more specifically, by an analysis of the number of managers required and the number available as identified through the management inventory. But there are other factors, internal and external, that influence the need for managers. The external forces influencing the demand for and supply of managers include economic, technological, social, political, and legal factors discussed in Chapter 3. For example, economic growth may result in increased demand for the product which requires an expansion of the work force, thus increasing the demand for managers. At the same time, competing companies may also expand and recruit from a common labor pool, thus reducing the supply of managers. One must also consider the trends in the labor market, the demographics, and the composition of the community with respect to knowledge and skills of the labor pool and the attitude toward the company. Information about the long-term trends in the labor market may be obtained from several sources. The United States government, for example, publishes the *Monthly Labor Review* and the annual *Manpower Report of the President*, which makes long-term projections. Some trade associations and unions also project the demand for labor.

Personnel actions matrix

The data about the need and the availability of personnel give rise to four demand and supply situations, each requiring a different emphasis in personnel actions. This is illustrated in the matrix shown as Figure 13-3.

With a *high supply* of managers and a *high demand,* the focus will be on selection, placement, and promotion. Consequently, particular efforts are made to match the available managers with enterprise needs most effectively.

A *low supply* of managers and a *high demand* requires a different emphasis. If the company favors internal promotions—and most alertly managed firms do—special emphasis would be placed on training and development to enlarge and

FIGURE 13-3

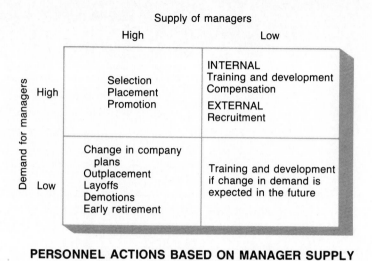

PERSONNEL ACTIONS BASED ON MANAGER SUPPLY
AND DEMAND WITHIN THE ENTERPRISE.

improve the pool of managers. But this takes time, and planning far in advance of actual needs is essential. Staffing should be based on open competition for available jobs, and managers from outside the firm should also be considered. Thus recruitment would be another option. In a situation with a high demand for managers within the enterprise, chances are that there is also a general demand for managers in the external environment. It is therefore crucial that compensation be competitive. This is important for retaining managers already employed by the enterprise, and it is also essential for recruiting managers.

A company with a *high supply* of managers and a *low demand* has several alternatives available. Either the firm can change plans to take advantage of the managerial assets, or it may resort to replacement or "outplacement" (a conscious attempt to help managers find and select other suitable employment), layoffs, demotions, or early retirements.

An enterprise with a *low supply* of managers and a *low demand* should be giving special attention to enterprise plans because this situation indicates a degree of stagnation in the firm. Since developing managers is a long process, the company should start developing managers early if there are prospects of growth and changes in demand for managers in the future.

Recruitment Selection, Placement, and Promotion

After the need for managerial personnel has been determined, a number of candidates may have to be recruited. This involves attracting qualified candidates to fill organizational roles. From these, managers or potential managers are selected; this is the process of choosing from among the candidates the most suitable ones. The aim is to place people in positions where they can utilize their personal strengths and, perhaps, overcome their weaknesses by getting experience or training in those skills in which they need improvement. Finally, placing a manager in a new position within the enterprise often results in a promotion, which normally involves more responsibility. Since recruitment, selection, placement, and promotion are complex processes, they will be discussed in greater detail in the next chapter.

Managerial Appraisal and Career Planning

Managerial appraisal is closely related to selection, placement, and promotion. One could even argue that appraisal should logically be placed before these other activities. It is true that appraisal serves as a basis for identifying persons within the enterprise who are ready for promotion. On the other hand, the candidates from outside the firm have first to be recruited, selected, and placed before their performance in a given position can be appraised. For this reason, managerial selection precedes appraisal in the model. But there is no doubt that appraisal is closely linked to selection, placement, and promotion, as is indicated by the feedback arrows in Figure 13-1. Career planning is often integrated with the appraisal process and will be discussed in Chapter 15.

Training and Development

In Chapter 16 on manager and organization development, a systematic approach to self-development and the utilization of managers' strengths and potentials, with emphasis on the integration of managerial needs and enterprise demands, will be discussed.

Leading and Controlling

Throughout this book, we have advocated the systems approach to managing. The model in Figure 13-1 shows that the activities in the staffing function must not be viewed in isolation; rather, they are related to leading (discussed in Part V) and controlling (Part VI of this book). For example, well-selected and well-trained managers provide good leadership and create an environment in which people are motivated and communicate effectively. Likewise, controlling is enhanced by effective staffing. Specifically, what better control is there than indirect control? This means that the higher the quality of selected managers and their subordinates, the lower the need for correcting undesirable deviations from performance standards.

Situational Factors Affecting Staffing

The actual process of staffing shown in Figure 13-1 is affected by many environmental factors. Specifically, external factors include the level of education, the prevailing attitudes in society (such as the attitude toward work), the many laws and regulations that directly affect staffing, economic conditions, and the supply of and demand for managers outside the enterprise.

But there are also many internal factors that affect staffing. They include, for example, organizational goals, tasks, technology, organization structure, the kinds of people employed by the enterprise, the demand for and the supply of managers within the enterprise, the reward system, and various kinds of policies. Some organizations are highly structured; others are not. For some positions—such as the position of a sales manager—skill in human relations may be of vital importance, while the same skill may be less critical for a research scientist working fairly independently in the laboratory. Effective staffing, then, requires recognition of many external and internal situational factors, but we will focus here on those that have a particular relevance to staffing.

The External Environment

Factors in the external environment do affect staffing to various degrees. These influences can be grouped into educational, sociocultural, legal-political, and economic constraints or opportunities. For example, the high technology used in many industries requires extensive and intensive education. Similarly, managers in our particular sociocultural environment generally do not accept orders blindly; they want to become active participants in the decision-making process. Furthermore, now and in the future, managers will have to be more oriented toward the public than they have been in the past, responding to the public's legitimate needs and adhering to high ethical standards.

The economic environment—including the competitive situation—determines the external supply of, and the demand for, managers. Legal and political constraints require firms to follow laws and guidelines issued by various levels of government. Table 13-1 summarizes major federal legislation and orders relating to fair employment that influence the staffing function. We will focus on equal employment opportunity and women in management. In addition, we will discuss the staffing of international businesses.

Equal employment opportunity   Several laws have been passed that provide for equal employment opportunity (EEO). The laws prohibit employment practices that discriminate on the basis of race, color, religion, national origin, sex, or age (in specified age ranges). EEO is based on federal, state, and local laws, and these laws impact on staffing. Recruitment and selection for promotion must be in compliance with these laws. This means that managers making decisions in these areas must be educated in the laws and how they apply to the staffing function.

Women in management   In the last decade or so, women have made significant progress in obtaining responsible positions in organizations. Among the reasons for this development are laws governing fair employment practices, changing societal attitudes toward women in the workplace, and the desire of companies to project a favorable image by placing qualified women in managerial positions.

But there appears to be some evidence that women also have some difficulty making it to the top. For example, there are no women on the way to the chief executive officer's job in the Fortune 500 corporations. Discrimination has been given as one reason according to a *Fortune* article.[6] On the other hand, Marissa Bellisario, as pointed out in Chapter 3, is one of the most successful executives in Italy with the press calling her "Lady Computer," and the "manager in jeans" (she occasionally wears jeans at work). In fact, companies such as IBM, AT&T, and GTE Corporation have unsuccessfully tried to recruit her.

---

[6]S. Fraker, "Why Women Aren't Getting to the Top," *Fortune*, Apr. 16, 1984, pp. 40–45.

TABLE 13-1   Major Federal Legislation and Orders Relating to Fair Employment Practices

Law/Order	Objectives	Applies to	Enforcement agency	Possible penalties
Civil Rights Act	Equal opportunity for races, religions, sexes, nationalities	Employers and unions with 15 employees/members; employment agencies; hiring halls; federal, state, and local governments	Equal Employment Opportunity Commission	Court-ordered affirmative action Back pay
Exec. Orders 11246, 11375	Equal opportunity and affirmative action	Government contractors in excess of $10,000; federal government agencies; U.S. Postal Service	Office of Federal Contract Compliance Programs Civil Service Commission	Contract cancellation
Age Discrimination in Employment Act	Equal opportunity for ages 40–70	Employers with 20 employees; unions with 25 members; employment agencies; federal, state, and local governments	EEOC (transferred from Labor Dept. July 1, 1979)	Court-ordered affirmative action Back pay; fines up to $10,000; possible imprisonment
Vocational Rehabilitation Act	Equal opportunity and affirmative action for handicapped personnel	Government contractors in excess of $2,500; federal government agencies	Office of Federal Contract Compliance Programs Civil Service Commission	Contract cancellation
Equal Pay Act	Equal pay for equal work regardless of sex	Employers subject to the Fair Labor Standards Act	EEOC (transferred from Labor Dept. July 1, 1979)	Back pay; fines up to $10,000; possible imprisonment

Source: E. B. Flippo and G. M. Munsinger, *Management,* 5th ed. (Boston, Allyn and Bacon, Inc., 1982), p. 287. Used with permission.

Staffing in the international environment   One must look beyond the immediate external environment and recognize the worldwide changes brought about primarily by advanced communication technology and by the existence of multinational corporations. In the future, it will not be unusual for large international firms to have top management teams composed of managers of many different nationalities. However, David A. Heenan and Howard V. Perlmutter state that only occasionally are foreign nationals included in human resource inventories while parent-country managers of multinational firms are usually included in the human resource pool.[7] In other words, one finds mostly Americans in crucial positions of American firms operating abroad. A notable exception is IBM, which has a truly geocentric management inventory. The geocentric attitude is the basis for viewing the organization as a worldwide entity with global decision making, including staffing decisions. The example of IBM may become the model for many multinational firms in which staffing has a worldwide scope.

[7]D. A. Heenan and H. V. Perlmutter, *Multinational Organization Development* (Reading, Mass.: Addison-Wesley Publishing Company, Inc., 1979), chap. 3.

**The Internal
Environment**

The internal factors selected for this discussion concern the staffing of managerial positions with personnel from within the firm as well as from the outside, determining the responsibility for staffing, and the need for top management support to overcome resistance to change.

Promotion from within   Originally, promotion from within implied that workers proceeded into front-line supervisory positions and then upward through the organizational structure. Thus, a firm was pictured as receiving a flow of nonmanagerial employees from which future managers emerged. As used to be said in the railroad industry, "When a president retires or dies, we hire a new office worker."

So long as the matter is considered in general terms, there is little doubt employees overwhelmingly favor a policy of promotion from within. The banning of outsiders places limits on competition for positions and gives employees of a firm an established monopoly on managerial openings. Employees come to doubt the wisdom of the policy, however, when they are confronted with a specific case of selection of one of their own for promotion. This feeling is present at all levels of the organization, largely because of rivalry for promotion or jelousy. The difficulty becomes most evident when selecting a general manager from among the sales, production, finance, or engineering managers. Top managers are often inclined to choose the easy way and avoid problems by selecting an outsider.

Some examples

Many companies advocate promotion from within. For example, William P. Given, when president of the American Brake Shoe Company, wrote, "It is our policy to give our own people the benefit of advancement as openings occur. We believe that unless we have no one who can possibly qualify it is not fair to our people to hire an outsider." Even more emphatic is the position taken by Sears, Roebuck and Company. In a booklet given to prospective employees is the statement, "At Sears the policy of 'promotion from within' is not just a phrase or slogan. It is a fact, insured by specific administrative measures to make sure that it happens." Similarly, Mobil Oil Company states that its policy is to fill all jobs, whenever possible, from within; and Procter & Gamble asserts that it adheres strictly to its policy of promotion from within, and that managers are required to train their successors. It is generally known that a good way to advance is to train subordinates so that they push their boss out of the current job. The policy of promotion from within is a part of the total approach to human resource management at Procter & Gamble that includes an intensive selection process, an extensive on-the-job training, and a good compensation system.

Such statements on promotion from within probably represent the general and official attitude of most corporate executives. There can be little question that many companies place heavy emphasis on the policy for the purpose of encouraging prospective managerial candidates to accept employment, and with the view of fostering long-run commitment and of bolstering employee morale. It is not always clear whether these same firms give similar assurance to their middle and top functional executives. The saving phrase "whenever possible" is quite sufficient to provide an escape.

Advantages

Promoting from within the enterprise not only has positive values relating to morale and reputation but also permits taking advantage of the presence of potentially fine managers among the firm's employees. However, even though these positive but unmeasurable values are important, executives should not be blind to the dangers of either overemphasizing this source or relying upon it exclusively.

Questionable assumptions

The assumption underlying the policy of promotion from within is either that new employees are hired with a view to their managerial potential or that, from among the new and old employees, there will emerge a sufficient number of qualified candidates for promotion. The latter assumption is unsafe for modern enterprise. It is increasingly dangerous as our population becomes differentiated in the degree to which its members seek education, since well-educated persons are more likely than the less well educated to be the successful candidates for managerial positions.

The assumption that all employees are hired with a view to their managerial potential is contrary to fact. Indeed, most employees are hired for their skills as machinists, electricians, typists, accountants, engineers, or statisticians. Those who are wanted because of such skills are seldom turned down because they may have low managerial potential.

Another danger presented by an exclusive policy of promoting from within is that it may lead to the selection of persons for promotion who have, perhaps, only imitated their superiors. This is not necessarily a fault, especially if only the best methods, routines, and viewpoints are cultivated; but this is likely to be an unapproachable ideal. The fact is that enterprises often need people from the outside to introduce new ideas and practices. Consequently, there is good reason to avoid a policy of exclusive promotion from within.

Promotion from within in large companies

On the other hand, a policy of promotion from within may be quite suitable for a very large company such as Sears, Du Pont, or General Motors. But even Sears looked outside when the company recruited Philip Purcell as vice-president for corporate planning from the well-known consulting firm of McKinsey & Co. Nevertheless, large business and nonbusiness organizations usually have so many qualified people that promotion from within actually approaches a condition similar to an open-competition policy. Even in these large companies, however, it may be necessary to go outside, as General Motors did when it hired a university professor as vice-president to head its environmental control staff.

The policy of open competition   Managers must decide whether the benefits of a policy of promotion from within outweigh its shortcomings. There are clear-cut reasons for implementing the **principle of open competition** by opening vacant positions to the best-qualified persons available, whether inside or outside the enterprise. It gives the firm, in the final analysis, the opportunity to secure the services of the best-suited candidates. It counters the shortcomings of an exclusive policy of promotion from within, permits a firm to adopt the best techniques in the recruiting of managers, and motivates the complacent heir apparent. To exchange these advantages for the morale advantages attributed to internal promotion would appear questionable.

Principle of open competition

A policy of open competition is a better and more honest means of ensuring managerial competence than obligatory promotion from within. However, it does put the managers who use it under a special obligation. If morale is to be protected in applying an open-competition policy, the enterprise must have fair and objective methods of appraising and selecting its people. It should also do everything possible to help people develop so that they can qualify for promotions.

When these requirements are met, it would be expected that every manager making an appointment to a vacancy or a new position, would have available a roster of qualified candidates within the entire enterprise. If people know that their qualifications are being considered, if they have been fairly appraised and have been given opportunities for development, they are far less likely to feel a sense of injustice if an opening goes to an outsider. Other things being equal, present employees *should* be able to compete with outsiders. If a person has the ability for a position, he or she has the considerable advantage of knowing the enterprise, its personnel, history, problems, policies, and objectives. For the superior candidate, the policy of open competition should be a challenge and not a hindrance to advancement.

Selection of key managers from outside   Key managers are the ones who spark a program and carry it to completion. Although these executives may be found at all organizational levels, key managers will most probably be found at or near the top of the organization structure. They provide the tone, imagination, and judgment which help an enterprise attain its objectives. Since subordinate managers tend to reflect the attitudes of their superiors, their contribution to a program may often be ascribed to the inspiration of outstanding personalities.

Reasons for selection of outside candidates

Often there are reasons for selecting key executives from outside the enterprise. Outside candidates may be considered superior to the internal contenders. For example, when firms reach a position in their development where the outstanding need is for their energies to be directed vigorously toward the solution of marketing problems, they are likely to turn to the outside. Promotion of insiders may not be advisable, since they have brought the enterprise to its stagnant position. Indeed, this is the situation that faced many firms during the 1960s when key marketing executives were brought in to guide firms through a highly competitive period. For similar reasons, production managers were imported during the early decades of the twentieth century, and engineers have more recently been brought into conspicious positions with firms in the electronics and plastics industries. Here the factors being sought were vision, new ideas, and new applications. And in the same time periods, financial executives seemed to be preferred because of their experience with money and controls and with looking at an organization as a whole.

Responsibility for staffing   While responsibility for staffing should rest with every manager at every level, the ultimate responsibility is with the chief executive officer and the policymaking group of top executives. They have the duty of developing policy, assigning its execution to subordinates, and making certain it is being properly carried out. Policy considerations, for example, include decisions about the development of a staffing program, whether to promote from within or to secure managers from the outside, where to seek candidates, which selection procedure to follow, the kind of appraisal program to use, the nature of manager and organization development, and what promotion and retirement policies to follow.

Line managers should certainly make use of the services of staff members—usually from the personnel department—to assist in recruiting, selecting, placing, promoting, appraising, and training people. In the final analysis, however, it is the manager's responsibility to fill positions with the best qualified persons.

Need for top management support in overcoming resistance to effective staffing
The prestige and power of top management must be brought to bear if staffing is to be effective. Some managers within the organization will resent losing promising subordinates, even though they can make a greater contribution to the enterprise in a different department. Others will resist changes required by managerial and organizational development efforts. There are also those who may be threatened by imaginative and achievement-oriented subordinates. Still others may not see staffing as a pressing matter and neglect it altogether. To overcome these human tendencies, top management involvement in staffing is necessary.

Summary

Staffing means filling positions in the organization structure. In staffing, we identify work-force requirements, inventory people available, recruit, select, place, promote, appraise, compensate, and train people.

We use a systems approach to staffing, with enterprise and organization plans becoming important inputs for staffing tasks. The number and quality of managers required to carry out crucial tasks depend on many different factors. One major step in staffing is to determine the people available by making a management inventory. This can be done by using an inventory chart, which, in turn, helps to make staffing decisions involving recruiting, selecting, placing, promoting, or dismissing people. To assess and improve managerial competency, we appraise, train, and develop managers.

Staffing does not take place in a vacuum and one must consider many situational factors—both internal and external ones. Staffing requires adherence to equal employment opportunity laws so that practices do not discriminate, for example, against minorities or women. Also, one must evaluate the pros and cons of promoting people from within the organization or selecting people from the outside.

Key Ideas and Concepts for Review

Staffing
Systems approach to staffing
Dynamic factors in staffing
Inventory chart
Situational factors affecting staffing
Promotion from within

Policy of open competition
Selection of key managers from outside
Equal employment opportunities
Women in management
Responsibility for staffing

For Discussion

1 What differences do you see between staffing for managers and for nonmanagers?

2 What rewards would you expect from becoming a manager? What are some of the negative aspects of being a manager?

3 Why is the function of staffing so seldom approached logically? Briefly describe the systems approach to staffing. How is staffing related to other managerial functions and activities?

4 List and evaluate external factors affecting staffing. Which ones are most critical today? Explain.

5 What are the key characteristics of a manager inventory chart? Discuss the advantages and limitations of such a chart.

6 What are the dangers and difficulties in applying a policy of promotion from within?

7 What is meant by a policy of open competition? Do you favor such a policy? Why, or why not?

8 Do you believe that a manager inventory should be kept confidential? Why, or why not?

9 Take an organization you know and evaluate the effectiveness of the enterprise's recruitment, selection, and appraisal of people. How systematically are these and other staffing activities carried out?

CASE 13-1

BELDEN ELECTRONICS COMPANY

The Belden Electronics Company (BEC) has an excellent national as well as international reputation and employees are proud to work for the firm. But the company demands complete loyalty from its employees and even tries to influence their behavior and appearance after work.

Christine Sharp was a bright young woman who had been working for BEC for over 10 years. She was highly respected by her colleagues, did an excellent job as a divisional sales manager, and it was generally agreed that she had excellent potential for advancement. For 2 months Ms. Sharp had dated Frank Simmons, who worked in the electronics division of a competing company. One day, Ralph Schmidt, Christine's boss, approached her about this matter, stating that there might be a possible conflict of interest in the association with an employee of the competitor. He made it clear that BEC has an unwritten policy that demands (and rewards) complete loyalty from all its employees.

Shortly after this emotional confrontation with her boss, Ms. Sharp was transferred to a non-managerial position without any loss in pay. She also noted that even her friends at BEC tried to avoid her. But Ms. Sharp felt very strongly that the company had no business suggesting whom she could and could not see after working hours; as a result, she quit her job.

1 Can a company demand loyalty to the extent indicated in the case? Would your answer be different if Ms. Sharp had access to important company trade secrets?

2 What would you have done in Ms. Sharp's position?

3 What would you have done in the supervisor's position?

CASE 13-2
TEXAS OIL COMPANY

Fred Jenkins and Barbara Eaton, both employees at the Texas Oil Company, sat in the cafeteria and discussed recent happenings in the company. A few months ago, Texas Oil was acquired by one of the largest conglomerate firms, causing a great deal of upheaval among its employees and considerable turnover in personnel. Top management of the conglomerate realized that in order to keep the employees of the newly acquired company happy, it had to provide large salary increases, bonuses, and other benefits. Yet, it lost many of Texas Oil's top managers, a fifth of its production people, and many persons involved in oil exploration. While some of the employees left the company for better pay outside the firm, there were also indications that money was not the primary motive for leaving. Becoming a part of a huge conglomerate might seem attractive, but it also involved closer supervision, more bureaucratic rules, and less discretion in decision making. The more formalized approach to managing also created additional paperwork and more formal procedures and controls.

The employees at Texas Oil had been accustomed to a rather laissez-faire managerial approach. This changed, however, when the company became a part of the conglomerate. Despite the conglomerate's attempts to decentralize, the chain of command became much longer, and many managers, especially those with entrepreneurial talent, were frustrated. Fred and Barbara talked about their preferences and whether or not they should leave the company to join a small oil firm known for its informal managerial style. Fred Jenkins favored the small-company atmosphere, but Barbara Eaton liked the status, prestige, and multinational character of the conglomerate.

1 What are the advantages and disadvantages of working for a large, prestigious multinational firm?

2 What are the advantages and disadvantages of working for a small company?

3 What are your preferences? Why?

For Further Information

Bartolomé, F. "The Work Alibi: When It's Harder to Go Home," *Harvard Business Review*, vol. 61, no. 2 (March–April 1983), pp. 67–74.

Bolt, J. F. "Job Security: Its Time Has Come," *Harvard Business Review*, vol. 61, no. 6 (November–December, 1983), pp. 115–123.

Cunningham, M. *Powerplay: What Really Happened at Bendix* (New York: Linden Press of Simon & Schuster, Inc., 1984).

Drucker, P. "Executives Are 'Aging' at 42," *Wall Street Journal*, Mar. 7, 1984.

Hackman, R. J., E. E. Lawler III, and L. W. Porter (eds.) *Perspectives on Behavior in Organizations*, 2nd ed. (New York: McGraw-Hill Book Company, 1983).

Likert, R. *The Human Organization: Its Management and Value* (New York: McGraw-Hill Book Company, 1967).

Mintzberg, H. "The Manager's Job: Folklore and Fact," *Harvard Business Review*, vol. 53, no. 4 (July–August 1975), pp. 49–61.

Riger, S., and P. Galligan. "Women in Management: An Explanation of Competing Paradigms," *American Psychologist*, vol. 35 (October 1980), pp. 902–910.

Robbins, S. S. *Personnel: The Management of Human Resources*, 2nd ed. (Englewood Cliffs, N.J.: Prentice-Hall, Inc., 1982).

Rosen, B., S. Rynes, and T. A. Mahoney. "Compensation, Jobs, and Gender," *Harvard Business Review*, vol. 61, no. 4 (July–August, 1983), pp. 170–190.

Schein, E. H. "Increasing Organizational Effectiveness Through Better Human Resource Planning and Development," in H. Koontz, C. O'Donnell, and H. Weihrich (eds.), *Management—A Book of Readings* (New York: McGraw-Hill Book Company, 1980), pp. 383–395.

Schwartz, S. J. "How to Dehire: A Guide for the Manager," *Human Resource Management*, vol. 19 (Winter 1980), pp. 22–25.

Skinner, W. "Big Hat, No Cattle: Managing Human Resources," *Harvard Business Review*, vol. 59, no. 5 (September–October 1981), pp. 106–114.

"Top Women Executives Find Path to Power is Strewn With Hurdles," *Wall Street Journal*, Oct. 15, 1984.

Walker, J. W. *Human Resource Planning* (New York: McGraw-Hill Book Company, 1980).

Werther, W. B., Jr., and K. Davis. *Personnel Management and Human Resources* (New York: McGraw-Hill Book Company, 1981).

"You've Come a Long Way, Baby—But Not as Far as You Thought," *Business Week*, Oct. 1, 1984.

"Young Executive Women Advance Farther, Faster Than Predecessors," *Wall Street Journal*, Oct. 26, 1984.

14

Selection: Matching the Person with the Job

CHAPTER OBJECTIVES

After reading this chapter, you should understand:

1 The important aspects of the systems approach to selection of managers
2 Position requirements for managerial jobs
3 Job design for individuals and work teams
4 Desired skills and personal characteristics for managers
5 The process of matching job requirements with manager qualifications
6 The selection process, techniques, and instruments
7 Important limitations in the selection process of managers
8 The importance of orienting and socializing new employees

Definition of selection

Plant, equipment, materials, and people do not make a business any more than airplanes, tanks, ships, and people make an effective military force. One other element is indispensable: effective managers. The quality of managers is one of the most important factors determining the continuing success of any organization. It necessarily follows, therefore, that the selection of managers is one of the most critical steps in the entire process of managing. We define *selection* as choosing from among candidates, from within the organization or from the outside, the most suitable person for the current position or for future positions.

Systems Approach to the Selection of Managers: An Overview

Since qualified managers are critical to the success of an enterprise, a systematic approach is essential to manager selection and to the assessment of present and future needs for managerial personnel.

Systems approach to selection

An overview of the systems approach to selection is illustrated in Figure 14-1. The variables that are closely related to selection, but are not discussed in this chapter, are marked with broken lines in the model. The *managerial requirements plan* is based on the firm's objectives, forecasts, plans, and strategies. This plan is translated into *position and job design* requirements which are matched with such *individual characteristics* as intelligence, knowledge, skills, attitudes, and experience. To meet organizational requirements, managers *recruit, select, place, and promote* people. This, of course, must be done with due consideration for the *internal environment* (for example, company policies, supply and demand of managers, and the organizational climate) and the *external environment* (laws, regulations, availability of managers). After people have been selected and placed in positions, they must be introduced to the new job. This *orientation* involves learning about the company, its operation, and its social aspects.

The newly placed managers then carry out their managerial and nonmanagerial functions (such as marketing), their *managerial performance* eventually determines *enterprise performance*. Subsequently, managerial performance is *appraised*, and managers are *rewarded*. (See Chapter 15.) Based on this evaluation, manager and organization *development* are initiated (Chapter 16). Finally, appraisal may also become the basis for *promotion, demotion, replacement, and retirement* decisions.

That is the selection model in brief; now each major variable in the model will receive closer attention.

Position Requirements and Job Design

To select a manager effectively requires a clear understanding of the nature and purpose of the position which is to be filled. An objective analysis of position requirements must be made, and, as far as possible, the job must be designed to meet organizational and individual needs. In addition, positions must be evaluated and compared so the incumbents can be treated fairly and equitably. Among other factors to consider are the skills required—technical, human, conceptual, and design—since these vary with the level in the organizational hierarchy and the personal characteristics needed by managers.

Identifying Job Requirements

In identifying job requirements, we must answer questions such as: What has to be done in this job? How is it done? What background knowledge, attitudes, and skills are required? Since positions are not static, we may have to consider additional questions: Can it be done differently? If so, what are the new requirements? To find answers to these and similar questions, we must analyze the job. This can be done through observation, interviews, questionnaires, or even a systems anal-

FIGURE 14-1

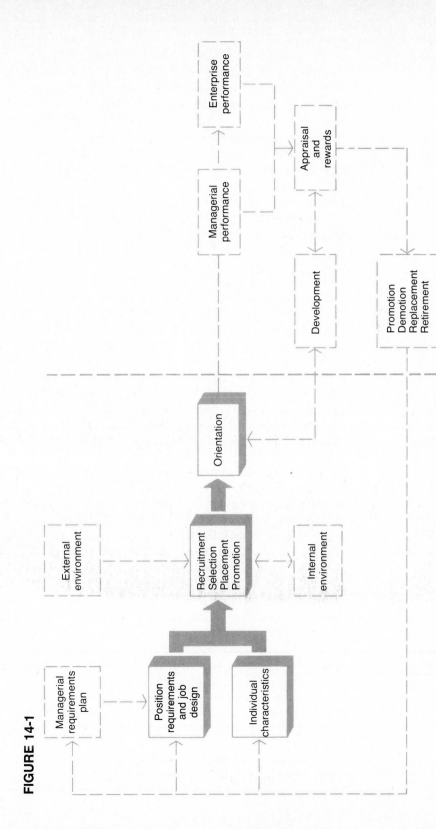

SYSTEMS APPROACH TO SELECTION.

Variables marked with broken lines are staffing and other activities that are discussed in other chapters.

ysis. Thus, a job description, based on job analysis, usually lists important duties, authority-responsibility relationships (although these can also be handled by reference to a chart of approval authorization, discussed in Chapter 11), and the relationship to other positions. More recently, some firms have also included objectives and expected results in job descriptions.

There is, of course, no foolproof rule for designing managerial jobs. Nevertheless, we can avoid mistakes by following some guidelines.

The scope of the job should be appropriate A job too narrowly defined provides no challenge, no opportunity for growth, and no sense of accomplishment. Consequently, good managers will be bored and dissatisfied. On the other hand, a job must not be so broad that it cannot be effectively handled. The result will be stress, frustration, and loss of control.

The position should involve a full-time, challenging job Sometimes managers are given a job that does not require their full time and effort. They are not challenged by their task and they feel underutilized. Consequently, they often meddle in the work of their subordinates, who then also feel that they do not have sufficient authority and discretion to do their jobs. Some time ago, when a utility company asked for help in solving organizational conflicts, it was found that people did not have full-time jobs; they were quarreling about jobs, duties, and tasks; they were in each other's way. Thus, they channeled their energy against one another instead of toward the aims of the company. The need to design jobs with challenging objectives, duties, and responsibilities should be obvious.

The job design should reflect required managerial skills Generally, the design of the job should start with the tasks to be accomplished. The design is usually broad enough to accommodate people's needs and desires. But some writers on management suggest that we may have to learn to design the job to fit the leadership style of a particular person. It may be especially appropriate to design jobs for exceptional persons, in order to utilize their potential. The problem, of course, is that such a position would probably have to be restructured every time a new manager occupied it. The job description, then, must provide a clear idea of the performance requirements for a person in a particular position, but must also allow some flexibility so that the employer can take advantage of individual characteristics and abilities.

Situational approach

Any position description is contingent on the particular job and the organization. For example, in a bureaucratic and fairly stable organization environment, the position may be described in relatively specific terms. In contrast, in a dynamic organization with an unstable, fast-changing environment, a job description may have to be more general and most likely will have to be reviewed more frequently. A situational approach to job descriptions and job designs is called for.

Job Design

People spend a great deal of time on the job, and it is therefore important to design jobs so that individuals feel good about their work. This requires an appropriate job structure in terms of content, function, and relationships.

Individual jobs

Design of jobs for individuals and work teams   The focus of job design can be on the individual position or on work groups.[1] First, *individual jobs* can be enriched by grouping tasks into natural work units. This means putting tasks that are related into one category and assigning an individual to carry out the tasks. A second related approach is to combine several tasks into one job. For example, rather than having the tasks of assembling a water pump carried out by several persons on the assembly line, work stations can be established with individuals doing the whole task of putting the unit together and even testing it. A third way of enriching the job is to establish direct relationships with the client. A systems analyst may present findings and recommendations directly to the managers involved in the systems change rather than reporting to his or her superior who would then make the recommendations to top management. Fourth, prompt and specific feedback should be built into the system whenever appropriate. In one retail store, for example, salespersons received the sales figures for each day and summary figures for each month. Fifth, individual jobs can be enriched through *vertical job loading*, which is increasing individuals' responsibility for planning, doing, and controlling their job.

Work teams

Similar arguments can be made for improving the design of jobs for *work teams*.[2] Jobs should be designed so that groups have a complete task to perform. Moreover, teams may be given authority and freedom to decide how well the jobs shall be performed, giving the groups a great deal of autonomy. Within the team, individuals can often be trained so that they can rotate to different jobs within the group. Finally, rewards may be administered on the basis of group performance, which tends to induce cooperation among team members rather than competition.

Factors influencing job design   In designing jobs, the requirements of the enterprise have to be taken into account. But other factors must be considered in order to realize maximum benefits; they include individual differences, the technology involved, the costs associated with restructuring the jobs, the organization structure, and the internal climate.

Individual needs

People have different needs. Those with unused capabilities and a need for growth and development usually want to have their job enriched and assume greater responsibility. While some people prefer to work by themselves, others with social needs usually work well in groups. The nature of the task and the technology related to the job must also be considered. While it may be possible for work teams to assemble automobiles, as is done at a Volvo plant in Sweden, it may not be efficient to use the same work design for the high production runs at General Motors in the United States. The costs of changing to new job designs must also be considered. It makes a great deal of difference whether a plant is newly designed or an old plant has to be redesigned and changed to accommodate new job design concepts.

---

[1]This discussion of job design is based in part on D. A. Nadler, J. R. Hackman, and E. E. Lawler III, *Managing Organizational Behavior* (Boston: Little, Brown and Company, 1979), chap. 5.
[2]Ibid. See also the discussion of sociotechnical systems in Chapter 2 of this book.

Work environment

The organization structure must also be taken into account. Individual jobs must fit the overall structure. Autonomous work groups, for example, may work well in a decentralized organization but they may be inappropriate in a centralized structure. Similarly, the organizational climate influences job design. Groups may function well in an atmosphere that encourages participation, job enrichment, and autonomous work, while they may not fit into an enterprise with an autocratic top-down approach to managerial leadership.

Job design at Volvo

Job design receives considerable attention abroad as well as in the United States. At the Volvo truck assembly plant in Sweden, work teams have a great deal of autonomy. For example, these teams choose their own supervisor, assign the work among themselves, set their own outputs within specified limits, and assume responsibility for quality control. In Kalmar, Sweden, Volvo designed an auto plant for teams of fifteen to twenty-five employees, each team handles a specific major task. Employees also receive immediate feedback on hourly production rates, which are displayed on screens.

Skills and Personal Characteristics Needed by Managers

To be effective, managers need various skills ranging from technical to design. The relative importance of these skills varies according to the level in the organization.

Managerial Skills and the Organizational Hierarchy

Robert L. Katz identified three kinds of skills for administrators.[3] We suggest a fourth—the ability to design solutions.

1 *Technical skill* is knowledge of and proficiency in activities involving methods, processes, and procedures. Thus it involves working with tools and specific techniques. For example, mechanics work with tools, and their supervisors should have the ability to teach these skills to their subordinates. Similarly, accountants apply specific techniques in doing their job.

2 *Human skill* is the ability to work with people; it is cooperative effort; it is teamwork; it is the creation of an environment in which people feel secure and free to express their opinions.

3 *Conceptual skill* refers to the ability to see the "big picture"; to recognize significant elements in a situation; to understand the relationships among the elements.

---

[3]R. L. Katz, "Skills of an Effective Administrator," *Harvard Business Review*, vol. 33, no. 1 (January–February 1955), pp. 33–42; and R. L. Katz, "Retrospective Commentary," *Harvard Business Review*, vol. 52, no. 5 (September–October 1974), pp. 101–102.

FIGURE 14-2

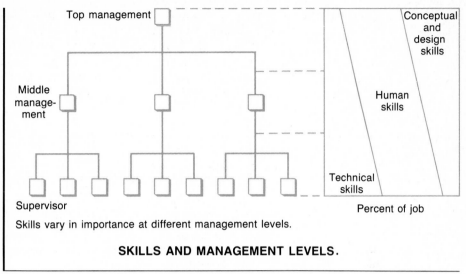

Skills vary in importance at different management levels.

SKILLS AND MANAGEMENT LEVELS.

4 *Design skill* connotes the ability to solve problems in ways that will benefit the enterprise. To be effective, particularly at upper organizational levels, managers must be able to do more than see a problem. They must have, in addition, the skill of a good design engineer in working out a practical solution to a problem. If managers merely see the problem and become "problem watchers," they will fail. Managers must also have that valuable skill of being able to design a workable solution to the problem in the light of the realities they face.

Skills in the hierarchy

The relative importance of these skills may differ at various levels in the organization hierarchy. As shown in Figure 14-2, technical skills are of greatest importance at the supervisory level. Human skills are also helpful in the frequent interactions with subordinates. Conceptual skills, on the other hand, are usually not critical for lower-level supervisors. At the middle-management level, the need for technical skills decreases; human skills are still essential; the conceptual skills gain in importance. At the top management level, conceptual and design abilities and human skills are especially valuable, but there is relatively little need for technical abilities. It is assumed, especially in large companies, that chief executives can utilize the technical abilities of their subordinates. In smaller firms, however, technical experience may be still quite important.

Analytical and Problem-Solving Abilities

One of the frequently mentioned skills desired of managers is analytical and problem-solving ability. But as Alan Stoneman, former president of the Purex Corporation, used to say: "We have no problems here; all are opportunities; all a problem should be is an opportunity." In other words, managers must be able to identify problems, analyze complex situations, and by solving the problems encountered, exploit the opportunities presented. They must scan the environment and identify, through a rational process, those factors that stand in the way of opportunities. Thus, analytical skills should be used to find needs of present customers—or potential ones—and then to satisfy these needs with a product or service. It has been amply demonstrated that this opportunity-seeking approach can mean corporate success. For example, Edwin H. Land of Polaroid filled the needs of people who wanted instant photographs. Similarly, Heinz Nordhoff of Volkswagen satisfied those customers in the late 1940s, 1950s, and 1960s who wanted a low-cost, reliable, and fuel-efficient automobile. But problem identification and analysis are not enough. Managers also need the will to implement the solutions; they must recognize the emotions, needs, and motivations of the people involved in initiating the required change as well as those who resist change.

Personal Characteristics Needed by Managers

In addition to the various skills that effective managers need, several personal characteristics are also important. They are (1) a desire to manage, (2) ability to communicate with empathy, (3) integrity and honesty, and (4) the person's experience—his or her past performance as a manager—which is a very significant characteristic and which should also be considered.

Desire to manage   The successful manager has a strong desire to manage, to influence others, and to get results through team efforts of subordinates. To be sure, many people want the privileges of the managerial positions, which include high status and salary, but they lack the basic motivation to achieve results by creating an environment in which people work together toward common aims. The desire to manage requires effort, time, energy, and usually long hours of work.

Communication skills and empathy   Another important characteristic of managers is the ability to communicate through written reports, letters, speeches, and discussions. Communication demands clarity, but even more, it demands empathy. This is the ability to understand the feelings of another person and to deal with the emotional aspects of communication. Communication skills are important for effective *intragroup* communication, that is, communication with people in the same organizational unit. As one goes up in the organization, however, *intergroup* communication becomes increasingly important. This kind of communication is not only with other departments but also with groups outside the enterprise: customers, suppliers, governments, the community, and, of course, the stockholders in business enterprises.

Integrity and honesty   Managers must be morally sound and worthy of trust. Integrity in managers includes honesty in money matters and in dealing with others, effort to keep superiors informed, adherence to the full truth, strength of character, and behavior in accordance with ethical standards.

Examples

Many of these qualities, and others, have been cited by top executives of major companies. Henry Ford II, former chairperson of Ford Motor Company, mentioned as appealing qualities honesty, candor, and openness. Similarly, Donald M. Kendall, chairperson of Pepsico, Inc., listed work ethics and integrity as essential characteristics of executives. Noah Dietrich, who ran the Howard Hughes empire for 32 years, identified honesty and candor as the top qualities of his subordinates. His attitude was: "I cannot do my job if the executives who report to me do not tell me the truth about their operations."

Past performance as a manager   One of the very important characteristics for selection is past performance as a manager. It is probably the most reliable forecast of a manager's future performance. Of course, an assessment of managerial experience is not possible in selecting first-line supervisors from the ranks, since they have not had such experience. But past accomplishments are important considerations in the selection of middle- and upper-level managers.

Matching Manager Qualifications with Position Requirements

After the organizational positions are identified, managers are obtained through recruitment, selection, placement, and promotion. (See variables in Figure 14-1.) There are basically two sources of managerial personnel: People from within the enterprise may be promoted or transferred, and managers may be hired from the outside. For *internal* promotions, a computerized information system may help to identify qualified candidates. It can be used in conjunction with a comprehensive human resource plan. Specifically, it can be utilized to anticipate staff requirements, new openings, attritions, development needs, and career planning.

Internal sources

There are also several *external* sources available, and the enterprise may use different methods in finding qualified managers. Many employment agencies—public and private—locate suitable candidates for positions. Other sources for managers are professional associations, educational institutions, referrals from people within the enterprise, and of course, unsolicited applications from persons interested in the firm.

External sources

Recruitment of Managers

Recruiting involves attracting candidates to fill the positions in the organization structure. Before recruiting begins, the position's requirements—which should relate directly to the task—must be clearly identified. This makes it easier to recruit suitable candidates from the outside. Enterprises with a favorable public image find it easier to attract qualified candidates. A company such as IBM (International Business Machines) has a well-recognized image, while small firms—which frequently offer excellent growth and development opportunities—may have to make great efforts to communicate to the applicant the kinds of products, services, and opportunities the firm offers.

Public sector

Recruitment in the public sector has many similarities to recruitment in the private sector. However, government regulations or policies may demand that managers adhere to special hiring guidelines. For example, legislation may require that potential employees live within a municipality's boundaries. Another difference is that applicants for public sector positions often have to take competitive

FIGURE 14-3

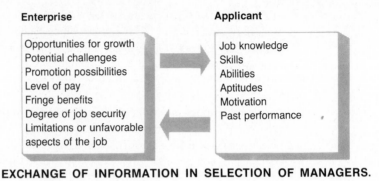

Enterprise

Opportunities for growth
Potential challenges
Promotion possibilities
Level of pay
Fringe benefits
Degree of job security
Limitations or unfavorable
aspects of the job

Applicant

Job knowledge
Skills
Abilities
Aptitudes
Motivation
Past performance

EXCHANGE OF INFORMATION IN SELECTION OF MANAGERS.

tests, such as civil service examinations, although an increasing number of privately owned enterprises are using written and oral tests.

Unfortunately, the selection process in government is not always as objective and rational as it should be, and the practice of making decisions on criteria other than competence is probably not unusual. Frederic V. Malek, a former special assistant to the President and now a business executive himself, reports that it is unthinkable for a major corporation to put a person without considerable managerial experience in charge of 5,000 people. Yet, in government this is not uncommon.[4] Thus, in order to improve the effectiveness and efficiency of government, a better selection process is required.

Information Exchange Contributing to Successful Selection

The exchange of information works two ways in recruitment and selection: an enterprise provides applicants with an objective description of the company and the position, while the applicants provide information about their capabilities. (See Figure 14-3.)

The enterprise

Business and other organizations attempt to project a favorable image, stress opportunities for personal growth and development, highlight potential challenges, and indicate promotion possibilities. They also convey information about pay, fringe benefits, and perhaps job security. The image can, of course, be overdone, raising unrealistic expectations in the applicant. In the long run, there may be undesirable side effects resulting in low job satisfaction, high turnover, and unfulfilled dreams. Certainly the enterprise should present itself in an attractive light, yet the opportunities should be discussed in a factual and realistic manner, mentioning limitations and even unfavorable aspects of the job.

The applicant

On the other hand, management should elicit from all the applicants an objective demonstration of their knowledge, skills, abilities, aptitudes, motivation, and past performance. A number of techniques and instruments can reveal this information; we will discuss them below. To be sure, the collection of data about

---

[4]F. V. Malek, *Washington's Hidden Tragedy* (New York: The Free Press, 1978), p. 68.

an applicant can go too far and can become an invasion of privacy. The managerial candidate will tolerate only a reasonable amount of interviewing, testing, and disclosure of personal information. Clearly, managers must exercise restraint and request information that is essential and relevant to the job.

Selection, Placement, and Promotion

Selecting a manager is choosing from among the candidates the one that best meets the position requirements. The selection may be for a specific job opening, or it may be for future managerial requirements. Thus, we can distinguish between the selection and placement approaches to filling organizational positions. In the *selection approach*, applicants are sought to fill a position with rather specific requirements, while in the *placement approach*, the strengths and weaknesses of the individual are evaluated and a suitable position is found or even designed.

Promotion

Promotion is a change within the organization to a higher position with greater responsibilities and requiring more advanced skills. It usually involves higher status and an increase in pay. The various facets of selection generally apply also to promotion, which may be a reward for outstanding performance or a result of the firm's desire to better utilize the individual's skills and abilities.

Balancing Skills and the Age Factor

There are other important considerations in selection. As we pointed out above, managerial positions demand a variety of skills: technical, human, conceptual, and problem-solving. Since one person may not have all the required abilities, others may have to be selected to compensate for any deficiencies. For example, a top manager with excellent conceptual and design skills may need assistance from persons with technical skills. Similarly, a manager with a strong marketing and financial background may have to be complemented by an operations expert.

Age must also be taken into account when selecting managers. It is not uncommon to find that all vice-presidents and middle managers in a company are in the same age bracket. Problems will thus occur when several managers on a similar organization level retire at the same time, a situation that can be avoided by considering age at the time appointments are made. Managers must be careful, however, to avoid illegal discrimination based on age. Systematic work-force planning can provide for fair distribution of managers in different age groups within the organizational structure.

The Peter Principle

Errors in selection are possible, perhaps even common. According to Laurence J. Peter and Raymond Hall, authors of *The Peter Principle*, managers tend to be promoted to the level of their incompetence.[5] Specifically, if a manager succeeds in a position, this very success may lead to promotion to a higher position, often one requiring skills that the person does not possess. Such a promotion may involve work that is over the manager's head. While we must not overlook the possibility of individual growth, the Peter Principle can serve as a warning not to take the selection and promotion process lightly.

---

[5]L. J. Peter and R. Hall, *The Peter Principle* (New York: Bantam Books, Inc., 1969).

Responsibility for Selection

The final decision in the selection of a person for a new position should rest with the candidate's prospective superior; only then can the selector be held accountable for the performance of the chosen candidate. It is also advisable to get the opinions of others, especially those with whom the candidate will have working relationships. In addition, the superior of the selector should be involved, approving, rather than actually making, the selection decision. This gives additional assurance that qualifications rather than friendships are the basic reasons for the choice. It also is a way of making more certain that the selecting manager is choosing people with adequate qualifications and potential for growth.

Selection Process, Techniques, and Instruments

In this section, we give an overview of the selection process, followed by the discussion of a number of instruments and techniques, including interviews, tests, and the assessment center. For good selection, the information about the applicant should be both *valid* and *reliable*. When we ask if data are *valid*, we raise the question: Are we measuring what we think we are measuring? In selection, validity is the degree to which the data predict the candidate's success as a manager. The information should also have a high degree of reliability, a term which refers to the accuracy and consistency of the measurement. For example, a reliable test if repeated under the same conditions, would give essentially the same results.

Validity

Reliability

The Selection Process

Steps in selection

There are some variations of the specific steps in the selection process. For example, the interview of a candidate for a first-level supervisory position may be relatively simple when compared with the rigorous interviews for a top-level executive. Nevertheless, the following broad outline is indicative of the typical process.

First, the selection criteria are established, usually based on the current—and sometimes future—job requirements. These criteria include such items as education, knowledge, skills, and experience. Second, the candidate is requested to complete an application form (this step may be omitted if the candidate for the position is from within the organization). Third, a screening interview is conducted to identify the more promising candidates. Fourth, additional information may be obtained by testing the candidate's qualifications for the position. Fifth, a series of formal interviews are conducted by the manager, his or her superior, and other persons within the organization. Sixth, the information provided by the candidate is checked and verified. Seventh, some organizations require a physical examination. Eighth, based on the results of previous steps, a job offer is made or the candidate is informed that he or she has not been selected for the position. Let us examine some parts of the selection process in greater detail.

Interviews

Virtually every manager hired or promoted by a company is interviewed by one or more people. Despite its general use, the interview is considerably distrusted as a reliable and valid means for selecting managers. Various interviewers may weigh or interpret the obtained information differently. Interviewers often do not ask the right questions. They may be influenced by the interviewee's general appearance, which may have little bearing on job performance. They also frequently make up their minds early in the interview, before they have all the information necessary to make a fair judgment.

Interviewer training

Several techniques can be used to improve the interviewing process and overcome some of these weaknesses. First, the interviewers should be trained so that they know what to look for. For example, in interviewing people from within the enterprise, they should analyze and discuss past records. They should study the results achieved as well as the way key managerial activities were performed. Chapter 15, on appraisal, shows in greater detail how this can be done. When selecting managers from outside the firm, interviewers find that these data are more difficult to obtain, and they usually get them by checking with the listed references.

Asking the right questions

Second, the interviewer should be prepared to ask the right questions. There are structured, semistructured, and unstructured interviews. In an *unstructured* interview, an interviewer may say something like, "Tell me about your last job." In the *semistructured* interview, the manager follows an interview guide but may also ask other questions. In a *structured* interview, a set of prepared questions is asked, such as:

What were your specific duties and responsibilities in your last job?

What did you achieve in this job and how does this compare with the normal output for this job?

Who could be asked to verify these achievements?

To what extent were these achievements due to your efforts?

What were the contributions of other people?

Who are they?

What did you like and dislike about your job?

What innovations did you make in your job?

Why do you want to change your job?

Multiple interviews

A third way to improve selection is to conduct multiple interviews utilizing several different interviewers. Thus, several people can compare their evaluations and perceptions. However, not all interviewers should vote in selecting the candidate; rather, this technique provides additional information to the manager who will be responsible for the final decision.

Supplemental data

Fourth, the interview is just one aspect of the selection process. It should be supplemented by data from the application form, the results of various tests, and the information obtained from persons listed as references. Reference checks and letters of recommendation may be necessary to verify the information given by the applicant. For a reference to be useful, the person giving the reference must know the applicant well and give a truthful and complete assessment of the applicant. Many people are reluctant to provide complete information, so an applicant's strong points are often overemphasized while his or her shortcomings may be glossed over. The Privacy Act of 1974 and related legislation and judicial rulings have made it even more difficult to obtain objective references. Under this act, the applicant has a legal right to inspect letters of reference unless this right is waived. This is one of the reasons that teachers are sometimes reluctant to make objective and accurate job referrals for their students.

Tests

The primary aim of testing is to obtain data about the applicants that help to predict their probable success as managers. Some of the benefits from testing include finding the best person for the job, obtaining a high degree of job satisfaction for the applicant, and reducing turnover. The most commonly used tests can be classified as follows:

1 *Intelligence tests* are designed to measure mental capacity and to test memory, speed of thought, and ability to see relationships in complex problem situations.

2 *Proficiency and aptitude tests* are constructed to discover interests, existing skills, and potential for acquiring skills.

3 *Vocational tests* are designed to show a candidate's most suitable occupation.

4 *Personality tests* are designed to reveal candidates' personal characteristics and the way candidates may interact with others, thereby giving a measure of leadership potential.

Limitations

Competent industrial psychologists agree that tests are not accurate enough to be used as the sole way of measuring candidates' characteristics and must be interpreted in the light of each individual's entire history. Second, any test user must know what tests do and what their limitations are; one of the major limitations is uncertainty about whether the tests are really applicable. Even psychologists are not yet highly confident that tests developed thus far are effective in measuring managerial abilities and potentials. Third, before any test is widely used, it should be tried out, if possible on personnel currently employed in an enterprise, to see whether it is valid for employees whose managerial abilities are already known. Fourth, it is also important that tests be administered and interpreted by experts in the field. Finally, tests should not discriminate unfairly and should be consistent with laws and government guidelines.

Assessment Centers

The assessment center is not a location but a technique for selecting and promoting managers. This approach may be used in combination with training. Assessment centers were first used for selecting and promoting lower-level supervisors, but now they are applied to middle-level managers as well. They seem, however, to be inappropriate for top executives. The assessment center technique is not new. It was used by the German and British military in World War II and the American Office of Strategic Services. But its first corporate use in the United States is generally attributed to the American Telephone and Telegraph Company about three decades ago. It has been estimated that more than 1100 business, government, and nonprofit organizations use this method, including General Electric, IBM, J. C. Penney, and Sears.[6]

Typical activities

Intended to measure how a potential manager will act in typical managerial situations, the usual center approach is to have candidates take part in a series of exercises. During this period they are observed and assessed by psychologists or experienced managers. A typical assessment center will have the candidates:

Take various psychological tests

Engage in small groups in management games

Engage in "in-basket" exercises, in which they are asked to handle a variety of matters that they might face in a managerial job

Participate in a leaderless group discussion of some problem

Give a brief oral presentation on a particular topic or theme, usually recommending a course of desirable action to a mythical superior

Engage in various other exercises, such as preparing a written report

During these exercises, the candidates are observed by their evaluators, who also interview them from time to time. At the end of the assessment center period, the assessors summarize their appraisals of each candidate's performance, compare their evaluations with those of other assessors, come to conclusions with them concerning a candidate's managerial potential, and write a summary report on the candidate. These reports are made available to appointing managers for their guidance. They are also often used as guides for management development. In many cases candidates are given feedback on their evaluation; in other cases feedback is given only when candidates request it. Sometimes the summary evaluation as to promotability remains confidential, even though candidates may be informed by assessors about their performance in the various exercises.

Evidence of the usefulness of the assessment center approach—although not conclusive—is encouraging. Specifically, its reliability seems high enough to suggest that further use is warranted.

Problems

Assessment centers do present some problems however. First, they are costly in terms of time, especially since many effective programs extend over a 5-day period. Second, training assessors is a problem, particularly in those companies which believe, with some justification, that the best assessors are likely to be experienced line managers rather than trained psychologists. Third, although a number of different exercises are used to cover the kinds of things a manager does, questions have been raised as to whether these exercises are the best criteria for evaluation. An even greater problem exists in determining what evaluation

---

[6]W. F. Cascio, *Applied Psychology in Personnel Management* (Reston, Va.: Reston Publishing Company, Inc., 1982), chap. 12.

measures should be applied to each exercise. Most assessment centers, being highly oriented to individual and interpersonal behavior under various circumstances, may be overlooking the most important element in selecting managers, especially those about to enter the managerial ranks for the first time. That element is motivation—whether or not a person truly wants to be a manager. To be so motivated, candidates must know what managing is, what it involves, and what is required to be a successful manager. Obviously, motivation is a difficult quality to evaluate. However, by making clear to a candidate what managing involves and requires and then asking the candidate to think this over, the interviewer can give the candidate a good basis on which to determine whether he or she really wants to be a manager.

Limitations of the Selection Process

The diversity of selection approaches and tests indicates that there is no one perfect way to select managers. Experience has shown that even carefully chosen selection criteria are still imperfect in predicting performance. Furthermore, there is a distinction between what persons can do, that is, their ability to perform, and what people will do, which relates to motivation. The latter is a function of the individual and the environment. For example, a person's needs may be different at various times. The organizational environment also changes. The climate of an enterprise may change from one that encourages initiative to a restrictive one because a new top management introduces a different managerial philosophy. Therefore, selection techniques and instruments are not a sure way to predict what people will do, even though they may have the ability to do it.

Testing itself, especially psychological testing, has limitations. Specifically, seeking of certain information may be considered an invasion of privacy. In addition, it has been charged that some tests unfairly discriminate against members of minority groups or women. These complex issues are not easily resolved, yet they cannot be ignored when selecting managers.

Still other concerns in selection and hiring are the time and cost involved in making personnel decisions. It is important to identify such factors as advertising expenses, agency fees, cost of test materials, time spent for interviewing candidates, costs for reference checks, medical exams, start-up time require for the new manager to get acquainted with the job, relocation, and orientation of the new employee. When recruiting costs are recognized, it becomes evident that turnover can be very expensive to an enterprise.

Orienting and Socializing New Employees

The selection of the best person for the job is only the first step in building an effective management team. Even companies that make great efforts in the recruitment and selection process often ignore the needs of new managers after they have been hired. Yet the first few days and weeks can be crucial for integrating the new person into the organization.

Orientation

Orientation involves the introduction of new employees to the enterprise, its functions, tasks, and people. Large firms usually have a formal orientation program which explains these features of the company: history, products and services, general policies and practices, organization (divisions, departments, and geographic locations), benefits (insurance, retirement, vacations), requirements for confidentiality and secrecy in defense contracts, safety and other regulations. These may be further described in detail in a company booklet, but the orientation meeting provides new employees with an opportunity to ask questions. Although these formal programs are usually conducted by persons from the personnel department, the primary responsibility for orienting the new manager still rests with the superior.

Organizational socialization

There is another and perhaps even more important aspect of orientation: the socialization of new managers. *Organizational socialization* is defined in several different ways. A global view includes three aspects: the acquisition of work skills and abilities, the adoption of appropriate role behaviors, and the adjustment to the norms and values of the work group.[7] So, in addition to meeting the specific requirements of the job, new managers will usually encounter new values, new personal relationships, and new modes of behavior. They do not know people they can ask for advice, they do not know how the organization works, and they have a fear of being unsuccessful in the new job. All this uncertainty can cause a great deal of anxiety for the new employee, especially the management trainee. Because the initial experience in an enterprise can be very important for future management behavior, the first contact of trainees should be with the best superiors in the enterprise, people who can serve as models for future behavior.

Example

One company that recognized these problems many years ago is Texas Instruments, which held 1-day anxiety-reducing sessions. The group participating in these sessions was compared with a control group that did not have the benefit of such a program. It was found that the session saved the company a great deal of money in training, absenteeism, tardiness, and rejection of already-hired trainees. Improvement in job performance resulted in an additional savings.[8]

Summary

The comprehensive managerial requirements plan is the basis for position requirements. In designing managerial jobs, we must see that the scope of the job is appropriate, that the position involves a full-time, challenging job, and that it reflects required managerial skills. The job structure must be appropriate in terms of content, function, and relationships. Jobs can be designed for individuals or work teams. The importance of technical, human, conceptual, and design skills varies with the level in the organizational hierarchy. The position requirements are matched with the various skills and characteristics of individuals. The matching is important in recruitment, selection, placement, and promotion.

---

[7]D. C. Feldman, "The Multiple Socialization of Organization Members," *Academy of Management Review*, vol. 6, no. 2 (April 1981), pp. 309–318.

[8]E. R. Gomersall and M. S. Myers, "Breakthrough in On-the-Job Training," *Harvard Business Review*, vol. 44, no. 4 (July–August 1966), pp. 62–72.

Effective staffing demands a balance of skills and of employee ages. Errors in selection can lead to actualization of the Peter Principle, which states that managers tend to be promoted to the level of their incompetence. Although the advice of several people may be sought, the selection decision should generally rest with the immediate superior of the candidate for the position.

The selection process may include interviews, various tests, and the use of assessment centers. To avoid dissatisfaction and employee turnover, new employees must be introduced to, and integrated with, other persons in the organization.

Key Ideas and Concepts for Review

Systems approach to selection of managers	Promotion
Position requirements	Peter Principle
Job design for individual jobs	Validity
Job design for work teams	Reliability
Managerial skills in the organization hierarchy	Selection process
	Kinds of tests
Recruitment	Assessment centers
Selection	Orientation of new employees
Placement	Socialization of new employees

For Discussion

1 What is the systems approach to selection of managers? Why is it called a systems approach? How does it differ from other approaches?

2 What are the important managerial skills? In what ways do you think the need for these skills differs at various levels in the organizational hierarchy?

3 What are some of the factors that are important in designing individual jobs and jobs for work teams? Which ones seem most important to you? Why?

4 What kinds of personal characteristics are important for managerial success?

5 What are the various approaches in the selection of managers? Which approach do you prefer? Why?

6 The Peter Principle has been widely quoted in management circles. What do you think of it? Do you think that it could ever apply to you? Does it mean that all chief executives are incompetent? Explain.

7 What kinds of tests may be used in selecting managers? What are the benefits and limitations of these tests?

8 What is an assessment center? How does it work? Would you like to participate in such a center? Why or why not?

9 Why are orientation and socialization important?

10 Take an organization you know and discuss how managers and nonmanagers are recruited and selected. How effective is the recruitment and selection?

CASE 14-1

CARL WENDOVER

Carl Wendover, an assistant manager of a well-run division, was selected as head of another division. He encountered trouble from the beginning—trouble becoming familiar with the information required by the executive vice-president, trouble with the subordinates he inherited, and trouble in really understanding that he was in trouble. Within a year he was terminated.

The man who selected him was concerned about how he came to make such a mistake. He analyzed the situation carefully and concluded that when Carl Wendover was an assistant manager, he was not trained to operate the division. His then superior simply used him as a staff man and

excluded him completely from division operations. The assistant certainly "looked good" to all, but he was merely reflecting the reputation of the well-run division.

1 Exactly why was the mistake in the instance of Carl Wendover made? What defense, if any, could Wendover advance in his behalf?

2 If you were the person who selected Wendover, what would you do to avoid making this mistake again?

3 If you were the executive vice-president, what action, if any, would you take so that such mistakes would be unlikely to occur?

CASE 14-2

THE DENIED PROMOTION

Jerry Nolan worked at the headquarters of the Worldwide Motorbike Company. His task was to process warranty claims and advise service engineers working in the field with distributors throughout the world. Then he heard of an opening for a field engineer.

As a first step, Jerry Nolan approached his immediate superior, Donald Brown, and asked to be considered as a field engineer in Jane Smith's department. The idea was rejected with the comment, "Let's talk about it later." When Mr. Brown left for a business trip, Jerry approached Jane Smith, the service manager for international oper-

ations, who was not only Brown's superior but was also responsible for the field engineers. During the discussion, Ms. Smith, who favored promoting young talent from within the company, recognized that Jerry Nolan was well qualified for the position of field engineer. She promised to talk to Mr. Brown after his return from the trip.

One week later Mr. Brown called Jerry Nolan into his office and opened the conversation as follows: "I heard that you talked to Ms. Smith while I was out of town, about the position of field engineer. I cannot let you take this position. We just switched to a computerized claim-processing system and I need you because you have the broadest experience of any of my seven subordinates." Jerry was shocked. Should he be denied the promotion because he was the best person in the group? Two weeks later, a field engineer was hired from outside the firm. Jerry Nolan wondered what he should do next.

1 If you were Jerry Nolan, what would you do?

2 What do you think about the staffing practices of the company? What policies, if any, would you recommend?

3 What do you think about Mr. Brown's managerial behavior?

For Further Information

Carrell, M. R., and F. E. Kuzmits. *Personnel: Management of Human Resources* (Columbus, Ohio: Charles E. Merrill Publishing Co., 1982).

Dipboye, R. L. "Self-Fulfilling Prophecies in the Selection-Recruitment Interview," *Academy of Management Review*, vol. 7, no. 4 (October 1982), pp. 579–586.

Fiedler, F. E. "Engineer the Job to Fit the Manager," *Harvard Business Review*, vol. 43, no. 5 (September–October 1965), pp. 115–122.

Greer, C. R. "Countercyclical Hiring as a Staffing Strategy for Managerial and Professional Personnel: Some Considerations and Issues," *Academy of Management Review*, vol. 9, no. 2 (April 1984), pp. 324–330.

Gyllenhammer, P. G. "How Volvo Adapts Work to People," *Harvard Business Review*, vol. 55, no. 4 (July–August 1977), pp. 102–113.

Leontiades, M. "Choosing the Right Manager to Fit the Strategy," in A. A. Thompson, Jr., A. J. Strickland III, and W. E. Fulmer (eds.), *Readings in Strategic Management* (Plano, Tex.: Business Publications, Inc., 1984), pp. 290–305.

McMurry, R. N. "Avoiding Mistakes in Selecting Executives," in H. Koontz, C. O'Donnell, and H. Weihrich (eds.), *Management—A Book of Readings*, 5th ed. (New York: McGraw-Hill Book Company, 1980), pp. 396–401.

Pascale, R. "Fitting New Employees into the Company Culture," *Fortune*, May 28, 1984, pp. 28–43.

Wanous, J. P. *Organizational Entry: Recruitment, Selection, and Socialization of Newcomers* (Reading, Mass.: Addison-Wesley Publishing Company, Inc., 1980).

15

Performance Appraisal and Career Strategy

CHAPTER OBJECTIVES

After reading this chapter, you should understand:

1 The importance of effective appraisal of managers
2 The qualities that should be measured in appraising managers
3 The problems of traditional trait appraisals
4 Effective managerial appraisal—that is, the measurement of performance in accomplishing goals and plans as well as performance as a manager
5 Important aspects of career planning

Managerial appraisal has sometimes been referred to as the Achilles' heel of managerial staffing. But it is probably a major key to managing itself. It is the basis for determining who is promotable to a higher position. It is also important to management development because if a manager's strengths and weaknesses are not known, it is difficult to determine whether development efforts are aimed in the right direction. Appraisal is, or should be, an integral part of a system of managing. Knowing how well a manager plans, organizes, staffs, leads, and controls is really the only way to ensure that those occupying managerial positions are actually managing effectively. If a business, a government agency, a charitable organization, or even a university is to reach its goals effectively and efficiently, ways of accurately measuring management performance must be found and implemented.

There are other reasons why effective managerial appraisal is important. One

Legal requirements
of the most compelling arises from the provisions of Title VII of the Civil Rights Act of 1964 (as amended) and the regulations of the Equal Employment Opportunity Commission and the Office of Federal Contract Compliance. These agencies have been highly critical of many appraisal programs, finding them often to result in discrimination, particularly in areas of race, age, and sex. Courts have supported the federal agencies in their insistence that, to be acceptable, an appraisal program must be reliable and valid. That these are rigorous standards is apparent.

Effective performance appraisal should also recognize the legitimate desire of employees for progress in their professions. One way to integrate organizational demands and individual needs is through career management, which can be a part of performance appraisal as we will see later in this chapter.

The Problem of Management Appraisal

Reluctance to appraise subordinates

Managers have long been reluctant to appraise subordinates. However, in an activity as important as managing, there should be no reluctance to measure performance as accurately as we can. In almost all kinds of group enterprise, whether in work or play, performance has usually been rated in some way. Moreover, most people, and particularly people of ability, want to know how well they are doing.

It is difficult to believe that the controversy, the misgivings, and even the disillusionment, still so widespread with respect to managerial performance appraisal have come from the practices of measuring and evaluating. Rather, it appears that they have arisen from the things measured, the standards used, and the way measurement is done.

Inadequate standards

Managers can understandably take exception, feel unhappy, or resist when they believe that they are evaluating, or being evaluated, inaccurately or against standards that are inapplicable, inadequate, or subjective. However, some light and hope have emerged in the past 30 years and offer promise of making evaluation effective. The interest in evaluating managers by comparing actual performance against preset verifiable objectives or goals is a development of considerable potential.

Even appraisal against verifiable objectives is not enough. It needs to be supplemented by an appraisal of managers as managers. Moreover, neither system is without difficulties and pitfalls, and neither can be operated by simply adopting the technique and doing the paperwork. We must do more. In the first place, it is essential that managing by verifiable objectives, as explained in Chapter 5, be a way of life in an enterprise. In the second place, managers need both a clear understanding of the managerial job and the fundamentals underlying it, and an ability to apply these fundamentals in practice.

Choosing the Appraisal Criteria

It hardly seems necessary to say that managerial appraisal should measure a person's performance as a manager in meeting goals for which a manager is responsible. Yet, obvious as this is, examination of many appraisal systems used by business, government, and other enterprises shows that many people do not understand this fact, or at least are unable or unwilling to translate understanding into practice.

Two sets
of criteria

Note, then, that appraisal should measure both performance in accomplishing goals and plans and performance as a manager. No one wants a person in a managerial role who appears to do everything right as a manager, but who cannot turn in a good record of profit making, marketing, controllership, or whatever the area of responsibility may be. Nor should we be satisfied to have a "performer" in a managerial position who cannot operate effectively as a manager. Some performers tend to be "flashes in the pan," that is, they are star performers who have succeeded through no fault of their own.

Performance in Accomplishing Goals

In assessing performance, systems of appraising against verifiable preselected goals have extraordinary value. Given consistent, integrated, and understood planning designed to reach specific objectives, probably the best criteria of managerial performance relate to the ability to set goals intelligently, to plan programs that will accomplish those goals, and to succeed in achieving them. Those who have operated under some variation of this system often claim that these criteria are adequate and that elements of luck or other factors beyond the manager's control are taken into account when arriving at any appraisal. But, in too many cases, managers who achieve results due to sheer luck are promoted, and others, who do not achieve expected results because of factors beyond their control, are blamed for failures. Thus, we need a supplement to appraisal against verifiable objectives.

Performance as Managers

Although an impressive record of setting and accomplishing goals is persuasive evidence of any group leader's ability, it should be supplemented by an appraisal of a manager *as a manager*. Managers at any level undertake nonmanagerial duties, and these cannot be overlooked. The primary purpose for which managers are hired and against which they should be measured, however, is their performance as managers—that is, they should be appraised on the basis of how well they understand and undertake the managerial functions of planning, organizing, staffing, leading, and controlling. For standards in this area we must turn to the fundamentals of management. But let us first look at some traditional appraisal programs.

Traditional Trait Appraisals

For many years, managers have been evaluated against standards of personal traits and work characteristics. Typical trait-rating evaluation systems may list ten to fifteen personal characteristics, such as ability to get along with people, leadership, analytical competence, industry, judgment, and initiative. The list may also include such work-related characteristics as job knowledge, ability to carry through on assignments, production or cost results, or success in seeing that plans and instructions are carried out. However, at least until recent years, personal traits have far outnumbered work related characteristics. Given these standards, the rater was then asked to appraise subordinates, rating them from unacceptable to outstanding.

Weaknesses of Trait Appraisals

Managers resist doing this type of evaluation or tend to go through the paperwork without knowing exactly how to rate. Even where earnest attempts have been made to "sell" such programs, to indoctrinate managers, and to train them in the meaning of traits so that they can improve their appraisal ability, few managers can or will do them well.

Subjectivity

One practical problem of the trait approach to appraisal is that because trait evaluation cannot be objective, serious and fair-minded managers do not wish to utilize their obviously subjective judgment on a matter so important as performance. And employees who receive less than the top rating almost invariably feel that they have been unfairly dealt with.

Another problem is that the basic assumption of trait appraisals is open to question. The connection between performance and possession of specific traits is doubtful. What is evaluated tends to be outside of—separated from—a manager's actual operations. Trait appraisal substitutes someone's opinion of an individual for what the person really does.

Many managers look upon trait rating as only a paperwork exercise that must be done because someone has ordered it. When people have this attitude, they go through the paperwork and tend to make ratings as painless (for the subordinate and themselves) as possible. Consequently, they tend not to be very discriminating. It is interesting, but hardly surprising, that a study of ratings of navy officers several years ago came up with an arithmetical paradox: that, of all officers of the United States Navy rated over a period of time, some 98.5 percent were outstanding or excellent, and only 1 percent were average!

Trait criteria are at best nebulous. Raters are dealing with a blunt tool, and subordinates are likely to be vague about what qualities they are being rated on. In the hands of most practitioners, it is a crude device, and since raters are painfully aware of this, they are reluctant to use it in a manner that would damage the careers of their subordinates. One of the principal purposes of appraisal is to provide a basis upon which to discuss performance and to plan for improvement. But trait evaluations provide few tangible things to discuss, little on which participants can agree as fact, and therefore little mutual understanding of what is required to obtain improvement.

Attempts to Strengthen Trait Rating

As the deficiencies of trait rating have come to be recognized, a number of changes and additions have been introduced. Some are aimed at making the traits more comprehensible to raters. In a rating form used by a well-known business corporation, a person's "judgment" is defined as his or her capability to recognize the significant from the less significant in arriving at sound conclusions. Likewise, attempts are made to give meanings to various grades under each category.

Often, too, trait and work-quality forms are supplemented by open-ended evaluations in which, without specific guidance, appraisers are asked to supply whatever evidence on performance they feel is pertinent. Sometimes, also, this approach is used for the entire appraisal. Appraisers may be given a broad outline to guide them; for example, they may be asked for comments under such categories as operations, organization, personnel, and financial, and they may be asked specifically to consider such things as quality, quantity, time required to complete work, customer relations, and subordinate employee morale. Although these categories are helpful, experience has shown that they do not greatly improve the quality of ratings.

Attempts have also been made to improve the effectiveness of the rating process. In some systems, subordinates are required to rate themselves, and superiors must compare their ratings with those made by subordinates. In other instances, the superior's superior is asked to rate the former's subordinate or at least to carefully review the evaluation made by the immediate superior. Sometimes, a rater is forced by an appraisal system to rank subordinates from the best to the least able. In still other cases, rating has been done through the use of critical incidents that are assumed to give meaning to the grades given.

These and other devices have been used to offset the disadvantages of trait rating. They have helped, but they cannot overcome the fact that traits and work qualities are subjective and are not correlated with what a manager's job really is.

Appraising Managers against Verifiable Objectives

One of the most promising tools of managerial appraisal is the system of evaluating managerial performance against the setting and accomplishing of verifiable objectives. As was noted in Chapter 5, a network of meaningful and attainable objectives is basic to effective managing. This is simple logic, since people cannot be expected to accomplish a task with effectiveness or efficiency unless they know what the end points of their efforts should be. Nor can any organized enterprise in business or elsewhere be expected to do so.

The Appraisal Process

Once a program of managing by verifiable objectives is operating, a major phase of appraisal is a fairly easy step. Supervisors determine how well managers set objectives and how well they have performed against them. Where appraisal by results has failed or been disillusioning, this failure has occurred especially because managing by objectives was seen only as an appraisal technique. The system is not likely to work if used only for this purpose. Management by objectives must be a way of managing, a way of planning, as well as the key to organizing, staffing, leading, and controlling. When this is the case, appraisal boils down to whether or not managers have established adequate but reasonably attainable objectives and how they have performed against them in a certain period.

System of managing and appraising by objectives

Look at the system of managing and appraising by objectives, as shown in Figure 5-3 (page 105). As you can see, appraising is merely a last step in the entire process.

There are other questions, too. Were the goals adequate? Did they call for "stretched" (high but reasonable) performance? These questions can be answered only by the judgment and experience of a person's superior, although this judgment can become sharper with time and experience, and it may be even more objective if the superior can use the goals of other managers in similar positions for comparison.

Appropriateness of goals

In assessing the accomplishment of goals, the evaluator must take into account such considerations as whether the goals were reasonably attainable in the first place, whether factors beyond a person's control unduly helped or hindered in accomplishing goals, and what the reasons for the results were. The reviewer should also note whether an individual continued to operate against obsolete goals when situations changed and revised goals were called for.

Frequent reviews

As in any case of control, progress toward goals should be fairly frequently reviewed, as it may be dangerous to limit appraisal to looking at performance once a year. For a top manager, such as a president or a division general manager, progress should probably be reviewed and appraised quarterly in fair detail and more broadly, in the light of probable accomplishment, for three or four additional quarters in the future. Alert and intelligent managers, hardly wishing to have obsolete objectives, naturally prefer to have both goal setting and evaluation be regular activities, and certainly, in most instances, will not wish to wait too long to know how they and their subordinates are doing.

For individuals below the top level, quarterly reviews may be enough. And they may not. The real factor is the time span necessary to determine whether a goal is still valid and whether satisfactory progress is being made. For certain positions, such as those of first-level supervisors, reviews probably could be usefully made each month. Note that this task does not necessarily involve much additional work by a superior. It is merely carrying on the function of managing, and actual appraising becomes a relatively easy by-product of the process if we have concentrated on objectives.

Strengths of Appraisal against Verifiable Objectives

The strengths of appraising against accomplishment of objectives are almost the same as those of managing by objectives. Both are part of the same process, both are basic to effective managing, and both are means of improving the quality of managing.

In the area of appraising, there are special and important strengths. Appraising on the basis of performance against verifiable objectives has the great advantage of being operational. Appraisals are not apart from the job that managers do but are a review of what they actually did as managers.

There are always questions of how well a person did; of whether goals were missed or accomplished, and for what reasons; and of how much in the way of goal attainment should be expected. But information about what a person has done, measured against what that individual agreed was a reasonable target, is available. This information furnishes strong presumptions of objectivity and reduces the element of pure judgment in appraisal. Moreover, the appraisal can be carried on in an atmosphere of superiors working with subordinates and not sitting in judgment on them.

Weaknesses of Appraisal against Verifiable Objectives

As we noted in Chapter 5, there are certain weaknesses in the implementation of managing by objectives. These, of course, apply with equal force to appraisal. One of them is that it is entirely possible for persons to meet or miss goals through no fault of their own. Luck often plays a part in performance. It is possible, for example, that a new product's acceptance will be far beyond expectations and its success will make a marketing manager look exceptionally good, even though the quality of the marketing program and its implementation might actually be poor. Or an unpredictable cancellation of a major military contract might make the record of a division manager look unsatisfactory.

Most evaluators will say that they always take uncontrollable or unexpected factors into account in assessing goal performance, and to a very great extent they do. But it is extremely difficult to do so. In an outstanding sales record, for example, how can anyone be sure how much was due to luck and how much to competence? Outstanding performers are rated highly, at least as long as they perform. Nonperformers can hardly escape having a cloud cast over them.

With its emphasis on accomplishing operating objectives, the system of appraising against these may overlook needs for individual development. Goal attainment tends to be short-run in practice. Even where longer-range goals are put into the system, seldom would they be so long-range as to allow for adequate long-term development of managers. Managers concerned primarily with results might be driven by the system to take too little time to plan, implement, and follow through with programs required for their development and that of their subordinates.

On the other hand, since managing by objectives gives better visibility to managerial needs, development programs can be better pinpointed. If individual development is to be assured, however, goals in this area should be specifically set.

From an appraisal as well as an operating management point of view, perhaps the greatest deficiency of management by objectives is that it appraises operating performance only. Not only is there the question of luck, mentioned previously, but also there are other factors to appraise, notably an individual's *managerial* abilities. This is why an adequate appraisal system must appraise performance as a manager as well as performance in setting and meeting goals.

Appraising Managers as Managers: A Suggested Program

The most appropriate standards to use for appraising managers as managers are the fundamentals of management. It is not enough to appraise a manager broadly, evaluating only performance of the basic functions of the manager; we should go further.

Techniques and principles of management

We believe that the best approach is to utilize the basic techniques and principles of management as standards. If they are basic, as they have been found to be in a wide variety of managerial positions and environments, they should serve as reasonably good standards. As crude as they may be and even though some judgment may be necessary in applying them to practice, they give the evaluator some bench marks to measure how well subordinates understand and are following the functions of managing. They are definitely more specific and more applicable than evaluations based on such broad standards as work and dress habits, cooperation, intelligence, judgment, or loyalty. They at least focus attention on what may be expected of a manager *as a manager*. And, when used in conjunction with appraisal of the performance of plans and goals, they can help remove much of the weakness in many management appraisal systems.

In brief, the program involves classifying the functions of the manager as done in this book and then dealing with each function by a series of questions. The questions are designed to reflect the most important fundamentals of managing in each area. Although the total list of key questions, the form used, the system of ratings, and the instructions for operating the program are too extensive to be treated in this book,[1] we can look at some sample "checkpoints."

Planning skills

For example, in the area of *planning*, a manager would be rated by such check questions as the following:

Does the manager—

set for the departmental unit both short-term and long-term goals in verifiable terms that are related in a positive way to those of superiors and of the company?

check plans periodically to see whether they are consistent with current expectations?

in choosing from among alternatives, recognize and give primary attention to those factors which are limiting or critical to the solution of a problem?

Organizing skills

In the area of *organizing*, such questions are asked as the following:

Does the manager—

delegate authority to subordinates on the basis of results expected of them?

refrain from making decisions in that area once authority has been delegated to subordinates?

regularly teach subordinates, or otherwise make sure that they understand, the nature of line and staff relationships?

Seventy-three checkpoints

In the three other areas of managing—in staffing, in leading, and in controlling—we ask similar questions. In all, there are seventy-three checkpoints. Semantics has always been a problem in management. Therefore, we suggest using a standard book on management (such as this one) and referring to the pages that correspond to the check questions.[2] This approach leads to a fair degree of managerial development.

Managers are rated on how well they perform the activities. The scale used is from 0 for "inadequate" to 5 for "superior." To give the numerical ratings more rigor, each rating is defined. For example, "superior" means "a standard of

---

[1]All the key questions are given in Harold Koontz, *Appraising Managers as Managers* (New York: McGraw-Hill Book Company, 1971), chaps. 5 and 6 and apps. 2–5.

[2]This has been done, for example, in the text booklet accompanying the cassette recording program "Measuring Managers: A Double-Barreled Approach," by Harold Koontz and Heinz Weihrich (New York: American Management Association, 1981).

performance which could not be improved under any circumstances or conditions known to the rater.''

To further reduce subjectivity and to increase the discrimination among performance levels, we include the requirements that (1) in the comprehensive annual appraisal, incident examples are given to support certain ratings, (2) the ratings are reviewed by the superior's superior and (3) the raters are informed that their own evaluation will depend in part on how well they discriminate on the ratings of performance levels when evaluating their subordinates. Obviously, objectivity is enhanced by the number (seventy-three) and the specificity of the checkpoint questions.

Advantages of the New Program

Experience with this program in a multinational company showed certain advantages. By focusing on the essentials of management, this method of evaluation gives operational meaning to what management really is. Also, the use of a standard reference text for interpretation of concepts and terms removes many of the semantic and communication difficulties so commonly encountered. Such things as variable budgets, verifiable objectives, staff, functional authority, and delegation take on consistent meaning. Likewise, many management techniques become uniformly understood.

The system, furthermore, has proved to be a tool for management development; in many cases, it has brought to managers' attention certain basics that they may have long disregarded or not understood. In addition, it has been found useful in pinpointing areas where weaknesses exist and to which development should be directed. Finally, as intended, the program acts as a supplement to and a check on appraisal of managers' effectiveness in setting and achieving goals. If a manager has an outstanding performance in goal accomplishment but is found to be a less-than-average manager, those in charge would look for the reason. Normally, we would expect a truly effective manager to be effective also in meeting goals.

Weaknesses of the New Program

There are, however, a number of weaknesses or shortcomings in the approach. It applies only to managerial aspects of a given position and not to such technical qualifications as marketing or engineering abilities that might also be important. These, however, can be weighed on the basis of goals selected and achieved. There is also the apparent complexity of the seventy-three checkpoints; to rate on all of them does take time, but the time is well spent.

Perhaps the major shortcoming of the proposed approach to appraising managers as managers is its subjectivity. As we mentioned earlier, some subjectivity in rating each checkpoint was found to be unavoidable. However, the program still has a high degree of objectivity and is far more objective than appraisal of managers only on the broader areas of the managerial functions. At least the checkpoints are specific and go to the essentials of managing.

An Illustration

One company that had used the management-by-objectives approach successfully in its appraisal program found it desirable to supplement the program with a performance appraisal based on common management responsibilities. The form used for this evaluation, shown as Table 15-1, was based on the ideas discussed

TABLE 15-1 Performance Appraisal: Common Management Responsibilities

Name	Rated by	Date

To be completed and included as a part of the overall appraisal for all unit level positions and above who have authority and responsibility for managing human resources.

Needs improvement or Unsatisfactory progress as well as corrective plans must be documented in REMARKS.

Importance weight assigned to Common Management Responsibilities ☐

1 Planning:

A Develops and implements effective plans that contain verifiable and realistic goals and objectives.

B Plans include long range considerations.

C Establishes specific quantitative / qualitative work goals or standards to be achieved by subordinates.

REMARKS:

2 Organization / Staffing:*

A Organizes and staffs consistent with a thorough understanding of job responsibilities.

B Identifies changes in job responsibilities and effects changes in Position Information Questionnaires.

C Selects qualified personnel to fill vacancies.

REMARKS:

3 Delegation / Control:

A Delegates authority and maintains control consistent with expectations.

B Control techniques and standards reflect plans and satisfy budget compliance as well as report exceptions in a timely way.

C Controls provide for optimizing resource utilization.

REMARKS:

Performance Progress Review

Month	J	F	M	A	M	J	J	A	S	O	N	D
A												
B												
C												

Performance Rating

Out-standing	Super-ior	Fully Compe-tent	Needs Improve-ment	Unsat-isfac-tory
5	4	3	2	1

*The "Performance Progress Review" and "Performance Rating" boxes have been omitted for the managerial responsibilities that follow.

TABLE 15-1 *(Continued)*

4 Decision Making / Directing:
A Accepts responsibility for making decisions.
B Decisions are timely and consistent with plans, programs, and policies.
C Qualifies decisions by considering all points of view (subordinates, peer, superior).
D Problem solving is effective.
REMARKS:

6 Compensation:
A Administration of Performance Planning and Appraisal Program.
B Performance appraisal is based on job related criteria.
C Salary administration is fair, equitable and consistent with corporate wage and salary administration guidelines.
D Performance Planning and Appraisal is used as an effective motivating tool and morale builder.
E Communicates Performance Planning and Appraisal program and expected results to subordinates effectively.
REMARKS:

Code:
☑ Fully meeting expectations or better
◉ Needs improvement
Ⓤ Unsatisfactory

5 Administration:
A Administration of policies and procedures.
B Contributes effectively to corporate goals such as: Affirmative Action, Safety, EEOC, Minority Contractor, etc.
C Sets and administers effective disciplinary standards.
REMARKS:

7 Human Resource Development:
A Provides for subordinate training and development and assists motivated subordinates prepare for additional responsibility.
B Human resource planning and career development procedures are current and realistic.
C Subordinates' developmental needs are specifically documented.
D Succession plans written for all subordinates.
E Actively pursues own personal plan for career development and/or improvement as agreed to with immediate supervisor.
REMARKS:

Calculation

Total		
Average		
× Importance wt.		
= Rating		

above; but it has been greatly simplified. You will note that the program covers all the managerial functions. However, the number of managerial activities graded has been substantially reduced from the seventy-three suggested above. The program provides for frequent performance review so that corrective actions can be taken without delay. Note also that this approach focuses on individual development; if performance of an activity either requires improvement or is unsatisfactory, this must be documented with plans shown for overcoming the weakness.

Formulating the Career Strategy[3]

The appraisal of performance should identify the strengths and weaknesses of an individual; this identification can be the starting point for a career plan. The personal strategy should be designed to utilize strengths and overcome weaknesses in order to take advantage of career opportunities. We will now look at the career-planning process by following the model shown as Figure 15-1.

1 Preparation of a Personal Profile

One of the most difficult tasks is to gain insight into oneself; yet, this is an essential first step in developing a career strategy. Managers should ask themselves: Am I an introvert or an extrovert? What are my attitudes toward time, achievement, work, material things, and change? The answer to these and similar questions and a clarification of values will help in determining the direction of the professional career.

2 Development of Long-Range Personal and Professional Goals

No airplane would take off without a flight plan including a destination. Yet, how clear are managers about the direction of their lives? One often resists career planning because it involves a commitment. By choosing one goal, one gives up opportunities to pursue others; if one becomes a lawyer, one cannot become a doctor. Managers also resist goal setting because uncertainties in the environment cause concern about making commitments. Furthermore, there is the fear of failure to achieve the goals because the nonachievement of objectives is a blow to one's ego.

But by understanding the factors that inhibit goal setting, one can take steps to increase commitment. First, when the setting of performance goals becomes a part of the appraisal process, identifying career goals is easier. Moreover, one does not set career goals all at once. Rather, goal setting is a continuing process that allows flexibility; professional goals can be revised in the light of changing circumstances. Another factor that reduces resistance to goal setting is the integration of long-term aims with the more immediate requirement for action. For example, the aim of becoming a doctor makes it easier to study boring subjects that are necessary for the medical degree.

---

[3]Adapted from H. Weihrich, *Management Excellence—Productivity Through MBO* (New York: McGraw-Hill Book Company, 1985).

FIGURE 15-1

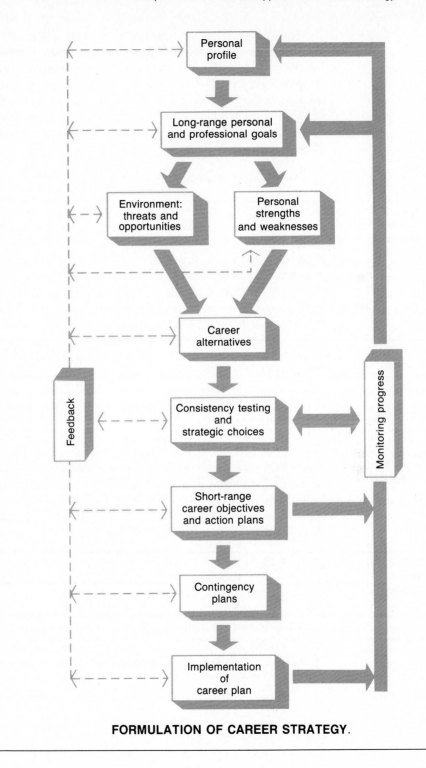

FORMULATION OF CAREER STRATEGY.

How far in advance should one plan? The answer may be found in the commitment principle discussed in the planning section. It states that planning should cover a period of time necessary for the fulfillment of commitments involved in the decision made today. Therefore, the time frame for career planning will differ with the circumstances. For example, if one wants to become a professor, it is necessary to plan for university studies of 7 to 9 years. On the other hand, if the career goal is to become a taxi driver, the time span is much shorter. At any rate, the long-term aim has to be translated into short-term objectives. Before we discuss these, however, we will make a careful assessment of the external environment with its threats and opportunities.

3 Analysis of the Environment: Threats and Opportunities

In the analysis of the environment within and outside the organization, many diverse factors need to be taken into account. They include economic, social, political, technological, and demographic factors; they also include the labor market, competition, and other factors relevant to a particular situation. For example, joining an expanding company usually provides more career opportunities than working for a mature company that is not expected to grow. Similarly, working for a mobile manager means an increased probability that the position of the superior will become vacant; or one might "ride the coattail" of a competent mobile manager. At any rate, successful career planning requires a systematic scanning of the environment for opportunities and threats.

One has not only to be concerned about the present but also to forecast the future. Since there are a great many factors that need to be analyzed, planning one's career necessitates being selective and concentrating on those factors critical to personal success.[4]

4 Analysis of Personal Strengths and Weaknesses

For successful career planning, the environmental opportunities and threats must be matched with the strengths and weaknesses of individuals. Capabilities may be categorized as technical, human, conceptual, or design. As you saw in Figure 14-2, the relative importance of these skills differs for the various positions in the organizational hierarchy, with technical skills being very important on the supervisory level and conceptual skills being crucial for top managers.

5 Development of Strategic Career Alternatives

In developing career strategies, several alternatives are available. The most successful strategy would be to build on one's strengths to take advantages of opportunities. For example, if one has an excellent knowledge of computers and many companies are looking for computer programmers, one should find many opportunities for a satisfying career. On the other hand, if one is interested in programming, but lacks the necessary skills, the proper approach would be a developmental strategy to overcome the weakness and develop these skills in order to take advantage of the opportunities.

---

[4]For sources that may help you in predicting where the job opportunities will be, see the suggested readings at the end of the chapter.

It may also be important to recognize the threats in the environment and to develop a strategy to cope with them. A person may have excellent managerial and technical skills, but work in a declining company or industry. The appropriate strategy may be to find employment in an expanding firm or in a growing industry.

6 Consistency Testing and Making Strategic Choices

In developing one's strategy, one must realize that the rational choice based on strengths and opportunities is not always the most fulfilling one. Although one may have certain skills demanded in the job market, a career in that field may not be congruent with personal values or interests. For example, a person may prefer dealing with people to programming computers. Some may find great satisfaction in specialization, while others prefer to broaden their knowledge and skills.

Strategic choices require tradeoffs. Some alternatives involve high risks, others low risks. Some choices demand action now; other choices can wait. Careers that were glamorous in the past may have an uncertain future. Rational and systematic analysis is just one step in the career-planning process, for a choice also involves personal preferences, personal ambitions, and personal values.

7 Development of Short-Range Career Objectives and Action Plans

So far our concern has been with the career direction. But the strategy has to be supported by short-term objectives and action plans which can be a part of the performance appraisal process. Thus, if the aim is to achieve a certain management position that requires a master of business degree, the short-term objective may be to complete a number of courses. Here is an example of a short-term verifiable objective: to complete the course Fundamentals of Management by May 30 with a grade of A. This objective is measurable as it states what will be done, by what time, and the quality of performance (the grade).

Objectives often must be supported by action plans. Continuing with our example, the completion of the management course may require a schedule for attending classes, doing the homework, and obtaining the support of the spouse who may suffer because taking classes takes time that might otherwise be spent with the family. As you can see, the long-term strategic career plan needs to be supported by short-term objectives and action plans.

8 Development of Contingency Plans

Career plans are developed in an environment of uncertainty, and the future cannot be predicted with great accuracy. Therefore, contingency plans based on alternative assumptions should be prepared. While one may enjoy working for a small, fast-growing venture company, it may be wise to prepare an alternative career plan based on the assumption that the venture may not succeed.

9 Implementation of the Career Plan

Career planning may start during the performance appraisal. At that time, the person's growth and development should be discussed. Career goals and personal ambitions can be considered in selecting and promoting, and in designing training and development programs.

10 Monitoring Progress

Monitoring is the evaluation of progress toward career goals and the making of necessary corrections in the aims or plans. While working for a company, an opportune time for assessing career programs would be at the performance appraisal. This is the time not only to review performance against objectives in the operating areas, but also to review the achievement of milestones in the career plan. In addition, progress should be monitored at other times such as at the completion of an important task or project.

Summary

Appraisal is essential for effective managing. Appraisal should measure performance in achieving goals and plans and performance as a manager, that is, how well the person carries out key managerial activities. Traditional appraisal methods that attempt to measure personality traits or work qualities have serious limitations.

An effective method is to appraise managers against verifiable objectives, as exemplified by the discussion of management by objectives (MBO) in Chapter 5. This approach is operational, related to the manager's job, and relatively objective. Still, persons may perform well (or badly) because of luck or factors beyond their control. Therefore, the management-by-objectives approach should be supplemented by appraisal of managers as managers, that is, appraisal of how well managers perform key managerial activities. In a suggested program, seventy-three of these activities are identified and stated as checklist questions. These questions are grouped under planning, organizing, staffing, leading, and controlling, categories that form the framework of this book.

Career planning can be effectively integrated with performance appraisal. Although the specific steps in developing a career strategy may vary, the process usually involves (1) preparing a personal profile, (2) developing professional goals, (3) analyzing the environment for threats and opportunities, (4) analyzing personal strengths and weaknesses, (5) developing strategic career alternatives, (6) testing for consistency of the alternatives and making strategic choices, (7) developing short-range career objectives and action plans, (8) developing contingency plans, (9) implementing the career plan, and (10) monitoring the progress of the career in accordance with the plan.

Key Ideas and Concepts for Review

Performance in accomplishing goals and plans

Performance as a manager

Weaknesses of trait appraisal

Strengths and weaknesses of appraisal against verifiable objectives

Suggested performance appraisal of managers

Strengths and weaknesses of the new program

Steps in developing a career strategy

For Discussion

1 Do you think managers should be appraised regularly? If so, how?

2 What problems may arise from the fact that different managers on the same level appraise differently, some generally rating higher than others?

3 Many firms evaluate managers on such personality factors as aggressiveness, cooperation, leadership, and attitude. Do you think this kind of rating makes sense?

4 An argument has been made in this book for appraising managers on their ability to manage. Should anything more be expected of them?

5 How do you feel about an appraisal system based upon results expected and realized? Would you prefer to be appraised on this basis? If not, why?

6 What is your assessment of the degree of objectivity or subjectivity of the appraisal approaches suggested in this chapter? Can you suggest any further means of making appraisals more objective?

7 On what basis should your performance in college be appraised?

8 What would you say to a student who tells you that he studied at least four hours every day in preparation for the midterm exam and still got only a C?

9 What is your career goal? Have you developed a plan to achieve your goal?

CASE 15-1

HARDSTONE CORPORATION

William Hardstone, president of the Hardstone Corporation, was interested in putting in a bonus plan for his top managers and their immediate subordinates. The management consultant whom he engaged to help him with the plan strongly recommended that the bonus plan be based on (1) establishing a bonus pool of 8 percent of profits after retaining 12 percent on stockholders' equity plus long-term borrowing, and (2) allocating bo-

nus shares to each person on the basis of position, salary level, and performance on the job.

Mr. Hardstone readily agreed to these principles. The consultant then pointed out that if such a plan were to be instituted, as objective as possible an appraisal of individual performance would be a necessary part of it.

Mr. Hardstone agreed, but told the consultant: "I don't want any formal plan of appraisal. I had one once, and all that paperwork was meaningless since everyone was marked 'outstanding' or 'excellent.' I will do my own evaluation and allocate the bonuses to each person. I know how they are all doing and how well they are performing."

1 Do you believe that bonuses should be based, at least in part, on every individual's performance?

2 How would you answer Mr. Hardstone? Is he right, or could he be? What would you suggest?

CASE 15-2

FORESITE INCORPORATED

Carl Fisher was the president of Foresite, Inc., a multidivisional company in the high-technology field. The large company was well-known for its technical innovations and the high caliber of its scientists and engineers. But competition was on the increase and the president realized that the success of the firm depended on effective management. It was felt that planning was one of the very weak areas where improvement was needed. Therefore, the president invited John Weigand, a management consultant, to "look at his company" and to explore alternative ways of improving the organization. At the first meeting considerable trust developed between Fisher and Weigand, and in the course of the discussion it was agreed that any major organization intervention should be based on facts (meaning, on data collected from the organization itself). As a first step, Weigand interviewed three major department heads—Ms. Albani, Mr. Johnson, and Mr. Baker—to get an overview of the firm and the quality of its managers. The president agreed, tentatively, to a long-range systematic organizational development effort. However, the immediate problem was to make some selections for key managerial positions.

Managers have to be well versed in all managerial functions, but at this point it was felt that aspects of planning were particularly important. With the guidance of the consultant, Carl Fisher assessed the planning activities of three managers considered for the position of (1) head of the corporate planning group and (2) division manager. He found useful the appraisal approach developed by Harold Koontz and described in the text.

The instructions for rating the subordinates were as follows: In rating each question, give the following marks for each (for each level of rating use only one of two numbers, such as 4.0 or 4.5 for *Excellent*, not other decimals).

The possible marks were:

X = Not applicable to position

N = Do not know accurately enough for rating

5.0 = *Superior*: A standard of performance which could not be improved upon under any circumstances or conditions known to the rater

4.0 or 4.5 = *Excellent*: A standard of performance which leaves little of any consequence to be desired

3.0 or 3.5 = *Good*: A standard of performance above the average and meeting all normal requirements of the position

2.0 or 2.5 = *Average*: A standard of performance regarded as average for the position involved and the people available

1.0 or 1.5 = *Fair*: A standard of performance which is below the normal requirements of the position, but one that may be regarded as marginally or temporarily acceptable

0.0 = *Inadequate*: A standard of performance regarded as unacceptable for the position involved

The results of the evaluations were as shown in the accompanying table.

Performance as a Manager

Planning	Florence Albani	Ted Johnson	George Baker
1 Does the manager set for the departmental unit both short-term and long-term goals in verifiable terms (either qualitative or quantitative) that are related in a positive way to those of the superior and the company?	N	3.5	4.5
2 To what extent does the manager make sure that the goals of the department are understood by those who report to him or her?	3.0	3.0	4.0
3 How well does the manager assist those who report to him or her in establishing verifiable and consistent goals for their operations?	3.5	3.0	4.5
4 To what extent does the manager utilize consistent and approved planning premises in planning and see that subordinates do likewise?	4.5	3.5	4.0
5 Does the manager understand the role of company policies in decision making and ensure that subordinates do likewise?	4.5	4.0	4.0
6 Does the manager attempt to solve problems of subordinates by policy guidance, coaching, and encouragement of innovation, rather than by rules and procedures?	4.0	3.0	4.5
7 Does the manager help subordinates get the information they need to assist them in their planning?	4.5	3.5	4.0
8 To what extent does the manager seek out applicable alternatives before making a decision?	4.0	4.0	3.5
9 In choosing from among alternatives, does the manager recognize and give primary attention to those factors which are limiting, or critical, to the solution of a problem?	4.0	N	3.5
10 In making decisions, how well does the manager bear in mind the size and length of commitment involved in each decision?	4.5	4.0	3.5
11 Does the manager check plans periodically to see if they are still consistent with current expectations?	3.0	4.5	4.0
12 To what extent does the manager consider the need for, as well as the cost of, flexibility in arriving at a planning decision?	4.0	4.5	4.5
13 In developing and implementing plans, does the manager regularly consider long-range implications of the decisions along with the short-range results expected?	4.0	4.5	4.0
14 When the manager submits problems to the superior, or when a superior seeks help in solving problems, does he or she submit considered analyses of alternatives (with advantages and disadvantages) and recommended suggestions for solution?	4.0	4.0	3.5
Total number of questions in which ratings are made:	13	13	14
Total score on questions given ratings:	51.5	49.0	56
Average of ratings in Planning:	4.0	3.8	4.0

To gain greater confidence in his judgment, Carl Fisher also asked two of his vice-presidents to rate the three candidates. Their evaluations were consistent with that of the president.

Assume that all three candidates have similar technical and managerial skills besides those shown in the table and the performance results are similar.

1 Whom would you select as a head of the corporate planning staff? Why?

2 Whom would you choose as manager of the division?

3 What other factors would you consider in making the selection?

4 What training and development would you recommend for each of the managers?

For Further Information

Bolles, R. N. *What Color Is Your Parachute?* (Berkeley, Calif.: Ten Speed Press, 1984).

Business Week's Guide to Careers (New York: McGraw-Hill Book Company. This guide is published several times a year by *Business Week*.)

Crystal, J., and R. Bolles. *Where Do I Go from Here with My Life?* (New York: The Seabury Press, Inc., 1974).

Hall, D. T. *Careers in Organizations* (Pacific Palisades, Calif.: Goodyear Publishing Company, Inc., 1976).

Latham, G. P., and K. N. Wexley. *Increasing Productivity through Performance Appraisal* (Reading, Mass.: Addison-Wesley Publishing Company, Inc., 1980).

London, M. *Managing Careers* (Reading, Mass.: Addison-Wesley Publishing Company, Inc., 1982).

Mihal, W. L., P. A. Sorce, and T. E. Comte, "A Process Model of Individual Career Decision Making," *Academy of Management Review*, vol. 9, no. 1 (January 1984), pp. 95–103.

Stoner, J. A. F., T. P. Ference, E. K. Warren, and H. K. Christensen. *Managerial Career Plateaus—An Exploratory Study* (New York: Center for Research in Career Development, Columbia University, 1980).

Von Glinow, M. A., M. J. Driver, K. Brousseau, and J. B. Prince. "The Design of a Career-Oriented Human Resource System," *Academy of Management Review*, vol. 8, no. 1 (January 1983), pp. 23–32.

Walker, J. W., and T. G. Gutteridge. *Career Planning Practices: An AMA Survey Report* (New York: AMACOM, 1979).

Weihrich, H. "Strategic Career Management—A Missing Link in Management by Objectives," *Human Resource Management*, vol. 21, no. 2 and 3 (Summer/Fall 1982), pp. 58–66.

Wright, J. W. *The American Almanac of Jobs and Salaries* (New York: Avon Books, 1982).

16

Manager and Organization Development

CHAPTER OBJECTIVES

After reading this chapter, you should understand:

1 Manager development, managerial training, and organization development
2 The premises underlying the operational-management approach to training and development
3 The manager development process and training
4 Approaches to on-the-job training
5 Internal and external approaches to managerial training and development
6 How to manage organizational conflict
7 The nature and processes of organization development
8 The major principles of staffing

Good executives look to the future and prepare for it. One important way to do this is to develop and train managers so that they are able to cope with new demands, new problems, and new challenges. Indeed, executives have a responsibility to provide training and development opportunities for their employees so that the employees can reach their full potential.

The costs of training represent major investments, and executives are justifiably concerned about the effectiveness of training. We share this concern and therefore emphasize in this chapter the need for a systematic approach to manager and organization development. We use the term *manager development* to refer to

Manager development

Managerial training

Organization development

the progress a manager makes in learning how to manage. *Managerial training*, on the other hand, pertains to the programs that facilitate the learning process. There is less agreement on the definition of organization development (OD). We view *organization development* as a systematic, integrated, and planned approach to improving the effectiveness of groups of people and of the whole organization. Organization development uses various techniques for identifying and solving problems.

Essentially, then, OD focuses on the total organization (or a major segment of it), while manager development concentrates on the progress individuals make. These approaches support each other and should be integrated to improve the effectiveness of both the managers and the enterprise.

The Need for Effective Manager Development

Many companies have substantial training budgets and large training staffs that design, develop, and "market" programs. Nevertheless, some companies do not get the results they seek.

Management Development Failures

Many of the failures in management development programs can be attributed to an unsystematic approach to training. Much time and money has been spent on management development that does not develop. Before we look at ways to avoid such costly mistakes, some typical problems are highlighted.

Development efforts may not support enterprise objectives The purpose of training is to achieve enterprise objectives and develop professional managers. Unfortunately, there often is little relationship between the training activities and the aims of the firm.

In an effective and efficient training program, managers determine enterprise objectives and integrate them with developmental needs of employees. An enterprise with a need for long-range planning, for example, should match this need with talents and aspirations of managers in the company. Such a situation is shown in Figure 16-1, with the large shaded area indicating a high degree of integration between the enterprise and the managers' development objectives.

Development efforts may place emphasis on programs instead of results Some executives take pride in the large number of employees enrolled in management development courses. Unfortunately, benefits derived from attending these meetings are negligible unless they satisfy a clearly defined training need; too often companies emphasize training *activities*, with little concern about training *results*. Many companies have had generous training and development budgets, with many employees participating in a great variety of programs, but make no effort to evaluate the effects, if any, on the performance of the employees. Clearly, there is a need for greater concern about the benefits derived from management development.

FIGURE 16-1

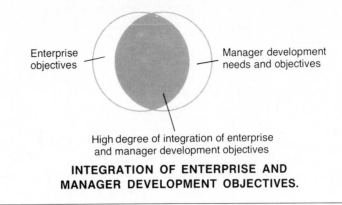

Enterprise objectives

Manager development needs and objectives

High degree of integration of enterprise and manager development objectives

INTEGRATION OF ENTERPRISE AND MANAGER DEVELOPMENT OBJECTIVES.

Manager development may be limited to a selected few   People sometimes think that manager development requires placing a few people with high potential in a training program, while ignoring the rest of the employees. It is, of course, difficult to identify the potential of prospective managers, but to rely on a few trainees is also a gamble. It is even more risky if the trainees are selected on the basis of friendship or kinship with executives, without regard for capabilities. Manager development programs should be available for all qualified employees who aspire to a career in management.

Operational-Management Premises

The operational-management approach to training and development is a situational one that integrates principles, concepts, theory, and behavioral knowledge with management practices to achieve the best results. This approach rests on several assumptions.

Top managers must actively support the program   The support of top executives is essential for any training and development program. But it is particularly important for programs that involve people from different levels of the enterprise, as many organization development efforts do. The support of top managers should go beyond a policy statement regarding training. For best results, it should include their active involvement and participation in development.

Training and development must involve managers at all levels   Training is not just for a selected few, nor is it only for those at lower levels. Top management may recognize the training needs of first-line supervisors, but not their own. Yet top managers should be trained first, to provide an example of their commitment to the continuing development of all people in the enterprise and also to show that they are up to date on management thinking and techniques before their subordinates know them.

Training and development needs vary   Needs vary not only for positions at different levels in the organization hierarchy but also for individuals, since background, requirements, aspirations, and potential are specific to the individual.

Consequently, training and development activities should be tailored to these specific and individual needs.

Training and development needs should determine methods   No program or method fits all needs. Programs and methods should be selected on the basis of how effectively and efficiently they satisfy personal needs and accomplish the developmental objectives of managers and the enterprise.

Theory and practice must go hand in hand   It has been said that nothing is as practical as good theory. There is little doubt that theory provides an excellent framework for learning, but theory and practice must be integrated. Training, which is the teaching of theory and the demonstration of techniques, is one side of the coin; the other side is the actual practice of managers. The need for management experience is obvious when applying training to practice.

Manager Development Process and Training

Three kinds of needs

Before deciding on specific training and development programs, three kinds of needs must be considered. The needs of the organization include such items as the objectives of the enterprise, the availability of managers, and turnover rates. Needs related to the operations and the job itself can be determined from job descriptions and performance standards. Data about individual training needs can be gathered from performance appraisals, interviews with the jobholder, tests, surveys, and career plans of individuals. Let us look more closely at the steps in the manager development process, focusing first on the present job, then on the next job in the career ladder, and finally on the long-term future needs of the organization. The steps in manager development are depicted in Figure 16-2.

Present Job

Example

Manager development and training must be based on a needs analysis derived from a comparison of actual performance and behavior with required performance and behavior. Such an analysis is shown in Figure 16-3. A district sales manager has decided that the selling of 1000 units is a reasonable expectation, but the actual sales are only 800, 200 units short of the sales target. Analysis of the deviation from the standard might indicate that the manager lacks the knowledge and skills for making a forecast, and that conflicts among subordinate managers hinder effective teamwork. Based on this analysis, training needs and methods for overcoming the deficiencies are identified. Consequently, the district sales manager enrolls in courses in forecasting and conflict resolution. Furthermore, organization development efforts are undertaken to facilitate cooperation among organization units.

Next Job

As shown in Figure 16-2, a similar process is applied in the identification of the training needs for the next job. Specifically, present competency is compared with the competency demanded by the next job. For instance, a person who has worked mainly in production may be under consideration for a job as a project manager.

FIGURE 16-2

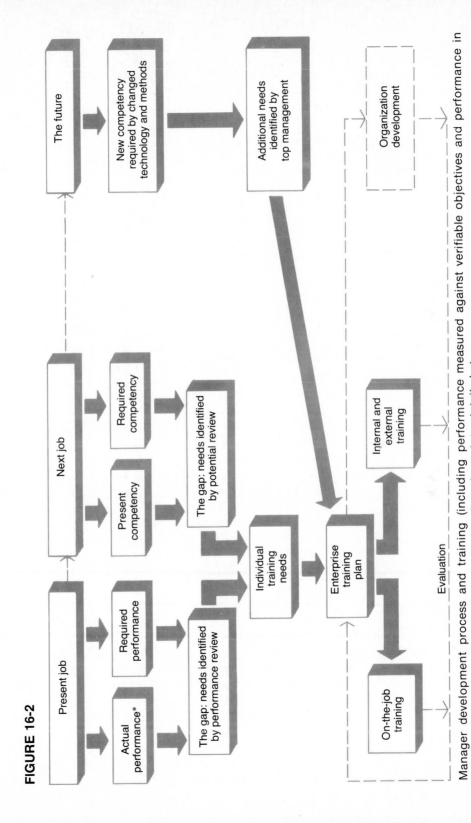

Manager development process and training (including performance measured against verifiable objectives and performance in carrying out managerial functions) can be broken down into detailed steps.

Adapted from John W. Humble, Improving Business Results *[Maidenhead, England: McGraw-Hill Book Company (UK), Ltd., 1968].*

FIGURE 16-3

TRAINING NEEDS ANALYSIS.

This position requires training in functional areas such as engineering, marketing, and even finance. This systematic preparation for a new assignment certainly is a more professional approach than simply thrusting a person into a new work situation without training.

Future Needs

Progressive organizations go one step further in their training and development approach; they prepare for the more distant future. This requires that they forecast what new competencies will be demanded by changing technology and methods. For example, expected energy shortages may require that managers be trained not only in the technical aspects of energy conservation but also in energy-related long-range planning and creative problem solving. These new demands—created by the external environment—have to be integrated into enterprise training plans which focus on the present and the future. These plans are contingent, on the one hand, on the training needs and, on the other hand, on the various approaches to manager development that are available.

Approaches to Manager Development: On-the-Job Training

There are many opportunities for development to be found on the job. Trainees can learn and at the same time contribute to the aims of the enterprise. However, because this approach requires competent higher-level managers who can teach and coach trainees, there are limitations to on-the-job training.

Planned Progression

Planned progression is a technique that gives managers a clear idea of their path of development. Managers know where they stand and where they are going. For example, a lower-level manager may have available an outline of the path from superintendent to works manager and eventually to production manager. The manager then knows the requirements for advancement and the means to achieve it. Unfortunately, there may be an overemphasis on the next job instead of on good performance of present tasks. Planned progression may be perceived by trainees as a smooth path to the top, but it really is a step-by-step approach which requires that tasks be done well at each level.

Job Rotation

Three kinds of rotation

The purpose of job rotation is to broaden the knowledge of managers or potential managers. The trainees learn about the different enterprise functions by rotating into different positions. They may rotate through (1) non-supervisory work, (2) observation assignments, (3) various managerial training positions, and (4) middle-level "assistant" positions; and there is even (5) unspecified rotation to various managerial positions.

The theory behind job rotation is good, but there are difficulties. As the term indicates, in some job rotation programs participants do not actually have managerial authority. Instead, they observe or assist line managers, but they do not have the responsibility they would have if they were actually managing. Even in rotations to managerial positions, the participants in the training program may not remain long enough in the position to prove their future effectiveness as managers. Furthermore, when the rotation program is completed, there may be no suitable positions available for the newly trained managers. Despite these drawbacks, if the inherent difficulties are understood by both managers and trainees, job rotation has positive aspects and should benefit trainees.

Creation of "Assistant-to" Positions

"Assistant-to" positions are frequently created to broaden the viewpoints of trainees by allowing them to work closely with experienced managers who can give special attention to the developmental needs of trainees. Managers can, among other things, give selected assignments to test the judgment of trainees. As in job rotation, this approach can be very effective when superiors are also qualified teachers who can guide and develop trainees until they are ready to assume full responsibilities as managers.

Temporary Promotions

Individuals are frequently appointed "acting" managers when, for example, the permanent manager is on vacation, is ill, or is making an extended business trip, or even when a position is vacant. Thus, temporary promotions are a developmental device as well as a convenience to the enterprise.

When the acting manager makes decisions and assumes full responsibility, the experience can be valuable. On the other hand, if such a manager is merely a figurehead, makes no decisions, and really does not manage, the developmental benefit may be minimal.

Committees and Junior Boards

Committees and "junior boards," also known as multiple management, are sometimes used as developmental techniques. These give trainees the opportunity to interact with experienced managers. Furthermore, trainees become acquainted with a variety of issues that concern the whole organization. They learn about the relationships among different departments and the problems created by the interaction of these organizational units. Trainees may be given the opportunity to submit reports and proposals to the committee or the board and to demonstrate their analytical and conceptual abilities. On the other hand, trainees may be treated in a paternalistic way by senior executives; although trainees are appointed to committees or junior boards, they may not be given opportunities to participate, an omission that might frustrate and discourage them. The program would then be detrimental to their development.

Coaching

On-the-job training is a never-ending process. A good example of on-the-job training is athletic coaching. To be effective, coaching, which is the responsibility of every line manager, must be done in a climate of confidence and trust between superior and trainees. Patience and wisdom are required of superiors, who must be able to delegate authority and give recognition and praise for jobs well done. Effective coaches will develop the strengths and potentials of subordinates and help them to overcome their weaknesses. To be sure, coaching requires time; but, if done well, it will save time and money, and will prevent costly mistakes by subordinates, and thus, in the long run, will benefit all—the superior, the subordinates, and the enterprise.

Approaches to Manager Development: Internal and External Training

Besides on-the-job training, there are many other approaches to developing managers. These programs may be conducted within the company or they may be offered externally by educational institutions and management associations, as indicated in Figure 16-2.

Sensitivity Training, T-Groups, and Encounter Groups

Objectives of sensitivity training

Sensitivity training, also called *T-group* ("T" stands for training), *encounter group,* or *leadership training,* is a controversial approach to manager development. Although popular in the 1960s and early 1970s, T-groups have lost favor as a managerial training technique in many companies. Still, certain aspects of sensitivity training may be used in team-building efforts. The objectives of sensitivity training generally include (1) better insight into one's own behavior and the way one "appears" to others; (2) better understanding of group processes; and (3) development of skills in diagnosing and intervening in group processes.

Although the sensitivity-training process has many variations, one general characteristic is that people interact and then receive feedback on their behavior from the trainer and other group members, who express their opinions freely and openly. The feedback may be candid and direct: "Jim, I do not get a good feeling when you approach the topic the way you just did. Could we talk about it?"

Jim may accept this comment and resolve to change his behavior. But he may also feel hurt and withdraw from the group. The T-group process may lead to personal anxieties and frustrations, but if properly administered, it can result in collaborative and supportive behavior.

Criticisms

The benefits of sensitivity training must be balanced against the criticisms of it.[1] For example, some people may be psychologically harmed because they simply cannot cope with the concurrent invasions of privacy. Owing to the group pressure and group dynamics, participants may reveal more about themselves than they actually intended to. There also is concern that some trainers may not be qualified to conduct sessions that become highly emotional. Finally, the relevancy of the outcomes of sensitivity training to the work situation has been questioned.

Despite the concerns of researchers and observers, many enterprises do use T-groups in their development efforts. The following guidelines can help to reduce potential harm and increase effectiveness:

Participation in T-groups should be voluntary.

Participants should be screened, and those who could be harmed, for example, highly defensive people, should be excluded from this experience.

Trainers should be carefully evaluated and their competence clearly established.

Potential participants should be informed about the goals and process before they commit themselves to sensitivity training.

Developmental objectives

Before using sensitivity training, organizations should clearly identify development and training needs and objectives. Based on these needs and objectives, other methods should also be considered.

Conference Programs

Conference programs may be used in internal or external training. During conference programs, managers or potential managers are exposed to the ideas of speakers who are experts in their field. Within the company, people may be instructed in the history of the firm, its purposes, policies, and relationships with customers, consumers, and other groups. External conferences may vary greatly, ranging from programs on specific managerial techniques to programs on broad topics, such as the relationship between business and society.

These programs can be valuable if they satisfy a training need and are thoughtfully planned. A careful selection of topics and speakers will increase the effectiveness of this training device. Furthermore, conferences can be made more successful by including discussions; two-way communication allows participants to ask for clarification of specific topics that are particularly relevant to them.

University Management Programs

Many universities now conduct courses, workshops, conferences, institutes, and formal programs for training managers. These offerings may include evening courses, short seminars, live-in programs, a full graduate curriculum, or even programs custom-designed for the needs of individual companies. Some executive development centers even provide career development assistance with programs de-

---

[1]For an evaluation of sensitivity training see A. C. Filley, R. J. House, and S. Kerr, *Managerial Process and Organizational Behavior* (Glenview, Ill.: Scott, Foresman and Company, 1976), pp. 498–503.

signed to fit typical training and development needs of first-line supervisors, middle managers, and top executives.

These programs expose managers to theories, principles, and new developments in management. In addition, there is usually a valuable interchange of experience among managers who, in similar positions, face similar challenges.

Readings

Another approach to development is planned reading of relevant and current management literature. This is essentially self-development. A manager may be aided by the training department, which often develops a reading list of valuable books. This learning experience can be enhanced through discussion of articles and books with other managers and the superior.

Special Training Programs

Management development must take an open-system approach that responds to the needs and demands of the external environment. Recently, government and industry have become aware of the need for training programs specifically designed for women, members of minority groups, and individuals who are physically handicapped. Many firms have made special efforts to train these people so that they may utilize their full potential while contributing to the aims of the enterprise.

Evaluation and Transfer

General developmental objectives

Determining the effectiveness of training programs is difficult. It requires measurements against standards and a systematic identification of training needs and objectives.

In general, developmental objectives include (1) an increase in knowledge, (2) development of attitudes conducive to good managing, (3) acquisition of skills, (4) improvement of management performance, and (5) achievement of enterprise objectives.

If training is to be effective, it is extremely important that the criteria used in the classroom situation resemble as closely as possible the criteria relevant in the working environment. One of the authors observed a T-group which had as its goals openness, "leveling," and feedback on each person's conduct in the group. The behavioral change of one of the participants would have had to be rated "excellent" when measured against the T-group criteria. However, when this person attempted to transfer his new values and behavior to the job, he met resistance and outright hostility. Arguments occurred and the result was that this person had to leave the company. Although the person changed, his boss did not; nor did his coworkers or the total work environment. This illustration shows that manager development requires a situational approach in which training objectives, techniques, and methods should be sufficiently congruent with the values, norms, and characteristics of the environment.

Organizational Conflict

Conflict is a part of organizational life and may occur within the individual, between individuals, between the individual and the group, and between groups. While conflict is generally perceived as being dysfunctional, it can also be beneficial because it may cause an issue to be presented in different perspectives. One top executive of a major company maintained that when there was no conflict on an issue, it could not have been sufficiently analyzed, and the final decision on the issue was usually postponed until all aspects were critically evaluated.

Sources of Conflict

There are many potential sources of conflict. Today's organizations are characterized by complex relationships and a high degree of interdependence of tasks that can cause frictions. Moreover, the goals of the parties are often incompatible, especially when the parties compete for limited resources. People also have different values and they have different perceptions of issues. A production manager, for example, may take the position that streamlining the product line and concentrating on a few products can make the organization more productive, while a sales manager may desire a broad product line that will satisfy diverse customer demands. An engineer may want to design the best product regardless of price or whether there is a demand for such a product.

There are other potentials for conflict. There may be conflicts between people in line and staff positions. The leadership style of the superior may cause conflicts. Differing educational backgrounds are potential sources of conflict. Perhaps most often mentioned is lack of communication. Many of these topics are discussed in various chapters of this book.

Managing Conflict

There are different ways of managing conflicts, focusing either on interpersonal relationships or on structural changes. *Avoidance* of the situation that causes the conflict is an example of an interpersonal approach.[2] Another way to cope with conflict is through *smoothing*, emphasizing the areas of agreement and common goals and deemphasizing disagreements. A third way is *forcing*—pushing one's own view on others; this, of course, will cause overt or covert resistance. A traditional way of coping with conflict is to *compromise*, agreeing in part to the other person's view or demand.

Attempts can also be made to *change the behavior* of individuals, a very difficult task indeed. At times, it may also be possible to *reassign* an individual to another organizational unit. In many situations, conflicts are resolved by a *person higher up in the organization* who has sufficient authority to decide an issue. The problem is that the loser may attempt to get even with the winner at a later time, thus perpetuating the conflict. In the *problem-solving* approach to organizational conflicts, differences are openly confronted and the issues are analyzed as objectively as possible.

Another way of coping with conflict is to make structural changes. This means modifying and integrating the *objectives* of groups with different viewpoints. Moreover, the *organization structure* may have to be changed and authority-responsibility relationships clarified. New ways of *coordinating* activities may have to be found. *Tasks* and *work locations* can also be rearranged. For example, in one workroom

---

[2]See R. R. Blake and J. S. Mouton, *Building a Dynamic Corporation Through Grid Organization Development* (Reading, Mass.: Addison-Wesley Publishing Company, 1969), chap. 6.

machines were placed in a way that prevented conflicting parties from interacting with one another. Often one must not only decide on the necessary changes but also select the appropriate process. For this reason we will turn our attention to organizational development.

Organization Development

OD defined

Organization development, typically shortened to OD, is a systematic, integrated, and planned approach to improve enterprise effectiveness. It is designed to solve problems that decrease operating efficiency at all levels. Such problems may include lack of cooperation, excessive decentralization, and poor communication.

The techniques of OD may involve laboratory training, managerial-grid training, and survey feedback. Some OD practitioners also use team building, process consultation, job enrichment, organizational behavior modification, and management by objectives as part of their approach.

Organization Development Process

Example

Organization development is a situational or contingency approach to improving enterprise effectiveness. Although various techniques are utilized, the process often involves the steps shown in Figure 16-4. An example can illustrate the application of the model.

Consider a firm that experiences certain problems: conflict among organizational units, low morale, customer complaints, and increasing costs (*problem recognition* in the model). The chief executive contacts an OD expert to discuss the situation. Both agree on the necessity of an *organizational diagnosis*. The consultant that collects information from several organizational units, using questionnaires, interviews, and observations. The data are analyzed and prepared for feedback.

FIGURE 16-4

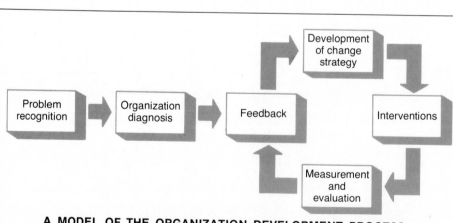

A MODEL OF THE ORGANIZATION DEVELOPMENT PROCESS.

Adapted from H. M. F. Rush, Organization Development: A Reconnaissance *(New York: National Industrial Conference Board, Inc., 1973), p. 6. Used by permission.*

The executive confers with other managers and sets up a meeting with them. At the meeting, after some introductory comments, the consultant presents the findings under the headings "relations between departments," "enterprise goals," and "customer relations" (*feedback*). The group then ranks the problems in order of their importance. With the guidance of the consultant, the group discusses the difficulties, identifies the underlying causes, and explores possible solutions.

The role of the consultant is that of a coach facilitating the process. Short lectures and exercises on decision making, team building, and problem solving are integrated into the process. At times, subgroups are established to deal with specific issues. The emphasis is on openness and objectivity. The meeting ends with an agreement on a *change strategy*.

The specific *interventions* may include a change in the organization structure, a more effective procedure for handling customer complaints, and the establishment of a team charged with the responsibility of implementing a cost reduction program. Furthermore, the group agrees to meet again in three months to measure and evaluate the effectiveness of the OD efforts.

Although these phases complete the OD cycle, the effort does not end. Instead, OD becomes a *continuous process*—planned, systematic, and focused on change—that aims at making the enterprise more effective.

Grid Organization Development and Other Methods

One systematic program in organization development is the grid approach.[3] Because the grid itself is discussed in Chapter 19, the emphasis here is on the six phases of grid organization development.

Six phases of grid OD

Phase 1 is an introduction to the basic concept of the grid. Robert Blake and Jane Mouton state that the concern for people and the concern for production are not mutually exclusive; they are complementary. The aim of the grid exercise is to develop a high concern for both.

Phase 2 is a continuation of Phase 1, but the focus is on the *team* instead of the individual. In this phase, group members set standards, develop ways to achieve objectives, and identify barriers to achievement of the full potential of the enterprise.

Phase 3 concerns *intergroup development*. It is in this phase that OD really begins. The focus is now on the organization, rather than on individuals. The aim is to reduce conflicts among groups that work together.

Phase 4 involves *organizational goal setting*. In this phase top managers identify the aims of the enterprise and *design an ideal strategic corporate model*. Managers from all enterprise functions, including production, engineering, sales, finance, and personnel, are usually members of this policy-setting team.

---

[3]Blake and Mouton, op. cit. and R. R. Blake and J. S. Mouton, *The Versatile Manager—A Grid Profile* (Homewood, Ill.: Richard D. Irwin, Inc., 1981), pp. 157–178.

Phase 5 is the *implementation of the strategic model*. This phase may extend over several years. Managers from all levels of the organization hierarchy have responsibilities in carrying out the activities necessary to achieve the goals set in the previous phase.

Phase 6 is a *systematic critique*. Managers evaluate achievements as well as mistakes made in the previous phases; they also discuss new challenges.

Survey feedback method

Process consultation

Team-building

The managerial grid is but one of several approaches to OD. Another one is the *survey feedback method*; it emphasizes the collection, organization, analysis, and feedback of data to participants. Still another technique of OD is *process consultation*, which is concerned with the role of the consultant in facilitating processes within and between groups. In *team building*, people who work together meet to identify barriers to effective functioning of the group. Then the team members develop change objectives and action plans to make the group more effective in achieving enterprise goals.

As these illustrations demonstrate, the parameters of OD are not clearly defined. Instead, OD is eclectic in the sense that it chooses from a variety of tools, methods, and techniques that facilitate the solving of particular enterprise problems.

OD in Action

Donnelly Mirror

Donnelly Mirror, Inc., of Holland, Michigan, used OD to improve enterprise effectiveness.[4] This moderate-sized firm employs about 350 people to produce a large percent of the "day-night" rearview mirrors for automobiles manufactured in the United States.

Interest in OD began when employees attended managerial grid seminars. Later, the company also sought the services of the Institute of Social Research at the University of Michigan; the Institute was asked to collect data on the organization, to feed back this information, and to act as a general change agent. The OD approach focused on participative management, with emphasis on problem solving and decision making at the organizational level where problems actually occurred. The company also utilized the "linking pin" concept with overlapping work teams. Basically, the linking pin is the person who is a subordinate in one group and a superior in another, thus linking the two groups.

The results of these and a number of other OD changes at Donnelly Mirror are impressive: considerable cost reductions, improved quality levels, and a noticeable increase in employee satisfaction.

General Motors

General Motors (GM) used OD to improve the effectiveness of its management system. OD as a long-range, situational effort is based on action research and problem-solving techniques. Scientific analysis was used to identify factors that bore on a particular problem. Based on the findings, improvements were made through interventions such as changes in the job content, the organization structure, and the enterprise environment.

---

[4]H. M. F. Rush, *Organization Development: A Reconnaissance* (New York: National Industrial Conference Board, Inc., 1973), pp. 42–50.

At GM's Oldsmobile division, the OD program reduced absenteeism and turnover; the Chevrolet group improved employee job satisfaction; and the Buick division, using a job enrichment program, increased productivity, reduced petty grievances, improved departmental morale, and facilitated better interpersonal relationships.[5]

Organization development is not restricted to business but is widely practiced in the military, which may be a surprise to those who perceive the military as an autocratic, mechanistic organization with values apparently incompatible with OD technologies.[6] The U.S. Army decided in the early 1970s to try a number of new

U.S. Army

managerial approaches, including OD, which they named "organizational effectiveness" (OE). Among the techniques employed were team building, goal setting, and developmental efforts based on surveys. These decentralized and flexible OE efforts had the strong support of top management, which may have been an important factor in the effectiveness of the program as perceived by respondents in a study.

U.S. Navy

The OD efforts in the U.S. Navy emphasized survey feedback. The pilot program, called "command development," was not a spectacular success. Nevertheless, the OD efforts were continued under the name "human resource management" (HRM). This program (summarized in Table 16-1) is quite standardized. Although a high percentage of participants felt positive about the program, others did not like the survey or felt that the process was too time-consuming.

U.S. Air Force

The U.S. Air Force does not have a centralized program, but relies on a variety of approaches such as laboratory training, team building, survey feedback, and job enrichment. Their results were also mixed. For example, the OD programs conducted for people on the shop floor had limited success but job enrichment was rather successful. Here, as elsewhere, most claims for the effectiveness of OD are based on testimonials and anecdotes. There is little solid empirical evidence that OD efforts changed the organizations or improved performance.

Need for research

Although the results of the various kinds of OD efforts in different organizations are mixed, some are encouraging. Still, more research needs to be done in a variety of companies under different conditions to make a definitive evaluation of OD. Today there is still a major gap in research on the cost and effectiveness of OD efforts. No doubt such research is a complex task because it is not easy to isolate cause and effect relationships. For instance, improved enterprise performance may be attributable to favorable market conditions and not to OD efforts. However, the great interest in measuring productivity—indicated by recent writings in management journals—may eventually result in development of more sophisticated tools for assessing the effects of OD and other managerial approaches.

---

[5]S. P. Robbins, *The Administrative Process* (Englewood Cliffs, N.J.: Prentice-Hall, Inc., 1976), pp. 340–345, 347–349.

[6]This discussion is drawn from D. D. Umstot, "Organization Development Technology and the Military: A Surprising Merger?" *Academy of Management Review*, vol. 5, no. 2 (April 1980), pp. 189–201.

TABLE 16-1   The Navy's Human Resource Management Cycle

Time phasing	Time to conduct		Step activity
Weeks 1–2	1½ days	1	Initial meetings between commanding officer (CO) and consultants
Week 2	½ day	2	Data-gathering planning meetings: Will interview be conducted? What questions? Are additional survey questions desired? Schedule the survey administration
Week 3	1 hour per person	3	Survey administration (mandatory): To all hands
Week 4	As required	4	Conduct interviews (optional)
Week 5	1 day	5	Return survey results to CO: Brief printout format, terms Study and analysis
Weeks 6–7	½ day per working group	6	Survey feedback to work groups (optional): Familiarization with data Source of perceptions? Supervisory self-knowledge Possible solutions/recommendations for action
Weeks 8–9	½ day	7	Action-planning meeting (optional): Develop plans for human resource availability week: OD, equal opportunity, alcohol, drug abuse, and overseas diplomacy
Week 10	1–3 days per group	8	Human resource workshops (optional): Vertical slice of ship or intact work group Modular training packages (standardized series of lectures, films, and exercises on such topics as motivation, communications, MBO, leadership, and race relations)
	2 days	9	Command action-planning workshop (optional): Selected members of crew normally (CO participates part-time) CO approves plan (a command action plan is mandatory)
Week 11	Indefinite	10	Action phase: Implement action plans
Weeks 25–30	½ day	11	Follow-up by consultant: Determine effect of human resource activities through interviews and discussions Meet with CO
Weeks 11–104	As negotiated	12	Follow-on activities (optional): Survey readministered Conduct additional workshops or training activities

Source: D. D. Umstot, "Organization Development Technology and the Military: A Surprising Merger?" *Academy of Management Review*, vol. 5, no. 2 (April 1980), p. 194. Used with permission.

Summary

Manager development is the progress a manager makes in learning how to manage effectively. Organization development, on the other hand, is a systematic, integrated, and planned approach to making a whole organization or an organization unit more effective.

There is a need for effective management development, as shown by the failures of managers. To aid in eliminating these failures, we suggest a systematic approach to manager development and training. On-the-job training includes planned progression, job rotation, the creating of "assistant-to" positions, temporary promotions, the use of committees and junior boards, and coaching. Manager development may include a variety of internal and external training programs.

There are many sources of conflicts; ways of managing conflict include avoidance of the situation, smoothing, forcing, compromising, changing behavior, reassigning individuals, resolving the conflict at higher levels, and problem solving. Other approaches include making structural changes: modifying objectives, developing new methods of coordination, and rearranging authority-responsibility relationships, tasks, and work locations.

The typical organization development process includes the recognition of problems, the diagnosis of an organization, feedback of information on the organization, the development of a change strategy, interventions, and measurement and evaluation of the change efforts. A variety of different OD programs are used to improve organizational effectiveness and efficiency.

Key Ideas and Concepts for Review

Manager development
Managerial training
Organization development
Premises of training and development
Manager development process
On-the-job training

Internal and external training and
 development
Sources of organizational conflict
Ways of managing organizational conflict
Organization development process
Grid organization development

For Discussion

1 It has been argued that firms have an obligation to train and develop all employees with managerial potential. Do you agree?

2 What are some typical failures in manager development and training? Can you explain these failures? What would you recommend to overcome the shortcomings?

3 Evaluate the advantages and limitations of different approaches to on-the-job training.

4 Evaluate sensitivity training as a technique for training managers. Do you think sensitivity training would make you a better manager? Explain.

5 In the job you now have or the one you expect to have in the future, what kind of coaching and management development would be most beneficial to you?

6 Take an organization you know and analyze its management development efforts.

7 What kinds of conflicts have you experienced in an organization with which you are familiar? What were the causes of the conflicts? What was done, if anything, about resolving these conflicts?

8 What are the main characteristics of organization development? How does OD differ from manager development? Do you think OD might work in your organization? Explain why or why not.

CASE 16-1

AEROSPACE, INC.

Jim Smith was the manager of the systems development department of Aerospace, Inc. During his fifteen years with the company, he trained many managers and encouraged their development, only to see many of them leave the firm after they got their advanced degrees. The company had a liberal policy of educational reimbursement (75 percent of tuition costs and books), and many engineers (about 50 percent of them have a master's degree in a technical field) took advantage of the educational opportunities.

Joan Harris, an electrical engineer, came to see her boss, Jim Smith, who congratulated Ms. Harris for obtaining her master's degree in business administration, which she received with the assistance of the firm's educational program.

Ms. Harris, to the surprise of Mr. Smith, said that she was leaving the company to go to a competitor because she did not see any opportunities for advancement in the firm.

Mr. Smith was furious because this had happened several times before. He immediately went to see the vice-president of operations and complained about the educational reimbursement policy and the lack of a systems approach to staffing.

1 What might be the reason that employees left after receiving their degrees with the help of educational reimbursements?

2 If you were the vice-president, what would you do?

3 How can such labor turnover be prevented?

CASE 16-2

MANAGEMENT DEVELOPMENT AT THE PENDLETON DEPARTMENT STORES CORPORATION

A consultant was discussing the problem of improving the quality of management with a group of executives at the Pendleton Department Stores Corporation headquartered in Chicago. The executive vice-president asked whether there were any broad guidelines in the field of management development. Addressing the consultant, he said, "We know you have had many and varied experiences in the development of managers at all levels in many types of enterprise. Have you reached any conclusions that might approach the quality of general truths or, perhaps, principles?"

"While I would not want to assert that there are principles in this field," the consultant replied, "there are certain convictions that I have about programs for manager development. In the first place, the top manager—whether head of a large division, a region, or the whole enterprise—must know specifically what the proposed program is expected to accomplish, must be convinced that this is the way to go, and must have the patience and willpower to insist that every manager will put the theory into practice.

"In the second place," he continued, "the program must be implemented by operating managers and not by a consultant or the personnel department. Third, every program should be evaluated on the basis of its contribution to company results. And finally, I am certain that when the key top manager loses direct interest in, and contact with, the program, the quality and effectiveness of the program will deteriorate."

"But," said the executive vice-president, "how can we take so direct a part in such programs? We have so many things to do. Anyway, that is the reason we have a training section of the personnel department."

1 Do you agree with the consultant? If so, just how would you accomplish what he suggests be done?

2 What of the executive vice-president's position—how can a top executive do all these things to ensure manager training and still have time to do the rest of his or her job?

For Further Information

Argyris, C. *Reasoning, Learning, and Action* (San Francisco: Jossey-Bass Inc., Publishers, 1982).

Badawy, M. K. *Developing Managerial Skills in Engineers and Scientists* (New York: Van Nostrand Reinhold Company, 1982).

Behrman, J. N., and R. I. Levin. "Are Business Schools Doing Their Job?" *Harvard Business Review*, vol. 62, no. 1 (January–February 1984), pp. 140–147.

French, W. L., and C. H. Bell, Jr. *Organization Development*, 2nd ed. (Englewood Cliffs, N.J.: Prentice-Hall, Inc., 1978).

French, W. L., C. H. Bell, Jr., and R. A. Zawacki, (eds.) *Organization Development—Theory, Practice, and Research* (Plano, Tex.: Business Publications, Inc., 1983).

Jenkins, R. L., R. C. Reizenstein, and F. G. Rodgers. "Report Cards on the MBA," *Harvard Business Review*, vol. 62, no. 5 (September–October 1984), pp. 20–30.

Kotter, J. P., and L. A. Schlesinger. "Choosing Strategies for Change," *Harvard Business Review*, vol. 57, no. 2 (March–April 1979), pp. 106–114.

Michael, S. R., F. Luthans, G. S. Odiorne, W. W. Burke, and S. Hayden. *Techniques of Organizational Change* (New York: McGraw-Hill Book Company, 1981).

Robey, D., and S. Altman, (eds.) *Organization Development—Progress and Perspectives* (New York: Macmillan Publishing Company, Inc., 1982).

Ulschak, F. L. *Human Resource Development; The Theory and Practice of Need Assessment* (Reston, Va.: Reston Publishing, Company, Inc., 1983).

Watson, C. E. "Getting Management Training to Pay Off," in H. Koontz, C. O'Donnell, and H. Weihrich (eds.), *Management—A Book of Readings*, 5th ed. (New York: McGraw-Hill Book Company, 1980), pp. 447–453.

Wexley, K. N., and G. P. Latham. *Developing and Training Human Resources in Organizations* (Glenview, Ill.: Scott, Foresman and Company, 1981).

White, L. P., and K. C. Wooten. "Ethical Dilemmas in Various Stages of Organizational Development," *Academy of Management Review*, vol. 8, no. 4 (October 1983), pp. 690–697.

Summary of Major Principles of Staffing

There are no universally accepted staffing principles. Nevertheless, those listed below are useful as guidelines for understanding the staffing function. These principles are grouped under the purpose and process of staffing.

The Purpose of Staffing
The purpose of staffing is summarized by the following principles.

Principle of the objective of staffing The objective of managerial staffing is to ensure that organization roles are filled by those qualified personnel who are able and willing to occupy them.

Principle of staffing The clearer the definition of organization roles and their human requirements, and the better the techniques of manager appraisal and training employed, the higher the managerial quality.

The first principle stresses the importance of desire and ability to undertake the responsibilities of management. There is considerable evidence of failure to achieve results when these qualities are lacking. The second principle rests upon an important body of knowledge concerning management practices. Those organizations that have no established job definitions, no effective appraisals, and no system for training and development will have to rely on coincidence or outside sources to fill positions with able managers. On the other hand, enterprises applying the systems approach to staffing will utilize the potentials of individuals in the enterprise more effectively and efficiently.

The Process of Staffing

The following principles indicate the means for effective staffing.

Principle of job definition The more precisely the results expected of managers are identified, the more the dimensions of their positions can be defined.

This principle is similar to the principle of functional definition discussed in Part III on organizing. Since organizational roles are occupied by people with different needs, these roles must have many dimensions—such as pay, status, power, discretion, and possibility of accomplishment—that induce managers to perform.

Principle of managerial appraisal The more clearly verifiable objectives and required managerial activities are identified, the more precise can be the appraisal of managers against these criteria.

This principle suggests that performance should be measured both against verifiable objectives—as in an appraisal approach based on management by objectives—and against standards of performance as managers. The appraisal of managers as managers considers how well the key managerial activities within the functions of planning, organizing, staffing, leading, and controlling are carried out.

Principle of open competition The more an enterprise is committed to the assurance of quality management, the more it will encourage open competition among all candidates for management positions.

Violation of this principle has led many firms to appoint managers with inadequate abilities. Although social pressures strongly favor promotion from within the firm, these forces should be resisted whenever better candidates can be brought in from the outside. At the same time, the application of this principle obligates an organization to appraise its people accurately and to provide them with opportunities for development.

Principle of management training and development The more management training and development are integrated with the management process and enterprise objectives, the more effective the development programs and activities will be.

This principle suggests that, in the systems approach, training and development efforts are related to the managerial functions, the aims of the enterprise, and the professional needs of managers.

Principle of training objectives The more precisely the training objectives are stated, the more likely are the chances of achieving them.

The analysis of training needs is the basis for training objectives that give direction to development and facilitate the measurement of the effectiveness of training efforts. This principle brings into focus the contribution that training makes to the purpose of the enterprise and the development of individuals.

Principle of continuing development The more an enterprise is committed to managerial competence, the more it requires managers to practice continuing self-development.

This principle suggests that in a fast-changing and competitive environment, managers cannot stop learning. Instead, they have to update their managerial knowledge continuously, reevaluate their approaches to managing, and improve their managerial skills and performance to achieve enterprise results.

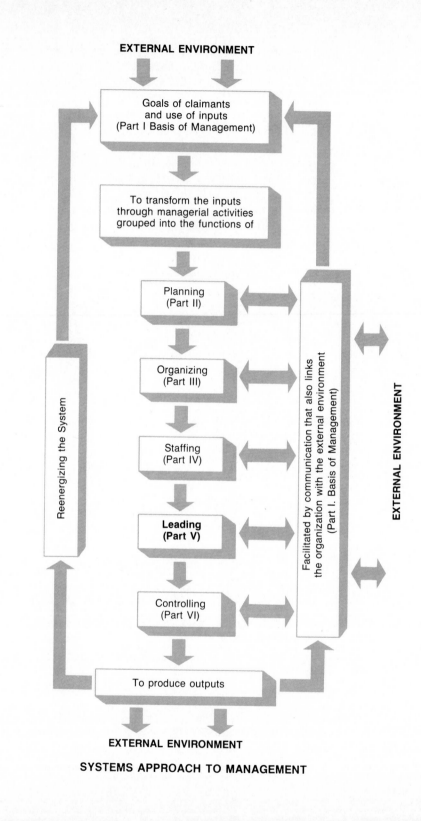

SYSTEMS APPROACH TO MANAGEMENT

Leading

17

Managing and the Human Factor

CHAPTER OBJECTIVES

After reading this chapter, you should understand:

1. The nature of the managerial function of leading
2. Basic human factors that affect managing in enterprises
3. Various models of the nature of people and their implications for managing
4. The need for an eclectic view of behavioral models
5. The importance of creativity and innovation in managing
6. The importance of harmonizing objectives

Management and leadership are often regarded as the same activity. Although it is true that the most effective manager will almost certainly be an effective leader and that leading is an essential function of managers, there is more to managing than just leading. As we indicated in previous chapters, managing involves planning carefully, setting up an organization structure that will aid people in achieving plans, and staffing the organization structure with people who are as competent as possible. You will see in Part VI that the measurement and correction of activities through controlling is also an important function of managing. However, all these managerial functions accomplish little if managers do not understand the human factor in their operations and do not know how to lead people in such a way as to produce desired results.

Followership

In a very fundamental sense, leadership also is followership, and we must discover why people follow. Basically, people tend to follow those who offer them a means of satisfying their own desires and needs. The task of managers is to encourage people to contribute effectively toward the accomplishment of enterprise goals, and to satisfy their own desires and needs in the process.

*Definition
of leading*

The managerial function of **leading** is defined as the process of influencing people so that they will strive willingly and enthusiastically toward the achievement of organizational goals. In our discussion of this function, we show that the behavioral sciences here make their major contribution to managing. As we analyze the pertinent behavioral science knowledge in managing, we will focus on the human factors, motivation, leadership, and communication.

The Human Factors in Managing

All organized effort is undertaken to achieve enterprise objectives; in general, the objective is to produce and make available some kind of goods or services. This effort is by no means restricted to business activity; we have stressed that it also applies to universities, hospitals, charitable associations, and governments. It is obvious that while enterprise objectives may differ somewhat in these various organizations, the individuals involved also have needs and objectives that are especially important to them. It is through the function of leading that managers help people see that they can satisfy their own needs and utilize their potential, while at the same time they contribute to the aims of the enterprise. Managers thus must have an understanding of the roles assumed by people, the individuality of people, and their personalities.

**Multiplicity
of Roles**

Individuals are much more than merely a productive factor in management's plans. They are members of social systems of many organizations; they are consumers of goods and services, and thus they vitally influence demand; they are members of families, schools, and churches; and they are citizens. In these different roles, they establish laws that govern managers, ethics that guide behavior, and a tradition of human dignity that is a major characteristic of our society. In short, managers and the people they lead are interacting members of a broad social system.

No Average Person

People act in different roles but they are also different themselves. There is no average person. Yet, in organized enterprises, the assumption is often made that there is. Firms develop rules, procedures, work schedules, safety standards, and position descriptions—all with the implicit assumption that people are essentially alike. Of course, this assumption is necessary to a great extent in organized efforts, but it is equally important to acknowledge that people are unique—they have different needs, different ambitions, different attitudes, different desires for responsibility, different levels of knowledge and skills, and different potentials.

Unless managers understand the complexity and individuality of people, they may misapply generalizations about motivation, leadership, and communication. Principles and concepts, although generally true, have to be adjusted to fit the specific situation. In an enterprise, not all the needs of individuals can be completely satisfied, but managers do have considerable latitude in making individual arrangements. Although position requirements are usually derived from enterprise and organization plans, this does not necessarily exclude the possibility of arranging the job to fit the person in a specific situation in order to make better use of management talent already existing in the enterprise.

Importance of Personal Dignity

Managing involves achieving enterprise objectives. Achieving results is important, but the means must never violate the dignity of people. The concept of individual dignity means that people must be treated with respect, no matter what their position in the organization. The president, vice-president, manager, first-line supervisor, and worker all contribute to the aims of the enterprise. Each person is unique, with different abilities and aspirations, but all are human beings and all deserve to be treated as such.

Importance of Considering the Whole Person

We cannot talk about human nature unless we consider the whole person, not just separate and distinct characteristics, such as knowledge, attitudes, skills, or personality traits. A person has them all to different degrees. Moreover, these characteristics interact with one another, and their predominance in specific situations changes quickly and unpredictably. The human being is a total person influenced by external factors such as family, neighbors, schools, churches, union or trade associations, political associations, and fraternal groups. People cannot divest themselves of the impact of these forces when they come to work. Managers must recognize these facts and be prepared to deal with them.

Behavioral Models

In order to understand the complexity of people, writers on management have developed several models. A model is an abstraction of reality. It includes variables that are considered important, but it also leaves out those factors less critical for explaining phenomena. Managers, whether they consciously know it or not, have in their minds a model of individual and organizational behavior that is based on assumptions about people. These assumptions and their related theories influence managerial behavior.

Over the years, various views of the basic nature of people have been suggested. To deal with all of them would not be practicable here. Therefore, we focus on the models of Schein and McGregor's classic assumptions about people.

From the Rational-Economic View to the Complex Person

Edgar H. Schein developed four conceptions about people. First, he noted *rational-economic assumptions* based on the idea that people are primarily motivated by economic incentives.[1] Since these incentives are controlled by the enterprise, people are essentially passive and are manipulated, motivated, and controlled by the organization. These assumptions are similar to those listed as Theory X by McGregor, to be discussed shortly.

---

[1] *Organizational Psychology*, 3d ed. (Englewood Cliffs, N.J.: Prentice-Hall, Inc., 1980), pp. 52–101.

The second model, concerning *social assumptions*, is based on Elton Mayo's idea that, basically, people are motivated by social needs. Thus, social forces of the peer group are more important than controls by management.

The third model, concerning *self-actualizing assumptions*, suggests that motives fall into five classes in a hierarchy ranging from simple needs for survival to the highest needs—for self-actualization with maximum use of a person's potential. According to this conception, people are self-motivated—they want to be, and can be, mature.

The fourth model, based on *complex assumptions*, presents Schein's own view of people. His underlying assumptions are that people are complex and variable and have many motives which combine into a complex motive pattern. In addition, people are able to learn new motives and to respond to different managerial strategies.

McGregor's Theory X and Theory Y

Another view of human nature has been expressed in two sets of assumptions developed by Douglas McGregor and commonly known as Theory X and Theory Y.[2] Managing, McGregor suggested, must start with the basic question of how managers see themselves in relation to others. This viewpoint requires some thought on the perception of human nature. Theory X and Theory Y are two sets of assumptions about human nature. McGregor chose these terms because he wanted neutral terminology without any connotation of "good" or "bad."

Theory X assumptions   The traditional assumptions about human nature, according to McGregor, are included in Theory X as follows:

1   Average human beings have an inherent dislike of work and will avoid it if they can.

2   Because of this human characteristic of dislike of work, most people must be coerced, controlled, directed, and threatened with punishment to get them to put forth adequate effort toward the achievement of organizational objectives.

3   Average human beings prefer to be directed, wish to avoid responsibility, have relatively little ambition, and want security above all.

Theory Y assumptions   The assumptions under Theory Y are seen by McGregor as follows:

1   The expenditure of physical effort and mental effort in work is as natural as play or rest.

2   External control and the threat of punishment are not the only means for producing effort toward organizational objectives. People will exercise self-direction and self-control in the service of objectives to which they are committed.

---

[2]*The Human Side of Enterprise* (New York: McGraw-Hill Book Company, 1960).

3 The degree of commitment to objectives is in proportion to the size of the rewards associated with their achievement.

4 Average human beings learn, under proper conditions, not only to accept but also to seek responsibility.

5 The capacity to exercise a relatively high degree of imagination, ingenuity, and creativity in the solution of organizational problems is widely, not narrowly, distributed in the population.

6 Under the conditions of modern industrial life, the intellectual potentialities of the average human being are only partially utilized.

These two sets of assumptions obviously are fundamentally different. Theory X is pessimistic, static, and rigid. Control is primarily external, that is, imposed on the subordinate by the superior. In contrast, Theory Y is optimistic, dynamic, and flexible, with an emphasis on self-direction and in the integration of individual needs with organizational demands. There is little doubt that each set of assumptions will affect the way managers carry out their managerial functions and activities. Let us look at their purposes in a little more detail.

Clarification of the theories   McGregor was apparently concerned that Theory X and Theory Y might be misinterpreted. The following points will clarify some of the areas of misunderstanding and keep the assumptions in proper perspective. First, Theory X and Theory Y assumptions are just that: they are assumptions only. They are *not* prescriptions or suggestions for managerial strategies. Rather, these assumptions must be tested against reality. Furthermore, these assumptions are intuitive deductions and are not based on research. Second, Theories X and Y do not imply "hard" or "soft" management. The "hard" approach may produce resistance and antagonism. The "soft" approach may result in laissez-faire management and is not congruent with Theory Y. Instead, the effective manager recognizes the dignity and capabilities, as well as the limitations, of people and adjusts behavior as demanded by the situation. Third, Theories X and Y are not to be viewed as opposite extremes of a continuum. They are not a matter of degree; rather, they are completely different views of people.

A fourth potential misunderstanding is that Theory Y is a case for consensus management. It is not an argument against the use of authority. Instead, under Theory Y, authority is seen as only one of the many ways a manager exerts leadership. Fifth, different tasks and situations require a variety of approaches to management. At times, authority and structure may be effective for certain tasks, and different approaches may be required in different situations. Thus, the productive enterprise is one that fits the task requirements to the people and the particular situation.

Toward an Eclectic View of Behavioral Models

Which of these many views of individuals is valid? We have noted that Schein suggested four conceptions, ranging from the rational-economic view to a view that stresses complex motivations. We have seen that McGregor grouped assumptions into Theory X and Theory Y. Which model, then, is valid?

It appears that no single model is sufficient to explain the full range of individual and organizational behavior. To repeat: People are different—there is no average person. Moreover, people also behave differently in diverse situations, and, to complicate matters, they even behave differently in similar situations at different times. In some situations, people act rationally; in other situations, they are guided by emotions. It is the manager's responsibility to create an environment in which people are induced to contribute to the aims of the enterprise. Yet to assume that people can be manipulated is to ignore their individuality and underestimate their intelligence. Economic rewards certainly are important in an enterprise, but people often want more than money from a job. They usually want to develop their capabilities, their competence, and their potential as well.

The effective manager will take an eclectic approach by drawing from different models that describe human nature. At the very least, he or she must recognize that people must be treated with respect and dignity, must be considered as whole persons, and must be seen in the context of their total environment, in which they assume many different roles. Different situations require a variety of managerial approaches for utilizing most effectively and efficiently the most valuable resource of the enterprise, namely, people.

Creativity and Innovation

Creativity vs. innovation

An important factor in managing people is creativity. We can make a distinction between creativity and innovation. The term **creativity** often refers to the ability to develop new ideas. **Innovation,** on the other hand, usually means the use of these ideas. In an organization, this can mean a new product, a new service, or a new way of doing things. Although this discussion centers on the creative process, it is implied that organizations not only generate new ideas but also translate them into practical applications.

The Creative Process

The creative process is seldom simple and linear. Instead it can be thought of as having several overlapping and interacting phases: (1) unconscious scanning, (2) intuition, (3) insight, and (4) logical formulation.[3]

Unconscious scanning

The first phase of unconscious scanning is difficult to explain as it is beyond consciousness. This scanning usually requires an absorption in the problem. Yet, managers working under time constraints often make decisions prematurely rather than dealing thoroughly with ambiguous, ill-defined problems.

Intuition

The second phase, intuition, connects the unconscious with the conscious. This stage may involve the combination of factors that may seem contradictory at first. For example, Alfred Sloan of General Motors conceived in the 1920s the idea of a decentralized division structure with centralized control. These concepts seem to contradict each other. Yet, they make sense when one recognizes the underlying principles: (1) giving responsibility for the operations to the chief ex-

---

[3]Much of the discussion of the creative process is based on M. B. McCaskey, *The Executive Challenge—Managing Change and Ambiguity* (Marshfield, Mass.: 1982), chap. 8.

ecutive of each division, and (2) maintaining centralized control for certain functions. It took the intuition of a great corporate leader to see these two principles interact in the managerial process.

Intuition needs time to work; the finding of new combinations and integration of diverse concepts and ideas takes time. One must think through the problem. Intuitive thinking is promoted by several techniques such as brainstorming and synectics which will be discussed below.

Insight

Insight is the third phase of the creative process. It may be likened to the exclamation "Eureka!" attributed to Archimedes on discovering the method for determining the purity of gold. Insight is mostly the result of hard work. It requires, for example, development of many ideas that result in a usable new product, service, or process. Interestingly, insight may come at times when the thoughts are not directly focused on the problem at hand. Moreover, new insights may last for only a few minutes; effective managers may benefit from having paper and pencil ready to make notes of their creative ideas.

Logical formulation

The last phase in the creative process is logical formulation or verification. The insight needs to be tested through logic or experiment. This may be accomplished by continued work on the idea or by inviting critiques from others. Sloan's idea of decentralization, for example, needed to be tested against organizational reality.

Techniques to Enhance Creativity

Creative thoughts are often the fruits of extensive efforts, and several techniques are available to nurture those kinds of thoughts, especially in the decision-making process. Some techniques focus on group interactions; others focus on individual actions. To illustrate, we will look at two of the most popular: brainstorming and synectics.

Brainstorming One of the best-known techniques to facilitate creativity has been developed by Alex F. Osborn, who has been called "the father of brainstorming."[4] The purpose of this approach is to improve problem solving by finding new and unusual solutions. In the brainstorming session, a multiplication of ideas is sought. The rules are:

1 No ideas are criticized.

2 The more radical the ideas are, the better.

3 The quantity of ideas produced is stressed.

4 The improvement of ideas by others is encouraged.

Brainstorming, which emphasizes group thinking, was widely accepted after its introduction. However, the enthusiasm was dampened by research which showed that individuals could develop better ideas working by themselves than when working in groups. Additional research, however, showed that in some situations the group approach may work well, specifically when the information is distributed

---

[4]A. F. Osborn, *Applied Imagination*, 3d rev. ed. (New York: Charles Scribner's Sons, 1963).

among various people and when a poorer group decision is more acceptable than a better individual decision. Also, the acceptance of new ideas is usually greater when the decision is made by the group charged with its implementation.[5]

Synectics   Originally known as the Gordon technique, after its creator, William J. Gordon, this system was further modified and became known as synectics.[6] In this approach, the members of the synectics team are carefully selected for their suitability to deal with the problem, a problem which may involve the entire organization.

   The leader of the group plays a vital role in synectics. In fact, only the leader knows the specific nature of the problem. This person narrows and carefully leads the discussion without revealing the problem itself. The main reason for this approach is to prevent the group from reaching a premature solution to the problem. The system involves a complex set of interactions from which a solution emerges—frequently the invention of a new product.

Limitations of Traditional Group Discussions

Although the techniques of brainstorming and synectics may result in creative ideas, it would be incorrect to assume that creativity flourishes only in groups. Indeed, the usual group discussion can inhibit creativity. For example, group members may pursue an idea to the exclusion of other alternatives. Experts on a topic may not be willing to express their ideas in a group for fear of being ridiculed. Also, lower-level managers may be inhibited in expressing their views in a group with higher-level managers. Pressures to conform can discourage the expression of deviant opinions. The need for getting along with others can be stronger than the need for exploring creative but unpopular alternatives to the solution of a problem. Finally, groups, with their need to arrive at a decision, may not make the effort of searching for data relevant to a decision.

The Creative Manager

All too often it is assumed that most people are noncreative and have little ability to develop new ideas. This assumption, unfortunately, can be detrimental to the organization, for in the appropriate environment virtually all people are capable of being creative, even though the degree of creativity varies considerably among individuals.

   Generally speaking, creative people are inquisitive and come up with many new and unusual ideas; they are seldom satisfied with the status quo. Although intelligent, they not only rely on the rational process but also involve the emotional aspects of their personality in problem solving. They appear to be excited about solving a problem, even to the point of tenacity. Creative individuals are aware of themselves and capable of independent judgment. They object to conformity and see themselves as being different.

---

[5]I. Summers and D. E. White, "Creativity Techniques: Toward Improvement of the Decision Process," *Academy of Management Review*, vol. 1, no. 2 (April 1976), pp. 99–107.

[6]W. J. J. Gordon, "Operational Approach to Creativity," *Harvard Business Review*, vol. 34, no. 6 (November–December 1956), pp. 41–51; and W. J. J. Gordon, *Synectics* (New York: Harper & Row, 1961).

Potential
difficulties

Unquestionably, creative people can make great contributions to an enterprise. At the same time, however, they may also cause difficulties in organizations. Change, as any manager knows, is not always popular. Moreover, change frequently has undesirable and unexpected side effects. Similarly, unusual ideas, pursued stubbornly, may frustrate others and inhibit the smooth functioning of an organization. Finally, creative individuals may be disruptive when they ignore established policies, rules, and regulations.

In conclusion, the creativity of most individuals is probably underutilized in many cases. Yet, unusual innovations can be of great benefit to a firm. Consequently, individual and group techniques should be effectively used to nurture creativity, especially in the area of planning. But, creativity is not a substitute for managerial judgment. It is the manager who must determine and weigh the risks involved in pursuing unusual ideas and translating them into innovative practices.

Harmonizing Objectives: The Key to Leading

Understanding the human factor in enterprises is important for the managerial function of leading. The way a manager views human nature influences his or her way of motivating and leading. A number of models presenting various conceptions of human nature have been proposed; however, no single view is sufficient to understand the whole person. Therefore, an eclectic view of human nature is the best approach.

People do not work in isolation; rather, to a great extent they work in groups toward the achievement of personal and enterprise objectives. Unfortunately, these objectives are not always in harmony with one another. Also, the goals of subordinates are not always the same as those of the superior. Therefore, one of the most important activities of managers is to make the needs of all individuals harmonize with the demands of the entire enterprise.

Leading bridges the gap between, on the one hand, logical and well-considered plans, carefully designed organization structures, good programs of staffing, and efficient control techniques, and, on the other hand, the need for people to understand, to be motivated, and to contribute all they are capable of to an enterprise and department goals. There is no way that a manager can utilize the desires and objectives of individuals to achieve enterprise objectives without knowing what individuals want. Even then, managers must be able to design an environment that will take advantage of these individual drives. Managers must know how to communicate with and guide their subordinates so that they will see how they serve their own interests by working efficiently for an organization.

Summary

Leading is the process of influencing people so that they will strive toward organizational goals. People assume many different roles and there is no average person. While working toward goals, the manager must take into account the dignity of the whole person.

There are different views and assumptions about human nature. Schein proposed four sets of assumptions: the rational-economic, social, self-actualizing, and complex assumptions. McGregor called his sets of assumptions about people Theory X and Theory Y. But no single model is sufficient to explain the complexities of people. Consequently, we suggest taking an eclectic view, drawing from different models to describe human nature.

Creativity, the ability and power to develop new ideas, is important for effective managing. The creative process consists of four overlapping phases: (1) unconscious scanning, (2) intuition, (3) insight, and (4) logical formulation. Two popular techniques for enhancing creativity are brainstorming and synectics.

Managers need to understand the various behavioral patterns of themselves and their subordinates that help in harmonizing objectives. This understanding is probably the key to effective leading.

Key Ideas and Concepts for Review

Leading	Eclectic view of people
Human factors in managing	Creative process
Individual dignity	Logical formulation
Schein's assumptions about people	Brainstorming
Theory X assumptions	Synectics
Theory Y assumptions	Harmonizing objectives

For Discussion

1 What are Theory X and Theory Y assumptions? State your agreements or disagreements with these assumptions. What are some misunderstandings of Theories X and Y?

2 What are some of the important human factors in an organization? How would you like to be treated by your superior?

3 Try to recall your most important creative insight. How did it come about?

4 Do you, as a student, an employee, or a manager, work at your full capacity? Why, or why not?

5 Why is the harmonizing of personal and enterprise objectives the key to leading?

6 Based on your experience, do you think that people are basically lazy, or are they eager to contribute to the goals of an organization? Give some examples supporting your view.

7 To what extent are your personal objectives the same as the objectives of the university you attend or the organization for which you work?

CASE 17-1

WHAT DO WE KNOW FOR SURE?

The class in management was nearing the conclusion of its study of human behavior. Several members had reported on the research and conclusions of prominent writers in the field. All were quite familiar with the work of Schein, McGregor, and others.

Hoping to focus attention on the conclusions that might be reached, the professor asked, "Do you feel that the research conducted by these scholars has enabled us to move from hypothesis to truth about the behavior of people?"

One thoughtful student, almost talking to herself, commented: "When I read the work of these investigators, I was convinced that each had a most telling case. I thought that here indeed was truth. Then I recalled that in each instance, these writers were inferring from observed behavior. While I was convinced that what people *did* was accurately reported, I could not help but feel that other observers, looking at the same behavior, would have different explanations. Perhaps we will never *know* why people behave as they do. Indeed, I don't understand myself; does the professor understand himself!"

The pragmatist in the class had little use for this line of thought. "What difference does it make," he said, "why people behave in a particular way? Isn't it enough to know that they do so behave? Using this, why can't we establish a motivation system within any enterprise that will work?"

A voice in the back of the room was heard to say, "I'm afraid of generalizations."

1 In your opinion, which of the theories explains best why people behave as they do? Why?

2 Select two theories by authors mentioned in the case and discuss the similarities and differences in their views about human nature.

CASE 17-2

CUSTOMER'S ELECTRIC APPLIANCE COMPANY

John Caldwell, the president of the Customer's Electric Appliance Company, had just received the latest report of the state of the firm. He did not like what he read: sales down, costs increased, profits decreased, customer complaints up, and labor turnover extremely high. He immediately asked his secretary to order all the vice-presidents from the functional areas, the controller, and other key staff personnel to come to his office. At the meeting, Mr. Caldwell stated, "I have just received the report on key indicators and I think the poor performance of the firm is directly attributable to your lack of leadership. This company has become a country club. When I walk through the corridors, I see people standing around as if they were at a cocktail party. Their concern is to do less for more money and more fringe benefits. They have completely forgotten that we are in business to make a profit. You must remember that people want to do as little as possible and to squeeze the last dime out of the company. What is needed is closer supervision and more control. When people are not performing, you warn them once—if they do not shape up, fire them. Recently, several customers complained that they could not get any service when their requests would not result in sales and commission for the salesperson. I want you to check the salespeople very closely on their dealings with our customers. Do not hesitate to listen in on their telephone conversations. Perhaps, you might even make recordings of these conversations and bring them to my attention.''

The executives at the meeting nodded approvingly at the president's remarks. Only Carolyn Jung, a 28-year-old staff assistant, raised some questions. She wondered whether the company should go that far in installing controls. In fact, she suggested that people basically want to work, they want to contribute, they want to do a good job, provided opportunities are given. She even suggested that the company perhaps did not really utilize people's potentials because employees to-

day are better educated than ever before and they want to participate in the decision-making process. She recommended that the president explain to the employees the company's poor performance and then solicit their help in improving productivity.

The president, stunned by Ms. Jung's comments, said that she must have been misled by some of the newfangled ideas she might have heard when she recently took courses to complete her M.B.A. degree. Mr. Caldwell then abruptly closed the meeting with the order that all officers come to a meeting scheduled for the following Monday and report on the specific steps each one would undertake to bring the company under control.

1   If you were employed by the firm and attended the meeting (let's say you had been employed for 6 months), what would you have said, if anything?

2   What is the president's view of human nature?

3   What are the assumptions about people underlying Ms. Jung's comments?

4   If you were an outside consultant attending this meeting, what recommendations would you make to the president to improve the human organization?

For Further Information

Davis, K., and J. Newstrom. *Human Behavior at Work—Organizational Behavior* 7th ed. (New York: McGraw-Hill Book Company, 1985).

Delbecq, A. L., A. H. Van de Ven, and D. H. Gustafson. *Group Techniques for Program Planning* (Glenview, Ill.: Scott, Foresman and Company, 1975).

Hackman, J. R., E. E. Lawler III, and L. W. Porter (eds.). *Perspectives on Behavior in Organizations*, 2nd ed. (New York: McGraw-Hill Book Company, 1983).

Isenberg, D. J. "How Senior Managers Think," *Harvard Business Review*, vol. 62, no. 6 (November–December 1984), pp. 80–90.

McGregor, D. *The Professional Manager*. (New York: McGraw-Hill Book Company, 1969).

Miner, J. B. *Theories of Organizational Behavior* (Hinsdale, Ill.: Dryden Press, 1980).

Morse, J., and J. W. Lorsch. "Beyond Theory Y," *Harvard Business Review*, vol. 48, no. 3 (May–June 1970), pp. 61–68.

Rush, H. M. F. *Behavioral Science—Concepts and Management Application.* (New York: National Industrial Conference Board, 1969).

Weihrich, H. "Games Organizational People Play," *Management International Review*, vol. 18, no. 4 (1978), pp. 33–40.

Motivation

After reading this chapter, you should understand:

1 The meaning of motivation, motivators, and satisfaction, and the reasons why motives are often complex and even conflicting
2 Various leading theories of motivation and their strengths and weaknesses
3 Special motivational techniques and job enrichment
4 The systems and contingency approach to motivation with special emphasis on developing an organizational climate to ensure motivation

Managing requires the creation and maintenance of an environment in which individuals work together in groups toward the accomplishment of a common objective. A manager cannot do this job without knowing what motivates people. The building of motivating factors into organizational roles, the staffing of these roles, and the entire process of leading people must be built on a knowledge of motivation. When we emphasize the importance of knowing and taking advantage of motivating factors, we are not trying to cast managers in the role of amateur psychiatrists. The managers' job is not to manipulate people but, rather, to recognize what motivates people.

The basic element of all human behavior is some kind of activity, whether physical or mental. We can look at human behavior as a series of activities. The question arises as to what activities human beings will undertake at any point of time, and why. We know that activities are goal-oriented; that is, people do things that lead them to accomplish something. But individual goals can be baffling. Sometimes people know exactly why they do things; often, however, individual drives lie buried in the subconscious. For example, do you know why you did what you did today and what all your various activities were designed to achieve?

The primary task of managers is to get people to contribute activities that help to achieve the mission and goals of an enterprise or of any department or other organized unit within it. Clearly, to guide people's activities in desired directions requires knowing, to the best of any manager's ability, what leads people to do things, what motivates them.

Motivation and Motivators

Human motives are based on needs, whether consciously or subconsciously felt. Some are primary needs, such as the physiological requirements for water, air, food, sleep, and shelter. Other needs may be regarded as secondary, such as self-esteem, status, affiliation with others, affection, giving, accomplishment, and self-assertion. As you can easily imagine, these needs vary in intensity and over time with various individuals.

Motivation

Motivation is a general term applying to the entire class of drives, desires, needs, wishes, and similar forces. To say that managers motivate their subordinates is to say that they do those things which they hope will satisfy these drives and desires and induce the subordinates to act in a desired manner.

The Need-Want-Satisfaction Chain

We can, then, look at motivation as involving a chain reaction—starting out with felt needs, resulting in wants or goals sought which give rise to tensions (that is, unfulfilled desires), then causing action toward achieving goals, and finally satisfying wants. This chain is shown in Figure 18-1.

The chain explanation is complex. In the first place, except for physiological needs, such as hunger, needs are not independent of a person's environment. We can easily see also that many physiological needs are stimulated by environmental factors: The smell of food may make us feel hungry, a high thermometer reading may make us suddenly feel hot, or the sight of a cold drink may cause an overwhelming thirst.

Environment has a major influence on our perception of secondary needs. The promotion of a colleague may kindle our desire for a higher position. A challenging problem may whet our desire to accomplish something by solving it.

FIGURE 18-1

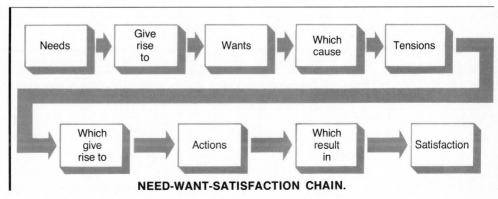

NEED-WANT-SATISFACTION CHAIN.

A congenial social group may increase our need for affiliation, and, of course, being alone more than we want to be can give us strong motivation for wanting to be with people.

In the second place, the need-want-satisfaction chain does not always operate as simply as portrayed. Needs do cause behavior. But needs also may result from behavior. Satisfying one need may lead to a desire to satisfy more needs. For example, a person's need for accomplishment may be made keener by the satisfaction gained from achieving a desired goal; or it may be dulled by failure. The one-way nature of the chain has also been challenged by the work of some biological scientists, especially in recent years, who have found that needs are not always the cause of human behavior, but may be a result of it. In other words, behavior is often what we do and not why we do it.

Complexity of Motivation

It takes only a moment's thought to realize that at any given time, an individual's motives may be quite complex and often conflicting. A person may be motivated by a desire for economic goods and services (groceries, a better house, a new car, or a trip), and even these desires may be complex and conflicting (should one buy a new house or a new car?). At the same time an individual may want self-esteem, status, a feeling of accomplishment, or relaxation (who has not felt a conflict between the time demands of a job and the desire to play golf or to go to a movie?).

Motivators   **Motivators** are things which induce an individual to perform. While motivations reflect wants, motivators are the identified rewards, or incentives, that sharpen the drive to satisfy these wants. They are also the means by which conflicting needs may be reconciled or one need heightened so that it will be given priority over another.

A manager can do much to sharpen motives by establishing an environment favorable to certain drives. For example, people in a business which has developed a reputation for excellence and high quality tend to be motivated to contribute to this reputation. Similarly, the environment of a business in which managerial performance is effective and efficient tends to breed a desire for high-quality management among most, or all, managers and personnel.

A motivator, then, is something that influences an individual's behavior. It makes a difference in what a person will do. Obviously, in any organized enterprise, managers must be concerned about motivators and also inventive in their use. People can often satisfy their wants in a variety of ways. A person can, for example, satisfy a desire for affiliation by being active in a social club rather than in a business, meet economic needs by performing a job just well enough to get by, or satisfy status needs by spending time working for a political party. What a manager must do, of course, is to use those motivators which will lead people to perform effectively for the enterprise that employs them. No manager can expect to hire the whole person since people always have desires and drives outside the enterprise. But if a company or any other kind of enterprise is to be efficient and successful, enough of every person's drives must be stimulated and satisfied to ensure effective performance.

FIGURE 18-2

DIFFERENCES BETWEEN MOTIVATION AND SATISFACTION.
Motivation is the drive to satisfy a want (achieve an outcome); satisfaction is experienced when the outcome has been achieved.

Motivation

Satisfaction

Difference between motivation and satisfaction *Motivation* refers to the drive and effort to satisfy a want or goal. *Satisfaction* refers to the contentment experienced when a want is satisfied. In other words, motivation implies a drive toward an outcome, and satisfaction is the outcome already experienced, as you can see in Figure 18-2.

From a management point of view, then, a person might have high job satisfaction but have a low level of motivation for the job, or the reverse might be true. There is understandably the probability that highly motivated persons with low job satisfaction will look for other positions. Likewise, those people who find their positions rewarding but are being paid considerably less than they desire or think they deserve will probably search for other jobs.

Motivation: The Carrot and the Stick

In examining the various leading theories of motivation and motivators, we seldom now hear reference to the carrot and the stick. This metaphor relates, of course, to the use of rewards and penalties in order to induce desired behavior and comes from the old story that the best way to make a donkey move is to put a carrot in front of him or jab him with a stick from behind.

Despite all the researchers and theories of motivation that have come to the fore in recent years, reward and punishment are still considered strong motivators. For centuries, however, they were too often thought of as the only forces that can motivate people. As we shall see in the succeeding sections, there are many other motivators.

At the same time, in all theories of motivation, the inducements of some kind of "carrot" are recognized. Often this is money in the form of pay or bonuses. Even though money is not the only motivating force, it has been and will continue to be an important one. The trouble with the money "carrot" approach is that

The carrot

too often everyone gets a carrot, regardless of performance, through such practices as salary increases and promotion by seniority, automatic "merit" increases, and executive bonuses not based on individual manager performance. It is as simple as this: If a person put a donkey in a pen full of carrots and then stood outside with a carrot, would the donkey be encouraged to come out of the pen?

The stick

The "stick" in the form of fear—fear of loss of job, loss of income, reduction of bonus, demotion, or some other penalty—has been and continues to be a strong motivator. Yet it is admittedly not the best kind. If often gives rise to defensive or retaliatory behavior, such as union organization, poor-quality work, executive indifference, failure of a manager to take any risks in decision making, or even dishonesty. But fear of penalty cannot be overlooked. And most managers never fully appreciate the power of their position. Whether they are first-level supervisors or chief executives, the power of their position to give or withhold rewards or impose penalties of various kinds gives them an ability to control, to a very great extent, the economic and social well-being of their subordinates. It is hardly a wonder that a substantial number of managers have "yes-sayers" reporting to them and seldom realize it.

The Hierarchy of Needs Theory

One of the most widely mentioned theories of motivation is the hierarchy of needs theory put forth by psychologist Abraham Maslow.[1] Maslow saw human needs in the form of a hierarchy, ascending from the lowest to the highest, and he concluded that when one set of needs was satisfied, this kind of need ceased to be a motivator.

The Need Hierarchy

The basic human needs placed by Maslow in an ascending order of importance and shown in Figure 18-3 are these:

1 **Physiological needs.** These are the basic needs for sustaining human life itself, such as food, water, warmth, shelter, and sleep. Maslow took the position that until these needs are satisfied to the degree necessary to maintain life, other needs will not motivate people.

2 **Security, or safety, needs.** These are the needs to be free of physical danger and the fear of loss of a job, property, food, or shelter.

3 **Affiliation, or acceptance, needs.** Since people are social beings, they need to belong, to be accepted by others.

4 **Esteem needs.** According to Maslow, once people begin to satisfy their need to belong, they tend to want to be held in esteem both by themselves and by others. This kind of need produces such satisfactions as power, prestige, status, and self-confidence.

---

[1]*Motivation and Personality* (New York: Harper & Row, Publishers, Incorporated, 1954).

FIGURE 18-3

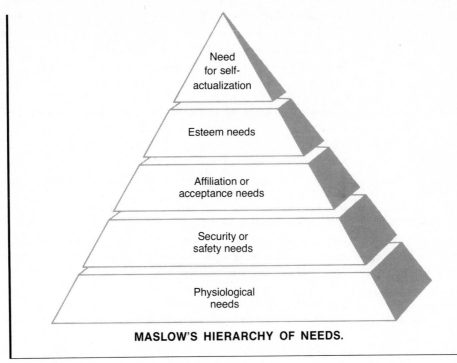

MASLOW'S HIERARCHY OF NEEDS.

(pyramid levels from top to bottom: Need for self-actualization; Esteem needs; Affiliation or acceptance needs; Security or safety needs; Physiological needs)

5 **Need for self-actualization.** Maslow regards this as the highest need in his hierarchy. It is the desire to become what one is capable of becoming—to maximize one's potential and to accomplish something.

Questioning the Needs Hierarchy

Maslow's concept of a hierarchy of needs has been subjected to considerable research. E. Lawler and J. Suttle collected data on 187 managers in two different organizations over a period of 6 months to 1 year.[2] They found little evidence to support Maslow's theory that human needs form a hierarchy. They did note, however, that there were two levels of needs—biological and other needs—and that the other needs would emerge only when biological needs were reasonably satisfied. They found, further, that at the higher level, the strength of needs varied with the individual; in some individuals, social needs predominated, and in others, self-actualization needs were strongest.

In another study of Maslow's needs hierarchy involving a group of managers over a period of five years, D. T. Hall and K. Nougaim did not find strong evidence of a hierarchy.[3] They found that as managers advance in an organization,

---

[2]E. Lawler and J. Suttle, "A Causal Correlation Test of the Need-Hierarchy Concept," *Organizational Behavior and Human Performance*, vol. 7, no. 2 (April 1972), pp. 265–287.
[3]D. T. Hall and K. Nougaim, "An Examination of Maslow's Hierarchy in an Organizational Setting," *Organizational Behavior and Human Performance*, vol. 3, no. 1 (February 1968), pp. 12–35.

their physiological and safety needs tend to decrease in importance, and their needs for affiliation, esteem, and self-actualization tend to increase. They insisted, however, that the upward movement of need prominence resulted from upward career changes and not from the satisfaction of lower-order needs.

The Motivation-Hygiene Approach to Motivation

Maslow's need approach has been considerably modified by Frederick Herzberg and his associates.[4] Their research purports to find a **two-factor theory** of motivation. In one group of needs are such things as company policy and administration, supervision, working conditions, interpersonal relations, salary, status, job security, and personal life. These were found by Herzberg and his associates to be only **dissatisfiers** and not motivators. In other words, if they exist in a work environment in high quantity and quality, they yield no dissatisfaction. Their existence does not motivate in the sense of yielding satisfaction; their lack of existence would, however, result in dissatisfaction. They were consequently referred to as "hygiene" factors.

Dissatisfiers

In the second group, Herzberg listed certain **satisfiers**—and therefore motivators—all related to job content. They included achievement, recognition, challenging work, advancement, and growth in the job. Their existence will yield feelings of satisfaction or no satisfaction (not dissatisfaction). As we can see from Figure 18-4, the factors identified by Herzberg are similar to those suggested by Maslow.

Satisfiers

Maintenance or hygiene factors

The first group of factors Herzberg called **maintenance** or **hygiene** factors. Their presence will not motivate people in an organization; yet, they must be present, or dissatisfaction will arise. The second group, or the job-content factors, he found to be the real **motivators** because they have the potential of yielding a sense of satisfaction. Clearly, if this theory of motivation is sound, managers must give considerable attention to upgrading job content.

Motivators

The Herzberg research has not gone unchallenged. Some question Herzberg's methods, saying that his questioning methods tended to prejudice his results. For example, the well-known tendency of people to attribute good results to their own efforts and to blame others for poor results is thought to have prejudiced Herzberg's findings. Other researchers, not following his methods, have found that the so-called hygiene factors actually yielded satisfaction or dissatisfaction.

The Expectancy Theory of Motivation

Another approach, one that many believe goes far in explaining how people are motivated, is the **expectancy** theory. One of the leaders in advancing and explaining this theory is the psychologist Victor H. Vroom. He holds that people will be

---

[4]F. Herzberg, B. Mausner, R. Peterson, and D. Capwell, *Job Attitudes: Review of Research and Opinion* (Pittsburgh: Psychological Services of Pittsburgh, 1957), and F. Herzberg, B. Mausner, and B. Synderman, *The Motivation to Work* (New York: John Wiley & Sons, Inc., 1959).

FIGURE 18-4

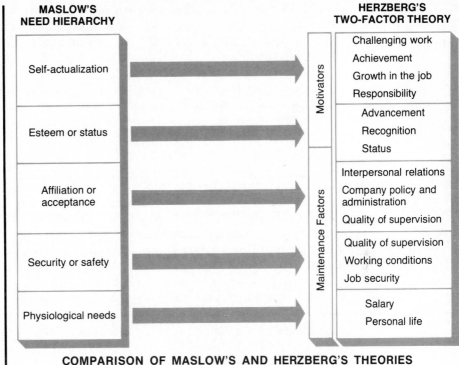

MASLOW'S NEED HIERARCHY

HERZBERG'S TWO-FACTOR THEORY

Maslow's Need Hierarchy	Herzberg's Two-Factor Theory	
Self-actualization	Motivators	Challenging work Achievement Growth in the job Responsibility
Esteem or status	Motivators	Advancement Recognition Status
Affiliation or acceptance	Maintenance Factors	Interpersonal relations Company policy and administration Quality of supervision
Security or safety	Maintenance Factors	Quality of supervision Working conditions Job security
Physiological needs	Maintenance Factors	Salary Personal life

COMPARISON OF MASLOW'S AND HERZBERG'S THEORIES OF MOTIVATION.

Note: Supervision can be a matter of satisfying both affiliation and security needs.

motivated to do things to reach a goal if they believe in the worth of that goal and if they can see that what they do will help them in achieving it.[5] In a sense, this is a modern expression of what Martin Luther observed centuries ago when he said that "everything that is done in the world is done in hope."

In greater detail, Vroom's theory is that people's motivation toward doing anything will be determined by the value they place on the outcome of their effort (whether positive or negative), multiplied by the confidence they have that their efforts will materially aid in achieving a goal. In other words, Vroom makes the point that motivation is a product of the anticipated worth that an individual places on a goal and the chances he or she sees of achieving these goals. Using his own terms, Vroom's theory may be stated as:

Force

Force = valence × expectancy

Valence

Expectancy

where *force* is the strength of a person's motivation, *valence* is the strength of an individual's preference for an outcome, and *expectancy* is the probability that a particular action will lead to a desired outcome.

---

[5]V. H. Vroom, *Work and Motivation* (New York: John Wiley & Sons, 1964).

When a person is indifferent about achieving a certain goal, a valence of zero occurs, and there is a negative valence when the person would rather not achieve the goal. The result of either would be, of course, no motivation. Likewise, a person would have no motivation to achieve a goal if the expectancy were zero or negative. The force exerted to do something will depend on *both* valence and expectancy. Moreover, a motive to accomplish some action might be determined by a desire to accomplish something else. For example, a person might be willing to work hard to get out a product for a valence in the form of pay. Or a manager might be willing to work hard to achieve company goals in marketing or production for a promotion or pay valence.

The Vroom Theory and Practice

One of the great attractions of the Vroom theory is that it recognizes the importance of various individual needs and motivations. It thus avoids some of the simplistic features of the Maslow and Herzberg approaches. It does seem more realistic. It fits the concept of harmony of objectives, explained in Chapter 17: that individuals have personal goals different from organization goals, but that these can be harmonized. Furthermore, Vroom's theory is completely consistent with the entire system of managing by objectives.

The strength of Vroom's theory is also its weakness. His assumption that senses of value vary among individuals at different times and in various places appears more accurately to fit real life. It is consistent also with the idea that a manager's job is to *design* an environment for performance, necessarily taking into account the differences in various situations. On the other hand, despite its logical accuracy, Vroom's theory is difficult to apply in practice. But this difficulty merely indicates that motivation is much more complex than the approaches of Maslow and Herzberg seem to imply.

The Porter and Lawler Model

L. W. Porter and E. E. Lawler have derived a substantially more complete model of motivation, built in large part on expectancy theory. In their study, they have applied this model primarily to managers.[6] It is summarized in Figure 18-5.

As this model indicates, the amount of effort (the strength of motivation and energy exerted) depends on the value of a reward plus the amount of energy a person believes is required and the probability of receiving the reward. The perceived effort and probability of actually getting a reward are, in turn, also influenced by the record of actual performance. Clearly, if people know they can do a job or if they have done it, they have a better appreciation of the effort required and know better the probability of rewards.

Actual performance in a job (the doing of tasks or the meeting of goals) is determined principally by effort expanded. But it is also greatly influenced by an individual's ability (knowledge and skills) to do the job and his or her perception of what the required task is (the extent to which the person understands the goals, required activities, and other elements of a task). Performance, in turn, is seen as

---

[6]L. W. Porter and E. E. Lawler, *Managerial Attitudes and Performance* (Homewood, Ill.: Richard D. Irwin, Inc., 1968).

FIGURE 18-5

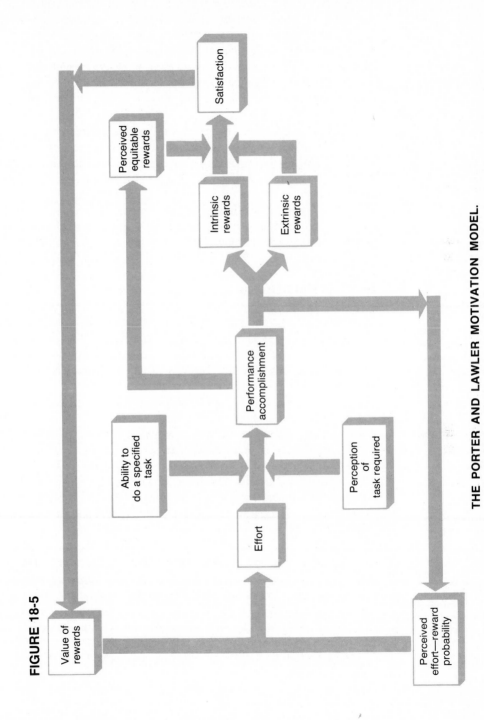

THE PORTER AND LAWLER MOTIVATION MODEL.

Source: Adapted from L. W. Porter and E. E. Lawler, Managerial Attitudes and Performance (Homewood, Ill.: Richard D. Irwin, Inc., 1968), p. 165.

leading to intrinsic rewards (such as a sense of accomplishment or self-actualization) and extrinsic rewards (such as working conditions and status). These rewards, tempered by what the individual sees as equitable, lead to satisfaction. But performance also influences sensed equitable rewards. As you can understand, what the individual sees as a fair reward for effort will necessarily affect the satisfaction derived. Likewise, the actual value of rewards will be influenced by satisfaction.

Implications for Practice

The Porter and Lawler model of motivation, while more complex than other theories of motivation, is almost certainly a more adequate portrayal of the system of motivation. To the practicing manager, this model means that motivation is not a simple cause and effect matter. It means, too, that managers should carefully assess their reward structures and that through careful planning, managing by objectives, and clear definition of duties and responsibilities by good organization structuring, the effort-performance-reward-satisfaction system can be integrated into an entire system of managing.

Reinforcement Theory

Psychologist B. F. Skinner of Harvard developed an interesting—but controversial—technique for motivation. This approach, called *positive reinforcement* or *behavior modification,* holds that individuals can be motivated by proper design of their work environment and praise for their performance, and that punishment for poor performance produces negative results.

Skinner and his followers do far more than praise good performance. They analyze the work situation to determine what causes workers to act the way they do, and then they initiate changes to eliminate troublesome areas and obstructions to performance. Specific goals are then set with workers' participation and assistance, prompt and regular feedback of results is made available, and performance improvements are rewarded with recognition and praise. Even when performance does not equal goals, ways are found to help people and praise them for the good things they do. It has also been found highly useful and motivating to give people full information on a company's problems, especially those in which they are involved.

This technique sounds almost too simple to work, and many behavioral scientists and managers are skeptical about its effectiveness. However, a number of prominent companies have found the approach beneficial. Emery Air Freight Corporation, for example, observed that this approach saved the company over $500,000 a year by merely inducing employees to take great pains to be sure that containers were properly filled with small packages before shipment.

Perhaps the strength of the Skinner approach is that it is so closely akin to the requirements of good managing. It emphasizes removal of obstructions to performance, careful planning and organizing, control through feedback, and the expansion of communication.

McClelland's Needs Theory of Motivation

David C. McClelland has contributed to the understanding of motivation by identifying three types of basic motivating needs.[7] He classified them as need for power (n/PWR), need for affiliation (n/AFF), and need for achievement (n/ACH). Considerable research has been done on methods of testing people with respect to these three types of needs, and McClelland and his associates have done substantial research, especially on the need for achievement.

All three drives—power, affiliation, and achievement—are of particular relevance to management since all must be recognized to make an organized enterprise work well. Because any organized enterprise and every department of it represent groups of individuals working together to achieve goals, the need for achievement is of paramount importance.

Need for Power

McClelland and other researchers have found that people with a high need for power have a great concern for exercising influence and control. Such individuals generally are seeking positions of leadership; they are frequently good conversationalists, though often argumentative; they are forceful, outspoken, hardheaded, and demanding; and they enjoy teaching and public speaking.

Need for Affiliation

People with a high need for affiliation usually derive pleasure from being loved and tend to avoid the pain of being rejected by a social group. As individuals, they are likely to be concerned with maintaining pleasant social relationships, to enjoy a sense of intimacy and understanding, to be ready to console and help others in trouble, and to enjoy friendly interaction with others.

Need for Achievement

People with a high need for achievement have an intense desire for success and an equally intense fear of failure. They want to be challenged, set moderately difficult (but not impossible) goals for themselves, and take a realistic approach to risk; they are not likely to be gamblers but, rather, prefer to analyze and assess problems, assume personal responsibility for getting a job done, like specific and prompt feedback on how they are doing, tend to be restless, like to work long hours, do not worry unduly about failure if it does occur, and tend to like to run their own shows.

How McClelland's Approach Applies to Managers

In researches made by McClelland and others, entrepreneurs—people who start and develop a business or other enterprise—showed very high need-for-achievement and fairly high need-for-power drives, but were quite low in their need for

---

[7]*The Achievement Motive* (New York: Appleton-Century-Crofts, 1953), *Studies in Motivation* (New York: Appleton-Century-Crofts, 1955), and *The Achieving Society* (Princeton, N.J.: D. Van Nostrand Company, Inc., 1961). See also his "Achievement Motivation Can Be Developed," *Harvard Business Review*, vol. 43, no. 1 (January–February 1965), pp. 6–24, 178, and (with David G. Winter) *Motivating Economic Achievement* (New York: The Free Press, 1969).

affiliation. Managers generally showed high on achievement and power and low on affiliation, but not so high or low as entrepreneurs.

McClelland found the patterns of achievement motivation clearest in people in small companies, with the president normally having very high achievement motivation. In large companies, interestingly enough, he found chief executives to be only average in achievement motivation and often stronger in drives for power and affiliation. Managers in the upper-middle level of management in such companies rated higher than their presidents in achievement motivation. Perhaps, as McClelland indicated, these scores are understandable. The chief executive has "arrived," and those below are striving to advance.

The question is often raised as to whether all managers should rate quite high on achievement motivation. People who do rate high tend to advance faster than those who do not. But, because so much of managing requires other characteristics besides achievement drive, every company should probably have many managers who, while possessing fairly strong achievement motivation, also have a high need for affiliation. This latter need is important for working with people and for co-ordinating the efforts of individuals working in groups.

Special Motivational Techniques

After looking at all the theories of motivation, we may well ask what they mean to managers. What are some of the major motivational techniques managers can use? While motivation is so complex and individualized that there can be no single best answer, we can identify some of the major motivational techniques.

Money

As we mentioned earlier in the discussion of the carrot and the stick, money can never be overlooked as a motivator. Whether in the form of wages, piecework or any other incentive pay, bonuses, stock options, company-paid insurance, or any of the other things that may be given to people for performance, money is important. And, as Patton pointed out, money is often more than money in that it can be a reflection of other motivators.

Economists and most managers have tended to place money high on the scale of motivators, while behavioral scientists tend to place it low. Probably neither view is right. But if money is to be the kind of motivator that it can and should be, managers must remember several things.

First, money, as money, is likely to be more important to people who are raising a family, for example, than to people who have "arrived" in the sense that their money needs are not so urgent. Money is an urgent means of achieving a minimum standard of living, although this minimum has a way of getting higher as people become more affluent. For example, an individual who was once satisfied with a small house and a low-priced car may now be able to derive the same satisfaction only from a large and comfortable house and a fairly luxurious automobile. And yet we cannot generalize in even these terms. For some people, money will always be of the utmost importance, while to others, it may never be.

Second, it is probably quite true that in most kinds of businesses and other enterprises, money is used as a means of keeping an organization adequately staffed and not primarily as a motivator. Various enterprises make wages and salaries competitive within their industry and their geographic area so as to attract and hold people.

Third money as a motivator tends to be dulled somewhat by the practice of making sure that salaries of various managers in a company are reasonably similar. In other words, we often take great care to be sure that people on comparable levels are given the same, or nearly the same, compensation. This is understandable, since people usually evaluate their compensation in the light of what their equals are receiving.

Fourth, if money is to be an effective motivator, people in various positions, even though at a similar level, must be given salaries and bonuses that reflect their individual performance. Perhaps we are committed to the practice of comparable wages and salaries. But a well-managed company need never be bound to the same practice with respect to bonuses. In fact, it appears that, unless bonuses to managers are based to a major extent on individual performance, an enterprise is not buying much motivation with them. The way to ensure that money has meaning as a reward for accomplishment and as a way of giving people pleasure from accomplishment is to base compensation as much as possible on performance.

It is almost certainly true that money can motivate only when the prospective payment is large relative to a person's income. The trouble with many wage and salary increases, and even bonus payments, is that they are not large enough to motivate the receiver. They may keep the individual from being dissatisfied and from looking for another job, but unless they are large enough to be felt, they are not likely to be a strong motivator.

Participation

One technique that has been given strong support as the result of motivation theory and research is the increased awareness and use of participation. There can be no doubt that only rarely are people not motivated by being consulted on action affecting them—by being "in on the act." There is also no doubt that most people in the center of an operation have knowledge both of problems and of solutions to them. As a consequence, the right kind of participation yields both motivation and knowledge valuable for enterprise success.

Participation is also a means of recognition. It appeals to the need for affiliation and acceptance. And, above all, it gives people a sense of accomplishment. As will be recalled, these are major advantages of a well-conceived and well-operated system of managing by objectives.

But encouraging participation should not mean that managers weaken their positions. Although they encourage participation of subordinates on matters where they can help and although they listen carefully, on matters requiring *their* decisions they must decide themselves. The best subordinates would not have it any other way, and few subordinates can ever have respect for a wishy-washy superior.

Quality of Working Life (QWL)

One of the most interesting approaches to motivation is the quality of working life (QWL) program. These represent a systems approach to job design and a promising development in the broad area of job enrichment, combined with a grounding in the sociotechnical systems approach to management (see Chapter 2). QWL is not only a very broad approach to job enrichment but also an interdisciplinary field of enquiry and action combining industrial and organization psychology and sociology, industrial engineering, organization theory and development, motivation and leadership theory, and industrial relations. Although QWL rose to prominence only in the 1970s, there are now hundreds of case studies and practical programs, and a number of QWL centers, primarily in the United States, Great Britain, and Scandinavia.[8]

QWL in action

QWL has received enthusiastic support from a number of sources. Managers have regarded it as a promising means of dealing with stagnating productivity, especially in the United States and Europe. Workers and union representatives have also seen it as a means of improving working conditions and productivity and as a means of justifying higher pay. Government agencies have been attracted to QWL as a means of increasing productivity and reducing inflation and as a way of obtaining industrial democracy and minimizing labor disputes.

In developing a QWL program, certain steps are normally undertaken. Usually, a labor-management steering committee is set up, ordinarily with a QWL specialist or staff, with the charge of coming up with ways of enhancing the dignity, attractiveness, and productivity of jobs through job enrichment and redesign. The participation of workers and their unions (if an operation is unionized) in the effort is thought to be very important, not only because of the exercise of industrial democracy but also the very great practical advantage that people on a job are best able to identify what would enrich the job for them and make it possible for them to be more productive. This typical QWL technique tends to solve the problem encountered in many job enrichment cases where workers have mistakenly not been asked what would make the job more interesting for them.

Out of the deliberations of this committee, a number of changes may be suggested in the design of jobs and in the entire working environment. The recommendations of the committees may extend to such matters as reorganization of the organization structure, means of improving communication, problems that may never have surfaced before and their solutions, changing work arrangements through technical modifications such as the redesign of an assembly line, better quality control, and other things that might improve organization health and productivity.

It is no wonder that QWL, with such possible important yields, has been spreading fast, especially in our larger companies. Nor is it a surprise that leaders in adopting QWL programs should be such well-managed companies as General Motors, Procter & Gamble, American Aluminum (ALCOA) and AT&T.

---

[8]For a pioneering work in this field, see L. E. Davis and A. R. Chernes, *Quality of Working Life*, vols. 1 and 2 (New York: The Free Press, 1975). Among the more prominent Quality of Working Life Centers are the Tavistock Institute in Great Britain under E. L. Trist; the Center at the University of California, Los Angeles, under L. E. Davis; and The Institute for Social Research in Industry in Trondheim, Norway, under M. Elder.

Job Enrichment

Research and analysis of motivation point to the importance of making jobs challenging and meaningful. This applies to the jobs of managers as well as to those of nonmanagers, and it is especially true of Herzberg's theory of motivation, where factors such as challenge, achievement recognition, and responsibility are seen as the real motivators. Even though Herzberg's theory has not gone unchallenged, it has led to a widespread interest in both the United States and overseas in developing ways to enrich job content, particularly for nonmanagerial employees.

Job enrichment

Job enrichment should be distinguished from job enlargement. Job enlargement attempts to make a job more varied by removing the dullness associated with performing repetitive operations. In **job enrichment,** the attempt is to build into jobs a higher sense of challenge and achievement. A job may be enriched by variety. But it also may be enriched by (1) giving workers more freedon in deciding about such things as work methods, sequence, and pace, or the acceptance or rejection of materials; (2) encouraging participation of subordinates and interaction between workers; (3) giving workers a feeling of personal responsibility for their tasks; (4) taking steps to make sure that workers can see how their tasks contribute to a finished product and the welfare of an enterprise; (5) giving people feedback on their job performance, preferably before their supervisors get it; and (6) involving workers in analysis and change of physical aspects of the work environment, such as layout of office or plant, temperature, lighting, and cleanliness.

**The Claims of
Job Enrichment**

A number of companies have introduced programs of job enrichment. The first company to do so on a fairly large scale was Texas Instruments, and other companies, such as AT&T, Procter & Gamble, and General Foods, have had considerable experience with it. In all these companies, claims have been made that productivity was increased, that absenteeism and turnover were reduced, and that morale improved.

Perhaps the most glowing claims for job enrichment are contained in the report of a study made by the U.S. Department of Health, Education, and Welfare, published in 1973.[9] As the result of an analysis of worker attitudes and the quality of working life, this study concluded that (1) the primary cause of dissatisfaction of workers is the nature of their work—the quality of their working life— and (2) blue-collar workers will work harder if their jobs are enriched and expanded so as to give them greater control over their work and more freedom from their supervisor.

**Limitations of
Job Enrichment**

Even the strongest supporters of job enrichment readily admit that there are limitations in its application. One of these is technology. With specialized machinery and assembly line techniques, it may not be possible to make all jobs very mean-

---

[9]*Work in America* (Washington: Government Printing Office, 1973).

ingful. Another limitation is cost. General Motors tried six-person and three-person teams in the assembly of motor homes but found that this approach was too difficult, slow, and costly. Two Swedish auto manufacturers, Saab and Volvo, have used the team approach and have found costs to be only slightly higher, but they believe that this increase was more than offset by reductions in absenteeism and turnover. Another problem has been the difficulty of enriching any job that requires low levels of skill.

There is also some question as to whether workers really want job enrichment, especially of the kind that changes the basic content of their jobs. Various surveys of worker attitudes, even the attitudes of assembly line workers, have shown that a high percentage of workers are not dissatisfied with their jobs and that few want "more interesting" jobs. What these workers seem to want above all is job security and pay. Moreover, there has been considerable feeling that when managers begin changing the nature of jobs, the increased productivity they seek may even mean loss of jobs.

The limitations of job enrichment apply mainly to jobs requiring low skill levels. The jobs of highly skilled workers, professionals, and managers already contain varying degrees of challenge and accomplishment. Perhaps these could be enriched considerably more than they are. But this can probably be done best by modern management techniques such as managing by objectives, utilizing more policy guidance with delegation of authority, introducing more status symbols in the form of titles and office facilities, and tying bonus and other rewards more closely to performance.

Problems with Job Enrichment

On the surface, job enrichment as a response to motivating factors is an attractive idea. But it apparently has not worked as well as anticipated. There do seem to be a number of problems in the way it has been approached.

One of the major problems appears to be the tendency for top managers and personnel specialists to apply their own scale of values of challenge and accomplishment to other people's personalities. Some people are challenged by jobs that would appear dull to many of us. In one company, an employee who had spent his life doing no more than keeping daily records of orders received honestly felt he had one of the most important jobs in the company. In another business, a woman who had had a job-enriched position with a variety of tasks told her supervisor that she was greatly relieved to be freed of such responsibility when she was given a repetitive assembly line job. Similarly, a woman who was found to have considerable leadership ability in her outside activities with the Girl Scouts and PTA turned down a supervisory position because her present job allowed her to think about the problems and programs she was interested in outside the company.

Another difficulty is that job enrichment is usually imposed on people; they are told about it, rather than asked whether they would like it and how their jobs could be made more interesting. This appeared to be, at least in part, the problem General Motors encountered in enlarging the jobs of assembly line workers at the Vega plant in Lordstown where workers interpreted the attempts to make jobs more varied and meaningful as only a scheme of the company to get them to work harder. We can never overlook the importance of consultation, of getting people involved.

Also, there has been little or no support of job enrichment by union leaders. If job enrichment were so important to workers, one would think that it would be translated into union demands, a move that apparently has seldom occurred.

**Making
Job Enrichment
Effective**

Several approaches can be used to make job enrichment appeal to higher-level motivations. First, we need a better understanding of what people want. As certain motivation researchers have pointed out, wants vary with people and situations. Research has shown that workers with few skills want such factors as job security, pay, benefits, less restrictive plant rules, and more sympathetic and understanding supervisors. As we move up the ladder in an enterprise, we find that other factors become increasingly important. But little job enrichment research has been done on high-level professionals and managers.

Benefit to workers

Second, if productivity increases are the main goal of enrichment, the program must show how workers will benefit. For example, in one company with fleets of unsupervised two-person service trucks, a program of giving these employees 25 percent of the cost savings from increased productivity, while still making it clear that the company would profit from their efforts, resulted in a startling rise in output and a much greater interest in these jobs.

*Consultation
with workers*

Third, people like to be involved, to be consulted, and to be given an opportunity to offer suggestions. They like to be considered as people. In one aerospace missile plant, increased morale and productivity, as well as greatly reduced turnover and absenteeism, resulted from the simple technique of having all employees' names on placards at their work stations and of having each program group—from parts production and assembly to inspection—work in an area in which machines and equipment were painted a different color.

Other factors

Fourth, people like to feel that their managers are truly concerned with their welfare. Workers like to know what they are doing and why. They like feedback on their performance. They like to be appreciated and recognized for their work.

A Systems and Contingency Approach to Motivation

The above analysis of theory, research, and application demonstrates that we must consider motivation from a systems and contingency point of view. Given the complexity of motivating people with varying personalities and in different situations, risks of failure exist when any single motivator or group of motivators is applied without taking into account these variables. Human behavior is not a simple matter but must be looked upon as a system of variables and interactions of which certain motivating factors are an important element.

**Dependence of
Motivation on
Organizational
Climate**

Motivating factors definitely do not exist in a vacuum. Even individual desires and drives are conditioned by physiological needs or by needs arising from a person's background. But what people are willing to strive for is also affected by the organizational climate in which they operate. At times a climate may curb motivations; at other times it may arouse them.

This is illustrated by the research of G. H. Litwin and R. A. Stringer.[10] Using McClelland's need for achievement, need for affiliation, and need for power as major types of motivation, they noted that the strength of these motives was affected by organizational climate. For example, in a sample of 460 managers in a highly structured organization, they found a strong relationship between such structure and power motivation and a negative relationship with achievement and affiliation motivation. In a climate with high responsibility and clear standards, they observed a strong relationship of this climate to the achievement motivation, a moderate correlation to power motivation, and no correlation or a negative correlation with affiliation motivation.

Litwin and Stringer found that their researches gave considerable support to the theory that there is a relationship between climate and the arousal or reduction of motivating forces. A summary of their research results is given in Table 18-1.

TABLE 18-1 Relationship of Climate to Motivation

Climate dimension	Effect on power motivation	Effect on achievement motivation	Effect on affiliation motivation
Structure (rigid structure with rules, regulations, and procedures)	Arousal	Reduction	Reduction
Responsibility (the feeling of being one's own boss)	Arousal	Arousal	No effect
Reward (emphasis on positive rewards rather than punishment)	No effect	Arousal	Arousal
Risk (emphasis on taking risks and assuming challenges)	Reduction	Arousal	Reduction
Warmth (friendly, informal group atmosphere)	No effect	No effect	Arousal
Support (mutual support; perceived helpfulness of managers and associates)	No effect	Arousal	Arousal
Standards (perceived importance of implicit and explicit goals and performance standards; emphasis on doing a good job; challenging goals)	Arousal	Arousal*	Reduction
Conflict (emphasis on hearing different opinions; getting problems out in the open)	Arousal	Arousal*	Reduction
Identity (feeling that a person belongs to a company and is a valuable team member)	No effect	Arousal	Arousal

*Proof of this effect on motivation was weak.
Source: Adapted from G. H. Litwin and R. A. Stringer, Jr., *Motivation and Organizational Climate* (Boston: Harvard Graduate School of Business Administration, 1968), pp. 81–82, 90–91.

[10]G. H. Litwin and R. A. Stringer, Jr., *Motivation and Organizational Climate* (Boston: Harvard Graduate School of Business Administration, 1968).

Motivation, Leadership, and Managership

The interaction of motivation and organizational climate not only underscores the systems aspects of motivation but also emphasizes how motivation both depends on and influences leadership styles and management practice. Both leaders and managers (who, if effective, will almost certainly be leaders) must respond to the motivations of individuals if they are to design an environment in which people will perform willingly. Likewise, they can design a climate that will arouse or reduce motivation.

We will discuss styles of leadership in Chapter 19. As for the ways and means by which managers design an environment for performance, they are really the subject of this entire book. In short, managers do this when they see that verifiable goals are set, strategies are developed and communicated, and plans to achieve objectives are made. They do it also in designing a system of organizational roles in which people can be effective (it should be pointed out in this connection that "organization structure" is not used here in the restrictive bureaucratic sense that Litwin and Stringer use the term "organization"). Managers do it also when they make sure that the structure is well-staffed. Their styles of leadership and their ability to solve communication problems are also central to managing. And managers do much to create an effective environment when they make sure that control tools, information, and approaches furnish people with the feedback knowledge they must have for effective motivation.

Summary

Motivation is not a simple concept; instead, motivation pertains to various drives, desires, needs, wishes, and other forces. Managers motivate by providing an environment that induces subordinates to contribute to the organization. The need-want-satisfaction chain is somewhat oversimplified. Indeed, motives are often conflicting.

Maslow's theory holds that human needs form a hierarchy ranging from the lowest-order needs (physiological needs) to that of the highest order (the need for self-actualization). According to Herzberg's two-factor theory, there are two sets of motivating factors. One set is called dissatisfiers and they are related to the job context. The absence of these factors results in dissatisfaction. The other set of factors (related to the content of the job) are the satisfiers or motivators.

Vroom's expectancy theory of motivation suggests that people are motivated to reach a goal if they think that the goal is worthwhile and people see that their activities help them to achieve the goal. The Porter and Lawler model has many variables. Essentially, performance is a function of ability, the perception of the task required, and effort. Effort is influenced by the value of rewards and the perceived effort-reward probability. Performance accomplishment, in turn, is related to rewards and satisfaction.

Reinforcement theory was developed by Skinner, who suggested that people are motivated by praise of desirable behavior; people should participate in setting their goals and should receive regular feedback with recognition and praise. McClelland's theory is based on the need for power, the need for affiliation, and the need for achievement.

In discussing special motivational techniques, we have also mentioned the role of money, the importance of participation, and approaches to improving the quality of working life. Job enrichment aims at making jobs challenging and meaningful. Although there have been some successes, certain limitations must not be overlooked.

The complexity of motivation requires a contingency approach that takes into account the environmental factors, including the organizational climate.

Key Ideas and Concepts for Review

Motivation	Positive reinforcement
Need-want-satisfaction chain	Behavior modification
Motivators	McClelland's needs theory
Maslow's need hierarchy	Quality of working life
Herzberg's motivation-hygiene approach	Job enrichment
Vroom's expectancy theory	Organizational climate and motivation
Porter and Lawler's motivation model	

For Discussion

1 What is motivation? How does effective managing take advantage of, and contribute to, motivation?

2 Why is the need-want-satisfaction chain too simplified an explanation of motivation?

3 Why has the Maslow theory of needs been criticized? To what extent, if any, is it valid?

4 Compare and contrast the Maslow and Herzberg theories of motivation. On what grounds has the Herzberg theory been criticized? Why would you suspect that Herzberg's approach has been so popular with practicing managers?

5 Explain Vroom's expectancy theory of motivation. How is it different from Porter and Lawler's approach? Which appeals to you as being more accurate? Which is more useful in practice?

6 Explain McClelland's theory of motivation. How does it fit into a systems approach? What does the impact of organizational climate show?

7 "You cannot motivate managers. They are self-propelled. You just get out of their way if you really want performance." Comment.

8 To what extent, and how, is money an effective motivator?

9 Take an organization you know and identify the reasons why people contribute to the goals of the enterprise.

10 What motivates you in striving toward excellence in your work at school? Are these motivating forces shown in any of the models discussed in this chapter?

CASE 18-1

MOTIVATION AT THE BRADLEY CLOTHING COMPANY

Alice Johnson, personnel manager of the Bradley Clothing Company, manufacturers of women's clothing and accessories, had just returned from a management development seminar where considerable attention had been given to motivation and especially the theories of Maslow and Herzberg. Impressed by Maslow's clear hierarchy of needs and Herzberg's motivator-hygiene theory, she felt that the company could immediately make practical use of them. She liked the simplicity of these two approaches to motivation and, feeling that the company's wage and salary levels were among the best in the industry, she was convinced that the company should concentrate on Herzberg's motivators.

As a result, she was able to convince the executive committee of the company to embark on various programs emphasizing recognition, advancement, greater personal responsibility, achievement, and making work more challenging. After the programs had been in operation for a number of months, she was puzzled to find that the results were not what she had expected.

Clothing designers did not seem to react enthusiastically to the programs. Some felt they already had a challenging job, that their sense of

achievement was fulfilled by exceeding their sales quotas, that their recognition was in their commission checks, and that all these new programs were a waste of time for them. Cutters, seamsters, pressers, and packagers had mixed feelings. Some responded favorably to the recognition they got as a result of the new programs, but others regarded them as a managerial scheme to get them to work harder without any increase in pay. Their union business agent, agreeing with the latter group, openly criticized the programs.

With reactions so variable, Ms. Johnson came under considerable criticism by the company's top officers, who believed they had been taken in by an overzealous personnel manager. On discussing the problem with the company's management consultant, Ms. Johnson was advised that she had taken too simple a view of human motivations.

1 Why do you believe this program caused so much difficulty?

2 Why did the management consultant say that Ms. Johnson had taken too simple a view of human motivation?

3 If you were Ms. Johnson, what would you have done?

CASE 18-2

CONSOLIDATED MOTORS CORPORATION

One of the problems that had long concerned the top managers of the Consolidated Motors Corporation was the lack of workers' interest in doing their jobs on both the components and the final

car assembly lines, with the result that quality had to be ensured by the inspection department. For those cars that could not meet final inspection, the company found its only answer to be the setting up of a group of highly skilled mechanics in a special shop where quality problems were fixed at the end of the line. Not only was this costly but it also caused considerable concern since most of the problems were the result of lack of care in assembling components and of the design of the automobile itself.

At the urging of the company president, the division general manager called a meeting of his key department heads to see what could be done about the problem.

Bill Burroughs, production manager, claimed that some of the problems were a matter of engineering. He held that if only engineering would design components and the automobile carefully enough, many quality problems would disappear. He also blamed the personnel department for not selecting workers more carefully and for not getting the union business agent involved in the problem. He pointed out especially that there was a high turnover, more than 5 percent per month among assembly workers, and that absenteeism on Mondays often reached 20 percent. His position was that no production department could operate effectively with this kind of labor force.

Charles Wilson, chief engineer, held that the components and cars were engineered well enough and that if engineering tolerances were any more strict, the fitting of parts would be so difficult and time-consuming that the company's automobiles would be too costly to make.

Alice Turner, the personnel manager, accounted for the personnel problems in several ways. First, she pointed out that her department had little or no control over whom the company hired or kept, in view of the strong labor union the company had. Second, she observed that assem-

bly work was dull, deadening drudgery and that the company should not expect people to have much interest in this work beyond their paychecks.

But Ms. Turner did say she was persuaded that the company could develop more worker interest and consequently higher-quality work and less absenteeism and turnover if assembly jobs could be enlarged. When asked what she would suggest, Ms. Turner recommended that the company do two things. One was to have workers handle several operations on the assembly line and work as a team, instead of doing only one simple task. A second was to rotate workers each week from one location on the line to a completely different one in order to give them new and more challenging work.

These suggestions were adopted and put into effect. To everyone's surprise, workers expressed great dissatisfaction with the new program. After a week, the assembly lines were closed down by a strike, the workers claiming that the new program was only a management scheme to get them to do more work than they had done before and to train them to replace other workers without any increase in pay.

The division manager and the personnel manager were surprised. When asked by the division manager what had happened, Ms. Turner could only say: "This is a mystery to me. We make their jobs more interesting, and they strike!"

1   What do you believe went wrong with the program?

2   What would you have done if you had been the personnel manager? Would you have used this program, a different one, or none at all? Why?

For Further Information

Alderfer, C. P. *Existence, Relatedness, and Growth: Human Needs in Organizational Settings* (New York: The Free Press, 1972).

Bylinsky, G. "America's Best-Managed Factories," *Fortune*, Mar. 28, 1984, pp. 16–24.

Guest, R. H. "Quality of Work Life—Learning from Tarrytown," *Harvard Business Review*, vol. 57. no. 4 (July–August 1979), pp. 76–87.

Haynes, R. S., R. C. Pine, and H. G. Fitch. "Reducing Accident Rates with Organizational Behavior Modification," *Academy of Management Journal*, vol. 25, no. 2 (June 1982), pp. 407–416.

Hofstede, G. "The Cultural Relativity of the Quality of Life Concept," *Academy of Management Review*, vol. 9, no. 3 (July 1984), pp. 389–398.

Klein, J. A. "Why Supervisors Resist Employee Involvement," *Harvard Business Review*, vol. 62, no. 5 (September–October 1984), pp. 87–95.

Lawler, E. E. "Merit Pay: Fact or Fiction?" *Management Review*, vol. 70, no. 4 (April 1981), pp. 50–53.

Miner, S. B. *Theory of Organization Behavior* (Hinsdale, Ill.: Dryden Press, 1980).

Mitchell, T. R. "Motivation: New Directions for Theory, Research, and Practice," *Academy of Management Review*, vol. 7, no. 1 (January 1982), pp. 80–88.

Patton, A. "The Motivations of an Executive," in H. Koontz, C. O'Donnell, and H. Weihrich (eds.), *Management—A Book of Readings*, 5th ed. (New York: McGraw-Hill Book Company, 1980), pp. 504–511.

Stanton, E. S. "A Critical Reevaluation of Motivation, Management and Productivity," in J. H. Donnelly, Jr., J. L. Gibson, and J. M. Ivancevich (eds.), *Perspectives on Management*, 5th ed. (Plano, Tex.: Business Publications, Inc., 1984), pp. 188–196.

19

Leadership

After reading this chapter, you should understand:

1 The nature and ingredients of leadership
2 The trait approaches to leadership and their limitations
3 Various leadership styles based on the use of authority
4 Likert's four systems of management
5 The two dimensions of Blake and Mouton's managerial grid and the resulting four extreme leadership styles
6 That leadership, according to Tannenbaum and Schmidt, should be seen as a continuum, with managerial power and influence ranging from low to high
7 Fiedler's contingency approach to leadership
8 The path-goal approach to leadership effectiveness developed by House

Although some people treat the terms "managership" and "leadership" as synonyms, we believe they should be distinguished. As a matter of fact, there can be leaders of completely unorganized groups, but there can be managers, as conceived here, only where organized structures create roles. There are also important analytical advantages in separating leadership from managership. It permits leadership to be singled out for study without the encumbrance of qualifications relating to the more general issues of managership.

Leadership is an important aspect of managing. As we will show in this chapter, the ability to lead effectively is one of the keys to being an effective manager; also, undertaking the other essentials of managing—doing the entire managerial job—has an important bearing on ensuring that a manager will be an effective leader. Managers must exercise all the functions of their role in order to combine human and material resources to achieve objectives. The key to doing this is the existence of a clear role and a degree of discretion or authority to support managers' actions.

Followership

The essence of leadership is followership. In other words, it is the willingness of people to follow that makes a person a leader. Moreover, as pointed out earlier, people tend to follow those whom they see as providing a means of achieving their own desires, wants, and needs.

An example of leadership-followership can be found in the story of the McDonald's hamburger franchise.[1] Although Ray Kroc, the founder, has passed away, his philosophy became a legend that continues. Chairman Fred Turner stays with hamburgers and fries even though other opportunities for company growth are available. He also continues to use Kroc's motto, expressed in the acronym QSCV (quality, service, cleanliness, and value). Leadership requires followership, and Turner has followed Kroc's footsteps since he joined the company at age 23.

We can see that leadership and motivation are closely interconnected. By understanding motivation, we can appreciate better what people want and why they act as they do. Also, as noted in the previous chapter, leaders may not only respond to subordinates' motivations but also arouse or dampen them by means of the organizational climate they develop. Both these factors are as important to leadership as they are to managership.

Defining Leadership

Definition of leadership

Leadership has different meanings to various authors. We define *leadership* as influence, the art or process of influencing people so that they will strive willingly and enthusiastically toward the achievement of group goals. Ideally, people should be encouraged to develop not only willingness to work but also willingness to work with zeal and confidence. Zeal is ardor, earnestness, and intensity in the execution of work; confidence reflects experience and technical ability. To lead is to guide, conduct, direct, and precede. Leaders act to help a group attain objectives through the maximum application of its capabilities. They do not stand behind a group to push and prod; they place themselves before the group as they facilitate progress and inspire the group to accomplish organizational goals. An example is the orchestra leaders, whose function is to produce coordinated sound and correct tempo through the integrated effort of the musicians. Depending upon the quality of the director's leadership, the orchestra will respond.

Let us consider the leadership style of Herbert Kelleher, the chairman of Southwest Airlines.[2] He attempts to create a family feeling among his employees by remembering their names and personally sending out birthday cards. In an

---

[1] M. J. Williams, "McDonald's Refuses to Plateau," *Fortune*, Nov. 12, 1984, pp. 34–40.
[2] "Why Herb Kelleher Gets So Much Respect from Labor," *Business Week*, Sept. 24, 1984, pp. 112–114.

attempt to stay competitive in the deregulated airline industry, he asked for, and received, considerable concessions from employees and their union. His hands-on leadership style won him the respect and followership of his employees. The austerity measures apply equally to management and employees. His office, for example, is in a barrack-style building. Leading by example those who follow him, he seems concerned about both the tasks to be done and the people who work for him.

Ingredients of Leadership

Every group of people that performs near its total capacity has some person as its head who is skilled in the art of leadership. This skill seems to be a compound of at least four major ingredients: (1) the ability to use power effectively and in a responsible manner; (2) the ability to comprehend that human beings have differing motivating forces at different times and in different situations; (3) the ability to inspire; and (4) the ability to act in a manner that will develop a climate conducive to responding to and arousing motivations.

Power

The first ingredient of leadership is power. The differences between power and authority and the nature of power were discussed in Chapter 10.

An understanding of people

The second ingredient of leadership is a fundamental understanding of people. As in all practices, it is one thing to know motivation theory, kinds of motivating forces, and the nature of a system of motivation, and another thing to be able to apply this knowledge to people and situations. A manager or any other leader who at least knows the present state of motivation theory and who understands the elements of motivation is more aware of the nature and strength of human needs and is more able to define and design ways of satisfying them and to administer so as to get the desired responses.

Inspiring followers

The third ingredient of leadership seems to be a rare ability to inspire followers to apply their full capabilities to a project. While the use of motivators seems to center on subordinates and their needs, inspiration also comes from group heads. They may have qualities of charm and appeal that give rise to loyalty, devotion, and a strong desire on the part of followers to promote what leaders want. This is not a matter of need-satisfaction; it is, rather, a matter of people giving unselfish support to a chosen champion. The best examples of inspirational leadership come from hopeless and frightening situations: an unprepared nation on the eve of battle, a prison camp with exceptional morale, or a defeated leader undeserted by faithful followers. Some may argue that such devotion is not entirely unselfish, that it is in the interests of those who face catastrophe to follow a person they trust. But few would deny the value of personal appeal in either case.

Style and climate

A fourth ingredient of leadership has to do with the style of the leader and the climate he or she develops. We have seen in Chapter 18 how much the strength of motivation depends on expectancies, perceived rewards, the amount of effort believed to be required, the task to be done, and other factors which are part of an environment. We have seen also how an organizational climate influences motivation. Awareness of these factors has led to considerable research on, and the development of various theories of, leadership behavior. The views of those who have long approached leadership as a psychological study of interpersonal relationships have tended to converge with ours. As will be recalled, we see the primary task of managers as the design and maintenance of an environment for performance.

Almost every role in organized enterprise is made more satisfying to participants and more productive for the enterprise by those who can help others fulfill their desire for such things as money, status, power, or pride of accomplishment. The fundamental principle of leadership is: *Since people tend to follow those who, in their view, offer them a means of satisfying their own personal goals, the more managers understand what motivates their subordinates and how these motivations operate, and the more they reflect this understanding in carrying out their managerial actions, the more effective they are likely to be as leaders.*

Principle of leadership

Because of the importance of leadership to all kinds of group action, there is a considerable volume of theory and research concerning it. It is difficult to summarize such a large volume of research in a form relevant to day-to-day management. However, in the succeeding pages we shall identify several major types of leadership theory and research and outline some basic kinds of leadership styles.

Trait Approaches to Leadership

Prior to 1949, studies of leadership were based largely on an attempt to identify the traits that leaders possess. Starting with the "great man" theory that leaders are born and not made, a belief dating back to the ancient Greeks and Romans, researchers tried to identify the physical, mental, and personality traits of various leaders. The "great man" theory lost much of its acceptability with the rise of the behaviorist school of psychology, which emphasizes that people are not born with traits other than inherited physical characteristics and perhaps tendencies toward good health.

Studies of leadership traits

Various studies of traits have been made. Ralph M. Stogdill found that various researchers identified five physical traits related to leadership ability (such as energy, appearance, and height), four intelligence and ability traits, sixteen personality traits (such as adaptability, aggressiveness, enthusiasm, and self-confidence), six task-related characteristics (such as achievement drive, persistence, and initiative), and nine social characteristics (such as cooperativeness, interpersonal skills, and administrative ability).[3] E. Ghiselli noted significant correlations between leadership effectiveness and the traits of intelligence, supervisory ability, initiative, self-assurance, and individuality in ways of doing work.[4] At the same time, ex-

---

[3]R. M. Stogdill, *Handbook of Leadership: A Survey of Theory and Research* (New York: The Free Press, 1974). See also his earlier study, "Personal Factors Associated with Leadership: A Survey of the Literature," *Journal of Psychology*, vol. 25 (1948), pp. 35–71.

[4]E. E. Ghiselli, "Managerial Talent," *American Psychologist*, vol. 16, no. 10 (October 1963), pp. 632–641.

tremely high or low intelligence reduces the leader's effectiveness.[5] In other words, the intelligence level of the leader should not be too different from that of the subordinates. In general, however, the study of leaders' traits has not been a very fruitful approach to explaining leadership. Not all leaders possess all the traits, and many nonleaders may possess most or all of them. Also, the trait approach gives no guidance as to *how much* of any trait a person should have. Furthermore the dozens of studies that have been made do not agree as to what traits are leadership traits or what their relationships are to actual instances of leadership. Most of these so-called traits are really patterns of behavior.

Leadership Behavior and Styles

It is difficult to separate theories of leadership. A number of researchers have concentrated on the behavior of leaders on the assumption that ability to lead and willingness to follow are based on leadership styles.

Styles Based on Use of Authority

Autocratic leadership

Some earlier explanations of leadership styles classified them on the basis of how leaders use their authority. Leaders were seen as applying three basic styles. The *autocratic leader* was defined as one who commands and expects compliance, who is dogmatic and positive, and who leads by the ability to withhold or give rewards and punishment. The *democratic*, or *participative*, leader consults with subordinates on proposed actions and decisions and encourages participation from them. This type of leader was seen as ranging from the person who does not take action without subordinates' concurrence to the one who makes decisions but consults with subordinates before doing so.

Democratic, participative leadership

Free rein leadership

The third type of leader uses his or her power very little, if at all, giving subordinates a high degree of independence, or *free rein,* in their operations. Such leaders depend largely on subordinates to set their own goals and the means of achieving them, and they see their role as one of aiding the operations of followers by furnishing them information and acting primarily as a contact with the group's external environment. Figure 19-1 illustrates the flow of influence in the three leadership situations.

Variations

There are variations within this simple classification of leadership styles. Some autocratic leaders are seen as "benevolent autocrats." Although they listen considerately to their followers' opinions before making a decision, the decision is their own. They may be willing to hear and consider subordinates' ideas and concerns, but when a decision is to be made, they may be more autocratic than benevolent.

A variation of the participative leader is the person who is supportive. Leaders in this category may look upon their task as not only consulting with followers and considering carefully their opinions but also doing all they can to support subordinates in accomplishing their duties.

---

[5]E. E. Ghiselli, *Explorations in Managerial Talent* (Pacific Palisades, Calif.: Goodyear Publishing Company, Inc., 1971).

FIGURE 19-1

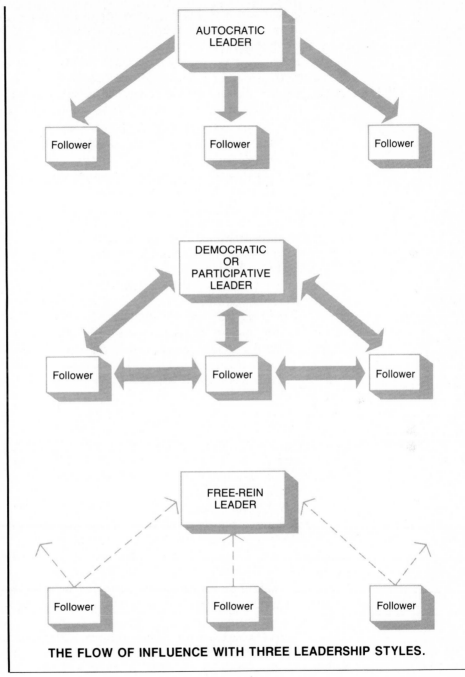

THE FLOW OF INFLUENCE WITH THREE LEADERSHIP STYLES.

Situational factors

The use of any style will depend on the situation. A manager may be highly autocratic in an emergency; one can hardly imagine a fire chief holding a long meeting with the crew to consider the best way of fighting a fire. Managers may also be autocratic when they alone have the answers to certain questions.

A leader may gain considerable knowledge and a better commitment on the part of persons involved by consulting with subordinates. We saw that this was true in developing verifiable objectives under systems of managing by objectives. Furthermore, a manager dealing with a group of research scientists may give them free rein in developing their inquiries and experiments. But the same manager might be quite autocratic in enforcing a rule concerning protective covering to be worn when handling certain potentially dangerous chemicals.

**Likert's
Four Systems of
Management**

Professor Rensis Likert and his associates at the University of Michigan have studied the patterns and styles of leaders and managers for three decades.[6] In the course of these researches, Likert has developed certain ideas and approaches important to understanding leadership behavior. He sees an effective manager as strongly oriented to subordinates, relying on communication to keep all parties working as a unit. All members of the group, including the manager or leader, adopt a supportive attitude in which they share in one another's common needs, values, aspirations, goals, and expectations. Since it appeals to human motivations, Likert views this approach as the most effective way to lead a group.

System 1

As guidelines for research and for the clarification of his concepts, Likert has posited four systems of management. System 1 management is described as "exploitive-authoritative"; these managers are highly autocratic, have little trust in subordinates, motivate people through fear and punishment with occasional rewards, engage in downward communication, and limit decision making to the top.

System 2

System 2 management is called "benevolent-authoritative"; these managers have a patronizing confidence and trust in subordinates, motivate with rewards and some fear and punishment, permit some upward communication, solicit some ideas and opinions from subordinates, and allow some delegation of decision making but with close policy control.

System 3

System 3 management is referred to as "consultive"; these managers have substantial but not complete confidence and trust in subordinates, usually try to make use of subordinates' ideas and opinions, use rewards for motivation with occasional punishment and some participation, engage in communication flow both down and up, make broad policy and general decisions at the top while allowing specific decisions to be made at lower levels, and act consultatively in other ways.

System 4

Likert saw System 4 management as the most participative of all and referred to it as "participative-group"; System 4 managers have complete trust and confidence in subordinates in all matters, always get ideas and opinions from subor-

---

[6]See especially his *New Patterns of Management* (New York: McGraw-Hill Book Company, 1961) and *The Human Organization* (New York: McGraw-Hill Book Company, 1967), from which material in this section has been drawn. Also see R. Likert and J. G. Likert, *New Ways of Managing Conflict* (New York: McGraw-Hill Book Company, 1976).

dinates and constructively use them, give economic rewards on the basis of group participation and involvement in such areas as setting goals and appraising progress toward goals, engage in much communication down and up and with peers, encourage decision making throughout the organization, and otherwise operate with themselves and their subordinates as a group.

In general, Likert found that those managers who applied the System 4 approach to their operations had greatest success as leaders. Moreover, he noted that departments and companies managed by the System 4 approach were most effective in setting goals and achieving them and were generally more productive. He ascribed this success mainly to the degree of participation and the extent to which the practice of supporting subordinates was maintained.

Figure 19-2 shows the profile of a new manager in a General Motors assembly plant. The organization operated previously in System 3, but moved toward System 4. This manager, aided by the survey feedback improvement approach, used the data of the profile to focus on those areas that needed improvement.

Reservations

Although there is considerable support for System 4 theory, it is not without its critics.[7] The research focus of this theory is on small groups, yet the discussion is frequently extrapolated and applied to the total organization. Furthermore, the research has primarily been conducted at lower organizational levels and may not be supported when data from top-level managers are separated.[8] Likert and his associates realized the need for clarity in role definitions, but at the same time they suggest, for example, cross-functional teams and matrix departmentation, which usually increase role conflict and uncertainty. Since System 4 approaches are often introduced when companies are profitable, the results attributed to the survey feedback method may actually be due to general prosperity of the firm. It appears, then, that those evaluating System 4 theories should take careful account of the surrounding circumstances. For the practicing manager this means that the benefits attributed to System 4 theory must be viewed with caution.

The Managerial Grid

One of the most widely known approaches to defining leadership styles is the *managerial grid,* developed some years ago by Robert Blake and Jane Mouton.[9] Building on previous research that showed the importance of a manager's having concern both for production and for people, Blake and Mouton devised a clever device to dramatize this concern. This grid, shown in Figure 19-3, has been used throughout the world as a means of managerial training and of identifying various combinations of leadership styles.

---

[7]J. B. Miner, *Theories of Organizational Structure and Process* (Hinsdale, Ill.: Dryden Press, 1982), chap. 2.

[8]D. G. Bowers, "Hierarchy, Function and the Generalizability of Leadership Practices," in J. G. Hunt and L. L. Larson (eds.), *Leadership Frontiers* (Kent, Ohio: Kent State University Press, 1975), pp. 167–180.

[9]*The Managerial Grid* (Houston, Tex.: Gulf Publishing Company, 1954) and *Building a Dynamic Corporation Through Grid Organization Development* (Reading, Mass.: Addison-Wesley Publishing Company, Inc., 1969). The grid concept has been further refined in R. R. Blake and J. S. Mouton, *The Versatile Manager: A Grid Profile* (Homewood, Ill.: Richard D. Irwin, Inc., 1981).

FIGURE 19-2

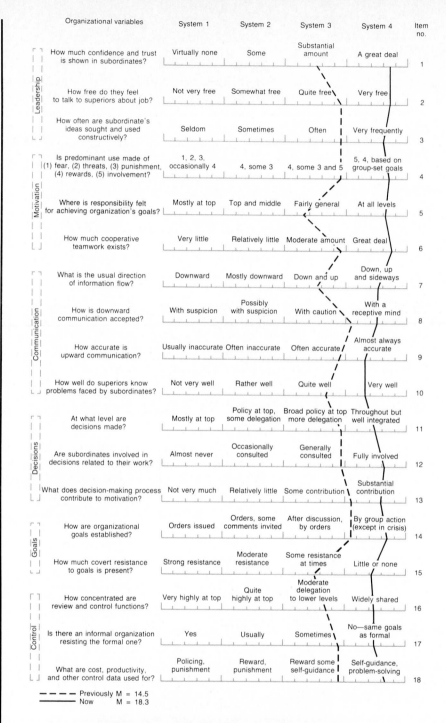

**PROFILE OF ORGANIZATIONAL CHARACTERISTICS OF A
NEW PLANT MANAGER AT A GENERAL MOTORS PLANT.**

Source: *R. Likert and J. G. Likert, New Ways of Managing Conflict (New York: McGraw-Hill Book
Company, 1976), p. 75. Used with permission.*

FIGURE 19-3

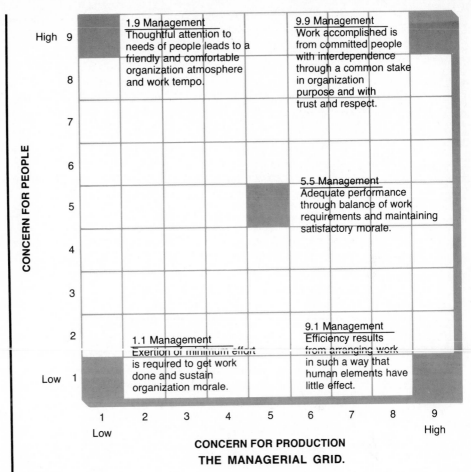

CONCERN FOR PEOPLE

High 9

1.9 Management
Thoughtful attention to
needs of people leads to a
friendly and comfortable
organization atmosphere
and work tempo.

8

9.9 Management
Work accomplished is
from committed people
with interdependence
through a common stake
in organization
purpose and with
trust and respect.

7

6

5

5.5 Management
Adequate performance
through balance of work
requirements and maintaining
satisfactory morale.

4

3

2

9.1 Management
Efficiency results
from arranging work
in such a way that
human elements have
little effect.

1.1 Management
Exertion of minimum effort
is required to get work
done and sustain
organization morale.

Low 1

1   2   3   4   5   6   7   8   9
Low   High

CONCERN FOR PRODUCTION
THE MANAGERIAL GRID.

Source: *Adapted from R. R. Blake and J. S. Mouton,* The Managerial Grid *(Houston, Texas: Gulf Publishing Company, 1964), p. 10.*

The grid dimensions   The grid has two dimensions, concern for people, and concern for production. As Blake and Mouton have emphasized, their use of the phrase "concern for" is meant to convey "how" managers are concerned about production or "how" they are concerned about people, and not such things as "how much" production they are concerned about getting out of a group.

"Concern for production" includes the attitudes of a supervisor toward a wide variety of things, such as the quality of policy decisions, procedures and processes, creativeness of research, quality of staff services, work efficiency, and volume of output. "Concern for people" is likewise interpreted in a broad way. It includes such elements as degree of personal commitment toward goal achievement, maintenance of the self-esteem of workers, placement of responsibility on the basis of trust rather than obedience, provision of good working conditions, and maintenance of satisfying interpersonal relations.

Style 1.1

Style 9.9

Style 1.9

Style 9.1

Style 5.5

The four extreme styles Blake and Mouton recognize four extremes of style. Under the 1.1 style (referred to as "impoverished management"), managers concern themselves very little with either people or production and have minimum involvement in their jobs; to all intents and purposes, they have abandoned their jobs and only mark time or act as messengers communicating information from superiors to subordinates. At the other extreme are the 9.9 managers, who display in their actions the highest possible dedication both to people and to production. They are the real "team managers" who are able to mesh the production needs of the enterprise with the needs of individuals.

Another style is 1.9 management (called "country club management" by some), in which managers have little or no concern for production but are concerned only for people. They promote an environment where everyone is relaxed, friendly, and happy and no one is concerned about putting forth coordinated effort to accomplish enterprise goals. At another extreme are the 9.1 managers (sometimes referred to as "autocratic task managers"), who are concerned only with developing an efficient operation, who have little or no concern for people, and who are quite autocratic in their style of leadership.

Using these four extremes as points of reference, every managerial technique, approach, or style can be placed somewhere on the grid. Clearly, 5.5 managers have medium concern for production and for people. They obtain adequate, but not outstanding, morale and production. They do not set goals too high, and they are likely to have a rather benevolently autocratic attitude toward people.

The managerial grid is a useful device for identifying and classifying managerial styles. But it does not tell us *why* a manager falls in one part or another of the grid. To find this out, we have to look at underlying causes, such as the personality of the leader or those of followers, the ability and training of managers, the enterprise environment, and other situational factors that influence how both leaders and followers act.

Leadership as a Continuum

The adaptation of leadership styles to different contingencies has been well-characterized by Robert Tannenbaum and Warren H. Schmidt, developers of the concept of a leadership continuum.[10] As is shown in Figure 19-4, they see leadership as involving a variety of styles, ranging from one that is highly boss-centered to one that is highly subordinate-centered. These vary with the degree of freedom a leader or manager grants to subordinates. Thus, instead of suggesting a choice between the two styles of leadership—authoritarian or democratic—this approach offers a range of style, with no suggestion that one is always right and another is always wrong.

The continuum theory recognizes that what style of leadership is appropriate

[10]R. Tannenbaum and W. H. Schmidt, "How to Choose a Leadership Pattern," *Harvard Business Review*, vol. 36, no. 2 (March–April 1958), pp. 95–101. See also H. Weihrich, "How to Change a Leadership Pattern," *Management Review*, vol. 68, no. 4 (April 1979), pp. 26–28, 37–40.

FIGURE 19-4

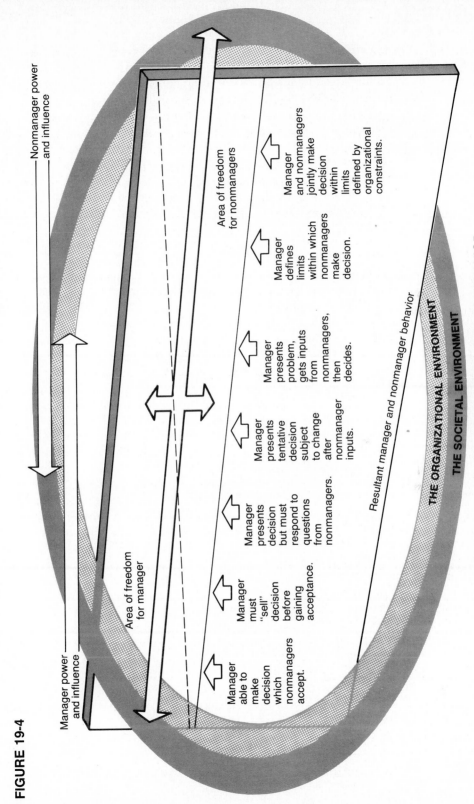

CONTINUUM OF MANAGER-NONMANAGER BEHAVIOR.

Source: *Reprinted with permission from R. Tannenbaum and W. H. Schmidt, "Retrospective Commentary" on "How to Choose a Leadership Pattern," Harvard Business Review, vol. 51, no. 3 (May–June 1973), p. 167.*

Four sets of forces

depends on the leader, the followers, and the situation. Tannenbaum and Schmidt saw the most important elements that may influence a manager's style along a continuum as (1) the forces operating in the manager's personality, including his or her value system, confidence in subordinates, inclination toward leadership, styles, and feelings of security in uncertain situations; (2) forces in subordinates that will affect the manager's behavior; and (3) forces in the situation, such as organization values and traditions, how effectively subordinates work as a unit, the nature of a problem and whether authority to handle it can be safely delegated, and the pressure of time.

In reviewing in 1973 their continuum model, which was first formulated in 1958, Tannenbaum and Schmidt placed circles around their model, as shown in Figure 19-4, to represent the influences on style imposed both by the organizational environment and the societal environment.[11] This was done to emphasize the open-system nature of leadership styles and the various impacts both of the organizational environment and of the social environment outside an enterprise. In their 1973 commentary, the authors put increased stress on the interdependency of leadership style and environmental forces—such as labor unions, greater pressures for social responsibility, the civil rights movement, and the ecology and consumer movements—that challenge the rights of managers to make decisions or handle their subordinates without considering interests outside the organization.

Situational, or Contingency, Approaches to Leadership

As disillusionment with the "great man" and trait approaches to understanding leadership increased, attention turned to the study of situations and the belief that leaders are the product of given situations. A large number of studies have been made on the premise that leadership is strongly affected by the situation from which the leader emerges and in which he or she operates. That this is a persuasive approach is indicated by the rise of Hitler in Germany in the 1930s, the earlier rise of Mussolini in Italy, the emergence of F. D. Roosevelt in the Great Depression of the 1930s in the United States, and the rise of Mao Tse-tung in China in the period after World War II. This approach to leadership recognizes that there exists an interaction between the group and the leader. It supports the follower theory that people tend to follow those whom they perceive (accurately or inaccurately) as offering them a means of accomplishing their own personal desires. The leader, then, is the person who recognizes these desires and does those things, or undertakes those programs, designed to meet them.

Situational, or contingency, approaches obviously have much meaning for managerial theory and practice. They also tie into the system of motivation discussed in the previous chapter, and have meaning for practicing managers who must take into account the situation when they design an environment for performance.

---

[11]Tannenbaum and Schmidt, op. cit., reprinted with a commentary by the authors in *Harvard Business Review*, vol. 51, no. 3 (May–June 1973), pp. 162–180.

**Fiedler's
Contingency
Approach
to Leadership**

Although their approach to leadership theory is primarily one of analyzing leadership style, Fred E. Fiedler and his associates at the University of Illinois have suggested a contingency theory of leadership.[12] Fiedler's theory implies that leadership is any process in which the ability of a leader to exercise influence depends upon the group task situation and the degree to which the leader's style, personality, and approach fit the group. In other words, according to Fiedler, people become leaders not only because of the attributes of their personalities but also because of various situational factors and the interaction between the leaders and the situation.

Critical dimensions of the leadership situation   On the basis of his studies, Fiedler described three *critical dimensions* of the leadership situation that help determine what style of leadership will be most effective:

1   **Position power.** This is the degree to which the power of a position, as distinguished from other sources of power, such as personality or expertise, enables a leader to get group members to comply with directions; in the case of managers, this is the power arising from organizational authority. As Fiedler points out, a leader with clear and considerable position power can more easily obtain good followership than one without such power.

2   **Task structure.** With this dimension, Fiedler had in mind the extent to which tasks can be clearly spelled out and people held responsible for them. Where tasks are clear (in contrast to situations where tasks are vague and unstructured), the quality of performance can be more easily controlled, and group members can be held more definitely responsible for performance.

3   **Leader-member relations.** This dimension, which Fiedler regarded as most important from a leader's point of view since position power and task structure may be largely under the control of an enterprise, has to do with the extent to which group members like and trust a leader and are willing to follow him or her.

Leadership styles   To approach his study, Fiedler set forth two major styles of leadership. One of these is primarily task-oriented, and a leader gains satisfaction from seeing tasks performed. The other is oriented primarily toward achieving good interpersonal relations and toward attaining a position of personal prominence.

*Favorableness
of the situation*

Favorableness of the situation was defined by Fiedler as the degree to which a given situation enables a leader to exert influence over a group. To measure leadership styles and determine whether a leader is chiefly task-oriented, Fiedler used an unusual testing technique. He based his findings on two types of scores:

---

[12]F. E. Fiedler, *A Theory of Leadership Effectiveness* (New York: McGraw-Hill Book Company, 1967). See also F. E. Fiedler and M. M. Chemers, *Leadership and Effective Management* (Glenview, Ill.: Scott, Foresman and Company, 1974).

(1) scores on the *least preferred coworker* (LPC)—these were ratings made by people in a group as to those with whom they would least like to work; and (2) scores on *assumed similarity between opposites* (ASO)—ratings based on the degree to which leaders see group members to be like themselves, on the assumption that people will like best, and work best with, those who are seen as most like themselves. Now the LPC scale is most commonly used in research. In developing this scale, respondents were asked the traits of a person with whom they could work least well.[13] The person was to be described on sixteen items that were scaled, such as:

LPC scale

Pleasant :____:____:____:____ | ____:____:____:____: Unpleasant

Rejecting :____:____:____:____ | ____:____:____:____: Accepting

In his studies using this method, supported also by studies of others, Fiedler found that people who rated their coworkers high (that is, in favorable terms) were those who derived major satisfaction from successful interpersonal relationships. People who rated their "least preferred coworker" low (that is, in unfavorable terms) were seen as deriving their major satisfaction from task performance. Likewise, he found that people who rated their coworkers as having high "assumed similarity between opposites" also rated them fairly high on the scale of "least preferred coworkers," and vice versa.

From his research, Fiedler came to some interesting conclusions. Recognizing that personal perceptions may be unclear and even quite inaccurate, Fiedler nonetheless found that:

> Leadership performance depends then as much on the organization as it depends on the leader's own attributes. Except perhaps for the unusual case, it is simply not meaningful to speak of an effective leader or an ineffective leader; we can only speak of a leader who tends to be effective in one situation and ineffective in another. If we wish to increase organizational and group effectiveness we must learn not only how to train leaders more effectively but also how to build an organizational environment in which the leader can perform well.[14]

Extreme situations

Fiedler's contingency model of leadership can be summarized by reference to Figure 19-5. As presented, this figure is really a summary of Fiedler's research, in which he found that in "unfavorable" or "favorable" situations the task-oriented leader would be the most effective. In other words, when leader position power is weak, the task structure is unclear and leader-member relations are moderately poor, the situation is unfavorable for the leader and the most effective leader will be one who is task-oriented. Likewise, at the other extreme, where position power is strong, the task structure is clear, and leader-member relations are good—a

---

[13]Fiedler, op. cit., p. 41.
[14]Ibid., p. 261.

FIGURE 19-5

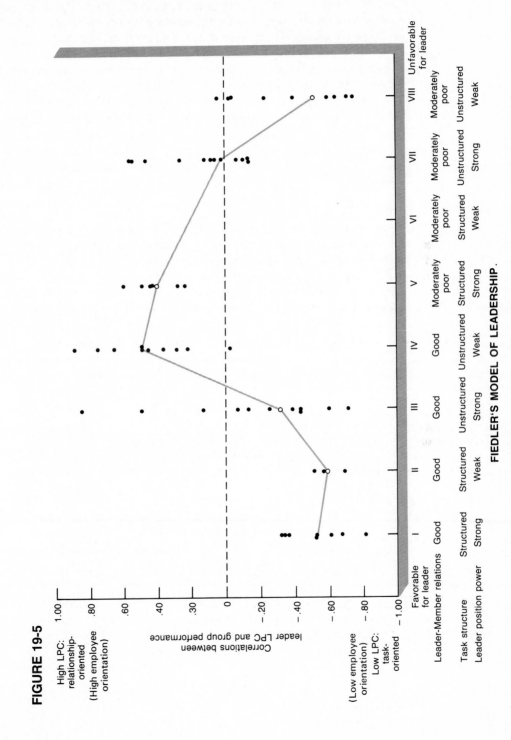

FIEDLER'S MODEL OF LEADERSHIP.

Source: *Adapted from F. E. Fiedler, A Theory of Leadership Effectiveness (New York: McGraw-Hill Book Company, 1967), p. 146. Used with permission.*

favorable situation for the leader—Fiedler found that the task-oriented leader was most effective. However, where the situation was only moderately unfavorable or favorable (the middle of the scale in the figure), the human relations-oriented leader was found to be most effective.

In a highly structured situation, such as in the military during a war, where the leader has a strong position power and good relations with members, there is a favorable situation in which task orientation is most appropriate. The other extreme, an unfavorable situation with moderately poor relations, an unstructured task, and weak position power, also suggests task orientation by the leader, who may reduce anxiety or ambiguity that could be created by the loosely structured situation. Between the two extremes (the middle of the scale in Figure 19-5), the suggested approach emphasizes cooperation and good relations with people.

Fieldler's research and management In reviewing Fiedler's research, one finds that there is nothing automatic or "good" in either the task-oriented or the people-satisfaction-oriented style. Leadership effectiveness depends upon the various elements in the group environment. This might be expected. Cast in the desired role of leaders, managers who apply knowledge to the realities of the group reporting to them will do well to recognize that they are practicing an art. But in doing so, they will necessarily take into account the motivations to which people will respond and their ability to satisfy them in the interest of attaining enterprise goals.

Several scholars have put Fiedler's theory to the test in various situations. Some have questioned the meaning of the LPC score, and others suggest that the model does not explain the causal effect of the LPC score on performance. Some of the findings are not statistically significant and situational measures may not be completely independent of the LPC score.

Despite criticism, it is important to recognize that effective leadership style depends on the situation. Although this idea may not be new, Fiedler and his colleagues drew attention to this fact and stimulated a great deal of research.

The Path-Goal Approach to Leadership Effectiveness

The path-goal theory suggests that the main function of the leader is to clarify and to set goals with subordinates, to help them to find the best path for achieving them, and to remove obstacles. Proponents of this approach have studied leadership in a variety of situations. As stated by Robert House, the theory builds on various motivational and leadership theories of others.[15]

---

[15]"A Path-Goal Theory of Leadership Effectiveness," *Administrative Science Quarterly*, vol. 16, no. 3 (September 1971), pp. 321–338, R. J. House and T. R. Mitchell, "Path-Goal Theory of Leadership," in H. Koontz, C. O'Donnell, and H. Weihrich (eds.), *Management—A Book of Readings*, 5th ed. (New York: McGraw-Hill Book Company, 1980), pp. 533–540, and A. C. Filley, R. J. House, and S. Kerr, *Managerial Process and Organizational Behavior* (Glenview, Ill.: Scott, Foresman and Company, 1976), chap. 12.

FIGURE 19-6

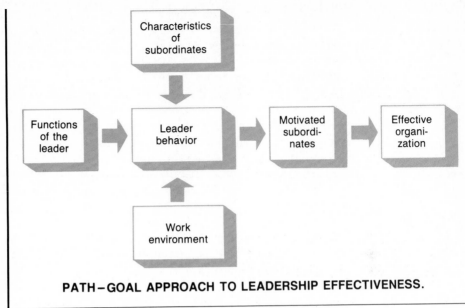

PATH—GOAL APPROACH TO LEADERSHIP EFFECTIVENESS.

Situational factors

In addition to the expectancy theory variables, other factors contributing to effective leadership should be considered. These situational factors include (1) characteristics of subordinates, such as their needs, self-confidence, and abilities; and (2) the work environment, including such components as the task, the reward system, and the relationship with coworkers (see Figure 19-6).

Leader behavior

Leader behavior is categorized into four groups:

1 Supportive leadership behavior gives consideration to the needs of subordinates, shows a concern for their well-being, and creates a pleasant organizational climate. It has the greatest impact on subordinates' performance when they are frustrated and dissatisfied.

2 Participative leadership allows subordinates to influence the decisions of their superiors and can result in increased motivation.

3 Instrumental leadership gives subordinates rather specific guidance and makes it clear what is expected of them; this includes aspects of planning, organizing, coordinating, and controlling by the leader.

4 Achievement-oriented leadership involves setting challenging goals, seeking improvement of performance, and having confidence that subordinates will achieve high goals.

Rather than suggesting that there is one best way to lead, this theory suggests that the appropriate style depends on the situation. Ambiguous and uncertain situations can be frustrating for subordinates and a more task-oriented style may be called for. In other words, when subordinates are confused, then the leader may tell them what to do, and show them a clear path to goals. On the other hand, in a routine task, such as can be found on the assembly line, additional structure (usually provided by a task-oriented leader) may be seen as redundant and subordinates may see this as overcontrolling. This, in turn, may be dissatisfying. To put it differently, employees want the leader to stay out of their way because the path is already clear enough.

The theory proposes that the behavior of the leader is acceptable and satisfies subordinates to the extent that they see it as a source for their satisfaction. Another proposition of the theory is that the behavior of the leader increases the effort of subordinates, that is, is motivating, insofar as (1) this behavior makes the satisfaction of the needs of subordinates dependent on effective performance, and (2) the behavior enhances subordinates' environment through coaching, directing, supporting, and rewarding.

The key to the theory is that the leader influences the paths between behavior and goals. The leader can do this by defining positions and task roles, by removing obstacles to performance, by enlisting the assistance of group members in setting goals, by promoting group cohesiveness and team effort, by increasing opportunities for personal satisfaction in work performance, by reducing stresses and external controls, by making expectations clear, and by doing other things that meet people's expectations.

The path-goal theory makes a great deal of sense to the practicing manager. At the same time one must realize that the model needs further testing before the approach can be used as a definite guide for managerial action.

Summary

Leadership is the art or process of influencing people so that they contribute willingly and enthusiastically toward group goals. Leadership requires followership. There are various approaches to the study of leadership ranging from the trait to the contingency approach. One such approach focuses on three styles: the autocratic, the democratic or participative, and the free-rein. Likert identified four systems of management ranging from System 1 (exploitive-authoritative) through System 4 (participative-group), which he considers the most effective system. The managerial grid identifies two dimensions: concern for production and concern for people. Based on these dimensions, four extreme styles are identified. Leadership can also be viewed as a continuum. One extreme of the continuum is the situation in which the manager has a great deal of freedom while subordinates have very little. The other extreme exemplifies the manager with very little freedom and a great deal of freedom given to subordinates.

Still another approach to leadership, built on the assumption that leaders are the product of given situations, focuses on the study of situations. Fiedler's contingency approach takes into account the position power of the leader, the structure of the task, and the relations between the leader and group members. The conclusion is that there is not one best leadership style and managers can be successful if placed in appropriate situations. The path-goal approach to leadership suggests that the most effective leaders help subordinates to achieve enterprise and personal goals.

Key Ideas and Concepts for Review

Leadership
Ingredients of leadership
Leadership traits
Leadership styles based on the use of authority
Likert's four systems of management

Managerial grid
Leadership as a continuum
Situational approach
Fiedler's contingency theory
Path-goal approach to leadership

For Discussion

1 What do you see as the essence of leadership?

2 How are leadership theory and styles related to motivation?

3 Why has the trait approach as a means of explaining leadership been so open to question?

4 Can you see why the managerial grid has been so popular as a training device?

5 For a business or political leader you admire, identify his or her style of leading by applying the managerial grid or the continuum-of-behavior model of Tannenbaum and Schmidt.

6 What is Fiedler's theory of leadership? Applying it to cases of leaders you have known, does it seem to be accurate?

7 What are the advantages and limitations of the path-goal approach to leadership?

8 Think of a situation in which you were the leader. Which leadership approach discussed in this chapter helps you to explain why you were a leader?

9 If you were selected the group leader for a class project (for example, to make a case study of a particular company), which leadership style or what behavior would you use? Why?

CASE 19-1

LEADERS IN GOVERNMENT DEPARTMENTS AND AGENCIES

"The trouble with government departments and agencies today," said Senator Paul Murphy, chairman of the Special Committee to Improve Government Management, "is that we have many managers, or administrators, who get high salaries, but too few leaders. I tell you that leaders are born and not made by any management development program you people have. We put people in positions of responsibility and expect them to be leaders. What we should do is to select people for government administrative positions who have demonstrated such personality traits as intelligence, energy, drive, initiative, enthusiasm, honesty, self-assurance, ability to get along with people, and ability to inspire confidence in their subordinates."

"But," responded Helen Baxter, Civil Service Commission management recruitment administrator, "you do not understand, Senator. We need people who are managers to head up our departments, divisions, and sections. Personal traits and qualities may be essential to political leaders. However, in government management we need persons who are concerned with getting tasks done as well as concerned with people. Well-known and respected psychologists, such as Dr. Fred Fiedler, Dr. Rensis Likert, Dr. Robert Blake, Dr. Jane Mouton, Dr. Robert Tannenbaum, and Dr. Warren Schmidt, have made all this clear in their theories and researches."

At that point, Senator Murphy declared: "I don't care what these psychologists say. What do they know about leaders? Our government departments and agencies have long suffered from lack of leadership at all levels and I want the Civil Service Commission to do something to ensure that we have leaders in administrative positions."

1 To what extent do you agree with Senator Murphy?

2 If you were Helen Baxter, how would you respond to the senator?

3 Combine the research and theories of Fiedler, Likert, Blake and Mouton, Tannenbaum and Schmidt, and others, and come up with an answer on how the government can be assured that government administrators will become effective leaders.

CASE 19-2

PALMER MACHINERY COMPANY

Palmer Machinery Company has encountered hard times, not only due to an economic recession, but also because of competition from products imported from Japan. In the past, labor relations have been rather poor. The unions usually asked for big pay increases for the workers and got them. But things have changed during the last few months, and labor and management have realized that they are in together for some bad times ahead.

The company maintains it is in a precarious

condition and asks labor for concessions and give-backs. The union calls a membership meeting and discusses the situation of the company. While Ann Stewart, an assembler, thinks that she is overpaid and argues for a wage reduction, the majority of those present disagree and do not want to make any concession. In fact, there is great mistrust of management's intentions, and the workers feel that giving concessions will encourage the company to ask for additional ones. After a long discussion some workers are more agreeable to concessions if management makes similar sacrifices. But management does not make any commitments. During the next few weeks the situation gets worse, and faced with a layoff, the union agrees to some cutbacks with an understanding that employees will share in some way in the profits of the company when things get better.

One month later, a survey of salaries of executives of major companies published in a national magazine shows that executives of their company received a substantial increase in compensation. One worker remarks: "You just cannot trust top management. I wish we had a situation as in Japan where in hard times the dividends are cut first, then the salary of top management is reduced, and later middle-level managers get a pay cut; the workers' pay is affected last."

1 Do you think the workers should have made concessions and agreed to givebacks?

2 If you were the president of the company, how would you have handled the situation?

3 What do you think of the Japanese approach of dealing with economic problems?

For Further Information

Bass, B. M. *Stogdill's Handbook of Leadership: A Survey of Theory and Research,* rev. ed. (New York: The Free Press, 1981).

Boyatzis, R. E. *The Competent Manager: A Model for Effective Performance* (New York: John Wiley & Sons, 1982).

Donnell, S. M., and J. Hall. "Men and Women As Managers: A Significant Case of No Significant Difference," *Organizational Dynamics,* vol. 9 (Spring 1980), pp. 60–77.

Hersey, P., and K. H. Blanchard. *Management of Organizational Behavior: Utilizing Human Resources,* 3rd ed. (Englewood Cliffs, N.J.: Prentice-Hall, Inc., 1977).

Hurst, D. K. "Of Boxes, Bubbles, and Effective Management," *Harvard Business Review,* vol. 62, no. 3 (May–June 1984), pp. 78–88.

Kotter, J. R. "Power to the Manager," *International Management,* (January 1980), pp. 19–21.

Lewis, A. M. "The Hall of Fame for U.S. Business Leadership," *Fortune,* Mar. 22, 1981, pp. 101–107.

McConkey, D. D. "Participative Management: What It Really Means in Practice," *Business Horizons,* vol. 23, no. 5 (October 1980), pp. 66–73.

Mintzberg, H. *Power in and around Organizations* (Englewood Cliffs, N.J.: Prentice-Hall, Inc., 1983).

Morris, T. D. "Taking Charge in Washington," *Harvard Business Review*, vol. 62, no. 4 (July–August 1984), pp. 24–40.

Yukl, G. M. *Leadership in Organizations* (Englewood Cliffs, N.J.: Prentice-Hall, Inc., 1981).

20

Communication

After reading this chapter, you should understand:

1   The nature of communication
2   The communication function in an organization
3   The basic communication process
4   The flow of communication in an organization
5   The characteristics of written, oral, and nonverbal communication
6   Barriers and breakdowns in communication
7   Approaches to effective communication
8   The role of the electronic media in communication
9   The major principles for leading

*Definition of
communication*

Although communication is important to all phases of managing, it is particularly important in the function of leading. There is general agreement about the necessity of effective communication, yet there is less agreement on an exact definition. We define **communication** as the transfer of information from the sender to the receiver with the information being understood by both the sender and the receiver. This definition becomes the basis for the communication process model—discussed in greater detail below—which focuses on the sender of the communication, the transmission of the message, and the receiver of the message. The model also draws attention to noise, which interferes with good communication, and feedback, which facilitates communication.

The Communication Function in an Organization

It is no exaggeration to say that the communication function is the means by which organized activity is unified. It may be looked upon as the means by which social inputs are fed into social systems. It is also the means by which behavior is modified, change is effected, information is made productive, and goals are achieved. Whether we are considering a church, a family, a scout troop, or a business enterprise, the transfer of information from one individual to another is absolutely essential.

The Importance of Communication

Over the years, the importance of communication in organized effort has been recognized by many authors. Some view communication as the means by which people are linked together in an organization to achieve a common purpose. This is still the fundamental function of communication. Indeed, group activity is impossible without communication which is needed for effecting coordination and change.

Psychologists have also been interested in communication. They emphasize human problems that occur in the communication process of initiating, transmitting, and receiving information. They have focused on the identification of barriers to good communication, especially those that involve interpersonal relationships. Sociologists and information theorists, as well as psychologists, have concentrated on the study of communication networks.

The Purpose of Communication

In its broadest sense, the purpose of communication in enterprise is to effect change—to influence action toward the welfare of the enterprise. Business, for example, requires information about prices, competition, technology, and finance, as well as information about the business cycle and government activity. This knowledge is the basis for decisions affecting product lines, production ratios, quality, marketing strategy, the mix of productive factors, and internal information flow. The immediate digestion of information and action in response to it, however, become extremely difficult in a large enterprise where several thousand or more people are involved.

Internal environment

Communication is essential for the *internal* functioning of enterprises because it integrates the managerial functions. Specifically, communication is needed:

To establish and disseminate goals of an enterprise

To develop plans for their achievement

To organize human and other resources in the most effective and efficient way

To select, develop, and appraise members of the organization

To lead, direct, and motivate, and to create a climate in which people want to contribute

To control performance

External environment

Figure 20-1 graphically shows that communication not only facilitates the managerial functions, but also relates the enterprise to its *external* environment. It is through information exchange that managers become aware of the needs of customers, the availability of suppliers, the claims of stockholders, the regulations of governments, and the concerns of a community. It is through communication

FIGURE 20-1

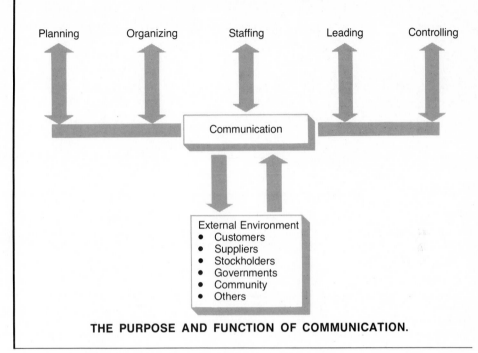

THE MANAGEMENT PROCESS

THE PURPOSE AND FUNCTION OF COMMUNICATION.

that any organization becomes an open system interacting with its environment, a fact whose importance is emphasized throughout this book.

Responsibility for Communication

It is generally known that managers determine the organizational climate and influence the attitudes of enterprise members. They do so mainly through communication initiated by top management. Although organizational leaders have a major responsibility to set the right tone for effective communication, every person in an organization also shares this responsibility.

Superiors must communicate with subordinates and vice versa. Communication is a two-way process in which everyone is both an originator and a receiver of communication. Information flows vertically along the chain of command and crosswise. Crosswise communication, as used here, involves the horizontal flow of information among persons on the same or similar organizational levels and diagonal flow of information among people at various levels, without superior-subordinate relationships. The best way to approach the analysis of the various facets of communication is through the introduction of a communication model.

The Communication Process

Simply stated, the communication process, diagrammed in Figure 20-2, involves the sender who transmits a message through a selected channel to the receiver. Let us examine closely the specific steps in the process.

FIGURE 20-2

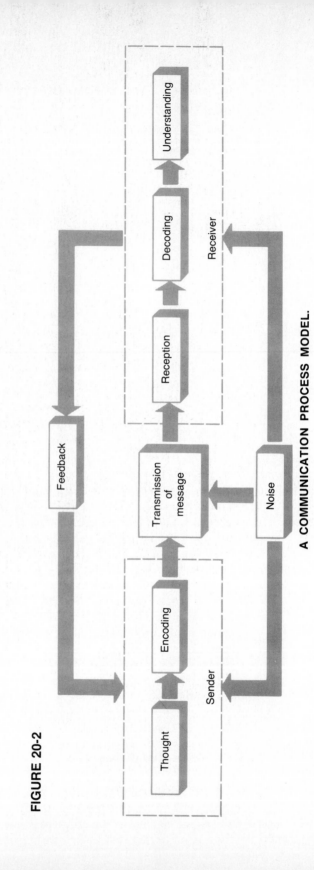

A COMMUNICATION PROCESS MODEL.

The Sender of the Message

Communication begins with the sender who has a thought or an idea, wh then encoded in a way that can be understood by both the sender and the receiver. We usually think of encoding a message into the English language, but there are many other ways of encoding, such as translating the thought into computer language.

The Transmission of the Message

The information is transmitted over a channel that links the sender with the receiver. The message may be oral or written, and it may be transmitted through a memorandum, a computer, the telephone, a telegram, or television. Television, of course, also facilitates the transmission of gestures and visual clues. At times, two or more channels are used. In a telephone conversation, for instance, two people may reach a basic agreement that they later confirm by a letter. Since many choices are available, each with advantages and disadvantages, the proper selection of the channel is vital for effective communication.

The Receiver of the Message

The receiver has to be ready for the message so that it can be decoded into thought. A person thinking about an exciting football game may pay insufficient attention to what is being said about an inventory report, for example, thus increasing the probability of a communication breakdown. The next step in the process is decoding, in which the receiver converts the message into thoughts. Accurate communication can occur only when both the sender and the receiver attach the same or at least similar meanings to the symbols that compose the message. A message encoded into French requires a receiver who understands French. This is obvious; less obvious, and frequently overlooked, is the use of technical or professional jargon that may not be understood by the recipient of the message. So communication is not complete unless it is understood. Understanding is in the mind of both the sender and the receiver. Persons with closed minds will normally not completely understand messages, especially if the information is contrary to their value system.

Noise and Feedback in Communication

Unfortunately, communication is affected by "noise," which is anything—whether in the sender, the transmission, or the receiver—that hinders communication. For example:

A noisy or confined environment may hinder the development of a clear thought.

Encoding may be faulty because of the use of ambiguous symbols.

Transmission may be interrupted by static in the channel, such as may be experienced in a poor telephone connection.

Inaccurate reception may be caused by inattention.

Decoding may be faulty because the wrong meaning may be attached to words and other symbols.

Understanding can be obstructed by prejudices.

Desired change may not occur because of fear of possible consequences of the change.

To check the effectiveness of communication, *feedback* is essential. We can never be sure whether or not a message has been effectively encoded, transmitted, decoded, and understood until it is confirmed by feedback. Similarly, feedback indicates whether individual or organizational change has taken place as a result of communication.

Situational and Organizational Factors in Communication

Many situational and organizational factors affect the communication process. Such factors in the external environment may be educational, sociological, legal-political, and economic. For example, a repressive political environment will inhibit the free flow of communication. Another situational factor is geographic distance. A direct face-to-face communication is different from a telephone conversation with another person on the other side of the globe and different from an exchange of cables or letters. Time must also be considered in communication. The busy executive may not have sufficient time to receive and send information accurately. Other situational factors that affect communication within the enterprise include the organization structure, managerial and nonmanagerial processes, and technology. An example of the latter is the pervasive impact of computer technology on the handling of very large amounts of data.

In summary, the communication model provides an overview of the communication process, identifies the critical variables, and shows their relationships. This, in turn, helps managers to pinpoint communication problems and to take steps to solve them, or even better, to prevent the difficulties from occurring in the first place.

Communication in the Enterprise

In today's enterprises, information must flow faster than ever before. Even a short stoppage on a fast-moving production line can be very costly in lost output. It is, therefore, essential that production problems be communicated quickly for corrective action. Another important element is the amount of information, which has greatly increased over the years, frequently causing an information overload. What is often needed is not more information, but relevant information. It is necessary to determine what kind of information the manager needs to have for effective decision making. To obtain this information frequently requires getting information from managers' superiors and subordinates and also from departments and people elsewhere in an organization.

The Manager's Need to Know

To be effective, a manager needs information necessary to carry out managerial functions and activities. Yet even a casual glance at communication systems shows that managers often lack vital information for decision making; or they may get too much information, resulting in overload. It is evident that managers must be discriminating in selecting information. A simple way for a manager to start is to ask: "What do I really need to know for my job?" Or, "What would happen if I did not get this information on a regular basis?" It is not maximum information a manager needs, but pertinent information. Clearly, there is no universally applicable communication system; rather the system must be tailored to the individual manager's needs.

The Communication Flow in the Enterprise

In an effective enterprise, communication flows in various directions: downward, upward, and crosswise. Traditionally, downward communication was emphasized, but there is ample evidence that if communication flows only downward, problems will develop. In fact, one could argue that effective communication has to start with the subordinate, and this means primarily upward communication. Communication also flows horizontally, that is, between people on the same or similar organizational levels, and diagonally, involving persons from different levels who are not in direct reporting relationships with one another. You can see the different kinds of information flows in Figure 20-3.

Downward communication   Downward communication flows from people at higher levels to those at lower levels in the organizational hierarchy. This kind of communication exists especially in organizations with an authoritarian atmosphere. The kinds of media used for downward oral communication include instructions, speeches, meetings, the telephone, loudspeakers, and even the grapevine. Examples of written downward communication are memoranda, letters, handbooks, pamphlets, policy statements, and procedures.

Unfortunately, information is often lost or distorted as it comes down the chain of command. Top management's issuance of policies and procedures does not ensure communication. In fact, many directives are not understood or even read. Consequently, a feedback system is essential for finding out whether information was perceived as intended by the sender.

Downward flow of information through the different levels of the organization is time-consuming. Indeed, delays may be so frustrating that some top managers insist that information be sent directly to the person or group requiring it.

FIGURE 20-3

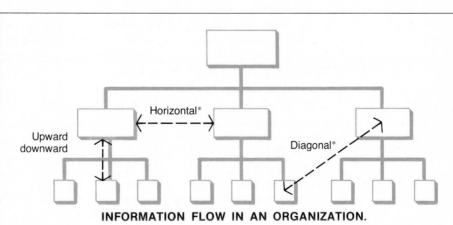

INFORMATION FLOW IN AN ORGANIZATION.

* Since horizontal and diagonal communication flows have some common characteristics, we call them crosswise communication and discuss them together later in this chapter.

Upward communication   Upward communication travels from subordinates to superiors and continues up the organizational hierarchy. Unfortunately, this flow is often hindered by managers in the communications chain who filter the messages and do not transmit all the information—especially unfavorable news—to their bosses. Yet, objective transmission of information is essential for control purposes. Upper management needs to know specifically about production performance, marketing information, financial data, what lower-level employees are thinking, and so on.

There is also a human perspective to upward communication, which is primarily nondirective and is usually found in participative and democratic organizational environments. Typical means for upward communication—besides the chain of command—are suggestion systems, appeal and grievance procedures, complaint systems, counseling sessions, joint setting of objectives in an effective MBO operation, the grapevine, group meetings, the practice of open-door policy, morale questionnaires, the exit interview, and the ombudsperson. The concept of the ombudsperson, used relatively little in the United States until recently, now seems to be gaining somewhat wider acceptance. Effective upward communication requires an environment in which subordinates feel free to communicate. Since the organizational climate is greatly influenced by upper management, the responsibility for creating a free flow of upward communication rests to a great extent—although not exclusively—with superiors.

Crosswise communication   Crosswise communication includes the horizontal flow of information between people on the same or similar organizational levels and diagonal flow between persons at different levels who have no direct reporting relationships. This kind of communication is used to speed information flow, to improve understanding, and to coordinate efforts for the achievement of organizational objectives. A great deal of communication does not follow the organizational hierarchy, but cuts across the chain of command.

The enterprise environment provides many occasions for *oral* communication. They range from the informal meeting of the company bowling team and lunch hours spent together to the more formal conferences and committee and board meetings. This kind of communication also occurs when individual members of different departments are grouped into task teams or project organizations. Finally, communication cuts across organizational boundaries when staff—which has an advisory function—interacts with line managers in different departments.

In addition, *written* forms of communication keep people informed about the enterprise. These written forms include the company newspaper or magazine and bulletin boards. Modern enterprises use many kinds of oral and written crosswise communication patterns to supplement the vertical flow of information.

Because information may not follow the chain of command, proper safeguards need to be taken to prevent potential problems. Specifically, crosswise communication should rest on the understanding that: (1) crosswise relationships will be encouraged wherever they are appropriate, (2) subordinates will refrain from making commitments beyond their authority, and (3) subordinates will keep superiors informed of important interdepartmental activities. In short, crosswise communication may create difficulties, but it is a necessity in many enterprises in order to respond to the needs of the complex and dynamic organizational environment.

Written, Oral, and Nonverbal Communication

Written and oral communication media have favorable and unfavorable characteristics; consequently, they are often used together so that the favorable qualities of each can complement the other. In addition, visual aids may be used to supplement both oral and written communications. For example, the lecture in the management training session may be more effective when written handouts, transparencies, and films are used. Evidence has shown that when a message is repeated in several media, the people receiving it will more accurately comprehend and recall it.

In selecting the media, we must consider the communicator, the audience, and the situation. An executive who feels uncomfortable in front of a large audience may choose written communication rather than a speech. On the other hand, certain people who may not read a memo may be reached and motivated by direct oral communication. Situations may also demand a specific medium. For example, President Carter would probably not have been able to handle the hostage crisis in Iran effectively through lengthy written communication. Face-to-face interaction, give-and-take with his advisers, was called for in this crisis situation.

Advantages

Written communication   Written communication has the advantage of providing records, references, and legal defenses. We can carefully prepare the message and direct it to a large audience through mass mailings. Written communication can also promote uniformity in policy and procedure and can reduce costs in some cases.

Disadvantages

The disadvantages are that written messages may create mountains of paper, may be poorly expressed by ineffective writers, and may provide no immediate feedback. Consequently, it may take a long time to know whether a message has been received and properly understood.

Oral communication   A great deal of information is communicated orally. One study found that 70 percent of the respondents stated that superiors gave 75 percent of their assignments orally.[1] Oral communication can take place in a face-to-face meeting of two people, or when a manager addresses a large audience; it can be formal or informal, and it can be planned or accidental.

Advantages

The advantages of oral communication are that it can provide for speedy interchange with immediate feedback. People can ask questions and clarify points. In a face-to-face interaction, the effect can be noted. Furthermore, a meeting with the superior may give the subordinate a feeling of importance. Clearly, informal or planned meetings can greatly contribute to the understanding of the issues.

Disadvantages

However, oral communication also has disadvantages. It does not always save time, as any manager knows who has attended meetings in which no results or

[1]M. H. Brenner and N. B. Sigband, "Organizational Communication—An Analysis Based on Empirical Data," *Academy of Management Journal*, vol. 16, no. 2 (June 1973), pp. 323–325.

agreements were achieved. These meetings can be costly in terms of time and money.

Nonverbal communication   We communicate in many different ways. What we say can be reinforced (or contradicted) by nonverbal communication, such as facial expressions and body gestures. Nonverbal communication is expected to support the verbal. But it does not always do so. For example, an autocratic manager who pounds a fist on the table while announcing that from now on participative management will be practiced certainly creates a credibility gap. Similarly, managers who state that they have an open-door policy, but then have a secretary carefully screen people who want to see the boss, create an incongruency between what they say and the way they behave. Clearly, nonverbal communication may support or contradict verbal communication, giving rise to the saying that actions often speak louder than words.

Barriers and Breakdowns in Communication

It is probably no surprise that managers frequently cite communication breakdowns as one of their most important problems. However, communication problems are often symptoms of more deeply rooted problems. For example, poor planning may be the cause for uncertainty about the direction of the firm. Similarly, a poorly designed organization structure may not clearly communicate organizational relationships. Vague performance standards may leave managers uncertain about what is expected of them. Thus, the perceptive manager will first look for the causes of communication problems instead of just dealing with the symptoms. Barriers can exist in the sender, in the transmission of the message, or in the receiver.

Lack of Planning

Good communication seldom happens by chance. Too often people start talking and writing without first thinking, planning, and stating the purpose of the message. Yet, giving the reasons for a directive, selecting the most appropriate channel, and choosing proper timing can greatly improve understanding and reduce resistance to change.

Unclarified Assumptions

Often overlooked, yet very important, are the uncommunicated assumptions that underlie messages. A customer may send a note that she will visit a vendor's plant. Then she may assume that the vendor will meet her at the airport, reserve a hotel room, arrange for transportation, and set up a full-scale review of the program at the plant. But the vendor may assume that the customer is coming to town mainly to attend a wedding and will make a routine call at the plant. The unclarified assumptions of both may result in confusion and the loss of good will.

Semantic Distortion

Another barrier to effective communication is semantic distortion, which can be deliberate or accidental. An advertisement saying "We sell for less" is deliberately ambiguous; it raises the question: Less than what? Words may evoke different responses. To some people, the word "government" may mean interference or deficit spending; to others, the same word may mean help, equalization, and justice.

Poorly Expressed Messages

No matter how clear the idea in the mind of the sender of communication, it may still be marked by poorly chosen words, omissions, lack of coherence, poor organization of ideas, awkward sentence structure, platitudes, unnecessary jargon, and a failure to clarify the implications of the message. This lack of clarity and precision, which can be costly, can be avoided through greater care in encoding the message.

Loss in Transmission and Poor Retention

In a series of transmissions from one person to the next, the message becomes less and less accurate. Poor retention of information is another serious problem. One study found, for example, that employees retain but 50 percent of the information they receive and supervisors only 60 percent.[2] This finding makes the necessity for repetition of the message and the use of several channels rather obvious. Consequently, companies often use more than one channel to communicate the same message.

Poor Listening and Premature Evaluation

There are many talkers but few listeners. Everyone probably has observed people entering a discussion with comments that have no relation to the topic. One reason may be that these persons are pondering their own problems—such as preserving their own egos or making a good impression on other group members—instead of listening to the conversaton.

Listening demands full attention and self-discipline. It also means avoiding premature evaluation of what the other person has to say. A common tendency is to judge, to approve or disapprove what is being said, rather than trying to understand the speaker's frame of reference. Yet listening without making a hasty judgment can make the whole enterprise more effective and more efficient. For example, sympathetic listening can result in better labor-management relations and greater understanding among managers; specifically, sales personnel may better understand the problems of production people, and the credit manager may realize that an overrestrictive credit policy may lead to a disproportionate loss in sales. In short, listening with empathy can reduce some of the daily frustrations of organized life and result in better communication.

Impersonal Communication

Effective communication is more than simply transmitting information to employees. It requires face-to-face communication in an environment of openness and trust. One story illustrates how this simple but effective communication technique may be overlooked.[3]

---

[2]R. Bellows, T. Q. Gilson, and G. S. Odiorne, *Executive Skills* (Englewood Cliffs, N.J.: Prentice-Hall, Inc., 1962), pp. 60–61.
[3]Roger D'Aprix, "The Oldest (and Best) Way to Communicate with Employees," *Harvard Business Review*, vol. 60, no. 5 (September–October, 1982), pp. 30–32.

A company was about to install a sophisticated $300,000 closed-circuit television system to improve the transmission of information to employees. When a management consultant recommended instead that the president join his people during the coffee break, rather than sipping his coffee in a closed group of top executives, he was skeptical. This suggestion seemed radical, but he agreed to try it. The experiment was a failure because the president found that his employees would not talk to him. After some soul-searching, the president tried once more meeting with his employees face-to-face during the coffee break, but at this time he talked about *their* concern (the opening of a European plant). To the president's surprise, employees talked openly about what was on their mind. In fact the communication went so well that the president requested that his executive group mingle with their people for kaffeeklatsches.

This occurrence illustrates that real improvement of communication often requires not expensive and sophisticated (and impersonal) communications media, but the willingness of superiors to engage in face-to-face communication. This informal gathering without status trappings or a formal authority base may be threatening to a top executive, but it may be worth taking the risk to benefit from better communication.

Distrust, Threat, and Fear

Distrust, threat, and fear undermine communication. In a climate containing these forces, any message will be viewed with skepticism. Distrust can be the result of inconsistent behavior by the superior, or it can be due to past experiences in which the subordinate was punished for honestly reporting unfavorable, but true, information to the boss. Similarly, in the light of threats—whether real or imagined—people tend to tighten up, become defensive, and distort information. What is needed is a climate of trust, which facilitates open and honest communication.

Insufficient Period for Adjustment to Change

The purpose of communication is to effect change which may seriously concern employees: shifts in the time, place, type, and order of work or shifts in group arrangements or skills to be used. Some communications point to the need for further training, career adjustment, or status changes. Changes affect people in different ways, and it may take time to think through the full meaning of a message. Consequently, it is important to efficiency not to force change before people can adjust to its implications.

Information Overload

One might think that more and unrestricted information flow would help to overcome communication problems. But unrestricted flow may result in too much information. People respond to information overload in various ways.[4] First, they may *disregard* certain information. A person getting too much mail may simply ignore letters that should be answered. Second, if they are overwhelmed with too

Reactions to information overload

---

[4]For a detailed discussion of this topic, see Miller's analysis of information overload in D. Katz and D. L. Kahn, *The Social Psychology of Organizations*, 2d ed. (New York: John Wiley & Sons, Inc., 1978), pp. 451–455.

much information, people *make errors* in processing it. For example, they may leave out the word "not" in a message, which reverses the intended meaning. Third, people may *delay* processing information either permanently or with the intention of catching up in the future. Fourth, a person may *filter* information. Filtering may be helpful when the most pressing and most important information is processed first and the less important messages receive lower priority. However, chances are that attention will be given first to matters that are easy to handle, while more difficult but perhaps critical messages are ignored. Finally, people respond to information overload by simply *escaping* from the task of communication. In other words, they ignore information or they do not communicate information because of an overload.

Some responses to information overload may be adaptive tactics that can, at times, be functional. For example, delaying the processing of information until the amount is reduced can be effective. On the other hand, withdrawing from the task of communicating is usually not a helpful response. Another way to approach the overload problem is to reduce the demands for information. Within an enterprise, this may be accomplished by insisting that only essential data be processed, such as information showing critical deviations from plans. Reducing the external demand for information is usually more difficult because these demands are less controllable by managers. An example is the government's demand for detailed documentation on government contracts. Companies that do business with the government simply have to comply with these requests.

Toward Effective Communication

The communication process model introduced at the beginning of this chapter (Figure 20-2) helps to identify the critical elements in the communication process. At each stage, breakdowns can occur—in the encoding of the message by the sender, in the transmission of the message, and in the decoding and understanding of the message by the receiver. Certainly noise can interfere with effective communication at each stage of the process.

As noted in the communication process model, effective communication requires that encoding and decoding be done with symbols that are familiar to the sender and the receiver of the message. Thus, the manager (and especially the staff specialist) should avoid technical jargon, which is intelligible only to the experts in their particular field.

Guidelines for Improving Communication

Effective communication is the responsibility of all persons in the organization, managers as well as nonmanagers, who work toward a common aim. Whether communication is effective can be evaluated by the intended results. The following guidelines can help to overcome the barriers to communication.

1 Senders of messages must clarify in their minds what they want to communicate. This means that one of the first steps in communicating is to clarify the purpose of the message and make a plan to achieve the intended end.

2   The planning of the communication should not be done in a vacuum. Instead others should be consulted and encouraged to participate: to collect the facts, analyze the message, and select the appropriate media. For example, you may ask a colleague to read an important memo before you distribute it throughout the organization. The content of the message should fit the level of knowledge of the recipients of the message and the organizational climate.

3   Consider the needs of the receivers of the information. Whenever appropriate, communicate something that is of value to them, in the short-run as well as in the more distant future. At times, unpopular actions that affect employees in the short-run may be more easily accepted if they are beneficial to them in the long run. For instance, shortening the workweek may be more acceptable if it is made clear that this action will strengthen the competitive position of the company in the long run.

4   There is a saying that the tone makes the music. Similarly in communication the tone of voice, the choice of language, and the congruency between what is said and how it is said influence the reactions of the receiver of the message. An autocratic manager ordering subordinate supervisors to practice participative management will create a credibility gap that will be difficult to overcome.

5   Too often information is transmitted without communicating, as communication is only complete when the message is understood by the receiver. And one never knows whether communication is understood unless the sender gets feedback. This can be accomplished by asking questions, requesting a reply to a letter, and encouraging receivers to give their reactions to the message.

6   The function of communication is more than transmitting information. It also deals with emotions that are very important in interpersonal relationships between superiors, subordinates, and colleagues in an organization. Furthermore, communication is vital for creating an environment in which people are motivated to work toward the goals of the enterprise, while, at the same time, they achieve their personal aims. Another function of communication is control. As we have seen in the discussion of management by objectives, control does not necessarily mean top-down control. Instead, the MBO philosophy emphasizes self-control, which demands clear communication with understanding of the criteria against which performance is measured.

7   Effective communication is not only the responsibility of the sender, but also of the receiver of the information. Thus, listening is an aspect that needs additional comment.

Listening: The Key to Understanding

Listening is a skill that can be developed. Professor Keith Davis proposed ten guides to improved listening: (1) stop talking, (2) put the talker at ease, (3) show the talker that you want to listen, (4) remove distractions, (5) empathize with the talker, (6) be patient, (7) hold your temper, (8) go easy on arguments and criticism,

(9) ask questions, and (10) stop talking![5] The first and the last guides are the most important; we have to stop talking before we can listen.

Carl R. Rogers and F. J. Roethlisberger suggest a simple experiment.[6] It goes like this. The next time you have an argument try to use the following simple rule: A person may only speak after the ideas and feelings of the previous speaker are repeated accurately to the speaker's satisfaction. This rule sounds simple, yet is difficult to practice. It requires listening, understanding, and empathy. But managers who have used this technique have reported a considerable number of cases in which they were not communicating accurately.

Some Tips for Improving Written Communication

Improving written communication

Effective writing may be the exception rather than the rule; nor do education and intelligence guarantee good writing. Many people fall into the habit of using technical jargon that can be understood only by experts in the same field. Common problems in written communication are that writers omit the conclusion or bury it in the report, are too wordy, and use poor grammar, ineffective sentence structure, and incorrect spelling. Yet a few guidelines suggested by Keith Davis may do much to improve written communication:[7]

Use simple words and phrases.

Use short and familiar words.

Use personal pronouns (such as "you") whenever appropriate.

Give illustrations and examples; use charts.

Use short sentences and paragraphs.

Use active verbs such as "The manager *plans* . . ."

Avoid unnecessary words

Writing style

Professor John Fielden suggests that the writing style should fit the situation and the effect you want to achieve.[8] Specifically, he recommends a forceful style when the writer has power; the tone should be polite, but firm. The passive style is appropriate when the writer is in a position lower than that of the recipient of the message. The personal style is recommended for communicating good news and making persuasive requests for action. The impersonal style is generally right for conveying negative information. The lively or colorful style is suitable for good-

---

[5]K. Davis and K. Newstrom, *Human Behavior at Work, Organizational Behavior*, 7th ed. (New York: McGraw-Hill Book Company, 1985), p. 438.

[6]"Barriers and Gateways to Communication," *Harvard Business Review*, vol. 30, no. 4 (July–August 1952), pp. 46–52.

[7]Davis and Newstrom, op. cit., p. 436.

[8]John S. Fielden, "What Do You Mean You Don't Like My Style?" *Harvard Business Review*, vol. 60, no. 3 (May–June 1982), pp. 128–138.

FIGURE 20-4

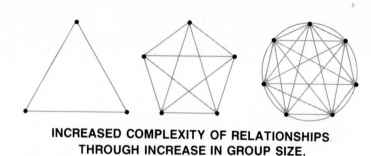

**INCREASED COMPLEXITY OF RELATIONSHIPS
THROUGH INCREASE IN GROUP SIZE.**

news items, advertisements, and sales letters. On the other hand, a less colorful style, combining the impersonal with the passive, may be appropriate for common business writing.

Effective Communication in the Group: The Committee

Managers spend a great deal of time in committees. The use of committees is not only due to the democratic tradition in American social life, but also to a growing emphasis on group management and group participation in organizations. In attempting to overcome some of the disadvantages of committees, managers may find the following guidelines to more effective communication useful.

1 Authority The committee's authority should be spelled out so that members know whether their responsibility is to make a decision, make a recommendation, or merely to deliberate and to give the chairperson some insights into the problem under discussion.

2 Size The size of the committee is very important. As shown in Figure 20-4, the complexity of interrelationships greatly increases with the size of the group. If the group is too large, there may not be enough opportunities for adequate communication among its members. On the other hand, if the group consists of only three persons, there is the possibility that two may form a coalition against the third member. No precise conclusions can be drawn here about the appropriate size. As a general rule, a committee should be large enough to promote deliberation and include the breadth of expertise required for the job but not so large as to waste time or foster indecision. The optimum committee size is thought by some to be at least five or six but not more than fifteen or sixteen. An analysis of small-group research indicates that the ideal committee size may be five when the five members possess adequate skills and knowledge to deal with problems facing the committee.[9] It is obvious that the larger the group, the greater the difficulty in obtaining a "meeting of the minds," and the more time necessary to allow everyone to contribute.

[9]See A. C. Filley, "Committee Management: Guidelines from Social Science Research," *California Management Review*, vol. 13, no. 1 (Fall 1970), pp. 13–21.

3 Membership The members of the committee must be selected carefully. If a committee is to be successful, the members must be representative of the interests they are intended to serve. They must also possess the required authority, and be able to perform well in a group. Finally, the members should have the capacity for communicating well and reaching group decisions by integrating group thinking rather than by inappropriate compromise.

4 Subject matter The subject matter must be carefully selected. Committee work should be limited to subject matter that can be handled in group discussion. Certain kinds of subjects lend themselves to committee action, while others do not. Jurisdictional disputes and strategy formulation, for example, may be suitable for group deliberation, while certain isolated, technical problems may be better solved by an expert in the specialized field. To make committees effective, an

Agenda

agenda and relevant information should be circulated well in advance so that the members can study the subject matter before the meeting.

5 Chairperson The selection of the chairperson is crucial for an effective committee meeting. Such a person can avoid the wastes and drawbacks of committees by planning the meeting, preparing the agenda, seeing that the results of research are available to the members ahead of time, formulating definite proposals for discussion or action, and conducting the meeting efficiently. The chairperson sets the tone of the meeting, integrates the ideas, and keeps the discussion from wandering.

6 Minutes Effective communication in committees usually requires circulating minutes and checking conclusions. At times, individuals leave the meeting with varying interpretations as to what was agreed. To avoid this, it is good to take careful minutes of the meeting and circulate them in draft form for correction or modification before the final copy is approved by the committee.

7 Cost effectiveness The committee must be worth its cost. It may be difficult to count the benefits, especially such intangible factors as morale, enhanced status of committee members, and the committee's value as a training device to enhance teamwork. But the committee can be justified only if the costs are offset by tangible and intangible benefits.

Electronic Media in Communication

Managers have studied and are gradually adopting various electronic devices that improve communication. Electronic equipment includes mainframe computers, minicomputers, and personal computers, electronic mail, electronic typewriters, the new cellular telephone that lets you make telephone calls from your car, and the beeper that keeps you in contact with the office. The impact of computers on all phases of the management process will be discussed later in connection with the management information system and will therefore be mentioned only briefly here. Let us first look at the increasing use of teleconferencing.

Teleconferencing

For some time now companies such as IBM, Bank of America, and Hughes have used teleconferencing.[10] However, the systems vary widely, including audio systems, audio systems with snapshots displayed on the video monitor, and live video systems. You can see, therefore, that the term "teleconferencing" is difficult to define. In general, most people think of a teleconference as a group of people interacting with each other using audio and video media with moving or still pictures.

Full-motion video is frequently used to hold meetings among managers. They not only hear each other, but they can also see each other's expression or discuss some visual display. This kind of communication is, of course, rather expensive, and audio in combination with still video may be used instead. This method of communicating may be useful for showing charts or illustrations when conducting a technical discussion.

Advantages

Some of the potential advantages of teleconferencing include savings in travel expenses and travel time. Also, conferences may be held when the need arises without making travel plans long in advance. Teleconferencing allows meetings to be held more frequently, improving communication between, for example, the headquarters and the geographically scattered divisions.

Drawbacks

But there are also drawbacks to teleconferencing. Because of its ease for arranging meetings, they may be held more often than necessary. Moreover, since this approach uses rather new technology, the equipment is subject to breakdowns. Most important, perhaps, teleconferencing is still a poor substitute for meeting with other persons face to face. Despite these limitations, we can expect increased use of teleconferencing in the future.

The Use of Computers for Information Handling

Electronic data processing now makes it possible to handle large amounts of data and to make information available to a large number of people. Thus, one can obtain, analyze, and organize timely data rather inexpensively. But it must never be forgotten that data is not necessarily information; to be this it must inform someone. The new computer graphics can inform visually, displaying important company information. At PepsiCo Inc., managers, instead of digging through reams of computer printouts, now can quickly display a colored map showing their competitive picture.[11] More about the impact of the computer on the process of managing later in Chapter 22.

Summary

Communication is the transfer of information from the sender to the receiver, with the information being understood by both the sender and the receiver. The communication process begins with the sender, who encodes an idea which is sent in

[10]R. Johansen and C. Bullen, "What to Expect from Teleconferencing," *Harvard Business Review*, vol. 62, no. 2 (March–April 1984), pp. 164–174.

[11]"Management Warms Up to Computer Graphics," *Business Week*, Aug. 13, 1984, pp. 96–101.

oral, written, or visual form to the receiver. The receiver decodes the message and gains an understanding of what the sender wants to communicate. This, in turn, may result in some change or action. But the communication process may be interrupted by "noise," that is, by anything that hinders communication. In an organization, managers should have the information necessary to doing a good job. The information may not only flow downward or upward in the organization structure, but may also flow horizontally or diagonally. Communication can be in written form; but even more information is communicated orally. In addition, people communciate through gestures and facial expressions.

Communication is hindered by barriers and breakdowns in communication. Understanding these barriers and applying the guides for effective communication and listening facilitates not only understanding but also managing. A great deal of time is spent communicating in committee meetings. Therefore guidelines are given to make them more productive. The electronic media can improve communication as illustrated by teleconferencing and the application of computers, two of many approaches to handling the increasing amount of information in organizations.

Key Ideas and Concepts for Review

Communication
Communication process model
"Noise" in communication
Downward communication
Upward communication
Crosswise communication
Written communication—advantages and
  disadvantages
Oral communication—advantages and
  disadvantages

Nonverbal communication
Barriers and breakdowns in
  communication
Responses to information overload
Guidelines for improving communication
Recommendations for making committees
  effective
Teleconferencing

For Discussion

1 Briefly describe the communication process model. Select a communication problem and determine the cause(s). Apply the model in your analysis.

2 List different channels for transmitting a message. Discuss the advantages and disadvantages of the various channels.

3 What are some kinds of downward communication? Discuss those used most frequently in an enterprise you are familiar with. How effective are the various types?

4 What are some problems in upward communication? What would you suggest to overcome the difficulties?

5   What are the advantages and disadvantages of written and oral communication? Which do you prefer? Under what circumstances?

6   What is information overload? Do you ever experience it? How do you deal with it?

7   How well do you listen? How could you improve your listening skills?

8   Think of a situation at home or at work and identify communication problems you have observed or experienced. Discuss how the communication model in this chapter can help you to locate the problems.

9   Take a public person who communicates well and discuss this person's characteristics as they relate to communication.

10   Describe one effective and one ineffective committee or group meeting in which you were a participant. Why was one effective and the other one ineffective?

CASE 20-1

HAYNES FASHION STORES, INCORPORATED

Joyce Haynes, just graduated from college, joined her father, Dudley Haynes, president of Haynes Fashion Stores, Incorporated, a chain of thirty women's apparel stores in the New England area. The company had been founded by Ms. Haynes grandfather over 50 years ago. With her grandfather's and, for the past 20 years, her father's drive and knowledge of women's fashions and of how to buy and sell them, the company had developed from a single store in Hartford, Connecticut, to a fairly large and highly profitable chain of stores. Dudley Haynes' management style was much like his father's. He knew what he was doing and how to do it and he prided himself on being able to keep his hands on details in buying, advertising, and store management. Every one of his store managers, as well as his top vice-presidents and headquarters staff people, met with the president every 2 weeks in Hartford. Between these meetings, Mr. Haynes spent 2 or 3 days each week visiting the stores and working with store managers.

But his major worries were communication and motivation. He felt that, at the conferences he held, all his managers and staff people listened carefully. But judging from what they did, he began to wonder whether they heard him or whether they had listened carefully. The results were that many of his policies were not being strictly followed in the stores; he often had to rewrite advertising copy; in some of the stores the employees had joined the clerks union; and he increasingly heard of things he did not like. Among them were reports that many of his employees and even some of his managers felt that they did not know what the Haynes company was trying to do and believed they could do better if they had a chance to communicate with Mr. Haynes and his headquarters vice-presidents. He also had a strong feeling that many of his managers in headquarters and in the stores, as well as most of the store clerks, were merely doing their jobs without showing any real imagination or drive. He was also concerned that some of his best people had quit and taken positions with a competitor.

When his daughter walked into his office to take a position as his special assistant, he said, "Joyce, I am worried about how things are going. Apparently, my two problems are communication and motivation. Now, I know that you took some courses in management in school. I have heard you talk of the problems, barriers, and techniques of communication. I have heard from you about some fellows—Maslow, Herzberg, Vroom, McClelland, and others—who you thought knew a great deal about motivation. While I doubt that these psychology types knew much about busi-

ness and I feel that I know what motivates people—primarily money, good bosses, and a good place to work—I wonder if you have learned anything that will help me. I hope so, for that college education of yours has cost me a lot of money. What do you suggest?"

1 If you were Ms. Haynes, what would you say to your father?

2 How would you go about analyzing the communication problem, and what problems do you see already from the case?

3 How would you suggest that the movivation theories of the various people you have studied might be applied to the Haynes Fashion Stores? Is there anything else you would want to know?

CASE 20-2

HOME RADIO AND TELEVISION COMPANY

Robert Gates founded a small radio manufacturing plant in Detroit in the 1930s. From this small start came one of the nation's largest radio, television, and allied products companies. By 1965 its sales approached $300 million annually, with 15,000 employees and ten manufacturing locations. Throughout its growth the founder remained active and imaginative, the driving force of the company. In earlier days every manager and worker knew him, and he was able to call most of them by their first names, so even after the company grew fairly large, people felt that they knew the founder and chief executive, and this strong feeling of personal loyalty had much to do with the fact that the company was never unionized.

However, as the company prospered and grew, Mr. Gates worried that it was losing its "small-

company" spirit. He also worried that communications were suffering, that his objectives and philosophy were not being understood in the company, that much wasteful duplication was occurring through poor knowledge of what others in the company were doing, and that new product development and marketing were suffering as a result. Likewise, he was concerned that he had lost touch with the people.

To solve the communication problem, he hired and had report to him a director of communication. Between the two, they put into effect every communication device they found other companies using: bulletin boards in every office and plant throughout the country; a revitalized company newspaper carrying much company and personal news affecting all locations; "Company Fact Books" for every employee, giving significant information about the company; regular profit sharing letters; company-sponsored courses to teach communication; monthly 1-day meetings at headquarters for the top 100 executives; annual 3-day meetings of 1200 managers of all levels at a resort area; and a large number of special committees to discuss company matters.

After much time, effort, and expense, Mr. Gates was disappointed to find that his problems of communication and of loss of the small-company feeling still existed and that the results of his programs did not seem to be significant.

1 Why do you believe that Mr. Gates was disappointed? Should he have been?

2 What do you see as the company's real communication problem?

3 What would you suggest to improve communication in the company?

4 Was Mr. Gates right in believing that communication would solve the problem of maintaining the small-company spirit?

For Further Information

"Ten Commandments of Good Communication," American Management Association. In H. Koontz, C. O'Donnell, and H. Weihrich (eds.), *Management—A Book of Readings*, 5th ed. (New York: McGraw-Hill Book Company, 1980) pp. 565–566.

Axley, S. R. "Managerial and Organizational Communication in Terms of the Conduit Metaphor," *Academy of Management Journal*, vol. 9, no. 3 (July 1984), pp. 428–437.

Fielden, J. "What Do You Mean I Can't Write?" in *Business Classics: Fifteen Key Concepts for Managerial Success* (Boston: President and Fellows of Harvard College, 1975), pp. 125–133.

Flesch, R. *The Art of Plain Talk* (New York: P. F. Collier & Son Corporation, 1967).

Greenbaum, H. H. "The Audit of Organizational Communication," *Academy of Management Journal*, vol. 17, no. 4 (December 1974), pp. 739–754.

"How Personal Computers Can Trip Up Executives," *Business Week*, Sept. 24, 1984, pp. 94–102.

"It's Rush Hour for 'Telecommuting'," *Business Week*, Jan. 23, 1984, pp. 99–102.

Josefowitz, N. "Management Men and Women: Closed vs. Open Doors," *Harvard Business Review*, vol. 58, no. 5 (September–October 1980), pp. 56–62.

Rowe, M. P., and M. Baker. "Are You Hearing Enough Employee Concerns?" *Harvard Business Review*, vol. 62, no. 3 (May–June 1984), pp. 127–135.

Schein, E. H. "Improving Face-to-Face Relationships," *Sloan Management Review*, vol. 22 (Winter 1981), pp. 43–52.

Strunk, W., Jr., and E. B. White. *The Elements of Style*, 3rd ed. (New York: Macmillan Publishing Company, Inc., 1979).

Tortoriello, T. R., S. J. Blatt, and S. De Wine. *Communication in the Organization: An Applied Approach* (New York: McGraw-Hill Book Company, 1978).

Wolf, M. P., D. F. Keyser, and R. R. Aurner. *Effective Communication in Business* (Cincinnati: South-Western Publishing Company, 1979).

Summary of Major Principles of Leading

In the area of managerial leading, there are a few major principles, or guidelines, that can be summarized. They are the following

Principle of harmony of objectives The more managers can harmonize the personal goals of individuals with the goals of the enterprise, the more effective and efficient the enterprise will be.

Principle of motivation Since motivation is not a simple cause-and-effect matter, the more managers carefully assess the reward structure, look upon it from a situation and contingency point of view, and integrate it into the entire system of managing, the more effective a motivational program will be.

Principle of leadership Since people tend to follow those who, in their view, offer them a means of satisfying their personal goals, the more managers understand what motivates their subordinates and how these motivations operate, and the more they reflect this understanding in carrying out their managerial actions, the more effective they are likely to be as leaders.

Principle of communication clarity Communication tends to be clear when it is expressed in a language and transmitted in a way that can be understood by the receiver.

The responsibility of the sender is to formulate the message so that it is understandable to the receiver. This responsibility pertains primarily to written and oral communication and points to the necessity for planning the message, stating the underlying assumptions, and applying the generally accepted rules for effective writing and speaking.

Principle of communication integrity The greater the integrity and consistency of written, oral, and nonverbal messages, as well as of the moral behavior of the sender, the greater the acceptance of the message by the receiver.

Principle of supplemental use of informal organization Communication tends to be more effective when managers utilize the informal organization to supplement the communication channels of the formal organization.

Informal organization is a phenomenon managers must accept. Information, true or not, flows quickly through the informal organization. Consequently, managers should take advantage of this device to correct misinformation and to provide information that cannot be effectively sent or appropriately received through the formal communication system.

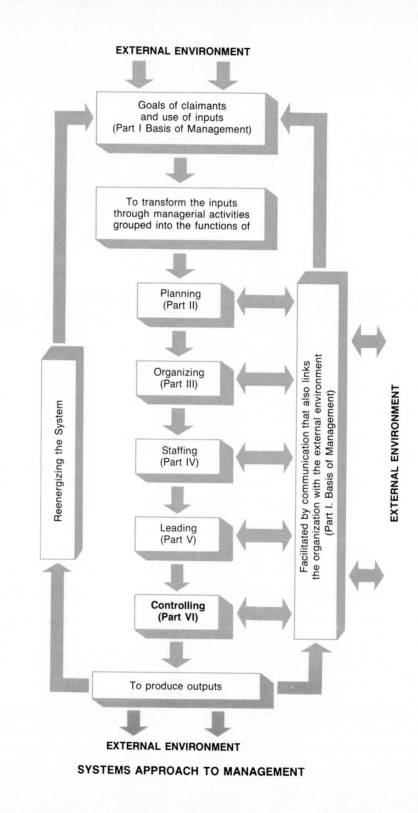

EXTERNAL ENVIRONMENT

Goals of claimants
and use of inputs
(Part I Basis of Management)

To transform the inputs
through managerial activities
grouped into the functions of

Planning
(Part II)

Organizing
(Part III)

Staffing
(Part IV)

Leading
(Part V)

**Controlling
(Part VI)**

Reenergizing the System

Facilitated by communication that also links
the organization with the external environment
(Part I. Basis of Management)

EXTERNAL ENVIRONMENT

To produce outputs

EXTERNAL ENVIRONMENT

SYSTEMS APPROACH TO MANAGEMENT

VI

Controlling

21

The System and Process of Controlling

CHAPTER OBJECTIVES

After reading this chapter, you should understand:

1 The steps in the basic control process
2 The importance of critical control points
3 Control as a feedback system
4 That because of time lags in feedback control, real-time information will not solve all the problems of management control
5 That feedforward control systems can make management control more effective
6 The requirements for effective controls

Definition of controlling

Planning and controlling

The managerial function of *controlling* is the measurement and correction of performance in order to make sure that enterprise objectives and the plans devised to attain them are accomplished. Planning and controlling are closely related. In fact, some writers on management think that these functions cannot be separated. We consider it wise to separate them conceptually, however, and therefore discuss them in Parts II and VI of this book. Still, planning and controlling may be viewed as the blades of a pair of scissors; the scissors cannot work unless there are two blades as illustrated in Figure 21-1. Without objectives and plans, control is not possible, because performance has to be compared against some established criteria.

Controlling is the function of every manager from president to supervisor.

FIGURE 21-1

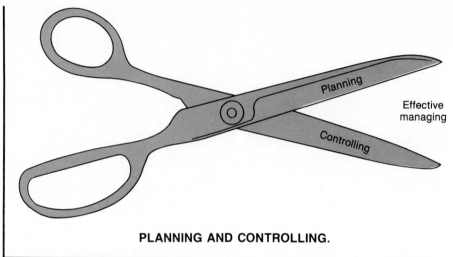

PLANNING AND CONTROLLING.

Some managers, particularly at lower levels, forget that the primary responsibility for the exercise of control rests in every manager charged with the execution of plans. Occasionally, because of the authority of upper-level managers and their resultant responsibility, top- and upper-level control is so emphasized that people assume that little controlling is needed at lower levels. Although the scope of control varies among managers, those at all levels have responsibility for the execution of plans, and control is therefore an essential managerial function at every level.

The Basic Control Process

Control techniques and systems are essentially the same for cash, office procedures, morale, product quality, or anything else. The basic control process, wherever it is found and whatever is being controlled, involves three steps: (1) establishing standards, (2) measuring performance against these standards, and (3) correcting variations from standards and plans.

1 Establishment of Standards

Because plans are the yardsticks against which managers devise controls, the first step in the control process logically would be to establish plans. However, since plans vary in detail and complexity and since managers cannot usually watch everything, special standards are established. Standards are by definition simply criteria of performance. They are the selected points in an entire planning program at which measures of performance are made so as to give managers signals as to how things are going without their having to watch every step in the execution of plans.

There are many kinds of standards. Among the best are verifiable goals or objectives as suggested in the discussion of managing by objectives. (See Chapter

5.) You will learn more about standards, especially about those that point out deviations at critical points, in the next section.

2 Measurement of Performance

Although such measurement is not always practicable, the measurement of performance against standards should ideally be on a forward-looking basis so that deviations may be detected in advance of their occurrence and avoided by appropriate actions. The alert, forward-looking manager can sometimes predict probable departures from standards. In the absence of such ability, however, deviations should be disclosed as early as possible.

If standards are appropriately drawn and if means are available for determining exactly what subordinates are doing, appraisal of actual or expected performance is fairly easy. But there are many activities for which it is difficult to develop accurate standards, and there are many activities that are hard to measure. It may be quite simple to establish labor-hour standards for the production of a mass-produced item, and it may be equally simple to measure performance against these standards, but if the item is custom-made, the appraisal of performance may be a formidable task because standards are difficult to set.

Moreover, in the less technical kinds of work, not only may standards be hard to develop but also appraisal will be difficult. For example, to control the work of the finance vice-president or the industrial relations director is not easy because definite standards are not easily developed. The superior of these managers often relies on vague standards, such as the financial health of the business, the attitude of labor unions, the absence of strikes, the enthusiasm and loyalty of subordinates, the expressed admiration of business associates, and the overall success of the department (often measured in a negative way by lack of evidence of failure). The superior's measurements are often equally vague. At the same time, if the department seems to be making the contribution expected of it at a reasonable cost and without too many serious errors, and if the measurable accomplishments give evidence of sound management, a general appraisal may be adequate. The point is that, as jobs move away from the assembly line, the shop, or the accounting machine, controlling them becomes more complex and often even more important.

3 Correction of Deviations

If standards are drawn to reflect the various positions in an organization structure and if performance is measured in these terms, it is easier to correct deviations, since the manager then knows exactly where, in the assignment of individual or group duties, the corrective measures must be applied.

Correction of deviations is the point at which control can be seen as a part of the whole system of management and can be related to the other managerial functions: Managers may correct deviations by redrawing their plans or by modifying their goals. (This is an exercise of the principle of navigational change.) Or they may correct deviations by exercising their organizing function through reassignment or clarification of duties. They may correct, also, by additional staffing, by better selection and training of subordinates, or by that ultimate restaffing measure—firing. Or, again, they may correct through better leading—fuller explanation of the job or more effective leadership techniques.

Critical Control Points and Standards

Standards are yardsticks against which actual or expected performance is measured. In a simple operation, a manager might control through careful personal observation of the work being done. However, in most operations this is not possible because of the complexity of the operations and the fact that a manager has far more to do than personally observe performance for a whole day. A manager must choose points for special attention and then watch them to be sure that the whole operation is proceeding as planned.

Critical points

The points selected for control should be *critical*, in the sense either of being limiting factors in the operation or of showing better than other factors whether plans are working out. With such standards, managers can handle a larger group of subordinates and thereby increase their span of management, with resulting cost savings and improvement of communication.

There are, however, no specific catalogs of controls available to all managers because of the peculiarities of various enterprises and departments, the variety of products and services to be measured, and the innumerable planning programs to be followed. At the same time, a number of types of critical-point standards have been used. Nonetheless, all managers must tailor their own controls and control standards to fit their individual needs.

The ability to select critical points of control is one of the arts of management, since sound control depends on them. In this connection, managers must ask themselves such questions as: What will best reflect the goals of my department? What will best show me when these goals are not being met? What will best measure critical deviations? What will inform me as to who is responsible for any failure? What standards will cost the least? For what standards is information economically available?

Types of Critical-Point Standards

Every objective, every goal of the many planning programs, every activity of these programs, every policy, every procedure, and every budget become standards against which actual or expected performance might be measured. In practice, however, standards tend to be of the following types: (1) physical standards, (2) cost standards, (3) capital standards, (4) revenue standards, (5) program standards, (6) intangible standards, and (7) goal standards.

1 Physical standards   Physical standards are nonmonetary measurements and are common at the operating level where materials are used, labor is employed, services are rendered, and goods are produced. They may reflect quantities such as labor-hours per unit of output, pounds of fuel per horsepower produced, ton-miles of freight traffic carried, units of production per machine-hour, or feet of wire per ton of copper. Physical standards may also reflect quality, such as hardness of bearings, closeness of tolerances, rate of climb of an airplane, durability of a fabric, or fastness of a color.

2 Cost standards   Cost standards are monetary measurements, and, like physical standards, are common at the operating level. They attach monetary values to the costs of operations. Illustrative of cost standards are such widely used measures as direct and indirect cost per unit produced, labor cost per unit or per hour, material cost per unit, machine-hour costs, costs per plane reservation, selling costs per dollar or unit of sales, and costs per foot of oil well drilled.

3 Capital standards   There are a variety of capital standards, all arising from the application of monetary measurements to physical items. They have to do with the capital invested in the firm rather than with operating costs and are therefore related to the balance sheet rather than to the income statement. Perhaps the most widely used standard for new investment, as well as for overall control, is return on investment. The typical balance sheet will disclose other capital standards, such as ratios of current assets to current liabilities, debt to net worth, fixed investment to total investment, cash and receivables to payables, and notes or bonds to stock, and the size and turnover of inventories.

4 Revenue standards   Revenue standards arise from attaching monetary values to sales. They may include such standards as revenue per bus passenger-mile, average sale per customer, or sales per capita in a given market area.

5 Program standards   A manager may be assigned to install a variable budget program, a program for formally following the development of new products, or a program for improving the quality of a sales force. Although some subjective judgment may have to be applied in appraising program performance, timing and other factors can be used as objective standards.

6 Intangible standards   More difficult to set are standards not expressed in either physical or monetary measurements. What standard can a manager use for determining the competence of the divisional purchasing agent or personnel director? What can one use for determining whether the advertising program meets both short- and long-term objectives? Or whether the public relations program is successful? Are supervisors loyal to the company's objectives? Is the office staff alert? Such questions show the difficulty of establishing standards for goals that cannot be given clear quantitative or qualitative measurement.

Many intangible standards exist in business, partially because adequate research into what constitutes desired performance has not been done above the level of the shop, the district sales office, the shipping room, or the accounting department. Perhaps a more important reason is that where human relationships count in performance, as they do above the basic operating levels, it is very hard to measure what is "good," "effective," or "efficient." Tests, surveys, and sampling techniques developed by psychologists and sociometrists have made it possible to probe human attitudes and drives, but many managerial controls over interpersonal relationships must continue to be based upon intangible standards, considered judgment, trial and error, and even, on occasion, sheer hunch.

7 Goals as standards   With the present tendency for better-managed enterprises to establish an entire network of verifiable qualitative or quantitative goals at every level of management, the use of intangible standards, while still important, is diminishing. In complex program operations as well as in the performance of managers themselves, modern managers are finding that through research and thinking, it is possible to define goals that can be used as performance standards. While the quantitative goals are likely to take the form of the standards outlined above, definition of qualitative goals represents a new development in the area of standards. For example, if the program of a district sales office is spelled out to include such elements as training salespeople in accordance with a plan with specific characteristics, the plan and its characteristics themselves furnish standards which tend to become objective and, therefore, "tangible."

Control as a Feedback System

Examples

Managerial control is essentially the same basic process as is found in physical, biological, and social systems. The steam engine governor is a simple mechanical feedback system; in other words, it is a system of feedback of information for control. In order to control an engine's speed under different load conditions, weights (balls) are whirled. As the speed increases, centrifugal force makes these weights exercise an outward thrust, which force in turn transmits a message to cut down the input of steam and thereby reduce the speed. As speed is reduced, the reverse occurs. Likewise, in the human body, a number of feedback systems control temperature, blood pressure, motor reactions, and other conditions. Another example of feedback is the grade a student receives on a midterm test. This is intended, of course, to give students information as to how they are doing, and if performance is less than desirable, to send a signal suggesting improvement. And in social systems, even excluding the managed formal organizations, one also finds feedback. For example, in the social system of baseball, there are such standards as three strikes and out, and even the seventh-inning stretch, which are accomplished, essentially, by the feedback of information which corrects those who would deviate.

Management control is usually perceived as a feedback system similar to that which operates in the usual household thermostat. This can be seen clearly by looking at the feedback process in management control shown in Figure 21-2. This system places control in a more complex and realistic light than would regarding it merely as a matter of establishing standards, measuring performance, and correcting for deviations. Managers do measure actual performance, compare this measurement against standards, and identify and analyze deviations. But then, to make the necessary corrections, they must develop a program for corrective action and implement this program in order to arrive at the performance desired.

Real-Time Information and Control

One of the interesting advances arising from the use of the computer and electronic gathering, transmission, and storage of data is the development of systems of real-time information. This is information about what is happening while it is happening. It is technically possible through various means to obtain real-time data

FIGURE 21-2

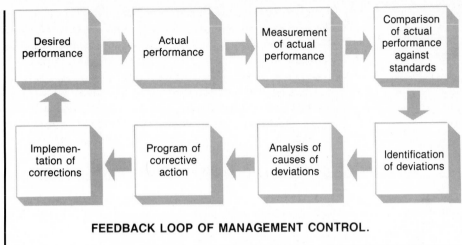

FEEDBACK LOOP OF MANAGEMENT CONTROL.

Examples

on many operations. For years, airlines have obtained information about vacant seats by simply pushing a flight number, trip segment (for example, Los Angeles to New York), and date into a memory system that immediately responds with information as to whether seats are available. Supermarkets and department stores have electronic cash registers in operation that transmit data on every sale immediately to a central data storage facility, where inventory, sales, gross profit, and other data can be obtained as they occur. A factory manager can have a system that reports at any time the status of production programs in terms of such things as the production point reached, labor-hours accumulated, and whether a project is late or on time in the manufacturing process. Some people see real-time information as a means of getting real-time control in areas of importance to managers; in other words, control effected at the very time information shows a deviation from plans. But reference to the management control feedback loop in Figure 21-2 will show that real-time information does not, except possibly in the simplest and most unusual cases, make possible real-time control. It is possible in many areas to collect real-time data measuring performance. It may also be possible in many of these cases to compare these data with standards and even to identify deviations. But the analysis of causes of deviations, the development of programs of correction, and the implementation of these programs are likely to be time-consuming tasks.

In the case of quality control, for example, it may take considerable time to discover what is causing factory rejects and more time to put corrective measures into effect. In the more complex case of inventory control, particularly in a manufacturing company where there are many items—raw materials, component parts, goods in process, and finished goods—the correction time may be very long. Once it is learned that an inventory is too high, the steps to get it back to the desired level may take a number of months. And so it goes with most instances of management control problems: time lags are unavoidable.

This does not mean that prompt measurement of performance is unimportant. The sooner managers know that activities for which they are responsible are not proceeding in accordance with plan, the faster they can take action to make corrections. But there is always the question of whether the cost of gathering real-time data is worth the few days saved. Often it is, as in the case of the airline business, where ready information on availability of seats is likely to be crucial to serving customers and filling airplanes. But in a major defense company producing one of the highest-priority defense equipment items, there was little real-time information in an otherwise highly sophisticated control information system. Even for this program, the benefit of gathering real-time data was thought not to be worth the expense because the correction process took so long.

Cost

Feedforward Control[1]

The time lag in the management control process shows that control must be directed toward the future if it is to be effective. It illustrates the problem of only using feedback from the output of a system and measuring this output as a means of control. It shows the deficiency of historical data such as those received from accounting reports. One of the difficulties with such historical data is that they tell business managers in November that they lost money in October (or even September) because of something that was done in July. At this late time, such information is only a distressingly interesting historical fact.

Insufficiency of feedback

What managers need for effective control is a system that will tell them, in time to take corrective action, that problems will occur if they do not do something about them now. Feedback of output of a system is not good enough for control. This kind of feedback is not much more than a postmortem, and no one has found a way to change the past.

Future-directed control is largely disregarded in practice, mainly because managers have been so dependent for purposes of control on accounting and statistical data. To be sure, in the absence of any means of looking forward, reference to history, on the questionable assumption that what is past is prologue, is admittedly better than no reference at all.

Techniques of Future-Directed Control

Neglect of future-directed control does not mean that nothing has been done. One common way many managers have practiced it is through careful and repeated forecasts using the latest available information, comparing what is desired with the forecasts, and introducing program changes so that forecasts can be made more promising. For example, a company may make a sales forecast that indicates that sales will be at a lower level than desirable. At this time, managers may develop new plans for advertising, sales promotion, or introduction of new products so as to improve the sales forecast.

Sales forecasts

[1]For a discussion of feedforward control techniques, see H. Koontz and R. W. Bradspies, "Managing through Feedforward Control," *Business Horizons*, vol. 15, no. 3 (June 1972), pp. 25–36. Much of the material in this section is drawn from that paper.

Cash flow planning

Likewise, most businesses and other enterprises engage in future-directed control when managers carefully plan the availability of cash to meet requirements. Businesses, for example, would hardly find it wise to wait for a report at the middle or end of May to find out whether they had enough cash in the banks to cover checks issued in April.

PERT

One of the better techniques of future-directed control in use today is the technique of network planning, exemplified by PERT (Program Evaluation and Review Technique) networks, to be discussed in the following chapter. This technique of planning and control enables managers to see that they will have problems in such areas as costs or on-time delivery unless they take action now.

Feedforward in Engineering

In recent years, particularly in chemical and electrical process systems, engineers have designed systems of feedforward control. For example, it was found that thermostatic control of water temperature with measurements at the outlet was not good enough for holding constant temperatures required for water being mixed into certain chemical compounds because of surges in water usage. As a result, process engineers designed systems whereby the needs for various quantities of water could be anticipated so that temperature could be controlled in advance of the outlet.

Feedforward in Human Systems

Interestingly enough, we find many examples of feedforward in human systems. A motorist, for example, who wishes to maintain a constant speed would not usually wait for the speedometer to signal a drop in speed before depressing the accelerator in going up a hill. Instead, knowing that the hill represents a disturbing variable in the system, the driver would likely correct for this by pressing the accelerator before speed falls. Likewise, a hunter will always aim ahead of a duck's flight to correct for the time lag between a shot and a hoped-for hit.

Feedforward versus Feedback Systems

Simple feedback systems measure outputs of a process and feed into the system or the inputs of a system corrective actions to obtain desired outputs. For most management problems, because of time lags in the correction process, this is not good enough. Feedforward systems monitor *inputs* into a process to ascertain whether the inputs are as planned; if they are not, the inputs, or perhaps the process, are changed in order to obtain desired results.

The nature of a feedforward as compared with a feedback system is depicted in Figure 21-3.

In a sense, we could say that a feedforward control system is really a kind of feedback system. This is true, but the information feedback is at the input side of the system so that corrections can be made before the system output is affected. Also, no one would deny that, even with a feedforward system, a manager would still want to measure final system output since nothing can be expected to work perfectly enough to ensure that the final output will always be exactly what is desired.

Feedforward in Management

To give you an idea of what feedforward means in management control, let us look at examples of cash and inventory planning systems. Figures 21-4 and 21-5 illustrate what is involved.

FIGURE 21-3

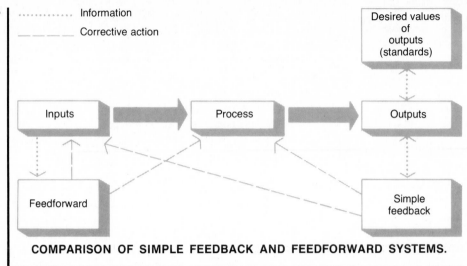

COMPARISON OF SIMPLE FEEDBACK AND FEEDFORWARD SYSTEMS.

The somewhat simplified schematic figures of input variables shown in the charts for cash and for inventory planning and control indicate that if managers are to exercise effective control over either cash or inventories, they must identify each as an interacting system. As can be seen in each instance, some of the variables interact, and some have either a negative or a positive effect on either cash or inventory.

Also, if the system of variables and their impact on a process are accurately portrayed—and each enterprise should design its own system appropriate to the realities of its situation—a deviation from any planned input can result in an unplanned output unless something is done about it in time. For example, in the case of the inventory model, if purchase deliveries are greater than planned or if factory usage turns out to be less than planned, the result will be a higher-than-planned inventory unless corrective action is taken. Of course, to make feedforward work in practice, inputs must be carefully monitored.

In the best kind of feedforward control program, the model of input variables should include inputs in the system model that materially influence the key inputs. For example, purchase deliveries tend to increase inventories. But these deliveries are, of course, dependent on orders placed, and the placing of orders is in turn dependent on other factors.

The system of feedforward may appear to be rather complex. But for major problem areas at least, it should not be difficult to identify system input variables, to see them as an interacting system, and to computerize the model. From that point it should be an easy matter to gather information on the inputs and to determine on a regular basis their effect on the desired end result. Certainly, in view of its importance to meaningful management control, this would not appear to be too much trouble to take.

One of the problems in all feedforward control systems is the necessity to watch for what engineers call "disturbances." These are factors which have not

FIGURE 21-4

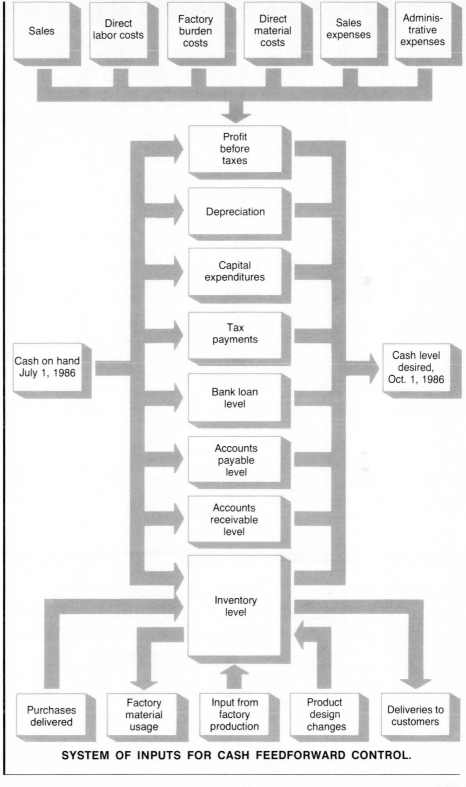

SYSTEM OF INPUTS FOR CASH FEEDFORWARD CONTROL.

FIGURE 21-5

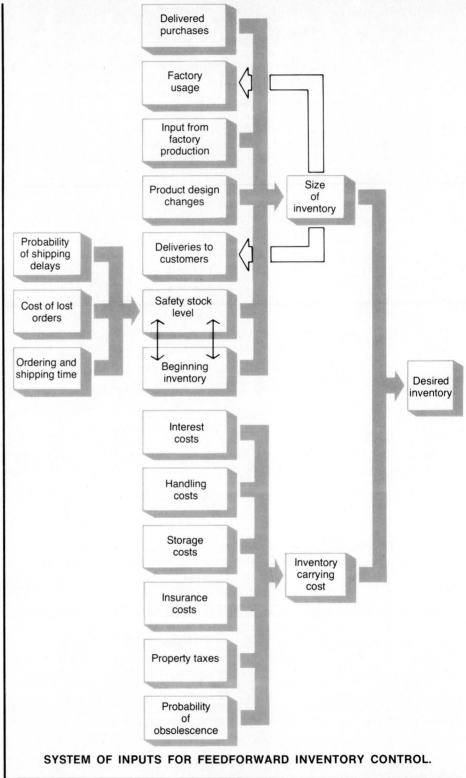

SYSTEM OF INPUTS FOR FEEDFORWARD INVENTORY CONTROL.

been taken into account in the input model but which may have an impact on the system and desired end results. Obviously, it would be impracticable to take into account in a model all inputs that might possibly affect the operation of a program. For example, for a company with a long history of adequate flow of bank loans for financing needs, the possibility that the company's bank may suddenly have to restrict credit might not have been a variable put into the input system. Or the bankruptcy of a large customer or supplier might be an unanticipated, and unprogrammed, input variable. Since unprogrammed events do sometimes occur and may upset a desired output, monitoring of regular inputs must be supplemented by watching for, and taking into account, unusual and unexpected "disturbances."

Requirements for Feedforward Control

The requirements for a workable feedforward control system may be summarized as follows:

1   Make a thorough and careful analysis of the planning and control system and identify the more important input variables.

2   Develop a model of the system.

3   Take care to keep the model up to date; in other words, the model should be reviewed regularly to see whether the input variables identified and their interrelationships continue to represent realities.

4   Collect data on input variables regularly and put them into the system.

5   Regularly assess the variations of actual input data from planned-for inputs and evaluate the impact on expected end results.

6   Take action. Like any other technique of planning and control, all that the system can do is to show people problems; they must obviously take action to solve them.

Requirements for Adequate Controls

All alert managers want to have an adequate and effective system of controls to assist them in making sure that events conform to plans. It is sometimes not realized that the controls used by managers must be designed for the specific task and person they are intended to serve. While the basic process and the fundamentals of control are universal, the actual system requires special design.

Indeed, we can say that if controls are to work, they must be specially tailored. In short, they must be tailored to plans and positions, to the individual managers and their personalities, and to the needs for efficiency and effectiveness.

Tailoring Controls to Plans and Positions

All control techniques and systems should reflect the plans they are designed to follow. Every plan and every kind and phase of an operation has unique characteristics. What managers need is the information that will tell them how the plans for which they are responsible are progressing. Certainly the information needed for following the progress of a marketing program will be quite different from that needed to check on a production plan.

Positions

In the same way, controls should be tailored to positions. What will do for a vice-president in charge of manufacturing will certainly not be appropriate for a shop supervisor. Controls for the sales department will differ from those for the finance department, and these from controls for the purchasing department. And a small business will need some controls different from those for a large business. The very nature of control emphasizes the fact that the more controls are designed to deal with and reflect the specific nature and structure of plans, the more effectively they will serve managerial needs.

Critical factors

Certain techniques, such as budgets, standard hours and costs, and various financial ratios, have general application in various situations. However, none of these widely used techniques is completely applicable in any given situation. Managers must always be aware of the critical factors in their plans and operations requiring control, and they must use techniques and information suited to them.

Organization structure

Controls should also reflect the organization structure. Being the principal means of clarifying the roles of people in an enterprise, organization structure shows who is responsible for the execution of plans and for any deviation from them. Controls must therefore reflect the organization structure, and the more carefully that controls are designed to reflect the place in the organization where responsibility for action lies, the more they will enable managers to correct deviations from plans. For example, unless product costs are accumulated, so as to fit the organization structure of the manufacturing department, and unless each factory superintendent and supervisor knows the costs incurred by his or her department in the production of an item, actual costs may be out of line without any of these managers knowing whether he or she is responsible. Fortunately, cost accountants have recognized the importance of relating cost data to organization structure, and the places where costs are incurred, now typically used in industry, provide data appropriate for each manager and his or her responsibility.

Tailoring Controls to Individual Managers

Controls must also be tailored to individual managers. Control systems and information are of course intended to help individual managers carry out their function of control. If they are not of a type that a manager can or will understand, they will not be useful. It really does not matter whether people cannot understand a control technique or control information or whether they are just unwilling to understand it. In either case, it is not understood. What individuals cannot understand they will not trust. And what they do not trust they will not use.

Different forms of information

Some people, for instance, certain statisticians and accountants, like their information in the form of complex tables of data or voluminous computer printouts. In such cases, let them have it that way. Other people like their information in chart form; if so, it should be furnished this way. And a few people, for instance, scientists and mathematicians, may even like their information in mathematical model form; in this event, it should be given to them that way. It is sometimes said that if people will not understand the information they need in any other way, we might consider giving it to them in comic-book form. The important thing is that people get the information they need in a form they will understand and use.

Tailoring techniques

What is said about tailoring information for understanding is true also of control techniques. Even quite intelligent people may be "turned off" by some of the sophisticated techniques of the expert. Sophisticated techniques of planning and control, like variable budgeting or network planning, can fail in practice solely because the systems either were not comprehensible to the people who had to use them or appeared to be too complex for them. Experts in these matters must not try to show others how expert they are, but should, rather, design a system at the level of ready comprehension so that people will use it. If we can get 80 percent of the benefit with a fairly crude system, this is far better than obtaining no benefit from a more perfect, but unworkable, system.

Controls Pointing Up Exceptions at Critical Points

One of the most important ways of tailoring controls to needs for efficiency and effectiveness is to make sure that they are designed to point up exceptions. In other words, by concentrating on exceptions from planned performance, managers can use controls based on the time-honored exception principle to detect those places where their attention is required.

But it is not enough merely to look at exceptions. Some deviations from standards have rather little meaning, and others have a great deal. Small deviations in certain areas may have greater significance than larger exceptions in other areas. A manager, for example, might be concerned if the cost of office labor deviated from budget by 5 percent, but be unworried if the cost of postage stamps deviated from budget by 20 percent.

Principle of critical-point control

Consequently, the exception principle must be accompanied in practice by the principle of critical-point control. It is not enough just to look for exceptions; we must also look for them at critical points. It is true that the more that managers concentrate their control efforts on exceptions, the more efficient their control will be. But this principle had best be considered in the light of the fact that effective control requires managers to pay primary attention to those things which are most important.

Objectivity of Controls

Management necessarily has many subjective elements, but whether a subordinate is doing a good job should ideally not be a matter for subjective determination. Where controls are subjective, a manager's or a subordinate's personality may influence judgments of performance and make them less accurate; but people have difficulty in explaining away control of their performance, particularly if the standards and measurements are kept up to date through periodic review. This requirement may be summarized by saying that effective control requires objective, accurate, and suitable standards.

Flexibility of Controls

Controls should remain workable in the face of changed plans, unforeseen circumstances, or outright failures. If controls are to remain effective despite failure or unexpected changes of plans, they must be flexible.

The need for flexible control can readily be illustrated. A budget system may project a certain level of expenses and grant authority to managers to hire labor and purchase materials and services at this level. If, as is usually the case, this budget is based on a forecast of a certain level of sales, it may become meaningless as a system of control if the actual sales volume is considerably above or below the forecast. Budget systems have been brought into ill repute among some companies because of inflexibility in such circumstances. What is needed, of course, is a system that will reflect sales variations as well as other deviations from plans. This requirement is provided by the flexible, or variable, budget, as we will see in Chapter 22.

| **Fitting the Control System to the Organizational Climate** | To be most effective, any control system or technique must fit the organizational climate. For example, a tight control system applied in an organization where people have been given considerable freedom and participation may go so strongly against the grain that it will be doomed to failure. On the other hand, if subordinates have been managed by a superior who allows little participation in decision making, a generalized and permissive control system would hardly succeed. People with a low desire to participate, or who have not been accustomed to participating, are likely to want to have clear standards and measurements and to want to be told what to do. |

Economy of Controls

Controls must be worth their cost. Although this requirement is simple, it is often difficult to accomplish in practice. A manager may have difficulty in ascertaining what a particular control system is worth or what it costs. Economy is relative, since the benefits vary with the importance of the activity, the size of the operation, the expense that might be incurred in the absence of control, and the contribution the system can make.

A limiting factor of control systems is their cost; this, in turn, will depend a great deal on managers' selecting for control only critical factors in areas important to them. If tailored to the job and to the size of the enterprise, control will probably be economical. One of the economies of large-scale enterprise is being able to afford expensive and elaborate control systems. Often, however, the magnitude of the problems, the wider area of planning, the difficulty of coordinating plans, and poor management communication in a large organization require such expensive controls that their overall efficiency suffers in comparison with lesser controls in a small business. Control techniques and approaches are efficient when they bring to light the causes of actual or potential deviations from plans with the minimum of costs.

Controls Leading to Corrective Action

An adequate system will disclose where failures are occurring and who is responsible for them, and it will ensure that some corrective action is taken. Control is justified only if deviations from plans are corrected through appropriate planning, organizing, staffing, and leading.

Summary

The managerial function of controlling is the measurement and correction of performance in order to ensure that enterprise objectives and the plans devised to attain them are being accomplished. It is a function of every manager from president to supervisor.

Control techniques and systems are basically the same regardless of what is being controlled. Wherever it is found and whatever is being controlled, the basic control process involves three steps: (1) establishing standards, (2) measuring performance against these standards, and (3) correcting variations from standards and plans. There are different kinds of standards and they should point out deviations at critical points.

Managerial control is usually perceived as a simple feedback system similar to the usual household thermostat. However, no matter how quickly information is available on what is happening (even real-time information, which is information on what is happening as it happens), there are unavoidable delays in analyzing deviations, developing programs for taking corrective action, and implementing these programs. In order to overcome these unavoidable time lags in control, it has been suggested that managers utilize a feedforward control approach and not rely on simple feedback alone. Feedforward control requires designing a model of a process or system and monitoring inputs with a view to detecting future deviations of results from plans and thereby giving managers time to take corrective action.

If controls are to work, they must be specially tailored (1) to plans and positions, (2) to individual managers, and (3) to the needs for efficiency and effectiveness. To be effective, controls also should be designed to point up exceptions at critical points, to be objective, to be flexible, to fit the organizational climate, to be economical, and to lead to corrective action.

Key Ideas and Concepts for Review

Controlling
Steps in controlling
Critical-point control
Types of critical-point standards
Feedback systems
Real-time information system

Techniques of future-directed control
Feedforward control in management
Requirements for feedforward control
Requirements for adequate controls
Exception principle

For Discussion

1 Planning and control are often thought of as a system; control is also often referred to as a system. What is meant by these observations? Can both statements be true?

2 Why is real-time information not good enough for effective control?

3 What is feedforward control? Why is it important to managers? Besides the examples of cash and inventory control mentioned in this chapter, can you think of any other areas where feedforward would be used? Selecting one of these, how would you proceed?

4 If you were asked to institute a system of "tailored" controls in a company, how would you go about it? What would you need to know?

5 Develop a set of standards for any area of interest to you where you might wish to exercise effective control.

6 Design a control system for measuring the progress you make in your course work. Apply the feedback and feedforward concepts discussed in this chapter.

CASE 21-1

THE KAPPA CORPORATION

As George House, vice-president of finance, and Helen Robbins, controller, walked into the office of Adrian Barnes, chairperson and chief executive officer of Kappa Corporation, they were met with the following outburst from the company's top officer:

"Why doesn't someone tell me things? Why can't I know what is going on around here? Why am I kept in the dark? No one informs me on how the company is going, and I never seem to hear of our problems until they become crises. Now, I want you both to work out a system where I can be kept informed, and I want to know by next Monday how you will do it. I am tired of being isolated from the things I must know if I am to take responsibility for this company."

After George House had left Mr. Barnes's office, he turned to his controller and muttered: "That silly jerk! Everything he wants to know or could possibly want to know is in that shelf of reports on the table in back of his desk."

1 Who was right—Adrian Barnes or George House? Was Barnes getting information?

2 What would you do to make sure that the chairperson did get the information he needed for control purposes?

CASE 21-2

HANOVER SPACE AND ELECTRONICS CORPORATION

Warren Hanover, president of Hanover Space and Electronics Corporation, and the presidents of other large defense contractors had just met with the Secretary of Defense in Washington. The secretary had impressed on the group of presidents the fact that the government must insist on better management and tighter control by defense con-tractors in order to get more product from increasingly scarce defense dollars, especially in view of the sharp inflation of recent years. The secretary had strongly emphasized that, from now on, the Defense Department would carefully examine management practices of contractors and, at the very least, would not give any major contract to a company that did not have a strong, effective control system.

Warren Hanover, as well as the other presidents, got the message. On his return to his headquarters in Kansas City, he immediately called in his administrative vice-president, told him of the secretary's position, and ordered him to install an effective control system. The administrative vice-president, in turn, called in the corporation controller and passed the order on to him. The controller then assigned the task to his staff assistant, asking her to scour the literature on control to find a system the company could adopt and to present a proposal to him within a week.

At the end of the week, the staff assistant had to report to the controller that she had not found a control system suitable for the company, despite the fact that she had reviewed dozens of books and journal articles.

1 Could the staff assistant have found a suitable control system if she had looked far enough?

2 If you were the staff assistant, what would you suggest be done to develop an effective control system?

For Further Information

Banks, R. L., and S. C. Wheelwright. "Operations vs. Strategy: Trading Tomorrow for Today," *Harvard Business Review*, vol. 57, no. 3 (May–June 1979), pp. 112–120.

Flamholtz, Eric. "Organizational Control Systems as a Managerial Tool," *California Management Review*, vol. 22, no. 2 (Winter 1979), pp. 50–59.

McFarlan, F. W., J. L. McKenney, and P. Pyburn. "The Information Archipelago—Plotting a Course," *Harvard Business Review*, vol. 61, no. 1 (January–February 1983), pp. 145–156.

McFarlan, F. W., and J. L. McKenney. "The Information Archipelago—Governing the New World." *Harvard Business Review*, vol. 61, no. 4 (July–August 1983), pp. 91–99.

Michael, S. R. "Feedforward versus Feedback Control," *Managerial Planning*, vol. 29, no. 3 (November–December 1980), pp. 34–38.

Mills, P. K. "Self-Management: Its Control and Relationship to Other Organizational Properties," *Academy of Management Review*, vol. 8, no. 3 (July 1983), pp. 445–453.

Smith, H. L., M. D. Fottler, and B. O. Saxberg. "Cost Containment in Health Care: A Model for Management Research," *Academy of Management Review*, vol. 6, no. 3 (July 1981), pp. 397–407.

22

Control Techniques and Information Technology

After reading this chapter, you should understand:

1 The nature of budgeting and types of budgets
2 Modern techniques of budgeting, including variable and zero-base budgets
3 Nonbudgetary control devices
4 Time-event networks as important techniques of planning and control
5 The nature and problems of program budgeting
6 The nature and applications of information technology

Although the basic nature and purpose of management control do not change, a variety of tools and techniques have been used over the years to help managers control. As you will see, all these techniques are in the first instance tools for planning. They illustrate the fundamental truth that the task of controls is to make plans succeed; naturally, in doing so, controls must reflect plans; and planning must precede control.

Some of these tools may be classed as traditional in the sense that they have long been used by managers, although variable budgeting and zero-base budgeting, for example, are refinements of traditional budgeting. Others, like Program

Evaluation and Review Technique (PERT) and program budgeting, represent a newer generation of planning and control tools. While there are many more of these than discussed here, the newer tools generally reflect the systems techniques long used in the physical sciences. Operations research, discussed in the next chapter, is such a technique. It uses mathematical and computing techniques to formulate a model that simulates a problem situation with its goal and variables and their relationships. If managers have such a model to guide them in their planning, they can use the same model for control purposes. They know what their goals are and what the variables are that influence performance. In this way, detecting variations and making corrections becomes somewhat easier.

In spite of all the newer techniques of planning and control, the traditional tools are still extremely important.

Control Techniques: The Budget[1]

A widely used device for managerial control is the budget. Indeed, it has sometimes been assumed that budgeting is *the* device for accomplishing control. However, many nonbudgetary devices are also essential.

Concept of Budgeting

Budgeting is the formulation of plans for a given future period in numerical terms. As such, budgets are statements of anticipated results, in financial terms—as in revenue and expense and capital budgets—or in nonfinancial terms—as in budgets of direct-labor-hours, materials, physical sales volume, or units of production. It has sometimes been said, for example, that financial budgets represent the "dollarizing" of plans.

Sometimes people do not understand how and why budgets must be based on plans. In fact, some enterprises, especially nonbusiness enterprises, do develop budgets without knowing plans. But when they do so, money allocated to pay for salaries, for office space and equipment, and for other expenses becomes a matter of negotiation between a top authority and the managers in an enterprise. The usual result is that funds are not intelligently allocated on the basis of what is really needed to accomplish desired goals. Many of us have seen this kind of uncertainty and consequent jockeying for position in government and university budgeting. Only when there are clear goals and action plans to accomplish them can anyone in a top position of authority know how much money is necessary to do what is desired.

Purpose of Budgeting

By stating plans in terms of numbers and breaking them into parts that parallel the parts of an organization, budgets correlate planning and allow authority to be delegated without loss of control. In other words, reducing plans to numbers forces a kind of orderliness that permits the manager to see clearly what capital will be

---

[1]Primarily because of the negative implications of budgeting in the past, the more positive phrase "profit planning" is sometimes used and the budget is then known as the "profit plan."

spent by whom and where, and what expense, revenue, or units of physical input or output the plans will involve. Having ascertained this, the manager can more freely delegate authority to effect the plan within the limits of the budget. Moreover, a budget, to be useful to a manager at any level, must reflect the organizational pattern. Only when plans are complete, coordinated, and developed enough to be fitted into departmental operations can a useful departmental budget be prepared as an instrument of control.

Types of Budgets

There are many types of budgets. They may be classified into several basic types, with a budget summary (discussed in Chapter 24) portraying the total planning picture of all the budgets: (1) revenue and expense budgets, (2) time, space, material, and product budgets, (3) capital expenditure budgets, and (4) cash budgets.

Revenue and expense budgets By far the most common budgets spell out plans for revenues and operating expenses in dollar terms. The most basic of these is the sales budget, the formal and detailed expression of the sales forecast. Just as the sales forecast is the cornerstone of planning, so is the sales budget the foundation of budgetary control. Although a company may budget other revenues, such as expected income from rentals, royalties, or miscellaneous sources, the revenue from sales of products or services furnishes the principal income to pay operating expenses and yield profits.

Operating expense budgets of the typical enterprise can be as numerous as the expense classifications in its chart of accounts and the units of organization in its structure. These budgets may deal with individual items of expense, such as travel, data processing, entertainment, advertising, telephone, insurance, and many others. Sometimes a department head will budget only major items and lump together other items in one control summary. For example, if the manager of a small department is expected to take one business trip a year at a cost of $720, budgeting this cost each month at $60 would mean little for monthly planning or control.

Time, space, material, and product budgets Many budgets are better expressed in physical than in monetary terms. Although such budgets are usually translated into monetary terms, they are much more significant at a certain stage in planning and control if they are expressed in terms of physical quantities. Among the more common of these are the budgets for direct-labor-hours, machine-hours, units of materials, square feet allocated, and units produced. Most firms budget product output, and most production departments budget their share of the output of components of the final product. In addition, it is common to budget labor, either in labor-hours or labor-days, by types of labor required. Obviously, such budgets cannot be well expressed in monetary terms, since the dollar cost would not accurately measure the resources used or the results intended.

Capital expenditure budgets Capital expenditure budgets outline specifically capital expenditures for plant, machinery, equipment, inventories, and other items. Whether for a short or a long term, these budgets require care since they give definite form to plans for spending the funds of an enterprise. Since capital is generally one of the most limiting factors of any enterprise and since a business takes a long time to recover its investment in plant and equipment through charges as costs, thereby leading to a high degree of inflexibility, capital expenditure budgets should usually be tied in with fairly long-range planning.

Cash budgets   The cash budget is simply a forecast of cash receipts and disbursements against which actual cash "experience" is measured. Whether called a budget or not, this is perhaps the most important single control of an enterprise. The availability of cash to meet obligations as they fall due is the first requirement of existence, and handsome business profits do little good when tied up in inventory, machinery, or other noncash assets. Cash budgeting also shows availability of excess cash, thereby making possible planning for profit-making investment of surpluses.

Dangers in Budgeting

Overbudgeting

Budgets should be used only as a tool of planning and control. Some budgetary control programs are so complete and detailed that they become cumbersome, meaningless, and unduly expensive. There is a danger in overbudgeting through spelling out minor expenses in detail and depriving managers of needed freedom in managing their departments. For example, a department head in a poorly budgeted company was hindered in an important sales promotion because expenditures for office supplies exceeded budgeted estimates; new expenditures had to be limited, even though his total departmental expenses were well within the budget and he had funds to pay personnel for writing sales promotion letters. In another department, expenses were budgeted in such useless detail that the cost of budgeting of many items exceeded the expenses controlled.

Overriding enterprise goals

Another danger lies in allowing budgetary goals to become more important than enterprise goals. In their zest to keep within budget limits, managers may forget that they owe primary loyalty to enterprise objectives. In one company with a budgetary control program, the sales department could not obtain needed information from the engineering department on the ground that the latter's budget would not stand such expense! This conflict between partial and overall control objectives, the excessive departmental independence generated, and the lack of coordination are symptoms of inadequate management since plans should constitute a supporting and interlocking network and every plan should be reflected in a budget in a way that will aid in achieving enterprise goals.

Hiding inefficiencies

Another danger in budgeting is that it may be used to hide inefficiencies. Budgets have a way of growing from precedent, and that a certain expenditure was made in the past can become evidence of its reasonableness in the present; if a department once spent a given amount for supplies, this cost becomes a minimum for future budgets. Also, managers sometimes learn that budget requests are likely to be pared down in the course of final approval, and therefore they ask for much more than they need. Unless budget making is accomplished by constant reexamination of standards and conversion factors by which planned action is translated into numerical terms, the budget may become an umbrella under which slovenly and inefficient management can hide.

Perhaps inflexibility is the greatest danger in budgets. Even if budgeting is not used to replace managing, the reduction of plans to numerical terms gives them a kind of misleading definiteness. It is entirely possible that events will prove that a larger amount should be spent for this kind of labor or that kind of material and a smaller amount for another, or that sales will exceed or fall below the amount forecast. Such differences may make a budget obsolete almost as soon as it is made; and, if managers must stay within the straitjacket of their budgets in the face of such events, the usefulness of budgets is reduced or nullified. This is especially true where budgets are made for long periods in advance.

Variable Budgets

Because of the dangers arising from inflexibility in budgets and because maximum flexibility consistent with efficiency underlies good planning, attention has been increasingly given to variable or flexible budgets. These are designed to vary usually as the volume of sales or some other measure of output varies and so are limited largely to expense budgets. The variable budget is based upon an analysis of expense items to determine how individual costs *should* vary with volume of output. Some costs do not vary with volume, particularly in so short a period as a month, six months, or a year. Among these are depreciation, property taxes and insurance, maintenance of plant and equipment, and costs of keeping a minimum staff of supervisory and other key personnel. Some of these standby, or period, costs—such as those of maintaining a minimum number of key or trained personnel for advertising or sales promotion and for research—depend upon managerial policy.

Costs that vary with volume of output range from those that are completely variable to those that are only slightly variable. The task of variable budgeting is to select some unit of measure that reflects volume, to inspect the various categories of costs (usually by reference to the chart of accounts), and, by statistical studies, methods engineering analyses and other means, to determine how these costs should vary with volume of output. At this stage, each category of cost is related to volume, sometimes with recognition of "steps" as volume increases. Each department is given these variable cost items, along with definite dollar amounts for its fixed, or standby, costs. Periodically—usually each month—department heads are then given the volume forecast for the immediate future, from which is calculated the dollar amounts of variable costs that make up the budget. In this way, a basic budget can be established for six months or a year in advance, but be made variable with shorter-term changes in sales and output.

This type of budget is illustrated by Figure 22-1, which depicts the fixed and variable portions of business cost. A chart of a department budget would have essentially the same appearance, with suitable cost elements. This chart uses units of monthly output as the base for volume, and direct labor and materials are included. However, many variable budgets assume that volume will automatically control direct labor and materials, and the budget is consequently used to control only indirect and general expenses.

As you can see, Figure 22-1 is based on the assumption that period costs will remain the same for a volume output of 0 to 6000 units. In most cases, a variable budget will represent a range of output where plant, managerial, organizational,

FIGURE 22-1

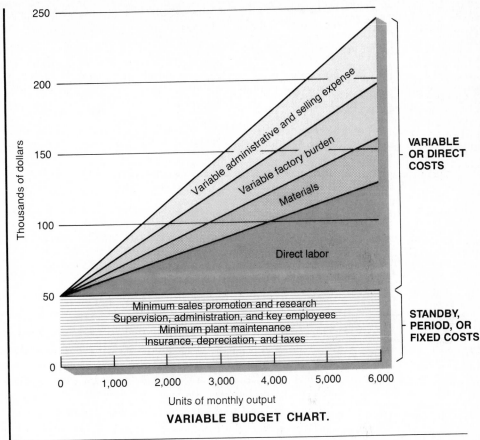

VARIABLE BUDGET CHART.

and other elements of period cost will be the same. But, in practice, this may be over a range of 3000 to 10,000 units. If it were less than 3000 units, a different variable budget would be required with the level of period costs more suitable for the smaller volume; if it were more than 10,000 units, another variable budget would be necessary to reflect the level of period costs necessitated by a larger operation.

A typical variable budget resulting from such an analysis is shown in Table 22-1. The table shows an expense budget for an entire company based on a range of expected monthly sales volume of $575,000 to $875,000. The assumption is that if sales were thought to be below $575,000, the company would probably have to reorganize its operations to profitably sustain this smaller volume. On the other hand, if monthly sales rose above $875,000, an expansion of company plant and organization would require a completely new variable budget.

Continuing need for other plans

When using the various kinds of variable budgets, department managers must still make future plans. It may be easy to tell a certain supervisor that during the month of May he can have twelve trained electronic assemblers, then, several

TABLE 22-1 A Typical Variable Budget for an Entire Company (In thousands of dollars)

Item of expense	Monthly sales volume						
	$575	$625	$675	$725	$775	$825	$875
Material	$184	$200	$216	$232	$248	$264	$280
Direct labor	70	76	82	88	94	100	106
Overhead costs	150	155	161	168	170	171	174
Cost of production	$404	$431	$459	$488	$512	$535	$560
Engineering	$ 35	$ 36	$ 38	$ 38	$ 38	$ 38	$ 40
Research and development	10	10	10	10	12	12	12
Sales and advertising	64	66	69	72	73	74	75
Administrative costs	60	62	63	63	64	65	66
Total costs	$573	$605	$639	$671	$699	$724	$753
Profit from operations	$2	$20	$36	$54	$76	$101	$122
Percentage of profit to sales	0.3%	3.2%	5.4%	7.5%	9.8%	12.3%	14%

weeks later, that he may have fifteen in June, and a month later, that his budget for July will permit his having only ten. But the problems of hiring and training competent personnel make accomplishing these variations more costly than they are worth. In other words, efficiency may demand that department managers not vary certain of their expenses with short-term variations in volume. In the search for flexibility in budgets, as with other tools of management, an intelligent manager will not lose sight of basic objectives and efficiencies by blindly following any system.

Variable budgets work best when sales or other measures of volume can be reasonably well forecast and reasonably long-range plans made, so that the level of expenses will not have to be changed so often and on such short notice as to make the job of supervisors intolerable. Under these circumstances, one might well ask: What are the advantages of variable budgeting? Although a fixed budget will work as well with good plans and sales forecasts, a variable budget *forces* study of, and preoccupation with, factors which translate work load into labor or expense needs. Carefully worked-out conversion factors—worked out and applied in advance—are necessary for any good budgeting. This, rather than flexibility itself, appears to be the principal advantage of variable budgeting.

Advantages

Alternative and Supplementary Budgets

Another method of obtaining variable budgeting is to establish alternative budgets. Sometimes a company will establish budgets for a high level of operation, a medium level, and a low level, and the three budgets will be approved for the company as a whole and for each organizational segment for six months or a year in advance. Then, at stated times, managers will be informed as to which budget to use in their planning and control. Alternative budgets are a modification of variable budgets, the latter being virtually infinitely variable instead of limited to a few alternatives.

Budget flexibility is also obtained with a plan referred to as the supplemental monthly budget. Under this plan, a 6-month or 1-year budget is prepared for the primary purpose of outlining the framework of the company's plans, coordinating them among departments, and establishing department objectives. This is a basic or minimum budget. Then a supplementary budget is prepared each month on the basis of the volume of business forecast for that month. This budget gives each manager authority for scheduling output and spending funds above the basic budget if, and to the extent that, the shorter-term plans so justify. It avoids some of the detailed calculations necessary under the typical variable budget. But these budget approaches do not usually have the advantage of forcing complete analysis of all costs and relating them to volume.

Zero-Base Budgeting

Another type of budgeting, the purpose of which has much in common with the purpose of a well-operated system of variable budgeting, is zero-base budgeting. The idea behind this technique is to divide enterprise programs into "packages" composed of goals, activities, and needed resources and then to calculate costs for each package from the ground up. By starting the budget of each package from base zero, costs are calculated afresh for each budget period, thus avoiding the common tendency in budgeting to look only at changes from a previous period.

Applications

This technique has generally been applied to so-called support areas, rather than to actual production areas, on the assumption that there is some room for discretion in expenditures for most programs in such areas as marketing, research and development, personnel, planning, and finance. The various programs thought to be desirable are costed and reviewed in terms of their benefits to the enterprise and are then ranked in accordance with those benefits and selected on the basis of which package will yield the benefit desired.

Advantage

The principal advantage of this technique is, of course, the fact that it forces managers to plan each program package afresh. As managers do so, they review established programs and their costs in their entirety, along with newer programs and their costs.

Effective Budgetary Control

If budgetary controls are to work well, managers must remember that budgets are designed only as tools and not to replace managing, that they have limitations, and that they must be tailored to each job. Moreover, they are the tools of all managers and not only of the budget administrator or the controller. The only persons who can administer budgets, since they are plans, are the managers responsible for budgeted programs. No successful budget program can be truly "directed" or "administered" by a budget director. This staff officer can assist in the preparation and use of budgets by the responsible managers, but, unless the entire company management is to be turned over to the budget officer, this person should not be given the job of making budget-commitment or expenditure decisions.

Top management support

To be most effective, budget making and administration must receive the wholehearted support of top management. To establish an office of budget administrator by decree and then forget about it leads to haphazard budget making and to saddling subordinate managers with another procedure or set of papers to prepare. On the other hand, if top management actively supports budget making and grounds a budget firmly on plans, requires divisions and departments to make and defend their budgets, and participates in this review, then budgets encourage alert management throughout the organization.

Participation

Related to the participation of top management, another means of making budgets work is to make sure that all managers expected to operate and live under budgets have a part in their preparation. Real participation in budget making is necessary to ensure success. Most budget administrators and controllers recognize this fact, but too often in practice participation amounts to managers being simply pressured to "accept" budgets.

Although budgets do furnish a means of delegating authority without loss of control, there is danger, as noted earlier, that they will be so detailed and inflexible that little real authority is, in fact, delegated. Some executives even believe that the best budget to give managers is one that lumps all their allowable expenditures for a period of time into a single amount and then gives them complete freedom as to how these funds are to be spent in pursuance of the company's goals. This kind of decentralization has much to recommend it, although better planning and control might be achieved by allowing the department manager real participation in budget making. It may be well, however, to allow department managers a reasonable degree of latitude in changing their budgets and in shifting funds, as long as they meet their *total* budgets.

Standards

One of the keys to making budgeting work is to develop and make available standards by which programs and work can be translated into needs for labor, operating expenses, capital expenditures, space, and other resources. Many budgets fail for lack of such standards, and some upper-level managers hesitate to allow subordinates to submit budget plans for fear that they may have no logical basis for reviewing budget requests. With conversion factors available, superior managers can review such requests and justify their approval or disapproval of them. Moreover, by concentrating on the resources required to do a planned job, managers can base their request on what they need to have for meeting output goals and improving performance. They no longer must cope with arbitrary across-the-board budget cuts—a technique more frustrating to the superior than to the subordinate who, on the occasion of the next request, has the foresight to pad for the inevitable slice. In fact, across-the-board cuts are the surest evidence of poor planning and loss of control.

Information

Lastly, if budgetary control is to work, managers need ready information as to actual and forecast performance under budgets by *their* departments. This information must be designed to show them how well *they* are doing. Unfortunately, however, such information is usually not available until it is too late for the manager to avoid budget deviations.

Traditional Nonbudgetary Control Devices

There are, of course, many traditional control devices not connected with budgets, although some may be related to, and used with, budgetary controls. Among the more important of them are statistical data, special reports and analyses, the operational audit, and personal observation.

Statistical Data

Chart form

Statistical analyses of the innumerable aspects of an operation and the clear presentation of statistical data, whether of a historical or forecast nature, are important to control. It is probably safe to say that most managers understand statistical data best when they are presented in chart form, since trends and relationships are not easily seen, except by those accountants and statisticians accustomed to them, in the tabular sheets of computer printouts. Moreover, if data are to be meaningful, even when presented on charts they should be formulated in such a way that comparisons to some standard can be made. What is the significance of a 3 or a 10 percent rise or fall in sales or costs? What was expected? What was the standard? How serious is the change? Who is responsible? Clear presentation of statistical data in tabular or chart form is an art that requires imagination.

Trends

Moreover, since no manager can do anything about history, it is essential that statistical reports show trends so that the viewer can extrapolate where things are going. This means that most data, when presented on charts, should be made available as averages to rule out variations due to accounting periods, seasonal factors, accounting adjustments, and other periodic variations. One of the simplest and best devices for giving perspective is the moving average. In the 12-month moving average, for example, the total for 12 consecutive months, divided by 12, is used. You can see the difference in clarity from the comparative data presented graphically in Figure 22-2.

Special Reports and Analyses

For control purposes, special reports and analyses help in particular problem areas. Although routine accounting and statistical reports furnish a good share of necessary information, there are often areas in which they are inadequate. One successful manager of a complicated operation hired a small staff of trained analysts and gave them no assignment other than that of investigating and analyzing operations under his control. This group developed a surprising sense for situations where things did not seem just right. Almost invariably, their investigation disclosed opportunities for cost improvement or better utilization of capital that no statistical chart would have revealed.

It may be that some of the funds being spent for elaborate information programs could be more profitably spent for special analyses. Their nonroutine nature can highlight the unusual and, in so doing, reveal places for significant improvement in efficiency. In the routine search for pennies and accounting for them, opportunities for saving dollars may be overlooked.

Operational Audit

Another effective tool of managerial control is the internal audit, or, as it is now coming to be called, the operational audit. **Operational auditing,** in its broadest sense, is the regular and independent appraisal, by a staff of internal auditors, of the accounting, financial, and other operations of a business. Although often limited to the auditing of accounts, in its most useful form operational auditing includes appraisal of operations generally, weighing actual results against planned results. Thus operational auditors, in addition to assuring themselves that accounts properly reflect the facts, also appraise policies, procedures, use of authority, quality of management, effectiveness of methods, special problems, and other phases of operations.

FIGURE 22-2

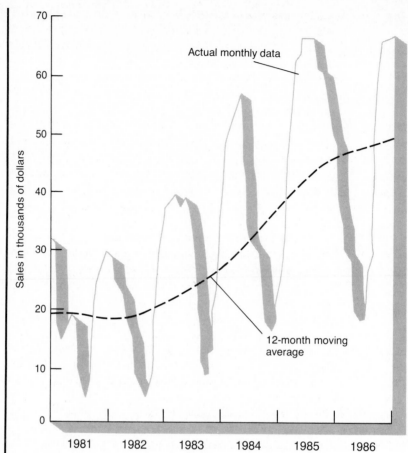

Actual monthly data versus twelve-month moving average. Sales of company X, 1981–1986.

Personal Observation

One should never overlook the importance of control through personal observation. Budgets, charts, reports, ratios, auditors' recommendations, and other devices are essential to control. But the manager who relies wholly on these devices and sits, so to speak, in a soundproof control room reading dials and manipulating levers can hardly expect to do a thorough job of control. Managers, after all, have the task of seeing that enterprise objectives are accomplished by *people*, and although many scientific devices aid in ensuring that people are doing that which has been planned, the problem of control is still one of measuring activities of human beings. It is amazing how much information an experienced manager can get from personal observation even from an occasional walk through a plant or an office.

Time-Event Network Analyses

Another planning and control technique is a time-event network analysis called Program Evaluation and Review Technique (PERT). Before the development of PERT, there were other techniques designed to watch how the parts of a program fit together during the passage of time and events.

Gantt Chart

The first of these techniques were the chart systems (see Figure 22-3) developed by Henry L. Gantt early in the twentieth century and culminating in the bar chart bearing his name. Although simple in concept, this chart, showing time relationships between "events" of a production program, has been regarded as revolutionary in management. What Gantt recognized was that total program goals should be regarded as a series of interrelated supporting plans (or events) that people can comprehend and follow. The most important developments of such control reflect this simple principle and also such basic principles of control as picking out the more critical elements of a plan to watch carefully.

Milestone Budgeting

As the result of the development of further techniques from the principles of the Gantt chart, and with better appreciation of the network nature of programs, "milepost" or "milestone" budgeting and PERT have been devised, contributing much to better control of many projects and operations. Used by an increasing number of companies in recent years in controlling engineering and development, milepost or milestone budgeting breaks a project down into controllable pieces and then carefully follows them. As we pointed out in the discussion of planning, even relatively simple projects contain a network of supporting plans or projects. In this approach to control, milestones are defined as identifiable segments. When accomplishment of a given segment occurs, cost or other results can be determined.

Engineering control was long hampered because people did not know how much progress was being made on a project. The difficulty with the common device of estimating completion time, with planned inputs of labor and materials, is that, although accurate records of personnel and material costs can be kept, estimates of percentage of completion tend to reach 85 or 90 percent and stay there, while time and costs continue.

Project events

The best way to plan and control an engineering project is to break it down into a number of events, for example, completion of preliminary drawings, an experimental model, a package design, a packaged prototype, and a production design. Or a project might be broken down vertically into subprojects—for example, the design of a circuit, a motor, a driving mechanism, a sensing device, a signal feedback device, and similar components—that can be designed individually, in a time sequence, to be ready when needed. Milestone budgeting allows a manager to see a complex program as a series of simpler parts and thus to maintain some control through knowing whether a program is succeeding or failing.

FIGURE 22-3

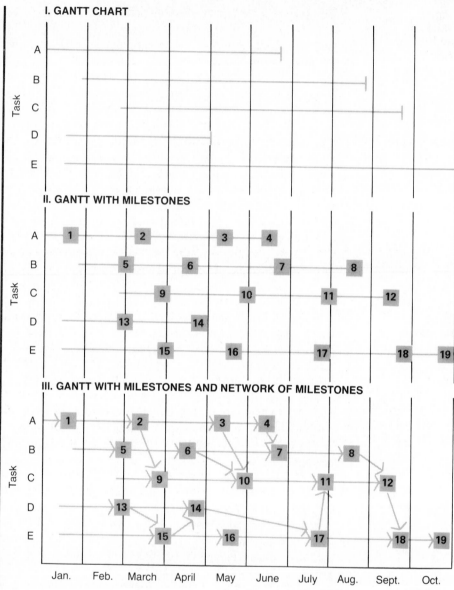

I. GANTT CHART

II. GANTT WITH MILESTONES

III. GANTT WITH MILESTONES AND NETWORK OF MILESTONES

Jan.   Feb.   March   April   May   June   July   Aug.   Sept.   Oct.

TRANSITION FROM A GANTT CHART TO PERT

The Gantt chart in I above shows the scheduled time of accomplishing a task, such as procurement (Task A), and the related schedules of doing other tasks, such as manufacture of parts (Task B). When each of these tasks is broken down into milestones, such as the preparation of purchase specifications (Task A-1), and when network relationships among the milestones of each task to those of other tasks are worked out, the result provides the basic elements of a PERT chart.

Program Evaluation and Review Technique

Developed by the Special Projects Office of the United States Navy,[2] PERT was first formally applied to the planning and control of the Polaris Weapon System in 1958 and worked well in expediting the successful completion of that program. For a number of years, it was so enthusiastically received by the armed services that it became virtually a required tool for major contractors and subcontractors in the armament and space industry. Although PERT is no longer much heard of in defense and space contracts for reasons that will be noted presently, its fundamentals are still essential tools of planning and control. Moreover, in a host of nongovernmental applications, including construction, engineering and tooling projects, and even such simple things as the scheduling of activities to get out monthly financial reports, PERT or its companion network technique, CPM (Critical Path Method), may be profitably used.

Major features   In a sense, PERT is a variation of milestone budgeting. It uses a time-event network analysis, as shown in Figure 22-4. This very simple example illustrates the basic nature of PERT. Each *circle* represents an event—a supporting plan whose completion can be measured at a given time. The circles are numbered in the order in which the events occur. Each *arrow* represents an activity—the time-consuming element of a program, the effort that must be made between events; *activity time* is the elapsed time required to accomplish an event represented by the numbers beside the arrows.

Three time estimates

In this example, only a single time is shown, but in the original PERT program there were three time estimates: "optimistic" time, an estimate of time required if everything goes exceptionally well; "most likely" time, an estimate of what the project engineer really believes necessary to do the job; and "pessimistic" time, an estimate based on the assumption that some logically conceivable bad luck—other than a major disaster—will be encountered. These estimates are often included in PERT because it is very difficult, in many engineering and development projects, to estimate time accurately, and partly, it is believed, because engineers will be willing to make a variety of estimates and will do their level best to beat the pessimistic estimate. When several estimates are made, they are usually averaged, with special weight given to the most likely estimate; a single estimate is then used for calculations.

Critical path

The next step is to compute the *critical path*, that sequence of events which takes the longest time and which involves, therefore, the least slack time. In Figure 22-4, the critical path is indicated as that following events 1–3–4–8–9–13. Over this path, the activity time for this sequence of events is 131.6 weeks; if promised delivery is in 135 weeks, even this critical path would have a slack of 3.4 weeks. Some of the other paths are almost as long as the critical path. For example, the path 1–2–9–13 is 129.4 weeks. This is not unusual in PERT charts, and it is customary to identify several critical paths in order of importance. Although the

---

[2]But also separately developed as the Critical Path Method by engineers at the Du Pont Company at virtually the same time. Only PERT is discussed here because the Critical Path Method, although different in some respects, utilizes the same basic principles.

FIGURE 22-4

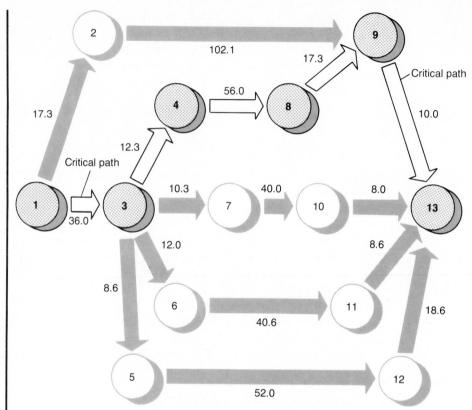

PERT FLOW CHART: TIME IN WEEKS.

Major assembly of an airplane. Events (major milestone of progress) are: (1) order program go-ahead; (2) initiate engine procurement; (3) complete plans and specifications; (4) complete fuselage drawings; (5) submit GFAE* requirements; (6) award tail assembly subcontract; (7) award wings subcontract; (8) complete manufacture of fuselage; (9) complete assembly of fuselage engine; (10) receive wings from subcontractors; (11) receive tail assembly from subcontractors; (12) receive GFAE; (13) complete aircraft.

Note: GFAE stands for government-furnished airplane equipment.

critical path has a way of changing as key events are delayed in other parts of the program, identifying it at the start makes possible close watching of this particular sequence of events to ensure the total program's being on schedule.

Typical PERT analyses run into hundreds or thousands of events. Even though smaller PERT analyses—including the input of event accomplishment and the frequent calculation of critical path—can be done manually, it is estimated that when upward of approximately 200 to 300 events are involved, it is virtually impossible to handle the calculations without an electronic computer.

It is customary to summarize very large and complex time-event networks by subnetworks and to prepare the summarized network for top-management consideration. Thus, the top-management network might include some forty or fifty major events, each a summary of a number of subsidiary events. In fact, it is possible to group, or to break down, events so as to have a PERT network appropriate to every level of management.

Advantages

Strengths and weaknesses   There are five important advantages of PERT. First, it forces managers to plan, because it is impossible to make a time-event analysis without planning and seeing how the pieces fit together. Second, it forces planning all down the line, because each subordinate manager must plan the event for which he or she is responsible. Third, it concentrates attention on critical elements that may need correction. Fourth, it makes possible a kind of forward-looking control; a delay will affect succeeding events and possibly the whole project, unless the manager can somehow make up the time by shortening that of some action in the future. Fifth, the network system with its subsystems permits managers to aim reports and pressure for action at the right spot and level in the organization structure at the right time.

Limitations

PERT also has certain limitations. Because of the importance of activity time to its operation, it cannot be useful when a program is nebulous and no reasonable "guesstimates" of schedule can be made; even here, however, insurance can be "bought" by such practices as puttng two or more groups of people to work on an event when costs permit. PERT is also not practicable for routine planning of recurring events, such as mass production; although it could be used here, once a repetitive sequence of events is clearly worked out, so elaborate a continuing control is not required. A major disadvantage of PERT has been its emphasis on time only, not on costs. While this focus is suitable for programs where time is of the essence or where, as so often is the case, time and costs have a close direct relationship, the tool is more useful when considerations other than time are introduced into it. (There is, however, another program called PERT/COST which does consider costs.)

PERT is not a cure-all. It will not *do* the planning, although it *forces* planning. It will not make control automatic, although it establishes an environment where sound control principles can be appreciated and used. And it apparently involves rather less expense than might be thought. Setting up the network, its analysis, its interpretation, and reporting from it probably require little, if any, more expense than most other planning and control techniques, unless, of course, these are made unduly complicated.

Program Budgeting

One of the widely publicized tools of planning and control, used primarily in government operation but applicable to any kind of enterprise, is program planning and budgeting (PPB), or, more simply, program budgeting. Although really not more, at least in its fundamentals, than what budgeting should always be, its emphasis and approach deserve analysis.

What Program Budgeting Is

Program budgeting is basically a means for providing a systematic method for allocating the resources of an enterprise in ways most effective to meet its goals. By emphasizing goals and programs to meet them, it overcomes the ordinary weakness of all kinds of budgets, even in business, of being too tied to the time frames of accounting periods of months, quarters, or years. By concentrating on goals and programs in the light of available resources, it stresses the desirability of assessing costs against benefits when selecting the best course toward accomplishing a program goal.

Special Application in Government

Program budgeting has offered particularly great actual and potential benefit in government where budgeting has too often been regarded as a mere control technique—with the objective of controlling the allocation and expenditure of funds—rather than as a planning *and* control tool. For too many years, government budgeting—at federal, state, and local levels—has been handled largely on a "line" basis, with allocation of funds to such functions as personnel, training, office supplies, transportation, and printing, rather than for programs designed to accomplish an identifiable goal. Also, with the fragmentation of program responsibility among various agencies, bureaus, or divisions, and with most objectives being set forth in such generalities as "providing adequate police protection," budgeting has tended to be an exercise by various government departments in competing and negotiating for funds, rather than in getting necessary support to accomplish specific desired program goals.

Problems in Applying Program Budgeting

In the Defense Department at least, program budgeting has worked fairly well, chiefly because it has been easier to make defense objectives and strategies fairly clear and definite. It has likewise appeared to work well in such essentially program-oriented agencies as those dealing with water resources and housing programs. However, for most government agencies, program budgeting has not been the great tool in practice that its logic would imply. There are a number of reasons why it has not.

In the first place, many federal, state, and local executives, particularly at the middle and lower levels of management, do not understand the philosophy and theory of the technique; they have been given directives and forms but have not really known what the system entails. A second major hurdle has been the lack of clearly defined goals; obviously, no one can plan and budget for an unknown or fuzzy goal. Another difficulty is the lack of attention to planning premises; even with clear program goals, the program budgeter is in the dark without knowledge of critical planning premises. Another problem arises from the long tradition in government of line budgeting, and most legislators, accustomed to line budgets, often will not tolerate other budgets unless they are recast in a line-item form. Also, many government budgetary divisions or staffs have been reluctant to make the change from their practice and procedures of annual budgets to longer-range program budgets. Other roadblocks include the fact that accounting data are seldom consistent with program budgeting, the lack of information in many areas to make meaningful cost effectiveness analyses, and the political problems of reorganizing government departments to improve concentration of program responsibility.

The problems in government have been such that there is some question whether program budgeting will ever be made to work as it should. But a tool that makes so much sense in an area where effective management is extremely important and difficult should not be allowed to fall into disuse. Unfortunately, those who introduced it in most government agencies, or ordered its introduction, apparently failed to realize that much teaching and other effort is required to make this technique successful.

Information Technology

The systems model of management shows that communication is needed for carrying out the managerial functions and to link the organization with its external environment. The Management Information System (MIS) provides the communication link and makes managing possible.

Electronic equipment permits fast and economical processing of huge amounts of data. The computer can, with proper programming, process data toward logical conclusions, classify them, and make them readily available for manager's use. In fact, data do not become information until they are processed into a usable form that informs.

Expanding Basic Data

The focus of attention on management information, coupled with its improved processing, has led to the reduction of long-known limitations. Managers for years have recognized that traditional accounting information, aimed at the calculation of profits, has been of limited value for control. Yet in many companies this has been virtually the only regularly collected and analyzed type of data. Managers have known that they need all kinds of nonaccounting information about the social, economic, political, and technical environment in which plans must operate, as well as information on internal operations. Such information should include both qualitative and quantitative data.

While not nearly enough progress has been made in meeting these requirements, the computer, plus operations research, has led to enormous expansion of available managerial information. One sees this especially in relation to data on marketing, competition, production and distribution, product cost, technological change and development, labor productivity, and goal accomplishment.

Information Indigestion

Managers who have experienced the impact of better and faster data processing are justly concerned with the danger of information indigestion. Their appetite for figures whetted, the data originators and processors are turning out material at an almost frightening rate. Managers are complaining of being buried under printouts, reports, projections, and forecasts which they do not have time to read or cannot understand or which do not fill their particular needs.

Intelligence Services

One attempt at solving the information overload is the establishment of an intelligence service and the development of a new profession of intelligence experts. The service would be provided by specialists who know (or find out) what information managers need and who would know how to digest and interpret such information for managerial use. Some companies have established organizational units under such names as "administrative services" or "management analyses and services" for making information understandable and useful.

Graphics

One way to overcome the resistance to computers is through the application of graphics. Rather than having to go through reams of computer outputs, information is displayed as easy-to-understand graphics. PepsiCo, for example, invested $250,000 in decision-support graphics over 3 years, generating 80,000 charts and slides.[3] The point is simply this: to be useful, managers must understand and use the information that is now available at low cost through the use of the computer.

The Use of Computers in Managing Information

Mainframe

Minicomputer

Microcomputer

The computer can store, retrieve, and process information. Often a distinction is made between kinds of computers. The *mainframe* is a full-scale computer, often called the central processing unit. The *minicomputer* has less memory and is smaller than the mainframe. The *microcomputer* is still smaller and may be a desk computer, home computer, personal computer, portable computer, or small business system.

Applications

Among the many business applications of the computer are material requirements planning, manufacturing resource planning, computer-aided control of manufacturing machinery, project costing, inventory control, and purchasing. The computer also aids design and engineering, an application which made the U.S. space program possible. Then there are the many uses in processing financial information such as accounts receivable and accounts payable, payroll, capital budgeting, and financial planning.

The Impact of Computers on Managers at Different Organizational Levels

Information needs differ at various organizational levels. Therefore, the impact of computers will also be different.

At the *supervisory level* activities are usually highly programmable and repetitive. Consequently, the use of the computer is widespread. Scheduling, daily planning, and controlling of the operation are just a few examples.

Low level

Middle level

Middle-level managers, such as department heads or plant managers, usually have responsibility for administration and coordination. But much of the information important to them is now also available to top management if the company has a comprehensive information system. For this reason, some people think that the need for middle-level managers will be reduced by the computer. Others predict that their roles may be expanded and changed.

Top level

Top managers are responsible for the strategy and overall policy of the organization. They are not only determining the general direction of the company, but also are responsible for the appropriate interaction between the enterprise and its environment. Clearly, the tasks of CEOs are not easily programmable. Yet, top managers can use the computer to retrieve information from a data base that aids the application of decision models. Thus, the company can make timely responses

---

[3]"Management Warms Up to Computer Graphics," *Business Week*, Aug. 13, 1984, pp. 96–101.

to changes in the external environment. Still, the use of the computer will probably less severely affect the jobs of top managers than those at the lower levels.

The Application and Impacts of Microcomputers

The personal computer (PC) is becoming increasingly appealing to managers because it is flexible and relatively inexpensive, and can be used more quickly than the mainframe computer. Its applications include:

- Budget preparation
- Graphic presentations
- Electronic spread sheets
- Financial analyses
- Word processing
- Simulation models
- Forecasting
- Electronic mail
- Tapping into data bases
- Time sharing

The implications of the increasing use of the microcomputer are manifold. There is a need for specialized staff support, education for managers and nonmanagers, and a redefinition of jobs. For example, the distinctions between line and staff will become less clear. The information that was formerly gathered by staff can now be obtained with ease by other managers accessing a common data base. On the other hand, information that was the prerogative of upper-level managers can also be made available to personnel at lower levels, possibly resulting in the shift of power to lower levels in the organization. But not all information should be accessible to all people in the company. Thus, one of the problems currently faced by many firms is maintaining the security of information.

The Fear of Computers

While high school students may feel comfortable using the computer, some managers fear it. One study revealed that the typical executive affected by this phobia is male, about 50 years old and has worked most of the time for the same company. This fear might explain why certain managers are reluctant to use the computer. Naturally, they do not want to look unskilled when they are not able to understand the new technology, and do not have the typing skills often necessary for submitting data to the computer. In the past, typing was considered the task of the secretary, not the manager.

Summary

A variety of tools and techniques have been used to help managers control. These techniques are generally, in the first instance, tools for planning and illustrate the fact that controls must reflect plans. Some of these tools may be classified as traditional in the sense that they have long been used by managers, although in the case of variable budgeting and zero-base budgeting, they are more recent refinements of traditional budgeting. Other techniques, like Program Evaluation and Review Technique (PERT) and program budgeting, represent a newer generation of planning and control tools.

One of the oldest control techniques is the budget. Budgeting is the formulation of plans in numerical terms. There are several types of budgets: (1) revenue and expense budgets, (2) time, space, material, and product budgets, (3) capital expenditure budgets, and (4) cash budgets. There are a number of dangers in budgeting, but the major danger, inflexibility, can be largely avoided by using variable, or flexible, budgets. These are budgets designed to vary with volume of output, with expenses divided among those that vary with output and those standby, period, or fixed costs that vary with time. Flexibility may also be obtained by providing alternative or supplementary budgets. Budgeting is made much more precise by zero-base budgeting, in which programs are divided into "packages" and costs for each package are calculated from a base of zero. In order to make budgetary control effective in practice, managers must always realize that budgets are tools and are not intended to replace managing.

Among the traditional nonbudgetary control devices, we find the use of statistical data and their analyses, special reports and analyses, the operational audit, and personal observation.

One of the newer techniques of planning and control is time-event-network analyses, called Program Evaluation and Review Technique (PERT). It is a refinement of the original Gantt charts, which were designed to show, in bar-chart form, the various things that must be done, and when, in order to accomplish a program. It is also a refinement of "milestone" budgeting, in which the things that have to be done to accomplish a program are broken down into identifiable and controllable pieces called milestones. When milestones are connected to form a network and the time required to complete each milestone is identified, we have a PERT/TIME network. From the sequence of events and times required for each, we can then find the sequence with the least slack time compared with a promised program completion date. This sequence is referred to as the critical path.

Program budgeting is a newer approach to budgeting. Generally used by government agencies, it involves tying budgets to the accomplishment of any given program, thus becoming a means of carefully calculating the resources necessary to accomplish that program.

Information technology facilitates communication within the organization and with the external environment. Managers need to have not necessarily more information, but the right kind in the right format. Different kinds of computers are put to various uses in the organization. Recently, personal computers have become increasingly popular with managers. But some managers fear the computer.

Key Ideas and Concepts for Review

Budgeting	PERT
Types of budgets	Critical path in PERT
Budgeting problems	Program budgeting
Variable budget	Information indigestion
Zero-base budgeting	Mainframe computer
Nonbudgetary control devices	Minicomputer
Operational audit	Microcomputer
Gantt chart	Applications of microcomputers
Milestone budgeting	

For Discussion

1 The techniques of control appear to be as much techniques of planning as they are of control. In what ways is this true? Why would you expect it to be so?

2 "Variable budgets are flexible budgets." Discuss.

3 It is often claimed that an operating expense budget must be set at a level lower than expected in order to ensure the attainment of cost and profit goals. Do you agree?

4 To what extent, and how, can budgeting be approached on a grass roots basis, that is, from the bottom of the organization upward?

5 If you were going to institute a program of special control reports and analyses for a top manager, how would you go about it?

6 PERT is a management invention that takes basic principles and knowledge and, through design to get a desired result, comes up with a useful technique of planning and control. Analyze PERT with this in mind.

7 Why has program budgeting been regarded as so important in government? If you were to introduce it in a government department, how would you proceed? What would you need to do so?

8 Take PERT and use it to plan your study program in your college. What are the advantages in using this technique? What are some problems?

9 Take an organization you know and show how it uses computers.

CASE 22-1

ANCHOR CONSOLIDATED INDUSTRIES, INC.

"I heard about this variable-budget idea in a management conference I attended last week," remarked Sidney Sims, president of Anchor Consolidated Industries, Inc., a small company whose clever new pleasure-boat products had given rise to growth since its founding 5 years ago to a level of $5 million in annual sales. "Some speaker said that the sound way to run a company is to let all the department and section heads develop their own budgets. But I can't imagine doing this in this company. If I did, these people would spend so much money that we would soon be bankrupt.

No! As long as I am in charge of this company, I will tell my people what they can spend. There will be no blank checks here. And I will hold my controller responsible for making sure this company makes the profits I want. I have heard of too many companies, with the fast growth we have had, that have gone broke because optimism and uncontrolled spending went through the ceiling. And this idea of variable budgets is even worse. Imagine what would happen if I let everyone vary his budgets each month, quarter, or year!"

1   To what extent do you agree or disagree with Sidney Sims?

2   Do you believe that his way of budget making will work? Why?

3   If you were going to suggest to Sims how he could have his department and section heads involved in budgeting, what would you suggest he do to avoid the problem now worrying him?

4   How would you assure effective control with variable budgets?

CASE 22-2

THE ELECTRICAL CONSTRUCTION COMPANY

Independent auditors had just completed the examination of the operations of a large electrical construction company. The item that they felt needed closer attention was the budget control of new construction work.

The audit showed that most electrical designs for new construction were carried out at the headquarters of the company by a project manager. In preparing a budget for a new project, he checked the expenses for similar jobs in the past, then simply multiplied them by various factors.

The auditors found that during the past 2 years, most budgets had been greatly overestimated. Incidentally, it was about 2 years ago that the project manager had been given the primary responsibility for budgeting. In this role, he would submit his budget to the Expenditure Control Committee, consisting of higher-level managers who had only a limited interest in budgeting. It was to this committee that the project manager submitted requests for additional money whenever needed. Most of the requests were approved.

The chief auditor felt that the project team tended to "expand" the time needed to complete the task whenever the members thought the budget made it possible. In other words, they "adjusted" their productivity to match the money allocated to the project.

The auditors noted that other contractors could do similar jobs for 20 percent less money. They concluded that a new control procedure was needed.

1   What do you think of the budgeting process?

2   What kind of control procedure should the auditors recommend?

For Further Information

Anthony, R., and J. Dearden. *Management Control Systems*, 4th ed. (Homewood, Ill.: Richard D. Irwin, Inc., 1980).

Churchill, N. C. "Budget Choice: Planning vs. Control," *Harvard Business Review*, vol. 62, no. 4 (July–August 1984), pp. 150–164.

Greenberg, K. "Executives Rate Their PCs," *PC World*, Sept. 1984, pp. 286–292.

Heintz, T. J. "Small Business Computers: A Management Primer," *Management World*, vol. 10, no. 8 (August 1981), pp. 12–15.

Karasik, M. S. "Selecting a Small Business Computer," *Harvard Business Review*, vol. 62, no. 1 (January–February 1984), pp. 26–30.

Keen, P. G. W., and L. A. Woodman. "What to Do With All Those Micros," *Harvard Business Review*, vol. 62, no. 5 (September–October 1984), pp. 142–150.

Kroeber, D. W. *Management Information Systems* (New York: The Free Press, 1982).

McFarlan, F. W. "Information Technology Changes the Way You Compete," *Harvard Business Review*, vol. 62, no. 3 (May–June 1984), pp. 98–103.

Wetherbe, J. C., and J. R. Montanari. "Zero Based Budgeting in the Planning Process," *Strategic Management Journal*, vol. 2 (January–March 1981), pp. 1–14.

Wilkinson, J. W. *Accounting and Information Systems* (New York: John Wiley & Sons, Inc., 1982).

Williams, J. J. "Designing a Budgeting System with Planned Confusion," *California Management Review*, vol. 24, no. 2 (Winter 1981), pp. 75–85.

Planning and Controlling Production and Operations Management

CHAPTER OBJECTIVES

After reading this chapter, you should understand:

1 The nature of production and operations management as an applied case of managerial planning and control.
2 The management techniques found to be especially useful for operations planning and control and also for planning and control of other areas of enterprise operation.
3 Certain techniques usually found in planning and control of operations.
4 Probable future developments in operations planning and control.

One of the major areas in any kind of enterprise, whether business, government, or others, is production and operations management. It is also the area where managing as a scientifically based art got its start. As we recall the interests and contributions of such pioneers in management as Taylor, Gantt, and Frank Gilbreth, to mention only a few, we note that their interest was largely in seeing how to make products most efficiently while still recognizing, as they did, the importance of the human factor as an indispensable input.

Production and Operations Management[1]

Production management

In the past, "production management" was the term used to refer to those activities necessary to manufacture products. However, in recent years, the area has been generally expanded to include such activities as purchasing, warehousing, transportation, and other operations from the procurement of raw materials through various activities until a product is available to the buyer. In addition, the term "operations management" refers to activities necessary to produce and deliver a service as well as a physical product.

Operations management

There are, of course, other essential activities undertaken by a typical enterprise. These enterprise functions often include, in addition to production or operations, research and development, engineering, marketing and sales, accounting, and financing. We have chosen in this chapter to deal only with what has come to be called "operations management" or "production management," and often "production and operations management" (POM). It should be pointed out that this is not, of course, the same thing as "operational" management theory. You should recall, as explained in Chapter 2, that operational-management theory is a study of the practice (managing) that theory or science is designed to underpin.

We single out operations for special attention mainly because it is in this area that most managerial functions (planning, organizing, staffing, leading, and controlling), theory, and techniques have been utilized. Therefore, it is an area which can be regarded as furnishing an excellent case study in the utilization of the scientific element and techniques of management.

Operations Management Systems

Figure 23-1 gives an overview of the operations function. Inputs are transformed to produce outputs. Inputs include needs of customers, information technology, labor and management, fixed assets, and variable assets that are relevant to the transformation process. Managers and workers use the information and physical factors to produce outputs. Some physical elements such as land, building, machines, and warehouses are relatively permanent. Other physical elements, such as materials and supplies, are consumed in the process of producing outputs. The transformation process incorporates planning, operating, and controlling the system. There are many tools and techniques available to facilitate the transformation

---

[1]In the preparation of this chapter, the authors have received considerable assistance from B. Chase and N. J. Aquilano, *Production and Operations Management* (Homewood, Ill.: Richard D. Irwin, Inc., 1981).

FIGURE 23-1

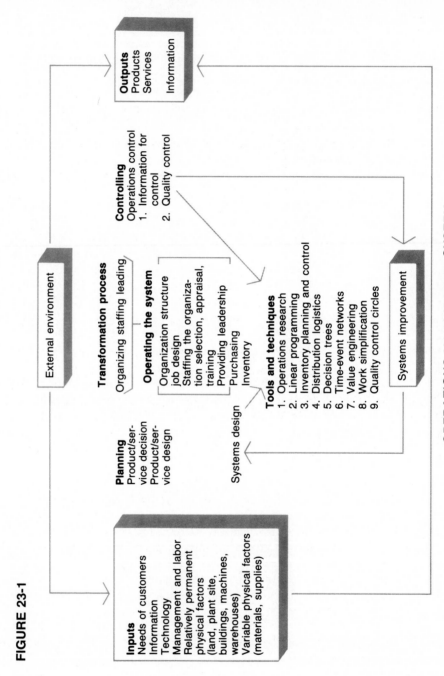

OPERATIONS MANAGEMENT SYSTEM.

TABLE 23-1   Illustrations of Operations Systems*

Inputs	Transformation	Outputs
1 Plant, factory machines, people, materials	Assembling bicycles	Completed bicycles
2 Students with limited knowledge, skills, and attitudes	Lectures, cases, experiential exercises, term papers	Students with enhanced knowledge, skills, and attitudes
3 Client problem	Consulting: data collection analysis, evaluation of alternatives, selection of alternative, recommendation	Consulting report recommending course of action

*The input-transformation-output model is widely used in the discussion of operations management. See, for example, Chase and Aquilano, op. cit.; H. Fearon, W. A. Ruch, P. G. Decker, R. R. Reck, V. G. Reuter, and C. D. Wieters, *Fundamentals of Production/Operations Management* (St. Paul: West Publishing Company, 1979); E. S. Buffa and J. S. Dyer, *Management Science/Operations Research* (New York: John Wiley & Sons, Inc., 1981).

process. The model also reflects a constant concern for improving the system. Outputs consist of products and services. These may even be information, such as may be provided by a consulting organization.

The last part of the model shows that operations are influenced by many external factors, such as safety regulations or fair labor practices. Since the external environment has been discussed before, especially in Chapter 3, we will not expand on it here, but simply point out that operations management must be an open system interacting with its surroundings.

The operations management model (Figure 23-1) serves as a framework for this chapter. Illustrations of operations systems with inputs, transformation (sometimes also called "process"), and outputs are shown in Table 23-1. As you can see, there is a close relationship between this model and the one introduced in Chapter 1, since this operations model may be regarded as a subsystem of a total management system.

Planning Operations

Objectives, premises, and strategies of an enterprise (discussed in Part II of this book) determine the search for and the selection of the product or service. In this discussion production of physical products is emphasized, but the concepts can also be applied to providing services. After an end product has been selected, the specifications are determined and the technological feasibility of producing it is considered. The design of an operation requires decisions concerning the location of facilities, the process to be used, the quantity to be produced, and the quality of the product.

Special interests in a product decision   One of the basic decisions an enterpise makes is to *select* a product or products it intends to produce and market. This requires gathering product ideas that will satisfy the needs of customers and contribute to the goals of an enterprise while being consistent with the strategy of the firm.[2] In a product decision, the various interests of functional managers must be considered. For example, a production manager may want a product that can be produced without difficulties, at a reasonable cost, and with long production runs. Engineers may share many of these aims, but they are often looking for engineering sophistication and not how the product can actually be produced at a reasonable cost.

The sales or marketing manager's interest is likely to be the needs of customers, and his or her aim is to increase the sales of products with ready availability and competitive prices. Moreover, sales managers may want to offer a broad product line without considering the engineering, production, transportation, and warehousing costs and problems involved. The finance manager's prejudices are likely to be in costs and profits, high return on investment, and low financial risks. The divergent interests of these functionally oriented managers and professionals influence what products will be produced and marketed, but it is the general manager who has to integrate the various interests and balance revenues with costs, profits with risks, long-term with short-term growth.

Steps in product design

Product and production design   The design of a product and its production require a number of activities. The following steps have often been suggested:

1 Create product ideas by searching for consumer needs and screening the various alternatives.

2 Select the product based on various considerations including data from market and economic analyses and make a general feasibility study.

3 Prepare a preliminary design by evaluating various alternatives, taking into consideration reliability, quality, and maintenance requirements.

4 Reach a final decision by developing, testing, and simulating the processes to see if they work.

5 Decide whether the enterprise's current facilities are adequate or if new or modified facilities are required.

6 Select the process for producing the product; consider the technology and the methods available.

7 After the product is designed, prepare the layout of the facilities to be used, plan the system of production, and schedule the various things that must be done.

Six kinds of production layouts

Systems design   In producing a product, several basic kinds of production layouts can be considered.[3] One alternative is to arrange the layouts in the order in

[2]For a discussion of the relationship between strategy and operations management, see W. Skinner, *Manufacturing in the Corporate Strategy* (New York: John Wiley & Sons, Inc., 1978) and S. C. Wheelwright, "Operations as Strategy Lessons from Japan," *Stanford GSB* (Fall 1981–1982), pp. 3–7.
[3]See Chase and Aquilano, op cit., sec 2. See also A. C. Laufer, *Operations Management* (Cincinnati: South Western Publishing Company, 1979), chap. 16.

which the *product* is produced or assembled. For example, a truck assembly line may be arranged so that the preassembled front and rear axles are attached to the frame, followed by the installation of the steering, the engine, and the transmission. Then the brake lines and electrical cables are connected and other parts are assembled and painted, before the truck is road tested.

A second alternative may be to lay out the production system according to the *process* employed. In a hospital, for example, specific steps are likely to be followed, beginning with the admission of the patient, the treatment of the patient—which usually involves specific subprocesses—billing for service, and dismissal. This may be followed up by posthospitalization treatment.

A third kind of layout can be selected in which the product stays in one place for assembly (sometimes called *fixed-position* layout). This layout is used for the assembly of extremely large and bulky items such as printing presses, large strip-mining machines, or ships.

The fourth kind of layout is arranged according to the nature of the *project*. Building a bridge or tunnel is normally a one-time project and designed to fit specific geographic requirements.

The fifth kind of layout we find is to arrange the production process to facilitate the *sale* of products. In a supermarket, basic food items, such as dairy products, are normally located away from the checkout counter. This requires customers to walk through the long aisles and, it is hoped, select other items on the way to the dairy section.

A sixth basic approach to a production layout is to design the process so as to facilitate *storage* or *movement* of products. Storage space is costly and an effective and efficient design can keep the storage costs low. Also, in order to reach an item it should not be necessary to move many other items.

Operating the System

After the products have been selected and the systems for producing them have been designed and built, the next major step is to operate the system. This requires setting up an organization structure, staffing the positions, and training people. Managers are needed who can provide the supervision and leadership to carry out activities necessary to produce desired products or provide services. Other activities, such as purchasing and maintaining the inventory, are also required in operating the system.

Controlling Operations

Controlling operations, as in any case of managerial control, requires the setting of performance criteria, measuring performance against them, and taking actions to correct undesirable deviations. Thus, one can control production, product quality and reliability levels, inventory levels, and work-force performance. A number of tools and techniques have been developed to do this. They, having wider application than operations or production, have been discussed previously but some are also important to operations. Our main concern here is with the role of information systems in operations control.

Information systems in operations control One type of planning and control system which has been available for several years, but not always used, integrates information on virtually an instantaneous basis, thereby reducing considerably the

Computers

delays that usually impede effective control. With the development of computer hardware and software, it is now possible for virtually any measurable data to be reported as events occur. Systems are available to provide for fast and systematic collection of data bearing on total operation, for keeping these data readily available, and for reporting without delay the status of any of a large number of projects at any instant. They are thus primarily information systems designed to provide effective planning and control.[4]

Example

Applied widely now to purchasing, storing, manufacturing, and shipping, those systems may operate through dispatch stations throughout a plant, and input centers, also located throughout a plant. At the dispatch centers, events are recorded as they occur and the information is dispatched immediately to a computer. For example, when a supervisor finishes an assigned task on the assembly of a product, the work-order timecard is put into a transactor which electrically transmits to a computer the information that item x has passed through a certain process, has accumulated y hours of labor, may or may not be on schedule, and other pertinent data. The input centers are equipped to originate information needed for a production plan automatically from programmed instructions, purchase orders, shop orders, and other authorizations. These data are fed into a computer and compared against plans which are used as standards against which actual operations, transmitted from the dispatch stations, can be compared.

In addition to fast entry, comparison, and retrieval of information, such an integrated operations control system furnishes needed information for planning programs in such areas as purchasing, production, and inventory control. Moreover, it permits almost instantaneous comparison of results with plans, pinpointing where they differ, and providing a regular (daily or more often, if needed) system of reports on deviations from plans on items that may be behind schedule or costs that are running above budget.

Other planning, control, and information systems have been developed to reflect quickly the interaction between production and distribution operations and such key financial measures as costs, profit, and cash flow. Companies with real-time computer models can give operating managers virtually instant analysis of such "what-if" questions as the effects of reducing or increasing output or of reduction in demand, the sensitivity of the system to labor cost increases, price changes, and new equipment additions. To be sure, system models, simulating actual operations and their impact on financial factors, are primarily planning tools. But so are most control techniques. However, by making possible exceptionally quick responses to the many "what-if" questions of operating managers, the time elapsed in correcting for deviations from plans can be greatly reduced and control materially improved.

These and other systems which use the technology of fast computation clearly promise to hasten the day when planning all the areas of production can be more precise and control more effective. The drawback is not cost, but rather the failure

---

[4]For a detailed discussion of information and control see E. E. Lawler and J. G. Rhode, *Information and Control in Organizations* (Santa Monica, Calif.: Goodyear Publishing Company, Inc., 1976).

of managers to spend the time and mental effort to conceptualize the system and its relationships or to see that someone in the organization does so. But because of the time delays in any feedback system, as pointed out in Chapter 21, fast information availability can never make for true real-time controls of the time delays in any feedback system. Only a feedforward approach can overcome these delays.

Operations Research for Planning and Controlling

A number of techniques employed in many kinds of planning and controlling are especially useful in managing operations. This is understandable, since most of the special techniques that have been developed are based on mathematical models and the use of quantitative data. Conceptual models and fairly exact quantitative data are available in many areas for production and operations management.

We have found it advantageous to discuss some of these techniques in Chapter 7 on decision making and in Chapter 22 on control techniques. Of special interest to managers of production and operations are the tools of operations research. Later in this chapter we will also discuss other techniques.

The Concept

Operations research is a product of World War II, although its forerunners in scientific method, higher mathematics, and such tools as probability theory go back far beyond that period. The accelerated growth of operations research in recent years has followed the trend of applying the methods of the physical scientist and the engineer to economic and political problems. It has also been made possible by the development of rapid computing machines, particularly those using electronics, since much of the advantage of operations research depends upon our being able to apply, at low cost, involved mathematical formulas and to use data with complex relationships. There are almost as many definitions of operations research as there are writers on the subject. For our purposes, the most acceptable

Definition of operations research

definition is that **operations research** is the applications of scientific method to the study of alternatives in a problem situation, with a view to obtaining a quantitative basis for arriving at a best solution. Thus the emphasis is on scientific method, on the use of quantitative data, on goals, and on the determination of the best means of reaching the goals. In other words, operations research might be called quantitative common sense.

The Essentials of Operations Research

Managers have long attempted to solve management problems scientifically, but operations researchers have supplied an element of novelty in the orderliness and completeness of their approach. They have emphasized defining the problem and goals, carefully collecting and evaluating data, developing and testing hypotheses, determining relationships among data, developing and checking predictions based on hypotheses, and devising measures to evaluate the effectiveness of a course of action.

Thus the essential characteristics of operations research as applied to decision making can be summarized as follows:

Six essential characteristics of O.R.

1 It emphasizes *models*—the logical physical representation of a reality or problem. Models can, of course, be simple or complex. For example, the accounting formula "Assets minus liabilities equals proprietorship" is a model, since it represents an idea and, within the limits of the terms used, symbolizes the relationship among the variables involved.

2 It emphasizes *goals* in a problem area and the development of measures of effectiveness in determining whether a given solution shows promise of achieving these goals. For example, if the goal is profit, the measure of effectiveness may be the rate of return on investment, and every proposed solution will arrange the variables so that the end result can be weighed against this measure.

3 It incorporates in a model the *variables* in a problem or at least those that appear to be important to its solution. Managers can control some variables; others may be uncontrollable factors in the problem.

4 It puts the model, and its variables, constraints, and goals, in *mathematical terms* so that they may be clearly identified, subjected to mathematical simplification, and readily utilized for calculation by substitution of quantities for symbols.

5 It *quantifies* the variables in a problem to the extent possible, since only quantifiable data can be inserted into a model to yield a measurable result.

6 It supplements much unavailable data with such usable mathematical and statistical devices as the *probabilities* in a situation, thus often making the mathematical and computing problem workable within a small margin of error despite gaps in accurate quantifiable data.

Kinds of models

Of all these characteristics, perhaps the basic tool—and the major contribution—of operations research is the construction and use of conceptual models. There are many types of models. Some assert logical relationships among variables. These may be referred to as "simulative" or "descriptive" if they are designed only to describe the relationship of elements in a situation. The models useful for planning are referred to as "decision" or "optimizing" models, designed to lead to the selection of a best course of action among available alternatives. They also simulate the problem.

Procedure

Applying operations research generally involves the following six steps:

1 Formulate the problem   As in any planning problem, the operations researcher must analyze the goals and the system in which the solution must operate. That complex of interrelated components in a problem area, referred to by operations researchers as a "system," is the environment of a decision and it represents planning premises. It may take in an entire business operation or be limited to planning production for presses and lathes. It is still, however, an interconnected complex of related human or material components. Obviously, unless managers can greatly simplify the problem by applying the principle of the limiting factor (that is, unless they eliminate alternatives that don't resolve the immediate problem), the more comprehensive the system, the more complex the problem.

Since the purpose of formulating a problem is to determine the best course of action among various alternatives, we must clearly define measures of effectiveness, as well as goals. Moreover, in a typical operations research problem, we should take into account as many goals as necessary and feasible. For example, in a production and distribution planning problem, we will probably wish to minimize both operating costs and investment in inventory, satisfy a level of consumer service, and make the best use of capital investments. To measure effectiveness in reaching these goals and to formulate the problem so that several objectives can be satisfied can become a very complex conceptual and computational matter. The simplest approach is to use certain goals as limitations by saying, for example, that the goal is to achieve minimum costs while maintaining a certain minimum level of customer service or a maximum level of inventory.

2 Construct a mathematical model   The next step is to restate the problem as a system of relationships in a mathematical model. For a single goal where at least some variables are subject to control, the general form of the operations research model is

$$E = f(x_i, y_j)$$

where E = measure of effectiveness of system
 x_i = controllable variables
 y_j = variables beyond control

Decision model

This model may be classified as either a decision model or a simulation model. When it is being used as a decision model, values inserted for the uncontrollable variables (y_j) and the controllable variables (x_i) are manipulated to yield the greatest measure of effectiveness (E). For example, suppose that marketing managers wish to find out what actions on their part would yield the most total sales dollars. The model might include such uncontrollable variables as competitors' prices, gross national product, or price-level changes, and such controllable variables as number of salespeople, commissions allowed, product prices, and advertising expenditures.

Simulation model

Although all models are intended to represent reality, "simulation models" are those where users put in the model a set of factual values for the controllable variables and assume a set of values for the uncontrollable variables. By using one or more sets of values for the uncontrollable variables (because often they cannot be known), we can compute various E's until we find one we believe to be satisfactory. In this event, of course, there is no way of knowing whether an optimal solution has been found. There is something to be gained by restating a problem in concrete (visible) terms. Often a decision model cannot be used because we lack input data and cannot accurately simulate reality (at least the important elements of reality), and because it may be very complex and difficult to build.

3 Derive a solution from the model   There are two basic procedures for arriving at a solution from a model. In the analytical procedure, we use mathematical deduction in order to reach, as nearly as possible, a mathematical solution before inserting quantities to get a numerical solution. This can be an important contribution to complex decision making. Variables can be reduced or restated in terms of common variables. Certain variables (for example, sales) can appear in a number of places in a model and we can factor some out or reduce them. In other cases, we can consolidate and simplify a series of mathematical equations. The result of this analytical procedure is that we have placed a complex series of relationships into as simple a mathematical form as possible. In addition, this analysis may disclose, mathematically, that certain variables are unimportant to a reasonable solution and may be dropped from consideration.

Analytical procedure

   The second procedure is referred to as "numerical." In this, the analyst simply tries different values for the controllable variables to see what the results will be, and from this develops a set of values which seems to give the best solution. The numerical procedure varies from pure trial and error to complex iteration. In iteration, we undertake successive trial runs to approach an optimal solution. In some complex cases, such as the iterative procedures used in linear programming, rules have been developed to help analysts more quickly undertake trials and identify the optimum solution when it is reached.

Numerical procedure

4 Test the model   Because a model, by its very nature, is only a representation of reality and because it is seldom possible to include all the variables, models should usually be tested. We can do so by using the model to solve a problem and comparing the results with what actually happens. These tests can be carried out by using past data or by trying the model out in practice to see how it measures up to reality.

5 Provide controls for the model and the solution   Because a once-accurate model may cease to represent reality, because the variables that are beyond our control may change, or because the relationships of variables may shift, provision must be made for control of the model and the solution. This is done in the same way any control is undertaken, by providing means for feedback so that significant deviations can be detected and changes made. In many complex models, such as those used for production or distribution planning, the effect of the deviations must be weighed against the cost of feeding in the correction or against the usually greater cost of revising the entire program. As a result, we may sometimes decide not to correct the model or the inputs.

6 Put the solution into effect   The final step is to put the model and the inputs into operation. In anything but the simplest programs, this will involve revising and clarifying procedures so that the inputs (including control feedback information) become available in an orderly fashion, and this, in turn, often requires reorganization of an enterprise's available information. What many users of operations research have found a major stumbling block is that no one is willing to undertake the hard work of developing better information to use with the models.

Accounting and other data normally available in a company are often not adequate to the requirements of successful operations research. Many managers, intrigued with the possibilities of operations research, wish that some of the research effort of experts, now so widely employed in constructing elegant models, could be channeled toward reorganizing information.

Other problems in making operations research useful for managers involve getting people to understand, appreciate, and use the techniques of operations research, and deciding such questions as what computing facilities to use, and how, and how the information outputs are to be made useful and understandable to those responsible for decisions. In this connection, operations researchers would do managers a real favor by frankly admitting the nature and margin of uncertainty in their solution.

All this is to say that operations researchers are not nearly done with their task when their model is reduced to paper and tested. Mathematical gymnastics may be interesting to the pure philosopher, but managers must make responsible decisions and the operations researcher who would be useful to managers must be more than a mathematical gymnast.

Linear Programming

A technique for determining the optimum combination of limited resources to obtain a desired goal, linear programming is one of the most successful applications of operations research. It is based upon the assumption that a linear, or straight-line, relationship exists between variables and that the limits of variations can be determined. For example, in a production shop, the variables may be units of output per machine in a given time, direct-labor costs or material costs per unit of output, number of operations per unit, and so forth. Most or all of these may have linear relationships, within certain limits, and by solving linear equations, the optimum in terms of cost, time, machine utilization, or other objectives can be established. Thus, this technique is especially useful where input data can be quantified and objectives are subject to definite measurement.

As one might expect, the technique has had its most promising use in such problem areas as production planning, shipping rates and routes, and the utilization of production and warehouse facilities to achieve lowest overall costs, including transportation costs. Because it depends on linear relationships and many decisions do not involve these or cannot be accurately enough simulated, newer and more complex systems of nonlinear programming have come into use.

Inventory Planning and Control

Perhaps in the history of operations research more attention has been directed to inventory control than to any other practical area of operations. If we wished to see the essential systems relationships as a little "black box" without going into detailed mathematics, we could depict them as is done in Figure 23-2.

Or, if these conceptual relationships were placed in one of the simpler mathematical forms covering approximately the system in Figure 23-2, it might look something like this:

$$Q = \sqrt{\frac{2R[S + E(s)]}{I}}$$

FIGURE 23-2

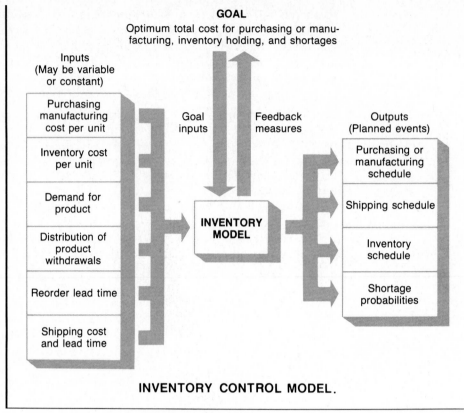

INVENTORY CONTROL MODEL.

where Q = reorder quantity
R = sales requirement per year
S = setup cost (per order)
I = interest and carrying cost, including storage, all expressed per piece, per year
$E(s)$ = expected cost of stockouts per order cycle

and where $E(s)$ is defined by this equation:

$$E(s) = \pi \sum_{u = r + 1}^{umax} (u - r)\, p\,(u)$$

where u = usage during any lead time
$p(u)$ = probability of usage greater than u
r = reorder point in units
u = expected usage during lead time
π = stockout cost per unit demanded but not available

As can be seen, even the simple "black box" representation of a subsystem of control can be very complex. Each of the inputs can be variable or constant, each can be discrete or continuous, and the rate of sales or material use over time can be variable or constant. Moreover, as this is a planning model, feedback of information—to make sure the model attains the goals desired—should be added to make it a planning and control system.

With all its complexities, the model illustrates several things. It forces consideration of the goals desired and of the need for placing definite values on outputs and inputs. It also furnishes a manager with the basis for plans and with standards by which to measure performance. However, with all its advantages, this is a subsystem and does not incorporate other subsystems, such as production planning, distribution planning, and sales planning.

Distribution Logistics

An exciting and profit-promising way of using systems logistics in planning and control is in the expansion of inventory control to include other factors, referred to here as "distribution logistics." In its most advanced form, currently in operation in a few companies, this treats the entire logistics of a business—from sales forecast through purchase and processing of material and inventorying to shipping finished goods—as a single system. The goal is usually to optimize the total costs of the system in operation, while furnishing a desired level of customer service and meeting certain constraints, such as financially limited inventory levels. This gathers into one system a large mass of relationships and information, so as to optimize the whole. It is entirely possible that transportation, manufacturing, or any other single area of cost will not be optimized, but the total cost of materials management will be.

Schematically, a distribution logistics system might appear as shown in Figure 23-3. This model, represented by a black box, would be expressed mathematically as an operating system. The figure shows the relationships between the goal desired, the input variables and limits, and the expected outputs. By optimizing *total* costs in a broad area of operation, the system might show that it would be cheaper to use more expensive transportation on occasion rather than to carry high inventories. Or it might show that production at less-than-economic order quantities would be justified in order to get better transportation or warehousing utilization or to meet customer service standards with limited inventories.

Limitations of Operations Research

Magnitude

So far, operations research has been used to solve only a fairly limited number of managerial problems. We should not overlook its limitations.

In the first place, there is the sheer magnitude of the mathematical and computing aspects. The number of variables and interrelationships in many managerial problems, plus the complexities of human relationships and reactions, calls for a higher order of mathematics than nuclear physics does. The late mathematical genius John von Neumann found, in his development of the theory of games, that his mathematical abilities soon reached their limit in a relatively simple strategic problem. Managers are, however, a long way from fully using the mathematics now available.

FIGURE 23-3

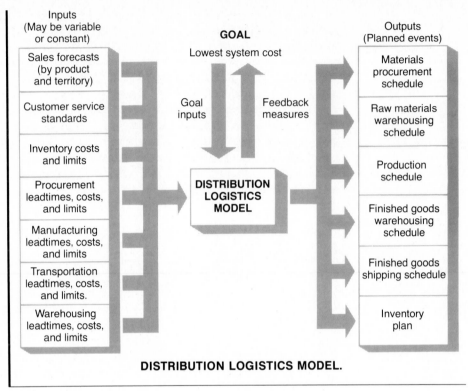

DISTRIBUTION LOGISTICS MODEL.

Qualitative factors

In the second place, although probabilities and approximations are being substituted for unknown quantities and although scientific method can assign values to factors we could never measure before, a major portion of important managerial decisions still involves qualitative factors. Until these can be measured, operations research will have limited usefulness in these areas, and decisions will continue to be based on nonquantitative judgments.

Lack of information

Related to the fact that many management decisions involve unmeasurable factors is the lack of information needed to make operations research useful in practice. When we conceptualize a problem area and construct a mathematical model to represent it, we discover variables about which we need information not now available. What we need is far more emphasis on the part of those interested in the practical applications of operations research on developing this required information.

Gap between managers and operations researchers

Still another limitation is the gap between practicing managers and trained operations researchers. Managers in general lack a knowledge and appreciation of mathematics, just as mathematicians lack understanding of managerial problems. This gap is being dealt with, to an increasing extent, by the business schools and, more often, by business firms that team up managers with operations researchers. But it is still the major reason why firms are slow to use operations research.

One of the specialists in operations research reported many years ago in a rather pessimistic tone about the actual use of this important tool. He had his graduate students write the authors of cases reported in the journal *Operations Research* over the first six years of its publication with a view to determining the extent to which recommendations of the studies had been carried out by practicing managers. He reported that there was not sufficient evidence in any case that the recommendations had been accepted. However, in recent years much more, but still fairly little, practical use is being made of this significant technique.

Expense

A final drawback of operations research—at least in its application to complex problems—is that analyses and programming are expensive, and many problems are not important enough to justify this cost. However, in practice this has not really been a major limitation.

Other Tools and Techniques

Besides operations research there are other techniques. We will discuss the application of decision trees, time-event networks, value engineering, work simplification, and quality circles.

Decision Trees

Although they have had a much wider use in planning and control, decision trees are nonetheless of interest in planning and controlling operations. Decision trees were discussed in Chapter 7 in connection with decision making, and no special discussion of their nature is needed here.

It can be seen, however, in any area of operations, how purchasing, fabrication, warehousing, or transport input variables may not always be certain, so that we may not be able to develop definite answers as to what we must do to make operations effective. Many uncertainties or chance events may arise in almost any system of production or operations. The failure of a supplier to deliver on time, a major machine breakdown, a labor dispute, a transportation strike, or a sudden change in customer demand may make any skillfully drawn operating plan obsolete.

Astute managers of any kind of operations will, therefore, find it to their advantage to develop contingency plans, and to consider the probability of unsettling chance events occurring. By being aware where disturbing chance events may occur and the probability of their occurrence, intelligent operations managers can know the nature of their risks and what path to follow when unexpected events do occur.

Time-Event Networks

In the previous chapter, we discussed time-event network analysis and saw how it is a logical extension of the famous Gantt chart. Often referred to as Program Evaluation and Review Technique (PERT) and in its essentials as Critical Path Method (CPM), this technique of planning and control has wide potential use in many applications. But PERT and its various refinements, like PERT/COST, have considerable potential for use in many aspects of planning and control of operations.

Perhaps the most useful application of time-event networks is in the planning and control of production. For example, the design of a typical assembly line, where parts and subassemblies must be fitted in at the right time and place, is a perfect example of such a network. It would be the rare assembly line where all activities were linear, that is, where an end product is assembled purely by a succession of sequential operations. One can hardly imagine an automobile assembly line, for example, where the assembly started with a frame, followed by assembly of the wheels, followed by assembly of the engine, and then the transmission. Indeed, assembly lines, in order to be at all efficient, must be based on a network of planned activities, many of them done simultaneously.

Much the same can be said for most other areas of production or operations. It is difficult to conceive of a warehousing and shipping operation where plans need not represent a network of events. Even warehousing finished goods and stacking them by model or style requires network planning if it is to be efficient. Loading a truck for delivery of various items to a number of customers in various locations is also likely to require a network of planned activities.

Students preparing term papers will clearly find it to their advantage to engage in network planning. It is hard to think of a student sitting down to write such a paper unless paper and a typewriter are available, the needed data have been gathered and analyzed, and an outline of the paper conceptualized.

By using network planning and control, those managing any phase of operations are forced to plan. In addition, if they do a fairly thorough job, they have a tool whereby critical paths may be identified, thus making possible pinpointing where corrective action can best be taken if deviations from plans become apparent.

Value Engineering

A product can be improved and its cost lowered through value engineering, which consists of analyzing the operation of the product or service, estimating the value of each operation, and attempting to improve that operation by trying to keep costs low at each step or part. The following specific steps are suggested:

1 Divide the product into parts and operations.

2 Identify the costs for each part and operation.

3 Identify the relative value or contribution of each part to the final part.

4 Find a new approach for those items which appear to have a high cost and low value.

Work Simplification

Work methods can also be improved through work simplification. The purpose is to obtain the participation of workers in simplifying their work. Training sessions are conducted to teach concepts and principles of techniques such as time and motion studies, work-flow analyses, and the layout of the work situation.

Quality Control Circles

For some time now, Japanese companies have been successful in marketing products. To a great extent this has been due to the quality of their products, but this has not always been the case. In fact, in the 1950s and 1960s many products made in Japan had the image of poor quality.

In order to compete in the world market, Japanese firms had to improve the quality of their products. The drive for improved quality of Japanese products was due first to regulatory action by the Japanese government. Shortly after World War II ended, the Japanese, realizing that their economic situation depended on increasing exports, encouraged their government to set up a system of regulations requiring all exporters to submit to a government agency a sample of a product to be exported and to meet demanding requirements for quality before a permit to export was issued.

The legislative drive for quality was supported by various management techniques encouraging or requiring product quality. One of the interesting techniques is the quality control circle, now in widespread use in Japan. At first employees were trained in the analysis of quality problems. But now other problems are also dealt with such as cost reduction, workshop facilities improvement, safety problems, employee morale, pollution control, and the education of employees.

Quality control circles evolved from suggestion programs. In both approaches, workers participate in solving work-related problems. Although in suggestion programs the problems are usually quite specific, those dealt with by quality control circles are often more complex and require the involvement of several members of the team. The team consists primarily of rank-and-file workers and sometimes also includes supervisors. So-called efficiency experts are usually excluded from the team.

It is interesting to note that while the concept of quality control originated in the United States, the Japanese appear to have perfected it. More recently, American firms have "rediscovered" the importance of quality as stressed, for example, in the advertisements for Chrysler and Ford automobiles. At any rate, there is no reason to doubt that quality control circles can be used by American companies who are now faced with a competitive situation in the world market that demands quality products.

The Future of Operations Management

Four trends

What factors show signs of influencing future developments in this field? Several major trends can be expected in operations management.[5]

1 The increased complexity of technology will be reflected in the products themselves as well as in the processes used to produce them. Fifteen years ago few people would have expected that sophisticated home computers could be produced at a price affordable by the usual consumers.

---

[5]Fearon et al., op. cit. (in Table 23-1).

2 Automation is becoming increasingly more important in the production process. General Motors, which pioneered the application of robots, is importing a new generation of robots from Japan. New machine tools, microprocessors, sensory technology, and computer controls now make it possible to reduce machine setup time and costs.[6] This means a greater variety of products at a lower cost. In the past, lower costs tended to be achieved through high-volume production of a particular model. Now through high technology setup times are reduced dramatically. This means a better use of machines with lower direct-labor costs. Moreover, work-in-process inventories can thereby be reduced. Finally, maintenance costs are reduced by simplifying processes, controls, and machines. These simplification technologies were pioneered by Toyota when it doubled its automobile model range without incurring the high costs traditionally associated with a variety of models.

3 The service industry in the United States is providing an increasingly important portion of the gross national product. This means that the concepts and principles of "production" have been advantageously adapted to such nonmanufacturing activities as banking, health care, and tourism.

4 The production function will become increasingly a global challenge. As we have recently seen, car engines produced in Japan and Germany are now installed in American cars. Moreover, major car manufacturers in the United States make arrangements to produce cars in Japan and market them under their own name in the United States and elsewhere.

Summary

Production management refers to those activities necessary to manufacture products or create services; they include activities such as purchasing, warehousing, transportation, and other operations from procurement of raw materials until the product or service is bought by the consumer. Operations management has a similar meaning, referring to activities necessary to produce and deliver a service as well as a physical product.

The operations management systems model (Figure 23-1) shows the inputs, transformation processes, outputs, and the feedback system. A variety of tools and techniques aid managers to make operations more productive. Seven steps have been suggested in planning and designing the product and its production. Six different kinds of production layouts have been identified. In order to operate the system, the functions of organizing, staffing, and leading must be carried out effectively. Controlling requires an information system often supported by computers.

---

[6]"The Big Revolution on the Factory Floor," *Wall Street Journal*, July 12, 1982.

Among the various tools for planning and controlling operations is operations research, which is the application of the scientific method to the study of alternatives in a problem situation to obtain a quantitative basis for arriving at a best solution. Examples are linear programming, inventory planning and control, and distribution logistics. Other tools and techniques are decision trees, time-event networks, value engineering, work simplification, and quality control circles.

Key Ideas and Concepts for Review

Production management

Operations management

Steps in product and production design

Production layouts

Information systems

Operations research

Essential characteristics of operations
  research

Operations research procedure

Linear programming

Inventory planning and control

Distribution logistics

Decision trees

Time-event networks

Value engineering

Work simplification

Quality control circles

Trends in operations research

For Discussion

1 Why is the field of production and operations management such a good one to use as a case example of planning and control techniques? Why do you believe that this was a favored area for analysis and suggested practice by the pioneers in the field of management?

2 Distinguish between planning and control techniques that are usually found only in production and operations management and those found to be useful in all areas of managing. Why is this so?

3 Explain the nature of and reasons for each step usually found in the development of a production and operations management program.

4 There are many typical layouts used in the design of a production program. Which one is ordinarily used for the manufacture of automobiles and why? Which one do you believe was used for construction of the trans-Alaska pipeline, and why?

5 Real-time information can be widely used in the area of production, but this does not solve the problem of control. Why?

6 What tools generally found in operations research have been widely used in production and operations management? Do they have anything in common? If so, what is it?

7 What makes distribution logistics a more useful and complex tool of planning and control than an inventory model?

8 Decision trees have been found to be useful in many other areas than production and operations management. Where? Why?

9 Why do you believe that quality control circles have been used so much in Japan?

10 Can you suggest any element that tends to be common in the summary of major trends expected in the future of production and operations planning and control?

CASE 23-1

LAMPERT & SONS COMPANY

John Lampert, president of Lampert & Sons Company, a small manufacturing firm producing electrical appliances, was an entrepreneur with a technical background. He recently moved into a new house, and his wife asked him to install some spotlights to accent certain items in the house such as bookshelves, a sculpture, and certain items in a wall unit.

A trip to the local lighting stores showed that the lamps that might fit the purpose cost far more than he was willing to pay. He felt that there was a real need for a low-cost, attractive spotlight or clamp-on lamp. He discussed his idea with a business colleague who raised a number of questions such as:

1 Is there really a need for such a product?

2 What should such a lamp look like?

3 How or where should it be produced (e.g., in his plant in the Midwest or abroad such as in Korea, Hong Kong, or Taiwan)?

4 What arrangements would have to be made if the lamp were to be produced by Lampert & Sons?

5 What kind of distribution channel(s) should be used to sell the product?

6 How would he maintain the quality if the price of the lamp was to be kept low?

After this discussion, Mr. Lampert realized that he really had not thought through his idea and could not satisfactorily answer several of the questions.

1 If you were a small-business consultant, how would you answer the questions Mr. Lampert's colleague raised?

2 What other actions would you recommend to make the product decision to design the product, to set up a production system, and to control the operation, especially the quality?

3 What decision-making tools and techniques could assist in making these decisions?

CASE 23-2

MANUFACTURING REQUIREMENTS PLANNING (MRP)

Proctor & Company, a high-technology supplier to the aerospace industry, had found itself in the enviable position of supplying some critical microwave components for the space shuttle. The business, which had started out in a garage, was founded and developed by two entrepreneurial partners, and had grown over a period of 10 years from $250,000 to $12 million in sales per year.

Along with the success of the operation had come some problems, and one of the most visible manifestations of the problems was the conflict between the partners, one of whom thought that the company should sell stock to the public, while the other thought that the company should remain privately owned. The former borrowed money from one of the principal banks in California, bought the other partner out, and proceeded to sell stock to the public.

The public offering was a great success, provided the company with all of the working capital it needed, and made the entrepreneur founder a millionaire in the process. However, while he was fulfilling his dreams, a lot of the basics in designing and producing the products had been overlooked or neglected, with the result that the operations of the company were running out of control.

Engineering changes proliferated and were always behind time in being documented and entered into document control records. Also, new products, which had been developed so easily in the early days and quickly brought to fruition, were now hopelessly bogged down in design and concept.

The president, who by instinct sensed that the flexibility and drive of the early days were no longer present, decided that he would have to move to impose some order upon the organization, much

as an assembly line brings order to manufacturing operations. Since the firm was heavily engineering and research oriented, the "order" for the program was at first perceived as something that could be readily purchased from specialists and which by its nature would ask the right questions and provide the essential elements in order to provide data necessary for planning and control.

The task of implementing the program was given to Jim Martin, the master scheduler. At the onset of program development, it was discovered that the parts master list—a complete listing of all parts used in manufacturing assemblies—was neither correct nor complete. Nor were engineering drawings or manufacturing bills of material in order. A general feeling of dismay set in as it became obvious why production schedules were so often overrun and deliveries late, and why parts seemed always to be in short supply: No one *knew* what component parts were really needed to make subassemblies and what end items were required in order to deliver products on time.

As a result, a single task such as compiling the data on parts contained in the storeroom, which should have taken 1 week to complete, ended up taking over 2 months. Each step uncovered problems of a similar magnitude: Bills of material and assembly structures were wrong. Part numbers were incorrect. Material and parts counts were off by a wide margin. Issues of parts to the plant and purchasing receipts were not recorded properly. Shop floor loading was done only for final assembly. Purchasing and material files were incorrect. Order quantities, lead times, and costs were out of date—and so forth throughout the system.

The master scheduler was in a quandary. The estimated few months' task of implementing an orderly control program was turning into a year-long nightmare. Worse still was the difficulty he was having discussing the scope of the problem with top management, since he knew that top management's policies had caused or contributed to the mess. On the one hand, he needed a large allocation of funds and labor-hours if the task was to be completed. On the other hand, he was paralyzed because of the limits of authority in the job's assignment and because of the fact that he was potentially bearing bad news to an optimistic president.

1 What do you think the key management issues were in the above situation?

2 What, if any, techniques or principles should have been effected?

3 What recommendations could you offer the master scheduler?

For Further Information

Adam, E. E., Jr., and R. J. Ebert. *Production and Operations Management: Concepts, Models, and Behavior*, 2nd ed. (Englewood Cliffs, N.J.: Prentice-Hall, Inc., 1982).

Buffa, E. S. *Elements of Productions/Operations Management* (New York: John Wiley & Sons, Inc., 1981).

Chase, R. B., and N. J. Aquilano. *Production and Operations Management* (Homewood, Ill.: Richard D. Irwin, Inc., 1981).

Hyer, N. L., and U. Wemmerloev. "Group Technology and Productivity," *Harvard Business Review*, vol. 62, no. 4 (July–August 1984), pp. 140–149.

Schonberger, R. J. "The Transfer of Japanese Manufacturing Management Approaches to U. S. Industry," *Academy of Management Review*, vol. 7, no. 3 (July 1982), pp. 479–487.

Shapiro, R. D. "Get Leverage from Logistics," *Harvard Business Review*, vol. 62, no. 3 (May–June 1984), pp. 119–126.

Sharman, G. "The Rediscovery of Logistics," *Harvard Business Review*, vol. 62, no. 5 (September–October 1984), pp. 71–79.

Weiss, A. "Simple Truths of Japanese Manufacturing," *Harvard Business Review*, vol. 62, no. 4 (July–August 1984), pp. 119–125.

Wheelwright, S. C., and R. B. Hayes. "Competing Through Manufacturing," *Harvard Business Review*, vol. 63, no. 1 (January–February 1985), pp. 99–109.

24

Control of Overall Performance

CHAPTER OBJECTIVES

After reading this chapter, you should understand:

1 The concept of overall control
2 The nature of budget summaries and reports
3 Profit and loss control
4 The concept of control through return on investment
5 The advantages and limitations of return-on-investment control

Most controls are designed for specific things: policies, wages and salaries, employee selection and training, research and development, product quality, costs, pricing, capital expenditures, cash, and other areas where we wish performance to conform to plans. Such controls are partial in the sense that they apply to a part of an enterprise and do not measure total accomplishments against total goals. Moreover, it is not possible to be precise about practical details of partial control without, at the very least, reference to a given plan, to the position and personality of the manager involved, and to specific enterprise goals.

Planning and control

Planning and control are increasingly being treated as an interrelated system. Along with techniques for partial control, control devices have been developed to measure the overall performance of an enterprise—or an integrated[1] division or project within it—against total goals.

Reasons for overall control

There are many reasons for control of overall performance. In the first place, as overall planning must apply to enterprise or major division goals, so must overall controls be applied. In the second place, decentralization of authority—especially in product or territorial divisions—creates semi-independent units, and these must be subjected to overall controls to avoid the chaos of complete independence. In the third place, overall controls permit measuring an integrated area manager's *total* effort, rather than parts of it.

Financial controls

Overall controls in business are, as one might expect, financial. Business owes its continued existence to profit making; its capital resources are a scarce, life-giving element; and, in the environment in which it operates, the best gauge of effectiveness is profits, costs, and money. Since finance is the binding force of business, financial controls are the most important single objective gauge of the success of plans.

Financial measurements also summarize, as a common denominator, the operation of a number of plans. Further, they accurately indicate total expenditures of resources in reaching goals. This is true in all forms of enterprise. Although the purpose of an educational or government enterprise is not to make monetary profits, any responsible manager must have some way of knowing what goal achievement has cost in terms of resources. Therefore, in all forms of enterprise, control of overall performance is likely to a great extent to be financial. Moreover, financial analyses furnish an excellent "window" through which accomplishment in nonfinancial areas can be seen. A deviation from planned costs, for example, may lead a manager to find the causes in poor planning, inadequate training of employees, or other nonfinancial factors.

Budget Summaries and Reports

Budget summary

A widely used control of overall performance takes the form of a summary of budgets. A **budget summary,** being a résumé of all the individual budgets, reflects company plans so that sales volume, costs, profits, utilization of capital, and return on investment may be seen in their proper relationship. In these terms it shows top management how the company as a whole is succeeding in meeting its objectives.

For the best control through a budget summary, a manager must first be satisfied that total budgets are an accurate and reasonably complete portrayal of

---

[1]"Integrated" here is used as meaning that an operation includes the functions necessary to gain an overall objective. Thus, a product division of a company would normally include engineering, manufacturing, and marketing, and these functions represent enough of a total operation for the division manager—even though subject to some direction and control from headquarters—to be held basically responsible for a profit. To a lesser degree, an engineering design operation might be regarded as integrated: If its head supervises all the engineering functions and specialities necessary for complete product design, he or she can then be held responsible for the efficient accomplishment of the project.

the company's plans. The manager should study the budget reports and any material accompanying them to determine whether the comparison of budget and actual costs shows the real nature of any deviations. As an example, a company head criticized his factory manager for being considerably over his labor budget in a month when the labor force had been materially reduced and the temporary increase in expenses was due to severance pay.

Minor discrepancies should receive appropriately little attention. The purpose of a control system is to draw attention to important variations, and both the budget reports and the attention paid to them should reflect this. Above all, a manager should never forget that a budget summary is no substitute for profitable operation. Budgeting is never more perfect than the planning behind it, and plans—especially long-range plans—are subject to the imperfections caused by change and uncertainty. There may even be times when a manager must forget the budget and take special action to meet unexpected events. Budgets are meant to be tools, and not masters, of managers.

On the other hand, managers should not underestimate the value of budget summaries in providing an effective means for overall control where there is decentralization of authority. Budget summaries furnish a means whereby enterprise objectives can be clearly and specifically defined, and departmental plans can be made to contribute toward such objectives. Should the budget summary and the reports of actual events indicate that the enterprise as a whole is not tending toward its objectives, top managers have a convenient and positive means of finding out where the deviations are occurring. The summaries thus furnish a useful guide for corrective action.

Profit and Loss Control

The profit and loss statement for an enterprise as a whole serves important control purposes, largely because it is useful for determining the immediate revenue or cost factors that have accounted for success or failure. Obviously, if it is first put in the form of a forecast, it is even a better control device in that it gives managers a chance, before things happen, to influence revenues, expenses, and, consequently, profits.

Nature and Purpose of Profit and Loss Control

Since the survival of a business usually depends on profits and since profits are a definite standard against which to measure success, many companies use the profit and loss statement for divisional or departmental control. Because this is a statement of all revenues and expenses for a given time, it is a true summary of the results of business operations. Profit and loss control, when applied to divisions or departments, is based on the premise that if it is the purpose of the entire business to make a profit, each part of the enterprise should contribute to this purpose. Thus, the ability of a part to make an expected profit becomes a standard for measuring its performance.

In profit and loss control, each major department or division details its revenues and expenses—normally including a proportionate share of company overhead—and calculates periodically its profit or loss. Some units have their own accounting group, whereas in others, the statement is prepared by the central accounting department. In either case, the organizational unit, in being expected to turn in a separate record of profitable operation, is considered by headquarters in much the same way that a holding company considers its subsidiary companies.

Use of profit and loss control

Profit and loss control usually is practicable only for major segments of a company, since the paperwork involved in building up profit and loss statements for smaller departments tends to be too heavy. Also, profit and loss control usually implies that managers of a division or department have a fairly wide authority to run their part of the business as they see fit, with profit the primary standard of success. However, many companies that do not so decentralize authority have nonetheless found profit and loss control valuable. The focus on profit and the sensitivity of the organizational unit to it are worthwhile even when managers have limited independence to seek profit as they wish.

The more integrated and complete the organization unit, the more accurate a measuring stick profit and loss control can be. For this reason, it works best in product or territorial divisions, where both sales and production functions for a product or service are under one general manager. For example, it is much easier to use the standard of profit for measuring the operations of the general manager of the Buick division of General Motors than it would be to use it for the supervisor of the motor-block-boring section of the manufacturing department of this division.

At the same time, companies organized on a functional basis do occasionally employ profit and loss control. The heat-treating department may produce and "sell" its service to the machining department, which in turn "sells" its product to the assembly department, which in turn "sells" a complete product to the sales department. This can be done, although the paperwork required is often not worth the effort, and the problem of determining the right transfer price may occasion much negotiation or many difficult executive decisions. If the transfer is made at cost, clearly only the sales department would show a profit or a loss. If it is made at a figure above cost, the question of what price to charge arises.

In most instances, profit and loss control is not applied to central staff and service departments. Although these departments could "sell" their services, the most satisfactory practice is to place them under some other form of control, such as the variable expense budget.

Limitations

Profit and loss control suffers its greatest limitations from the cost of accounting and paper transactions involving intracompany transfer of costs and revenues. Duplication of accounting records, efforts involved in allocating the many overhead costs, and time and effort required to calculate intracompany sales can make this control too costly if it is carried too far.

Profit and loss control also may be inadequate for overall performance. Top managers may not wish to yield so much authority to division managers as to make their division completely integrated, and they may desire the additional assurances of good budgetary control. In addition, profit and loss control in and of itself does not provide a standard of desirable profits or policy controls in the areas of product line development or in other matters of long-term overall company concern.

Another limitation of profit and loss control, especially if it is carried very far in the organization, is that departments may come to compete with an aggressive detachment not helpful to enterprise coordination. On the other hand, in many companies there is not enough feeling of departmental responsibility for company profit, and departments may develop the smugness of a monopolist with an assured market. The parts fabrication department that knows its products must be "bought" by the assembly department, the manufacturing or the service department that can force its output on the sales department, and the engineering group that has a monopolistic hold on both production and sales are dangerous monopolists indeed. Profit and loss control can break down these islands of monopoly. So, in spite of limitations—and especially if accompanied by an intracompany pricing policy requiring departments to meet competitive prices of suppliers outside the enterprise rather than being based on cost—profit and loss control can give top managers an extraordinary measure of overall control.

Control Through Return on Investment (ROI)

One of the most successfully used control techniques is that of measuring both the absolute and the relative success of a company or a company unit by the ratio of earnings to investment of capital. The return-on-investment approach, often referred to as simply ROI, has been the core of the control system of the Du Pont Company since 1919. A large number of companies have adopted it as their key measure of overall performance especially in the past decade. This yardstick is the rate of return that a company or a division can earn on the capital allocated to it. This tool, therefore, does not look at the profit as an absolute, but as a return on capital employed in the business. The goal of a business is seen, accordingly, not necessarily as optimizing profits but as optimizing returns from capital devoted to business purposes. This standard recognizes the fundamental fact that capital is a critical factor in almost any enterprise and, through its scarcity, limits progress. It also emphasizes the fact that the job of managers is to make the best possible use of assets entrusted to them.

Some Examples   As the system has been used by the Du Pont Company, return on investment involves consideration of several factors. Return is computed on the basis of capital turnover (that is, total sales divided by capital, or total investment) multiplied by earnings as a percentage of sales. This formula recognizes that a division with a high capital turnover and low percentage of earnings to sales may be more profitable in terms of return on investment than another with a high percentage of profits to sales but with low capital turnover. As can be seen, the system measures effectiveness in the use of capital. Investment includes not only the permanent plant facilities but also the working capital of the unit. In the Du Pont system, investment and working capital represent amounts invested without reduction for liabilities or reserves, on the ground that such a reduction would result in a fluctuation in operating investments as reserves or liabilities change, which would distort the rate of return and render it less meaningful. Earnings are, however, calculated after normal depreciation charges, on the basis that true profits are not earned until allowance is made for the write-off of depreciable assets.

Return-on-investment control is perhaps best summarized in chart form, as in Figure 24-1. Here, analysis of variations in rate of return leads into every financial aspect of the business. Rate of return is the common denominator used in comparing divisions, and differences can easily be traced to their causes.

A different view

However, other companies have taken the position that the return on investment should be calcualted on fixed assets less depreciation. Such companies hold that the depreciation reserve represents a write-off of the initial investment and that funds made available through such charges are reinvested in other fixed assets or used as working capital. Such a treatment appears more realistic to operating people, partly because it places a heavier rate-of-return burden on new fixed assets than on worn or obsolete ones.

In any control through return on investment, the number of ratios and comparisons behind the yardstick figure cannot be overlooked. Although improvement in rate of return can come from a higher percentage of profit to sales, improvement may also come from increasing the rate of turnover by lowering price and reducing return on sales. Moreover, the ratio of return on investment might be improved by getting more product (and sales) out of a given plant investment or by reducing the cost of sales for a given product.

Application to Product Lines

Functional-line organizations without integrated product divisions have applied return-on-investment control to their various product lines. By grouping its many products into a number of major classifications, a typical company follows through with the allocation of sales, costs, and investment in fixed assets and working capital to arrive at the same kind of rate-of-return analysis used by multidivision companies. A simplified example of these results is shown in Table 24-1.

To use the rate-of-return yardstick (as return on assets employed) for product lines, the company has allocated certain expenses and assets, but these allocations apparently have not caused much difficulty. Most production costs are maintained by product, and common costs, such as sales branch expenses, are allocated by volume of sales. More difficulty is incurred in determining asset usage by product lines, but cash, accounts receivable, and administrative and sales facilities are allocated in accordance with sales, while inventories and factory and plant equipment are prorated to the various products on the basis of special analyses.

In addition to comparing rates of return on assets of products, as indicated in Table 24-1, this company compares actual experience with trends for the various products (identified for purposes of simplicity as the "base year" in the table). An advantage of these comparisons is that the company is able to keep a sharp eye on its product lines, with a view to determining where capital is being most efficiently employed and as a guide toward obtaining a balanced use of capital for greatest overall profit. Thus, the company has been able to identify products that

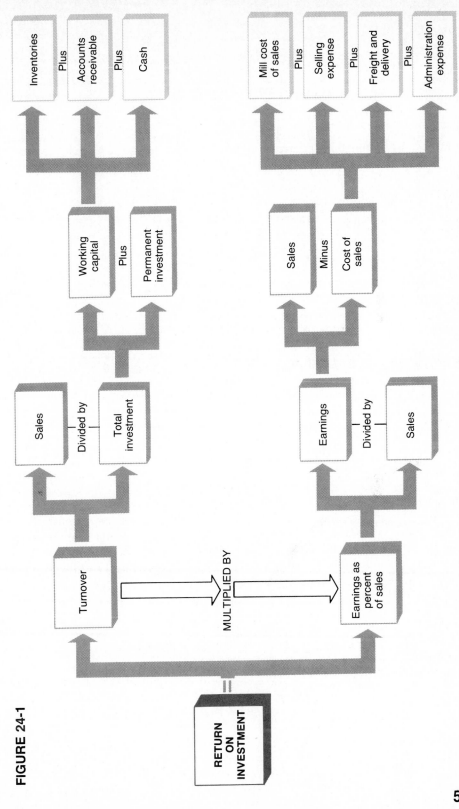

FIGURE 24-1

THE RELATIONSHIP OF FACTORS AFFECTING RETURN ON INVESTMENT.

TABLE 24-1   Comparative Rates of Return on Assets Employed: Multiproduct Company (In thousands of dollars)

	Total sales		Assets employed		Operating income*		
	Amount	Percent of total	Amount	Per dollar of sales	Amount	Percent return on sales	Percent return on assets
Base year:							
Product A	$ 39,300	40	$ 20,700	52.9%	$ 4,800	12.2	23.1
Product B	29,500	30	16,900	57.3	2,800	9.4	16.4
Product C	19,600	20	8,900	45.1	2,100	10.8	23.9
Product D	9,800	10	2,700	27.5	500	5.1	18.5
Total	$ 98,200	100	$ 49,200	50.1%	$10,200	10.4	20.8
Current year:							
Product A	$ 48,100	25	$ 28,400	59.0%	$ 5,600	11.6	19.7
Product B	96,200	50	75,300	78.3	8,500	8.8	11.2
Product C	38,500	20	19,500	50.7	3,900	10.2	20.1
Product D	9,600	5	2,900	29.9	500	5.2	17.2
Total	$192,400	100	$126,100	65.5%	$18,500	9.6	14.6

*Before interest on borrowed money and federal income taxes.

are either strong and established, new and improved, or past their peak in growth and profitability.

Advantages

Focus on central objectives

One of the principal advantages of using return on investment to control overall performance is that it, like profit and loss control, focuses managerial attention on the central objective of the business—to make the best profit possible on the capital available. It measures the efficiency of the company as a whole and of its major divisions or departments, its products, and its planning. It takes attention away from mere increase in sales volume or asset size or even from the level of costs, and draws attention to the combination of factors making for successful operation.

Effectiveness in decentralized structures

Another advantage of control by return on investment is that it is effective where authority is decentralized. It not only is an absolute guide to capital efficiency but also offers the possibility of comparing efficiency in the use of capital within the company and with other enterprises. By holding departmental managers responsible for performance in terms of the dollars invested in their parts of the business, it forces them to look at their operations from the point of view of top management. Managers often insist on heavy capital investments for new equipment or drive for lower prices to increase sales without taking into account the possible effect of their requests on the company as a whole. They also often feel isolated, particularly in large businesses, with respect to their performance. If managers are furnished a guide to efficiency that applies to a business as a whole, they develop a keener sense of responsibility for their department or division and top managers can more easily hold subordinate managers responsible.

A further advantage of return-on-investment control, if it is complete and shows all the factors bearing upon the return, is that it enables managers to locate weaknesses. If inventories are rising, the rate of return will be affected, or if other factors camouflage inventory variations and leave the rate looking good, tracing back influences will disclose any weakness of the inventory situation and open the way for consideration of a remedy.

Identification
of weaknesses

Limitations

Availability
of information

With all its advantages and with its widespread use by well-managed and successful companies, this method of control is not foolproof. Difficulties involve availability of information on sales, costs, and assets and proper allocation of investment and return for commonly sold or produced items. Does the present accounting system give the needed information? If not, how much will it cost to get it, through either changes in the system or special analyses? Where assets are jointly used or costs are common, what method of allocation between divisions or departments shall be used? Should a manager be charged with assets at their original costs, their replacement costs, or their depreciated values? Setting up a return-on-investment control system is no simple task.

Difficulties
in comparing

Another question is: What constitutes a reasonable return? Comparisons of rates of return are hardly enough, because they do not tell the top manager what the rate of return *should* be. Perhaps as good a standard as any is one that meets or surpasses the level of competing firms, since, in a practical sense, the best tends to be measured not by an absolute level but, rather, by the level of the competition for capital.

Resulting
inflexibility

One of the dangers of overemphasis on the rate of return is that it may lead to undesirable inflexibility in investing capital for new ventures. Many companies using this important measuring tool have set minimum rates which a division, new product program, or investment must meet before the allocation of additional capital would be approved. It is said that even Du Pont, for many years, would not approve a new product program which would not promise a minimum of 20 percent return on investment. According to one executive of the company, this rigid minimum caused it to pass up such great product opportunities as xerography and the Land (Polaroid) camera. More recently, the company has used a more flexible minimum rate of return, requiring a higher rate when risks are greater and a lower rate when results are very promising or more certain, or when an investment supplements an established business.

Preoccupation with
financial factors

Perhaps the greatest danger in return-on-investment control, as with any system of control based on financial data, is that it can lead to excessive preoccupation with financial factors within a firm or an industry. Undue attention to ratios and financial data can cause a firm to overlook environmental factors such as social and technical developments. It might also lead a company to overlook the fact that capital is not the only scarce resource from which a business can grow, prosper, and endure. Every bit as scarce are competent managers, good employee morale, and good customer and public relations. A well-managed company would never regard any financially based control as the sole gauge of overall performance.

Summary

Most controls are designed for specific things, such as wages and salaries, costs, prices, capital expenditures, and other areas where it is desired that performance conform to plans. These controls are partial; they do not measure total accomplishments against total goals. To provide measures against total goals, controls of overall performance of an enterprise, an integrated division, or other part of the enterprise may be used.

To a very great extent, overall controls are financial in that financial measures summarize, through the common denominator of money, the operation of a number of plans. The most widely used control of overall performance is the summary budget, that is, a summary of all operating revenue and expense budgets.

For businesses at least, another kind of overall control is profit and loss control. This control approach is based on the idea that if the objective of a business is to make a profit, then, to the extent we can do so, each part (division, department, or project) of a business operation should be evaluated on its ability to show a profit. To be sure, this control is very likely to be used only for major segments of a company, since the paperwork involved in constructing profit and loss statements for smaller units may be very heavy.

One of the most successfully used overall control techniques is the exercise of control through calculating and comparing return on investment. This approach is based on the belief that profit should not be considered as an absolute measure but as a return on the capital employed in a segment of a business. The famous Du Pont return-on-investment (ROI) model may be summarized in chart form showing sales, expenses, profits, and capital investments, and then calculating the percentage rate of return on capital invested. This device has been particularly useful for companies with highly integrated divisions or departments. But some companies without such divisions have been able to use ROI of product lines effectively by allocating sales, expenses, and assets employed to product lines.

Key Ideas and Concepts for Review

Budget summaries
Profit and loss control
Limitations of profit and loss control
Return on investment (ROI)

Advantages of ROI control
Limitations of ROI control
Use of ROI for product lines

For Discussion

1 Why do most controls of overall performance tend to be financial? Should they be? What else would you suggest?

2 "Profit and loss control is defective in that it does not emphasize return on investment; the latter is defective in that it places too great an emphasis on present results, possibly endangering future results." Discuss.

3 In applying rate of return on investment as a control tool, would you favor using an undepreciated or a depreciated asset base?

4 Selecting any federal, state, or local government agency you wish, could you develop a system or program for evaluating overall performance?

CASE 24-1
WESTERN PETROLEUM CORPORATION

Western Petroleum Corporation was founded in 1957 with an investment of $250,000 by multi-millionaire Victor Eastman and the same amount by several of his friends. With a few young geologists, recruited from several major oil companies, who saw a real chance for action in the company and with the daring of Mr. Eastman, the company embarked on a vigorous exploration program in northern California. Their approach was quickly rewarded by the discovery of a large gas field and several good oil wells. With large profits from these fields and Mr. Eastman's ability to get a concession from a country in northern Africa, the brilliance of the young team of geologists paid off when the company discovered a large oil field in the African country.

As profits accumulated, as banks rushed to lend money to Western, and as investors eagerly bought its stock, Western acquired a number of fairly large companies. They included (1) the Master Chemical Company, one of the largest producers of industrial chemicals and agricultural fertilizers in the United States, with annual sales of $500 million; (2) the Beverly Coal Company, third largest miner of coal in the country, with sales of more than $300 million per year; (3) the Pennant Gas and Oil Company, with refineries and retail oil products outlets in Europe and annual sales of $350 million per year; and (4) several other companies in such fields as oil marketing, real estate development, and plastics materials. In addition, Western continued its program of searching for oil both in the United States and overseas.

The company had an extraordinary history of growth. From sales of less than $500,000 in 1957, it grew to the remarkable size of $2.7 billion in sales by 1974. Profits kept pace with growth and, although Western had heavy loans from banks and others and had sold more than 40 million new shares of stock to the public, stock prices increased more than 20 times in the period.

Although profits leveled off in 1974, sales still rose by 15 percent over 1973. This was not regarded as a problem by Western's top management since the company was investing heavily in new oil exploration, and its industrial chemical profits had almost disappeared because of the overbuilding and severe price competition of all companies in this field. But, obviously, the stock market had some misgivings about Western. The company's shares, which had risen to $105 in 1972, fell to $25 in 1974. But the top management of Western was not too concerned since all oil and industrial chemicals stocks had suffered a drop in price.

However, toward the end of 1974, a number of adverse events occurred which did shock and surprise Western's management. Among the most important were the following:

1 Profits in industrial chemicals continued their decline as the new and larger competitors fought for business to keep their chemical plants operating at capacity or as near to it as possible.

2 An industrywide coal strike closed down the coal mines for almost 2 months in October and November of 1974, with an impact on profits of more than $11 million.

3 In addition, a new national coal Mine and Safety Act imposed stringent controls on mining procedures, reducing productivity and requiring the employment of many new miners in an industry where there were few experienced miners to be hired, so that inexperienced miners had to be employed.

4 With a new labor union contract, mine labor wages went up considerably. The Beverly Coal Company found it could not pass on these increased costs, along with the higher costs from lower productivity, to most of its large public utility customers, with whom it had entered long-term contracts at fixed prices per ton. The coal company management had defended these fixed-price contracts on the ground that past history had shown that cost increases had always been offset by productivity increases.

5 The plastic film, sheeting, and fabrics division suffered losses in 1974 exceeding $10 million primarily because (a) the new plant was poorly designed and more expensive to operate than had been anticipated; (b) the new and promising plastic coating material failed to meet specifications, with the result that buyers shipped it back to the company by the carload; and (c) large losses were incurred in raw material costs because of inadequate weighing, inspection, and storage procedures and facilities.

6 The largest loss charged against 1974's earnings was $88 million to charge off potential losses from some $200 million of 3- to 5-year oil-tanker charters. The general manager of the European operation had embarked on an ambitious program of chartering tankers so that the company could be assured of bringing oil to Europe from Saudi Arabia and other Persian Gulf sources in the event that problems in the Mideast resulted in loss of supply from the North Africa fields. When the size of these commitments was learned in 1974 and it became evident that the tanker charters would not be needed, and when tanker charter rates dropped considerably, the company was forced to take this large write-down. When the huge loss exposure was questioned, it was found that the European general manager had proceeded on his own to get these tanker charters. When he was called upon to resign as the result of his costly decision, he defended himself on the ground that he had suggested this idea to Mr. Eastman on one of his overseas trips and that the president had commented that he "thought it was a good idea" to get some tanker charters.

7 Other disappointments came as the result of write-downs of a number of other unsuccessful investments. The general manager of a small division approved the construction of a new office building in the headquarters city of his division at a cost of $6 million, only to find, as the building neared completion, that his division was being combined with another division and the headquarters moved to another city. An executive in charge of drilling a well in a foreign oil field ran into unexpected difficulties and went over his budget by more than $5 million before anyone at Western's headquarters even knew that the money had been spent and the well abandoned.

Mr. Eastman was a strong believer in a lean and streamlined headquarters organization. He felt that he could keep his eye on Western's operations and that the job of the president was to keep in close touch with operations of the various divisions and subsidiaries. Mr. Eastman would make the company's major decisions and especially would negotiate new acquisitions and new oil-exploration leases and concessions. It was his firm conviction that each subsidiary and division top manager should run his own operation and be judged primarily on the earnings statement and balance sheet of the operation.

The principal control tool at headquarters was the budget for capital expenditures. Each year, the vice-president in charge of finance would sit down with division and subsidiary top managers, hear their needs for capital expenditures, and then use his own judgment in allocating funds for these expenditures. In addition, all divisions and subsidiaries submitted balance sheets and earnings statements to headquarters every 3 months; these statements were reviewed by the financial department and then used to produce consolidated statements of the company for bankers and investors.

1 What is your evaluation of Western's management control approach and techniques?

2 To what extent and in which ways were Western's problems in 1974 due to lack of effective management control?

3 Precisely what program of controls would you recommend for Western?

CASE 24-2

HOSPITAL SERVICES, INC.

In past decades considerable interest was generated in hospital care. The aged and the poor were heavily subsidized by government programs aimed, among other things, at helping those in need to get adequate hospital care. During the same time, the cost of hospital services doubled, and still there were not enough beds for patients. Federal and state governments saw the need to distinguish among the most suitable types of care. It was clear that not everyone needed the full-service care of general hospitals. The law contemplated that once discharged from such a facility, patients would be sent to a convalescent hospital for a limited time, where the service level and costs were much lower. And, theoretically, having completed the allowed time, or as much of it as was needed, in this institution, patients would be returned to their homes, where they could receive needed services.

Jules McDonald was among several people who had the idea of building or buying a chain of convalescent hospitals to fill the growing need for beds. He thought that a chain could probably achieve some economies of operation that a single hospital would not find possible. He intended to broaden his business by purchasing land, securing a mortgage to take care of the hospitals, and selling the whole package to investors. He would place his own optical stores and drugstores within each hospital, have his own wholesalers in drugs and hospital equipment, and create his own construction companies.

McDonald needed money to do these things. He knew that the shares of convalescent hospital chains were being traded in multiples from 60 to 200 times earnings, and so he determined to tap the investment market for capital. He got together a few scattered assets, packaged them attractively, and took his business public. It could not be said that he could show any earnings, but he stressed his prospective earnings per share. Amazingly, the idea sold, and he raised about $15 million.

With cash in the bank and an attractive vi-

sion in his head, McDonald was ready to go with his Hospital Services, Inc. Plush offices came first. Then a group of lawyers and tax accountants was added. A salesman sold him a computer. Convalescent hospitals were purchased at high prices; land was bought across the country and construction was begun; and acquisitions were eagerly sought. McDonald did not do this all by himself. He was specially gifted in his public relations, government relations, and negotiations skills and tended to specialize in them. Managers were hired to take care of construction, hospital management, and finance.

As the months passed, the cash raised from the public issue was fast used. On paper, the cash flow from operations seemed to be adequate, but it did not actually materialize. No one, it seemed, was able to get a reading on hospital finances. In some cases, there were no profits; in other cases, the individual institution kept its own cash balance; and in others, there was a heavy drain of funds to cover expenses. The government did not help, either. Its agencies were new at this activity; new interpretations of the law were being made so frequently that no one knew what practice to follow.

Throughout this period of operation there was no slowdown in activity. McDonald was in his element, but his controller failed to warn him of imminent bankruptcy. There did come a day when he ran out of money. This occurred at a time when bankers were tightening up credit and the stock market was falling fast.

As he looked over his wreck, he inquired. "What control system should I have had?"

1 How did Hospital Services, Inc., get out of control?

2 Exactly what controls should have been used and how?

3 To assess the success of the company, what other things should have been done?

For Further Information

Brigham, E. F. *Financial Management: Theory and Practice*. Hinsdale, Ill.: Dryden Press, 1979.

Rhode, J. G., E. E. Lawler III, and G. L. Sundem. "Human Resource Accounting: A Critical Assessment," *Industrial Relations*, (February 1976), pp. 13–25.

Ernst, H. B. "New Balance Sheet for Managing Liquidity and Growth," *Harvard Business Review*, vol. 62, no. 2 (March–April 1984), pp. 122–136.

Kaplan, R. S. "Yesterday's Accounting Undermines Production," *Harvard Business Review*, vol. 62, no. 4 (July–August 1984), pp. 95–101.

Weston, J. R., and E. F. Brigham. *Managerial Finance*. Hinsdale, Ill.: Dryden Press, 1981.

25

Preventive Control: Ensuring Effective Managing

After reading this chapter, you should understand:

1 The concept and assumptions of direct control
2 The principle of preventive control
3 The assumptions and advantages of preventive control
4 The nature and purpose of the management audit and the enterprise self-audit
5 The problem of managerial obsolescence
6 Essentials for developing effective managers
7 The major principles of controlling

The preceding analysis of controls stresses the variety of approaches that managers follow to make results conform to plans. At the basis of control is the fact that the outcome of plans is dependent on the people who carry them out. For instance, a poor educational system cannot be controlled by criticizing its product, the unfortunate graduate; a factory turning out inferior products cannot be controlled by consigning products to the scrap heap; and a firm plagued with customer complaints cannot be controlled by ignoring the complainers. Responsibility for controllable deviations lies with whoever has made unfortunate decisions. Any hope of abolishing unsatisfactory results lies in changing the future actions of the responsible person, through additional training, modification of procedures, or new policy. This is the crux of controlling the quality of management.

Direct control

There are two ways of seeing to it that the responsible people modify future action. The normal procedure is to trace the cause of an unsatisfactory result back to the persons responsible for it and get them to correct their practices. This may be called "direct control." The alternative in the area of management is to develop better managers who will skillfully apply concepts, techniques, and principles and who will look at managing and managerial problems from a systems point of view, thus eliminating undesirable results caused by poor management. This will be referred to as "preventive control."[1]

Preventive control

Direct Control

In every enterprise, hundreds, and even thousands, of standards are developed to compare the actual output of goods or services—in terms of quantity, quality, time, and cost—with plans. A negative deviation indicates—in terms of goal achievement, cost, price, personnel, labor-hours, or machine-hours—that performance is less than good or normal or standard and that results are not conforming to plans.

Causes of Negative Deviations from Standards

The causes of negative deviations will often determine whether control measures are possible. Although an incorrect standard may cause deviations, if the standard is correct, plans may fail because of (1) uncertainty and (2) lack of knowledge, experience, or judgment by those who make the decisions or take actions.

Uncertainty   Elements affecting a given plan may be grouped into facts, risks, and uncertainty. Facts, such as number of employees, costs, or machine capacity are known. Considerably less is known about the element of risk. Insurable risks are readily converted to factual status through the payment of a known premium, and costs of certain noninsurable risks may be included in a business decision on the basis of probability. But most risks arise from uncertainty. The total of facts and risks is small, compared with the element of uncertainty, which includes everything about which nothing is certain. For instance, the success of a plan to manufacture aluminum pistons will depend not only on known facts and risks but also on such uncertainties as future world conditions, competition of known and yet unknown metals, and power technology that may eliminate all piston prime movers. Not even probability can be estimated for all the uncertain factors, and yet they can wreck a plan.

---

[1]In previous editions we used a different terminology. Following the recommendations of our colleagues, we use now "preventive" and "direct" control.

Managerial errors caused by unforeseeable events cannot be avoided. The fixing of personal responsibility by direct control techniques is of little avail in such situations.

Lack of knowledge, experience, or judgment   Plans may misfire and negative deviations occur when people appointed to managerial posts lack the necessary background. The higher in the organizational structure managers are placed, the broader the knowledge and experience they need. Long years as an engineer, a sales manager, a production executive, or a controller may be inadequate qualifications for a top manager.

Good judgment marks the mature person who intelligently applies educational and enterprise experience and is known for common sense. Unfortunately, some top managers who have gone through the motions of formal education, training of various kinds, and practical experience seem incapable of sound decisions and display poor judgment about such matters as product lines, expansion policy, innovation, and decentralization. At the top level, the chance of correction through separation from the firm tends to be fairly small. On the other hand, continuing errors of judgment at middle and lower levels are often followed by demotion, transfer, or separation.

If the cause of error is poor judgment, whether due to inadequate training or experience or to failure to use appropriate information in decision making, correction can be made. Managers can improve their education, be transferred to acquire broader experience, or be cautioned to take better stock of the situation before making decisions.

Questionable Assumptions Underlying Direct Control   In addition to its cost, the shortcomings of direct control may also sometimes be the result of questionable assumptions: (1) that performance can be measured, (2) that personal responsibility for performance exists, (3) that the time expenditure is warranted, (4) that mistakes can be anticipated or discovered in time, and (5) that the person responsible will take corrective steps.

1 That performance can be measured   At first glance, almost any enterprise appears to be a maze of controls. Input, output, cost, price, time, complaints, and quality are subject to numerous standards; and the standards may be expressed in terms of goal achievement, time, weight, tolerances, averages, ratios, dollars, and indexes. In terms of usefulness, the standards may be correct, acceptable, or merely better than nothing. Close analysis will often reveal shortcomings of two

Difficulty in measuring

types. In the first place, the ability of a manager to develop potential managers, the effectiveness of research, the amount of creativity, foresight, and judgment in decision making can seldom be measured accurately.

Location of control

The second shortcoming concerns the location of the control. Managers know that critical stages exist in acquiring input factors, manipulating them to produce a finished product, and selling and delivering the product. In a factory operation, for example, critical stages would include receiving inspection, inspection for each assembly process, shipping, and billing. These are critical because effective control here will minimize costs. No amounts of control at other points can make up for lack of control at these stages.

2 That personal responsibility exists   Sometimes no manager is responsible for poor results. Increase in interest rates or inflation may cause the costs of many activities to rise precipitously. Scarcity of a particular fuel may necessitate use of less economical sources of power. And markets may shrink for reasons unconnected with the firm.

3 That the time expenditure is warranted   Whether managers undertake the inquiry themselves or assign it to others, executive time must be spent in ferreting out causes of poor results. Large scrap losses, for example, may call for meetings attended by persons representing quality control, production planning, engineering, purchasing, and manufacturing. Passage of time may make the recall of facts quite different. These drawbacks may convince managers that the cost of investigation exceeds any benefit they may derive. This often precludes investigation of clear violations of standards.

4 That mistakes can be discovered in time   Discovery of deviations from plans often comes too late for effective action. Although true control can be applied only to future action, most controls depend on historical data—all that most managers have available. Managers should, of course, interpret such data in terms of their implications for the future.

   The costs of errors in major areas—such as cash or inventories—have led to the use of feedforward techniques as the basis for control. Since these are often difficult to use, the natural tendency to rely on historical reports seriously blocks adequate controls. Feedforward control techniques offer hope, but as yet they have not been widely developed or utilized. No manager really has control unless he or she can correct mistakes. And the best way to correct mistakes is to avoid them.

5 That the person responsible will take corrective steps   Fixing the responsibility may not lead to correction. High production costs, for example, might be traced back to a marketing manager who insists that "slight" product modification will make selling easier and that this involves "really" no change in a production run. If the marketing manager is a member of top management, a subordinate investigator may be intimidated. Although great effort may be made to correct subordinate managers, it is sometimes very difficult to correct an executive to whom one reports.

The Principle of Preventive Control

The principle of preventive control embraces the idea that most of the responsibility for negative deviations from standards can be fixed by applying fundamentals of management. It draws a sharp distinction between performance reports, essential in any case, and determining whether managers act in accordance with established principles in carrying out their functions. The **principle of preventive control,** then, can be stated as follows: *The higher the quality of managers and their subordinates, the less will be the need for direct controls.*

*Principles of
preventive control*

The extensive adoption of preventive control must await a wider understanding of managerial principles, functions, and techniques as well as management philosophy. While such an understanding is not achieved easily, it can be gained through university training, through on-the-job experience, through coaching by a knowledgeable superior, and by means of constant self-education. Moreover, as progress is made in appraising managers as managers, we can expect preventive control to have more practical meaning and effectiveness.

Assumptions of the Principle of Preventive Control

The desirability of preventive control rests upon three assumptions: (1) that qualified managers make a minimum of errors; (2) that managerial performance can be measured and that management concepts, principles, and techniques are useful diagnostic standards in measuring managerial performance; and (3) that the application of management fundamentals can be evaluated.

1 That qualified managers make a minimum of errors   J. P. Morgan has often been quoted as saying that the decisions of good managers are right two-thirds of the time. However, an accurate analysis of the quality of decision making should not rely upon quantity of errors but be concerned with the nature of the error. As J. Paul Getty once told one of the authors, his concern in his worldwide empire was not the percentage of decisions in which an executive was right or wrong; he could be wrong on only 2 percent of them and seriously endanger a company if the errors were critical. Managers can logically be held strictly accountable for the performance of their functions because these functions should be undertaken in conformance with the fundamentals of management. However, accountability cannot be exacted for errors attributable to factors beyond managers' authority or ability reasonably to forecast the future.

2 That management fundamentals can be used to measure performance   The chief purpose of this book has been to draw together concepts, principles, theory, and basic techniques or approaches of management and relate them to a system of managerial functions. As we stated in previous chapters, the completeness and certitude of these vary considerably, depending largely upon the state of knowledge concerning managing. There is, for instance, greater general acceptance of some of the principles of organizing than there is of the principles relating to other functions. Nevertheless, we are convinced that the fundamentals set forth here are useful in measuring managerial performance even though our statement will undoubtedly be refined and better verified by future specialists.

3 That the application of management fundamentals can be evaluated   Evaluation can provide for periodic measurement of the skill with which managers apply management fundamentals. This can be done not only by judging performance against these but also by casting them into a series of fairly objective questions. An approach to the proper evaluation of managers as managers was set forth in Chapter 15. The ability to set and achieve verifiable objectives is one measure of a manager's performance. But much depends on being able to evaluate the performance of a manager as a manager. As crude as these standards of measurement may be at the present state of the art of managing, they can still highlight the extent to which an individual has the knowledge and ability required to fill the managerial role.

Advantages

Accuracy

Controlling the quality of managers and thus minimizing errors has several advantages. In the first place, greater accuracy is achieved in assigning personal responsibility. The ongoing evaluation of managers is practically certain to uncover deficiencies and should provide a basis for specific training to eliminate them.

Corrective action and self-control

In the second place, preventive control should hasten corrective action and make it more effective. It encourages control by self-control. Knowing that errors will be uncovered in an evaluation, managers will themselves try to determine their responsibility and make voluntary corrections. For example, a report of excessive scrap will probably cause the department supervisor to determine quickly whether the excess was due to poor direction of subordinates or to other factors. The same report will cause the chief inspector to look into whether inspection employees acted properly, the purchasing agent to check the material purchased with engineering specifications, and the engineers to determine whether appropriate material was specified. All this action can be immediate and voluntary. Managers who conclude privately that they were in error are likely to do their best to prevent recurrence, for they realize their responsibility.

Lightening burden

The third advantage of preventive control is the potential for lightening the burden now caused by direct controls. This is a net gain, since the evaluation of managers is already part of staffing. The amount of potential savings is as yet unknown, although it must be considerable.

Psychological advantage

Last, the psychological advantage of preventive control is impressive. The feeling of subordinates that superiors do not rate fairly, rely on hunch and personality, and use improper measuring standards is almost universal, but preventive control of the kind suggested in Chapter 15 can go far in removing this feeling. Subordinate managers know what is expected of them, understand the nature of managing, and feel a close relationship between performance and measurement.

Management Audit and Enterprise Self-Audit

Enterprise self-audit

A question might be raised as to how a management audit may be distinguished from an enterprise self-audit. The latter emphasizes where a company is and is probably going in the face of present and future economic, political, and social developments. The **enterprise self-audit,** then, is really an audit of an organization's operations and only indirectly an audit of its managerial system.

Management audit

The **management audit** is not nearly as broad as the enterprise self-audit in that it aims only at evaluating the quality of managing and the quality of managing as a system. It will be discussed first.

Management Audit

Application of the principle of preventive control has led to action in several directions. One of the most promising and effective has been the improvement of programs in recent years to appraise individual managers. Primarily, this has taken the form of appraising performance against the standard of setting and achieving verifiable goals. However, much must still be done to make even this widely accepted approach effective. A second essential aspect of this process, still done only on a limited and experimental basis, is the appraisal of managers in their role as *managers*. Both these approaches were discussed in Chapter 15.

Another direction in which the principle of preventive control has led is in a developing interest in management audits. Compared with the practice of other forms of management evaluation, these do not aim at evaluating managers as individuals but rather at looking at the entire system of managing an enterprise. While little progress has been made in such management audits, some pioneering programs have been undertaken.

Management audits and accounting firms   Although many management consulting firms have undertaken various kinds of appraisal of management systems, usually as a part of an organization study, the greatest interest in pursuing management audits has been demonstrated by accounting audit firms. One of the significant developments of recent years has been their entry into the field of management services of a broad consultancy nature. While this has been an attractive field of expansion for these auditing companies, since they are already inside an organization and financial information furnishes a ready window on problems of managing, it does open some question of conflict of interest. In other words, the question is often raised whether the same firm can be in the position of a management consultant furnishing both advice and services and still be completely objective as an accounting auditor. To be sure, accounting firms have attempted to avoid this problem by organizationally separating these two activities.

Regardless of whether auditing firms should be in management services, the fact is that they are. Since many are experienced in both auditing and management services, it is only a short step to management auditing. If it is possible for these firms to set up a completely detached and objective management auditing operation and if this can be staffed by individuals with truly professional knowledge and ability in management, it is very possible that this may result in acceleration in the practice of management auditing. At least, as long as the various professional and academic associations with a specific interest in management seem to be doing little in this field, perhaps accounting firms will show the way.

The certified management audit   Another possibility for the future is the development of a certified management audit, an independent appraisal of a company's management by an outside firm. For years investors and others have relied on an independent certified accounting audit designed to make certain that the company's records and reports reflect sound accounting principles. From the standpoint of investors and even from that of managers and those desiring to work for a company, an independent audit of management quality would be extremely important. It is probably not too much to say that an investor would get more value from a certified management audit than from a certified accounting audit, since the future of a company is likely to depend more on the qualilty of its managers than on any other single factor.

To ensure objectivity, the certified management audit should be the respon-

Outside firm

sibility of a recognized outside firm, staffed with individuals qualified to appraise a company's managerial system and the quality of its managers. Although this would require considerable study from the inside and a set of reasonably objective standards, it probably would take little more time than a thorough accounting audit. Moreover, except for the audit of top-level managers, and the preparation of a final analysis of the company's management as a total system, much work on the management audit could be done, as in the case of accounting audits, with the help of suitable inside managerial and staff personnel. Furthermore, as with the accounting audit, when a group of special auditors once becomes familiar with a company, subsequent audits take less time than the first. In order to ensure real objectivity, a management audit should be made by a recognized and qualified group of management appraisers with a reporting responsibility, like that of most accounting auditors, to the board of directors or another responsible top management group.

Quality of managers

It is quite obvious that any management audit report must go far behind the typical accounting auditor's statements. It must do more than say that a management group has followed "generally accepted standards of management." To be meaningful it would require that the quality of managers and the system within which they manage be assessed objectively in fairly specific terms. This, as one can see, gives rise to problems. How many accounting or management consulting firms can really be expected to be objective where, as so often occurs, managerial deficiencies exist at the top and when the firms are retained by, and report to, these same top managers? This is not an easy hurdle to overcome, at least until almost completely objective standards can be agreed upon, learned by true professionals, and applied impartially. One cannot help but wonder whether this might not necessitate a specially licensed group independent of present accounting and management consulting firms and reporting, as professionals, to some agency independent of the organization being audited.

The Enterprise Self-Audit

J. O. McKinsey, who achieved an outstanding position in the realm of management about five decades ago, came to the conclusion that a business enterprise should periodically make a "management audit," an appraisal of the enterprise in all its aspects, in the light of its present and probable future environment. Although McKinsey called this a management audit, it is actually an audit of the entire enterprise.

Company's position

The enterprise self-audit appraises the company's position to determine where it is, where it is heading under present programs, what its objectives should be, and whether revised plans are needed to meet those objectives. In most enterprises, objectives and policies become obsolete. If the enterprise does not change course to suit the changing social, technical, and political environment, it loses markets, personnel, and other requirements for continued existence. The enterprise self-audit is designed to force managers to meet this situation.

Outlook

Procedure   The self-audit may be made annually or, more likely, once every 3 or 5 years. The first step is to study the outlook of the firm's industry. What are recent trends and prospects? What is the outlook for the product? Where are the markets? What technical developments are affecting the industry? How may demand be changed? What political or social factors may affect the industry?

Position in the industry

A second step in the self-audit is to appraise the position of the firm in the industry, both current and prospective. Has the company maintained its position? Has it expanded its influence and markets? Or has competition reduced its position? What is the competitive outlook? To answer such questions, the company may undertake studies on competitor standing, development of competition, customer reactions, and other factors bearing on its position within the industry.

Basic objectives and policies

On the basis of such studies, the next logical step for the company would be to reexamine its basic objectives and major policies to decide where the company wishes to be in, say, 5 or 10 years. After this reexamination, the company may audit its organization, policies, procedures, programs, facilities, financial position, personnel, and management. This examination should identify any deviations from objectives and facilitate the revision of many major and minor plans.

Contribution of the self-audit   Most top managers do not think in terms of an enterprise's future or evaluate overall performance in relation to long-range objectives. The enterprise self-audit has the distinct advantage of forcing them to appraise overall performance in terms not only of current goals but also of future ones. Top managers who expend mental effort for this kind of audit will almost certainly be well repaid and will be surprised at how many day-to-day decisions will be simplified by a clear picture of where the business is attempting to go.

To a very considerable extent, this is often done when a company evaluates a firm it wishes to acquire. Without in any way detracting from the major importance of financial performance, it is realized that a firm's value depends upon its future rather than its past. To make this evaluation, financial factors need to be supplemented by such consideration of such factors as product lines and basic competition, marketing strengths, research and development record, personnel and public relations, and the quality of management. If this is of importance to a buyer of a company one cannot help but wonder why it should not be significant on a regular and continuing basis to a firm.

Managerial Obsolescence

There can be no question that the manager's role—in every kind of enterprise and at every level—is expanding and changing materially. As new knowledge and techniques become better known and applied, and as they lead to the creation of environments in which it is possible for people to perform more effectively and efficiently, the varied demands of society will force managers to take increasing advantage of this science and its tools. Virtually every manager will increasingly be faced with requirements and opportunities for improvement and for a far more intellectual approach to managing.

This means for those who manage that the danger of becoming obsolete for the task will continually be greater. As long as managing was a task learned only from experience, obsolescence was fairly unimportant. But now experience and new knowledge have been distilled into meaningful principles, theory, concepts, and basic techniques which can be made useful to the manager who does not wish to risk the danger of becoming relatively more ignorant. There is no longer time for individuals to reach the state of required managerial excellence through trial and error. Absorption of new knowledge on a continuing basis, *plus* the ability to use it for practical purposes, is surely the only insurance against obsolescence.

Developing Excellent Managers

Although the introductory analyses of the task of the manager are presented in this book as a start toward understanding the science underlying managerial practice, more is required. Among the more important considerations in ensuring the development of excellent managers, we would like to offer the following. Surely effective future managerial practice will depend at least on these.

A Willingness to Learn

If managers are to avoid the stultifying effect of basing too much of their learning on experience, they must be aware of the dangers of experience. As was indicated earlier in this book, undistilled experience can lead an individual toward assuming that events or programs of the past will or will not work in a different future. But managers need more than this. They need to be *willing* to learn and to take advantage of new knowledge and new techniques. This necessitates a humble approach to their successes and limitations. It demands a recognition that there is no finishing school or terminal degree for management.

Acceleration of Management Development

The above discussion underlines the urgent importance of accelerated programs of management development. This implies not only more pertinent management seminars and conferences but also other means of transmitting to practicing managers in as simple and useful a way as possible the new knowledge and tools in the field of management.

One of the major challenges in this connection is that of compressing and transmitting the available knowledge. Every field of art based on a burgeoning science has the same problem. No field has completely solved it, although certain areas, such as specialized aspects of medicine and dentistry, have made considerable progress.

We have no adequate answer for this problem. It does appear that those on the management faculties of our universities have an obligation to practicing managers to do much of the task of compressing and transmitting this knowledge as easily and quickly as possible. There is still inadequate evidence that many university professors see the social importance of this role. Also, one might expect a greater contribution from various management associations, as well as from management consultants, who can certainly greatly improve their value to clients by doing this. Perhaps more can be done through intelligent digesting of articles and books. Also, it is entirely possible that there might be regularly established a series of special management clinics in which managers at all levels in alert companies would spend a day every few weeks being brought up to date on a specific area of new knowledge and techniques.

Importance of Planning for Innovation

As competition becomes sharper, as problem solving grows in complexity, and as knowledge expands, one expects that the manager of the future will have to place greater importance on planning for innovation. Even now it is widely recognized that a business enterprise, at least, must "innovate or die," that new products just do not happen, and that new marketing ideas do not often occur by luck. The manager of the future must place more emphasis than ever before on developing an environment for effective planning. This means, even more than at present, planning goals which call for stretch, creating policy guidelines to channel thinking toward them without stifling imagination, designing roles where people can be creative and yet constructive, keeping abreast of the entire external environment which affects every kind of organization, and recognizing the urgency of channeling research toward desired ends.

Measuring and Rewarding Management

One of the significant areas of concern to the manager of the future will be the importance both of objectively measuring managerial performance and of rewarding good performance, imposing sanctions on a poor operation, and providing corrective action where it is indicated. Managers must be willing to work toward establishing objective measures of performance through both a verifiable results approach and the measurement of abilities of individuals as managers.

Tailoring Information

Another important area for the manager of the future will be to obtain the right information in the right form and at the right time. Tailoring information, as outlined in this book, requires a high order of intelligence and design. Until more managers realize that very little of their operation can be planned and controlled through "handbook" approaches, and until more managers recognize that they themselves must become involved in tailoring the information they require, progress will continue to be slow in this area. As long as information design is confused with the clerical work of information gathering and summarizing, managers will understandably continue to fret about the inadequacy of the data on which they are forced to act.

Need for Research and Development in Tools and Techniques

All these areas should command greater managerial attention. In addition, a great need exists for more real research and development in management tools and techniques themselves. The level of research effort and support in the field of management is woefully low. It is also not particularly great in the disciplines underlying management or, for that matter, in the entire area of social science. Nevertheless, it is probable that research in underlying disciplines far outpaces that in the central area of management.

There are many reasons for this. General management research is a difficult, exceedingly complex, and dynamic field. It is one where facts and proved relationships are hard to come by and where the controlled experiment of the laboratory is difficult to use without dangerous oversimplification. Likewise, management research is expensive, and the funds that have gone into it are abysmally inadequate. It has been estimated that not more than 1½ percent of the total being spent annually for all research in this country, or less than one-twentieth of 1 percent of gross national product, goes into research in *all* social sciences. If funds spent on management and management-related research are more than one-twentieth of this, or two-thousandths of 1 percent of gross national product, we would be surprised.

Still another reason for the low state of management research is that there are few clinical analyses, despite a considerable volume of clinical experience. Consulting efforts of both professional consultants and individual academics, extensive management case collections, and studies and analyses made internally in business, government, and other enterprise almost certainly encompass a huge mass of undigested, largely unsummarized, and relatively useless information. If this clinical experience could be given the analytical and summarizing work so common in the health sciences, there might be now considerable evidence of what is workable in practice and where deficiencies exist.

In undertaking this research, patience and understanding are needed. Perfection of analysis to include all kinds of variables is a laudable goal for a researcher. But, particularly in the field of management, a little light can be a massive beam in a hitherto dark area. We must often settle for small advances so that cumulatively, and over time, we may gain larger ones.

Need for Managerial Inventions

But research without development is insufficient. One of the major challenges for the manager of the future is the need for developing more managerial inventions. It is interesting that so much creative talent has been channeled into the invention of physical designs and chemical compositions and how little into social inventions. The Gantt chart has sometimes been regarded as the most important social invention of the first half of the twentieth century. Other management inventions include the variable budget, rate-of-return-on-investment analysis, and PERT. Mere reference to these inventions underscores the fact that they are creative tools developed from a base of principles on the one hand and needs on the other. Reference to them indicates also that they are useful devices in improving the art of managing.

Inventions tend to reflect the cultural level of an art. There are few of them in management. Surely even the present inadequate cultural level can be coupled with urgent needs to give rise to many more management innovations, particularly if those concerned are willing to spend some time and money to direct their energies toward these inventions. It is very easy to see that one significant management invention, such as those mentioned in the previous paragraph, can make important contributions to management effectiveness and economy of operation. Applied research and development in this field surely justify a considerable expenditure of time and money.

Need for Strong Intellectual Leadership

That intellectual leadership in management is urgently needed can hardly be denied. Managing can no longer be only a practical art requiring merely native intelligence and experience. The rapid growth of underlying knowledge and the obvious need for even more, particularly that knowledge which is organized and useful for improvement of practice, are requirements which have tremendous significance.

For people in every type of enterprise, at any part of the globe, the challenge to create a highly productive society is great. History teaches us that when needs exist and are recognized, leadership usually arises to inspired solutions. The challenging needs are here awaiting the application of knowledge discussed in this book, which was aimed to make you more effective as a person and a manager so that you can lead the productive organization.

Summary

In carrying out the controlling function, managers have two basic approaches. The most usual one, which we refer to as "direct" control, is to develop standards for desired performance and to compare against these standards actual outputs of goods and services—in terms of quantity, quality, time, and cost. The normal procedure is to trace the cause of an unsatisfactory result back to the persons responsible for it and get them to correct their practices. We regard controls as "preventive" when negative deviations from standards are avoided by assuring that managers at all levels apply effectively the fundamentals of management. The principle of preventive control may then be stated as follows: The higher the quality of managers and their subordinates, the less will be the need for direct controls.

Even if control standards are correctly drawn, plans may fail for a number of reasons: uncertainty, lack of knowledge, poor judgment, inexperience, or simply poor performance. Most of the shortcoming ascribable to direct control rest with certain questionable assumptions: (1) that performance can be measured, (2) that personal responsibility for performance exists, (3) that the total expenditure to evaluate and correct deviations is warranted, (4) that mistakes can be anticipated or discovered in time, and (5) that the persons responsible will actually take corrective action.

The assumptions that underlie the principle of preventive control, all of which have a high degree of truth, are: (1) that qualified managers make a minimum of errors, (2) that management fundamentals can be used to measure performance, and (3) that the application of management fundamentals to practice can be evaluated.

Application of the principle of preventive control has given rise to interest in management audits, that is, in evaluating the entire system of managing in an enterprise. A stimulating possibility for the future is the development of a certified management audit. The enterprise self-audit appraises the company's position to determine where it is, where it is heading under the present program, and where it should be going.

There can be no question that the manager's role is expanding and changing. With new knowledge being developed and social forces requiring managers to take advantage of it, the danger of managers becoming obsolete for their task is growing more serious. To avoid managerial obsolescence, we need managers willing to learn, acceleration of programs of management development, more effective planning for innovation, better methods of evaluating and rewarding managerial performance, more tailored information, and greater emphasis on managerial research, development, and inventions. We urgently require the best intellectual leadership in management to meet these needs.

Key Ideas and Concepts for Review

Direct control
Assumptions of direct control
Principle of preventive control
Assumptions of preventive control
Advantages of preventive control

Enterprise self-audit
Management audit
Certified management audit
Essentials for developing effective
   managers

For Discussion

1 If preventive control were completely effective, would a company need any direct controls?

2 What distinction would you draw between management appraisal, as dealt with in Chapter 15, and the management audit discussed in this chapter?

3 How would you proceed to make a management audit? Are there any similarities between it and an accounting audit or an enterprise audit?

4 J. O. McKinsey's enterprise self-audit has seldom been used in industry. Why do you feel this has happened? Do you believe this device would be worth its cost?

5 Taking any major area of management theory and principles, how can it be applied to reality?

6 By reference to specific management problem areas, such as new product development, organization structure, or budgets, what are the ways managers can introduce flexibility, and what are the inflexibilities usually encountered in each?

7 How may a manager design an environment to encourage imaginativeness and creativity?

8 How would you anticipate that the computer will affect the manager's role at the top-management level? The middle-management level? First-level supervision?

9 If you were asked to organize and operate an effective management research and development staff, how would you proceed?

10 What can be done about the problem of top-level executive malnutrition?

CASE 25-1

McALLISTER-STRONG
PUBLISHING COMPANY

The president of McAllister-Strong Publishing Company and his friend slowly concluded their lunch. "The trouble with manager development training," the friend remarked, "is that the only one who gets smart is the trainer."

"It seems a bit harsh to say so, but I'm afraid that is true." The president took up the thought. "Let me tell you about one experience I had.

"I have attended a great many conferences, seminars, and other executive-type meetings in my time. I guess I was just an easy mark for anything that sounded like education. Anyway, times were good, we could afford the expense, and I was truly convinced that the way to develop good managers was to expose them to the best available information sources. Of course, this worked out very well in technical areas where we had a specific need. But in manager development, things were different. I had a staff survey made of what other businesses were doing in this area and what universities and others recommended. I chose to get behind a vigorous and comprehensive program. I installed an internal sensitivity program and required all my managers to attend. We regularly attended the American Management Association offerings. We had our top executives attend a highly recommended university program. And we even rented a small country club for

3 weeks where we reviewed our experiences. I would say we had about the best exposure in our industry."

"Should we order aspirin?" his friend asked solicitously.

"That effort in manager development cost us over $300,000 in 2 years' time. But as far as I can see, I don't have a single thing to show for it."

"For an expenditure of that size, I should think you would have established a control system," his friend said.

"If this were in marketing, or production, or engineering, you bet I would have done so. But how do you control a training program? I'm convinced that you have to *make* managers manage, but all I can think of doing is to pray for luck."

"By the way," his friend inquired, "do you think that anyone in these management associations, training firms, or university executive programs has ever established controls for the operations of his or her own organization and programs?"

1 Do you believe that a control system could be established for management training? How?

2 What are the strengths and weaknesses of the program you would suggest?

CASE 25-2

FURNITURE STORES, INC.

Doris Chang is the store manager of a furniture company with stores throughout the state. Her staff consists of seven salespersons and support personnel. Each salesperson is paid commissions based on sales. But everybody has to do other tasks, such as assisting the merchandise manager, arranging the displays, handling customer complaints, and straightening out merchandise. These tasks, and a few others, should be shared equally among the salespersons.

The store's sales quota is established at the headquarters of the furniture chain. This quota is divided by the number of salespersons and each is expected to meet his or her personal quota.

Jim Eagon, age fifty, is the top salesperson. When he misses his sales goal, which seldom happens, the store's quota is usually not met. Jim, however, often does not help in doing the common tasks, much to the frustration of the other six salespeople, who feel that if they do not handle the common tasks, they will be fired.

Recently, Ms. Chang noticed that one of her salespeople, Betty Patterson, made careless errors, neglected clients, and did not do her share of the common tasks. When confronted by the store manager, she complained about Jim Eagon who, in her opinion, got away with doing almost nothing. After this discussion, Ms. Chang began to observe the salespersons more closely and noticed that most of them neglected their work and were not cooperative.

The store manager felt that something had to be done. A talk with Jim Eagon had little effect. Yet, the store needed Jim because of his excellent sales record. On the other hand, the morale of the other salespersons had begun to deteriorate.

1 What should Ms. Chang do?

2 What are the standards of performance? Should they be changed? If so, in what ways?

3 How can the store manager restore the morale?

For Further Information

Behrman, J. N., and R. I. Levin. "Are Business Schools Doing Their Job?" *Harvard Business Review*, vol. 62, no. 1 (January–February 1984), pp. 140–147.

Deal, T. E., and A. A. Kennedy. *Corporate Cultures: The Rites and Rituals of Corporate Life* (Reading Mass.: Addison-Wesley Publishing Company, Inc., 1982).

Donnell, S. M., and J. Hall. "Men and Women as Managers: A Significant Case of No Significant Difference," in J. H. Donnelly, Jr., J. L. Gibson, and J. M. Ivancevich (eds.), *Perspectives on Management*, 5th ed. (Plano, Tex.: Business Publications, Inc., 1984), pp. 377–396.

Main, J. "Work Won't Be the Same Again," *Fortune*, June 28, 1982, pp. 58–65.

"Management Challenges for the 80's." *Association Management*, vol. 32 (April 1980), pp. 83–89.

Miller, D., P. H. Friesen, and H. Mintzberg (collaborator). *Organizations: A Quantum View* (Englewood Cliffs, N.J.: Prentice-Hall, Inc., 1984).

Naisbitt, J. *Megatrends* (New York: Warner Books, Inc., 1982).

Ouchi, W. *The M-Form Society* (Reading, Mass.: Addison-Wesley Publishing Company, Inc., 1984).

Ohmae, K. "Foresighted Management Decision Making: See the Options before Planning Strategy," *Management Review*, vol. 71, no. 5 (May 1982), pp. 46–55.

Peters, T. J., and R. H. Waterman, Jr. *In Search of Excellence* (New York: Harper & Row, Publishers, Incorporated, 1982).

Schmidt, W. H., and B. Z. Posner. *Management Values and Expectations* (New York: American Management Association, 1982).

Weihrich, H. *Management Excellence—Productivity Through MBO* (New York: McGraw-Hill Book Company, 1985).

Yang, C. Y. "Demystifying Japanese Management Practices," *Harvard Business Review*, vol. 62, no. 6 (November–December 1984), pp. 172–182.

Summary of Major Principles of Controlling

From the discussions in the previous chapters on management control, there have emerged certain essentials, or basic truths. These, which are referred to as "principles," are designed to highlight aspects of control that are regarded as especially important. In view of the fact that control, even though representing a system itself, is a subsystem of the larger area of management, certain of these principles are understandably similar to those identified in discussing the other managerial functions. Principles of control, like those in other managerial functions, can be grouped into three categories, reflecting their purpose and nature, structure, and process.

The Purpose and Nature of Control

The purpose and nature of control may be summarized by the following principles:

Principle of the purpose of control The task of control is to ensure that plans succeed by detecting deviations from plans and furnishing a basis for taking action to correct potential or actual undesired deviations.

Principle of future-directed controls Because of time lags in the total system of control, the more a control system is based on feedforward rather than simple feedback of information, the more managers have the opportunity to perceive undesirable deviations from plans before they occur and to take action in time to prevent them.

These two principles emphasize the purpose of control in any system of managerial action as one of ensuring that objectives are achieved through detecting deviations and taking corrective action designed to attain them. Moreover, control, like planning, should ideally be forward-looking. This principle is often disregarded in practice, largely because the present state of the art in managing has not regularly provided for systems of feedforward control. Managers have generally been dependent on historical data, which may be adequate for tax collection and determination of stockholders' earnings, but are not good enough for the most effective control. Lacking means of looking forward, reference to history, on the questionable assumption that "what is past is prologue," is better than not looking at all. But time lags in the system of management control make it imperative that greater efforts be undertaken to make future-directed control a reality.

Principle of control responsibility The primary responsibility for the exercise of control rests in the manager charged with the performance of the particular plans involved.

Since delegation of authority, assignment of tasks, and responsibility for certain objectives rest in individual managers, it follows that control over this work should be exercised by each of these managers. An individual manager's responsibility cannot be waived or rescinded without changes in the organization structure.

Principle of efficiency of controls Control techniques and approaches are efficient if they detect and illuminate the nature and causes of deviations from plans with a minimum of costs or other unsought consequences.

Control techniques have a way of becoming costly, complex, and burdensome. Managers may become so engrossed in control that they spend more than it is worth to detect a deviation. Detailed budget controls that hamstring a subordinate, complex mathematical controls that thwart innovation, and purchasing controls that delay deliveries and cost more than the item purchased are instances of inefficient controls.

Principle of preventive control The higher the quality of managers in a managerial system, the less will be the need for direct controls.

Most controls are based in large part on the fact that human beings make mistakes and often do not react to problems by undertaking their correction adequately and promptly. The more qualified managers are, the more they will perceive deviations from plans and take timely action to prevent them.

The Structure of Control

The principles that follow are aimed at pointing out how control systems and techniques can be designed to improve the quality of managerial control.

Principle of reflection of plans The more that plans are clear, complete, and integrated, and the more that controls are designed to reflect such plans, the more effectively controls will serve the needs of managers.

It is not possible for a system of controls to be devised without plans since the task of control is to ensure that plans work out as intended. There cannot be doubt that the more clear, complete, and integrated these plans are the more that control techniques are designed to follow the progress of these plans, the more effective they will be.

Principle of organizational suitability The more that an organizational structure is clear, complete, and integrated, and the more that controls are designed to reflect the place in the organization structure where responsibility for action lies, the more they will facilitate correction of deviations from plans.

Plans are implemented by people. Deviations from plans must be the responsibility primarily of managers who are entrusted with the task of executing planning programs. Since it is the function of an organization structure to define a system of roles, it follows that controls must be designed to affect the role where responsibility for performance of a plan lies.

Principle of individuality of controls The more that control techniques and information are understandable to individual managers who must utilize them, the more they will be actually used and the more they will result in effective control.

Although some control techniques and information can be utilized in the same form by various kinds of enterprises and managers, as a general rule controls should be tailored to meet the individual needs of managers. Some of this individuality is related to position in the organization structure, as noted in the previous principle. Another aspect of individuality is the tailoring of controls to the kind and level of understanding of managers. We have seen both company presidents and supervisors throw up their hands in dismay (often for quite different reasons) at the unintelligibility and inappropriate form of control information that was a delight to the figure- and table-minded controller. Control information which a manager cannot or will not use has little practical value.

The Process of Control

Control, often being so much a matter of technique, rests heavily on the art of managing, on know-how in given instances. However, there are certain propositions or principles which experience has shown have wide applicability.

Principle of standards Effective control requires objective, accurate, and suitable standards.

There should be a simple, specific, and verifiable way to measure whether a planning program is being accomplished. Control is accomplished through people. Even the best manager cannot help being influenced by personal factors, and actual performance is sometimes camouflaged by a dull or a sparkling personality or by a subordinate's ability to "sell" a deficient performance. By the same token, good standards of performance, objectively applied, will more likely be accepted by subordinates as fair and reasonable.

Principle of critical-point control Effective control requires attention to those factors critical to appraising performance against an individual plan.

It would ordinarily be wasteful and unnecessary for managers to follow every detail of plan execution. What they must know is that plans are being implemented. Therefore, they concentrate attention on salient factors of performance that will indicate, without watching everything, any important deviations from plans. Perhaps all managers can ask themselves what things in *their* operations will best show *them* whether the plans for which they are responsible are being accomplished.

The exception principle The more managers concentrate control efforts on exceptions, the more efficient will be the results of their control.

This principle holds that managers should concern themselves only with significant deviations, the especially good or the especially bad situations. It is often confused with the principle of critical-point control, and they do have some kinship. However, critical-point control has to do with recognizing the points to be watched, while the exception principle has to do with watching the size of deviations, logically at these points.

Principle of flexibility of controls If controls are to remain effective despite failure or unforeseen changes of plans, flexibility is required in their design.

According to this principle, controls must not be so inflexibly tied in with a plan as to be useless if the entire plan fails or is suddenly changed. Note that this principle applies to failures of plans, not failures of people operating under plans.

Principle of action Control is justified only if indicated or experienced deviations from plans are corrected through appropriate planning, organizing, staffing, and leading.

There are instances in practice where this simple truth is forgotten. Control is a wasteful use of managerial and staff time unless it is followed by action. If deviations are found in experienced or projected performance, action is indicated, in the form of either redrawing plans or making additional plans to get back on course. It may call for reorganization. It may require replacement of subordinates or training them to do the task desired. Or there may be no other fault than a lack of direction and leadership in getting a subordinate to understand the plans or to be motivated to accomplish them. But, in any case, action is implied.

Indexes

Name Index

Adam, E. E., Jr., 512
Alderfer, C. P., 395
Altman, S., 353
Anderson, C. R., 133
Ansoff, H., 133
Anthony, R., 488
Aquilano, N. J., 491n., 493n., 494n., 512
Archer, E. R., 136
Argyris, Chris, 27, 351
Athos, A. G., 42n., 43
Aurner, R. R., 441
Avery, Sewell, 92
Axley, S. R., 440

Badawy, M. K., 351
Baker, M., 440
Ball, Robert, 63n.
Banks, R. L., 465
Barnard, Chester I., 21, 27–28, 40, 154, 163, 178, 263
Bartlett, C. A., 178
Bartolomé, F., 292
Bass, B. M., 417
Beam, R. D., 179
Bedeian, A. G., 179
Behrman, J. N., 351, 542
Bell, C. H., Jr., 352
Bellisario, Marissa, 63, 284
Bellows, R., 429n.
Birnbaum, P. H., 179, 223

Blake, Robert R., 343n., 345, 396, 403–406, 416
Blanchard, K. H., 417
Blatt, S. J., 441
Bolles, R. N., 332
Bolt, J. F., 292
Bowers, D. G., 403
Boyatzis, R. E., 417
Bradshaw, Thornton, 75
Bradspies, R. W., 454n.
Brenner, M. H., 427n.
Brenner, S. N., 52n., 55n.
Brigham, E. F., 526
Brousseau, K., 332
Brown, A., 250
Brown, R. V., 155
Buehler, V. M., 21
Buffa, E. S., 493n., 512
Bullen, C., 436n.
Burke, W. W., 352
Bylinsky, G., 394

Capwell, D., 378n.
Carrell, M. R., 312
Carroll, D. T., 6n.
Carter, Jimmy, 427
Cascio, W. F., 307n.
Cavanaugh, G. P., 268
Chandler, Alfred D., Jr., 120, 133, 178
Chase, B., 491n., 493n., 494n., 512

Chemers, M. M., 409n.
Chernes, A. R., 386n.
Christensen, H. K., 332
Churchill, N. C., 488
Churchman, C. West, 41–42
Cobb, A. T., 223
Comte, T. E., 332
Cummings, L. L., 155
Cunningham, M., 292
Crystal, J., 332

Dale, E., 223, 237n., 250
Dalton, D. R., 204
D'Aprix, Roger, 429n.
David, F. R., 179
Davis, Keith, 50n., 69, 163–164, 268, 292, 370, 432–433
Davis, L. E., 386n.
Davis, S. M., 268
Deal, T. E., 263n., 268, 542
Dearden, J., 488
Decker, P. G., 493n.
Declerck, R. P., 133
Delbecq, A. L., 155, 370
Dewar, R. D., 172n.
De Wine, S., 441
Dickson, W. J., 11n.
Diebold, J., 69
Dietrich, Noah, 301
Dipboye, R. L., 312
Donaldson, L., 268

Donnell, S. M., 417, 542
Donnelly, J. H., Jr., 21, 395, 542
Driver, M. J., 332
Drucker, Peter F., 98, 102, 124, 178, 292
Dublin, R., 21
Duncan, J., 154
Durant, W. C., 120
Dyer, J. S., 493n.

Ebert, R. J., 512
Eisenhower, Dwight D., 170
Elder, M., 386n.
Ernst, H. B., 526

Fayol, Henri, 9–11, 17, 18, 34, 47, 250
Fearon, H., 493n., 507n.
Feldman, D. C., 309n.
Ference, T. P., 332
Fiedler, Fred E., 312, 396, 409–412, 415, 416
Fielden, John S., 433–434, 440
Fielding, G. J., 204
Filley, A. C., 341n., 412n., 434n.
Fitch, H. G., 395
Flamholtz, Eric, 465
Flax, S., 223
Flesch, R., 440
Flippo, E. B., 285
Ford, Henry, Sr., 236
Ford, Henry, II, 300
Fottler, M. D., 465
Fraker, S., 284n.
Frederick, W. C., 50n., 69
Fredrickson, J. W., 133
French, W. L., 352
Friesen, P. H., 543
Fulmer, W. E., 43, 312

Gabarro, J. J., 223
Galbraith, J. R., 204
Galligan, P., 292
Gantt, Henry L., 477, 490–491
Getty, J. Paul, 531
Ghiselli, E. E., 399–400
Gibson, J. L., 21, 395, 542
Gilbreth, Frank, 490–491
Gilson, T. Q., 429n.
Given, William P., 286
Gladwin, T. N., 69
Glueck, W. F., 77n., 133

Gomersall, E. R., 309n.
Gordon, William J., 366
Greenbaum, H. H., 440
Geenberg, K., 489
Greer, C. R., 312
Guest, R. H., 395
Gustafson, D. H., 370
Gutteridge, T. G., 332
Gyllenhammer, P. G., 312

Hackman, R. J., 292, 297n., 370
Hall, D. T., 332, 377–378
Hall, J., 417, 542
Hall, Raymond, 303
Hall, W. K., 96, 197
Hammermesh, R. G., 125n.
Harrigan, K. R., 133
Hayden, S., 352
Hayes, R. B., 512
Hayes, R. L., 133
Haynes, R. S., 395
Headly, B., 124n.
Healey, J. H., 167n.
Heenan, David A., 63n., 285
Heintz, T. J., 489
Henderson, B. D., 124n.
Henning, D. A., 223
Herbert, T. T., 204
Hersey, P., 417
Herzberg, Frederick, 40, 378, 380, 387, 391–393, 439
Hitler, Adolf, 408
Hofer, C. W., 125n.
Hofstede, G., 395
Homans, G. C., 8
House, Robert J., 341n., 396, 412
Hout, T., 96
Humble, J., 116
Hunger, J. D., 134
Hunt, J. G., 403n.
Hurst, D. K., 21, 417
Hyer, N. L., 512

Isenberg, D. J., 370
Ivancevich, J. M., 21, 47, 395, 542

Jackson, J. S., 179, 204
Jauch, L. R., 77n., 133
Jenkins, R. L., 352
Johansen, R., 436n.
Jones, T. M., 69
Josefowitz, N., 440

Kahn, D. L., 430n.
Kaplan, R. S., 526
Karasik, M. S., 489
Katz, D., 179, 430n.
Katz, Robert L., 179, 298
Keen, P. G. W., 489
Kelleher, Herbert, 397–398
Kendall, Donald M., 300–301
Kennedy, A. A., 263n., 268, 542
Kepner, C. H., 154
Kerr, S., 341n., 412n.
Keyser, D. F., 441
Kiechel, W., III, 125n., 223
King, Martin Luther, Jr., 206
Klein, J. A., 395
Koontz, Harold, 23n., 47, 58, 69, 96, 104n., 105, 116, 120n., 154, 155, 179, 204, 223, 245, 250, 268, 292, 312, 320n., 330, 353, 395, 412n., 440, 454n.
Kotter, J. P., 223, 352
Kotter, J. R., 417
Krein, T. J., 250
Kroc, Ray, 397
Kroeber, D. W., 489
Kuhn, A., 179
Kujawa, D., 69
Kuznits, F. E., 312

Land, Edwin H., 265, 300
Larson, L. L., 403n.
Latham, G. P., 332, 353
Laufer, A. C., 494n.
Laurent, A., 223
Lawler, E. E., III, 292, 297n., 370, 377, 380–382, 391, 392, 395, 496n., 526
Lawrence, P. R., 21, 179, 268
Lehner, V. C., 79n.
Leontiades, M., 133, 312
Levin, R. I., 351, 542
Lewis, A. M., 417
Likert, J. G., 402n., 404
Likert, Rensis, 292, 396, 402–404, 414, 415
Litwin, G. H., 390, 391
Logan, H. H., 223
London, M., 332
Longenecker, J. G., 112n.
Lorange, P., 96, 133
Lorsch, Jay W., 21, 39, 179, 268, 371
Luce, S. R., 268
Luthans, F., 352
Luther, Martin, 379

McCaskey, M. B., 364*n.*
McClelland, David C., 383–384, 390–392, 439
McConkey, D. D., 417
McConkie, M. L., 103*n.*
McCoy, B. H., 69
McCreary, E. A., 154
Mace, L. M., 96
McFarlan, F. W., 465, 489
McFarland, D. E., 69
McGregor, Douglas, 102–103, 361–363, 368–370
McKenney, J. L., 465
McMurry, R. N., 312
Magaziner, I. C., 69
Mahoney, T. A., 292
Main, J., 69, 542
Makridakis, S., 96
Malek, Frederic V., 108–109, 302
Mao Tse-tung, 408
March, J. G., 21, 154, 179, 223
Mark, M. A., 116
Maslow, Abraham, 40, 376–378, 380, 391–393, 439
Mathews, G. H., 268
Matteson, M. T., 21, 47
Mausner, B., 378*n.*
Mayo, Elton, 10–12, 17, 18, 362
Mendleson, J., 99, 116
Meyer, Alan D., 154
Michael, S. R., 352, 465
Mihal, W. L., 332
Miller, D., 543
Mills, P. K., 465
Miner, J. B., 134, 179, 371, 395, 403*n.*
Mintzberg, Henry, 31–33, 154, 179, 204, 223, 276, 292, 418, 543
Mitchell, T. R., 179, 223, 395, 412*n.*
Moberg, D. J., 268
Molander, E. A., 52*n.,* 55*n.*
Montanari, J. R., 489
Morgan, C. P., 179, 204
Morgan, J. P., 531
Morris, T. D., 418
Morrisey, G. L., 116
Morse, J., 371
Mosely, R. L., 223
Moses, 165–166, 181
Mouton, Jane S., 343*n.,* 345, 396, 403–406, 416
Munsinger, G. M., 285
Mussolini, Benito, 408
Myers, M. S., 309*n.*

Nadler, D. A., 297*n.*
Naisbitt, John, 86, 87, 96, 543
Newstrom, J., 164*n.,* 268, 370, 433*n.*
Nordhoff, Heinz, 300
Nougaim, K., 377–378

Odiorne, George S., 103, 116, 352, 429*n.*
O'Donnell, C., 47, 58, 69, 96, 154, 155, 179, 204, 223, 250, 268, 292, 312, 353, 395, 412*n.,* 440
Oh, T. K., 56*n.*
Ohmae, K., 543
Osborn, Alex F., 365
Ouchi, W. G., 58*n.,* 543
Oxenfeldt, A. R., 155

Paine, F. T., 133
Pareto, Vilfredo, 11
Parkinson, C. Northcote, 9, 18
Pascale, R. T., 42*n.,* 43, 312
Patton, A., 384, 395
Pearce, J. A., 96, 133, 179
Perlmutter, Howard V., 63*n.,* 285
Perrow, C., 250
Peter, Laurence J., 303
Peters, Thomas J., 6, 7, 21, 42*n.,* 263, 268, 543
Peterson, R., 378*n.*
Petre, P., 119*n.*
Pine, R. C., 395
Porter, L. W., 204, 292, 370, 380–382, 391, 392
Porter, M. E., 96, 133
Posner, B. Z., 543
Prince, J. B., 332
Pringle, C. D., 112 *n.*
Proctor, William Cooper, 265
Purcell, Philip, 287
Purcell, T. V., 54
Pyburn, P., 465

Raia, A. P., 103*n.,* 117
Raisinghani, D., 154
Reck, R. R., 493*n.*
Reich, R. B., 69
Reizenstein, R. C., 352
Reuter, V. G., 493*n.*
Rhode, J. G., 496*n.,* 526
Richards, M. D., 47
Riger, S., 292

Robbins, S. P., 292, 347*n.*
Robey, D., 353
Robinson, R. B., Jr., 133
Rodgers, F. G., 352
Roethlisberger, F. J., 10, 11, 17, 18, 433
Rogers, Carl R., 433
Roosevelt, Franklin D., 408
Rosen, B., 292
Rowe, M. P., 440
Ruch, W. A., 493*n.*
Rudder, E., 96
Rush, H. M. F., 344, 346*n.,* 371
Rynes, S., 292

Sathe, V., 263*n.*
Saxberg, B. O., 465
Schein, Edgar H., 292, 361–363, 368, 369, 441
Schendel, D., 125*n.*
Schlesinger, L. A., 352
Schmidt, Warren H., 396, 406–408, 415, 416, 543
Schonberg, R. J., 69
Schonberger, R. J., 512
Schwartz, S. J., 292
Scott, W. G., 47, 179, 223
Shafritz, J. M., 47
Shapiro, R. D., 512
Sharman, G., 512
Shetty, Y. K., 21
Shull, 155
Sigband, N. B., 427*n.*
Simet, D. P., 172*n.*
Simon, Herbert A., 21, 28, 136, 154, 155, 179, 223
Skinner, B. F., 382, 391
Skinner, W., 292, 494*n.*
Sloan, Alfred, 246–247, 364
Smith, H. L., 465
Smith, Roger, 75
Sorce, P. A., 332
Spendolini, M. J., 204
Staiger, J. G., 250
Stanton, E. S., 395
Staw, B. M., 155
Steiner, G. A., 50*n.,* 96, 134
Stieglitz, H., 204
Stodgill, Ralph M., 399, 417
Stoneman, Alan, 299
Stoner, J. A. F., 332
Strickland, A. J., III, 43, 134, 312
Stringer, R. A., Jr., 390, 391
Strunk, W., Jr., 441

Sullivan, J., 69
Summers, I., 366n.
Sundem, G. L., 526
Suttle, J., 377

Tannenbaum, Robert, 396,
    406–408, 415, 416
Taylor, Frederick W., 9–11, 17, 18,
    490–491
Theoret, A., 154
Thomson, A. A., Jr., 43, 134, 312
Thurston, P. H., 134
Todor, W. D., 204
Tortoriello, T. R., 441
Tregoe, B. B., 154
Treybig, Jim, 265
Trist, E. L., 28, 366n.
Turner, Fred, 397

Ulschak, F. L., 353
Ulvila, J. W., 155
Umstot, D. D., 347n., 348
Urwick, Lyndall, 166, 256

Vail, Theodor, 265
Van de Ven, A. H., 370
Van Fleet, D. D., 179
Velasquez, M., 268
Von Glinow, M. A., 332
von Neumann, John, 503
Vroom, Victor H., 378–380, 391,
    392, 439

Walker, J. W., 292, 332
Walter, I., 69
Walton, C., 54n., 56n.
Wanous, J. P., 312
Warren, E. K., 332
Waterman, Robert H., Jr., 6, 7, 21,
    42n., 43, 263, 268, 543
Watson, C. E., 353
Weber, J., 54, 55n.
Weihrich, H., 47, 58, 69, 96, 98n., 99,
    103n., 104n., 116, 117, 134, 154,
    155, 179, 204, 223, 250, 268,
    292, 312, 320n., 324n., 332,
    353, 371, 395, 412n., 440, 543
Weiss, A., 512
Wemmerloev, U., 512
Werther, W. B., Jr., 292

Weston, J. R., 526
Wetherbe, J. C., 489
Wexley, K. N., 332, 353
Wheelen, T. L., 134
Wheelwright, S. C., 96, 465, 494n.,
    512
Whitbeck, P. H., 47
White, E. B., 441
White, D. E., 366n.
White, L. P., 353
White, R. E., 125n.
Wieters, C. D., 493n.
Wilkinson, J. W., 489
Williams, J. J., 489
Williams, M. J., 397n.
Winter, David G., 383n.
Wood, Robert E., 237
Woodman, L. A., 489
Wooten, K. D., 353
Worf, M. P., 441
Wright, J. W., 332

Yang, C. Y., 69, 543
Yukl, G. M., 418

Zawacki, R. A., 352

Subject Index

ABC Airlines (case), 221
Acceptance needs, 376
Accounting firms, management
    audits by, 533
Achievement, need for, 383
Action, principle of, 547
Action plans, 129, 327
Adverse situations, generating
    alternatives in, 137
Aerospace, Inc. (case), 350
Affiliation needs, 376, 383
Air Force, U.S., 139–140, 347
Allied Chemical Corporation, 54
Alternatives, 137–143
    determination of, 87–88
    development of, 137–138
    evaluation of, 88, 138–140
    selection of, 140–143
    strategic, 126
American Aircraft Company (case),
    178
American Aluminum (ALCOA), 386
American Business Computers and
    Equipment Company (case),
    248–249
American Management Association,
    166n., 266
American Motors, 126
American Telephone & Telegraph
    (AT&T), 63, 264, 265, 306, 386,
    387
Analytical ability, 299–300

Anchor Consolidated Industries, Inc.
    (case), 487–488
Apple Computer, Inc., 143
Appraisal, 102–103
    of internal environment, 121, 126
    managerial, 277, 283
    by objectives, 105
    (See also Performance appraisal)
Approval authorization chart,
    242–246, 261
Aptitude tests, 306
Army, U.S., 216, 347
Art of Japanese Management, The
    (Pascale and Athos), 42
Assessment centers, 306–308
"Assistant-to" positions, 339
Assistants, unnecessary, 256
Audi, 143
Authority, 11, 270
    of committees, 434
    decentralization of, 224–250
        balance in, 243, 246–247
        clarification of, 242–243
        definition of, 224
        factors determining degree of,
          235–240
        forces favoring, 243
        limitations of, 243, 246
        obtaining desired degree of,
          241–242
        (See also Delegation of
          authority)

Authority (Cont.):
    functional (see Functional
        authority)
    leadership styles and, 400–402
    lines of, confusion of lines of
        information and, 253
    parity of responsibility and, 231,
        270
    power and, 206
    recentralization of, 240
    without responsibility, 253, 254
    (See also Line and staff
        relationships)
Authority-level principle, 229, 230
Autocratic leadership, 400
Automation, 508

Balance:
    in decentralization of authority,
        243, 246–247
    principle of, 271
Bank of America, 436
Behavior:
    group, 27
    influence of values and
        performance criteria on, 53
    interpersonal, 26
    leadership, 276, 400–408, 413
Behavior modification, 382
Behavioral models, 361–364
Behavioral science, 26

Belden Electronics Company (case), 290–291
Bible, 165–166
Boston Consulting Group (BCG), 124
"Bounded" rationality, 136
Bradley Clothing Company (case), 393
Brainstorming, 365–366
Branches, international, 61
Bridgestone Tire Company, 60
Budget summaries, 514–515
Budgets, 84, 467–474
  alternative, 472–473
  concept, 467
  dangers of, 469–470
  numberizing plans in, 88–89
  purpose of, 467–468
  supplementary, 472–473
  types of, 468–469
  variable, 470–472
  zero-based, 473
Business Cycle Developments, 86
Business failure, causes of, 4
Business Portfolio Matrix, 124–125
Business Week, 7, 86

Capital expenditure budgets, 468–469
Capital standards, 451
Career strategy, 283, 324–328
Carlton Plywood Company (case), 46
Case analysis, 23, 26
Cash budgets, 469
Cash flow planning, 455
Caterpillar tractor, 264
Centralization, 225
Certified management audits, 533–534
Chairpersons of committees, 435
Change:
  adjustment to, insufficient period for, 430
  rate of, 170
    decentralization and, 239
  strategy for, 345
  tradition of, 258
Chrysler Corporation, 507
Civil Rights Act (1964), Title VII of, 314
Claimants, 14
Clarification, avoiding conflict through, 258–261

Coaching, 340
Coercive power, 207
Command, unity of, 11, 229–230, 270
Commitment:
  personal, 111
  principle of, 90–91
  of resources, 119
  size and length of, 150
Committees:
  communication in, 434–435
  excess of, 256
  manager development in, 339–340
Communication, 16, 419–443
  barriers to, 428–431
  clarity of, 442
  definition of, 419
  effectiveness of, 170–171
  electronic media in, 435–436
  flow of, 425–426
  in groups, 434–435
  guidelines for improvement of, 431–432
  importance of, 420
  integrity of, 443
  listening and, 432–433
  manager's need to know and, 424–425
  nonverbal, 428
  oral, 427–428
  organization levels and, 168
  of premises, 129
  process of, 421–424
  purpose of, 420–421
  responsibility for, 421
  skills in, 300
  of strategies, 128–129
  written, 427
    tips for, 433–434
Competition, decision trees with, 146–148
Complex motive pattern, 362
Computers, 436, 484–485
  in operations management, 496
Concentration, 126
Conceptual models in operations research, 498
Conceptual skills, 298
Conference programs, 341
Conflict, 342–344
  interdepartmental, 100
  management of, 343–344
  sources of, 343
Congress, U.S., 56

Consolidated Computers, Inc., 68
Consolidated Motors Corporation (case), 393
Contingency approach, 12–13, 31, 39
  to leadership, 408–414
  to motivation, 389–391
Contingency plans, 327
Contingency strategies, 122, 128, 129
Control, 37, 277, 283, 447–465
  basic process of, 448–449
  critical points for, 450–452, 461
  decentralization and, 238
  decision trees in, 505
  delegation of authority and, 233
  direct, 528–530
  efficiency of, 545
  as feedback system, 452, 453
  feedforward, 454–459
  financial, 514
  future-directed, 454–455, 544–545
  individuality of, 546
  inventory, 501–503
  management by objectives and, 111
  of operations (*see* Operations management; Operations research)
  organization levels and, 168
  overall, 513–526
    budget summaries, 514–515
    (*See also* Return on investment)
  planning and, 74, 76, 447–448
  preventive, 527–543, 545
    enterprise self-audits, 534–535
    management audits, 532–534
    principle of, 530–532
  process of, 546–547
  profit and loss, 515–517
  purpose of, 544
  real-time information and, 452–454
  requirements for, 459–462
  responsibility for, 545
  structure of, 545–546
  techniques of, 466–489
    budgetary (*see* Budgets)
    operational audit, 475
    personal observation, 476
    program budgeting, 481–483
    special reports and analysis, 475

Control, techniques of (*Cont.*):
  statistical analysis, 475
  time-event network analysis,
    477–481
Controlling:
  definition of, 447
  principles of, 544–547
  (*See also* Control)
Cooperative social systems, 27–28
Coordination, 38
Corporate self-appraisal, 121
Corrective action, 532
  controls leading to, 462
Cost benefit analysis, 139
Cost effectiveness:
  analysis of, 139–140
  of committees, 435
  of controls, 462
Cost standards, 450–451
CPM (Critical Path Method), 479,
  505
Creativity, 364–367
  process of, 364–365
  techniques to enhance, 365–366
Critical Path Method (CPM), 479,
  505
Critical point control, 450–452, 461,
  546
Crosswise communication, 426–427
Culture of enterprise (*see*
  Organization culture)
Customer departmentation, 188–190
Customer's Electric Appliance
  Company (case), 369–370

Dayton-Hudson, 58
Decentralization:
  return on investment and,
    520–521
  (*See also* Authority,
    decentralization of)
Decision making, 135–155, 276
  alternatives in, 137–143
    development of, 137–138
    evaluation of, 138–140
    selection of, 140–143
  decentralization and, 234–235
  decision trees for, 145–148
  importance of, 136
    evaluation of, 140
  in Japan, 57
  limitations of, 136
  preference theory for,
    148–150

Decision making (*Cont.*):
  programmed and
    nonprogrammed, 143
  risk analysis for, 144–145
  systems approach and, 150–151
Decision models, 499
Decision roles, 33
Decision theory, 29
Decision trees, 145–148, 505
Defense Department, U.S.,
  139–140, 482
Delegation of authority, 226–234
  clarity of, 169, 227–229
  failures in, 253
  functional, 209–211, 214–215
  personal attitudes toward,
    231–233
  principles of, 228–231
  recovery of delegated authority,
    228
  by results expected, 228, 270
  steps in, 226–227
  weak, guidelines for overcoming,
    233–234
Delta Airlines, 264
Democratic leadership, 400
Departmentation, 180–204, 270
  aim of, 199
  customer, 188–190
  by enterprise function, 182, 184
  equipment, 192
  line and staff versus, 207–209
  market-oriented, 190–192
  mixing types of, 200
  by numbers, 181
  process, 192
  by product, 186–188
  by territory, 184–186
  by time, 181–182
Departments:
  conflicts among, 100
  definition of, 164
  procedures and, 82
  service, misuse of, 225
  (*See also* Departmentation)
Derivative plans, 88
Descriptive principles, 8–9
Design skills, 299
Deviations:
  correction of, 449
  negative, causes of, 528–529
Diagnosis, organization, 344
Dignity, personal, 361
Direct control, 528–530
Dissatisfiers, 378

Distribution logistics, 503
Distrust, communication undermined
  by, 430
Diversification, 126
Divisions, 164
Donnelly Mirror, Inc., 346
Downward communication, 425
DuPont Company, 77, 120, 264,
  479*n.*, 517

Eastern Electric Corporation (case),
  94–95
Economic Indicators, 86
Effectiveness, 6
Efficiency, 6
  organizational, 269
  of plans, 75–76
Electrical Construction Company
  (case), 488
Electronic Data Systems
  Corporation, 79
Electronic media, 435–436
Empathy, 300
Empirical analysis, 23, 26
  distilling basics with, 39
Employment, lifetime, 56–57
Encounter groups, 340–341
Engineering:
  feedforward in, 455
  project organization in, 192, 194,
    196
Enterprise profile, 126
Enterprise self-audit, 532, 534–535
Entertainment policy, 80
Entrepreneurial aspects of
  management, 276
Environment (*see* External
  environment; Internal
  environment)
Equal employment opportunity
  (EEO), 284
Equal Employment Opportunity
  Commission, 314
Equipment departmentation, 192
Esprit de corps, 11
Esteem needs, 376
Ethics, 54–56
  codes of, implementation of,
    54–55
  institutionalization of, 54
  raising standards of, 55
  in various societies, 55–56
Ethnocentrism, 61
Exception principle, 547

Expectancy theory, 378–382
Expense budgets, 468
Experience:
  decision making based on,
      140–141
  lack of, 529
Experimentation, 141–142
Expertness, 206
Exportation, 61
External environment, 3–4, 48–70
  assessment of, 120–121, 126
  career strategy and, 326
  communication and, 420–421
  decentralization and, 239–240
  ethics of, 54–56
  pluralistic, 50
  social responsibility and, 50–53
  staff knowledge of, 216
  staffing and, 284–285
  in systems approach, 15, 16, 70
Exxon, 77

Fanuc Ltd., 79
Fear, communication undermined
      by, 430
Feasibility, 89
Federal Reserve Board, 185
Feedback, 89, 345, 423–424
  control as system of, 452, 453
  feedforward versus, 455, 456
Feedforward control, 454–459
Financial control, 514
Financial strategy, 123
Firestone Tire & Rubber Company,
      60
Fixed-position production layout,
      495
Flexibility:
  in budgeting, 84, 470–473
  of controls, 461–462, 547
  delegation of authority and,
      227–228
  of plans, 150
  principle of, 271
Followership, 397
Forbes, 4
Ford Motor Company, 236, 300,
      507
Forecasting, 86–87, 120
  in feedforward control, 454
Foresite Incorporated (case),
      330–332
Formal organization, 162–163
Free rein leadership, 400

Functional authority, 209–215, 270
  area of, 212–213
  clarification of, 213–214
  complications in exercising, 213
  delegation of, 209–211, 214–215
  misuse of, 254
  of operating managers, 212
Functional definition, principle of,
      228
Functional departmentation,
      182–184
Functions of the Executive, The
      (Bernard), 27
Furniture Stores, Inc. (case), 542
Future-directed control, 454–455,
      544–545

Gantt charts, 477, 478
General Electric, 54, 63, 246, 264,
      307, 387
General Motors, 75, 79, 120, 126,
      128, 166, 246, 346–347, 386,
      388, 508
General Savings and Loan
      Association (case), 132
Geocentrism, 63
Geographic departmentation,
      184–186
German automobile industry, 508
Gifts from suppliers, policy on, 80
Goals, 38
  of organization (*see* Objectives)
  personal and professional, 324
Government:
  ethical codes in, 54–55
  leaders in departments and
      agencies of (case), 416
  management by objectives in,
      108–109
  program budgeting in, 482
  regulations imposed by, 239
  role of, 53
  staffing and, 285
Graphics, computer, 484
Great man school of leadership,
      276
Grid organization development,
      345–346
  (*See also* Matrix organization)
Group behavior, 27
Groups, communication in,
      434–435
Growth strategies, 123
GTE Corporation, 63

Hallmark Corporation, 77
Hanover Space and Electronics
      Corporation (case), 464–465
Hardstone Corporation (case),
      329–330
Hart Electronics (case), 18–19
Harvard Business Review, 52, 102
Hawthorne Studies, 11–12
Haynes Fashion Stores, Inc. (case),
      438–439
Health, Education, and Welfare,
      U.S. Department of, 387
Hewlett-Packard, 57–58, 190
Hierarchy of needs, 376–378
Home Radio and Television
      Company (case), 439–440
Honesty, 300–301
Hospital Services, Inc. (case), 525
Hughes Corporation, 436
Human impact of decisions, 150
Human relations, 26
Human resources needs, 252
  (*See also* Staffing)
Human skills, 298
Hygiene factors in motivation, 378

IBM Corporation, 54, 57, 63, 119,
      190, 264, 285, 301, 307, 436
Implementation of plans, 128
In Search of Excellence (Peters and
      Waterman), 6*n.,* 7, 42
Independence, desire for, 237
Inflexibility, avoidance of, 257–258
Influence, 276
Informal organization, 163–164, 443
Information:
  budgets and, 474
  forms of, 460
  lines of, confusion of lines of
      authority and, 253
  in operations control, 495–497
  overload of, 430–431
  real-time, 452–454
  tailoring, 537
Information systems for planning, 89
Information technology, 483–485
Informational roles, 32
Innovation, 364
  planning for, 537
Input-output model, 14
Insight, 365
Intangible factors, 138
Intangible standards, 451
Integrity, 300–301

Intellectual leadership, 538–539
Intelligence services, 483–484
Intelligence tests, 306
Internal environment, 3–4
　appraisal of, 121, 126
　career strategy and, 326
　communication and, 420
　staffing and, 286–289
Internal Revenue Service, 53, 185
International business, 60–65, 128
　production function in, 508
　staffing and, 285
International Business Machines
　(see IBM Corporation)
International Harvester Company,
　236
International Machine Corporation
　(case), 95
International Supermarkets, Inc.
　(case), 222–223
Interpersonal behavior, 26
Interpersonal roles, 32
Interviews with prospective
　managers, 304–306
Intuition, 364–365
Inventions, managerial, 538
Inventory planning and control,
　501–503
Isuzu Motors Ltd., 79
Italtel Societa Italiana, 63

Japan, 6, 75
　automation in, 508
　automobile industry in, 79, 508
　management approach in, 56–60
　quality control circles in, 507
Job definition, 261, 355
Job design, 296–298
Job enrichment, 387–389
Job rotation, 339
Joint ventures, 61, 178
Judgment, lack of, 529
Junior boards, 339–340

Kappa Corporation (case), 464
Key result areas, 98
Kimberly-Clark, 77
King's Supermarkets (case),
　153–154
K-Mart, 75
Knowledge, lack of, 529
Kodak, 143
Korea, 75

Lampert & Sons Company (case),
　510
Leader-member relations, 409
Leadership, 396–418, 442
　as continuum, 406–408
　definition of, 397
　facilitation of, 271
　great man school of, 276
　ingredients of, 398–399
　intellectual, 538–539
　motivation and, 391
　path-goal approach to, 412–414
　principle of, 399
　situational approach to, 408–414
　styles of, 400–408
　　authority and, 400–402
　　managerial grid, 403–406
　trait approaches to, 399–400
Leadership theory, 26
　motivation and, 40–41
Leading, 37, 277, 283
　definition of, 360
　harmonizing objectives as key to,
　　367
　human factor and, 359–371
　　behavioral models, 361–364
　　creativity and innovation,
　　　364–367
　principles of, 442–443
　(See also Leadership)
Legitimate power, 206
Lever Brothers, 91
Libby, McNeil & Libby, 196
Licensing agreements, 61
Lifetime employment, 56–57
Limited rationality, 136
Limiting factor, principle of, 137–138
Line and staff relationships,
　205–223
　dangers in, 216–217
　departmentation versus, 207–209
　effective, 218–220
　example of, 210
　nature of, 207
　(See also Functional authority)
Linear programming, 501
Liquidation, 128
Listening skills, 429, 432–433
Litton Industries, 78
LMT, Incorporated (case), 47
Logical formulation, 365
Logistics, 503
Long-range plans, 91–92
Long-term trends, 87
Loyalty, employee, 56

McAllister-Strong Publishing
　Company (case), 541
McDonald's, 397
Macintosh computers, 143
McKinsey & Company, 42–43
Mainframe computers, 484
Maintenance factors in motivation,
　378
Management:
　critics of, 4–5
　definition of, 13
　span of (see Span of
　　management)
Management analysis, 22–47
　approaches to, summarized,
　　24–25
　contingency approach to, 31
　convergence of approaches to,
　　38–44
　cooperative social systems
　　approach to, 27–28
　decision theory approach to, 29
　empirical approach to, 23, 26
　group behavior approach to, 27
　interpersonal behavior approach
　　to, 27
　managerial roles approach to,
　　31–33
　mathematical approach to, 30–31
　operational approach to, 33–35
　　implementation of, 35
　situational approach to, 31
　sociotechnical systems approach
　　to, 28–29
　systems approach to, 29–30
Management audits, 532–535
Management by objectives (MBO),
　102–104
　benefits of, 110–111
　checklist for, 110
　in government, 108–109
　guidelines for, 109
　process of, 104–107
　quantitative and qualitative
　　objectives in, 107–108
　weaknesses in, 111–113
Management contracts, 61
Management Information System
　(MIS), 483
Management inventory, 277,
　279–281
Management philosophy, 236–237
"Management process" school,
　34
Management Science, 30

"Management science" approach, 30–31, 41–42
Management techniques, 9
Management theory:
  evolution of, 9–12
  role of, 8–9
Manager development, 333–342, 355
  acceleration of, 536
  definition of, 333–334
  failures of, 334–335
  operational-management approach to, 335–336
  (*See also* Training)
Managerial grid, 403–406
Managerial inventions, 538
Managerial obsolescence, 535–536
Managerial roles, 31–33
Managerial systems, 30
Managerial tasks, 5
Managers:
  aim of, 5–7
  analysis of need for, 281–283
  appraisal of (*see* Performance appraisal)
  availability of, 237–238
  controls tailored to, 460–461
  creative, 366–367
  defining job of, 276
  functions of, 35–38, 54
  new, orientation and socialization of, 308–309
  number and kinds required, 277
  product, 196
  quality of, 534
  selection of, 277, 282–283, 293–312
    assessment centers, 306–308
    definition of, 293
    information exchange contributing to, 302–303
    interviews, 304–306
    job design, 296–298
    limitations of, 308
    from outside, 288
    personal characteristics, 300–301
    position requirements, 294–296
    process of, 304
    responsibility for, 304
    skill requirements, 298–300
    systems approach to, 294, 295
    tests, 306
  top (*see* Top managers)

Managing:
  as art and science, 7–8
  definition of, 3
Manpower Report of the President, 281
Manufacturing requirements planning (MRP), 511–512
Marginal analysis, 139
Market-oriented departmentation, 190–192
Marketing strategies, 123, 124
Marshall Field and Company, 236
Material budgets, 468
Mathematical analysis, 30–31, 41–42
Mathematical models:
  construction of, 499
  solutions to, 500–501
  tests of, 500
Matrix organization, 192–197
  in future, 197
  variations in practice of, 195–196
Maytag Corporation, 264
Measurement Instruments Corporation (case), 176–177
Medium-range planning, 128
Megatrends (Naisbitt), 86
Membership, committee, 435
Microcomputers, 484
  application and impact of, 485
Milestone budgeting, 477
Minicomputers, 484
Minutes of committee meetings, 435
Miracle Products Company (case), 249–250
Mission of enterprise, 52
  planning of, 77–78
Model building, 142
  (*See also* Mathematical models)
Money as motivator, 384–385
Montgomery Ward, 92
Monthly Labor Review, 281
Motivation, 40, 372–395, 442
  complexity of, 374–375
  definition of, 373
  expectancy theory of, 378–382
  hierarchy of needs theory of, 376–378
  job enrichment and, 387–389
  leadership theory and, 40–41
  motivation-hygiene approach to, 378
  need-want-satisfaction chain in, 373–374
  needs theory of, 383–384

Motivation (*Cont.*):
  reinforcement theory of, 382
  short-term objectives and, 103
  systems and contingency approach to, 389–391
  techniques of, 384–386
Movement of products, layout to facilitate, 495
Multinational corporations (MNCs), 60–65
  advantages of, 63
  challenges for, 63–64
  characteristics and practices of, 64–65
  staffing of, 285
Municipal Water District (case), 115–116

NASA, 77
National Research Council, 11
Navy, U.S., 139–140, 316, 347, 348
  Special Projects Office of, 479
Need-want-satisfaction chain, 373–374
Needs:
  hierarchy of, 376–378
  motivating, 383–384
New-product program, 101
  strategy for, 122–124
New York Central Railroad, 132
Noise, 423
Nonmanagerial tasks, 5
Nonprogrammed decisions, 143
Nonverbal communication, 428
Northern Chemical Corporation, Agricultural Fertilizer Division of (case), 202

Objective standards, 170
Objectives, 78, 97–117
  action plans and, 129
  certainty of, 150
  departmentation and, 199
  establishing, 86
  harmony of, 442
    as key to leading, 367
  hierarchy of, 98
  of manager development, 335
  nature of, 97–98
  network of, 100
  planning and, 74
  rational approach to achievement of, 89–93

Objectives (*Cont.*):
  recycling, 107
  setting, 98–100
  of staffing, 354
  as standards, 451–452
  strategies and, 126
  unity of, 269
  verifiable, 97, 107–108
    appraisal against, 315, 317–319
    decentralization and, 241
    (*See also* Management by
      objectives)
Objectivity of control, 461
Obsolescence, managerial, 535–536
Occidental Chemical Company, 197,
  199
Office of Federal Contract
  Compliance, 314
Office of Strategic Services, 306
Olivetti, 63
Olympic Toy Company (case), 153
On-the-job training, 338–340
Open competition, principle of,
  287–288, 355
Operating expense budgets, 468
Operational auditing, 475
Operational management, 11,
  33–35
  implementation of, 35
  span of management in, 168
  systems approach to, 13–17
Operational planning, 119
Operations management, 490–512
  controlling in, 495–497
  decision trees in, 505
  future of, 507–508
  planning in, 493–495
  quality control circles and, 507
  time-event networks in,
    505–506
  value engineering and, 506
  work simplification in, 505
Operations research, 497–505
  definition of, 497
  distribution logistics in, 503
  essentials of, 497–498
  limitations of, 503–505
  linear programming in, 501
  procedure for, 498–501
Operations Research, 505
Operations Research Society, 42
Opportunities, awareness of,
  85–86
Oral communication, 427–428
Oral delegation, 227

Organization:
  formal, 162–163
  informal, 163–164
  uses of term, 162
Organization behavior, 27
Organization charts, 259–261
Organization culture, 236
  definition of, 263
  illustrations of, 264
  influence of leader on, 264–265
Organization development, 41,
  344–347
  definition of, 334, 344
  examples of, 346–347
  grid, 345–346
  process of, 344–345
Organization hierarchy:
  objectives and, 98–100
  skills in, 299
Organization levels, 5, 164–168
  problems with, 167–168
  variations in span of management
    by, 172
Organization structure, 270
  control and, 460, 545–546
  job design and, 298
  strategy and, 120–122, 129–130
Organization theory, 40
Organizational conflict, 342–344
Organizational climate:
  controls and, 462
  leadership and, 398–399
  motivation and, 389–390
  for planning, 130
Organizational roles, 162
  clarification of, 106, 111
Organizational strategy, 123
Organizing, 36–37, 161–179,
  251–271
  appraisal of, 320
  cause of, 269
  into departments, 164
    (*See also* Departmentation)
  logic of, 173
  misconceptions about, 173
  mistakes in, 252–256
    planning to avoid, 256–257
  process of, 172–174, 270–271
  purpose of, 269
  steps in, 36
Orientation of new managers,
  308–309
Outputs, 16–17
Outside employment, policy on, 80
Overall control (*see* Control, overall)

Overorganization, 255–256

Palmer Machine Company (case),
  416–417
Paragon Radar Corporation (case),
  19–20
Parkinson's Law, 9
Participation:
  in budget making, 474
  leadership and, 400
  as motivator, 385
Path-goal approach to leadership,
  412–414
Pendleton Department Stores
  Corporation (case), 351
Penn Central Transportation
  Company (case), 132–133
Penney, J. C., Inc., 307
Pennsylvania Railroad, 132
PepsiCo, Inc., 301, 436, 484
Performance:
  decentralized, 238
  evaluation of, 531–532
  measurement of, 449, 537
    difficulty in, 529
    with management
      fundamentals, 531
  rewarding, 537
Performance appraisal, 102–103,
  313–332, 355
  criteria for, 53, 314–315
  legal requirements for, 314
  problem of, 314
  program for, 319–324
  trait approach to, 315–317
  against verifiable objectives,
    317–319
Personal commitment, 111
Personal computers (PCs), 485
Personal contact, need for, 171
Personal dignity, importance of, 361
Personal goals, 324
Personal profile, preparation of, 324
Personal risk, 149–150
Personality tests, 306
Personnel actions matrix, 281–282
Personnel strategies, 123
PERT (Program Evaluation and
  Review Technique), 455,
  477–481, 505
Peter Principle, The (Peter and
  Hall), 303
Physical standards, 450
Physiological needs, 376

Placement, 277, 282–283, 303
Planned progression, 338–339
Planning, 35–36, 73–96
  appraisal of, 320
  cash flow, 455
  clarity of, 170
  of communication, 428
  controlling and, 447–448,
    459–460, 513, 545
  decision trees in, 505
  definition of, 73
  efficiency of, 75–76
  failures in, 252
  flexibility in, 150
  hierarchy of plans, 77
  implementation of plans, 128
  for innovation, 537
  inventory, 501–503
  mistakes in organizing avoided by,
    256–257
  of operations (see Operations
    management; Operations
    research)
  organization levels and, 168
  organization structure and,
    121–122, 129–130
  organizational climate for, 130
  pervasiveness of, 74–75
  primacy of, 74
  process of, 89–93
  purpose of, 74
  steps in, 84–89
  strategies and policies to direct,
    119–120
  types of plans, 76–84
    budgets, 84
    missions, 77–78
    objectives, 78
    policies, 79–81
    procedures, 81–82
    programs, 83–84
    rules, 82–83
    strategies, 78–79
Pluralistic society, U.S. as, 50
Polaroid, 264, 265, 300
Policies, 79–81
  definition of, 118
  of open competition, 287–288
  planning and, 119–120
  procedures versus, 82
  promotion, 242
  uniformity of, decentralization and,
    235
Portfolio Matrix, 124–125
Position descriptions, 261, 355

Position requirements, 294–296
  matching qualifications with,
    301–304
Positions, controls tailored to,
  459–460
Positive reinforcement, 382
Postal Service, U.S., 185
Power, 276
  authority and, 206
  coercive, 207
  need for, 383
  position, 409
Predictive principles, 8–9
Preference theory, 148–150
Premises:
  certainty of, 150
  critical, 89
  development of, 86–87
    communication and, 129
Preventive control (see Control,
  preventive)
Pricing policy, 80
Principles:
  descriptive and predictive, 8–9
  scientific, 8
Privacy Act (1974), 306
Probabilities:
  decision tree with, 146–148
  estimation of, 144
Probability distribution curve,
  144–145
Problem formulation, 498–499
Problem recognition, 344
Problem-solving ability, 299–300
Procedures:
  excessive, 256
  planning of, 81–82
Process consultation, 346
Process departmentation, 192
Process production layout, 495
Procter & Gamble Company, 196,
  265, 387
Proctor & Company (case),
  511–512
Product budgets, 468
Product departmentation, 186–188
Product design, 493–494
Product lines, return on investment
  applied to, 518–520
Product management (see Matrix
  organization)
Product strategies, 122–124
Production design, 494–495
Production management (see
  Operations management)

Productivity, definition of, 6
Professional goals, 324
Proficiency tests, 306
Profit, 5
Profit and loss control, 515–517
Program budgets, 84, 481–483
Programmed decisions, 143
Programs, 83–84
  contingency, 129
  network of, 101
  standards for, 451
Project management (see Matrix
  organization)
Promotion, 277, 282–283, 303
  policy on, 242
  temporary, 339
  from within, 286–287
Prospective managers, tests of, 306
Psychological advantage of
  perventive control, 532
Public relations strategies, 123
Purex Corporation, 190, 299
Purposes (see Mission of
  enterprise)

Quaker Oats Company, 56
Qualitative factors, 138
Quality of working life (QWL)
  programs, 385–386
Quality control circles, 507
Quantifiable variables, 150
Quantitative factors, 138

Rational-economic view of behavior,
  361
Rationality, 136
RCA Corporation, 75
Reading in training programs, 342
Real-time information, 452–454
Receptiveness, 232
Recruitment, 277, 282–283,
  301–302
Recycling of objectives, 107
Referent power, 206
Reinforcement theory, 382
Relationships:
  failure to clarify, 252–253
  (See also Line and staff
    relationships)
Reorganization, 257–258
Research:
  and analysis, 142–143
  and development, 537–538
    matrix organization in, 196

Resources:
  allocation of, 124–125
  commitment of, 119
Responsibility, 11
  absoluteness of, 230–231, 270
  authority without, 253, 254
  for communication, 421
  for control, 545
  parity of authority and, 231, 270
  for poor results, 530
  for selection of managers, 304
  social, 50–53, 67
  of staff, lack of, 217
  for staffing, 288–289
Results expected, delegation by, 228, 270
Retrenchment, 128
Return on investment (ROI), 517–521
  advantages of, 520–521
  application to product lines of, 518–520
  examples of, 517–518
  factors affecting, 519
  limitations of, 521
Revenue budgets, 468
Revenue standards, 451
Reward power, 206
Risk:
  analysis of, 144–145
  attitudes toward, 148–149
  personal, 149–150
Roles:
  managerial, 31–33
  multiplicity of, 360
Roman Catholic Church, 170
Rules, 82–83

Saab, 388
Safety needs, 376
Sales, production layout to facilitate, 495
Sales budgets, 468
Sales forecasts, 454
Satisfaction, difference between motivation and, 375
Satisficing, 136
Satisfiers, 378
Scalar chain, 11
Scalar principle, 207, 228–229, 270
Scientific approach, 8–9
Scientific management, 10–11
Sears, Roebuck and Company, 120n., 237, 242, 264, 307

Securities and Exchange Commission, 56
Security needs, 376
Self-actualization, 362
  need for, 377
Self-audits, 532, 534–535
Self-control, 532
Semantic clarification, 42–43
Semantic distortions, 428–429
Seniority, 57
Sensitivity training, 340–341
Separation, 277
Service departments, misuse of, 255
Service industry, 508
Service strategies, 123–124
7-S framework, 42–43
Short-range plans, 91–92, 128
Short-term objectives, 103
Simulation models, 499
Situational approach, 12–13, 31, 39
  in communication, 424
  to leadership, 408–414
  to position descriptions, 296
  to span of management, 168
Size of organization, degree of decentralization and, 235–236
Skills, managerial, 298–300
  balancing age factor and, 303
Small business, staff in, 215–216
Small Business Reporter, 4
Social needs, 362
Social responsibility, 50–53, 67
Social systems, cooperative, 27–28
Socialization of new managers, 308–309
Sociotechnical systems, 28–29
Sony, 59
Southwest Airlines, 397
Space budgets, 468
Span of management, 164–168, 269
  choosing, 166–167
  decentralization and, 242
  factors influencing, 168–172
  narrow versus wide, 165
Spanish-American War, 216
Specialization, 126
Staff, 207
  benefits of, 216
  careless use of, 254
  effective, 218–220
  lack of responsibility of, 217
  limitations of, 216–218
  line distinguished from, 209
  planning, 121–122
  in small business, 215–216

Staffing, 37, 275–292
  definition of, 275–276
  process of, 354–355
  purpose of, 354
  responsibility for, 288–289
  situational factors affecting, 283–289
    external environment, 284–285
    internal environment, 286–289
    international environment, 285
  systems approach to, 277–283
    appraisal and career planning, 283
    leading and controlling, 283
    management inventory, 279–281
    personnel actions matrix, 281–282
    recruitment, selection, placement, and promotion, 282–283, 294, 295
  training and development, 283
Standard Oil Company, 120n.
Standards:
  budgets and, 474
  critical point, 450–452
  deviation from, 528–529
  establishment of, 448–449
  objective, 170
  principle of, 546
Statistical analysis, 475
Storage, production layout to facilitate, 495
Strategic business units (SBUs), 125, 197–199
Strategies, 78–79, 118–134
  career, 283, 324–328
  for change, 345
  definition of, 118
  implementation of, 128–130
  in management by objectives, 103
  planning and, 75, 119–120
  process of developing, 126–128
  requirements for, 120–122
  for resource allocation, 124–125
  types of, 122–124
Subordinates:
  objective setting by, 106–107
  reluctance to appraise, 314
  training of, 169
  willingness to trust, 232–233
Subordination, multiple, 254–255
Subsidiaries, 61
Successful companies, attributes of, 6

Surplus, 5–6
Survey feedback method of
    organization development, 346
Suzuki Motors Company, 79
Synectics, 366
Systems approach, 13–17, 29–30, 39
    decision making and, 150–151
    definition of, 13
    external environment in, 70
    in management by objectives,
        103–104
    to motivation, 389–391
    to staffing (see Staffing, systems
        approach to)

Tactics, 119
Tandom Corporation, 265
Task structure, 409
Tax systems, centralizing influence
    of, 240
Team building, 346
Technical skills, 298
Technology:
    impact of, 41
    increased complexity of, 507
Teleconferencing, 436
Temporary promotions, 339
Territorial departmentation, 184–186
Tests of prospective managers, 306
Texas Instruments, 387
Texas Oil Company (case), 291
T-groups, 340–341
Theory, definition of, 8
Theory X, 361–363
Theory Y, 362–363
Theory Z, 56–60
Threats, communication undermined
    by, 430
Time budgets, 468
Time-event networks, 477–481,
    505–506

Top managers:
    in budget process, 473–474
    computers and, 484–485
    influence on organization culture
        of, 264–265
    objective setting by, 104, 106
    orientation of, 126
    planning by, 75
    staffing and, 289
Toyota Motor Corporation, 79,
    128
Training, 277, 283, 336–338, 355
    analysis of needs for, 338
    definition of, 334
    internal and external, 340–342
    of interviewers, 305
    on-the-job, 338–340
    operational-management
        approach to, 335–336
    of subordinates, 169
Trait appraisals, 315–317
Traits, leadership, 399–400
Transformation process, 14, 16
Trends, long-term, 87

Uncertainty:
    decision making under, 144–150
    managerial errors due to,
        528–529
Unconscious scanning, 364
Underorganization, 255–256
Unions, centralizing influence of,
    240
Unity of command, 11, 229–230,
    270
Universal Food Products Company
    (case), 203
University management programs,
    341–342
Upward communication, 426
Utility theory, 148–150

Value engineering, 506
Values:
    corporate, 264–265
    social, 53
Variable budgets, 84, 470–472
Variables, quantifiable, 150
Verifiable objectives (see
    Objectives, verifiable)
VGI Company (case), 267–268
Vocational tests, 306
Volkswagen, 300
Volvo, 298, 388

Western Electric Company, 11
Western Petroleum Corporation
    (case), 523–524
Willingness to learn, 536
Women:
    in international business, 63
    in management, 284
Work activities of managers, 276
Work simplification, 505
Work teams, 297
World War II, 170, 306
Worldwide Motorbike Company
    (case), 311–312
Written communication, 427,
    433–434
Written delegation, 227

Xerox Information Systems Group,
    190

YKK, Inc., 59–60

Zero-based budgets, 84, 473